Readings in _____
SOCIAL PSYCHOLOGY
General, Classic, and Contemporary Selections

FIFTH EDITION

WAYNE A. LESKO
Marymount University

Boston   New York   San Francisco
Mexico City   Montreal   Toronto   London   Madrid   Munich   Paris
Hong Kong   Singapore   Tokyo   Cape Town   Sydney

Executive Editor: Carolyn O. Merrill
Editorial Assistant: Kate Edwards
Marketing Manager: Wendy Gordon
Editorial-Production Administrator: Annette Joseph
Editorial-Production Service: Susan Freese, Communicáto, Ltd.
Electronic Composition: Cabot Computer Services
Composition Buyer: Linda Cox
Manufacturing Buyer: JoAnne Sweeney
Cover Designer: Kristina Mose-Libon

For related titles and support materials, visit our online catalog at www.ablongman.com

Library of Congress Cataloging-in-Publication Data

Readings in social psychology : general, classic, and contemporary
    selections / [compiled by] Wayne A. Lesko. — 5th ed.
        p.   cm.
      Includes bibliographical references and index.
      ISBN 0-205-33807-0
      1. Social psychology.   I. Lesko, Wayne A.

HM1033.R43   2003
302—dc21

                                                                                    2002023211

Printed in the United States of America

10 9 8 7 6 5 4 3 2 1   RRD-VA   08 07 06 05 04 03 02

With love
To Matt, as you go out into the world
To Marlaine, as you join me as my wife

Brief Contents

Contents

Preface

THE TYPICAL SOCIAL psychology class ranges from sophomore through graduate levels, and the members may include majors who are required to take the course as well as nonmajors who have elected to do so. Regardless of the level or the audience, many instructors—myself included—feel that a collection of readings is a valuable means of promoting an understanding of the discipline.

Most collections of readings typically fall into two categories: professional articles from journals in the field or popular articles reprinted from such magazines as *Psychology Today*. The category of professional readings may include contemporary articles, classic articles, or a combination of the two. These articles provide excellent insight into the core of social psychology by describing not only the research outcomes but also the detailed methodology for how the results were obtained. Popular articles, on the other hand, lack the scientific rigor of journal articles but often present a broad overview of a number of findings pertaining to a particular topic. Clearly, both types of readings have advantages and disadvantages associated with them, depending on the particular level at which the course is taught.

In nearly three decades of teaching social psychology at both the undergraduate and graduate levels, I have found that students seem to respond best to a variety of reading formats. Popular articles are easy to understand and provide a good overview, while also generating critical thinking about an issue. Research articles provide insight into the methodological issues in social psychology and help the student develop a critical attitude in evaluating research contributions and conclusions. Classic research articles familiarize the student with early research that has had a lasting impact on social psychology, while contemporary works illustrate issues currently being studied and the methods used to investigate them.

Like the first four editions, this fifth edition of *Readings in Social Psychology: General, Classic, and Contemporary Selections* is designed to provide exactly that breadth of exposure to the different sources of information available in the field. In response to feedback from users of the last four editions of the book, as well as the need to update the selection of contemporary articles, more than half of the articles in this edition are new.

As in the previous editions, each chapter begins with an introduction to the topic, which is followed by three articles: one general (popular), one classic, and one contemporary. Each article begins with a short introduction that sets the stage, or provides a context for the article. Each article is followed by a set of Critical Thinking Questions, which ask the student to examine critically some part of the article presented, to speculate about generalizations and implications of the research, and, in some cases, to suggest new studies based on the information in the article. The classic articles are also followed by a list of Additional

Related Readings for students who may wish to examine more contemporary articles on the same topic.

The topical organization of *Readings in Social Psychology: General, Classic, and Contemporary Selections* (fifth edition) directly parallels that of Baron and Byrne's *Social Psychology* (tenth edition). Even so, this edition of *Readings in Social Psychology* can be adapted readily for use with any other text or used in lieu of a text, depending on how the course is taught. Likewise, the book can be used with classes of varying levels, by structuring which articles will be emphasized and in how much detail they will be examined.

Finally, all articles are presented verbatim, in their entirety, since it is my firm belief that one valuable skill gained by students from reading research articles is the ability to abstract pertinent information from an original source. The only exception to this, necessitated by copyright ownership, is found in Table 1 of Article 14, which is an abbreviation of the Bem Sex Role Inventory.

A Note to the Reader, which follows this Preface, offers some suggestions on how to get the most out of this book. It is especially recommended for students who do not have an extensive background in reading research articles.

At this point, perhaps some notice is in order about several of the articles. Understandably, everything is representative of the time in which it was written, both in terms of the ideas presented and the language used. Some of the classic articles in this collection were written 30 or more years ago and are out of step with current language style. Moreover, some of the descriptions made and observations offered would be considered condescending and even offensive by today's standards. Please keep this in mind, and consider the context in which each of the articles was written.

ACKNOWLEDGMENTS

At Allyn and Bacon, I would like to thank Carolyn Merrill, Executive Editor, and Jonathan Bender, Editorial Assistant, for their guidance and help with the format of the book. I likewise wish to extend my gratitude to Sue Freese, of Communicáto, Ltd., for her excellent copyediting of this book. Thanks also go to Robert A. Baron, Rensselaer Polytechnic Institute, and Donn Byrne, State University of New York–Albany, who provided input about organization and content of the various editions.

I am especially indebted to my graduate and undergraduate students in social psychology at Marymount University, whose honest feedback on the contents of the first four editions helped me create a new, improved book of readings.

I also want to thank the various friends, colleagues, and graduate assistants who helped me and provided encouragement and advice over the many editions of this collection of readings. Without their input, this work would not have been possible.

Last but not least, I thank all of the authors and publishers of the articles contained in this book for their permission to reprint these materials. Their fine work in advancing the field of social psychology is what literally made this book possible.

W. L.

A Note to the Reader

As YOU EMBARK on your study of social psychology, you will soon discover that the field is broad indeed. Many different topics will be encountered, but they all are related by the common thread that defines social psychology—namely, the study of individual behavior in social situations.

As a collection of readings, this book is designed to expose you to some of the most important areas of study within social psychology. Just as the topics found in the area of social psychology are diverse, so, too, are the ways in which social psychological knowledge is disseminated. If you are new to the field, most likely you have encountered one common source of information: articles in nonprofessional sources. For example, newspaper and magazine articles may present the information from some study in social psychology. Typically nontechnical pieces directed to the general public, these articles summarize a number of studies on a given topic and are fairly easy to comprehend. Each of the 14 chapters that comprise this book begins with such an article—what I have termed a *general* reading.

A second source of information is actually the backbone of social psychology: articles that appear in professional journals of the field. These articles are the primary means by which new ideas and the results of research are shared with the professional community. While they tend to be more technical and difficult to read compared to the general works, professional articles have the advantage of providing readers with sufficient detail to draw their own conclusions, rather than be forced to rely on someone else's interpretation of the information. Some of these articles represent research that has stood the test of time and are generally regarded as *classics* in the field; the second reading found in each chapter is such an article.

Finally, the last type of article found in each chapter is labeled *contemporary*. These articles are fairly recent examples of research currently being conducted in social psychology.

The format of each chapter is the same. Each opens with a brief introduction to the chapter topic; one general, one classic, and one contemporary article are then presented, in that order. Each article begins with an introduction written by me, which serves to focus your perspective before reading. Every article is then followed by Critical Thinking Questions. In some cases, these questions directly refer to information contained in the articles; in others, the questions are more speculative, asking you to go beyond the data presented. Finally, the classic articles contain Additional Related Readings. The references included here are either recent articles that address the same issues discussed in the classic article (a way of updating the current status of research on the topic) or a topic similar to the one discussed in the original. In either case, the interested student can use these references to find more information on the topic.

All of the articles in this collection are reprinted in their entirety. Not a word has been abridged or altered. (Again, the only exception is Table 1 of Article 14, which has been abbreviated due to a copyright restriction.) For the general articles, this should not be a problem for anyone. However, if this is the first time that you are reading journal articles from their primary sources, some assistance might be in order. First of all, do not allow yourself to be overwhelmed or intimidated. New students often are confused by some of the terminology that is used and are left totally dumbfounded by the detailed statistics that are usually part of such articles. Approached in the right way, these articles need not be intimidating and should be comprehensible to any reader willing to expend a little effort.

In reading a research article, I would like to make the following suggestions:

- Most articles begin with an Abstract or end with a Summary. If these are provided, begin by carefully reading them; they will give you an overview of why the study was conducted, what was done, and what the results were.

- Next, read the Introduction fairly carefully; this is where the authors describe previous research in the area and develop the logic for why they are conducting the experiment in the first place.

- The Methods section describes in detail the techniques used by the researchers to conduct their study; read this section thoroughly in order to understand exactly what was done.

- The next section, Results, is where the authors describe what was found in the study. This is often the most technically difficult part of the article; from your standpoint, you might want to skim over this part, focusing only on the sections that verbally describe what the results were. Do not worry about the detailed statistical analyses that are presented.

- Finally, you might want to read the Discussion section in some detail; here, the authors discuss the findings and implications of the study and perhaps suggest avenues for further study.

To summarize: Each article is fairly straightforward to comprehend, provided that you do not allow yourself to get too bogged down in the details and thus frustrated. The journey may seem difficult at times, but the end result—an appreciation and understanding of the complex issues of human social behavior—will be worth it. Enjoy!

W. L.

Chapter One

THE FIELD OF SOCIAL PSYCHOLOGY

AN INTRODUCTION TO a course such as social psychology often includes a section on research methods. Nonmajors confronting this topic often wonder why they need to know about research methods when in all likelihood they will never actually conduct research. Whether you are majoring in psychology or not, familiarity with research methods will benefit you, for several reasons.

First, it will help you understand the studies that make up the knowledge base of social psychology. Familiarity with methodology will allow you to make informed decisions about the conclusions drawn by various studies. Second, and perhaps more important, some knowledge of research issues will allow you to be an intelligent consumer of research information. Results of studies often are reported to the general public in newspapers and magazines. Knowing something about the methods used to produce these results will better prepare you to decide whether the conclusions drawn are warranted. Finally, it is useful to fully appreciate why the results of experimental data are needed instead of just relying on common sense. Article 1, "Folk Wisdom: Was Your Grandmother Right?" shows how folk wisdom (i.e., common sense) often is contradictory and hence not very useful as a guideline for behavior.

Research is the basic underpinning of psychological science. Given the subject matter of social psychology, it is often difficult, if not impossible, to get unbiased results if subjects know what is being observed. For that reason, psychologists, in general, and social psychologists, in particular, often have relied on deception as a means of obtaining naive subjects. But what ethical issues are involved in the use of deception? And what if deception is so widely used that subjects expect to be deceived whenever they participate in a research study? What, if any, are the alternatives to the use of deception? These are some of the questions addressed in Article 2, "Human Use of Human Subjects: The Problem of Deception in Social Psychological Experiments."

Finally, Article 3 examines the public perception of social psychological research. As discussed in the contemporary article, "'That's Completely Obvious . . . and Important': Lay Judgments of Social Psychological Findings," what the general public and what social psychology researchers each deems to be interesting and important may not be in harmony. Instead of simply being variations of opinions and values, these differences between social psychology researchers and the lay public may have important implications for issues such as how money is allocated for various research projects.

ARTICLE 1 _____

At the heart of all the articles you will read in this book is *research methodology.* Given a question you want to investigate, how do you go about actually collecting data?

There are a number of different ways of conducting social psychological research. One broad distinction is between *experimental methods* and *correlational (nonexperimental) methods.* Each method has potential advantages and disadvantages. One is not necessarily better than the other; it depends on what you are investigating.

Students encountering research methods literature for the first time are often surprised at the difficulty of designing and conducting a good piece of research. It is not as easy as it might seem on the surface. Numerous artifacts that can affect the outcome of a study need to be accounted for and controlled. An examination of the introductory chapters of most social psychology texts will give you a better understanding of some of these issues.

Sometimes, a study obtains results that are quite unexpected and surprises readers. Other times, however, readers may feel that the outcome of a study was totally expected—indeed, that it was just common sense. The reaction to such an article often is to question why it is even necessary to test the obvious.

The only problem with common sense is that it is often contradictory. For example, to whom are people most attracted: people like themselves or people different from themselves? Common sense would predict that "Birds of a feather flock together"; on the other hand, "Opposites attract." So which is it? As it turns out, common sense is not such a good predictor of actual behavior. The only way to know for sure is to go out and empirically test the concept.

The following article by Robert Epstein examines a number of common-sense ideas that have been passed down to us in light of what current research tells us about their validity. The article underscores the necessity of testing ideas empirically and why even supposedly obvious notions must be exposed to scientific scrutiny.

Folk Wisdom
Was Your Grandmother Right?
■ Robert Epstein

The table next to me at Fillipi's restaurant was a noisy one. Two men and two women in their 20s and 30s were arguing about a relationship issue. One of the men—call him Male #1—would soon be leaving the country for six months. Would the passion he shared with his beloved survive? The exchange went something like this:

Female #1 (probably the girlfriend): "When you really love someone, being apart makes you care even more. If someone is good to you, you sometimes take that for granted when the person is around every day. But when he's gone, all that good treatment is gone, too, and you realize just how much you had. You really start to yearn for him."

Male #2 (looking lustfully at Female #1, even though he seemed to be with the other woman): "That's right. The same thing happens when your parents die. You really start to miss and appreciate them. You even rewrite the past, forgetting the bad things and focusing on the good times and the kindness they showed you."

Female #1 (starting to look lovingly at Male #2): "Exactly. Everyone knows that absence makes the heart grow fonder."

Then Male #1, the one probably on his way to Thailand, spoke up. "Well, but . . ." He faltered, thinking hard about going on. All eyes were on him. He took a deep breath.

And then he said, slowly and deliberately, "But don't we also say, 'Out of sight, out of mind'?"

This was not good for anyone's digestion. Female #1's face turned the color of marinara sauce. Male #2 smiled mischievously, presumably imagining himself in bed with Female #1. Female #2 looked back and forth between her date and Female #1, also apparently imagining them in bed together. And Male #1, not wanting to face the carnage, lowered his eyes and tapped out a strange rhythm on the table top with his fork. Was he thinking about the classy Thai brothels he had read about on the Internet?

TRUTH OR POPPYCOCK?

"Absence makes the heart grow fonder" and "Out of sight, out of mind" are examples of folk wisdom—folk psychology, you might say. All cultures pass along wisdom of this sort—sometimes in the form of proverbs; sometimes through songs (remember Paul Simon's "Fifty Ways to Leave Your Lover"?), rhymes (Mother Goose), or stories (Aesop's fables); sometimes through laws and public information campaigns ("Stay alive, don't drink and drive"); and always through religion ("Do unto others as you would have them do unto you").

But folk wisdom is an unreliable, inconsistent kind of wisdom. For one thing, most proverbs coexist with their exact opposites, or at least with proverbs that give somewhat different advice. Does absence truly make the heart grow fonder, or are loved ones out of mind when they're out of sight? And isn't variety the spice of life? (If Male #1 had come up with *that* one, he might have been murdered on the spot.)

Do opposites attract, or do birds of a feather flock together? Should you love the one you're with, or

would that be like changing horses in midstream? We all know that he who hesitates is lost, but doesn't haste make waste, and isn't patience a virtue, and don't fools rush in, and aren't you supposed to look before you leap?

And, sure, money is power, but aren't the best things in life supposed to be free? And since time is money, and money is power, and power corrupts, does that mean time also corrupts? Well, maybe so. After all, the Devil finds work for idle hands.

I've only covered a few well-known proverbs from the English-speaking world. Each culture passes along its own wisdom, which is not always meaningful to outsiders. In India, for example, people say, "Call on God, but row away from the docks," and Romanians advise, "Do not put your spoon into the pot that does not boil for you." In Bali they say, "Goodness shouts and evil whispers," while in Tibet the message is, "Goodness speaks in a whisper, but evil shouts."

You get the idea. Proverbs that relay wisdom about how we're supposed to live do not necessarily supply useful or reliable advice. In fact, proverbs are sometimes used merely to justify what we already do or believe, rather than as guidelines for action. What's more, we tend to *switch* proverbs to suit our current values and ideals. A young man might rationalize risky action by pointing out that "You only live once"; later in life—if he's still around—he'll probably tell you, "Better safe than sorry."

Is the situation hopeless? Can we glean any truths at all from the wisdom of the ages?

The behavioral sciences can help. Science is a set of methods for testing the validity of statements about the world—methods for getting as close to "truth" as we currently know how to get. Psychologists and other scientists have spent more than a century testing the validity of statements about human behavior, thinking, and emotions. How well does folk psychology stand up to scientific inquiry? What do we find when we test a statement like "Absence makes the heart grow fonder"? If, as I do, you sometimes rely on folk wisdom to guide your actions or teach your children, this is a question well worth considering.

Here's how five common proverbs measure up to behavioral research.

CONFESSION IS GOOD FOR THE SOUL

Psychologists don't study the soul, of course. But, says psychologist James W. Pennebaker, Ph.D., "If we define 'soul' loosely as who you are, how you feel about yourself, and how healthy you are, then confession is good for the soul." Pennebaker, a researcher at the University of Texas at Austin, is one of several behavioral scientists who have looked carefully at the results of "self-disclosure"—talking or writing about private feelings and concerns. His research suggests that for about two-thirds of us, self-disclosure has enormous emotional and physical benefits. Pennebaker's newly revised book, *Opening Up: The Healing Power of Expressing Emotion,* summarizes 15 years of compelling research on this subject.

Self-disclosure, as you might expect, can greatly reduce shame or guilt. In fact, studies of suspected criminals showed that they acted far more relaxed after confessing their crimes—despite the fact that punishment now awaited them. Self-disclosure may also provide the power behind talk therapy. "The fact that self-disclosure is beneficial," says Pennebaker, "may explain why all forms of psychotherapy seem to be helpful. Whether the therapy is behavioral or psychoanalytic, in the beginning the clients tell their stories."

Perhaps most intriguing are the physical effects of "confession." Pennebaker has found that self-disclosure may actually boost the immune system, spurring production of white blood cells that attack invading microorganisms, increasing production of antibodies, and heightening the body's response to vaccination.

But what about those other proverbs that advise us to keep our mouths shut? "Let sleeping dogs lie." "Least said is soonest mended." "Many have suffered by talking, few by silence." Can self-disclosure do harm? According to Pennebaker, self-disclosure is not likely to be beneficial when it's forced. University of Notre Dame psychologist Anita Kelly, Ph.D., has suggested, moreover, that revealing secrets may be harmful if the confidant is likely to be judgmental. And a 1989 study conducted by Maria Sauzier, M.D., of Harvard Medical School, showed that people often regret disclosures of child abuse. Sauzier found that nearly half of the parents whose children had disclosed sexual abuse (usually to the other parent or a therapist) felt that both the children and the families were

harmed by the disclosures. And 19 percent of the adolescents who confessed that they had been abused regretted making the disclosures. In general, however, confession seems to be a surprisingly beneficial act.

ALL WORK AND NO PLAY MAKES JACK A DULL BOY

To me, the most frightening scene in the movie *The Shining* was the one in which actress Shelley Duvall, concerned that her husband (Jack Nicholson) was going crazy, approached the desk at which he had spent several months supposedly writing a novel. There she found hundreds of pages containing nothing but the sentence, "All work and no play makes Jack a dull boy" typed thousands of times on a manual typewriter. I've always wondered who did all that typing! And I've also wondered about the truth of the proverb. Once again, we're also faced with contradictory bits of folk wisdom that urge us to work until we drop: "Rest makes rusty." "Labor warms, sloth harms." "Labor is itself a pleasure."

Is too much work, without the balance of leisure activity ("play"), actually harmful? Research suggests that the answer is yes, with one possible exception: if you love your work—in other words, if you've been able to make your *avocation* your *vocation*—then work may provide you with some of the benefits of play.

In the 1940s, anthropologist Adam Curle pointed out that the distinction between work and leisure seems to be an unfortunate product of modern society. In many traditional cultures, he wrote, "there is not even a word for work." Work and play "are all of a piece," part of the integrated structure of daily living. But modern society has created the need for people to earn a living, an endeavor that can be difficult and can easily get out of hand. Hence, the modern pursuit of "leisure time" and "balance"—correctives for the desperate measures people take to pay their bills.

Study after study confirms the dangers of overwork. It may or may not make you a dull person, but it clearly dulls your mind. For example, recent research on fire fighters by Peter Knauth, Ph.D., shows that long work shifts increase reaction time and lower alertness. And studies with emergency room physicians show that overwork increases errors and impedes judgment. Indeed, a Hollywood cameraman, coming off an 18-hour work shift, made news recently when he lost control of his car and died in a crash.

Conversely, leisure activities have been shown in numerous studies by researchers Howard and Diane Tinsley, Virginia Lewis, and others, to relieve stress, improve mood, increase life satisfaction, and even boost the immune system.

Curiously, the hard-driven "type A" personalities among us are not necessarily Dull Jacks. According to a recent study of more than 300 college students by Robert A. Hicks, Ph.D., and his colleagues, type-A students claim to engage in considerably more leisure activities than their relaxed, type-B counterparts. Type As may simply live "more intensely" than type Bs, whether they're on the job or goofing off.

The distinction between work and play is, to some extent, arbitrary. But it's clear that if you spend too much time doing things you don't want to do, your performance, health, and sense of well-being will suffer.

BOYS WILL BE BOYS

The widely held (though politically incorrect) belief that boys are predisposed from birth to feel, learn, and perform differently from girls is strongly supported by research. For example, boys are, on average, considerably more aggressive than girls. They are left-handed more frequently than girls and tend to be better at math and at spatial rotation tasks. Girls, meanwhile, may perform certain kinds of memory tasks better. They also start talking earlier than boys, and, at the playground, they're more likely to imitate boys than boys are to imitate girls. And boys tend to listen more with their right ear, while girls tend to listen with both ears equally. These findings generally hold up cross-culturally, which suggests that they are at least somewhat independent of environmental influences. Upbringing plays an important role in gender differences, of course—even in the first days after birth, parents treat boy babies differently from girls—but converging evidence from psychology, neuroscience, and evolutionary biology suggests that many gender differences are actually programmed from birth, if not from conception.

Since the brain is the mechanism that generates behavior, where we find behavioral differences, we should also find neurological differences. Indeed, recent research suggests a host of differences between male and female brains. For example, although, on average, male brains are larger than female brains, the hemispheres of the brain seem to be better connected in females, which may help explain why females are more sensitive and emotional than males.

Behavior is also driven by hormones. Here, too, there are significant gender differences. From birth, testosterone levels are higher in males, which helps to account for males' aggressiveness. June Reinisch, Ph.D., then at Indiana University, studied boys and girls whose mothers had been exposed to antimiscarriage drugs that mimic testosterone. Not surprisingly, she found that these children of both sexes were considerably more aggressive than their counterparts with normal testosterone levels. But even among the exposed children, the boys were more aggressive than the girls.

So boys will indeed be boys (and, by implication, girls will be girls). But this is only true "on average." Male and female traits overlap considerably, which means that a particular male could be more emotional than most females and a particular female could be better at math than most males. To be fair, you have to go case by case.

EARLY TO BED, AND EARLY TO RISE, MAKES A MAN HEALTHY, WEALTHY, AND WISE

This proverb, often attributed to Ben Franklin, actually seems to have originated in the late 1400s, and Franklin may have lifted it from a collection of adages published in 1656. Historical trivia aside, research on sleep suggests that the proverb gives sound advice—but only because our culture is out-of-synch with the biology of nearly half the population.

Here's how it works: it's long been known that the body has natural rhythms. Those that occur on a 24-hour cycle are called "circadian" and include cycles of temperature change, wakefulness, and eating. For most people, these cycles are highly resistant to change. This much you probably have heard, but what you might not know is that there are two distinctly different circadian rhythm patterns. "Larks"—who show what researchers call "morningness" (honest!)—are people whose cycles peak early in the day. Not surprisingly, larks awaken early and start the day strong. "Owls"—people inclined toward "eveningness"—peak late in the day. In both cases, the peaks are associated with better performance on memory tasks, quicker reaction times, heightened alertness, and cheerful moods. Some people are extreme larks or owls, others are moderates, and a few fit neither category.

There's a problem here, especially if, like me, you're an extreme owl. The trouble is that many important human activities—business meetings, job interviews, weddings, classes, and so on—are conducted during daylight hours, when larks have a distinct advantage. Not surprisingly, owls spend much of their time griping about how out-of-synch they seem to be. A 1978 study of college students by Wilse B. Webb, Ph.D., and Michael H. Bonnet, Ph.D., of the University of Florida, paints a grim picture for people like me: "Larks reported waking up when they expected to, waking up feeling more rested, and waking up more easily than the owls." Larks also reported having "fewer worries" and getting "more adequate sleep," and they awakened feeling physically better than owls. The differences were even greater, moreover, when owls tried to adapt to the lark sleep pattern. What's more, these problems can impair not only owls' sense of restedness but also their bank account; a study of Navy personnel suggests that people who sleep well make considerably more money than people who sleep poorly.

The long and short of it is that if your biorhythms allow you easily to "go to bed with the lamb and rise with the lark" (another old proverb), you may indeed end up with more money, better health, and more life satisfaction—but only because your internal clock is more in-synch with the stock exchange.

SPARE THE ROD
AND SPOIL THE CHILD

A recent headline in my local newspaper proclaimed, "Spanking Backfires, Latest Study Says." I cringe when I see stories like this, because I believe they ultimately harm many children. People have come to confuse discipline with "abuse," which is quite a different beast. "Discipline"—whether in the form of "time outs," reprimands, or spankings—is absolutely

necessary for parenting. Extensive research by psychologist Diana Baumrind, Ph.D., and others, has shown that permissive parenting produces children who can't handle independence and are unable to behave in a socially responsible manner. A great many social problems that we face today may be the inadvertent product of a generation of well-meaning, misinformed, overly-permissive parents.

However, if all you provide is discipline, without affection and emotional support—the "authoritarian" parenting style—you can damage your children. Offspring of authoritarian parents tend to be hostile and defiant, and, like the victims of permissive parents, they too have trouble with independence.

The most effective parenting style involves both a high level of discipline and ample affection and support. That's the best approach for producing children who are self-reliant, socially responsible, and successful in their own relationships, research shows.

In the latest anti-spanking study, published in August by University of New Hampshire sociologist Murray Straus, Ph.D., children between the ages of 6 to 9 who were spanked more than three times a week displayed more misbehavior two years later. Doesn't this show that spanking causes misbehavior? Not at all. Correlational studies are difficult to interpret. Perhaps without those spankings, the kids would have been even worse off. It's also possible that many of these spankings were unnecessary or excessive, and that it was this inappropriate discipline that sparked the later misbehavior.

Conversely, at least eight studies with younger kids show that spanking can indeed improve behavior. The age of the child, in fact, is probably important. Children under the age of six seem to regard spanking as a parent's right. But older kids may view it as an act of aggression, and in such cases spanking's effects may not be so benign.

Punishment, verbal or physical, applied in moderation and with the right timing, is a powerful teaching tool. It should not be the first or the only tool that a parent uses, but it has its place.

TRUTH À LA CARTE

But what about the restaurant debate? Does absence make the heart grow fonder or not? Alas, not enough research has been conducted to shed much light on this question. We do know that "out of sight, out of mind" is true when we're fresh from the womb; young babies will behave as if a toy has vanished into thin air when the toy is moved out of sight. But our memories quickly improve. Research conducted by Julia Vormbrock, Ph.D., and others, shows that children grow more fond of their caregivers when they're separated from them—at least for a few days. After two weeks of separation, however, most children become "detached," reports Vormbrock.

Psychologist Robert Pelligrini, Ph.D., once asked 720 young adults about separation, and two-thirds said that "absence makes the heart grow fonder" seemed more true than "out of sight, out of mind." A poll, however, doesn't tell us much about the truth of the matter. To settle things, we'll need an experiment. Hmmm. First we'll need 100 couples, whom we'll give various tests of "fondness." Then we'll assign, at random, half of the couples to a Control Group and half to an Absence Group. Next we'll separate the partners in each couple in our Absence Group by, say, 1,000 miles for six months—somehow providing jobs, housing, and social support for every person we relocate. Finally, we'll readminister our fondness tests

---

Rating the Proverbs

Here's a quick rundown on how well some other common proverbs measure up to research findings:

★★★★★ Looks good
★★★★ Some evidence supports it
★★★ Not clear
★★ Some evidence casts doubt
★ Scrap heap

"Once bitten, twice shy." Behind almost every dog or cat phobia, there's a bite or scratch. ★★★★★

"Practice makes perfect." Even the brain-injured can often learn new material with sufficient repetition. ★★★★

"Misery loves company." Depressed people often shun company, which unfortunately is part of the problem. ★★

"Two heads are better than one." Teams or groups typically produce better solutions than individuals do. ★★★★

"Cold hands, warm heart." Cold hands, poor circulation. See your physician. ★

"Every cloud has a silver lining." Not really, but therapy techniques like cognitive restructuring can get you to think so, and that can get you through the day. ★★★

"Old habits die hard." When we fail at a task, we tend to resort to old behavior patterns, even those from childhood. ★★★★

"You can't teach an old dog new tricks." You'll feel better, think more clearly, and may even live longer if you keep learning throughout life. ★★

"Familiarity breeds contempt." People tend to like what's familiar. ★

"Blood will tell." For better or worse, genes really do set limits on both physical characteristics and behavior. ★★★★

"A woman's place is in the home." Only when artificial barriers keep her there. ★

"When the cat's away, the mice will play." Kids and employees tend to slack off when their parents or supervisors are out of sight. ★★★★

"There's no accounting for tastes." Until you look at upbringing, biochemistry, evolutionary influences, and so on. ★★

to all 100 couples. If we find significantly greater levels of fondness in the separated couples than in the unseparated couples, we'll have strong support for the idea that absence makes the heart grow fonder.

Any volunteers? What? You would never subject yourself to such an absurd procedure? Well, fortunately, no one would ever conduct such research, either.

And that's the bottom line: the behavioral sciences can provide useful insights about how we should lead our lives, but there are limits to the kind of research that can be conducted with people. Folk wisdom may be flawed, but, in some instances, it's all we've got or will ever have. So don't put all you eggs in one basket.

CRITICAL THINKING QUESTIONS

1. A number of proverbs are rated in the box at the end of the article. Select one of the proverbs, and design a study that would test its validity.
2. Select one of the proverbs referred to in Question 1, and find a study that has been conducted on the topic. Summarize the results.
3. In addition to the folk wisdom mentioned in the article, what are other examples of common-sense ideas that contradict one another?
4. Many people rely on folk wisdom to guide their actions or explain certain situations. Is doing so ineffective or even dangerous? Or does folk wisdom (or common sense) still play a useful role in helping people manage their lives? Summarize the pros and cons of relying on folk wisdom as a guide to behavior.

ARTICLE 2 _____

Have you ever participated in a social psychology experiment? What were you thinking while you were participating? Were you accepting of the situation and the explanation you were given by the researcher, or were you trying to figure out the real purpose of the experiment? If you were doing the latter, you would be in good company, as many people have come to associate psychological research (and in particular, social psychology research) with the use of deception.

Deception has always been a staple in the research conducted in the field. But what exactly is *deception?* Is it simply another term for lying? In practice, deception in research can be located on a continuum from simply withholding from the subjects the true nature of the experiment to actively creating a cover story to try to keep the subjects from determining the actual purpose of the study. Deception is largely based on the assumption that if subjects knew the true nature of the experiment (the hypothesis being tested, that is), then they would not act naturally and hence contaminate the results.

This next classic article by Herbert C. Kelman explores the use of deception in social psychological experiments. After discussing some of the ethical issues involved in the use of deception, Kelman goes on to suggest how the use of deception should be handled, as well as alternatives to deception. In the years since the publication of this article in 1967, many changes in the ethical guidelines for the treatment of human subjects have been made. For example, it is now standard policy for institutions to have ethical review boards for the approval of any study involving human subjects. Nonetheless, deception in one form or another is still a common feature in social psychological research.

Human Use of Human Subjects
The Problem of Deception in Social Psychological Experiments[1]

■ Herbert C. Kelman

Though there is often good reason for deceiving Ss in social psychological experiments, widespread use of such procedures has serious (a) ethical implications (involving not only the possibility of harm to S, but also the quality of the E-S relationship), (b) methodological implications (relating to the decreasing naïveté of Ss), and (c) implications for the future of the discipline. To deal with these problems, it is necessary (a) to increase active awareness of the negative implications of deception and use it only when clearly justified, not as a matter of course; (b) to explore ways of counteracting and minimizing negative consequences of deception when it is used; and (c) to

develop new experimental techniques that dispense with deception and rely on S's positive motivations.

In 1954, in the pages of the *American Psychologist*, Edgar Vinacke raised a series of questions about experiments—particularly in the area of small groups—in which "the psychologist conceals the true purpose and conditions of the experiment, or positively misinforms the subjects, or exposes them to painful, embarrassing, or worse, experiences, without the subjects' knowledge of what is going on [p. 155]."

Reprinted from *Psychological Bulletin*, 1967, *67*, 1–11. Copyright © 1967 by the American Psychological Association. Reprinted with permission.

He summed up his concerns by asking, "What . . . is the proper balance between the interests of science and the thoughtful treatment of the persons who, innocently, supply the data? [p. 155]." Little effort has been made in the intervening years to seek answers to the questions he raised. During these same years, however, the problem of deception in social psychological experiments has taken on increasingly serious proportions.[2]

The problem is actually broader, extending beyond the walls of the laboratory. It arises, for example, in various field studies in which investigators enroll as members of a group that has special interest for them so that they can observe its operations from the inside. The pervasiveness of the problem becomes even more apparent when we consider that deception is built into most of our measurement devices, since it is important to keep the respondent unaware of the personality or attitude dimension that we wish to explore. For the present purposes, however, primarily the problem of deception in the context of the social psychological experiment will be discussed.

The use of deception has become more and more extensive, and it is now a commonplace and almost standard feature of social psychological experiments. Deception has been turned into a game, often played with great skill and virtuosity. A considerable amount of the creativity and ingenuity of social psychologists is invested in the development of increasingly elaborate deception situations. Within a single experiment, deception may be built upon deception in a delicately complex structure. The literature now contains a fair number of studies in which second- or even third-order deception was employed.

One well-known experiment (Festinger & Carlsmith, 1959), for example, involved a whole progression of deceptions. After the subjects had gone through an experimental task, the investigator made it clear—through word and gesture—that the experiment was over and that he would now "like to explain what this has been all about so you'll have some idea of why you were doing this [p. 205]." This explanation was false, however, and was designed to serve as a basis for the true experimental manipulation. The manipulation itself involved asking subjects to serve as the experimenter's accomplices. The task of the "accomplice" was to tell the next "subject" that the experiment in which he had just participated (which was

in fact a rather boring experience) had been interesting and enjoyable. He was also asked to be on call for unspecified future occasions on which his services as accomplice might be needed because "the regular fellow couldn't make it, and we had a subject scheduled [p. 205]." These newly recruited "accomplices," of course, were the true subjects, while the "subjects" were the experimenter's true accomplices. For their presumed services as "accomplices," the true subjects were paid in advance—half of them receiving $1, and half $20. When they completed their service, however, the investigators added injury to insult by asking them to return their hard-earned cash. Thus, in this one study, in addition to receiving the usual misinformation about the purpose of the experiment, the subject was given feedback that was really an experimental manipulation, was asked to be an accomplice who was really a subject, and was given a $20 bill that was really a will-o'-the-wisp. One wonders how much further in this direction we can go. Where will it all end?

It is easy to view this problem with alarm, but it is much more difficult to formulate an unambiguous position on the problem. As a working experimental social psycholgist, I cannot conceive the issue in absolutist terms. I am too well aware of the fact that there are good reasons for using deception in many experiments. There are many significant problems that probably cannot be investigated without the use of deception, at least not at the present level of development of our experimental methodology. Thus, we are always confronted with a conflict of values. If we regard the acquisition of scientific knowledge about human behavior as a positive value, and if an experiment using deception constitutes a significant contribution in such knowledge which could not very well be achieved by other means, then we cannot unequivocally rule out this experiment. The question for us is not simply whether it does or does not use deception, but whether the amount and type of deception are justified by the significance of the study and the unavailability of alternative (that is, deception-free) procedures.

I have expressed special concern about second-order deceptions, for example, the procedure of letting a person believe that he is acting as experimenter or as the experimenter's accomplice when he is in fact serving as the subject. Such a procedure undermines the relationship between experimenter and subject even further than simple misinformation about the purposes of the experiment; deception does not merely take place *within* the experiment, but encompasses the whole definition of the relationship between the parties involved. Deception that takes place while the person is within the role of subject for which he has contracted can, to some degree, be isolated, but deception about the very nature of the contract itself is more likely to suffuse the experimenter-subject relationship as a whole and to remove the possibility of mutual trust. Thus, I would be inclined to take a more absolutist stand with regard to such second-order deceptions—but even here the issue turns out to be more complicated. I am stopped short when I think, for example, of the ingenious studies on experimenter bias by Rosenthal and his associates (e.g., Rosenthal & Fode, 1963; Rosenthal, Persinger, Vikan-Kline, & Fode, 1963; Rosenthal, Persinger, Vikan-Kline, & Mulry, 1963). These experiments employed second-order deception in that subjects were led to believe that they were the experimenters. Since these were experiments about experiments, however, it is very hard to conceive of any alternative procedures that the investigators might have used. There is no question in my mind that these are significant studies; they provide fundamental inputs to present efforts at reexamining the social psychology of the experiment. These studies, then, help to underline even further the point that we are confronted with a conflict of values that cannot be resolved by fiat.

I hope it is clear from these remarks that my purpose in focusing on this problem is not to single out specific studies performed by some of my colleagues and to point a finger at them. Indeed, the finger points at me as well. I too have used deception, and have known the joys of applying my skills and ingenuity to the creation of elaborate experimental situations that the subjects would not be able to decode. I am now making active attempts to find alternatives to deception, but still I have not forsworn the use of deception under any and all circumstances. The questions I am raising, then, are addressed to myself as well as to my colleagues. They are questions with which all of us who are committed to social psychology must come to grips, lest we leave their resolution to others who have no understanding of what we are trying to accomplish.

What concerns me most is not so much that deception is used, but precisely that it is used without question. It has now become standard operating procedure in the social psychologist's laboratory. I sometimes feel that we are training a generation of students who do not know that there is any other way of doing experiments in our field—who feel that deception is as much de rigueur as significance at the .05 level. Too often deception is used not as a last resort, but as a matter of course. Our attitude seems to be that if you can deceive, why tell the truth? It is this unquestioning acceptance, this routinization of deception, that really concerns me.

I would like to turn now to a review of the bases for my concern with the problem of deception, and then suggest some possible approaches for dealing with it.

IMPLICATIONS OF THE USE OF DECEPTION IN SOCIAL PSYCHOLOGICAL EXPERIMENTS

My concern about the use of deception is based on three considerations: the ethical implications of such procedures, their methodological implications, and their implications for the future of social psychology.

1. *Ethical implications.* Ethical problems of a rather obvious nature arise in the experiments in which deception has potentially harmful consequences for the subject. Take, for example, the brilliant experiment by Mulder and Stemerding (1963) on the effects of threat on attraction to the group and need for strong leadership. In this study—one of the very rare examples of an experiment conducted in a natural setting—independent food merchants in a number of Dutch towns were brought together for group meetings, in the course of which they were informed that a large organization was planning to open up a series of supermarkets in the Netherlands. In the High Threat condition, subjects were told that there was a high probability that their town would be selected as a site for such markets, and that the advent of these markets would cause a considerable drop in their business. On the advice of the executives of the shopkeepers' organizations, who had helped to arrange the group meetings, the investigators did not reveal the experimental manipulations to their subjects. I have been worried about these Dutch merchants ever since I heard about this study for the first

time. Did some of them go out of business in anticipation of the heavy competition? Do some of them have an anxiety reaction every time they see a bulldozer? Chances are that they soon forgot about this threat (unless, of course, supermarkets actually did move into town) and that it became just one of the many little moments of anxiety that must occur in every shopkeeper's life. Do we have a right, however, to add to life's little anxieties and to risk the possibility of more extensive anxiety purely for the purposes of our experiments, particularly since deception deprives the subject of the opportunity to choose whether or not he wishes to expose himself to the risks that might be entailed?

The studies by Bramel (1962, 1963) and Bergin (1962) provide examples of another type of potentially harmful effects arising from the use of deception. In the Bramel studies, male undergraduates were led to believe that they were homosexually aroused by photographs of men. In the Bergin study, subjects of both sexes were given discrepant information about their level of masculinity or femininity; in one experimental condition, this information was presumably based on an elaborate series of psychological tests in which the subjects had participated. In all of these studies, the deception was explained to the subject at the end of the experiment. One wonders, however, whether such explanation removes the possibility of harmful effects. For many persons in this age group, sexual identity is still a live and sensitive issue, and the self-doubts generated by the laboratory experience may take on a life of their own and linger on for some time to come.

Yet another illustration of potentially harmful effects of deception can be found in Milgram's (1963, 1965) studies of obedience. In these experiments, the subject was led to believe that he was participating in a learning study and was instructed to administer increasingly severe shocks to another person who after a while began to protest vehemently. In fact, of course, the victim was an accomplice of the experimenter and did not receive any shocks. Depending on the conditions, sizable proportions of the subjects obeyed the experimenter's instructions and continued to shock the other person up to the maximum level, which they believed to be extremely painful. Both obedient and defiant subjects exhibited a great deal of stress in this

situation. The complexities of the issues surrounding the use of deception become quite apparent when one reads the exchange between Baumrind (1964) and Milgram (1964) about the ethical implications of the obedience research. There is clearly room for disagreement, among honorable people, about the evaluation of this research from an ethical point of view. Yet, there is good reason to believe that at least some of the obedient subjects came away from this experience with a lower self-esteem, having to live with the realization that they were willing to yield to destructive authority to the point of inflicting extreme pain on a fellow human being. The fact that this may have provided, in Milgram's (1964) words, "an opportunity to learn something of importance about themselves, and more generally, about the conditions of human action [p. 850]" is beside the point. If this were a lesson from life, it would indeed constitute an instructive confrontation and provide a valuable insight. But do we, for the purpose of experimentation, have the right to provide such potentially disturbing insights to subjects who do not know that this is what they are coming for? A similar question can be raised about the Asch (1951) experiments on group pressure, although the stressfulness of the situation and the implications for the person's self-concept were less intense in that context.

While the present paper is specifically focused on social psychological experiments, the problem of deception and its possibly harmful effects arises in other areas of psychological experimentation as well. Dramatic illustrations are provided by two studies in which subjects were exposed, for experimental purposes, to extremely stressful conditions. In an experiment designed to study the establishment of a conditioned response in a situation that is traumatic but not painful, Campbell, Sanderson, and Laverty (1964) induced—through the use of a drug—a temporary interruption of respiration in their subjects. "This has no permanently harmful physical consequences but is nonetheless a severe stress which is not in itself painful . . . [p. 628]." The subjects' reports confirmed that this was a "horrific" experience for them. "All the subjects in the standard series said that they thought they were dying [p. 631]." Of course the subjects, "male alcoholic patients who volunteered for the experiment when they were told that it was connected with a possible therapy for alcoholism [p. 629]," were not warned in advance about the effect of the drug, since this information would have reduced the traumatic impact of the experience.[3] In a series of studies on the effects of psychological stress, Berkun, Bialek, Kern, and Yagi (1962) devised a number of ingenious experimental situations designed to convince the subject that his life was actually in danger. In one situation, the subjects, a group of Army recruits, were actually "passengers aboard an apparently stricken plane which was being forced to 'ditch' or crash-land [p. 4]." In another experiment, an isolated subject in a desolate area learned that a sudden emergency had arisen (accidental nuclear radiation in the area, or a sudden forest fire, or misdirected artillery shells—depending on the experimental condition) and that he could be rescued only if he reported his position over his radio transmitter, "which has quite suddenly failed [p. 7]." In yet another situation, the subject was led to believe that he was responsible for an explosion that seriously injured another soldier. As the authors pointed out, reactions in these situations are more likely to approximate reactions to combat experiences or to naturally occurring disasters than are reactions to various laboratory stresses, but is the experimenter justified in exposing his subjects to such extreme threats?

So far, I have been speaking of experiments in which deception has potentially harmful consequences. I am equally concerned, however, about the less obvious cases, in which there is little danger of harmful effects, at least in the conventional sense of the term. Serious ethical issues are raised by deception per se and the kind of use of human beings that it implies. In our other interhuman relationships, most of us would never think of doing the kinds of things that we do to our subjects—exposing others to lies and tricks, deliberately misleading them about the purposes of the interaction or withholding pertinent information, making promises or giving assurances that we intend to disregard. We would view such behavior as a violation of the respect to which all fellow humans are entitled and of the whole basis of our relationship with them. Yet we seem to forget that the experimenter-subject relationship—whatever else it is—is a *real* interhuman relationship, in which we have responsibility toward the subject as another

human being whose dignity we must preserve. The discontinuity between the experimenter's behavior in everyday life and his behavior in the laboratory is so marked that one wonders why there has been so little concern with this problem, and what mechanisms have allowed us to ignore it to such an extent. I am reminded, in this connection, of the intriguing phenomenon of the "holiness of sin," which characterizes certain messianic movements as well as other movements of the true-believer variety. Behavior that would normally be unacceptable actually takes on an aura of virtue in such movements through a redefinition of the situation in which the behavior takes place and thus of the context for evaluating it. A similar mechanism seems to be involved in our attitude toward the psychological experiment. We tend to regard it as a situation that is not quite real, that can be isolated from the rest of life like a play performed on stage, and to which, therefore, the usual criteria for ethical interpersonal conduct become irrelevant. Behavior is judged entirely in the context of the experiment's scientific contribution and, in this context, deception—which is normally unacceptable—can indeed be seen as a positive good.

The broader ethical problem brought into play by the very use of deception becomes even more important when we view it in the light of present historical forces. We are living in an age of mass societies in which the transformation of man into an object to be manipulated at will occurs "on a mass scale, in a systematic way, and under the aegis of specialized institutions deliberately assigned to this task [Kelman, 1965]." In institutionalizing the use of deception in psychological experiments, we are, then, contributing to a historical trend that threatens values most of us cherish.

2. *Methodological implications.* A second source of my concern about the use of deception is my increasing doubt about its adequacy as a methodology for social psychology.

A basic assumption in the use of deception is that a subject's awareness of the conditions that we are trying to create and of the phenomena that we wish to study would affect his behavior in such a way that we could not draw valid conclusions from it. For example, if we are interested in studying the effects of failure on conformity, we must create a situation in which the subjects actually feel that they have failed, and in which they can be kept unaware of our interest in observing conformity. In short, it is important to keep our subjects naïve about the purposes of the experiment so that they can respond to the experimental inductions spontaneously.

How long, however, will it be possible for us to find naïve subjects? Among college students, it is already very difficult. They may not know the exact purpose of the particular experiment in which they are participating, but at least they know, typically, that it is *not* what the experimenter says it is. Orne (1962) pointed out that the use of deception "on the part of psychologists is so widely known in the college population that even if a psychologist is honest with the subject, more often than not he will be distrusted." As one subject pithily put it, "'Psychologists always lie!'" Orne added that "This bit of paranoia has some support in reality [pp. 778–779]." There are, of course, other sources of human subjects that have not been tapped, and we could turn to them in our quest for naïveté. But even there it is only a matter of time. As word about psychological experiments gets around in whatever network we happen to be using, sophistication is bound to increase. I wonder, therefore, whether there is any future in the use of deception.

If the subject in a deception experiment knows what the experimenter is trying to conceal from him and what he is really after in the study, the value of the deception is obviously nullified. Generally, however, even the relatively sophisticated subject does not know the exact purpose of the experiment; he only has suspicions, which may approximate the true purpose of the experiment to a greater or lesser degree. Whether or not he knows the *true* purpose of the experiment, he is likely to make an effort to figure out its purpose, since he does not believe what the experimenter tells him, and therefore he is likely to operate in the situation in terms of his own hypothesis of what is involved. This may, in line with Orne's (1962) analysis, lead him to do what he thinks the experimenter wants him to do. Conversely, if he resents the experimenter's attempt to deceive him, he may try to throw a monkey wrench into the works; I would not be surprised if this kind of Schweikian game among subjects became a fairly well-established part of the culture of sophisticated campuses. Whichever course the subject uses, however, he is operating in terms of

his own conception of the nature of the situation, rather than in terms of the conception that the experimenter is trying to induce. In short, the experimenter can no longer assume that the conditions that he is trying to create are the ones that actually define the situation for the subject. Thus, the use of deception, while it is designed to give the experimenter control over the subject's perceptions and motivations, may actually produce an unspecifiable mixture of intended and unintended stimuli that make it difficult to know just what the subject is responding to.

The tendency for subjects to react to unintended cues—to features of the situation that are not part of the experimenter's design—is by no means restricted to experiments that involve deception. This problem has concerned students of the interview situation for some time, and more recently it has been analyzed in detail in the writings and research of Riecken, Rosenthal, Orne, and Mills. Subjects enter the experiment with their own aims, including attainment of certain rewards, divination of the experimenter's true purposes, and favorable self-presentation (Riecken, 1962). They are therefore responsive to demand characteristics of the situation (Orne, 1962), to unintended communications of the experimenter's expectations (Rosenthal, 1963), and to the role of the experimenter within the social system that experimenter and subject jointly constitute (Mills, 1962). In any experiment, then, the subject goes beyond the description of the situation and the experimental manipulation introduced by the investigator, makes his own interpretation of the situation, and acts accordingly.

For several reasons, however, the use of deception especially encourages the subject to dismiss the stated purposes of the experiment and to search for alternative interpretations of his own. First, the continued use of deception establishes the reputation of psychologists as people who cannot be believed. Thus, the desire "to penetrate the experimenter's inscrutability and discover the rationale of the experiment [Riecken, 1962, p. 34]" becomes especially strong. Generally, these efforts are motivated by the subject's desire to meet the expectations of the experimenter and of the situation. They may also be motivated, however, as I have already mentioned, by a desire to outwit the experimenter and to beat him at his own game, in a spirit of genuine hostility or playful one-upmanship. Second, a situation involving the use of deception is inevitably highly ambiguous since a great deal of information relevant to understanding the structure of the situation must be withheld from the subject. Thus, the subject is especially motivated to try to figure things out and likely to develop idiosyncratic interpretations. Third, the use of deception, by its very nature, causes the experimenter to transmit contradictory messages to the subject. In his verbal instructions and explanations he says one thing about the purposes of the experiment; but in the experimental situation that he has created, in the manipulations that he has introduced, and probably in covert cues that he emits, he says another thing. This again makes it imperative for the subject to seek his own interpretation of the situation.

I would argue, then, that deception increases the subject's tendency to operate in terms of his private definition of the situation, differing (in random or systematic fashion) from the definition that the experimenter is trying to impose; moreover, it makes it more difficult to evaluate or minimize the effects of this tendency. Whether or not I am right in this judgment, it can, at the very least, be said that the use of deception does not resolve or reduce the unintended effects of the experiment as a social situation in which the subject pursues his private aims. Since the assumptions that the subject is naïve and that he sees the situation as the experimenter wishes him to see it are unwarranted, the use of deception no longer has any special obvious advantages over other experimental approaches. I am not suggesting that there may not be occasions when deception may still be the most effective procedure to use from a methodological point of view. But since it raises at least as many methodological problems as any other type of procedure does, we have every reason to explore alternative approaches and to extend our methodological inquiries to the question of the effects of using deception.

3. Implications for the future of social psychology. My third concern about the use of deception is based on its long-run implications for our discipline and combines both the ethical and methodological considerations that I have already raised. There is something disturbing about the idea of relying on massive deception as the basis for developing a field of inquiry. Can one really build a discipline on a foundation of such research?

From a long-range point of view, there is obviously something self-defeating about the use of deception. As we continue to carry out research of this kind, our potential subjects become more and more sophisticated, and we become less and less able to meet the conditions that our experimental procedures require. Moreover, as we continue to carry out research of this kind, our potential subjects become increasingly distrustful of us, and our future relations with them are likely to be undermined. Thus, we are confronted with the anomalous circumstance that the more research we do, the more difficult and questionable it becomes.

The use of deception also involves a contradiction between our experimental procedures and our long-range aims as scientists and teachers. In order to be able to carry out our experiments, we are concerned with maintaining the naïveté of the population from which we hope to draw our subjects. We are all familiar with the experimenter's anxious concern that the introductory course might cover the autokinetic phenomenon, need achievement, or the Asch situation before he has had a chance to complete his experimental runs. This perfectly understandable desire to keep procedures secret goes counter to the traditional desire of the scientist and teacher to inform and enlighten the public. To be sure, experimenters are interested only in temporary secrecy, but it is not inconceivable that at some time in the future they might be using certain procedures on a regular basis with large segments of the population and thus prefer to keep the public permanently naïve. It is perhaps not too fanciful to imagine, for the long run, the possible emergence of a special class, in possession of secret knowledge—a possibility that is clearly antagonistic to the principle of open communication to which we, as scientists and intellectuals, are so fervently committed.

DEALING WITH THE PROBLEM OF DECEPTION IN SOCIAL PSYCHOLOGICAL EXPERIMENTS

If my concerns about the use of deception are justified, what are some of the ways in which we, as experimental social psychologists, can deal with them? I would like to suggest three steps that we can take: increase our active awareness of the problem, explore ways of counteracting and minimizing the negative effects of deception, and give careful attention to the development of new experimental techniques that dispense with the use of deception.

1. *Active awareness of the problem.* I have already stressed that I would not propose the complete elimination of deception under all circumstances, in view of the genuine conflict of values with which the experimenter is confronted. What is crucial, however, is that we always ask ourselves the question whether deception, in the given case, is necessary and justified. How we answer the question is less important than the fact that we ask it. What we must be wary of is the tendency to dismiss the question as irrelevant and to accept deception as a matter of course. Active awareness of the problem is thus in itself part of the solution for it makes the use of deception a matter for discussion, deliberation, investigation, and choice. Active awareness means that, in any given case, we will try to balance the value of an experiment that uses deception against its questionable or potentially harmful effects. If we engage in this process honestly, we are likely to find that there are many occasions when we or our students can forego the use of deception—either because deception is not necessary (that is, alternative procedures that are equally good or better are available), because the importance of the study does not warrant the use of an ethically questionable procedure, or because the type of deception involved is too extreme (in terms of the possibility of harmful effects or of seriously undermining the experimenter-subject relationship).

2. *Counteracting and minimizing the negative effects of deception.* If we do use deception, it is essential that we find ways of counteracting and minimizing its negative effects. Sensitizing the apprentice researcher to this necessity is at least as fundamental as any other part of research training.

In those experiments in which deception carries the potential of harmful effects (in the more usual sense of the term), there is an obvious requirement to build protections into every phase of the process. Subjects must be selected in a way that will exclude individuals who are especially vulnerable; the potentially harmful manipulation (such as the induction of stress) must be kept at a moderate level of intensity; the experimenter must be sensitive to danger signals in the reactions of his subjects and be prepared to deal with crises when they arise; and, at the conclusion of the session, the experimenter must take time not only to reassure the subject, but also to help him work through his feelings about the experience to whatever degree may be required. In general, the principle that a subject ought not to leave the laboratory with greater anxiety or lower self-esteem than he came with is a good one to follow. I would go beyond it to argue that the subject should in some positive way be enriched by the experience, that is, he should come away from it with the feeling that he has learned something, understood something, or grown in some way. This, of course, adds special importance to the kind of feedback that is given to the subject at the end of the experimental session.

Postexperimental feedback is, of course, the primary way of counteracting negative effects in those experiments in which the issue is deception as such, rather than possible threats to the subject's well-being. If we do deceive the subject, then it is our obligation to give him a full and detailed explanation of what we have done and of our reasons for using this type of procedure. I do not want to be absolutist about this, but I would suggest it as a good rule of thumb to follow: Think very carefully before undertaking an experiment whose purposes you feel unable to reveal to the subjects even after they have completed the experimental session. It is, of course not enough to give the subject a perfunctory feedback, just to do one's duty. Postexperimental explanations should be worked out with as much detail as other aspects of the procedure and, in general, some thought ought to be given to ways of making them meaningful and instructive for the subject and helpful for rebuilding his relationship with the experimenter. I feel very strongly that to accomplish these purposes, we must keep the feedback itself inviolate and under no circumstance give the subject false feedback or pretend to be giving him feedback while we are in fact introducing another experimental manipulation. If we hope to maintain any kind of trust in our relationship with potential subjects, there must be no ambiguity that the statement "The experiment is over and I shall explain to you what it was all about" means precisely that and nothing else. If subjects have reason to suspect even that statement, then we have lost the whole basis for a decent human relationship with our subjects and all hope for future cooperation from them.

3. *Development of new experimental techniques.* My third and final suggestion is that we invest some of the creativity and ingenuity, now devoted to the construction of elaborate deceptions, in the search for alternative experimental techniques that do not rely on the use of deception. The kind of techniques that I have in mind would be based on the principle of eliciting the subject's positive motivations to contribute to the experimental enterprise. They would draw on the subject's active participation and involvement in the proceedings and encourage him to cooperate in making the experiment a success—not by giving the results he thinks the experimenter wants, but by conscientiously taking the roles and carrying out the tasks that the experimenter assigns to him. In short, the kind of techniques I have in mind would be designed to involve the subject as an active participant in a joint effort with the experimenter.

Perhaps the most promising source of alternative experimental approaches are procedures using some sort of role playing. I have been impressed, for example, with the role playing that I have observed in the context of the Inter-Nation Simulation (Guetzkow, Alger, Brody, Noel, & Snyder, 1963), a laboratory procedure involving a simulated world in which the subjects take the roles of decision-makers of various nations. This situation seems to create a high level of emotional involvement and to elicit motivations that have a real-life quality to them. Moreover, within this situation—which is highly complex and generally permits only gross experimental manipulations—it is possible to test specific theoretical hypotheses by using data based on repeated measurements as interaction between the simulated nations develops. Thus, a study carried out at the Western Behavioral Sciences Institute provided, as an extra, some interesting opportunities for testing hypotheses derived from balance theory, by the use of mutual ratings made by decision-makers of Nations A, B, and C, before and after A shifted from an alliance with B to an alliance with C.

A completely different type of role playing was used effectively by Rosenberg and Abelson (1960) in their studies of cognitive dilemmas. In my own research program, we have been exploring different kinds of role-playing procedures with varying degrees of success. In one study, the major manipulation consisted in informing subjects that the experiment to

which they had just committed themselves would require them (depending on the condition) either to receive shocks from a fellow subject, or to administer shocks to a fellow subject. We used a regular deception procedure, but with a difference: We told the subjects before the session started that what was to follow was make-believe, but that we wanted them to react as if they really found themselves in this situation. I might mention that some subjects, not surprisingly, did not accept as true the information that this was all make-believe and wanted to know when they should show up for the shock experiment to which they had committed themselves. I have some questions about the effectiveness of this particular procedure. It did not do enough to create a high level of involvement, and it turned out to be very complex since it asked subjects to role-play subjects, not people. In this sense, it might have given us the worst of both worlds, but I still think it is worth some further exploration. In another experiment, we were interested in creating differently structured attitudes about an organization by feeding different kinds of information to two groups of subjects. These groups were then asked to take specific actions in support of the organization, and we measured attitude changes resulting from these actions. In the first part of the experiment, the subjects were clearly informed that the organization and the information that we were feeding to them were fictitious, and that we were simply trying to simulate the conditions under which attitudes about new organizations are typically formed. In the second part of the experiment, the subjects were told that we were interested in studying the effects of action in support of an organization on attitudes toward it, and they were asked (in groups of five) to role-play a strategy meeting of leaders of the fictitious organization. The results of this study were very encouraging. While there is obviously a great deal that we need to know about the meaning of this situation to the subjects, they did react differentially to the experimental manipulations and these reactions followed an orderly pattern, despite the fact that they knew it was all make-believe.

There are other types of procedures, in addition to role playing, that are worth exploring. For example, one might design field experiments in which, with the full cooperation of the subjects, specific experimental variations are introduced. The advantages of dealing with motivations at a real-life level of intensity might well outweigh the disadvantages of subjects' knowing the general purpose of the experiment. At the other extreme of ambitiousness, one might explore the effects of modifying standard experimental procedures slightly by informing the subject at the beginning of the experiment that he will not be receiving full information about what is going on, but asking him to suspend judgment until the experiment is over.

Whatever alternative approach we try, there is no doubt that it will have its own problems and complexities. Procedures effective for some purposes may be quite ineffective for others, and it may well turn out that for certain kinds of problems there is no adequate substitute for the use of deception. But there *are* alternative procedures that, for many purposes, may be as effective or even more effective than procedures built on deception. These approaches often involve a radically different set of assumptions about the role of the subject in the experiment: They require us to *use* the subject's motivation to cooperate rather than to bypass it; they may even call for increasing the sophistication of potential subjects, rather than maintaining their naïveté. My only plea is that we devote some of our energies to active exploration of these alternative approaches.

REFERENCES

Asch, S. E. Effects of group pressure upon the modification and distortion of judgments. In H. Guetzkow (Ed.), *Groups, leadership, and men.* Pittsburgh: Carnegie Press, 1951. Pp. 117–190.

Baumrind, D. Some thoughts on ethics of research: After reading Milgram's "Behavioral Study of Obedience." *American Psychologist,* 1964, **19,** 421–423.

Bergin, A. E. The effect of dissonant persuasive communications upon changes in a self-referring attitude. *Journal of Personality,* 1962, **30,** 423–438.

Berkun, M. M., Bialek, H. M., Kern, R. P., & Yagi, K. Experimental studies of psychological stress in man. *Psychological Monographs,* 1962, **76**(15, Whole No. 534).

Bramel, D. A dissonance theory approach to defensive projection. *Journal of Abnormal and Social Psychology,* 1962, **64,** 121–129.

Bramel, D. Selection of a target for defensive projection.

Journal of Abnormal and Social Psychology, 1963, **66,** 318–324.

Campbell, D., Sanderson, R. E., & Laverty, S. G. Characteristics of a conditioned response in human subjects during extinction trials following a single traumatic conditioning trial. *Journal of Abnormal and Social Psychology,* 1964, **68,** 627–639.

Festinger, L., & Carlsmith, J. M. Cognitive consequences of forced compliance. *Journal of Abnormal and Social Psychology,* 1959, **58,** 203–210.

Guetzkow, H., Alger, C. F., Brody, R. A., Noel, R. C., & Snyder, R. C. *Simulation in international relations.* Englewood Cliffs, N.J.: Prentice-Hall, 1963.

Kelman, H. C. Manipulation of human behavior: An ethical dilemma for the social scientist. *Journal of Social Issues,* 1965, **21**(2), 31–46.

Milgram, S. Behavioral study of obedience. *Journal of Abnormal and Social Psychology,* 1963, **67,** 371–378.

Milgram, S. Issues in the study of obedience: A reply to Baumrind. *American Psychologist,* 1964, **19,** 848–852.

Milgram, S. Some conditions of obedience and disobedience to authority. *Human Relations,* 1965, **18,** 57–76.

Mills, T. M. A sleeper variable in small groups research: The experimenter. *Pacific Sociological Review,* 1962, **5,** 21–28.

Mulder, M., & Stemerding, A. Threat, attraction to group, and need for strong leadership. *Human Relations,* 1963, **16,** 317–334.

Orne, M. T. On the social psychology of the psychological experiment: With particular reference to demand characteristics and their implications. *American Psychologist,* 1962, **17,** 776–783.

Riecken, H. W. A program for research on experiments in social psychology. In N. F. Washburne (Ed.), *Decisions, values and groups.* Vol. 2. New York: Pergamon Press, 1962. Pp. 25–41.

Rosenberg, M. J., & Abelson, R. P. An analysis of cognitive balancing. In M. J. Rosenberg et al., *Attitude organization and change.* New Haven: Yale University Press, 1960. Pp. 112–163.

Rosenthal, R. On the social psychology of the psychological experiment: The experimenter's hypothesis as unintended determinant of experimental results. *American Scientist,* 1963, **51,** 268–283.

Rosenthal, R., & Fode, K. L. Psychology of the scientist: V. Three experiments in experimenter bias. *Psychological Reports,* 1963, **12,** 491–511. (Monogr. Suppl. 3-V12)

Rosenthal, R., Persinger, G. W., Vikan-Kline, L., & Fode, K. L. The effect of early data returns on data subsequently obtained by outcome-biased experimenters. *Sociometry*, 1963, **26**, 487–498.

Rosenthal, R., Persinger, G. W., Vikan-Kline, L., & Mulry, R. C. The role of the research assistant in the mediation of experimenter bias. *Journal of Personality*, 1963, **31**, 313–335.

Vinacke, W. E. Deceiving experimental subjects. *American Psychologist*, 1954, **9**, 155.

ENDNOTES

1. Paper read at the symposium on "Ethical and Methodological Problems in Social Psychological Experiments," held at the meetings of the American Psychological Association in Chicago, September 3, 1965. This paper is a product of a research program on social influence and behavior change supported by United States Public Health Service Research Grant MH-07280 from the National Institute of Mental Health.

2. In focusing on deception in *social* psychological experiments, I do not wish to give the impression that there is no serious problem elsewhere. Deception is widely used in most studies involving human subjects and gives rise to issues similar to those discussed in this paper. Some examples of the use of deception in other areas of psychological experimentation will be presented later in this paper.

3. The authors reported, however, that some of their other subjects were physicians familiar with the drug; "they did not suppose they were dying but, even though they knew in a general way what to expect, they too said that the experience was extremely harrowing [p. 632]." Thus, conceivably, the purposes of the experiment might have been achieved even if the subjects had been told to expect the temporary interruption of breathing.

CRITICAL THINKING QUESTIONS

1. Which of the studies mentioned in the article involves the greatest ethical issues? Why? Select one of the studies cited in this article, and suggest an alternative to the type of deception that was employed.

2. Should the use of deception be banned? Why or why not? If not, under what conditions should it be allowed? What impact would such a limitation have on social psychological research? Defend your position.

3. Who should determine what constitutes an ethically appropriate experiment? Professors? Students? Outside laypeople? Explain your answer. What would be the ideal composition of a board charged with reviewing research proposals? Why?

4. Obtain a copy of the current "American Psychological Association Guide for the Ethical Treatment of Human Subjects." Review these guidelines, considering how comprehensive they are. What criteria should be used in determining what is in the best interests of the subjects of an experiment?

5. What do you think of Kelman's position on "second-order" deception? Do you agree that it is of even greater concern than standard ("first-order") deception practices? Why or why not?

6. What do you think of Kelman's suggestions for the development of new experimental techniques as an alternative to deception? Find a research study that tried such a technique in lieu of deception. Alternatively, find a research study reported in this book of readings and suggest an alternative to the deception that was used. In either case, what might be lost and what might be gained by not deceiving subjects? Explain your answer.

ADDITIONAL RELATED READINGS

Russo, N. F. (1999). Putting the *APA Publication Manual* in context. *Psychology of Women Quarterly, 23*(2), 399–402.

Thompson, A., & Fata, M. (1997). Relating the psychological literature to the American Psychological Association ethical standards. *Ethics & Behavior, 7*, 79–88.

ARTICLE 3 ⎯⎯⎯⎯⎯⎯⎯⎯⎯⎯⎯⎯⎯⎯⎯⎯⎯

Social psychology can be defined as the "scientific field of study that investigates how people's feelings, thoughts, and behaviors are influenced by other people." Given this rather broad definition, the scope of what comes under the heading of social psychology is large, indeed. Think, for a second, about your own life. What aspects of your life are truly independent of social influences? Obviously, when you are with other people, social factors are likely operating. But what about when you are alone?

To take an extreme example, suppose you were stranded on a deserted island. Would your behavior still be influenced by social factors? The answer is yes and no: No, because no one would be around to have an immediate impact on your behaviors, thoughts, and feelings. But yes, because you already would have acquired your beliefs, your emotional responses to the world, and your tendency to act in certain ways. The fact is, we are social creatures, and what we are now is the product of all the social encounters that we have experienced in the past.

Given that the domain of social psychology is the whole realm of human social interaction, what questions should the discipline address? For example, social psychology could investigate obvious social phenomena, such as the tendency for people to be more attracted to physically appealing individuals. Or at the other extreme, social psychology could investigate aspects of social phenomena that are obscure and even superfluous, such as why people tend to be more willing to believe their own lies if someone gives them $1 for telling the lie than if they are given $20 for telling the same lie. Thus, social psychology can address questions that range from the trivial to the critically important.

The following article by F. D. Richard, Charles F. Bond, Jr., and Juli J. Stokes-Zoota examines the issue of what the general public thinks of social psychological research. Do laypeople share the same views as social psychologists as to what research topics are important? Furthermore, do laypeople often think that social psychological research only investigates and confirms the obvious? And how do social psychologists compare in terms of what they find important? Since laypeople include both members of the general public and decision makers such as politicians, who often determine how funding will be allocated for the social sciences, the implications of the findings presented in this article are very important.

"That's Completely Obvious . . . and Important"
Lay Judgments of Social Psychological Findings

■ F. D. Richard, Charles F. Bond, Jr., and Juli J. Stokes-Zoota

Many social psychologists believe that if research results are obvious, they are unimportant and uninteresting. The current study evaluated lay perceptions of social psychological research findings. Results from three studies reveal differences between lay evaluations of research and scientific evaluations. In Study 1, students with no prior

Reprinted from F. D. Richard, C. F. Bond, Jr., and J. J. Stokes-Zoota, *Personality and Social Psychology Bulletin, 27*(4) pp. 497–505, copyright © 2001 by Sage Publications, Inc. Reprinted by permission of Sage Publications, Inc.

exposure to social psychology judge the most obvious research findings to be the most important. In Study 2, students can predict findings, and the most predictable findings are judged most important. In Study 3, students judge the most obvious findings to be most important to establish with research. Results address the accuracy of lay judgments of research, judgmental strategies, and the process by which social psychologists select research topics.

Many social psychologists seek novel research results. Milgram's studies of obedience to authority, Asch's experiments on conformity, and LaPiere's test of attitude-behavior consistency produced some of the early novelties of the field. A social psychologist may spend years attempting to nullify or reverse a commonly accepted research observation (Lepper, Keavney, & Drake, 1996). Many counterintuitive discoveries are published in the most prestigious journals.

Scientists often judge the scientific impact of a research finding from its obviousness (Miller & Pollock, 1994). Abelson (1995), in fact, listed "surprisingness" as one of the criteria that determine the interestingness and importance of psychological research findings. In an influential discussion of social psychological research, Aronson, Ellsworth, Carlsmith, and Gonzales (1990) noted that people view scientific conclusions as "trivial" if the research finding is "common knowledge" (p. 79). Many journal reviewers and editors discourage research findings that simply rediscover what was already known (Miller & Pollock, 1994).

Despite social psychologists' search for extraordinary and surprised findings, much social psychological research was historically viewed as obvious and uninformative. Humphrey and Argyle (1962) noted a common reaction to social psychology—"the results of much social research are not surprising, that we knew them all before" (p. 14). Critiques of social research conducted during World War II suggested that the resulting information could have been deduced with "far greater psychological insight" from the writings of nonpsychologists (Schlessinger, 1949, p. 854). Critics argue that social psychology is a pseudo-science that provides little knowledge beyond common sense (see Furnham, 1983).

THE LAY PERSON'S REACTION TO RESEARCH

Similar to social psychologists, lay people have beliefs about human social behavior (Kruglanski, 1989). Some scientists claim that "the layman's understanding of human nature is both extensive and reliable" (Joynson, 1974, p. 16). Heider (1958) provided considerable insight into lay persons' use of social knowledge to explain and predict events in their life. A college student might, for example, attempt to determine why he or she was not invited to a particular party. The college student may investigate several alternative explanations and draw inferences about his or her own behavior and the behavior of others. Indeed, the use of common knowledge to conduct a form of lay social psychology may saturate the human experience.

Many other examples of lay persons using common knowledge in a form of lay psychology can be provided. People develop naïve theories about their social environment to assist them in making predictions about future social encounters (Anderson & Lindsay, 1998; Wegener & Petty, 1998). Implicit personality theory (Schneider, 1973) and theories on the role of others' views of one's self-concept (see Kinch, 1963) imply that people can be accurate about the traits and views of acquaintances. A recent program of research (Kenny, 1994) showed that people make consensual, accurate judgments of others' personality characteristics.

Given the many intuitions that people have about social psychology, one might expect the lay person to find the conclusions of scientific social psychology to be relatively obvious. Instructors of social psychology courses, for example, may have experienced such "obvious" reactions to the research presented in textbooks and in lectures. Students have casually gained knowledge of social behavior through everyday experiences and through the transmission of cultural folklore (Lee, 1988; Ziman, 1978). Research findings that match intuition may seem trivial to the lay person and be viewed as uninformative and of little personal relevance (Slovic & Fischhoff, 1977; Townsend, 1995).

Although many people have reservations about social psychological research findings, their reservations may not be valid. People may regard research findings as obvious because of a hindsight bias (Miller & Pollock, 1994). After the fact, people may interpret an event as though they "knew it all along," regardless of their prior expectations (Davies, 1987; Slovic & Fischhoff, 1977). Lazarsfeld (1949) exploited the hindsight bias in his review of the research results presented in *The American Soldier* series. After presenting several seemingly obvious findings and supporting arguments, Lazarsfeld informed the reader that the actual results are exactly opposite the ones previously presented.

OBVIOUSNESS INVESTIGATED

Several studies have assessed the obviousness and predictability of research results. One study (Gordon, Kleiman, & Hanie, 1978) assessed the predictability of research findings in industrial-organizational psychology. Gordon et al. (1978) abstracted 61 research findings from articles published in refereed industrial-organizational journals. Half of the findings were changed to reflect the opposite of the research result. Nonpsychologists, on average, correctly identified 67% of the research findings in industrial-organizational psychology (with 50% representing chance responding). As Gordon et al. noted, these results demonstrate the common sense character of industrial-organizational research.

Other studies have demonstrated that people with limited psychological training know many of the research findings presented in textbooks. Barnett (1986), for example, selected findings from psychology of personality textbooks, including findings on aggression, self-esteem, and gender roles. Nonpsychologists made true or false judgments of these research findings as well as foils developed from the findings. High school students correctly identified 66% of the findings (with 50% representing chance responding). Students show similar levels of knowledge of findings presented in textbooks on developmental psychology (Barnett, Knust, McMillan, Kaufman, & Sinisi, 1988).

Although students can accurately predict some of the findings of psychological research, they are not invariably accurate. Relevant studies indicate that people have a large number of misconceptions about psychology (e.g., Brown, 1983; Lamal, 1979;

Vaughan, 1977). Brown (1983), for example, provided 37 true or false statements about psychology to college students. Approximately half of the statements were answered incorrectly by the majority of the students. Of the students, 84%, for example, agreed with the statement that "people who are weak in some academic subjects are usually good in others."

Students are not able to predict research results on the processes and products of teaching (Wong, 1995). In a recent study, Wong provided students with brief descriptions of research findings on the psychology of teaching with foils that expressed the opposite of each finding. Students considered both the finding and the opposite statement and were to indicate which statement reflected the actual finding. Many of the foils were chosen more often than the corresponding finding.

Empirical investigations to date on the obviousness of research have focused only on a small number of findings from a few areas of psychology. The research presented by Barnett (1986), for example, was restricted to 60 findings that had been presented in textbooks on personality. Although research in social psychology is believed to be relatively obvious (Gordon et al., 1978; Schlessinger, 1949), no large-scale empirical investigation into the obviousness of social psychological findings has been reported.

The goal of the current research is to address two questions about social psychology. First, how obvious are social psychological research findings? Second, how do people react to social psychological research findings that are perceived as obvious? The obviousness of social psychological research findings and the reaction of the nonscientists to such research are investigated. Results should elucidate the relationships between different components of lay evaluations of research and may have implications for cognitive mechanisms involved in judgments of obviousness. Studies 1 and 3 solicit lay judgments of social psychological research findings. Study 2 assesses the predictability of social psychological results.

STUDY 1

College students evaluated a large number of research findings on a broad range of topics in social psychology. Study 1 examined students' judgments of the obviousness, importance, and interestingness of these research findings. These judgments will provide information regarding the obviousness of social psychological research and may suggest more generally how the lay person responds to research findings in the social sciences.

Method

Participants. The participants were 204 introductory psychology students. Twenty-four students assessed statements of social psychological findings for clarity, and 180 students judged the findings for obviousness, importance, and interestingness. Study 1 was conducted early in an academic semester, prior to research participants' receiving any course exposure to social psychological research. Students received credit toward their final grade in the introductory psychology course for participation in the experiment.

Materials. Social psychological findings published in meta-analyses served as the set of materials to be evaluated by participants. The meta-analyses were obtained from a search of various computer databases and through browsing issues of *Psychological Bulletin*. A meta-analytic finding was selected if the topic of the analysis appeared in a recent encyclopedia of social psychology (Manstead & Hewstone, 1995). Perusing the Abstract, Results, and Discussion sections of each meta-analysis, we generated statements of the broadest conclusions reached in the meta-analysis.

These conclusions were worded in everyday language. A meta-analytic conclusion about aggression (Paik & Comstock, 1994), for example, was stated as follows: "Exposure to mass media violence increases aggression." A finding on the recognition of emotional facial expressions (Russell, 1994) was phrased as follows: "People can recognize facial expressions of emotion across cultures." The search resulted in 398 distinct social psychological findings from 322 meta-analytic documents. The 398 findings concerned 18 different social psychological topics. For the current study, three sets of findings were prepared. Set 1 contained 128 findings on aggression, gender roles, group processes, motivation, relationships, and social cognition; set 2 contained 135 findings on expectancy effects, health psychology, law, leadership, nonverbal

communication, and personality; and set 3 contained 135 findings on attitudes, attribution, helping, intergroup relations, methodology, and social influence.

Each set of findings was presented in one of two orders. Half of the participants received the six topics in random order, whereas the other half of the participants received these six topics in the opposite order. In each set, the findings on a given topic were presented in conjunction with one another; findings from different topics were listed on different pages. Within each topic heading, half of the participants received the findings in one random order; the other half of the participants received them in the opposite order. For clarity, a few statements were always presented in immediate succession. For example, the following three research findings on Fiedler's (1964) Contingency Theory were presented consecutively under the topic area of leadership: "In favorable situations, task-oriented leaders are most effective"; "In unfavorable situations, task-oriented leaders are most effective"; "In intermediate situations, morale-oriented leaders are most effective."

Procedure. One experimenter obtained judgments over several 1-hour sessions with no more than 16 participants per session. The participants made judgments while seated in a small classroom. After arriving at a classroom, participants were given a consent form, an answer sheet, and a set of findings. The experimenter informed the participants that they would be making judgments about findings of social psychological research. The experimenter then described a judgment task.

Clarity Judgment. Twenty-four students evaluated the clarity of each finding. Each student received a set of findings in one of the orders described above. The experimenter instructed the students to "indicate whether you can or cannot understand each of these social psychological research findings." The experimenter instructed the students "not to indicate whether they agreed with the finding." The experimenter gave the students course credit following the completion of these judgments.

On average, participants judged 89% of the findings to be understandable. Although we attempted to avoid professional jargon in wording all 398 social psychological findings, 16 of the findings were judged not to be understandable by at least half of the participants making these judgments. These 16 findings were rephrased and included among the 398 findings to be evaluated for obviousness, importance, and interestingness by other students.

Evaluative Judgments. Students provided evaluative judgments of social psychological findings. Each experimental session included one of three judgment tasks. At some sessions, participants were told to indicate "whether each research finding is obvious or not obvious." At other sessions, participants were told to indicate "whether each research finding is important or not important." At other sessions, participants were told to indicate "whether each research finding is interesting or not interesting." The terms "obvious," "important," and "interesting" were not defined for the participants; however, students were instructed to refrain from evaluating the findings on any dimension other than the one requested (e.g., "Do not indicate if you agree or disagree with the statement."). Each participant made only one type of judgment and was unaware that any other judgments of the findings were being made. All participants gave a binary response to each finding and completed their judgment task in less than 60 minutes.

Results and Discussion

A preliminary analysis was conducted to assess the reliability of lay judgments of research. The percentage of times a research finding was judged as obvious, important, or interesting by participants who saw the findings in one order was correlated with the percentage of times the same judgment was made by participants who saw the findings in the reverse order. Based on the split-half method, the effective interrater reliability (by the Spearman-Brown formula) was .87, .66, and .57 for judgments of obviousness, importance, and interestingness, respectively. Judgments of obviousness show high interrater reliability. Judgments of importance and interestingness show moderate interrater reliability.

Critics have charged that social psychological research findings are obvious, unimportant, and uninteresting. If these charges are correct, one might expect most of the findings to be judged obvious and only a few to be judged important and interesting. To

see whether students have the same reaction, judgments were accumulated across participants for each of the 398 research findings. The average finding was judged to be obvious by 51.88% of the students, important by 64.06% of the students, and interesting by 58.64% of the students, cross-finding SDs = 27.05%, 17.08%, and 16.54%, respectively. Students judge half of these social psychological findings to be obvious. They judge more than half of the findings to be important and interesting. These data do not support the usual criticisms of social psychological research. See Table 1 for judgments of a few illustrative findings.

Although the obviousness, importance, and interestingness of research findings were judged by three separate groups of students, one might imagine that the judgments would be interrelated. Psychologists suggest that the most interesting and important findings are those that violate expectations, transcend existing knowledge, and are least obvious. To determine whether students have the same view, we checked for relationships among the obviousness, the importance, and the interestingness of the 398 social psychological research findings. We did so by noting for each of the findings the percentage of students who judged the finding to be obvious, the percentage who judged that finding to be important, and the percentage who judged it to be interesting.

A surprising relationship emerged: Findings that are judged to be highly obvious are judged to be highly important, $r(396) = +.47$ $p < .0005$, for the correlation between the percentage of students who judge a finding obvious and those who judge it important. In addition, obvious research findings are judged to be somewhat less interesting than nonobvious findings, $r(396) = -.20$, $p < .0005$. The percentage of students who judge a finding important and the percentage of students who judge a finding interesting are not significantly interrelated, $r(396) = +.04$, $p = .43$.

Lay consumers have different reactions to research than do research practitioners. Psychologists consider obvious social psychological research to be unimportant and uninteresting. By contrast, the lay public seems to consider the most obvious research to be the most important. The positive relationship between perceived obviousness and perceived importance

TABLE 1 / Statements of Social Psychological Research Findings Extracted from Meta-Analyses and Judged to Be Least Obvious, Most Important, and Most Interesting by Introductory Psychology Students

Statements Judged Least Obvious	Percentage Judged Obvious
Nonmasculine men are at risk for assaulting their wives.	0
The people who are good at understanding others' nonverbal behavior are from nonexpressive families.	0
People who participate in a group are likely to become the leader of that group.	0

Statements Judged Most Important	Percentage Judged Important
People attribute their successes to effort.	100
Students achieve the most if their teachers interact with them, display warmth, and give them positive feedback.	100
Leaders are most effective if they offer rewards that are contingent on performance.	95

Statements Judged Most Interesting	Percentage Judged Interesting
Men are more likely than women to be satisfied if they remarry.	95
Children who are helpful can infer others' motives and thoughts.	95
Men touch women more than women touch men.	95

documented in this study is not just statistically significant but appreciable in size ($r = +.47$). Indeed, this raw correlation coefficient may underestimate the magnitude of the relationship between the obviousness and importance of a finding because the r is attenuated by measurement error. Corrected for attenuation, the relationship yields an r of $+.62$. These results were unexpected and motivated further investigation.

STUDY 2

One might assume that findings judged to be obvious by lay persons could easily be predicted, making research on these topics unnecessary. Taking the results of Study 1 at face value, one might conclude that a large percentage of social psychological findings are predictable and that the most predictable findings in social psychology are the most important. The judged obviousness of a finding, however, may not be a good indicator of the extent to which the finding could be predicted. Judgments of obviousness may reflect a hindsight bias (Davies, 1987). Wong (1995), for example, found that 33% of research findings on teaching were judged to be less obvious than foils for those findings.

People often hold beliefs that are mutually contradictory (Aronson et al., 1990). People may believe, for example, that "opposites attract" while also believing that "birds of a feather flock together" (Feingold, 1988). Perhaps the opposite of many research findings in social psychology would seem just as plausible to the lay observer as the findings themselves. Study 2 addresses the extent to which lay persons are able to predict social psychological research findings and to discriminate them from nonfindings. Analyses also will be conducted to determine whether findings that are highly predictable are judged to be obvious, unimportant, and uninteresting.

Method

Participants. The participants in Study 2 were 72 introductory psychology students who had not participated in Study 1. The data were collected prior to the students' exposure to social psychological research in their introductory psychology course. Students received credit toward their final grade for participation in the experiment.

Materials.   For a discrimination task, a large number of social psychological nonfindings were generated. In particular, a foil was created for each of the 398 social psychological findings that had been judged in Study 1. Each foil reflected the opposite of 1 of the 398 research findings. The research finding that "men are more aggressive than women," for example, resulted in a foil of "women are more aggressive than men."

Three sets of social psychological statements were generated. One set included 135 statements, a second set included 132 statements, and a third set included 131 statements. Each set included statements from each of 18 social psychological topic areas. Roughly half of the statements in each set were research findings; the other statements were foils for other findings. Each set of statements was represented on two complementary stimulus forms. Each time a research finding appeared on one of the forms, the foil for that finding appeared on the other form. For each set of statements, participants viewed approximately half of the statements on one social psychological topic as the finding and the remaining statements from the topic as the foil. If a participant read 8 statements about attribution, for example, 4 of the statements would be research findings, and the others would be foils for 4 other findings.

Half of the participants received the statements on a form in one random order; the other half received the statements in the opposite order. The statements were not grouped by topic. However, for interpretability, a few statements were always presented consecutively and in the same orientation (i.e., either all research findings or all research foils). A research finding was never judged by the same student who judged the foil corresponding to that finding; the two statements were placed on complementary stimulus forms.

Procedure.   Students made judgments in a small classroom with no more than 10 other students. The various stimulus forms mentioned above were randomly distributed to students. The experimenter noted that the students would be reading a series of statements, that some of the statements were research findings discovered by social psychologists, and that other statements were not research findings. The students were to indicate on an answer sheet "whether each statement is or is not a social psychological research finding." Students making these binary discrimination judgments were unaware of the judgments made in earlier studies. Each student completed the discrimination task in less than 60 minutes, then received course credit.

Results and Discussion

Each participant attempted to discriminate research findings from nonfindings. The proportion of students who judged a research finding to be a research finding and the proportion of students who judged the corresponding foil not to be a finding were aggregated across participants. These two proportions served as measures of the discriminability of each finding. The interrater reliability of the discrimination judgments across different forms was relatively high: By the Spearman-Brown formula, effective rs = .71 and .77 for the proportion of participants judging a research finding to be a finding and the proportion of participants judging a foil not to be a finding, respectively.

Previous research suggests that people are inaccurate in selecting research findings from their opposites (Wong, 1995). Others suggest that social research findings are quite obvious and easy to predict (Gordon et al., 1978). In the current study, participants judged 68.40% of 398 social psychological research findings to be findings and judged 68.49% of 398 research foils not to be findings. Students with limited knowledge of social psychology were accurate in discriminating social psychological findings from foils more than two thirds of the time; for a comparison of the percentage correct judgments to the 50% that would be expected by chance, $ts(396)$ = 15.22 and 14.92, for findings and foils, respectively, each $p <$ .00001. Participants were not completely accurate, however. In 72 of 398 cases, participants were more likely to regard the foil to be a finding than the finding itself.

Researchers have questioned the validity of obviousness judgments as an indicator of the predictability of research findings (Wong, 1995). As a test of validity, the discriminability of a finding (as measured in the current study) was compared to the perceived obviousness of the findings, as measured in Study 1. Results showed that the higher the percentage of students who judge a finding to be obvious, the higher the percentage who can distinguish that research finding from a foil, $r(396) = +.58$, $p < .0005$. The judged obviousness of a research finding was more strongly related to the percentage of students who judged a finding to be a finding, $r(396) = +.66$, $p < .0005$, than to the percentage of students who judged the corresponding foil to be a nonfinding, $r(396) = +.29$, $p < .0005$.

For social psychological findings taken from the broadest conclusions of published meta-analyses, obviousness is a valid predictor of the ability of the lay person to correctly identify true findings. Lay judgments of obviousness also seem to be more related to participants' ability to identify findings than their ability to reject foils. Perhaps people find it easier to accept a statement than to reject the statement (see Gilbert, 1991).

The earlier studies showed that the judged importance of a finding was positively related to its judged obviousness. We wondered whether judged importance also would be related to a finding's predictability. It is. The greater the proportion of participants who judge a finding to be important, the greater the proportion who can discriminate that finding from its opposite, $r(396) = +.36$, $p < .0005$. Students may have the most lay knowledge about the most important research topics (Joynson, 1974; Kruglanski, 1989). The discriminability of a finding is not related to its judged interestingness, $r(396) = -.08$, $p = 11$.

STUDY 3

The results of Studies 1 and 2 would seem to imply that students' judgments of research differ from social psychologists' judgments in some fundamental way. Perhaps, though, the difference is not so profound. Here, students have been asked to judge the importance of social psychological *phenomena*. Social psychologists, by contrast, are trained to evaluate *research* on these phenomena. In characterizing a commonsensical research result as trivial, social psychologists

may not mean to imply that the corresponding phenomenon is unimportant but only that it need not have been established by research. In labeling the same result "important," students may not mean to imply that the phenomenon required scientific documentation but only that it has societal (or personal) significance. In this interpretation, students would make the same judgments as social psychologists if the objects of their judgments did not differ.

To assess this possibility, we conducted a third study. In Study 3, students evaluated the importance of conducting research to establish social psychological findings. Perhaps students will consider it unimportant to conduct research to establish the findings of social psychology. Perhaps (like social psychologists) they will judge the most obvious findings to be the ones least important to research.

Method

Participants. The participants in Study 3 were 60 introductory psychology students who had not participated in either of the earlier studies. The data were collected prior to the students' exposure to social psychological research in their introductory psychology course. Students received credit toward their final grade for participating.

Materials. Participants viewed the research findings that had been evaluated in Study 1. Thus, each participant read one of three sets of statements, each set containing approximately 130 of 398 social psychological research findings. Each finding was judged by 20 of the Study 3 research participants. As before, the statements were listed under topic headings. The order of the topics and the order of the statements within each topic were varied across students.

Procedure. Students made judgments in a small classroom with no more than 10 other students. Sets of research statements were randomly distributed to students. The experimenter noted that the students would be reading a series of social psychological statements. The experimenter explained that participants were to indicate for each statement "whether it is important to conduct research to determine if the statement is true." Students made a binary judgment indicating whether it was important or not important to conduct research to establish whether a given statement was true. Students were unaware that any other judgments of the statements had been made. Students completed the judgment task in less than 60 minutes. Afterward, participants indicated whether they had taken a psychology course prior to the one in which they were enrolled.

Results and Discussion

The percentage of students who indicated that a research finding was important to research was accumulated. There was moderate interrater reliability in these judgments: By the Spearman-Brown formula, effective $r = .50$ for the percentage of students judging a finding as important to research across different forms. Students judged that 64.12% of the findings were important to research. This is nearly identical to the mean percentage of findings judged important in Study 1 (the latter = 64.06%, as reported above). The greater the judged importance of a research statement in Study 1, the more the current students thought it was important to conduct research to determine if the statement was true, $r(396) = .55$, $p < .0001$.

As shown in Study 1, the research findings that are most obvious to students are the findings they regard as most important. Perhaps, though, college students believe that it is unnecessary to establish obvious conclusions with research. If so, there should be a negative relationship between the obviousness of a finding and students' judgments of the importance to research that finding. No such correlation was observed. In fact, students consider it more important to conduct research to establish obvious findings than nonobvious findings; $r(396) = +.21$, $p < .0005$, for the relationship between the percentage of students in Study 1 who judged a finding obvious and the percentage in Study 3 who judged it important to research. Students also consider it more important to conduct research to establish highly predictable than unpredictable findings; $r(396) = +.22$, $p < .0005$, for the relationship between the Study 3 judgments of a finding and the predictability of that finding in Study 2. According to lay judges, the more obvious a research finding, the more important the research *fact* and the more important it is to *conduct research* to

establish that fact. Apparently, highly obvious facts concern issues of special societal (or personal) significance, and students believe that such issues warrant investigation.

Perhaps these results are somehow influenced by formal coursework in psychology. To minimize this possibility, students participated in Study 3 at the beginning of an introductory psychology course. Participants also reported on earlier psychology courses they had taken. Of the 60 participants, 20 (33.3%) indicated taking a psychology course prior to their current course. In judgments of importance to conduct research, there was no significant difference between students who had taken a previous psychology course and those who had not. Students with and without prior coursework in psychology judged the same number of findings to be important to research ($Ms = 65.14$% vs. 63.38% for those who had and had not taken a prior course, respectively), $t(58) = -.48$, $p > .60$. Students with and without prior coursework in psychology judged it more important to conduct research on obvious than nonobvious phenomena ($rs = +.20$ and $+.14$ for the two groups, respectively, each $p < .005$) and more important to conduct research on highly predictable phenomena than nonpredictable phenomena ($rs = +.18$ and $+.19$ for the two groups, respectively, each $p < .005$). Correlations involving students who had taken a prior course in psychology did not differ significantly from correlations involving students who had not taken a prior course ($p > .20$ in each of two significance tests).

GENERAL DISCUSSION

Some have claimed that social science research is hardly surprising to anyone (Lamal, 1991) and amounts to nothing more than common knowledge (e.g., Gordon et al., 1978). Others suggest that evaluations of research are questionable and susceptible to bias (Davies, 1987; Wong, 1995). The results presented above allow an evaluation of these claims. To the lay person, social psychological research findings are not completely obvious, nor are they also not completely unimportant and uninteresting. Although some researchers have questioned the validity of the obvious reaction to research findings (Wong, 1995), the results outlined above indicate that feelings of obviousness have some validity. College students can discriminate social psychological findings from nonfindings, and the judged obviousness of a finding is related to its predictability.

Although many scientists think that predictable findings are trivial (see Aronson et al., 1990; Townsend, 1995), the lay person does not share this view. In lay judgments, the most important findings are obvious and easily predictable. Three explanations for these unexpected results will be explored: a heuristic processing explanation, a research motives explanation, and a differential dissemination explanation.

Lay persons may employ heuristics to evaluate research. Lay strategies for evaluating research findings may be quite different from scientific strategies. Novices are less likely to use information that is inconsistent with expectations (Fiske, Kinder, & Larter, 1983) and are more likely to engage in heuristic processing (Wood, Kallgren, & Priesler, 1985). The novice may overlook contradictions to a presented finding and base their evaluations on a simple strategy.

Perhaps the direct relationship observed in the current research between novices' judgments of obviousness and importance emerged because both judgments were made using an availability heuristic (Slovic & Fischhoff, 1977; Tversky & Kahneman, 1982). Novices may judge a psychological statement as obvious if they can quickly think of an example. Moreover, the accessibility of examples in memory may indicate the number, salience, or importance of these events in the novices' lives. The positive relationship between judgments of obviousness and research predictability suggests that people use lay knowledge to evaluate the obviousness and validity of research claims.

A second possibility concerns scientists' motives for conducting research. Social psychologists must have some motivation for choosing a particular research topic (Gergen, 1982). One possible motive is that the topic is widely regarded as important. An alternative motive is that the research hypothesis is novel or counterintuitive (Abelson, 1995). In this view, no research would ever be conducted on an "unimportant" topic unless the topic had a counterintuitive appeal. It also follows that researchers would not pursue a patently obvious result unless the result

was generally considered important. Thus, most research considered not important is by default motivated by its nonobviousness. In labeling unimportant findings nonobvious, lay judges are simply acknowledging the tension between these two research motives.

Lay evaluations of the importance of a research finding should not, of course, be uncritically accepted. Indeed, each of the findings in the current research was taken from meta-analyses and had been addressed in a number of primary studies. Apparently, social psychologists find all of these findings important. Perhaps research topics considered unimportant by social psychologists would be viewed differently by the lay person. Researchers pursue a line of inquiry for many reasons. Although it is useful for researchers to be aware of cultural perceptions of research, lay judgments should not dictate their choice of research topics. Understanding how lay people respond to research conclusions, however, provides insight into how researchers can effectively communicate research results to the lay public.

A third possible explanation of the observed relationship between lay judgments of obviousness and importance involves the public dissemination of research results. Some findings are publicly disseminated, whereas others are not. Perhaps the most important findings are the ones most widely disseminated. Findings with immense social importance likely are reported in the media and become known by the public at large (Basil & Brown, 1994). Although an important finding may initially be counterintuitive, once the finding is disseminated, it is gradually incorporated into common knowledge and comes to seem obvious.

CONCLUSION

The social sciences have received criticism for providing little knowledge beyond what is known by the lay person (Bode, 1922; Shwayder, 1965). Methodologists agree that social psychologists should pursue knowledge that transcends common sense (Lee, 1988). Some argue that the goal of psychology should be to demonstrate the inadequacy of common sense knowledge (Aronson et al., 1990). The current research suggests that persons relying on lay knowledge of human social behavior can predict a large portion of scientific knowledge in social psychology. However, the most predictable of these findings do not seem trivial to the lay person. Predictable results are the most important results, lay judgments imply.

Many social psychologists are reluctant to pursue obvious research findings, preferring research results they consider surprising. Researchers who confine their attention to nonobvious phenomena may neglect research that lay persons find important. Instructors of courses in social psychology often emphasize the most surprising (or nonobvious) findings to motivate student interest. In doing so, they may fail to cover research that students find important.

People who have limited knowledge of research, like politicians and administrators, must make decisions about the allocation of resources for research. The current results may help illuminate these decisions. Scientists need to consider lay reactions to their research. Further research will be needed to clarify why students find obvious results to be important. In addition, work should seek to determine whether nonstudents make similar judgments. This work may suggest ways to reduce bias in lay evaluations of psychological research and enhance public appreciation of research results.

REFERENCES

Abelson, R. P. (1995). *Statistics as principled argument.* Hillsdale, NJ: Lawrence Erlbaum.

Anderson, C. A., & Lindsay, J. J. (1998). The development, perseverance, and change of naive theories. *Social Cognition, 16,* 8–30.

Aronson, E., Ellsworth, P. C., Carlsmith, J. M., & Gonzales, M. H. *(1990). Methods of research in social psychology* (chap. 2, pp. 40–82). New York: McGraw-Hill.

Barnett, M. A. (1986). Commonsense and research findings in personality. *Teaching of Psychology, 13,* 62–64.

Barnett, M. A., Knust, J., McMillan, T., Kaufman, J., & Sinisi, C. (1988). Research findings in developmental psychology: Common sense revisited. *Teaching of Psychology, 15,* 195–197.

Basil, M. D., & Brown, W. J. (1994). Interpersonal communication in news diffusion: A study of "Magic" Johnson's announcement. *Journalism Quarterly, 71,* 305–320.

Bode, B. H. (1922). What is psychology? *Psychological Review, 29,* 250–258.

Brown, L. T. (1983). Some more misconceptions about psychology among introductory psychology students. *Teaching of Psychology, 10,* 207–210.

Davies, M. F. (1987). Reduction of hindsight bias by restoration of foresight perspective: Effectiveness of foresight-encoding and hindsight-retrieval strategies. *Organizational Behavior and Human Decision Processes, 40,* 50–68.

Feingold, A. (1988). Matching for attractiveness. *Psychological Bulletin, 104,* 226–235.

Fiedler, F. E. (1964). A contingency model of leadership effectiveness. *Advances in Experimental Social Psychology, 1,* 149–190.

Fiske, S. T., Kinder, D. R., & Larter, W. M. (1983). The novice and the expert: Knowledge-based strategies in political cognition. *Journal of Experimental Social Psychology, 19,* 381–400.

Furnham, A. (1983). Social psychology as common sense. *Bulletin of the British Psychological Society, 36,* 105–109.

Gergen, K. J. (1982). *Toward transformation in social knowledge.* New York: Springer-Verlag.

Gilbert, D. T. (1991). How mental systems believe. *American Psychologist, 46,* 107–119.

Gordon, M. E., Kleiman, L. S., & Hanie, C. A. (1978). Industrial-organizational psychology: Open thy ears o house of Israel. *American Psychologist, 33,* 893–905.

Heider, F. (1958). *The psychology of interpersonal relations.* New York: John Wiley.

Humphrey, G., & Argyle, M. (Eds.). (1962). *Social psychology through experiment.* London: Methuen.

Joynson, R. B. (1974). *Psychology and common sense.* London: Routledge Kegan Paul.

Kenny, D. A. (1994). *Interpersonal perception: A social relations analysis.* New York: Guilford.

Kinch, J. W. (1963). A formal theory of the self-concept. *American Journal of Sociology, 68,* 481–486.

Kruglanski, A. W. (1989). *Lay epistemics and human knowledge: Cognitive and motivational bases.* New York: Plenum.

Lamal, P. A. (1979). College students' common beliefs about psychology. *Teaching of Psychology, 6,* 155–158.

Lamal, P. A. (1991). Psychology as common sense: The case of findings concerning work motivation and satisfaction. *Psychological Science, 2,* 129–130.

Lazarsfeld, P. F. (1949). The American soldier: An expository review. *Public Opinion Quarterly, 13,* 377–404.

Lee, V. L. (1988). *Beyond behaviorism.* Hillsdale, NJ: Lawrence Erlbaum.

Lepper, M. R., Keavney, M., & Drake, M. (1996). Intrinsic motivation and extrinsic rewards: A commentary on Cameron and Pierce's meta-analysis. *Review of Educational Research, 66,* 5–32.

Manstead, A. S. R., & Hewstone, M. (1995). *The Blackwell*

encyclopedia of social psychology. Cambridge, MA: Blackwell.

Miller, N., & Pollock, V. E. (1994). Meta-analysis and some science-compromising problems of social psychology. In W. R. Shadish & S. Fuller (Eds.), *The social psychology of science* (pp. 230–261). New York: Guilford.

Paik, H., & Comstock, G. (1994). The effects of television violence on antisocial behavior. *Communication Research, 21,* 516–546.

Russell, J. A. (1994). Is there universal recognition of emotion from facial expression? A review of the cross-cultural studies. *Psychological Bulletin, 115,* 102–141.

Schlessinger, A., Jr. (1949). The statistical soldier. *Partisan Reviews, 16,* 852–856.

Schneider, D. J. (1973). Implicit personality theory: A review. *Psychological Bulletin, 79,* 294–309.

Shwayder, D. S. (1965). *The stratification of behaviour* (Part 1, pp. 1–19). New York: Humanities Press.

Slovic, P., & Fischhoff, B. (1977). On the psychology of experimental surprises. *Journal of Experimental Psychology: Human Perception and Performance, 3,* 544–551.

Townsend, M. A. R. (1995). Effects of accuracy and plausibility in predicting results of research findings on teaching. *British Journal of Educational Psychology, 65,* 359–365.

Tversky, A., & Kahneman, D. (1982). Availability: A heuristic for judging frequency and probability. In D. Kahneman, P. Slovic, & A. Tversky (Eds.), *Judgment under uncertainty: Heuristics and biases* (pp. 163–178). New York: Cambridge University Press.

Vaughan, E. D. (1977). Misconceptions about psychology among introductory psychology students. *Teaching of Psychology, 4,* 138–141.

Wegener, D. T., & Petty, R. E. (1998). The naive scientist revisited: Naive theories and social judgment. *Social Cognition, 16,* 1–7.

Wong, L. Y. (1995). Research on teaching: Process-product research findings and the feeling of obviousness. *Journal of Educational Psychology, 87,* 504–511.

Wood, W., Kallgren, C., & Priesler, R. (1985). Access to attitude relevant information in memory as a determinant of persuasion. *Journal of Experimental Social Psychology, 21,* 73–85.

Ziman, J. (1978). *Reliable knowledge: An exploration of the grounds for belief in science.* London: Cambridge University Press.

Author's Note: The authors would like to express their gratitude to the editor and two anonymous reviewers for their helpful comments in the preparation of this article. The authors also would like to thank Russell Matthews and Wyndy Wiitala for their assistance in data collection and analysis.

CRITICAL THINKING QUESTIONS

1. Create a list of five facts of social behavior—things that you believe are true. Then do research from a social psychology textbook or database to determine if these beliefs are, indeed, supported by the social psychological literature.

2. According to the article, social psychologists are not always motivated to investigate topics that the lay public finds intrinsically important but for which the results seem obvious. Develop a list of what you consider to be the most important questions that social psychology should try to answer. As you go through the course, keep track of which topics have been investigated and what the findings were. If a topic you listed has not been investigated, why do you think that may be the case?

3. All of the subjects involved in the research described in the article were college students. Do you think subjects who were not college students would show similar patterns of responding? Why or why not? Outline a study to compare and contrast college and non–college subject responses on the topics investigated in this article.

4. The article states that "People who have limited knowledge of research, like politicians and administrators, must make decisions about the allocation of resources for research." What implications do the findings presented in this article have for how research monies may be distributed? For example, what types of studies seem most likely to be funded? Least likely? What might help decision makers come up with the best decisions regarding funding? Explain.

Chapter Two

SOCIAL PERCEPTION

HOW DO WE form impressions of other people? What information do we use in forming those impressions? How important are first impressions? How do we make judgments about why people act the way they do? These are some of the questions addressed by the readings in this chapter on social perception.

When we interact with another person, we are literally bombarded with information. What the person looks like, what he or she is saying, and how he or she is acting comprise but a fraction of the information available to us that we may use in forming an impression of the individual. One judgment we may make about another individual concerns his or her overall character. In other words, we want to know how honest, trustworthy, likeable, or good the person is. But exactly what are we looking for? And are some of us better than others at making accurate judgments?

One topic of study in this area is how long it takes for us to form an impression of someone. Do we do so almost immediately, or do we hold off until we know more about the individual? Article 4, "The New-Boy Network: What Do Job Interviews Really Tell Us?" discusses how we form impressions of people in a remarkably short period of time. But are such snap judgments accurate? In fact, they are perhaps more so than many of us realize. The applications of these findings to the typical job interview situation are discussed further in the article.

Another topic of interest is whether all the information that is available about someone is equally relevant in forming our impression of him or her. Or are some factors more important than others? Article 5, "The Warm-Cold Variable in First Impressions of Persons," examines some of the important factors that influence our judgments of other people. This classic article is a fine example of the power of first impressions and the impact that they have on how we relate to others.

Finally, Article 6, "Detecting Deceit via Analysis of Verbal and Nonverbal Behavior," offers a contemporary look at research on one particular aspect of impression formation: the ability to detect whether someone is lying. The article examines variables and techniques that may be important in accurately detecting deception. It turns out that some commonly assumed correlates of lying, such as not being able to look a person in the eye, may not be true, while other factors may be much more accurate.

ARTICLE 4 _____

What information do we use in forming impressions of other people? When meeting someone for the first time, we rely on a variety of information, such as how he or she acts, looks, and dresses, and what he or she says. Some of this information is nonverbal. We pay a lot of attention to facial expressions, for example, as well as body postures and movements. Most of us have some sort of intuitive rules for decoding nonverbal behavior. For example, what does it mean when someone is standing upright with his or her arms folded across the chest? Is that person being defensive? Not very warm and open? Some popularizations of psychology maintain that certain nonverbal cues have specific meanings, such as in the example just given. However, the example used also might mean nothing more than that the person was cold or that he or she habitually stands that way. Regardless of any supposedly clearcut meanings of nonverbal behavior, we all have our own intuitive means for making judgments about the people we meet.

So, how long does it take for us to make a judgment about someone? An hour? Fifteen minutes? Two seconds? The following article by Malcolm Gladwell discusses research that shows that people make judgments about others in a remarkably short period of time. Furthermore, these quick judgments tend to be amazingly similar to those made by people interacting over a much longer time period or even by trained interviewers. But the question is: How accurate are the judgments made by *any* of these people?

Although we may have confidence in our own judgments, the concept known as the *fundamental attribution error* suggests that we only see what we want to see. According to this concept, we have a basic tendency to make global, personality generalizations based upon observations made in specific situations. For example, if we meet someone at a party who seems warm, outgoing, and confident, we assume that this is what his or her personality is like in other situations, as well. In other words, we think that we know the real person and ignore or downplay the fact that he or she may act quite differently in other situations. Worse yet, once we form this initial impression, it may be hard to change, since we may persist in only seeing what is consistent with our initial judgment. All of these issues are problematic for anyone interested in accurately assessing others, whether in daily life or, as is the context of the following article, in making hiring decisions.

The New-Boy Network
What Do Job Interviews Really Tell Us?

■ Malcolm Gladwell

Nolan Myers grew up in Houston, the elder of two boys in a middle-class family. He went to Houston's High School for the Performing and Visual Arts and then Harvard, where he intended to major in History and Science. After discovering the joys of writing code, though, he switched to computer science. "Programming is one of those things you get involved in, and you just can't stop until you finish," Myers says. "You get involved in it, and all of a sudden you look at your watch and it's four in the morning! I love the elegance of it." Myers is short and slightly stocky and has pale-blue eyes. He smiles easily, and when he speaks he moves his hands and torso for emphasis. He plays in a klezmer band called the Charvard Chai Notes. He talks to his parents a lot. He gets B's and B-pluses.

This spring, in the last stretch of his senior year, Myers spent a lot of time interviewing for jobs with technology companies. He talked to a company named Trilogy, down in Texas, but he didn't think he would fit in. "One of Trilogy's subsidiaries put ads out in the paper saying that they were looking for the top tech students, and that they'd give them two hundred thousand dollars and a BMW," Myers said, shaking his head in disbelief. In another of his interviews, a recruiter asked him to solve a programming problem, and he made a stupid mistake and the recruiter pushed the answer back across the table to him, saying that his "solution" accomplished nothing. As he remembers the moment, Myers blushes. "I was so nervous. I thought, Hmm, that sucks!" The way he says that, though, makes it hard to believe that he really was nervous, or maybe what Nolan Myers calls nervous the rest of us call a tiny flutter in the stomach. Myers doesn't seem like the sort to get flustered. He's the kind of person you would call the night before the big test in seventh grade, when nothing made sense and you had begun to panic.

I like Nolan Myers. He will, I am convinced, be very good at whatever career he chooses. I say those two things even though I have spent no more than ninety minutes in his presence. We met only once, on a sunny afternoon in April at the Au Bon Pain in Harvard Square. He was wearing sneakers and khakis and a polo shirt, in a dark-green pattern. He had a big backpack, which he plopped on the floor beneath the table. I bought him an orange juice. He fished around in his wallet and came up with a dollar to try and repay me, which I refused. We sat by the window. Previously, we had talked for perhaps three minutes on the phone, setting up the interview. Then I E-mailed him, asking him how I would recognize him at Au Bon Pain. He sent me the following message, with what I'm convinced—again, on the basis of almost no evidence—to be typical Myers panache: "22ish, five foot seven, straight brown hair, very good-looking.:)." I have never talked to his father, his mother, or his

little brother, or any of his professors. I have never seen him ecstatic or angry or depressed. I know nothing of his personal habits, his tastes, or his quirks. I cannot even tell you why I feel the way I do about him. He's good-looking and smart and articulate and funny, but not so good-looking and smart and articulate and funny that there is some obvious explanation for the conclusions I've drawn about him. I just like him, and I'm impressed by him, and if I were an employer looking for bright young college graduates, I'd hire him in a heartbeat.

I heard about Nolan Myers from Hadi Partovi, an executive with Tellme, a highly touted Silicon Valley startup offering Internet access through the telephone. If you were a computer-science major at M.I.T., Harvard, Stanford, Caltech, or the University of Waterloo this spring, looking for a job in software, Tellme was probably at the top of your list. Partovi and I talked in the conference room at Tellme's offices, just off the soaring, open floor where all the firm's programmers and marketers and executives sit, some of them with bunk beds built over their desks. (Tellme recently moved into an old printing plant—a low-slung office building with a huge warehouse attached—and, in accordance with new-economy logic, promptly turned the old offices into a warehouse and the old warehouse into offices.) Partovi is a handsome man of twenty-seven, with olive skin and short curly black hair, and throughout our entire interview he sat with his chair tilted precariously at a forty-five-degree angle. At the end of a long riff about how hard it is to find high-quality people, he blurted out one name: Nolan Myers. Then, from memory, he rattled off Myers's telephone number. He very much wanted Myers to come to Tellme.

Partovi had met Myers in January, during a recruiting trip to Harvard. "It was a heinous day," Partovi remembers. "I started at seven and went until nine. I'd walk one person out and walk the other in." The first fifteen minutes of every interview he spent talking about Tellme—its strategy, its goals, and its business. Then he gave everyone a short programming puzzle. For the rest of the hour-long meeting, Partovi asked questions. He remembers that Myers did well on the programming test, and after talking to him for thirty to forty minutes he became convinced that Myers had, as he puts it, "the right stuff." Partovi spent even less time with Myers than I did. He didn't talk to Myers's family, or see him ecstatic or angry or depressed, either. He knew that Myers had spent last summer as an intern at Microsoft and was about to graduate from an Ivy League school. But virtually everyone recruited by a place like Tellme has graduated from an élite university, and the Microsoft summer-internship program has more than six hundred people in it. Partovi didn't even know why he liked Myers so much. He just did. "It was very much a gut call," he says.

This wasn't so very different from the experience Nolan Myers had with Steve Ballmer, the C.E.O. of Microsoft. Earlier this year, Myers attended a party for former Microsoft interns called Gradbash. Ballmer gave a speech there, and at the end of his remarks Myers raised his hand. "He was talking a lot about aligning the company in certain directions," Myers told me, "and I asked him about how that influences his ability to make bets on other directions. Are they still going to make small bets?" Afterward, a Microsoft recruiter came up to Myers and said, "Steve wants your E-mail address." Myers gave it to him, and soon he and Ballmer were E-mailing. Ballmer, it seems, badly wanted Myers to come to Microsoft. "He did research on me," Myers says. "'He knew which group I was interviewing with, and knew a lot about me personally. He sent me an E-mail saying that he'd love to have me come to Microsoft, and if I had any questions I should contact him. So I sent him a response, saying thank you. After I visited Tellme, I sent him an E-mail saying I was interested in Tellme, here were the reasons, that I wasn't sure yet, and if he had anything to say I said I'd love to talk to him. I gave him my number. So he called, and after playing phone tag we talked—about career trajectory, how Microsoft would influence my career, what he thought of Tellme. I was extremely impressed with him, and he seemed very genuinely interested in me."

What convinced Ballmer he wanted Myers? A glimpse! He caught a little slice of Nolan Myers in action and—just like that—the C.E.O. of a four-hundred-billion-dollar company was calling a college senior in his dorm room. Ballmer somehow knew he liked Myers, the same way Hadi Partovi knew, and the same way I knew after our little chat at Au Bon Pain. But what did we know? What could we know?

By any reasonable measure, surely none of us knew Nolan Myers at all.

It is a truism of the new economy that the ultimate success of any enterprise lies with the quality of the people it hires. At many technology companies, employees are asked to all but live at the office, in conditions of intimacy that would have been unthinkable a generation ago. The artifacts of the prototypical Silicon Valley office—the videogames, the espresso bar, the bunk beds, the basketball hoops—are the elements of the rec room, not the workplace. And in the rec room you want to play only with your friends. But how do you find out who your friends are? Today, recruiters canvas the country for résumés. They analyze employment histories and their competitors' staff listings. They call references, and then do what I did with Nolan Myers: sit down with a perfect stranger for an hour and a half and attempt to draw conclusions about that stranger's intelligence and personality. The job interview has become one of the central conventions of the modem economy. But what, exactly, can you know about a stranger after sitting down and talking with him for an hour?

Some years ago, an experimental psychologist at Harvard University, Nalini Ambady, together with Robert Rosenthal, set out to examine the nonverbal aspects of good teaching. As the basis of her research, she used videotapes of teaching fellows which had been made during a training program at Harvard. Her plan was to have outside observers look at the tapes with the sound off and rate the effectiveness of the teachers by their expressions and physical cues. Ambady wanted to have at least a minute of film to work with. When she looked at the tapes, though, there was really only about ten seconds when the teachers were shown apart from the students.

"I didn't want students in the frame, because obviously it would bias the ratings," Ambady says. "So I went to my adviser, and I said, 'This isn't going to work.'"

But it did. The observers, presented with a ten-second silent video clip, had no difficulty rating the teachers on a fifteen-item checklist of personality traits. In fact, when Ambady cut the clips back to five seconds, the ratings were the same. They were even the same when she showed her raters just two seconds of videotape. That sounds unbelievable unless you actually watch Ambady's teacher clips, as I did, and realize that the eight seconds that distinguish the longest clips from the shortest are superfluous: anything beyond the first flash of insight is unnecessary. When we make a snap judgment, it is made in a snap. It's also, very clearly, a judgment: we get a feeling that we have no difficulty articulating.

Ambady's next step led to an even more remarkable conclusion. She compared those snap judgments of teacher effectiveness with evaluations made, after a full semester of classes, by students of the same teachers. The correlation between the two, she found, was astoundingly high. A person watching a two-second silent video clip of a teacher he has never met will reach conclusions about how good that teacher is that are very similar to those of a student who sits in the teacher's class for an entire semester.

Recently, a comparable experiment was conducted by Frank Bernieri, a psychologist at the University of Toledo. Bernieri, working with one of his graduate students, Neha Gada-Jain, selected two people to act as interviewers, and trained them for six weeks in the proper procedures and techniques of giving an effective job interview. The two then interviewed ninety-eight volunteers, of various ages and backgrounds. The interviews lasted between fifteen and twenty minutes, and afterward each interviewer filled out a six-page, five-part evaluation of the person he'd just talked to. Originally, the intention of the study was to find out whether applicants who had been coached in certain nonverbal behaviors designed to ingratiate themselves with their interviewers—like mimicking the interviewers' physical gestures or posture—would get better ratings than applicants who behaved normally. As it turns out, they didn't. But then another of Bernieri's students, an undergraduate named Tricia Prickett, decided that she wanted to use the interview videotapes and the evaluations that had been collected to test out the adage that "the handshake is everything."

"She took fifteen seconds of videotape showing the applicant as he or she knocks on the door, comes in, shakes the hand of the interviewer, sits down, and the interviewer welcomes the person," Bernieri explained. Then, like Ambady, Prickett got a series of strangers to rate the applicants based on the handshake clip, using the same criteria that the interviewers had used.

Once more, against all expectations, the ratings were very similar to those of the interviewers. "On nine out of the eleven traits the applicants were being judged on, the observers significantly predicted the outcome of the interview," Bernieri says. "The strength of the correlations was extraordinary."

This research takes Ambady's conclusions one step further. In the Toledo experiment, the interviewers were trained in the art of interviewing. They weren't dashing off a teacher evaluation on their way out the door. They were filling out a formal, detailed questionnaire, of the sort designed to give the most thorough and unbiased account of an interview. And still their ratings weren't all that different from those of people off the street who saw just the greeting.

This is why Hadi Partovi, Steve Ballmer, and I all agreed on Nolan Myers. Apparently, human beings don't need to know someone in order to believe that they know someone. Nor does it make that much difference, apparently, that Partovi reached his conclusion after putting Myers through the wringer for an hour, I reached mine after ninety minutes of amiable conversation at Au Bon Pain, and Ballmer reached his after watching and listening as Myers asked a question.

Bernieri and Ambady believe that the power of first impressions suggests that human beings have a particular kind of prerational ability for making searching judgments about others. In Ambady's teacher experiments, when she asked her observers to perform a potentially distracting cognitive task—like memorizing a set of numbers—while watching the tapes, their judgments of teacher effectiveness were unchanged. But when she instructed her observers to think hard about their ratings before they made them, their accuracy suffered substantially. Thinking only gets in the way. "The brain structures that are involved here are very primitive," Ambady speculates. "All of these affective reactions are probably governed by the lower brain structures." What we are picking up in that first instant would seem to be something quite basic about a person's character, because what we conclude after two seconds is pretty much the same as what we conclude after twenty minutes or, indeed, an entire semester. "Maybe you can tell immediately whether someone is extroverted, or gauge the person's ability to communicate," Bernieri says. "Maybe these clues or cues are immediately accessible and apparent." Bernieri and Ambady are talking about the existence of a powerful form of human intuition. In a way, that's comforting, because it suggests that we can meet a perfect stranger and immediately pick up on something important about him. It means that I shouldn't be concerned that I can't explain why I like Nolan Myers, because, if such judgments are made without thinking, then surely they defy explanation.

But there's a troubling suggestion here as well. I believe that Nolan Myers is an accomplished and likable person. But I have no idea from our brief encounter how honest he is, or whether he is self-centered, or whether he works best by himself or in a group, or any number of other fundamental traits. That people who simply see the handshake arrive at the same conclusions as people who conduct a full interview also implies, perhaps, that those initial impressions matter too much—that they color all the other impressions that we gather over time.

For example, I asked Myers if he felt nervous about the prospect of leaving school for the workplace, which seemed like a reasonable question, since I remember how anxious I was before my first job. Would the hours scare him? Oh no, he replied, he was already working between eighty and a hundred hours a week at school. "Are there things that you think you aren't good at, which make you worry?" I continued.

His reply was sharp: "Are there things that I'm not good at, or things that I can't learn? I think that's the real question. There are a lot of things I don't know anything about, but I feel comfortable that given the right environment and the right encouragement I can do well at." In my notes, next to that reply, I wrote "Great answer!" and I can remember at the time feeling the little thrill you experience as an interviewer when someone's behavior conforms with your expectations. Because I had decided, right off, that I liked him, what I heard in his answer was toughness and confidence. Had I decided early on that I didn't like Nolan Myers, I would have heard in that reply arrogance and bluster. The first impression becomes a self-fulfilling prophecy: we hear what we expect to hear. The interview is hopelessly biased in favor of the nice.

When Ballmer and Partovi and I met Nolan Myers, we made a prediction. We looked at the way he behaved in our presence—at the way he talked and seemed to think—and drew conclusions about how he would behave in other situations. I had decided, remember, that Myers was the kind of person you called the night before the big test in seventh grade. Was I right to make that kind of generalization?

This is a question that social psychologists have looked at closely. In the late nineteen-twenties, in a famous study, the psychologist Theodore Newcomb analyzed extroversion among adolescent boys at a summer camp. He found that how talkative a boy was in one setting—say, lunch—was highly predictive of how talkative that boy would be in the same setting in the future. A boy who was curious at lunch on Monday was likely to be curious at lunch on Tuesday. But his behavior in one setting told you almost nothing about how he would behave in a different setting: from how someone behaved at lunch, you couldn't predict how he would behave during, say, afternoon playtime. In a more recent study, of conscientiousness among students at Carleton College, the researchers Walter Mischel, Neil Lutsky, and Philip K. Peake showed that how neat a student's assignments were or how punctual he was told you almost nothing about how often he attended class or how neat his room or his personal appearance was. How we behave at any one time, evidently, has less to do with some immutable inner compass than with the particulars of our situation.

This conclusion, obviously, is at odds with our intuition. Most of the time, we assume that people display the same character traits in different situations. We habitually underestimate the large role that context plays in people's behavior. In the Newcomb summer-camp experiment, for example, the results showing how little consistency there was from one setting to another in talkativeness, curiosity, and gregariousness were tabulated from observations made and recorded by camp counsellors on the spot. But when, at the end of the summer, those same counsellors were asked to give their final impressions of the kids, they remembered the children's behavior as being highly consistent.

"The basis of the illusion is that we are somehow confident that we are getting what is there, that we are able to read off a person's disposition," Richard Nisbett, a psychologist at the University of Michigan, says. "When you have an interview with someone and have an hour with them, you don't conceptualize that as taking a sample of a person's behavior, let alone a possibly biased sample, which is what it is. What you think is that you are seeing a hologram, a small and fuzzy image but still the whole person."

Then Nisbett mentioned his frequent collaborator, Lee Ross, who teaches psychology at Stanford. "There was one term when he was teaching statistics and one term he was teaching a course with a lot of humanistic psychology. He gets his teacher evaluations. The first referred to him as cold, rigid, remote, finicky, and uptight. And the second described this wonderful warm-hearted guy who was so deeply concerned with questions of community and getting students to grow. It was Jekyll and Hyde. In both cases, the students thought they were seeing the real Lee Ross."

Psychologists call this tendency—to fixate on supposedly stable character traits and overlook the influence of context—the Fundamental Attribution Error, and if you combine this error with what we know about snap judgments the interview becomes an even more problematic encounter. Not only had I let my first impressions color the information I gathered about Myers, but I had also assumed that the way he behaved with me in an interview setting was indicative of the way he would always behave. It isn't that the interview is useless; what I learned about Myers—that he and I get along well—is something I could never have got from a résumé or by talking to his references. It's just that our conversation turns out to have been less useful, and potentially more misleading, than I had supposed. That most basic of human rituals—the conversation with a stranger—turns out to be a minefield.

Not long after I met with Nolan Myers, I talked with a human-resources consultant from Pasadena named Justin Menkes. Menkes's job is to figure out how to extract meaning from face-to-face encounters, and with that in mind he agreed to spend an hour interviewing me the way he thinks interviewing ought to be done. It felt, going in, not unlike a visit to a shrink, except that instead of having months, if not years, to work things out, Menkes was set upon stripping away my secrets in one session.

Consider, he told me, a commonly asked question like "Describe a few situations in which your work was criticized. How did you handle the criticism?"

The problem, Menkes said, is that it's much too obvious what the interviewee is supposed to say. "There was a situation where I was working on a project, and I didn't do as well as I could have," he said, adopting a mock-sincere singsong. "My boss gave me some constructive criticism. And I redid the project. It hurt. Yet we worked it out." The same is true of the question "What would your friends say about you?"—to which the correct answer (preferably preceded by a pause, as if to suggest that it had never dawned on you that someone would ask such a question) is "My guess is that they would call me a people person—either that or a hard worker."

Myers and I had talked about obvious questions, too. "What is your greatest weakness?" I asked him. He answered, "I tried to work on a project my freshman year, a children's festival. I was trying to start a festival as a benefit here in Boston. And I had a number of guys working with me. I started getting concerned with the scope of the project we were working on—how much responsibility we had, getting things done. I really put the brakes on, but in retrospect I really think we could have done it and done a great job."

Then Myers grinned and said, as an aside, "Do I truly think that is a fault? Honestly, no." And, of course, he's right. All I'd really asked him was whether he could describe a personal strength as if it were a weakness, and, in answering as he did, he had merely demonstrated his knowledge of the unwritten rules of the interview.

But, Menkes said, what if those questions were rephrased so that the answers weren't obvious? For example: "At your weekly team meetings, your boss unexpectedly begins aggressively critiquing your performance on a current project. What do you do?"

I felt a twinge of anxiety. What would I do? I remembered a terrible boss I'd had years ago. "I'd probably be upset," I said. "But I doubt I'd say anything. I'd probably just walk away." Menkes gave no indication whether he was concerned or pleased by that answer. He simply pointed out that another person might well have said something like "I'd go and see my boss later in private, and confront him about why he embarrassed me in front of my team." I was saying that I would probably handle criticism—even inappropriate criticism—from a superior with stoicism; in the second case, the applicant was saying he or she would adopt a more confrontational style. Or, at least, we were telling the interviewer that the workplace demands either stoicism or confrontation—and to Menkes these are revealing and pertinent pieces of information.

Menkes moved on to another area—handling stress. A typical question in this area is something like "Tell me about a time when you had to do several things at once. How did you handle the situation? How did you decide what to do first?" Menkes says this is also too easy. "I just had to be very organized," he began again in his mock-sincere singsong. "I had to multitask. I had to prioritize and delegate appropriately. I checked in frequently with my boss." Here's how Menkes rephrased it: "You're in a situation where you have two very important responsibilities that both have a deadline that is impossible to meet. You cannot accomplish both. How do you handle that situation?"

"Well," I said, "I would look at the two and decide what I was best at, and then go to my boss and say, 'It's better that I do one well than both poorly,' and we'd figure out who else could do the other task."

Menkes, immediately seized on a telling detail in my answer. I was interested in what job I would do best. But isn't the key issue what job the company most needed to have done? With that comment, I had revealed something valuable: that in a time of work-related crisis I start from a self-centered consideration. "Perhaps you are a bit of a solo practitioner," Menkes said diplomatically, "That's an essential bit of information."

Menkes deliberately wasn't drawing any broad conclusions. If we are not people who are shy or talkative or outspoken but people who are shy in some contexts, talkative in other situations, and outspoken in still other areas, then what it means to know someone is to catalogue and appreciate all those variations. Menkes was trying to begin that process of cataloguing. This interviewing technique is known as "structured interviewing," and in studies by industrial psychologists it has been shown to be the only kind of interviewing that has any success at all in predicting performance in the workplace. In the structured interviews, the format is fairly rigid. Each applicant is treated in precisely the same manner. The questions are scripted. The interviewers are carefully trained, and each applicant is rated on a series of predetermined scales.

What is interesting about the structured interview is how narrow its objectives are. When I interviewed Nolan Myers I was groping for some kind of global sense of who he was; Menkes seemed entirely uninterested in arriving at that same general sense of me—he seemed to realize how foolish that expectation was for an hour-long interview. The structured interview works precisely because it isn't really an interview; it isn't about getting to know someone, in a traditional sense. It's as much concerned with rejecting information as it is with collecting it.

Not surprisingly, interview specialists have found it extraordinarily difficult to persuade most employers to adopt the structured interview. It just doesn't feel right. For most of us, hiring someone is essentially a romantic process, in which the job interview functions as a desexualized version of a date. We are looking for someone with whom we have a certain chemistry, even if the coupling that results ends in tears and the pursuer and the pursued turn out to have nothing in common. We want the unlimited promise of a love affair. The structured interview, by contrast, seems to offer only the dry logic and practicality of an arranged marriage.

Nolan Myers agonized over which job to take. He spent half an hour on the phone with Steve Ballmer, and Ballmer was very persuasive. "He gave me very, very good advice," Myers says of his conversations with the Microsoft C.E.O. "He felt that I should go to the place that excited me the most and that I thought would be best for my career. He offered to be my mentor." Myers says he talked to his parents every day about what to do. In February, he flew out to California and spent a Saturday going from one Tellme executive to another, asking and answering questions. "Basically, I had three things I was looking for. One was long-term goals for the company. Where did they see themselves in five years? Second, what position would I be playing in the company?" He stopped and burst out laughing. "And I forget what the third one is." In March, Myers committed to Tellme.

Will Nolan Myers succeed at Tellme? I think so, although I honestly have no idea. It's a harder question to answer now than it would have been thirty or forty years ago. If this were 1965, Nolan Myers would have gone to work at I.B.M. and worn a blue suit and sat in a small office and kept his head down, and the particulars of his personality would not have mattered so much. It was not so important that I.B.M. understood who you were before it hired you, because you understood what I.B.M. was. If you walked through the door at Armonk or at a branch office in Illinois, you knew what you had to be and how you were supposed to act. But to walk through the soaring, open offices of Tellme, with the bunk beds over the desks, is to be struck by how much more demanding the culture of Silicon Valley is. Nolan Myers will not be provided with a social script, that blue suit and organization chart. Tellme, like any technology startup these days, wants its employees to be part of a fluid team, to be flexible and innovative, to work with shifting groups in the absence of hierarchy and bureaucracy, and in that environment, where the workplace doubles as the rec room, the particulars of your personality matter a great deal.

This is part of the new economy's appeal, because Tellme's soaring warehouse is a more productive and enjoyable place to work than the little office boxes of the old I.B.M. But the danger here is that we will be led astray in judging these newly important particulars of character. If we let personality—some indefinable, prerational intuition, magnified by the Fundamental Attribution Error—bias the hiring process today, then all we will have done is replace the old-boy network, where you hired your nephew, with the new-boy network, where you hire whoever impressed you most when you shook his hand. Social progress, unless we're careful, can merely be the means by which we replace the obviously arbitrary with the not so obviously arbitrary.

Myers has spent much of the past year helping to teach Introduction to Computer Science. He realized, he says, that one of the reasons that students were taking the course was that they wanted to get jobs in the software industry. "I decided that, having gone through all this interviewing, I had developed some expertise, and I would like to share that. There is a real skill and art in presenting yourself to potential employers. And so what we did in this class was talk about the kinds of things that employers are looking for—what are they looking for in terms of personality. One of the most important things is that you have to come across as being confident in what you are doing and in who you are. How do you do that? Speak clearly and smile." As he said that, Nolan Myers smiled. "For a lot of people, that's a very hard skill to learn. But for some reason I seem to understand it intuitively."

CRITICAL THINKING QUESTIONS

1. In everyday situations, what can be done to help minimize the power of first impressions? Or is it even possible *not* to form first impressions? Defend your position with data regarding impression formation and impression management.

2. What advice have you received about how to make a good first impression on other people? How consistent (or inconsistent) is that advice with the information contained in this article?

3. How might the findings in this article about the power of first impressions be applicable to jury trials? Dating situations? Is the process involved in forming a first impression fundamentally the same in all situations, or does it depend on the context in which the impression is being made? Defend your position.

4. The concept of *emotional intelligence* has attracted a good deal of interest in recent years . Find information on this concept, and relate it to the ideas presented in this article.

5. Based upon the information in this article, what advice would you give to someone about how to make a favorable initial impression on a prospective employer?

ARTICLE 5 _____

A variety of sources of information may be available for use in forming an impression of a person. However, that does not mean that all of the information will be used or hold equal value. Some sources of information may carry more weight than others. For example, we may notice how the person acts, or we may have heard something about him or her from someone else. How do we use this information to develop an impression of the person?

Building on the classic work of S. E. Asch, Harold H. Kelley examines what can be called a *central organizing trait*, one that is important in influencing the impressions that we form. By examining the effect of changing just one adjective in describing a person (i.e., *warm* versus *cold*), the study demonstrates that this initial difference influenced how the subjects actually rated the person. Even more interesting is that these differences in initial impression carried over into how the subjects interacted with the person. The implication is that perhaps our initial impressions lead us to act in certain ways toward others, perhaps creating a self-fulfilling prophecy by giving us what we expected to see in the first place.

The Warm-Cold Variable in First Impressions of Persons

■ Harold H. Kelley

This experiment is one of several studies of first impressions (3), the purpose of the series being to investigate the stability of early judgments, their determinants, and the relation of such judgments to the behavior of the person making them. In interpreting the data from several nonexperimental studies on the stability of first impressions, it proved to be necessary to postulate inner-observer variables which contribute to the impression and which remain relatively constant through time. Also some evidence was obtained which directly demonstrated the existence of these variables and their nature. The present experiment was designed to determine the effects of one kind of inner-observer variable, specifically, *expectations* about the stimulus person which the observer brings to the exposure situation.

That prior information or labels attached to a stimulus person make a difference in observers' first impressions is almost too obvious to require demonstration. The expectations resulting from such preinformation may restrict, modify, or accentuate the impressions he will have. The crucial question is: What changes in perception will accompany a given expectation? Studies of stereotyping, for example, that of Katz and Braly (2), indicate that from an ethnic label such as "German" or "Negro," a number of perceptions follow which are culturally determined. The present study finds its main significance in relation to a study by Asch (1) which demonstrates that certain crucial labels can transform the entire impression of the person, leading to attributions which are related to the label on a broad cultural basis or even, perhaps, on an autochthonous basis.

Asch read to his subjects a list of adjectives which purportedly described a particular person. He then asked them to characterize that person. He found that the inclusion in the list of what he called *central* qualities, such as "warm" as opposed to "cold," produced a widespread change in the entire impression. This effect was not adequately explained by the halo effect since it did not extend indiscriminately in a positive or negative direction to all characteristics.

Rather, it differentially transformed the other qualities, for example, by changing their relative importance in the total impression. Peripheral qualities (such as "polite" versus "blunt") did not produce effects as strong as those produced by the central qualities.[1]

The present study tested the effects of such central qualities upon the early impressions of *real* persons, the same qualities, "warm" vs. "cold," being used. They were introduced as preinformation about the stimulus person before his actual appearance; so presumably they operated as expectations rather than as part of the stimulus pattern during the exposure period. In addition, information was obtained about the effects of the expectations upon the observers' behavior toward the stimulus person. An earlier study in this series has indicated that the more incompatible the observer initially perceived the stimulus person to be, the less the observer initiated interaction with him thereafter. The second purpose of the present experiment, then, was to provide a better controlled study of this relationship.

No previous studies reported in the literature have dealt with the importance of first impressions for behavior. The most relevant data are found in the sociometric literature, where there are scattered studies of the relation between choices among children having some prior acquaintance and their interaction behavior. For an example, see the study by Newstetter, Feldstein, and Newcomb (8).

PROCEDURE

The experiment was performed in three sections of a psychology course (Economics 70) at the Massachusetts Institute of Technology.[2] The three sections provided 23, 16, and 16 subjects respectively. All 55 subjects were men, most of them in their third college year. In each class the stimulus person (also a male) was completely unknown to the subjects before the experimental period. One person served as stimulus person in two sections, and a second person took this role in the third section. In each case the stimulus person was introduced by the experimenter, who posed as a representative of the course instructors and who gave the following statement:

Your regular instructor is out of town today, and since we of Economics 70 are interested in the general problem of how various classes react to different instructors, we're going to have an instructor today you've never had before, Mr. ____. Then, at the end of the period, I want you to fill out some forms about him. In order to give you some idea of what he's like, we've had a person who knows him write up a little biographical note about him. I'll pass this out to you now and you can read it before he arrives. Please read these to yourselves and don't talk about this among yourselves until the class is over so that he won't get wind of what's going on.

Two kinds of these notes were distributed, the two being identical except that in one the stimulus person was described among other things as being "rather cold" whereas in the other form the phrase "very warm" was substituted. The content of the "rather cold" version is as follows:

Mr. ____ is a graduate student in the Department of Economics and Social Science here at M.I.T. He has had three semesters of teaching experience in psychology at another college. This is his first semester teaching Ec. 70. He is 26 years old, a veteran, and married. People who know him consider him to be a rather cold person, industrious, critical, practical, and determined.

The two types of preinformation were distributed randomly within each of the three classes and in such a manner that the students were not aware that two kinds of information were being given out. The stimulus person then appeared and led the class in a twenty-minute discussion. During this time the experimenter kept a record of how often each student participated in the discussion. Since the discussion was almost totally leader-centered, this participation record indicates the number of times each student initiated verbal interaction with the instructor. After the discussion period, the stimulus person left the room, and the experimenter gave the following instructions:

Now, I'd like to get your impression of Mr. ____. This is not a test of you and can in no way affect your grade in this course. This material will not be identified as belonging to particular persons and will be kept strictly confidential. It will be of most value to us if you are completely honest in your evaluation of Mr. _____. Also, please understand that what you put down will not be used against him or cause him to lose his job or anything like that. This is not a test of him but merely a study of how different classes react to different instructors.

The subjects then wrote free descriptions of the stimulus person and finally rated him on a set of 15 rating scales.

RESULTS AND DISCUSSION

1. *Influence of warm-cold variable on first impressions.* The differences in the ratings produced by the warm-cold variable were consistent from one section to another even where different stimulus persons were used. Consequently, the data from the three sections were combined by equating means (the S.D.'s were approximately equal) and the results for the total group are presented in Table 1. Also in this table is presented that part of Asch's data which refers to the qualities included in our rating scales. From this table it is quite clear that those given the "warm" preinformation consistently rated the stimulus person more favorably than those given the "cold" preinformation. Summarizing the statistically significant differences, the "warm" subjects rated the stimulus person as more considerate of others, more informal, more sociable, more popular, better natured, more humorous, and more humane. These findings are very similar to Asch's for the characteristics common to both studies. He found more frequent attribution to his hypothetical "warm" personalities of sociability,

TABLE 1 / Comparison of "Warm" and "Cold" Observers in Terms of Average Ratings Given Stimulus Persons

Item	Low End of Rating Scale	High End of Rating Scale	Average Rating		Level of Significance of Warm-Cold Difference	Asch's Data: Per Cent of Group Assigning Quality at Low End of Our Rating Scale*	
			Warm N = 27	Cold N = 28		Warm	Cold
1	Knows his stuff	Doesn't know his stuff	3.5	4.6			
2	Considerate of others	Self-centered	6.3	9.6	1%		
3†	Informal	Formal	6.3	9.6	1%		
4†	Modest	Proud	9.4	10.6			
5	Sociable	Unsociable	5.6	10.4	1%	91%	38%
6	Self-assured	Uncertain of himself	8.4	9.1			
7	High intelligence	Low intelligence	4.8	5.1			
8	Popular	Unpopular	4.0	7.4	1%	84%	28%
9†	Good natured	Irritable	9.4	12.0	5%	94%	17%
10	Generous	Ungenerous	8.2	9.6		91%	08%
11	Humorous	Humorless	8.3	11.7	1%	77%	13%
12	Important	Insignificant	6.5	8.6		88%	99%
13†	Humane	Ruthless	8.6	11.0	5%	86%	31%
14†	Submissive	Dominant	13.2	14.5			
15	Will go far	Will not get ahead	4.2	5.8			

*Given for all qualities common to Asch's list and this set of rating scales.
†These scales were reversed when presented to the subjects.

popularity, good naturedness, generosity, humorousness, and humaneness. So these data strongly support his finding that such a central quality as "warmth" can greatly influence the total impression of a personality. This effect is found to be operative in the perception of real persons.

This general favorableness in the perceptions of the "warm" observers as compared with the "cold" ones indicates that something like a halo effect may have been operating in these ratings. Although his data are not completely persuasive on this point, Asch was convinced that such a general effect was *not* operating in his study. Closer inspection of the present data makes it clear that the "warm-cold" effect cannot be explained altogether on the basis of simple halo effect. In Table 1 it is evident that the "warm-cold" variable produced differential effects from one rating scale to another. The size of this effect seems to depend upon the closeness of relation between the specific dimension of any given rating scale and the central quality of "warmth" or "coldness." Even though the rating of intelligence may be influenced by a halo effect, it is not influenced to the same degree to which considerateness is. It seems to make sense to view such strongly influenced items as considerateness, informality, good naturedness, and humaneness as dynamically more closely related to warmth and hence more perceived in terms of this relation than in terms of a general positive or negative feeling toward the stimulus person. If first impressions are normally made in terms of such general dimensions as "warmth" and "coldness," the power they give the observer in making predictions and specific evaluations about such disparate behavior characteristics as formality and considerateness is considerable (even though these predictions may be incorrect or misleading).

The free report impression data were analyzed for only one of the sections. In general, there were few sizable differences between the "warm" and "cold" observers. The "warm" observers attributed more nervousness, more sincerity, and more industriousness to the stimulus person. Although the frequencies of comparable qualities are very low because of the great variety of descriptions produced by the observers, there is considerable agreement with the rating scale data.

Two important phenomena are illustrated in these free description protocols, the first of them having been noted by Asch. *Firstly,* the characteristics of the stimulus person are interpreted in terms of the precognition of warmth or coldness. For example, a "warm" observer writes about a rather shy and retiring stimulus person as follows: "He makes friends slowly but they are lasting friendships when formed." In another instance, several "cold" observers described him as being, ". . . intolerant: would be angry if you disagree with his view. . ."; while several "warm" observers put the same thing this way: "Unyielding in principle, not easily influenced or swayed from his original attitude." *Secondly,* the preinformation about the stimulus person's warmth or coldness is evaluated and interpreted in the light of the direct behavioral data about him. For example, "He has a slight inferiority complex which leads to his coldness," and "His conscientiousness and industriousness might be mistaken for coldness." Examples of these two phenomena occurred rather infrequently, and there was no way to evaluate the relative strengths of these countertendencies. Certainly some such evaluation is necessary to determine the conditions under which behavior which is contrary to a stereotyped label resists distortion and leads to rejection of the label.

A comparison of the data from the two different stimulus persons is pertinent to the last point in so far as it indicates the interaction between the properties of the stimulus person and the label. The fact that the warm-cold variable generally produced differences in the same direction for the two stimulus persons, even though they are very different in personality, behavior, and mannerisms, indicates the strength of this variable. However, there were some exceptions to this tendency as well as marked differences in the *degree* to which the experimental variable was able to produce differences. For example, stimulus person A typically appears to be anything but lacking in self-esteem and on rating scale 4 he was generally at the "proud" end of the scale. Although the "warm" observers tended to rate him as they did the other stimulus person (i.e., more "modest"), the difference between the "warm" and "cold" means for stimulus person A is very small and not significant as it is for stimulus person B. Similarly, stimulus person B was seen as "unpopular" and "humorless," which agrees with his typical classroom behavior. Again the "warm" observers rated him more favorably on these items, but their ratings were not significantly different from those of the "cold" observers, as was true for the other stimulus person. Thus we see that the strength or compelling-ness of various qualities of the stimulus person must be reckoned with. The stimulus is not passive to the forces arising from the label but actively resists distor-tion and may severely limit the degree of influence exerted by the preinformation.[3]

2. *Influence of warm-cold variable on interaction with the stimulus person.* In the analysis of the fre-quency with which the various students took part in the discussion led by the stimulus person, a larger proportion of those given the "warm" preinformation participated than of those given the "cold" preinfor-mation. Fifty-six per cent of the "warm" subjects entered the discussion, whereas only 32 per cent of the "cold" subjects did so. Thus the expectation of warmth not only produced more favorable early perceptions of the stimulus person but led to greater initiation of interaction with him. This relation is a low one, significant at between the 5 per cent and 10 percent level of confidence, but it is in line with the general principle that social perception serves to guide and steer the person's behavior in his social environment.

As would be expected from the foregoing findings, there was also a relation between the favorableness of the impression and whether or not the person partici-pated in the discussion. Although any single item yielded only a small and insignificant relation to par-ticipation, when a number are combined the trend becomes clear cut. For example, when we combine the seven items which were influenced to a statistically significant degree by the warm-cold variable, the total score bears considerable relation to participation, the relationship being significant as well beyond the 1 per cent level. A larger proportion of those having favor-able total impressions participated than of those hav-ing unfavorable impressions, the bi-serial correlation between these variables being .34. Although this relation may be interpreted in several ways, it seems most likely that the unfavorable perception led to a curtailment of interaction. Support for this comes from one of the other studies in this series (3). There it was found that those persons having unfavorable impressions of the instructor at the end of the first class meeting tended less often to initiate interactions with him in the succeeding four meetings than did those having favorable first impressions. There was

also some tendency in the same study for those per-sons who interacted least with the instructor to change least in their judgments of him from the first to later impressions.

It will be noted that these relations lend some support to the autistic hostility hypothesis proposed by Newcomb (7). This hypothesis suggests that the possession of an initially hostile attitude toward a person leads to a restriction of communication and contact with him which in turn serves to preserve the hostile attitude by preventing the acquisition of data which could correct it. The present data indicate that a restriction of interaction is associated with unfavor-able preinformation and an unfavorable perception. The data from the other study support this result and also indicate the correctness of the second part of the hypothesis, that restricted interaction reduces the like-lihood of change in the attitude.

What makes these findings more significant is that they appear in the context of a discussion class where there are numerous *induced* and *own* forces to enter the discussion and to interact with the instructor. It seems likely that the effects predicted by Newcomb's hypothesis would be much more marked in a setting where such forces were not present.

SUMMARY

The warm-cold variable had been found by Asch to produce large differences in the impressions of per-sonality formed from a list of adjectives. In this study the same variable was introduced in the form of expec-tations about a real person and was found to produce similar differences in first impressions of him in a classroom setting. In addition, the differences in first impressions produced by the different expectations were shown to influence the observers' behavior to-ward the stimulus person. Those observers given the favorable expectation (who, consequently, had a fa-vorable impression of the stimulus person) tended to interact more with him than did those given the unfavorable expectation.

REFERENCES

1. Asch, S. E., Forming impressions of personality. *J. Abnorm. Soc. Psychol.,* 1946, 41, 258–290.

2. Katz, D., and Braly, K. W. Verbal stereotypes and racial prejudice. In Newcomb, T. M. and Hartley, E. L. (eds.), *Readings in social psychology*. New York: Holt, 1947. Pp. 204–210.

3. Kelley, H. H. First impressions in interpersonal relations. Ph.D. thesis, Massachusetts Institute of Technology, Cambridge, Mass. Sept., 1948.

4. Krech, D., and Crutchfield, R. S. *Theory and problems of social psychology*. New York, McGraw-Hill, 1948.

5. Luchins, A. S. Forming impressions of personality: A critique. *J. Abnorm. Soc. Psychol.*, 1948, 43, 318–325.

6. Mensch, I. N., and Wishner, J. Asch on "Forming impressions of personality": further evidence. *J. Personal.*, 1947, 16, 188–191.

7. Newcomb, T. M. Autistic hostility and social reality. *Hum. Relations.*, 1947, 1, 69–86.

8. Newstetter, W. I., Feldstein, M. H., and Newcomb, T. M. *Group adjustment: A study in experimental sociology*. Cleveland: Western Reserve University, 1938.

ENDNOTES

1. Since the present experiment was carried out, Mensch and Wishner (6) have repeated a number of Asch's experiments because of dissatisfaction with his sex and geographic distribution. Their data substantiate Asch's very closely. Also, Luchins (5) has criticized Asch's experiments for their artificial methodology, repeated some of them, and challenged some of the kinds of interpretations Asch made from his data. Luchins also briefly reports some tantalizing conclusions from a number of studies of first impressions of actual persons.

2. Professor Mason Haire, now of the University of California, provided valuable advice and help in executing the experiment.

3. We must raise an important question here: Would there be a tendency for "warm" observers to distort the perception in the favorable direction regardless of how much the stimulus deviated from the expectation? Future research should test the following hypothesis, which is suggested by Gestalt perception theory (4, pp. 95–98): If the stimulus differs but slightly from the expectation, the perception will tend to be *assimilated* to the expectation; however, if the difference between the stimulus and expectation is too great, the perception will occur by contrast to the expectation and will be distorted in the opposite direction.

CRITICAL THINKING QUESTIONS

1. Reread the information that was presented to the subjects to manipulate the warm-cold variable. The manipulation obviously produced a significant effect on the subjects' subsequent evaluations of the teacher. Do you feel that the manipulation was realistic? For example, how realistic is it to have a guest teacher described as "rather cold" in a brief biographical sketch? Could this particular manipulation have resulted in any experimental demand characteristics? Address the issue of the relative importance of experimental versus mundane realism as it pertains to this study.

2. How long lasting do you think first impressions are? For example, would they persist over the course of a semester or even longer? How could you test this?

3. What are the practical implications of this study? If you were working in a setting where you were interviewing and hiring applicants for a job, how could you use this information to help you make better, more accurate decisions?

4. The warm-cold information was provided by the instructor of the course, a person who presumably had high credibility. Do you think the credibility of the source of the information would affect how influenced the individuals were? How could you test this?

ADDITIONAL RELATED READINGS

Singh, R., & Teoh, J. B. P. (2000). Impression formation from intellectual and social traits: Evidence for behavioural adaptation and cognitive processing. *British Journal of Social Psychology, 39*(4), 537–554.

Stapel, D. A., & Koomen, W. (2000). The impact of opposites: Implications of trait inferences and their antonyms for person judgment. *Journal of Experimental Social Psychology, 36*(5), 439–464.

ARTICLE 6 _____

What information do we use in forming impressions of other people? When meeting people for the first time, we certainly rely on outward characteristics, such as how they look and dress. We also give a lot of weight to how they act. Do they seem friendly and trustworthy? Or does something about them seem aloof or hostile?

Some of the information that we use in forming initial impressions of people is based upon stereotypes of what they look like or whom they remind us of, but even more information is obtained from watching their nonverbal cues. Why is this the case? Simply put, many of the things that people do are under their direct control. For example, the words that we choose to speak are subject to our conscious influence and hence can be readily manipulated. But our nonverbal behavior, such as the body movements that accompany our words, are somewhat less under conscious control. Furthermore, while we are better able to select the words we speak, we may be less aware of—and thus able to control—changes in our speech patterns (known as *paralanguage*), such as pausing, pitch of voice, and rate of speech. An observer may give the nonverbal and paralanguage cues more weight than what we actually say because those cues may seem a more honest reflection of what we are really all about.

One obvious practical application of the use of nonverbal and paralanguage cues is to detect deception. Being able to tell when someone is lying to us has real advantages. Research suggests that lying is a fairly common part of human interaction. Occasionally, these falsehoods take the form of bold-faced lies, such as making up a story to get out of trouble for something we have done. More commonly, however, we use so-called white lies to skirt the truth and perhaps not hurt someone's feelings ("Yes, dear, I really loved the vacuum cleaner you gave me for Christmas").

But how accurate are most of us in detecting such deceptions? Furthermore, are trained professionals, such as police and customs agents, better at detecting deception than the average person? A good deal of research suggests that most people, including law-enforcement professionals, are not particularly accurate in determining when someone is lying. The following article by Aldert Vrij, Katherine Edward, Kim P. Roberts, and Ray Bull examines what factors actually may be most important in detecting deception and which detection techniques may be the most useful in identifying lies.

Detecting Deceit via Analysis of Verbal and Nonverbal Behavior

■ Aldert Vrij, Katherine Edward, Kim P. Roberts, and Ray Bull

Abstract: *We examined the hypotheses that (1) a systematic analysis of nonverbal behavior could be useful in the detection of deceit and (2) that lie detection would be most accurate if both verbal and nonverbal indicators of deception are taken into account. Seventy-three nursing students participated in a study about "telling lies" and either told the truth or lied about a film they had just seen. The interviews were videotaped and audiotaped, and the nonverbal behavior (NVB) and speech content of the liars and truth tellers were analyzed, the latter with*

Reprinted from *Journal of Nonverbal Behavior, 24*(4), 239–263. Copyright © 2000 by Plenum Publishers. Reprinted by permission.

the Criteria-Based Content Analysis technique (CBCA) and the Reality Monitoring technique (RM). Results revealed several nonverbal and verbal indicators of deception. On the basis of nonverbal behavior alone, 78% of the lies and truths could be correctly classified. An even higher percentage could be correctly classified when all three detection techniques (i.e., NVB, CBCA, RM) were taken into account.

There are, in principle, three ways to catch liars: (1) by observing how they behave (the movements they make, whether or not they smile or show gaze aversion, their pitch of voice, their speech rate, whether or not they stutter, and so on), (2) by listening to what they say (analyzing the speech content), and (3) by measuring their physiological responses. In order to measure physiological responses, several polygraph test procedures have been developed such as the Control Question Test (Raskin, 1979, 1982, 1986; Reid, 1947) and the Guilty Knowledge Test (Lykken, 1960, 1998). Deception detection techniques based on what a person says include Content-Based Criteria Analysis (CBCA) (Köhnken, 1990, 1996; Steller & Köhnken, 1989) and Reality Monitoring (RM) (Porter & Yuille, 1996; Sporer, 1997). David Raskin and Gunter Köhnken—leading experts in lie detection via physiological responses and via what is said, respectively—both believe that detecting deception via nonverbal behavioral cues is a precarious exercise on which people cannot rely (Köhnken, 1997, personal communication; Raskin, 1996, personal communication).

Research, so far seems to support this pessimistic view. When detecting deceit via nonverbal cues, accuracy rates (percentage of correct answers) usually vary between 45 and 60 percent, when a 50% accuracy rate would be obtained by tossing a coin (DePaulo, Stone, & Lassiter, 1985a; Kraut, 1980; Vrij, 2000). If accuracy at detecting lies is computed separately from accuracy at detecting truths, it emerges that people are particularly poor at detecting lies. In a recent review including approximately 40 studies, Vrij (2000) found a 67% accuracy rate for detecting truths and a 44% accuracy rate for detecting lies. (The high accuracy rate for truths and the low accuracy rate for lies is the result of a 'truth-bias: People's tendency to judge other's messages as being truthful' [Levine, Park, & McCornack, 1999; Vrij, 2000]). Although the average hit rate for detecting truths (67%) is

reasonably high, it says little about lie detection skills. Good lie detection implies high accuracy rates for both detecting truths and detecting lies. Research has shown that it is possible to detect *both* lies and truths above the level of chance (on average around 70% or above) when conducting polygraph tests (Ekman, 1992; Vrij, 2000) or when using CBCA or RM (Vrij, 2000; Vrij & Akehurst, 1998).

Although observers seem to perform relatively poorly in detecting deceit while paying attention to nonverbal cues compared to detecting deceit by analyzing with CBCA or RM or by measuring physiological responses, we are reluctant to draw any firm conclusions on the basis of such comparisons as those comparisons are unfair and inappropriate. Studies of detecting deceit via examining physiological responses or via CBCA and RM always include well-trained experts as lie detectors (because they are the only ones who know how to conduct such examinations), whereas lay persons (e.g., college students) are often used as lie detectors in studies involving nonverbal behavior. Some nonverbal behavior studies, however, used professionals such as police officers and customs officers as lie detectors. Although several studies showed that even those professionals perform around the level of chance (DePaulo & Pfeifer, 1986; Köhnken, 1987; Vrij, 1993). Ekman and his colleagues (Ekman & O'Sullivan, 1991; Ekman, O'Sullivan, & Frank, 1999) found that some groups of professionals perform above the level of chance, such as members of the Secret Service and a group of federal officers with a special interest and experience in deception. The latter group obtained an accuracy rate (truths and lies combined) of 73% (Ekman et al., 1999). However, even these hit rates are within the range of scores reported in the literature for untrained human lie detectors with no special experience (DePaulo, Anderson, & Cooper, 1999).

An explanation why professionals also seem to perform poorly in detecting lies via examining nonverbal behavior is that they do not know where to look and have false beliefs about which behaviors might be clues to deception (Akehurst, Köhnken, Bull, & Vrij, 1996; Vrij & Semin, 1996). Vrij and Semin (1996) found that 75% of professional lie detectors (police officers, customs officers and so on) believe that liars look away, although gaze aversion has not been found to be a reliable indicator of deception (DePaulo et al.,

1985; Vrij, 2000; Zuckerman, DePaulo, & Rosenthal, 1981). Research has shown that observers improve their skills in detecting deceit if they receive some information about the relationship between nonverbal behavior and deception. Lie detectors in deTurck's (1991) study obtained an accuracy rate of 70% after they were informed to ignore looking at eye contact but to focus their attention on message duration, response latency, pauses, nonfluencies, adaptors and hand gestures. These accuracy rates are probably still not at their potential level due to the fact that judges do not always use the information with which they are provided. Vrij (1994) informed judges that liars generally display fewer subtle hand and finger movements than truth tellers. He then showed judges videoclips of twenty different people. For each person, two video fragments were presented simultaneously (on two different TV screens located next to each other). In one fragment the person was lying and in the other fragment the person was telling the truth. The judges were asked to indicate for each person in which fragment the person was lying. By consequently using the information provided, 75% of the answers could have been correct. The average accuracy rate, however, was only 60%, suggesting that the judges did not consistently apply the information provided.

It is therefore possible that even higher accuracy rates could be obtained when a more sophisticated nonverbal behavior deception detection method is used, excluding any subjective interpretations. The present experiment examines this issue.

The crucial question is to which behaviors attention should be paid. This question is difficult to answer, as research has shown that deception itself is not related to a unique pattern of specific behaviors (DePaulo et al., 1985; Ekman, 1992; Vrij, 1998, 2000; Zuckerman et al., 1981). In other words, there is nothing like Pinocchio's nose. However, liars might experience emotions while lying. The three most common types of emotion associated with deceit are fear, excitement ('duping delight') and guilt (Ekman, 1989, 1992). Liars might be afraid of getting caught, they might become excited at having the opportunity of fooling someone, or they might feel guilty (Ekman, 1992). In some situations, liars also might find it difficult to lie. They have to think of plausible answers, should not contradict themselves, should tell a lie that is consistent with everything the other person knows, should avoid making slips of the tongue, and have to remember what they have said, so that they can say the same things when someone asks them to repeat their story. Experiencing emotions and cognitive load might result in signs of emotion and cognitive load which then gives the lie away (Ekman, 1992; Vrij, 1998, 2000). Experimental studies concerning how people behave under stress have been mainly conducted by Ekman and his colleagues (Ekman, 1992; Frank & Ekman, 1997). They found that under these circumstances it is possible to detect deceit (they reported hit rates around 80%) by paying attention to signs of emotions which emerge via (micro) facial expressions (Frank & Ekman, 1997) or by observing smiles and pitch of voice (Ekman, O'Sullivan, Friesen, & Scherer, 1991). The strongest evidence for the effects of raising the stakes would be obtained by experimentally manipulating the stakes. In a series of experiments conducted by DePaulo and her colleagues in which the stakes were manipulated, it was found that high stake lies were indeed easier to detect than low stake lies (DePaulo, Kirkendol, Tang, & O'Brien, 1988; DePaulo, Lanier, & Davis, 1983; DePaulo, LeMay, & Epstein, 1991; DePaulo, Stone, & Lassiter, 1985b; Lane & DePaulo, 1999). In one of our own recent studies (Vrij, Harden, Terry, Edward, & Bull, in press) this finding was replicated.

The present experiment deals with cognitive load. All participants watched a videotape of a theft in a hospital. In a subsequent interview specific questions about the film were asked. Some participants were requested to recall what they had seen, whereas others were asked to lie without having much time to prepare their lies. The fact that the participants had to lie almost spontaneously makes this task difficult for the liars and we therefore expected liars, compared to truth tellers, to show more behaviors that indicate cognitive load. In particular, we expected liars to show a longer latency period, more 'ah' and 'non-ah' speech disturbances, a slower speech rate and fewer illustrators and hand/finger movements (Hypothesis 1) as these behaviors are associated with thinking hard (Burgoon, Kelly, Newton, & Keely-Dyreson, 1989; Ekman & Friesen, 1972; Goldman-Eisler, 1968; Köhnken, 1989; Vrij, 1998). See the Method section for a description of these behaviors. In order to find out to what extent truth tellers and liars can be correctly classified on the basis of these behaviors, discriminant analyses were conducted with objective truth status as the classifying variable and these six nonverbal behaviors as independent variables. It was expected that the analysis would reveal an accuracy rate (percentage of correct classifications of truth tellers and liars) above the level of chance (Hypothesis 2).

Differences between liars and truth tellers in what they say are often assessed using Criteria-Based Content Analysis (CBCA) (Ruby & Brigham, 1997; Steller & Köhnken, 1989; Vrij, 2000; Vrij & Akehurst, 1998). CBCA was developed in Germany by Steller and Köhnken (Steller & Köhnken, 1989) in order to evaluate statements from children who are witnesses or alleged victims, most commonly of sexual abuse. Many authors still describe CBCA as a technique solely developed to evaluate statements made by children in sexual offense trials (Honts, 1994; Horowitz, Lamb, Esplin, Boychuk, Krispin, & Reiter-Lavery, 1997). Others, however, advocate the additional use of the technique to evaluate the testimonies of adults who talk about issues other than sexual abuse (Köhnken, Schimossek, Aschermann, & Höfer, 1995; Porter & Yuille, 1996; Ruby & Brigham, 1997; Steller & Köhnken, 1989). In CBCA, trained evaluators examine a statement and judge the presence or absence of each of 19 criteria. Appendix 1 provides a brief description of the CBCA criteria used in this study. Vrij and Akehurst (1998) and Vrij (2000) give more detailed descriptions of the CBCA criteria. The underlying hypothesis of CBCA is that a statement derived from an actual memory of an experience differs in content and quality from a statement based on invention or fantasy, and that only a person who has actually experienced an event is likely to incorporate certain types of content into a statement about it. In other words, the presence of each criterion strengthens the hypothesis that the account is based on genuine personal experience. This hypothesis is originally stated by Undeutsch (1967, 1989) and is therefore known as the *Undeutsch-Hypothesis* (Steller, 1989). Following the Undeutsch-hypothesis, it was expected that liars would obtain lower CBCA scores than truth tellers (Hypothesis 3), and that liars and truth tellers could be correctly classified above the level of chance on the basis of their CBCA scores (Hypothesis 4).

Recently, Reality Monitoring has been used as an alternative method to measure verbal differences between responses believed to be true and false (Alonso-Quecuty, 1992, 1996; Hernandez-Fernaud & Alonso-Quecuty, 1997; Höfer, Akehurst, & Metzger, 1996; Manzanero & Diges, 1996; Roberts, Lamb, Zale, & Randall, 1998; Sporer, 1997). The core of Reality Monitoring is that memories of real experiences are obtained through perceptual processes and are therefore likely to contain *perceptual information* (visual details and details of sound, smell, taste, or physical sensations), *contextual information* (details about where and when the event took place), and *affective information* (details about how someone felt during the event). Accounts of imagined events are derived from in internal source and are therefore likely to contain *cognitive operations,* such as thoughts and reasonings ('I can only remember my thinking of what my friend would like to have for a present') (Johnson, Hashtroudi, & Lindsay, 1993; Johnson & Raye, 1981, 1998). It was therefore expected that truth tellers would obtain a higher Reality Monitoring score than liars (Hypothesis 5) and would include more perceptual, contextual and affective information in their statements than liars (Hypothesis 6). Liars, on the other hand, are likely to include more cognitive operations in their statements than truth tellers (Hypothesis 7). It was also expected that liars and truth tellers could be correctly classified above the level of chance on the basis of their Reality Monitoring scores (Hypothesis 8).

Finally, it was investigated whether a combination of the two verbal techniques and the nonverbal technique would classify liars and truth tellers more accurately than the individual techniques. We expected this to be the case. A combined technique takes more information into account than do individual techniques, and, the more aspects of liars that will be scrutinized, the more likely it is that their lies can be detected (Hypothesis 9).

METHOD

Participants

A total of 73 nursing students participated, 20 males and 53 females. Their average age was $M = 28.89$ years

(*SD* = 7.9 years). Originally, 79 participants took part in the experiment. Three participants, however, gave answers which lasted less than 10 seconds. As it is impossible to perform CBCA assessments on very short statements, these participants were disregarded in the analyses. Another two participants did not lie when requested to do so and one participant lied when asked to tell the truth. These participants were also disregarded in the analyses.

Procedure

Nursing students were recruited at the University of Portsmouth nursing school. They were asked to participate in a study about "telling lies." Each student participated individually and received £5 for their participation. First of all, in order to motivate the nurses to try to perform well in the study they were told that the ability to lie successfully is extremely important to nurses and that good nurses may need to be good liars. Previous research has indicated that this information does increase participants' motivation to perform well (DePaulo, Kirkendol, Tang, & O'Brien, 1988; DePaulo, Lanier, & Davis, 1983). They were then told that they would see a video and that they would be interviewed twice about this video. In one interview they had to recall what they had seen and in the other interview they had to lie. The order in which the truthful and deceptive interviews took place was counterbalanced. Only the first interviews (deceptive for some participants and truthful for others) were analyzed, creating a between-subjects design. We introduced the study to the participants as a within-subjects design because we wanted all participants to lie. We did this for motivation purposes: (1) in this case nobody could think that they were allocated to a 'control condition' and (2) the information about the good liar-good nurses relationship was relevant to all participants. The nurses were then shown a video of 118 seconds in length. This videotaped event featured a colour presentation of the theft of a bag from a patient by a visitor. In the video, a woman enters a hospital and walks to the first floor. While walking down the corridor, she notices a patient lying in bed with a handbag next to her. The visitor enters her room, looks at the patient's name plate and pretends that she knows the patient. She then takes the bag and

starts to walk out of the room. The patient notices the theft and asks the visitor to return the handbag. A nurse comes in and asks what is going on. The patient tells the nurse that she does not know the visitor and that the visitor is trying to steal her bag. The visitor tells the nurse that she is the patient's neighbour and that the patient is confused. The nurse then leaves the room. The video finishes with the visitor smiling as she opens the patient's purse and notices money in it.

After watching the video, participants in the *truthful condition* (*N* = 34) were asked the following three general and open-ended questions: What did the nurse do? What did the patient do? and What did the visitor do? They were asked to answer all questions truthfully. Participants in the *deception condition* (*N* = 39) were asked to lie while answering the same three questions. In order to make the task not too difficult for the participants they were informed about two of the three questions that would be asked before the interview started and they were given approximately 15 seconds to think about an answer. Which questions were told beforehand was counterbalanced. Analyses showed that this manipulation had no effect on either the verbal or nonverbal behavior displayed by the participants and will therefore be disregarded in this article. All interviews were videotaped and audiotaped and were transcribed verbatim from the audiotapes (the transcripts included the stutters made by the participants). The answers of truth tellers were significantly longer (*M* = 89 seconds, *SD* = 46) than the answers of liars (*M* = 42 seconds, *SD* = 19), $F(1, 71) = 34.06$, $p < .01$).

Dependent Variables

Two observers coded the behavior of the participants independently, and Pearson's correlations were conducted between the two sets of data from the two coders to detect any differences in judgement. The observers were not informed as to whether the participants were lying or telling the truth and had not seen the stimulus video. They employed a coding system used by us in previous studies (Akehurst & Vrij, 1999; Vrij, 1991, 1995; Vrij, Semin, & Bull, 1996; Vrij, Akehurst, & Morris, 1997). The following ten behaviors were coded (the 'ah' and 'non-ah' speech disturbances were scored on the basis of a typed verbatim text):

- *gaze aversion:* number of seconds for which the participant looked away from the interviewer (2 coders, $r = .95$, $p < .01$)
- *smiling:* frequency of smiles and laughs (2 coders, $r = .90$, $p < .01$)
- *illustrators:* frequency of arm and hand movements which were designed to modify and/or supplement what was being said verbally (Ekman & Friesen, 1969) (2 coders, $r = .96$, $p < .01$)
- *adaptors:* frequency of scratching the head, wrists etc. Rubbing one's hands together were not coded as adaptors but as hand and finger movements (2 coders, $r = .94$, $p < .01$)
- *frequency of hand and finger movements:* Movements of the hands or fingers without moving the arms (2 coders, $r = .92$, $p < .01$)
- *frequency of foot and leg movements:* Movements of feet or legs. Simultaneous movements of feet and legs were scored as one movement (2 coders, $r = .93$, $p < .01$)
- *speech hesitations:* frequency of saying 'ah' or 'mm' between words (2 coders, $r = .95$, $p < .01$)
- *speech errors:* frequency of word and/or sentence repetition, sentence change, sentence incompletion, and slips of the tongue (2 coders, $r = .91$, $p < .01$).
- *latency period:* period of time between the question being asked and the answer being given (2 coders, $r = .98$, $p < .01$)
- *speech* rate: number of spoken words (using the count option in WordPerfect) divided by the length of interview minus latency period (2 coders, $r = .98$, $p < .01$).

The Pearson's correlations show evidence of a strong consistency between the two coders. Thus, the behavioral scores were based on the average scores of the two coders and are presented in Table 1. The reported duration and frequencies of all categories of nonverbal behavior were corrected for the length of the interviews or for the number of spoken words. Patterns listed from gaze aversion down to foot and leg movements were calculated on a per minute basis. Patterns for ah and non-ah disturbances were calculated per 50 words. Latency period scores represent the average latency period per question. Two independent raters received training in CBCA scoring. First, both raters read all the major published papers about CBCA. Second, they were trained in CBCA scoring by a British CBCA expert. Third, both the trainee raters and the expert rater evaluated several example transcripts (from a different study). Fourth, the three raters compared their results and feedback was given by the expert rater. Following common procedure (Craig, 1995; Hershkowitz, Lamb, Sternberg, & Esplin, 1997; Lamb, Sternberg, Esplin, Hershkowitz, Orbach, & Hovav, 1997; Lamb, Sternberg, Esplin, Hershkowitz, & Orbach, 1997; Landry & Brigham, 1992; Ruby & Brigham, 1998; Vrij, Kneller, & Mann, 2000; Winkel & Vrij, 1995; Zaparniuk, Yuille, & Taylor, 1995) the two observers in the present study scored for each of the three answers the presence or absence of each of the CBCA criteria[1] used in this study, with exception of criterion 3 (quantity of details): '1' was assigned when the criterion was present and '0' when the criterion was absent. Per criterion a total score for the whole interview was calculated by adding the three scores for the three individual answers and then dividing this total score by three. In order to score criterion 3, the raters counted per interview the number of details mentioned. Ratings took place by using the transcripts, and the raters were blind to the experimental conditions. Correlations between the two coders for each of the criteria were satisfactory. They were lower than the correlations with regard to nonverbal behaviors, but higher than found by some others in CBCA research (Anson, Golding, & Gully, 1993): logical structure: $r = .55$, $p < .01$; unstructured production: $r = .65$, $p < .01$; quantity of details: $r = .90$, $p < .01$; contextual embedding: $r = .85$, $p < .01$; description of interactions: $r = .90$, $p < .01$; reproduction of speech: $r = .97$, $p < .01$; unusual details: $r = .77$, $p < .01$; superfluous details: $r = .69$, $p < .01$; accounts of mental state: $r = .58$, $p < .01$; attribution of perpetrator's mental state: $r = .71$, $p < .01$; spontaneous corrections: $r = .54$, $p < .01$; admitting lack of memory: $r = .89$, $p < .01$; raising doubts about one's own memory: $r = .70$, $p < .01$; pardoning the perpetrator: $r = 1.00$, $p < .01$. The scores for each of the criteria were therefore based on the average scores of the two coders.

TABLE 1 / Nonverbal Behavior as a Function of Deception

Behavior	Condition				
	Truth		Lie		
	m	(sd)	m	(sd)	F(1, 71)
gaze aversion	4.66	(6.5)	6.33	(8.2)	.91
smiles	.66	(1.0)	1.66	(3.1)	3.24
illustrators	6.74	(8.1)	1.64	(5.0)	10.86**
adaptors	1.97	(3.8)	.86	(3.0)	1.93
hand/finger movements	15.73	(13.7)	9.17	(13.0)	4.42*
foot/leg movements	11.62	(9.7)	13.78	(16.9)	.43
ah speech disturbances	2.73	(2.7)	4.64	(3.4)	7.00**
non-ah speech disturbances	.98	(1.8)	1.62	(2.3)	1.73
latency period	2.24	(1.4)	3.65	(4.3)	5.73*
speech rate	130.23	(49.4)	142.11	(64.3)	.76
CBCA	5.32	(2.0)	3.31	(1.5)	23.44**
RM	3.20	(1.3)	2.00	(1.1)	14.58**

$**p < .01$; $*p < .05$.

The next step was to calculate a total CBCA score, which is common in CBCA research (Craig, 1995; Esplin, Boychuk, & Raskin, 1988, cited in Raskin & Esplin, 1991; Hershkowitz et al., 1997; Lamb et al., 1997a, b; Vrij et al., 2000; Winkel & Vrij, 1995). In order to calculate the CBCA score, the scores for the 14 criteria were dichotomized. With regard to number of details, a median split (N = 13.50) was used. Those 50% of the participants (N = 37) with a score higher than 13.50 obtained '1' on this criterion, the other 50% obtained a score of '0.' Dichotomizations for the other criteria occurred on the basis of presence or absence of a criterion in the whole interview. A score of '0' was assigned when the criterion was absent, and a score of '1' was assigned when the criterion was present. The total CBCA score was the total score of the 14 criteria and could range from 0 to 14.

Two independent raters received training in RM-scoring. A British RM expert provided the judges with a detailed description of how the criteria should be scored, including some case examples. On the basis of this information the judges felt capable of scoring the transcripts without any further instructions. This is in agreement with Sporer (1997) who also found that it is much easier to teach (and to learn) Reality Monitoring scoring than CBCA scoring. With regard to the present study, the two raters scored per interview the frequency of occurrence of visual details (which

includes actions) ("The visitor[a] came in[b] and kissed[c] the patient[d]" are four visual details (a, b, c, and d), sound details ("She said that is my bag" is one sound detail), time details ("When the nurse came in, the patient . . ." is one time detail), details about location ("The visitor walked through the corridor" is one location detail), and cognitive operations ('the patient didn't believe she knew the visitor' is one cognitive operation). Affective information is similar to CBCA criterion 12 (accounts of subjective mental state) and therefore was not scored again, the CBCA score for this criterion being used in the Reality Monitoring scores. Ratings took place using the transcripts and the raters were blind to the experimental conditions. Intercoder reliability scores (Pearson's correlations) were calculated for all the individual criteria (visual details: $r = .96$, $p < .01$ sound details: $r = .77$, $p < .01$; details about location: $r = .72$, $p < .01$ time details: $r = .85$, $p < .01$; cognitive operations: $r = .75$, $p < .01$). The correlations showed consistency amongst the two coders and scores for each of the criteria were therefore based on the average scores of the two coders. Table 2 provides the results for the individual Reality Monitoring criteria. In order to create the Reality Monitoring scale each variable was dichotomized. A median split (N = 10.50) was used for visual details. Those 50% of the participants with a score higher than 10.50 obtained '1' on this criterion, the other

50% obtained a score of '0.'[2] Dichotomizations for the other criteria occurred on the basis of absence or presence of each of the criteria in the interview. A score of '0' was assigned when the criterion was absent, and a score of '1' when the criterion was present. Cognitive operations were not included in the total Reality Monitoring score as the presence of this criterion does not indicate truth telling (as is the case with the other criteria). The Reality Monitoring scale therefore contained five criteria (visual details, sound details, details about locations, details about time and affective information) and the total score could range from 0 to 5.

RESULTS

In order to test Hypothesis 1 (liars display a longer latency period, more ah and non-ah speech disturbances, a slower speech rate and fewer illustrators and hand/finger movements than truth tellers), Hypothesis 3 (truth tellers will obtain a higher CBCA score than liars) and Hypothesis 5 (truth tellers will obtain a higher RM score than liars) a MANOVA was conducted with Deception (yes or no) as factor and the nonverbal behaviors, total CBCA score and total RM score as dependent variables. The MANOVA revealed a significant effect, $F(12, 60) = 5.11, p < .01$. Table 1 provides the univariate outcomes. As can be seen in Table 1, several significant differences emerged between liars and truth tellers. Compared to truth tellers, liars made fewer illustrators and hand and finger movements, had more ah-speech disturbances, and waited longer before giving an answer. These findings support Hypothesis 1. Furthermore, truth tellers obtained a higher CBCA[3] score and a higher RM score than liars. Therefore, Hypotheses 3 and 5 are also supported.

In order to test Hypothesis 6 (truth tellers will include more perceptual, contextual and affective information in their statements than liars) and Hypothesis 7 (liars are likely to include more cognitive operations in their statements than truth tellers) a MANOVA was conducted with Deception (yes or no) as factor and the individual (not dichotomized) Reality Monitoring criteria as dependent variables. The MANOVA showed a significant effect, $F(5, 67) = 9.61, p < .01$. Table 2 gives the results for the individual Reality Monitoring criteria. As can be seen in Table 2, truth tellers included more perceptual details (vision and sound), more information about locations and more information about time in their accounts than liars. This supports Hypothesis 6. In contrast to what was predicted in Hypothesis 7, liars mentioned fewer cognitive operations than truth tellers.

In order to test Hypotheses 2, 4, 8 and 9, four discriminant analyses were conducted determining the accuracy of the detection techniques in classifying liars and truth tellers. In these analyses, the objective truth status was the classifying variable and the six nonverbal behaviors mentioned in Hypothesis 1, total CBCA score and total RM score were the variables. The results are given in Table 3. First of all, it can be seen that the analysis with nonverbal behaviors as variables yielded a highly significant discriminant function, $\chi^2(4, n = 73) = 23.57, p < .01$. Four variables contributed to this function: Illustrators (Wilks' lambda = .87), ah-speech disturbances (Wilks' lambda .78), hand and finger movements (Wilks' lambda = .73), and latency period (Wilks' lambda = .71). In total, 70.6% of the truth tellers and 84.6% of the liars were correctly classified resulting in a total accuracy score of 78.08%. This supports Hypothesis 2.[4] Also the discriminant analyses with the total CBCA scores and RM scores as variables resulted in highly significant discriminant functions (see Table 3) and correct classifications of the majority of participants (72.60% with CBCA and 67.12% with RM respectively). This supports Hypotheses 4 and 8.

The fourth discriminant analysis revealed that, as was predicted in Hypothesis 9, the combination of the two verbal techniques with the nonverbal technique resulted in the highest accuracy scores, in particular a higher accuracy rate for detecting truths was obtained. In that case, 76.5% of the truth tellers and 84.6% of the liars were correctly classified, resulting in a total accuracy score of 80.82%. The discriminant function was highly significant, $\chi^2(6, n = 73) = 38.79, p < .01$. Six variables contributed to this function: CBCA score (Wilks' lambda = .74), latency period (Wilks' lambda = .67), hand and finger movements Wilks' lambda = .63), ah-speech disturbances (Wilks' lambda = .60), illustrators (Wilks' lambda = .58) and speech rate (Wilks' lambda = .57).

TABLE 2 / Reality Monitoring Criteria as a Function of Deception

| | Condition | | | | |
| | Truth | | Lie | | |
Criteria	m	(sd)	m	(sd)	F(1, 71)
Perceptual information: vision	13.13	(6.3)	9.45	(3.7)	9.39**
Perceptual information: sound	3.31	(2.2)	1.26	(1.4)	22.88**
Spatial information	2.03	(2.1)	1.30	(1.2)	3.53*
Temporal information	1.35	(1.4)	.28	(.7)	18.57**
Cognitive operations	3.32	(2.1)	1.71	(1.7)	12.88**

**p < .01; *p < .05.

DISCUSSION

Previous research has created a pessimistic view about the possibility of detecting lies by analyzing nonverbal behavior. We argued that it might be possible to detect lies when the appropriate behaviors are taken into account and subjective interpretations are disregarded. We defined appropriate behaviors as signs of emotion or signs of cognitive load. As mentioned in the introduction, DePaulo's work revealed that high stake lies are easier to detect than low stake lies, and Ekman's work showed that up to 80% of truths and lies can be detected in high stake situations while paying attention to behavioral signs of emotion. Our findings revealed similar high percentages of accurately detecting truths and lies in situations which require hard thinking while taking signs of cognitive load into account.[5] The findings suggest that, if properly applied, analyzing nonverbal behavior might be an accurate tool to detect deceit.

The liars in this study were facing a difficult task. They had to make up a story (had to tell a so-called 'bold-faced lie' [McCornack, 1997]) and had to do this almost spontaneously. It is therefore perhaps not surprising that they showed signs of cognitive load. To what extent are these bold-faced lies realistic? McCornack (1997) argues that bold-faced lies comprise only a small portion of the deceptive messages and that most deceptive messages in daily life involve subtle and complex packaging of both false and truthful elements. We have no reason to dispute this view, but would like to emphasize that bold-faced lies do occur in daily life settings. They also take place in police interviews. For example, in our analysis of

police interviews with a convicted murderer (Vrij & Mann, in press) we came across a bold-faced lie, which is related to how he met the victim. Substantial evidence (several independent eye witnesses and physical evidence) has shown that he went to *location A* and that *he made contact with the victim*. He strongly denied this and told the police instead that he met the victim at *location B* (which was totally different from location A) and that *the victim approached him*. He described in detail how the victim contacted him, a story which was entirely fabricated. Another of our studies (Vrij & Mann, in press, b) involved two more apparently bold-faced lies. In one case, a man who was found guilty of the murder of his wife claimed that people forced themselves into his house, killed his wife, beat him until he was unconscious and tied him up. He had several injuries which, he claimed, were the result of the attack. The man, however, had injured himself in an attempt to make his story more plausible. In another case, a woman who was found guilty of killing her boyfriend told the police that they were the victims of road rage and that a stranger chased their car and eventually killed her boyfriend. All these seem to be examples of bold-faced lies. One might argue that even bold-faced lies are often not total fabrications as people, when fabricating a story, could simply describe a situation they had experienced before. It is unlikely that the liars in the present study could do this, as they were forced to fabricate about a specific situation, namely the activities of a patient, nurse, and visitor in a hospital. We acknowledge that some bold-faced lies are probably not total fabrications, but we believe that some are. For example, had the woman ever experienced a road rage

TABLE 3 / Discriminant Analyses with Nonverbal Behavior, Criteria-Based Content Analysis and Reality Monitoring

Detection Technique	Hit Rates			Eigenvalue	Lambda	df	χ^2
	Truth	Lie	Total				
Nonverbal behavior	70.6%	84.6%	78.08%	.41	.71	4	23.57**
CBCA	64.7%	79.5%	72.60%	.35	.74	1	20.91**
RM	70.6%	64.1%	67.12%	.25	.80	1	13.17**
CBCA + RM + nonverbal behavior	76.5%	84.6%	80.82%	.77	.57	6	38.79**

**p < .01, *p < .05.

event in her life before? Similarly, was the man beaten until unconscious and tied up in his life before? We do not know the answers to these questions but their stories might well have been total fabrications.

We instructed the liars in our study to tell total fabrications not because we are particularly interested in this type of lie, but because we wanted to create a situation in which the lie requires mental effort. We acknowledge that in real life telling lies often does not require more mental effort than telling the truth. McCornack (1997, p. 102) convincingly argued that deception possesses fundamental cognitive efficiency advantages over truth telling within certain contexts. For example, by receiving a present which you do not like from an acquaintance it is often easier to lie and to say that you like the present than to express your true opinion. We believe that in real life some lies do require mental effort, as our own study with the convicted murderer revealed (Vrij & Mann, in press, a). When the police interviewed him the first time, he was asked 'What did you do on that particular day?' He described his activities in detail and in chronological order but his behavior changed as soon as he started to describe his activities during the afternoon. The police later discovered that he lied in that part of the interview. While lying, the man showed more gaze aversion, had longer pauses, spoke slower and made more speech errors than when he was telling the truth. This behavioral pattern is typical for somebody who has to think hard. Perhaps it was surprising that the man gave the impression that he had to think hard. As he told the police, he knew he was a suspect in this case and expected to be interviewed. There is also evidence that he had prepared himself for the police interviews. A possible explanation is that he was not

very bright, thus not fully taking advantage of the preparation time that was available to him. As Ekman and Frank (1993) have pointed out, preparation probably does not benefit liars who are not so clever. If intelligence really affects preparations, then criminals or guilty suspects might be in a disadvantageous position during police interviews as their IQ is often rather low (Gudjonsson, 1992).

It also might explain the preliminary findings of our current analyses of interviews with suspects in police interviews (Mann, Vrij, & Bull, 1998). They reveal that when suspects lie they show a decrease in illustrators, all increase in pauses and an increase in latency period. In other words, suspects, seem to show signs of cognitive load. In our view, systematic and detailed analyses of nonverbal behavior displayed by suspects and looking for signs of cognitive load are therefore useful to detect deceit.

Obviously, signs of cognitive load per se do not necessarily indicate deception, as truth tellers might have to think hard as well. Detecting deceit by paying attention to nonverbal behavior in real life settings is a two stage process (Vrij, 2000). First, signs of emotion (guilt, fear, excitement or any other emotion) or cognitive load need to be detected and, second, explanations for these signs should be given, where deceit is only one possible explanation. This process may reveal lies. As was mentioned above, the convicted murderer changed his behavior as soon as he started describing his activities during the afternoon (Vrij & Mann, in press, a). We wondered why and hypothesized that he was lying at that particular moment. Our intuition turned out to be correct.

In theory it is possible that in the present experiment the behavior of an extraordinary sample of people was examined whose lies are easy to detect. There is evidence that this was not the case. In a recent study (Vrij & Baxter, 1999), we randomly selected fragments of 10 interviews out of the 73 interviews analyzed in the present study and showed these interviews to 50 college students, We asked the students to indicate for each person in the interview whether the person was lying or not. The students achieved an accuracy rate of 56% for truths and 50% for lies. These outcomes are typically found in this type of detection of deception experiment.

The results of the present experiment further revealed that accuracy rates above the level of chance were obtained with both CBCA assessments and Reality Monitoring assessments. It is difficult to make a comparison of both methods at this stage. CBCA might well have been in a disadvantageous position in this comparison, as it was used in a context other than the one for which it was designed. As stated earlier, CBCA was originally designed for assessing statements of children in sexual abuse cases. In this study it has been used to assess adults' statements. Some researchers have advocated the use of the CBCA technique to also evaluate the testimonies of adults who talk about issues other than sexual abuse. The reasonably high accuracy rate obtained in the present study (72.6%) supports their view. Reality Monitoring might have been in a disadvantageous position as well. One important aspect of Reality Monitoring is looking for perceptual information, such as cues of sound, vision, smell, taste or touch. As participants did not actually take part in an event—they were only watching a videotape—they could not smell, taste or touch anything (and therefore did not mention any of these cues). Finally, the comparison of both verbal methods was not entirely fair because accounts of mental state were counted only under CBCA. These scores were then added in the Reality Monitoring lie detection scale as well. CBCA was hereby given a potential advantage.

A logical step is to combine both verbal methods. An interesting addition to the CBCA list of criteria would be the Reality Monitoring criterion 'perceptual information' (criterion 2). For example, pornographic films may increase children's knowledge about sexual acts. As a result, an unexperienced child may give a detailed account about a non-experienced sexual encounter after watching a pornographic film. However, in such a recall details about smell and taste will be missing, as genuine experiences are required for such details. Details about smell and taste in statements about sexual abuse may therefore be a strong indication that the statements are based upon real experiences (unless smell and taste were mentioned by people in the pornographic film).

There was no support for Hypothesis 7 which suggested that liars would include more cognitive operations in their accounts than truth tellers. Previous deception research with Reality Monitoring also could not support this hypothesis (Alonso-Quecuty, 1992, 1996; Hofer et al., 1996; Roberts et al., 1998; Sporer, 1997). One explanation is that people use cognitive operations in order to facilitate and enhance later memory for experienced events (Roediger, 1996). For example, a person who drove fast in Germany might try to remember this in two different ways. First, the person could remember having actually looked at the speedometer to find out how fast he or she was driving. Alternatively, they could remember this by logical reasoning, for example, by thinking that he or she must have driven fast because they used the motorway. The latter alternative, in which a cognitive operation is included, is an easier way of remembering having driven fast than the first alternative. When the person is asked a couple of years later whether he or she drove fast through Germany it is therefore more likely that the person will remember this by thinking that he or she drove on the motorway than by remembering having checked the speedometer. As a result, the person's memory about this experienced event will contain a cognitive operation. Due to the lack of support for cognitive operations found in the present and previous studies, we suggest this variable should not be included in a Reality Monitoring lie detection scale. As was mentioned in the method section, cognitive operations was not included in the Reality Monitoring scale in the present study either. Including this variable in the Reality Monitoring scale and rerunning the discriminant analysis led to a significant discriminant function ($\chi^2(1, n = 73) = 8.53, p < .01$, eigenvalue = .13, Wilks' lambda = .89) but to lower hit rates (truth: 70.6%, lie: 53.8%, total: 61.64%) than the hit rates obtained without cognitive operations (see Table 3).

Although previous studies suggest that verbal cues (CBCA and RM) are more powerful discriminators between truths and lies than nonverbal cues (see introduction), such studies typically do not compare verbal cues and nonverbal cues directly, making it impossible to determine the relative power of both sets of discriminators. Such a direct comparison was made in the present experiment. Interestingly, the present findings did not show superiority of verbal cues above nonverbal cues. However, we acknowledge that more research needs to be done. Such studies should incorporate different types of lie.

Instead of comparing verbal and nonverbal detection methods, in our view a more fruitful approach would be to investigate to what extent a combination of verbal and nonverbal detection methods lead to higher accuracy rates than the two types of method independently. The present study showed that the highest accuracy rates were obtained by combining the verbal and nonverbal techniques. The discriminant analysis that took all three techniques into account could correctly classify 80.82% of the liars and truth tellers and both verbal (CBCA) and nonverbal cues contributed to the significant discriminant function. Some Reality Monitoring researchers (Porter & Yuille, 1996; Roberts et al., 1998) already use a combined instrument by including speech disturbances in their Reality Monitoring scale. Our findings support this idea. In the discriminant analysis in which the three techniques were included, both speech disturbances and verbal cues (CBCA score) contributed to the discriminant function. The discriminant function, however, revealed that in addition to speech disturbances, behaviors such as illustrators, hand and finger movements, and latency period made an important contribution to detecting deceit as well. We therefore recommend to also take behaviors other than speech disturbances into account when attempting to detect deceit.

Concerning the methodology of the study, one issue merits attention. All participants watched the same 2 minute video of a theft in a hospital. It might be that the truths told by the participants bore more similarity to one another than the lies they told. On the basis of this, it might be that a coder could probably tell after a few trials of coding which narrative they were coding were probably truthful and which

were lies. This 'knowledge' might have affected their codings. Although this sounds reasonable, we do not think that this actually happened, as the stories of truth tellers did not show too much similarity. Some truth tellers used a 'global approach' and just mentioned in a few sentences what, in their view, were the main events in the video. However, different truth tellers who applied this approach phrased the events differently and mentioned different events. Other truth tellers used a more detailed approach and discussed the video in more detail. Even in this situation the stories of different truth tellers varied, as different truth tellers mentioned different details.

With regard to the ecological validity of the present study, probably the most obvious criticism is that we asked our participants to describe an event they had watched on a video rather than describing a live event in which they had actually participated. There were two reasons why we chose a videotaped event. First, we wanted to create a highly controlled and standardised situation. We believe that it is essential to test innovative ideas (such as comparing different detection of deception techniques) in highly controlled situations first, as the exact impact can only be determined in such situations. Second, recent research has shown that watching an event on a video or actually taking part in such an event results in similar CBCA scores (Akehurst, Köhnken, & Höfer, 1995). This suggests that a method utilizing a videotaped event has a positive effect on the standardization of the study without compromising its ecological validity too much. Despite this, we do acknowledge that deception research should also include studies with higher ecological validity than that of the present study.

APPENDIX 1

A Brief Description of the CBCA Criteria Used in This Study

1. Logical structure. Logical structure is present if the statement essentially makes sense, that is, if the statement is coherent and logical and the different segments fit together, that is, for example different segments are not inconsistent or discrepant. *2. Unstructured production.* Unstructured production is present if the information is scattered throughout the statement instead of mentioned in a structured, coherent and chronological order. The incoherent and unorganized manner of presentation is, for instance, caused by digressions or spontaneous shifts of focus. *3. Quantity of details.* This criterion requires that the statement must be rich in detail, that is, specific descriptions of place, time, persons, objects and events should be present. *4. Contextual embedding.* Contextual embedding is present if the events are placed in time and location, and when the actions are connected with other daily activities and/or customs. *5. Descriptions of interactions.* This criterion is fulfilled if the statement contains information about interactions involving at least the accused and witness, and if this information consists of three parts, i.e. an action of actor A leads to a reaction of actor B which leads to a reaction of actor A again. *6. Reproduction of speech.* Reproduction of speech is present if speech, or parts of the conversation, is reported in its original form and if the different speakers are recognizable in the reproduced dialogues. This criterion is not satisfied by a report about the content of a dialogue; it is only satisfied when there is a virtual replication of the utterances of at least one person. *8. Unusual details.* Unusual details refer to details of persons, objects, or events which are unusual and/or unique but meaningful in the context. *9. Superfluous details.* Superfluous details are present if the witness describes details in connection with the allegations which are not essential for the accusation, such as a child who says that the adult tried to get rid of the cat which entered the bedroom because he (the adult) is allergic to cats. *12. Accounts of subjective mental state.* This criterion is present when the witness describes feelings or thoughts experienced at the time of the incident, as well as reports of cognitions, such as thinking about how to escape while the event was in progress. *13. Attribution of perpetrator's mental state.* This criterion is present if the witness describes her or his perceptions of the perpetrator's feelings, thoughts or motives during the incident. *74. Spontaneous corrections.* This criterion is fulfilled if corrections are spontaneously offered or information is spontaneously added to material previously provided in the statement (spontaneous means without any interference by the interviewer). *15. Admitting lack of memory.* This criterion is

present if a witness admits lack of memory by either saying "I don't know" or "I don't remember" or by giving a more extensive answer. *16. Raising doubts about one's own testimony.* This criterion is present if the witness expresses concern that some part of the statement seems incorrect or unbelievable. *18. Pardoning the perpetrator.* Pardoning the perpetrator is present if the witness tends to favour the alleged perpetrator in terms of making excuses for the alleged perpetrator or failing to blame the alleged perpetrator.

NOTES

1. Given the fact that in this study statements of adults were used, we thought that several criteria would be inappropriate and were therefore ignored. These criteria were: accurately reported details misunderstood (criterion 10), related external associations (criterion 11) and details characteristic of the offense (criterion 19). Unexpected complications (criterion 7) and self deprecations (criterion 17) were initially scored but were never present. They were therefore disregarded, leaving a total of 14 CBCA criteria to be assessed.

2. The number of details in the Reality Monitoring scoring differed from the number of details in the CBCA scoring because different definitions are used in both coding systems. For example, "The young nurse . . ." results in two details in CBCA scoring and in one detail in Reality Monitoring scoring.

3. A MANOVA was conducted examining differences between liars and truth tellers with regard to the 14 individual CBCA criteria used in this study. The MANOVA, which was performed on the original, not dichotomized data, showed a significant main effect, $F(14, 58) = 4.74$, $p < .01$. Univariate tests revealed that compared to liars, truth tellers included more details ($M = 21.25$ ($SD = 8.5$) vs = M 11.30 ($SD = 4.1$), $F(1, 71) = 42.59$, $p < .01$), more contextual embeddings ($M = .18$ ($SD = .2$) vs $M = .09$ ($SD = .1$), $F(1, 71) = 3.92$, $p < .05$), more reproductions of conversations ($M = .20$ ($SD = .2$) vs $M = .09$, ($SD = .1$), $F(1, 71) = 4.75$, $p < .05$), more unusual details ($M = .07$ ($SD = .1$) vs $M = .00$ ($SD = .0$), $F(1, 71) = 9.02$, $p < .01$, more accounts of other's mental state ($M = .49$ ($SD = .3$) vs $M = .23$ ($SD = .3$), $F(1, 71) = 15.83$, $p < .01$, and more spontaneous corrections ($M = .23$ ($SD = .2$) vs $M = .11$ ($SD = .2$), $F(1, 71) = 5.74$, $p < .05$).

4. It is important to note that it is the combination of nonverbal behaviors that is powerful, not any one individual behavior. Illustrators obtained a high individual hit rate (69.86%, eigenvalue .15, Wilks' lambda = 87, $\chi^2(1, n = 73) = 10.03$, $p < .01$). However, a distinction between truths and lies resulted in a high hit rate for lies (89.7%) but a particularly low hit rate for truths (47.1%).

5. We assume that our findings are caused by cognitive load. However, as we did not experimentally manipulate cognitive load in this study, we cannot say this for certain.

REFERENCES

Akehurst, L., Köhnken, G., Vrij, A., & Bull, R. (1996). Lay persons' and police officers' beliefs regarding deceptive behavior. *Applied Cognitive Psychology, 10,* 461–473.

Akehurst, L., Köhnken, G., & Höfer, E. (1995). *The analysis and application of Statement Validity Assessment.* Paper presented at the Fifth European Conference on Psychology and Law, Budapest, Hungary.

Akehurst, L., & Vrij, A. (1999). Creating suspects in police interviews. *Journal of Applied Social Psychology, 29,* 192–210.

Alonso-Quecuty, M. L. (1992). Deception detection and Reality Monitoring: A new answer to an old question? In F. Lösel, D. Bender, & T. Bliesener (Eds.), *Psychology and law: International perspectives* (pp. 328–332). Berlin: de Gruyter.

Alonso-Quecuty, M. L. (1996). Detecting fact from fallacy in child and adult witness accounts. In G. Davies, S. Lloyd-Bostock, M. McMurran, & C. Wilson (Eds.), *Psychology, law, and criminal justice: International developments in research and practice* (pp. 74–80). Berlin: de Gruyter.

Anson, D. A., Golding, S. L., & Gully, K. J. (1993). Child sexual abuse allegations: Reliability of Criteria-Based Content Analysis. *Law and Human Behavior, 17,* 331–341.

Burgoon, J. K., Kelly, D. L., Newton, D. A., & Keely-Dyreson, M. P. (1989). The nature of arousal and nonverbal indices. *Human Communication Research, 16,* 217–255.

Craig, R. A. (1995). *Effects of interviewer behavior on children's statements of sexual abuse.* Unpublished manuscript.

DePaulo, B. M., Anderson, D. E., & Cooper, H. (1999, October). *Explicit and implicit deception detection.* Paper presented at the annual conference of the Society of Experimental Social Psychologists, St. Louis, Missouri.

DePaulo, B. M., Kirkendol, S. E., Tang, J., & O'Brien, T. P. (1988). The motivational impairment effect in the communication of deception: Replications and extensions. *Journal of Nonverbal Behavior, 12,* 177–202.

DePaulo, B. M., Lanier, K., & Davis, T. (1983). Detecting deceit of the motivated liar. *Journal of Personality and Social Psychology, 45,* 1096–1103.

DePaulo, B. M., LeMay, C. S., & Epstein, J. A. (1991). Effects of importance of success and expectations for success on effectiveness at deceiving. *Personality and Social Psychology Bulletin, 17,* 14–24.

DePaulo, B. M., & Pfeifer, R. L. (1986). On-the-job experience and skill at detecting deception. *Journal of Applied Social Psychology, 16,* 249–267.

DePaulo, B. M., Stone, J. L., & Lassiter, G. D. (1985a). Deceiving and detecting deceit. In B. R. Schenkler (Ed.), *The self and social life* (pp. 323–370). New York: McGraw-Hill.

DePaulo, B. M., Stone, J. L., & Lassiter, G. D. (1985b). Telling ingratiating lies: Effects of target sex and target attractiveness on verbal and nonverbal deceptive success. *Journal of Personality and Social Psychology, 48,* 1191–2103.

deTurck, M. A. (1991). Training observers to detect spontaneous deception: Effects of gender. *Communication Reports, 4,* 81–89.

Ekman, P. (1989). Why lies fail and what behaviors betray a lie. In J. C. Yuille (Ed.), *Credibility assessment* (pp. 71–82). Dordrecht, the Netherlands: Kluwer.

Ekman, P. (1992). *Telling lies: Clues to deceit in the marketplace, politics and marriage.* New York: W. W. Norton.

Ekman, P., & Frank, M. G. (1993). Lies that fall. In M. Lewis & C. Saarni (Eds.), *Lying and deception in everyday life* (pp. 184–201). New York: Guildford Press.

Ekman, P., & Friesen, W. V. (1969). The repertoire of nonverbal behavior: Categories, origins, usage, and coding. *Semiotica, 1,* 49–97.

Ekman, P., & Friesen, W. V. (1972). Hand movements. *Journal of Communication, 22,* 353–374.

Ekman, P., & O'Sullivan, M. (1991). Who can catch a liar? *American Psychologist, 46,* 913–920.

Ekman, P., O'Sullivan, M., & Frank, M. G. (1999). A few can catch a liar. *Psychological Science, 10,* 263–266.

Ekman, P., O'Sullivan, M., Friesen, W. V., & Scherer, K. (1991). Face, voice, and body in detecting deceit. *Journal of Nonverbal Behavior, 15,* 125–135.

Frank, M. G., & Ekman, P. (1997). The ability to detect deceit generalizes across different types of high-stake lies. *Journal of Personality and Social Psychology, 72,* 1429–1439.

Goldman-Eisler, F. (1968). *Psycholinguistics: Experiments in spontaneous speech.* New York: Doubleday.

Gudjonsson, G. H. (1992). *The psychology of interrogations, confessions and testimony.* Chichester, England: Wiley.

Hernandez-Fernaud, E., & Alonso-Quecuty, M. (1997). The cognitive interview and lie detection: A new magnifying glass for Sherlock Holmes? *Applied Cognitive Psychology, 11,* 55–68.

Hershkowitz, I., Lamb, M. E., Sternberg, K. J., & Esplin, P. W. (1997). The relationships among interviewer utterance type, CBCA scores and the richness of children's responses. *Legal and Criminological Psychology, 2,* 169–176.

Höfer, E., & Akehurst, L., & Metzger, G. (1996, August). *Reality monitoring: A chance for further development of CBCA?* Paper presented at the Annual meeting of the European Association on Psychology and Law, Siena, Italy.

Honts, C. R. (1994). Assessing children's credibility: Scientific and legal issues in 1994. *North Dakota Law Review, 70,* 879–903.

Horowitz, S. W., Lamb, M. E., Esplin, P. W., & Boychuk, T. D., Krispin, O., & Reiter-Lavery, L. (1997). Reliability of criteria-based content analysis of child witness statements. *Legal and Criminological Psychology, 2,* 11–21.

Johnson, M. K., Hashtroudi, S., & Lindsay, D. S. (1993). Source monitoring. *Psychological Bulletin, 114,* 3–28.

Johnson, M. K., & Raye, C. L. (1981). Reality monitoring. *Psychological Review, 88,* 67–85.

Johnson, M. K., & Raye, C. L. (1998). False memories and confabulation. *Trends in Cognitive Sciences, 2,* 137–145.

Köhnken, G. (1987). Training police officers to detect deceptive eyewitness statements. Does it work? *Social Behavior, 2,* 1–17.

Köhnken, G. (1989). Behavioral correlates of statement credibility: Theories, paradigms and results. In H. Wegener, F. Lösel, & J. Haisch (Eds.), *Criminal behavior and the justice system: psychological perspectives* (pp. 271–289). New York: Springer-Verlag.

Köhnken, G. (1990). *Glaubwürdigkeit: Untersuchungen zu einem psychologischen konstrukt.* München, Germany: Psychologie Verlags Union.

Köhnken, G. (1996). Social psychology and the law. in G. R. Semin, & K. Fiedler (Eds.), *Applied Social Psychology* (pp. 257–282). London: Sage Publications.

Köhnken, G., Schimossek, E., Aschermann, E., & Höfer, E. (1995). The cognitive interview and the assessment of the credibility of adult's statements. *Journal of Applied Psychology, 80,* 671–684.

Kraut, R. E. (1980). Humans as lie detectors: Some second thoughts. *Journal of Communication, 30,* 209–216.

Lamb, M. E., Sternberg, K. J., Esplin, P. W., Hershkowitz, I., Orbach, Y., & Hovav, M. (1997a). Criterion-based content analysis: A field validation study. *Child Abuse and Neglect, 21,* 255–264.

Lamb, M. E., Sternberg, K. J., & Esplin, P. W. Hershkowitz, I., & Orbach, Y. (1997b). Assessing the credibility of children's allegations of sexual abuse: A survey of recent research. *Learning and Individual Differences, 9,* 175–194.

Landry, K., & Brigham, J. C. (1992). The effect of training in Criteria-Based Content Analysis on the ability to detect deception in adults. *Law and Human Behavior, 16,* 663–675.

Lane, J. D., & DePaulo, B. M. (1999). Completing Coyne's cycle: Dysphorics' ability to detect deception. *Journal of Research in Personality, 33,* 311–329.

Levine, T. R., Park, H. S., & McCornack, S. A. (1999). Accuracy in detecting truths and lies. Documenting the "veracity effect." *Communication Monographs, 66,* 125–144.

Lykken, D. T. (1960). The validity of the guilty knowledge technique: The effects of faking. *Journal of Applied Psychology, 44,* 258–262.

Lykken, D. T. (1998). *A tremor in the blood: Uses and abuses of the lie detector.* New York: Plenum Trade.

Mann, S., Vrij, A., & Bull, R. (1998, September). *Telling and detecting true lies.* Paper presented at the eighth annual meeting of the European Association on Psychology and Law, Cracow, Poland.

Manzanero, A. L., & Diges, M. (1996). Effects of preparation on internal and external memories, In G. Davies, S. Lloyd-Bostock, M. McMurran, & C. Wilson (Eds.), *Psychology, law, and criminal justice: International developments in research and practice* (pp. 56–63). Berlin: de Gruyter.

McCornack, S. A. (1997). The generation of deceptive messages: Laying the groundwork for a viable theory of interpersonal deception. In J. O. Greene (Ed.), *Message production: Advances in communication theory.* Mahwah, NJ: Lawrence Erlbaum Associates.

Porter, S., & Yuille, J. C. (1996). The language of deceit: An investigation of the verbal clues to deception in the interrogation context. *Law and Human Behavior, 20,* 443–459.

Raskin, D. C. (1979). Orienting and defensive reflexes in the detection of deception. In H. D. Kimmel, E. H. Van Olst, & J. F. Orlebeke (Ed.), *The orienting reflex in humans* (pp. 587–605). Hillsdale, NJ: Erlbaum.

Raskin, D. C. (1982). The scientific basis of polygraph techniques and their uses in the judicial process. In A. Trankell (Ed.), *Reconstructing the past* (pp. 317–371). Stockholm: Norsted & Soners.

Raskin, D. C. (1986). The polygraph in 1986: Scientific, professional, and legal issues surrounding acceptance of polygraph evidence. *Utah Law Review, 29,* 29–74.

Raskin, D. C., & Esplin, P. W. (1991). Statement Validity Assessment: Interview procedures and content analysis of children's statements of sexual abuse. *Behavioral Assessment, 13,* 265–291.

Reid, J. E. (1947). A revised questioning technique in lie detection tests. *Journal of Criminal Law, Criminology, and Police Science, 37,* 542–547.

Roberts, K. P., Lamb, M. E., Zale, J. L., & Randall, D. W. (1998). *Qualitative differences in children's accounts of confirmed and unconfirmed incidents of sexual abuse.* Paper presented at the biennial meeting of the American Psychology-Law Society, Redondo Beach, LA.

Roediger, H. L. (1996). Memory illusions. *Journal of Memory and Language, 35,* 76–100.

Ruby, C. L., & Brigham, J. C. (1997). The usefulness of the criteria-based content analysis technique in distinguishing between truthful and fabricated allegations. *Psychology, Public Policy, and Law, 3,* 705–737.

Ruby, C. L., & Brigham, J. C. (1998). Can Criteria-Based Content Analysis distinguish between true and false statements of African-American speakers? *Law and Human Behavior, 22,* 369–388.

Sporer, S. L. (1997). The less travelled road to truth: Verbal cues in deception detection in accounts of fabricated and self-experienced events. *Applied Cognitive Psychology, 11,* 373–397.

Steller, M. (1989). Recent developments in statement analysis. In J. C. Yuille (Ed.), *Credibility Assessment* (pp. 135–154). Deventer, the Netherlands: Kluwer.

Steller, M., & Köhnken, G. (1989). Criteria-Based Content Analysis. In D. C. Raskin (Ed.), *Psychological methods in criminal investigation and evidence* (pp. 217–245). New York: Springer-Verlag.

Undeutsch, U. (1967). Beurteilung der Glaubhaftigkeit von Aussagen. In U. Undeutsch (Ed.), *Handbuch der Psychologie Vol. II: Forensische Psychologie* (pp. 26–181). Gottingen, Germany: Hogrefe.

Undeutsch, U. (1989). The development of statement reality analysis. In J. C. Yuille (Ed.), *Credibility Assessment* (pp. 101–121). Dordrecht, The Netherlands: Kluwer.

Vrij, A. (1991). *Misverstanden tussen politie en allochtonen: Sociaal-psychologische aspecten van verdacht zijn.* Amsterdam: VU Uitgeverij.

Vrij, A. (1993). Credibility judgments of detectives: The impact of nonverbal behavior, social skills and physical characteristics on impression formation. *Journal of Social Psychology, 133,* 601–611.

Vrij, A. (1994). The impact of information and setting on detection of deception by police detectives. *Journal of Nonverbal Behavior, 18,* 117–137.

Vrij, A. (1995). Behavioral correlates of deception in a simulated police interview. *Journal of Psychology: Interdisciplinary and Applied, 129,* 15–29.

Vrij, A. (1998). Nonverbal communication and credibility. In A. Memon, A. Vrij, & R. Bull, *Psychology and law: Truthfulness, accuracy and credibility* (pp. 32–59). Maidenhead, Great Britain: McGraw-Hill.

Vrij, A. (2000). *Detecting lies and deceit: The psychology of lying and implications for professional practice.* Chichester: John Wiley & Sons.

Vrij, A., & Akehurst, L. (1998). Verbal communication and credibility: Statement Validity Assessment. In A. Memon, A. Vrij, & R. Bull, *Psychology and law: Truthfulness, accuracy and credibility* (pp. 3–31). Maidenhead, Great Britain: McGraw-Hill.

Vrij, A., Akehurst, L., & Morris, P. M. (1997). Individual differences in hand movements during deception. *Journal of Nonverbal Behavior, 21,* 87–102.

Vrij, A., & Baxter, M. (1999). Accuracy and confidence in detecting truths and lies in elaborations and denials: Truth bias, lie bias and individual differences. *Expert Evidence, 7,* 25–36.

Vrij, A., Harden, F., Terry, J., Edward, K., & Bull, R. (in press). The influence of personal characteristics, stakes and lie complexity on the accuracy and confidence to detect deceit. In R. Roesch, R. R. Corrado, & R. J. Dempster (Eds.), *Psychology in the courts: International advances in knowledge.* Amsterdam: Harwood Academic.

Vrij, A., Kneller, W., & Mann, S. (2000). The effect of informing liars about Criteria-Based Content Analysis on their ability to deceive CBCA-raters. *Legal and Criminological Psychology, 5,* 57–70.

Vrij, A., & Mann, S. (in press, a). Telling and detecting lies in a high-stake situation: The case of a convicted murderer. *Applied Cognitive Psychology.*

Vrij, A., & Mann, S. (in press, b). Who killed my relative? Police officers' ability to detect real-life high stake lies. *Psychology, Crime, & Law.*

Vrij, A., & Semin, G. R. (1996). Lie experts' beliefs about nonverbal indicators of deception. *Journal of Nonverbal Behavior, 20,* 1, 65–81.

Vrij, A., Semin, G. R., & Bull, R. (1996). Insight in behavior displayed during deception. *Human Communication Research, 22,* 544–562.

Winkel, F. W., & Vrij, A. (1995). Verklaringen van kinderen in interviews: Een experimenteel onderzoek naar de diagnostische waarde van Criteria Based Content Analysis. *Tijdschrift voor Ontwikkelingspsychologie, 22,* 61–74.

Zaparniuk, J., Yuille, J. C., & Taylor, S. (1995). Assessing the credibility of true and false statements. *International Journal of Law and Psychiatry, 18,* 343–352.

Zuckerman, M., DePaulo, B. M., & Rosenthal, R. (1981). Verbal and nonverbal communication of deception. In L. Berkowitz (Ed.), *Advances in experimental social psychology,* volume 14 (pp. 1–57). New York: Academic Press.

This study was sponsored by a grant from the Leverhulme Trust given to the first author.

CRITICAL THINKING QUESTIONS

1. What implications does the information presented in this article have for situations such as therapy sessions and courtroom proceedings? Is it feasible to teach people to be more aware of the nonverbal messages they send? Can people learn how to interpret such messages more accurately? How might either or both of these goals be accomplished? Explain your answers.

2. "You cannot *not* communicate." Discuss what this statement means in terms of nonverbal communication.

3. From the information contained in this article, develop a list of specific nonverbal and paralanguage cues that are useful in detecting deception. Which commonly assumed correlates of lying are not really useful?

4. How useful are the findings from this study for detecting lying in real-world, day-to-day interactions (e.g., when you do not have a videotape of an event to review)? Explain your answer.

5. The nursing students who participated in this experiment were asked to lie, and in order to motivate them, the researchers told them that "The ability to lie successfully is extremely important to nurses and that good nurses may need to be good liars." Do you see any problems with the researchers issuing this statement? Were the student nurses debriefed after the session? Do you think they should have been debriefed? Discuss your answers.

Chapter Three

SOCIAL COGNITION

THE WORLD AROUND us presents a complex array of information. Due simply to sheer volume, it is humanly impossible to pay attention to all the information available to us. So, given all of this information, how do we make sense of it? This chapter on social cognition examines some of the ways that people process information about themselves and others in order to make judgments.

A major interest of social psychologists is how people mentally process the information they receive. Decisions are not always based on a thorough analysis of the information at hand. Instead, people sometimes rely on mental shortcuts or intuition in reaching decisions. These mental shortcuts, or *heuristics,* are commonly employed strategies that people use for making sense of the world. The problem is, these mental strategies often get us into trouble by shading how we interpret events in the world around us. Article 7, "Some Systematic Biases of Everyday Judgment," examines how heuristics and other forms of cognitive bias may hinder effective decision making.

Social cognition also deals with how we make sense of ourselves. One interesting line of research has addressed the relationship between cognition and emotion. Specifically, do our mental processes influence what we feel, or do our feelings shape our mental processes? Article 8, "Cognitive, Social, and Physiological Determinants of Emotional State," is a classic investigation of the relationship between thought processes and emotion. The methods and findings of the study make interesting reading, but its implications are even more important: Is it possible to change the emotions we experience simply by changing the cognitive labels that we attach to them?

Finally, the last article in this chapter returns to the question of how we try to make sense of the world. Once we see the outcome of an event, what happens to our initial beliefs about the possibility that outcome would occur? *Hindsight bias,* or the tendency to distort prior beliefs in light of current knowledge, appears to be a fairly common process in social cognition. This topic, along with the serious implications of this tendency, is explored in Article 9, "'I Knew We Would Win': Hindsight Bias for Favorable and Unfavorable Team Decision Outcomes."

ARTICLE 7 _____

Social cognition is concerned with the processes that people use to make sense of the social world. One finding from research in this area is that people tend to be *cognitive misers;* that is, all things being equal, people prefer to think as little as possible in reaching decisions. To help them achieve this goal, they employ cognitive strategies such as *heuristics* (i.e., mental short-cuts for understanding the world).

For example, why are some people afraid of flying? If you asked them whether they know that statistics show that airplane travel actually is safer than other modes of transportation, the majority undoubtedly would say that yes, they know that. Yet their fear persists. Why? One contributing factor may be the *availability heuristic,* a mental shortcut that involves judging the probability of something happening by how easily it comes to mind. We all can vividly recall the images of airplane crashes that appear in the media every time an accident occurs. The pictures are terrifying, so they readily come to mind. Even though automobile accidents are more common, how often do we see detailed (and repeated) images of car crashes? Rarely. So even though airplane crashes occur much less frequently than fatal automobile accidents, it is easier to recall images of the former. Hence, we have a greater tendency to fear them, as well.

We use many types of heuristics to help us explain and understand our world. What all of these mental shortcuts do, however, are create biases in how we interpret the events around us. Many of these biases involve inconsequential events, and no harm comes from believing them. But in other situations, using this biased information processing to make important decisions about our lives may lead to problems.

The following article by Thomas Gilovich examines some of the biases in everyday judgment that cloud our ability for accurate, critical thinking.

Some Systematic Biases of Everyday Judgment

■ Thomas Gilovich

Skeptics have long thought that everyday judgment and reasoning are biased in predictable ways. Psychological research on the subject conducted during the past quarter century largely confirms these suspicions. Two types of explanations are typically offered for the dubious beliefs that are dissected in *Skeptical Inquirer.* On one hand, there are motivational causes: Some beliefs are comforting, and so people embrace that comfort and convince themselves that a questionable proposition is true. Many types of religious beliefs, for example, are often explained this way. On the other hand, there are cognitive causes: faulty processes of reasoning and judgment that lead people to

misevaluate the evidence of their everyday experience. The skeptical community is convinced that everyday judgment and reasoning leave much to be desired.

Why are skeptics so unimpressed with the reasoning abilities and habits of the average person? Until recently, this pessimism was based on simple observation, often by those with a particularly keen eye for the foibles of human nature. Thus, skeptics often cite such thinkers as Francis Bacon, who stated:

> . . . *all superstition is much the same whether it be that of astrology, dreams, omens, retributive judgment, or the like . . . [in that] the deluded believers observe events which are fulfilled, but neglect or pass*

Reprinted from *The Skeptical Inquirer,* March 13, 1997, 21(2), p. 31. Copyright © 1997, CSICOP, Inc. Reprinted with permission.

over their failure, though it be much more common.
(Bacon 1899/1620)

John Stuart Mill and Bertrand Russell are two other classic scholars who, along with Bacon, are often quoted for their trenchant observations on the short-comings of human judgment. It is also common to see similar quotes of more recent vintage—in *Skeptical Inquirer* and elsewhere—from the likes of Richard Feynman, Stephen Jay Gould, and Carl Sagan. During the past twenty-five years, a great deal of psychological research has dealt specifically with the quality of everyday reasoning, and so it is now possible to go beyond simple observation and arrive at a truly rigorous assessment of the shortcomings of everyday judgment. In so doing, we can determine whether or not these scholars we all admire are correct. Do people misevaluate evidence in the very ways and for the very reasons that Bacon, Russell, and others have claimed? Let us look at the research record and see.

THE "COMPARED TO WHAT?" PROBLEM

Some of the common claims about the fallibility of human reasoning stand up well to empirical scrutiny. For example, it is commonly argued that people have difficulty with what might be called the "compared to what" problem. That is, people are often overly impressed with an absolute statistic without recognizing that its true import can only be assessed by comparison to some relevant baseline.

For instance, a 1986 article in *Discover* magazine (cited in Dawes 1988) urges readers who fly in airplanes to "know where the exits are and rehearse in your mind exactly how to get to them." Why? The article approvingly notes that someone who interviewed almost two hundred survivors of fatal airline accidents found that ". . . more than 90% had their escape routes mentally mapped out beforehand." Good for them, but note that whoever did the study cannot interview anyone who perished in an airplane crash. Air travel being as scary as it is to so many people, perhaps 90 percent or more of those who died in airline crashes rehearsed their escape routes as well. Ninety percent sounds impressive because it is so close to 100 percent. But without a more pertinent comparison, it really does not mean much.

Similarly, people are often impressed that, say, 30 percent of all infertile couples who adopt a child subsequently conceive. That is great news for that 30 percent to be sure, but what percentage of those who do not adopt likewise conceive? People likewise draw broad conclusions from a cancer patient who goes into remission after steadfastly practicing mental imagery. Again, excellent news for that individual, but might the cancer have gone into remission even if the person had not practiced mental imagery?

This problem of failing to invoke a relevant baseline of comparison is particularly common when the class of data that requires inspection is inherently difficult to collect. Consider, for example, the commonly expressed opinion, "I can always tell that someone is wearing a hairpiece." Are such claims to be believed, or is it just that one can tell that someone is wearing a hairpiece . . . when it is obvious that he is wearing a hairpiece? After all, how can one tell whether some have gone undetected? The goal of a good hairpiece is to fool the public, and so the example is one of those cases in which the confirmations speak loudly while the disconfirmations remain silent.

A similar asymmetry should give pause to those who have extreme confidence in their "gaydar," or their ability to detect whether someone is gay. Here, too, the confirmations announce themselves. When a person for whatever reason "seems gay" and it is later determined that he is, it is a salient triumph for one's skill at detection. But people who elude one's gaydar rarely go out of their way to announce, "By the way, I fooled you: I'm gay."

At any rate, the notion that people have difficulty invoking relevant comparisons has received support from psychological research. Studies of everyday reasoning have shown that the logic and necessity of control groups, for example, is often lost on a large segment of even the educated population (Boring 1954; Einhorn and Hogarth 1978; Nisbett and Ross 1980).

THE "SEEK AND YE SHALL FIND" PROBLEM

Another common claim that stands up well to empirical research is the idea that people do not assess hypotheses even-handedly. Rather, they tend to seek out confirmatory evidence for what they suspect to be true, a tendency that has the effect of "seek and ye shall find." A biased search for confirmatory information frequently turns up more apparent support for a hypothesis than is justified.

This phenomenon has been demonstrated in numerous experiments explicitly designed to assess people's hypothesis-testing strategies (Skov and Sherman 1986; Snyder and Swann 1978). But it is so pervasive that it can also be seen in studies designed with an entirely different agenda in mind. One of my personal favorites is a study in which participants were given the following information (Shafir 1993):

> *Imagine that you serve on the jury of an only-child sole-custody case following a relatively messy divorce. The facts of the case are complicated by ambiguous economic, social, and emotional considerations, and you decide to base your decision entirely on the following few observations. To which parent would you award sole custody of the child?*

> **Parent A:**
> *average income*
> *average health*
> *average working hours*
> *reasonable rapport with the child*
> *relatively stable social life*

> **Parent B:**
> *above-average income*
> *minor health problems*
> *lots of work-related travel*
> *very close relationship with the child*
> *extremely active social life*

Faced with this version of the problem, the majority of respondents chose to award custody to Parent B, the "mixed bag" parent who offers several advantages (above-average income), but also some disadvantages (health problems), in comparison to Parent A. In another version of the problem, however, a different group is asked to which parent they would deny custody of the child. Here, too, a majority selects Parent B. Parent B, then, is paradoxically deemed both more and less worthy of caring for the child.

The result is paradoxical, that is, unless one takes into account people's tendencies to seek out confirming information. Asked which parent should be awarded the child, people look primarily for positive qualities that warrant being awarded the child—looking less vigilantly for negative characteristics that would lead one to favor the other parent. When asked which parent should be denied custody, on the other hand, people look primarily for negative qualities that would disqualify a parent. A decision to award or deny, of course, should be based on a comparison of the positive and negative characteristics of the two parents, but the way the question is framed channels respondents down a narrower path in which they focus on information that would confirm the type of verdict they are asked to render.

The same logic often rears its head when people test certain suppositions or hypotheses. Rumors of some dark conspiracy, for example, can lead people to search disproportionately for evidence that supports the plot and neglect evidence that contradicts it.

THE SELECTIVE MEMORY PROBLEM

A third commonly sounded complaint about everyday human thought is that people are more inclined to remember information that fits their expectations than information at variance with their expectations. Charles Darwin, for example, said that he took great care to record any observation that was inconsistent with his theories because "I had found by experience that such facts and thoughts were far more apt to escape from the memory than favourable ones" (cited in Clark 1984).

This particular criticism of the average person's cognitive faculties is in need of revision. Memory research has shown that often people have the easiest time recalling information that is inconsistent with their expectations or preferences (Bargh and Thein 1985; Srull and Wyer 1989). A little reflection indicates that this is particularly true of those "near misses" in life that become indelibly etched in the brain. The novelist Nicholson Baker (1991) provides a perfect illustration:

> *[I] told her my terrible story of coming in second in the spelling bee in second grade by spelling keep "c-e-e-p" after successfully tossing off microphone, and how for two or three years afterward I was pained every time a yellow garbage truck drove by on Highland Avenue and I saw the capitals printed on it, "Help Keep Our*

City Clean," with that impossible irrational K that had made me lose so humiliatingly. . . .

Baker's account, of course, is only an anecdote, possibly an apocryphal one at that. But it is one that, as mentioned above, receives support from more systematic studies. In one study, for example, individuals who had bet on professional football games were later asked to recall as much as they could about the various bets they had made (Gilovich 1983). They recalled significantly more information about their losses—outcomes they most likely did not expect to have happen and certainly did not prefer to have happen (see Figure 1).

Thus, the simple idea that people remember best that which they expect or prefer needs modification. Still, there is something appealing and seemingly true about the idea, and it should not be discarded prematurely. When considering people's belief in the accuracy of psychic forecasts, for example, it certainly seems to be fed by selective memory for successful predictions. How then can we reconcile this idea with the finding that often inconsistent information is better recalled? Perhaps the solution lies in considering when an event is eventful. With respect to their capacity to grab attention, some events are one-sided and others two-sided. Two-sided events are those that stand out and psychologically register as events regardless of how they turn out. If you bet on a sporting event or an election result, for example,

either outcome—a win or a loss—has emotional significance and is therefore likely to emerge from the stream of everyday experience and register as an event. For these events, it is doubtful that confirmatory information is typically better remembered than disconfirmatory information.

In contrast, suppose you believe that "the telephone always rings when I'm in the shower." The potentially relevant events here are one-sided. If the phone happens to ring while showering, it will certainly register as an event, as you experience great stress in deciding whether to answer it, and you run dripping wet to the phone only to discover that it is someone from AT&T asking if you are satisfied with your long-distance carrier. When the phone does not ring when you are in the shower, on the other hand, it is a non-event. Nothing happened. Thus, with respect to the belief that the phone always rings while you are in the shower, the events are inherently one-sided: Only the confirmations stand out.

Perhaps it is these one-sided events to which Bacon's and Darwin's comments best apply. For one-sided events, as I discuss below, it is often the outcomes consistent with expectations that stand out and are more likely to be remembered. For two-sided events, on the other hand, the two types of outcomes are likely to be equally memorable; or, on occasion, events inconsistent with expectations may be more memorable.

But what determines whether an event is one- or two-sided? There are doubtless several factors. Let's consider two of them in the context of psychic predictions. First, events relevant to psychic predictions are inherently one-sided in the sense that such predictions are disconfirmed not by any specific event, but by their accumulated failure to be confirmed. Thus, the relevant comparison here is between confirmations and non-confirmations, or between events and non-events. It is no surprise, surely, that events are typically more memorable than non-events.

In one test of this idea, a group of college students read a diary purportedly written by another student, who described herself as having an interest in the prophetic nature of dreams (Madey 1993). To test whether there was any validity to dream prophecy, she decided to record each night's dreams and keep a record of significant events in her life, and later

FIGURE 1 / Gamblers' Recall of Information about Bets Won and Lost. (From Gilovich 1983.)

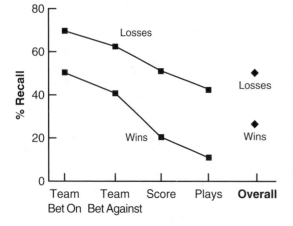

determine if there was any connection between the two. Half of the dreams (e.g., "I saw lots of people being happy") were later followed by events that could be seen as fulfilling ("My professor cancelled our final, which produced cheers throughout the class"). The other half went unfulfilled.

After reading the entire diary and completing a brief "filler" task, the participants were asked to recall as many of the dreams as they could. As figure 2 shows, they recalled many more of the prophecies that were fulfilled than those that were not (see Figure 2). This result is hardly a surprise, of course, because the fulfillment of a prophecy reminds one of the original prediction, whereas a failure to fulfill it is often a non-event. The relevant outcomes are therefore inherently one-sided, and the confirmations are more easily recalled. The end result is that the broader belief in question—in this case, dream prophecy—receives spurious support.

The events relevant to psychic predictions are one-sided in another way as well. Psychic predictions are notoriously vague about when the prophesied events are supposed to occur. "A serious misfortune will befall a powerful leader" is a more common prophecy than "The President will be assassinated on March 15th." Such predictions are temporally unfocused, in that there is no specific moment to which interested parties are to direct their attention. For such predictions, confirmatory events are once again more likely to stand out because confirmations are more likely to prompt a recollection of the original prophecy. The events relevant to temporally unfocused expectations, then, tend to be one-sided, with the confirmations typically more salient and memorable than disconfirmations.

Temporally focused expectations, on the other hand, are those for which the timing of the decisive outcome is known in advance. If one expects a particular team to win the Super Bowl, for example, one knows precisely when that expectation will be confirmed or refuted—at the end of the game. As a result, the events relevant to temporally focused expectations tend to be two-sided because one's attention is focused on the decisive moment, and both outcomes are likely to be noticed and remembered.

In one study that examined the memory implications of temporally focused and unfocused expectations, participants were asked to read the diary of a student who, as part of an ESP experiment, was required to try to prophesy an otherwise unpredictable event every week for several weeks (Madey and Gilovich 1993). The diary included the student's weekly prophecy as well as various passages describing events from that week. There were two groups of participants in the experiment. In the temporally unfocused condition, the prophecies made no mention of when the prophesied event was likely to occur ("I have a feeling that I will get into an argument with my Psychology research group"). In the temporally focused condition, the prediction identified a precise day on which the event was to occur ("I have a feeling that I will get into an argument with my Psychology research group on Friday"). For each group, half of the prophecies were confirmed (e.g., "Our professor assigned us to research groups, and we immediately disagreed over our topic") and half were disconfirmed (e.g., "Our professor assigned us to research groups, and we immediately came to a unanimous decision on our topic"). Whether confirmed or disconfirmed, the relevant event was described in the diary entry for the day prophesied in the temporally focused condition. After reading the diary and completing a short distracter task, the participants were asked to recall as many prophecies and relevant events as they could.

FIGURE 2 / Participants' Recall of Dream Prophecies That Were Either Confirmed or Unconfirmed. (Adapted from Madey 1993.)

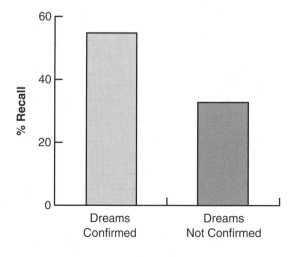

Knowing when the prophesied events were likely to occur helped the respondents' memories, but only for those prophecies that were disconfirmed (see Figure 3). Confirmatory events were readily recalled whether temporally focused or not. Disconfirmations, on the other hand, were rarely recalled unless they disconfirmed a temporally focused prediction. When one considers that most psychic predictions are temporally unfocused, the result, once again, is that the evidence for psychic predictions can appear more substantial than it is.

CONCLUSION

There is, of course, much more psychological research on the quality of everyday judgment than that reviewed here (see, for example, Baron 1988; Dawes 1988; Gilovich 1991; Nisbett and Ross 1980; Kahneman, Slovic, and Tversky 1982). But even this brief review is sufficient to make it clear that some of the reputed biases of everyday judgment turn out to be real, verifiable shortcomings. Systematic research

by and large supports the suspicions of much of the skeptical community that everyday judgment is not to be trusted completely. At one level, this should not come as a surprise: It is precisely because everyday judgment cannot be trusted that the inferential safeguards known as the scientific method were developed. It is unfortunate that those safeguards are not more widely taught or more generally appreciated.

REFERENCES

Bacon, F. 1899. *Advancement of Learning and the Novum Organum* (rev. ed.). New York: Colonial Press. (Original work published 1620).

Baker, N. 1991. *Room Temperature*. New York: Vintage.

Bargh, J. A., and R. D. Thein. 1985. Individual construct accessibility, person memory, and the recall-judgment link: The case of information overload. *Journal of Personality and Social Psychology* 49: 1129–1146.

Baron, J. 1988. *Thinking and Deciding*. New York: Cambridge University Press.

Boring, E. G. 1954. The nature and history of experimental control. *American Journal of Psychology* 67: 573–589.

Clark, R. W. 1984. *The Survival of Charles Darwin: A Biography of a Man and an Idea*. New York: Random House.

Dawes, R. M. 1988. *Rational Choice in an Uncertain World*. San Diego, Calif.: Harcourt Brace Jovanovich.

Einhorn, H. J., and R. M. Hogarth. 1978. Confidence in judgment: Persistence in the illusion of validity. *Psychological Review* 85: 395–416.

Gilovich, T. 1983. Biased evaluation and persistence in gambling. *Journal of Personality and Social Psychology* 44: 1110–1126.

———.1991. *How We Know What Isn't So: The Fallibility of Human Reason in Everyday Life*. New York: Free Press.

Kahneman, D., P. Slovic, and A. Tversky. 1982. *Judgment under Uncertainty: Heuristics and Biases*. Cambridge: Cambridge University Press.

Madey, S. F. 1993. Memory for expectancy-consistent and expectancy-inconsistent information: An investigation of one-sided and two-sided events. Unpublished doctoral dissertation, Cornell University.

Madey, S. F., and T. Gilovich. 1993. Effect of temporal focus on the recall of expectancy-consistent and expectancy-inconsistent information. *Journal of Personality and Social Psychology* 65: 458–468.

Nisbett, R. E., and L. Ross. 1980. *Human Inference: Strategies and Shortcomings of Social Judgment*. Englewood Cliffs, N.J.: Prentice-Hall.

FIGURE 3 / Participants' Recall of Prophecies That Were Confirmed or Disconfirmed, as a Function of Whether or Not the Prophecies Specified When the Critical Events Were to Occur. (Adapted from Madey and Gilovich 1993.)

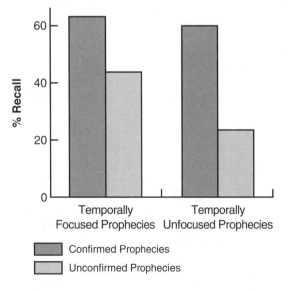

Shafir, E. 1993. Choosing versus rejecting: Why some options are both better and worse than others. *Memory and Cognition* 21: 546–556.

Skov, R. B., and S. J. Sherman. 1986. Information-gathering processes: Diagnosticity, hypothesis-confirmatory strategies, and perceived hypothesis confirmation. *Journal of Experimental Social Psychology* 22: 93–121.

Synder, M., and W. B. Swann. 1978. Hypothesis-testing processes in social interaction. *Journal of Personality and Social Psychology* 36: 1202–1212.

Srull, T. K., and R. S. Wyer. 1989. Person memory and judgment. *Psychological Review* 9: 58–83.

CRITICAL THINKING QUESTIONS

1. Find sources from various media that illustrate the "compared to what" problem discussed in the article. Discuss how your examples illustrate erroneous reasoning.

2. The article states that "Studies of everyday reasoning have shown that the logic and necessity of control groups, for example, is often lost on a large segment of even the educated population." Explain what is meant by the "logic and necessity of control groups."

3. Do you agree or disagree with the concept expressed in the quote in Question 2 that many people have poor critical-thinking skills? If you agree, what suggestions do you have for how people can handle life's issues most effectively? If you disagree, defend your position.

4. Give a personal example of some sort of biased thinking that you have witnessed. What bias or biases were involved?

5. Check your horoscope at the beginning of the day to see what it says is in store for you. Then record events at the end of the day that either confirm or disconfirm the predictions in your horoscope. Use the information contained in the article to discuss your findings.

ARTICLE 8 _____

How do you know what emotion you are experiencing? Ask that question of someone who has just learned that he or she has won the lottery, and the answer would undoubtedly be "thrilled," "excited," "overjoyed," or some such adjective to describe a very positive emotional state. Ask if it is actually anger that the winner is feeling, and he or she probably would look at you as if you were crazy. But how does that person *know* what emotion he or she is feeling?

The work that follows by Schachter and Singer is a classic study that addresses what determines a person's emotional state. Briefly, the authors' findings suggest that what we call *emotion* is partly due to some sort of physiological arousal. However, what we feel is also determined by the cognitive label that we attach to that physiological arousal. According to this approach, a person who experiences some sort of physiological arousal might subjectively experience one of two very different emotional states, either anger or euphoria, depending on how he or she labeled the experience. The article discusses the process as well as some of the conditions that result when this process occurs.

While reading the article, think of its implications: Is cognition a necessary part of emotion? Without it, what (if anything) would we feel? What about newborn children? Since their cognitive abilities are not yet fully developed, does that mean that they don't experience emotions?

Cognitive, Social, and Physiological Determinants of Emotional State[1]

■ Stanley Schachter and Jerome E. Singer

The problem of which cues, internal or external, permit a person to label and identify his own emotional state has been with us since the days that James (1890) first tendered his doctrine that "the bodily changes follow directly the perception of the exciting fact, and that our feeling of the same changes as they occur *is* the emotion" (p. 449). Since we are aware of a variety of feeling and emotion states, it should follow from James' proposition that the various emotions will be accompanied by a variety of differentiable bodily states. Following James' pronouncement, a formidable number of studies were undertaken in search of the physiological differentiators of the emotions. The results, in these early days, were almost uniformly negative. All of the emotional states experimentally manipulated were characterized by a general pattern of excitation of the sympathetic nervous system but there appeared to be no clear-cut physiological

discriminators of the various emotions. This pattern of results was so consistent from experiment to experiment that Cannon (1929) offered, as one of the crucial criticisms of the James-Lange theory, the fact that "the same visceral changes occur in very different emotional states and in non-emotional states" (p. 351).

More recent work, however, has given some indication that there may be differentiators. Ax (1953) and Schachter (1957) studied fear and anger. On a large number of indices both of these states were characterized by a similarly high level of autonomic activation but on several indices they did differ in the degree of activation. Wolf and Wolff (1947) studied a subject with a gastric fistula and were able to distinguish two patterns in the physiological responses of the stomach wall. It should be noted, though, that for many months they studied their subject during and

Reprinted from *Psychological Review*, 1962, 69, 379–399.

following a great variety of moods and emotions and were able to distinguish only two patterns.

Whether or not there are physiological distinctions among the various emotional states must be considered an open question. Recent work might be taken to indicate that such differences are at best rather subtle and that the variety of emotion, mood, and feeling states are by no means matched by an equal variety of visceral patterns.

This rather ambiguous situation has led Ruckmick (1936), Hunt, Cole, and Reis (1958), Schachter (1959) and others to suggest that cognitive factors may be major determinants of emotional states. Granted a general pattern of sympathetic excitation as characteristic of emotional states, granted that there may be some differences in pattern from state to state, it is suggested that one labels, interprets, and identifies this stirred-up state in terms of the characteristics of the precipitating situation and one's apperceptive mass. This suggests, then, that an emotional state may be considered a function of a state of physiological arousal[2] and of a cognition appropriate to this state of arousal. The cognition, in a sense, exerts a steering function. Cognitions arising from the immediate situation as interpreted by past experience provide the framework within which one understands and labels his feelings. It is the cognition which determines whether the state of physiological arousal will be labeled as "anger," "joy," "fear," or whatever.

In order to examine the implications of this formulation let us consider the fashion in which these two elements, a state of physiological arousal and cognitive factors, would interact in a variety of situations. In most emotion inducing situations, of course, the two factors are completely interrelated. Imagine a man walking alone down a dark alley; a figure with a gun suddenly appears. The perception-cognition "figure with a gun" in some fashion initiates a state of physiological arousal; this state of arousal is interpreted in terms of knowledge about dark alleys and guns and the state of arousal is labeled "fear." Similarly a student who unexpectedly learns that he has made Phi Beta Kappa may experience a state of arousal which he will label "joy."

Let us now consider circumstances in which these two elements, the physiological and the cognitive, are, to some extent, independent. First, is the state of physiological arousal alone sufficient to induce an emotion? Best evidence indicates that it is not. Marañon[3] (1924), in a fascinating study (which was replicated by Cantril & Hunt, 1932, and Landis & Hunt, 1932), injected 210 of his patients with the sympathomimetic agent adrenalin and then simply asked them to introspect. Seventy-one percent of his subjects simply reported their physical symptoms with no emotional overtones; 29% of the subjects responded in an apparently emotional fashion. Of these the great majority described their feelings in a fashion that Marañon labeled "cold" or "as if" emotions, that is, they made statements such as "I feel *as if* I were afraid" or "*as if* I were awaiting a great happiness." This is a sort of emotional "déjà vu" experience; these subjects are neither happy nor afraid, they feel "as if" they were. Finally a very few cases apparently reported a genuine emotional experience. However, in order to produce this reaction in most of these few cases, Marañon (1924) points out:

> One must suggest a memory with strong affective force but not so strong as to produce an emotion in the normal state. For example, in several cases we spoke to our patients before the injection of their sick children or dead parents and they responded calmly to this topic. The same topic presented later, during the adrenal commotion, was sufficient to trigger emotion. This adrenal commotion places the subject in a situation of "affective imminence." (pp. 307–308)

Apparently, then, to produce a genuinely emotional reaction to adrenalin, Marañon was forced to provide such subjects with an appropriate cognition.

Though Marañon (1924) is not explicit on his procedure, it is clear that his subjects knew that they were receiving an injection and in all likelihood knew that they were receiving adrenalin and probably had some order of familiarity with its effects. In short, though they underwent the pattern of sympathetic discharge common to strong emotional states, at the same time they had a completely appropriate cognition or explanation as to why they felt this way. This, we would suggest, is the reason so few of Marañon's subjects reported any emotional experience.

Consider now a person in a state of physiological arousal for which no immediately explanatory or appropriate cognitions are available. Such a state could result were one covertly to inject a subject with adrenalin or, unknown to him, feed the subject a sympathomimetic drug such as ephedrine. Under such conditions a subject would be aware of palpitations, tremor, face flushing, and most of the battery of symptoms associated with a discharge of the sympathetic nervous system. In contrast to Marañon's (1924) subjects he would, at the same time, be utterly unaware of why he felt this way. What would be the consequence of such a state?

Schachter (1959) has suggested that precisely such a state would lead to the arousal of "evaluative needs" (Festinger, 1954), that is, pressures would act on an individual in such a state to understand and label his bodily feelings. His bodily state grossly resembles the condition in which it has been at times of emotional excitement. How would he label his present feelings? It is suggested, of course, that he will label his feelings in terms of his knowledge of the immediate situation.[4] Should he at the time be with a beautiful woman, he might decide that he was wildly in love or sexually excited. Should he be at a gay party, he might, by comparing himself to others, decide that he was extremely happy and euphoric. Should he be arguing with his wife, he might explode in fury and hatred. Or, should the situation be completely inappropriate, he could decide that he was excited about something that had recently happened to him or, simply, that he was sick. In any case, it is our basic assumption that emotional states are a function of the interaction of such cognitive factors with a state of physiological arousal.

This line of thought, then, leads to the following propositions:

1. Given a state of physiological arousal for which an individual has no immediate explanation, he will "label" this state and describe his feelings in terms of the cognitions available to him. To the extent that cognitive factors are potent determiners of emotional states, it could be anticipated that precisely the same state of physiological arousal could be labeled "joy" or "fury" or "jealousy" or any of a great diversity of emotional labels depending on the cognitive aspects of the situation.

2. Given a state of physiological arousal for which an individual has a completely appropriate explanation (e.g., "I feel this way because I have just received

an injection of adrenalin") no evaluative needs will arise and the individual is unlikely to label his feelings in terms of the alternative cognitions available.

Finally, consider a condition in which emotion inducing cognitions are present but there is no state of physiological arousal. For example, an individual might be completely aware that he is in great danger but for some reason (drug or surgical) remain in a state of physiological quiescence. Does he experience the emotion "fear"? Our formulation of emotion as a joint function of a state of physiological arousal and an appropriate cognition, would, of course, suggest that he does not, which leads to our final proposition.

3. Given the same cognitive circumstances, the individual will react emotionally or describe his feelings as emotions only to the extent that he experiences a state of physiological arousal.[5]

PROCEDURE

The experimental test of these propositions requires (a) the experimental manipulation of a state of physiological arousal, (b) the manipulation of the extent to which the subject has an appropriate or proper explanation of his bodily state, and (c) the creation of situations from which explanatory cognitions may be derived.

In order to satisfy the first two experimental requirements, the experiment was cast in the framework of a study of the effects of vitamin supplements on vision. As soon as a subject arrived, he was taken to a private room and told by the experimenter:

In this experiment we would like to make various tests of your vision. We are particularly interested in how certain vitamin compounds and vitamin supplements affect the visual skills. In particular, we want to find out how the vitamin compound called "Suproxin" affects your vision.

What we would like to do, then, if we can get your permission, is to give you a small injection of Suproxin. The injection itself is mild and harmless; however, since some people do object to being injected we don't want to talk you into anything. Would you mind receiving a Suproxin injection?

If the subject agrees to the injection (and all but 1 of 185 subjects did) the experimenter continues with instructions we shall describe shortly, then leaves the room. In a few minutes a physician enters the room, briefly repeats the experimenter's instructions, takes the subject's pulse and then injects him with Suproxin.

Depending upon condition, the subject receives one of two forms of Suproxin—epinephrine or a placebo.

Epinephrine or adrenalin is a sympathomimetic drug whose effects, with minor exceptions, are almost a perfect mimicry of a discharge of the sympathetic nervous system. Shortly after injection systolic blood pressure increases markedly, heart rate increases somewhat, cutaneous blood flow decreases, while muscle and cerebral blood flow increase, blood sugar and lactic acid concentration increase, and respiration rate increases slightly. As far as the subject is concerned the major subjective symptoms are palpitation, tremor, and sometimes a feeling of flushing and accelerated breathing. With a subcutaneous injection (in the dosage administered to our subjects), such effects usually begin within 3–5 minutes of injection and last anywhere from 10 minutes to an hour. For most subjects these effects are dissipated within 15–20 minutes after injection.

Subjects receiving epinephrine received a subcutaneous injection of 1/2 cubic centimeter of a 1:1000 solution of Winthrop Laboratory's Suprarenin, a saline solution of epinephrine bitartrate.

Subjects in the placebo condition received a subcutaneous injection of 1/2 cubic centimeter of saline solution. This is, of course, completely neutral material with no side effects at all.

Manipulating an Appropriate Explanation

By "appropriate" we refer to the extent to which the subject has an authoritative, unequivocal explanation of his bodily condition. Thus, a subject who had been informed by the physician that as a direct consequence of the injection he would feel palpitations, tremor, etc. would be considered to have a completely appropriate explanation. A subject who had been informed only that the injection would have no side effects would have no appropriate explanation of his state. This dimension of appropriateness was manipulated in three experimental conditions which shall be

called: Epinephrine Informed (Epi Inf), Epinephrine Ignorant (Epi Ign), and Epinephrine Misinformed (Epi Mis).

Immediately after the subject had agreed to the injection and before the physician entered the room, the experimenter's spiel in each of these conditions went as follows:

Epinephrine Informed. *I should also tell you that some of our subjects have experienced side effects from the Suproxin. These side effects are transitory, that is, they will only last for about 15 or 20 minutes. What will probably happen is that your hand will start to shake, your heart will start to pound, and your face may get warm and flushed. Again these are side effects lasting about 15 or 20 minutes.*

While the physician was giving the injection, she told the subject that the injection was mild and harmless and repeated this description of the symptoms that the subject could expect as a consequence of the shot. In this condition, then, subjects have a completely appropriate explanation of their bodily state. They know precisely what they will feel and why.

Epinephrine Ignorant In this condition, when the subject agreed to the injection, the experimenter said nothing more relevant to side effects and simply left the room. While the physician was giving the injection, she told the subject that the injection was mild and harmless and would have no side effects. In this condition, then, the subject has no experimentally provided explanation for his bodily state.

Epinephrine Misinformed. *I should also tell you that some of our subjects have experienced side effects from the Suproxin. These side effects are transitory, that is, they will only last for about 15 or 20 minutes. What will probably happen is that your feet will feel numb, you will have an itching sensation over parts of your body, and you may get a slight headache. Again these are side effects lasting 15 or 20 minutes.*

And again, the physician repeated these symptoms while injecting the subject.

None of these symptoms, of course, are consequences of an injection of epinephrine and, in effect, these instructions provide the subject with a completely inappropriate explanation of his bodily feelings. This condition was introduced as a control condition of sorts. It seemed possible that the description of side effects in the Epi Inf condition might turn the subject introspective, self-examining, possibly slightly troubled. Differences on the dependent variable between the Epi Inf and Epi Ign conditions might, then, be due to such factors rather than to differences in appropriateness. The false symptoms in the Epi Mis condition should similarly turn the subject introspective, etc., but the instructions in this condition do not provide an appropriate explanation of the subject's state.

Subjects in all of the above conditions were injected with epinephrine. Finally, there was a placebo condition in which subjects, who were injected with saline solution, were given precisely the same treatment as subjects in the Epi Ign condition.

Producing an Emotion Inducing Cognition

Our initial hypothesis has suggested that given a state of physiological arousal for which the individual has no adequate explanation, cognitive factors can lead the individual to describe his feelings with any of a diversity of emotional labels. In order to test this hypothesis, it was decided to manipulate emotional states which can be considered quite different—euphoria and anger.

There are, of course, many ways to induce such states. In our own program of research, we have concentrated on social determinants of emotional states and have been able to demonstrate in other studies that people do evaluate their own feelings by comparing themselves with others around them (Schachter 1959; Wrightsman 1960). In this experiment we have attempted again to manipulate emotional state by social means. In one set of conditions, the subject is placed together with a stooge who has been trained to act euphorically. In a second set of conditions the subject is with a stooge trained to act in an angry fashion.

Euphoria

Immediately[6] after the subject had been injected, the physician left the room and the experimenter returned with a stooge whom he introduced as another subject, then said:

> Both of you have had the Suproxin shot and you'll both be taking the same tests of vision. What I ask you to do now is just wait for 20 minutes. The reason for this is simply that we have to allow 20 minutes for the Suproxin to get from the injection site into the bloodstream. At the end of 20 minutes when we are certain that most of the Suproxin has been absorbed into the bloodstream, we'll begin the tests of vision.

The room in which this was said had been deliberately put into a state of mild disarray. As he was leaving, the experimenter apologetically added:

> The only other thing I should do is to apologize for the condition of the room. I just didn't have time to clean it up. So, if you need any scratch paper or rubber bands or pencils, help yourself. I'll be back in 20 minutes to begin the vision tests.

As soon as the experimenter had left, the stooge introduced himself again, made a series of standard icebreaker comments, and then launched his routine. For observation purposes, the stooge's act was broken into a series of standard units, demarcated by a change in activity or a standard comment. In sequence, the units of the stooge's routine were the following:

1. Stooge reaches for a piece of paper and starts doodling saying, "They said we could use this for scratch, didn't they?" He doodles a fish for some 30 seconds, then says:

2. "This scrap paper isn't even much good for doodling" and crumples paper and attempts to throw it into wastebasket in far corner of the room. He misses but this leads him into a "basketball game." He crumples up other sheets of paper, shoots a few baskets, says "Two points" occasionally. He gets up and does a jump shot saying, "The old jump shot is really on today."

3. If the subject has not joined in, the stooge throws a paper basketball to the subject saying, "Here, you try it."

4. Stooge continues his game saying, "The trouble with paper basketballs is that you don't really have any control."

5. Stooge continues basketball, then gives it up saying, "This is one of my good days. I feel like a kid

again. I think I'll make a plane." He makes a paper airplane saying, "I guess I'll make one of the longer ones."

6. Stooge flies plane. Gets up and retrieves plane. Flies again, etc.

7. Stooge throws plane at subject.

8. Stooge, flying plane, says, "Even when I was a kid, I was never much good at this."

9. Stooge tears off part of plane saying, "Maybe this plane can't fly but at least it's good for something." He wads up paper and making a slingshot of a rubber band begins to shoot the paper.

10. Shooting, the stooge says, "They [paper ammunition] really go better if you make them long. They don't work right if you wad them up."

11. While shooting, stooge notices a sloppy pile of manila folders on a table. He builds a tower of these folders, then goes to the opposite end of the room to shoot at the tower.

12. He misses several times, then hits and cheers as the tower falls. He goes over to pick up the folders.

13. While picking up, he notices, behind a portable blackboard, a pair of hula hoops which have been covered with black tape with a few wires sticking out of the tape. He reaches for these, taking one for himself and putting the other aside but within reaching distance of the subject. The stooge tries the hula hoop, saying, "This isn't as easy as it looks."

14. Stooge twirls hoop wildly on arm, saying, "Hey, look at this—this is great."

15. Stooge replaces the hula hoop and sits down with his feet on the table. Shortly thereafter the experimenter returns to the room.

This routine was completely standard, though its pace, of course, varied depending upon the subject's reaction, the extent to which he entered into this bedlam and the extent to which he initiated activities of his own. The only variations from this standard routine were those forced by the subject. Should the subject originate some nonsense of his own and request the stooge to join in, he would do so. And, he would, of course, respond to any comments initiated by the subject.

Subjects in each of the three "appropriateness" conditions and in the placebo condition were submitted to this setup. The stooge, of course, never knew in which condition any particular subject fell.

Anger

Immediately after the injection, the experimenter brought a stooge into the subject's room, introduced the two and after explaining the necessity for a 20 minute delay for "the Suproxin to get from the injection site into the bloodstream" he continued, "We would like you to use these 20 minutes to answer these questionnaires." Then handing out the questionnaires, he concludes with, "I'll be back in 20 minutes to pick up the questionnaires and begin the tests of vision."

Before looking at the questionnaire, the stooge says to the subject,

I really wanted to come for an experiment today, but I think it's unfair for them to give you shots. At least, they should have told us about the shots when they called us; you hate to refuse, once you're here already.

The questionnaires, five pages long, start off innocently requesting face sheet information and then grow increasingly personal and insulting. The stooge, sitting directly opposite the subject, paces his own answers so that at all times subject and stooge are working on the same question. At regular points in the questionnaire, the stooge makes a series of standardized comments about the questions. His comments start off innocently enough, grow increasingly querulous, and finally he ends up in a rage. In sequence, he makes the following comments.

1. Before answering any items, he leafs quickly through the questionnaire saying, "Boy, this is a long one."

2. Question 7 on the questionnaire requests, "List the foods that you would eat in a typical day." The stooge comments, "Oh for Pete's sake, what did I have for breakfast this morning?"

3. Question 9 asks, "Do you ever hear bells? _____ How often? _____" The stooge remarks, "Look at Question 9. How ridiculous can you get? I hear bells every time I change classes."

4. Question 13 requests, "List the childhood diseases you have had and the age at which you had them"

to which the stooge remarks, "I get annoyed at this childhood disease question. I can't remember what childhood diseases I had, and especially at what age. Can you?"

5. Question 17 asks, "What is your father's average annual income?" and the stooge says, "This really irritates me. It's none of their business what my father makes. I'm leaving that blank."

6. Question 25 presents a long series of items such as "Does not bathe or wash regularly," "Seems to need psychiatric care," etc. and requests the respondent to write down for which member of his immediate family each item seems most applicable. The question specifically prohibits the answer "None" and each item must be answered. The stooge says, "I'll be damned if I'll fill out Number 25. 'Does not bathe or wash regularly'—that's a real insult." He then angrily crosses out the entire item.

7. Question 28 reads: "How many times each week do you have sexual intercourse?" 0–1 _____ 2–3 _____ 4–6 _____ 7 and over _____. The stooge bites out, "The hell with it! I don't have to tell them all this."

8. The stooge sits sullenly for a few moments then he rips up his questionnaire, crumples the pieces and hurls them to the floor, saying, "I'm not wasting any more time. I'm getting my books and leaving" and he stamps out of the room.

9. The questionnaire continues for eight more questions ending with: "With how many men (other than your father) has your mother had extramarital relationships?" 4 and under _____; 5–9 _____; 10 and over _____.

Subjects in the Epi Ign, Epi Inf and Placebo conditions were run through this "anger" inducing sequence. The stooge, again, did not know to which condition the subject had been assigned.

In summary, this is a seven condition experiment which, for two different emotional states, allows us (a) to evaluate the effects of "appropriateness" on emotional inducibility and (b) to begin to evaluate the effects of sympathetic activation on emotional inducibility. In schematic form the conditions are the following:

Euphoria	*Anger*
Epi Inf	Epi Inf
Epi Ign	Epi Ign
Epi Mis	Placebo
Placebo	

The Epi Mis condition was not run in the Anger sequence. This was originally conceived as a control condition and it was felt that its inclusion in the Euphoria conditions alone would suffice as a means of evaluating the possible artifactual effect of the Epi Inf instructions.

Measurement

Two types of measures of emotional state were obtained. Standardized observation through a one-way mirror was the technique used to assess the subject's behavior. To what extent did he act euphoric or angry? Such behavior can be considered in a way as a "semi-private" index of mood for as far as the subject was concerned, his emotional behavior could be known only to the other person in the room—presumably another student. The second type of measure was self-report in which, on a variety of scales, the subject indicated his mood of the moment. Such measures can be considered "public" indices of mood for they would, of course, be available to the experimenter and his associates.

Observation

Euphoria   For each of the first 14 units of the stooge's standardized routine an observer kept a running chronicle of what the subject did and said. For each unit the observer coded the subject's behavior in one or more of the following categories:

Category 1: Joins in activity.   If the subject entered into the stooge activities, e.g., if he made or flew airplanes, threw paper basketballs, hula hooped, etc., his behavior was coded in this category.

Category 2: Initiates new activity.   A subject was so coded if he gave indications of creative euphoria, that is, if, on his own, he initiated behavior outside of the stooge's routine. Instances of such behavior would be the subject who threw open the window and, laughing, hurled paper basketballs at passersby; or, the subject who jumped on a table and spun one hula hoop on his leg and the other on his neck.

Categories 3 and 4: Ignores or watches stooge. Subjects who paid flatly no attention to the stooge or who, with or without comment, simply watched the stooge without joining in his activity were coded in these categories.

For any particular unit of behavior, the subject's behavior was coded in one or more of these categories. To test reliability of coding two observers independently coded two experimental sessions. The observers agreed completely on the coding of 88% of the units.

Anger   For each of the units of stooge behavior, an observer recorded the subject's responses and coded them according to the following category scheme:

Category 1: Agrees.   In response to the stooge the subject makes a comment indicating that he agrees with the stooge's standardized comment or that he, too, is irked by a particular item on the questionnaire. For example, a subject who responded to the stooge's comment on the "father's income" question by saying, "I don't like that kind of personal question either" would be so coded (scored +2).

Category 2: Disagrees.   In response to the stooge's comment, the subject makes a comment which indicates that he disagrees with the stooge's meaning or mood; e.g., in response to the stooge's comment on the "father's income" question, such a subject might say, "Take it easy, they probably have a good reason for wanting the information" (scored −2).

Category 3: Neutral.   A noncommittal or irrelevant response to the stooge's remark (scored 0).

Category 4: Initiates agreement or disagreement.   With no instigation by the stooge, a subject, so coded, would have volunteered a remark indicating that he felt the same way or, alternatively, quite differently than the stooge. Examples would be "Boy I hate this kind of thing" or "I'm enjoying this" (scored +2 or −2).

Category 5: Watches.   The subject makes no verbal response to the stooge's comment but simply looks directly at him (scored 0).

Category 6: Ignores.   The subject makes no verbal response to the stooge's comment nor does he look at

him; the subject, paying no attention at all to the stooge, simply works at his own questionnaire (scored −1).

A subject was scored in one or more of these categories for each unit of stooge behavior. To test reliability, two observers independently coded three experimental sessions. In order to get a behavioral index of anger, observation protocol was scored according to the values presented in parentheses after each of the above definitions of categories. In a unit-by-unit comparison, the two observers agreed completely on the scoring of 71% of the units jointly observed. The scores of the two observers differed by a value of 1 or less for 88% of the units coded and in not a single case did the two observers differ in the direction of their scoring of a unit.

Self-Report of Mood and Physical Condition

When the subject's session with the stooge was completed, the experimenter returned to the room, took pulses and said:

Before we proceed with the vision tests, there is one other kind of information which we must have. We have found, as you can probably imagine, that there are many things beside Suproxin that affect how well you see in our tests. How hungry you are, how tired you are, and even the mood you're in at the time—whether you feel happy or irritated at the time of testing will affect how well you see. To understand the data we collect on you, then, we must be able to figure out which effects are due to causes such as these and which are caused by Suproxin.

The only way we can get such information about your physical and emotional state is to have you tell us. I'll hand out these questionnaires and ask you to answer them as accurately as possible. Obviously our data on the vision tests will only be as accurate as your description of your mental and physical state.

In keeping with this spiel, the questionnaire that the experimenter passed out contained a number of mock questions about hunger, fatigue, etc., as well as questions of more immediate relevance to the experiment. To measure mood or emotional state the following two were the crucial questions:

1. How irritated, angry or annoyed would you say you feel at present?

I don't feel at all irritated or angry	I feel a little irritated and angry	I feel quite irritated and angry	I feel very irritated and angry	I feel extremely irritated and angry
(0)	(1)	(2)	(3)	(4)

2. How good or happy would you say you feel at present?

I don't feel at all happy or good	I feel a little happy and good	I feel quite happy and good	I feel very happy and good	I feel extremely happy and good
(0)	(1)	(2)	(3)	(4)

To measure the physical effects of epinephrine and determine whether or not the injection had been successful in producing the necessary bodily state, the following questions were asked:

1. Have you experienced any palpitation (consciousness of your own heart beat)?

Not at all	A slight amount	A moderate amount	An intense amount
(0)	(1)	(2)	(3)

2. Did you feel any tremor (involuntary shaking of the hands, arms or legs)?

Not at all	A slight amount	A moderate amount	An intense amount
(0)	(1)	(2)	(3)

To measure possible effects of the instructions in the Epi Mis condition, the following questions were asked:

1. Did you feel any numbness in your feet?
2. Did you feel any itching sensation?
3. Did you experience any feeling of headache?

To all three of these questions was attached a four-point scale running from "Not at all" to "An intense amount."

In addition to these scales, the subjects were asked to answer two open-end questions on other physical or emotional sensations they may have experienced during the experimental session. A final measure of bodily state was pulse rate which was taken by the physician or the experimenter at two times—immediately before the injection and immediately after the session with the stooge.

When the subjects had completed these questionnaires, the experimenter announced that the experiment was over, explained the deception and its necessity in detail, answered any questions, and swore the subjects to secrecy. Finally, the subjects answered a brief questionnaire about their experiences, if any, with adrenalin and their previous knowledge or suspicion of the experimental setup. There was no indication that any of the subjects had known about the experiment beforehand but 11 subjects were so extremely suspicious of some crucial feature of the experiment that their data were automatically discarded.

Subjects

The subjects were all male, college students taking classes in introductory psychology at the University of Minnesota. Some 90% of the students in these classes volunteer for a subject pool for which they receive two extra points on their final exam for every hour that they serve as experimental subjects. For this study the records of all potential subjects were cleared with the Student Health Service in order to insure that no harmful effects would result from the injections.

Evaluation of the Experimental Design

The ideal test of our propositions would require circumstances which our experiment is far from realizing. First, the proposition that: "A state of physiological arousal for which an individual has no immediate explanation will lead him to label this state in terms of the cognitions available to him" obviously requires conditions under which the subject does not and cannot have a proper explanation of his bodily state. Though we toyed with such fantasies as ventilating the experimental room with vaporized adrenalin, reality forced us to rely on the disguised injection of Suproxin—a technique which was far from ideal for no matter what the experimenter told them, some subjects would inevitably attribute their feelings to the injection. To the extent that subjects did so, differences between the several appropriateness conditions should be attenuated.

Second, the proposition that: "Given the same cognitive circumstances the individual will react emotionally only to the extent that he experiences a state of physiological arousal" requires for its ideal test the manipulation of states of physiological arousal and of physiological quiescence. Though there is no question that epinephrine effectively produces a state of arousal, there is also no question that a placebo does not prevent physiological arousal. To the extent that the experimental situation effectively produces sympathetic stimulation in placebo subjects, the proposition is difficult to test, for such a factor would attenuate differences between epinephrine and placebo subjects.

Both of these factors, then, can be expected to interfere with the test of our several propositions. In presenting the results of this study, we shall first present condition by condition results and then evaluate the effect of these two factors on experimental differences.

RESULTS

Effects of the Injections on Bodily State

Let us examine first the success of the injections at producing the bodily state required to examine the propositions at test. Does the injection of epinephrine produce symptoms of sympathetic discharge as compared with the placebo injection? Relevant data are presented in Table 1 where it can be immediately seen that on all items subjects who were in epinephrine conditions show considerably more evidence of sympathetic activation than do subjects in placebo conditions. In all epinephrine conditions pulse rate increases significantly when compared with the decrease characteristic of the placebo conditions. On the scales it is clear that epinephrine subjects experience considerably more palpitation and tremor than do placebo subjects. In all possible comparisons on these symptoms, the mean scores of subjects in any of the epinephrine conditions are greater than the corresponding scores in the placebo conditions at better than the .001 level of significance. Examination of the absolute values of these scores makes it quite clear that subjects in epinephrine conditions were, indeed, in a state of physiological arousal, while most subjects in placebo conditions were in a relative state of physiological quiescence.

The epinephrine injection, of course, did not work with equal effectiveness for all subjects; indeed for a few subjects it did not work at all. Such subjects reported almost no palpitation or tremor, showed no increase in pulse and described no other relevant physical symptoms. Since for such subjects the necessary experimental conditions were not established, they were automatically excluded from the data and all further tabular presentations will not include such subjects. Table 1, however, does include the data of these subjects. There were four such subjects in euphoria conditions and one of them in anger conditions.

In order to evaluate further data on Epi Mis subjects it is necessary to note the results of the

TABLE 1 / Effects of the Injections on Bodily State

Condition	N	Pulse		Self-Rating of				
		Pre	Post	Palpitation	Tremor	Numbness	Itching	Headache
Euphoria								
Epi Inf	27	85.7	88.6	1.20	1.43	0	0.16	0.32
Epi Ign	26	84.6	85.6	1.83	1.76	0.15	0	0.55
Epi Mis	26	82.9	86.0	1.27	2.00	0.06	0.08	0.23
Placebo	26	80.4	77.1	0.29	0.21	0.09	0	0.27
Anger								
Epi Inf	23	85.9	92.4	1.26	1.41	0.17	0	0.11
Epi Ign	23	85.0	96.8	1.44	1.78	0	0.06	0.21
Placebo	23	84.5	79.6	0.59	0.24	0.14	0.06	0.06

"numbness," "itching," and "headache" scales also presented in Table 1. Clearly the subjects in the Epi Mis condition do not differ on these scales from subjects in any of the other experimental conditions.

Effects of the Manipulations on Emotional State

Euphoria   Self-report. The effects of the several manipulations on emotional state in the euphoria conditions are presented in Table 2. The scores recorded in this table are derived, for each subject, by subtracting the value of the point he checks on the irritation scale from the value of the point he checks on the happiness scale. Thus, if a subject were to check the point "I feel a little irritated and angry" on the irritation scale and the point "I feel very happy and good" on the happiness scale, his score would be +2. The higher the positive value, the happier and better the subject reports himself as feeling. Though we employ an index for expositional simplicity, it should be noted that the two components of the index each yield results completely consistent with those obtained by use of this index.

Let us examine first the effects of the appropriateness instructions. Comparison of the scores for the Epi Mis and Epi Inf conditions makes it immediately clear that the experimental differences are not due to artifacts resulting from the informed instructions. In both conditions the subject was warned to expect a variety of symptoms as a consequence of the injection. In the Epi Mis condition, where the symptoms were inappropriate to the subject's bodily state the self-report score is almost twice that in the Epi Inf condition where the symptoms were completely appropriate to the subject's bodily state. It is reasonable, then, to attribute differences between informed subjects and those in other conditions to differences in manipulated appropriateness rather than to artifacts such as introspectiveness or self-examination.

It is clear that, consistent with expectations, subjects were more susceptible to the stooge's mood and consequently more euphoric when they had no explanation of their own bodily states than when they did. The means of both the Epi Ign and Epi Mis conditions are considerably greater than the mean of the Epi Inf condition.

It is of interest to note that Epi Mis subjects are somewhat more euphoric than are Epi Ign subjects. This pattern repeats itself in other data shortly to be presented. We would attribute this difference to differences in the appropriateness dimension. Though, as in the Epi Ign condition, a subject is not provided with an explanation of his bodily state, it is, of course, possible that he will provide one for himself which is not derived from his interaction with the stooge. Most reasonably he could decide for himself that he feels this way because of the injection. To the extent that he does so he should be less susceptible to the stooge. It seems probable that he would be less likely to hit on such an explanation in the Epi Mis condition than in the Epi Ign condition for in the Epi Mis condition both the experimenter and the doctor have told him that the effects of the injection would be quite different from what he actually feels. The effect of such instructions is probably to make it more difficult for the subject himself to hit on the alternative explanation described above. There is some evidence to support this analysis. In open-end questions in which subjects described their own mood and state, 28% of the subjects in the Epi Ign condition made some connection between the injection and their bodily state compared with the 16% of subjects in the Epi Mis condition who did so. It could be considered, then, that these three conditions fall along a dimension of appropriateness, with the Epi Inf condition at one extreme and the Epi Mis condition at the other.

TABLE 2 / Self-Report of Emotional State in the Euphoria Conditions

Condition	N	Self-Report Scales	Comparison	p
Epi Inf	25	0.98	Epi Inf vs. Epi Mis	< .01
Epi Ign	25	1.78	Epi Inf vs. Epi Ign	.02
Epi Mis	25	1.90	Placebo vs. Epi Mis, Ign, or Inf	ns
Placebo	26	1.61		

All *p* values reported throughout paper are two-tailed.

Comparing the placebo to the epinephrine conditions, we note a pattern which will repeat itself throughout the data. Placebo subjects are less euphoric than either Epi Mis or Epi Ign subjects but somewhat more euphoric than Epi Inf subjects. These differences are not, however, statistically significant. We shall consider the epinephrine-placebo comparisons in detail in a later section of this paper following the presentation of additional relevant data. For the moment, it is clear that, by self-report manipulating appropriateness has had a very strong effect on euphoria.

Behavior. Let us next examine the extent to which the subject's behavior was affected by the experimental manipulations. To the extent that his mood has been affected, one should expect that the subject will join in the stooge's whirl of manic activity and initiate similar activities of his own. The relevant data are presented in Table 3. The column labeled "Activity index" presents summary figures on the extent to which the subject joined in the stooge's activity. This is a weighted index which reflects both the nature of the activities in which the subject engaged and the amount of time he was active. The index was devised by assigning the following weights to the subject's

activities: 5—hula hooping; 4—shooting with slingshot; 3—paper airplanes; 2—paper basketballs; 1—doodling; 0—does nothing. Pretest scaling on 15 college students ordered these activities with respect to the degree of euphoria they represented. Arbitrary weights were assigned so that the wilder the activity, the heavier the weight. These weights are multiplied by an estimate of the amount of time the subject spent in each activity and the summed products make up the activity index for each subject. This index may be considered a measure of behavioral euphoria. It should be noted that the same between-condition relationships hold for the two components of this index as for the index itself.

The column labeled "Mean number of acts initiated" presents the data on the extent to which the subject deviates from the stooge's routine and initiates euphoric activities of his own.

On both behavioral indices, we find precisely the same pattern of relationships as those obtained with self-reports. Epi Mis subjects behave somewhat more euphorically than do Epi Ign subjects who in turn behave more euphorically than do Epi Inf subjects. On all measures, then, there is consistent evidence that a subject will take over the stooge's euphoric mood to the extent that he has no other explanation of his bodily state.

Again it should be noted that on these behavioral indices, Epi Ign and Epi Mis subjects are somewhat more euphoric than placebo subjects but not significantly so.

Anger   Self-report. Before presenting data for the anger conditions, one point must be made about the anger manipulation. In the situation devised, anger, if manifested, is most likely to be directed at the experimenter and his annoyingly personal questionnaire. As we subsequently discovered, this was rather unfortunate, for the subjects, who had volunteered for the experiment for extra points on their final exam, simply refused to endanger these points by publicly blowing up, admitting their irritation to the experimenter's face or spoiling the questionnaire. Though as the reader will see, the subjects were quite willing to manifest anger when they were alone with the stooge, they hesitated to do so on material (self-ratings of mood and questionnaire) that the experimenter might

TABLE 3 / Behavioral Indications of Emotional State in the Euphoria Conditions

Condition	N	Activity Index	Mean Number of Acts Initiated
Epi Inf	25	12.72	.20
Epi Ign	25	18.28	.56
Epi Mis	25	22.56	.84
Placebo	26	16.00	.54

p value			

Comparison		Activity Index	Initiates
Epi Inf vs. Epi Mis		.05	.03
Epi Inf vs. Ipi Ign		ns	.08
Plac vs. Epi Mis. Ign. or Inf		ns	ns

Tested by χ^2 comparison of the proportion of subjects in each condition initiating new acts.

see and only after the purposes of the experiment had been revealed were many of these subjects willing to admit to the experimenter that they had been irked or irritated.

This experimentally unfortunate situation pretty much forces us to rely on the behavioral indices derived from observation of the subject's presumably private interaction with the stooge. We do, however, present data on the self-report scales in Table 4. These figures are derived in the same way as the figures presented in Table 2 for the euphoria conditions, that is, the value checked on the irritation scale is subtracted from the value checked on the happiness scale. Though, for the reasons stated above, the absolute magnitude of these figures (all positive) is relatively meaningless, we can, of course, compare condition means within the set of anger conditions. With the happiness-irritation index employed, we should, of course, anticipate precisely the reverse results from those obtained in the euphoria conditions; that is, the Epi Inf subjects in the anger conditions should again be less susceptible to the stooge's mood and should, therefore, describe themselves as in a somewhat happier frame of mind than subjects in the Epi Ign condition. This is the case; the Epi Inf subjects average 1.91 on the self-report scales while the Epi Ign subjects average 1.39.

Evaluating the effects of the injections, we note again that, as anticipated, Epi Ign subjects are somewhat less happy than Placebo subjects but, once more, this is not a significant difference.

Behavior. The subject's responses to the stooge, during the period when both were filling out their questionnaires, were systematically coded to provide a

behavioral index of anger. The coding scheme and the numerical values attached to each of the categories have been described in the methodology section. To arrive at an "Anger index" the numerical value assigned to a subject's responses to the stooge is summed together for the several units of stooge behavior. In the coding scheme used, a positive value to this index indicates that the subject agrees with the stooge's comment and is growing angry. A negative value indicates that the subject either disagrees with the stooge or ignores him.

The relevant data are presented in Table 5. For this analysis, the stooge's routine has been divided into two phases—the first two units of his behavior (the "long" questionnaire and "What did I have for breakfast?") are considered essentially neutral revealing nothing of the stooge's mood; all of the following units are considered "angry" units for they begin with an irritated remark about the "bells" question and end with the stooge's fury as he rips up his questionnaire and stomps out of the room. For the neutral units, agreement or disagreement with the stooge's remarks is, of course, meaningless as an index of mood and we should anticipate no difference between conditions. As can be seen in Table 5, this is the case.

For the angry units, we must, of course, anticipate that subjects in the Epi Ign condition will be angrier than subjects in the Epi Inf condition. This is indeed the case. The Anger index for the Epi Ign condition is positive and large, indicating that these subjects have

TABLE 4 / Self-Report of Emotional State in the Anger Conditions

Condition	N	Self-Report Scales	Comparison	p
Epi Inf	22	1.91	Epi Inf vs. Epi Ign	.08
Epi Ign	23	1.39	Placebo vs. Epi Ign or Inf	*ns*
Placebo	23	1.63		

TABLE 5 / Behavioral Indications of Emotional State in the Anger Conditions

Condition	N	Neutral Units	Anger Units
Epi Inf	22	+0.07	−0.18
Epi Ign	23	+0.30	+2.28
Placebo	22[a]	−0.09	+0.79

Comparison for Anger Units	p
Epi Inf vs. Epi Ign	< .01
Epi Ign vs. Placebo	< .05
Placebo vs. Epi Inf	*ns*

[a]For one subject in this condition the sound system went dead and the observer could not, of course, code his reactions.

become angry, while in the Epi Inf condition the Anger index is slightly negative in value indicating that these subjects have failed to catch the stooge's mood at all. It seems clear that providing the subject with an appropriate explanation of his bodily state greatly reduces his tendency to interpret his state in terms of the cognitions provided by the stooge's angry behavior.

Finally, on this behavioral index, it can be seen that subjects in the Epi Ign condition are significantly angrier than subjects in the Placebo condition. Behaviorally, at least, the injection of epinephrine appears to have led subjects to an angrier state than comparable subjects who received placebo shots.

Conformation of Data to Theoretical Expectations

Now that the basic data of this study have been presented, let us examine closely the extent to which they conform to theoretical expectations. If our hypotheses are correct and if this experimental design provided a perfect test for these hypotheses, it should be anticipated that in the euphoria conditions the degree of experimentally produced euphoria should vary in the following fashion:

Epi Mis ≥ Epi Ign > Epi Inf = Placebo

And in the anger conditions, anger should conform to the following pattern:

Epi Ign > Epi Inf = Placebo

In both sets of conditions, it is the case that emotional level in the Epi Mis and Epi Ign conditions is considerably greater than that achieved in the corresponding Epi Inf conditions. The results for the Placebo condition, however, are ambiguous for consistently the Placebo subjects fall between the Epi Ign and the Epi Inf subjects. This is a particularly troubling pattern for it makes it impossible to evaluate unequivocally the effects of the state of physiological arousal and indeed raises serious questions about our entire theoretical structure. Though the emotional level is consistently greater in the Epi Mis and Epi Ign conditions than in the Placebo condition, this difference is significant at acceptable probability levels only in the anger conditions.

In order to explore the problem further, let us examine the experimental factors identified earlier, which might have acted to restrain the emotional level in the Epi Ign and Epi Mis conditions. As was pointed out earlier, the ideal test of our first two hypotheses requires an experimental setup in which the subject has flatly no way of evaluating his state of physiological arousal other than by means of the experimentally provided cognitions. Had it been possible to physiologically produce a state of sympathetic activation by means other than injection, one could have approached this experimental ideal more closely than in the present setup. As it stands, however, there is always a reasonable alternative cognition available to the aroused subject—he feels the way he does because of the injection. To the extent that the subject seizes on such an explanation of his bodily state, we should expect that he will be uninfluenced by the stooge. Evidence presented in Table 6 for the anger condition and in Table 7 for the euphoria conditions indicates that this is, indeed, the case.

As mentioned earlier, some of the Epi Ign and Epi Mis subjects in their answers to the open-end questions clearly attributed their physical state to the injection, e.g., "the shot gave me the shivers." In Tables 6 and 7 such subjects are labeled "Self-informed." In Table 6 it can be seen that the self-informed subjects are considerably less angry than are the remaining subjects; indeed, they are not angry at all. With these self-informed subjects eliminated the difference between the Epi Ign and the Placebo conditions is significant at the .01 level of significance.

Precisely the same pattern is evident in Table 7 for the euphoria conditions. In both the Epi Mis and the Epi Ign conditions, the self-informed subjects have considerably lower activity indices than do the

TABLE 6 / The Effects of Attributing Bodily State to the Injection on Anger in the Anger Epi Ign Condition

Condition	N	Anger Index	p
Self-informed subjects	3	−1.67	ns
Others	20	+2.88	ns
Self-informed vs. Others			.05

TABLE 7 / The Effects of Attributing Bodily State to the Injection on Euphoria in the Euphoria Epi Ign and Epi Mis Conditions

Epi Ign			
	N	Activity Index	p
Self-informed subjects	8	11.63	ns
Others	17	21.14	ns
Self-informed vs. Others			.05

Epi Mis			
	N	Activity Index	p
Self-informed subjects	5	12.40	ns
Others	20	25.10	ns
Self-informed vs. Others			.10

remaining subjects. Eliminating self-informed subjects, comparison of both of these conditions with the Placebo condition yields a difference significant at the .03 level of significance. It should be noted, too, that the self-informed subjects have much the same score on the activity index as do the experimental Epi Inf subjects (Table 3).

It would appear, then, that the experimental procedure of injecting the subjects, by providing an alternative cognition, has, to some extent, obscured the effects of epinephrine. When account is taken of this artifact, the evidence is good that the state of physiological arousal is a necessary component of an emotional experience for when self-informed subjects are removed, epinephrine subjects give consistent indications of greater emotionality than do placebo subjects.

Let us examine next the fact that consistently the emotional level, both reported and behavioral, in Placebo conditions is greater than that in the Epi Inf conditions. Theoretically, of course, it should be expected that the two conditions will be equally low, for by assuming that emotional state is a joint function of a state of physiological arousal and of the appropriateness of a cognition we are, in effect, assuming a multiplicative function, so that if either component is at zero, emotional level is at zero. As noted earlier this expectation should hold if we can be sure that there is no sympathetic activation in the Placebo conditions.

This assumption, of course, is completely unrealistic for the injection of placebo does not prevent sympathetic activation. The experimental situations were fairly dramatic and certainly some of the placebo subjects gave indications of physiological arousal. If our general line of reasoning is correct, it should be anticipated that the emotional level of subjects who give indications of sympathetic activity will be greater than that of subjects who do not. The relevant evidence is presented in Tables 8 and 9.

As an index of sympathetic activation we shall use the most direct and unequivocal measure available—change in pulse rate. It can be seen in Table 1 that the predominant pattern in the Placebo condition is a decrease in pulse rate. We shall assume, therefore, that those subjects whose pulse increases or remains the same give indications of sympathetic activity while those subjects whose pulse decreases do not. In Table 8, for the euphoria condition, it is immediately clear that subjects who give indications of sympathetic activity are considerably more euphoric than are subjects who show no sympathetic activity. This relationship is, of course, confounded by the fact that euphoric subjects are considerably more active than non-euphoric subjects—a factor which independent of mood could elevate pulse rate. However, no such factor operates in the anger condition where angry subjects are neither more active nor talkative than calm subjects. It can be seen in Table 9 that Placebo subjects who show signs of sympathetic activation give indications of considerably more anger than do subjects who show no such signs. Conforming to expectation, sympathetic activation accompanies an increase in emotional level.

TABLE 8 / Sympathetic Activation and Euphoria in the Euphoria Placebo Condition

Subjects Whose:	N	Activity Index	p
Pulse decreased	14	10.67	ns
Pulse increased or remained same	12	23.17	ns
Pulse decrease vs. pulse increase or same			.02

TABLE 9 / Sympathetic Activation and Anger in Anger Placebo Condition

Subjects Whose:	N^a	Activity Index	p
Pulse decreased	13	+0.15	ns
Pulse increased or remained same	8	+1.69	ns
Pulse decrease vs. pulse increase or same			.01

[a] N reduced by two cases owing to failure of sound system in one case and experimenter's failure to take pulse in another.

It should be noted, too, that the emotional levels of subjects showing no signs of sympathetic activity are quite comparable to the emotional level of subjects in the parallel Epi Inf conditions (see Tables 3 and 5). The similarity of these sets of scores and their uniformly low level of indicated emotionality would certainly make it appear that both factors are essential to an emotional state. When either the level of sympathetic arousal is low or a completely appropriate cognition is available, the level of emotionality is low.

DISCUSSION

Let us summarize the major findings of this experiment and examine the extent to which they support the propositions offered in the introduction of this paper. It has been suggested, first, that given a state of physiological arousal for which an individual has no explanation, he will label this state in terms of the cognitions available to him. This implies, of course, that by manipulating the cognitions of an individual in such a state we can manipulate his feelings in diverse directions. Experimental results support this proposition for following the injection of epinephrine, those subjects who had no explanation for the bodily state thus produced, gave behavioral and self-report indications that they had been readily manipulable into the disparate feeling states of euphoria and anger.

From this first proposition, it must follow that given a state of physiological arousal for which the individual has a completely satisfactory explanation, he will not label this state in terms of the alternative cognitions available. Experimental evidence strongly

supports this expectation. In those conditions in which subjects were injected with epinephrine and told precisely what they would feel and why, they proved relatively immune to any effects of the manipulated cognitions. In the anger condition, such subjects did not report or show anger; in the euphoria condition, such subjects reported themselves as far less happy than subjects with an identical bodily state but no adequate knowledge of why they felt they way they did.

Finally, it has been suggested that given constant cognitive circumstances, an individual will react emotionally only to the extent that he experiences a state of physiological arousal. Without taking account of experimental artifacts, the evidence in support of this proposition is consistent but tentative. When the effects of "self-informing" tendencies in epinephrine subjects and of "self-arousing" tendencies in placebo subjects are partialed out, the evidence strongly supports the proposition.

The pattern of data, then, falls neatly in line with theoretical expectations. However, the fact that we were forced, to some extent, to rely on internal analyses in order to partial out the effects of experimental artifacts inevitably makes our conclusions somewhat tentative. In order to further test these propositions on the interaction of cognitive and physiological determinants of emotional state, a series of additional experiments, published elsewhere, was designed to rule out or overcome the operation of these artifacts. In the first of these, Schachter and Wheeler (1962) extended the range of manipulated sympathetic activation by employing three experimental groups—epinephrine, placebo, and a group injected with the sympatholytic agent, chlorpromazine. Laughter at a slapstick movie was the dependent variable and the evidence is good that amusement is a direct function of manipulated sympathetic activation.

In order to make the epinephrine-placebo comparison under conditions which would rule out the operation of any self-informing tendency, two experiments were conducted on rats. In one of these Singer (1961) demonstrated that under fear inducing conditions, manipulated by the simultaneous presentation of a loud bell, a buzzer, and a bright flashing light, rats injected with epinephrine were considerably more frightened than rats injected with a placebo.

Epinephrine-injected rats defecated, urinated, and trembled more than did placebo-injected rats. In nonfear control conditions, there were no differences between epinephrine and placebo groups, neither group giving any indication of fear. In another study, Latané and Schachter (1962) demonstrated that rats injected with epinephrine were notably more capable of avoidance learning than were rats injected with a placebo. Using a modified Miller-Mowrer shuttle-box, these investigators found that during an experimental period involving 200 massed trials, 15 rats injected with epinephrine avoided shock an average of 101.2 trials while 15 placebo-injected rats averaged only 37.3 avoidances.

Taken together, this body of studies does give strong support to the propositions which generated these experimental tests. Given a state of sympathetic activation, for which no immediately appropriate explanation is available, human subjects can be readily manipulated into states of euphoria, anger, and amusement. Varying the intensity of sympathetic activation serves to vary the intensity of a variety of emotional states in both rats and human subjects.

Let us examine the implications of these findings and of this line of thought for problems in the general area of the physiology of the emotions. We have noted in the introduction that the numerous studies on physiological differentiators of emotional states have, viewed en masse, yielded quite inconclusive results. Most, though not all, of these studies have indicated no differences among the various emotional states. Since as human beings, rather than as scientists, we have no difficulty identifying, labeling, and distinguishing among our feelings, the results of these studies have long seemed rather puzzling and paradoxical. Perhaps because of this, there has been a persistent tendency to discount such results as due to ignorance or methodological inadequacy and to pay far more attention to the very few studies which demonstrate *some* sort of physiological differences among emotional states than to the very many studies which indicate no differences at all. It is conceivable, however, that these results should be taken at face value and that emotional states may, indeed, be generally characterized by a high level of sympathetic activation with few if any physiological distinguishers among the many emotional states. If this is correct, the findings of the present study may help to resolve the problem.

Obviously this study does *not* rule out the possibility of physiological differences among the emotional states. It is the case, however, that given precisely the same state of epinephrine-induced sympathetic activation, we have, by means of cognitive manipulations, been able to produce in our subjects the very disparate states of euphoria and anger. It may indeed be the case that cognitive factors are major determiners of the emotional labels we apply to a common state of sympathetic arousal.

Let us ask next whether our results are specific to the state of sympathetic activation or if they are generalizable to other states of physiological arousal. It is clear that from our experiments proper, it is impossible to answer the question for our studies have been concerned largely with the effects of an epinephrine created state of sympathetic arousal. We would suggest, however, that our conclusions are generalizable to almost any pronounced internal state for which no appropriate explanation is available. This suggestion receives some support from the experiences of Nowlis and Nowlis (1956) in their program of research on the effects of drugs on mood. In their work the Nowlises typically administer a drug to groups of four subjects who are physically in one another's presence and free to interact. The Nowlises describe some of their results with these groups as follows:

> At first we used the same drug for all 4 men. In those sessions seconal, when compared with placebo, increased the checking of such words as expansive, forceful, courageous, daring, elated, and impulsive. In our first statistical analysis we were confronted with the stubborn fact that when the same drug is given to all 4 men in a group, the N that has to be entered into the analysis is 1, not 4. This increases the cost of an already expensive experiment by a considerable factor, but it cannot be denied that the effects of these drugs may be and often are quite contagious. Our first attempted solution was to run tests on groups in which each man had a different drug during the same session, such as 1 on seconal, 1 on benzedrine, 1 on dramamine, and 1 on placebo. What does seconal do? Cooped up with, say, the egotistical benzedrine partner, the withdrawn, indifferent dramamine partner, and the slightly bored lactose man, the seconal subject reports that he is distractible, dizzy, drifting, glum, defiant, languid, sluggish, discouraged, dull, gloomy,

lazy, and slow! This is not the report of mood that we got when all 4 men were on seconal. It thus appears that the moods of the partners do definitely influence the effect of seconal. (p. 350)

It is not completely clear from this description whether this "contagion" of mood is more marked in drug than in placebo groups, but should this be the case, these results would certainly support the suggestion that our findings are generalizable to internal states other than that produced by an injection of epinephrine.

Finally, let us consider the implications of our formulation and data for alternative conceptualizations of emotion. Perhaps the most popular current conception of emotion is in terms of "activation theory" in the sense employed by Lindsley (1951) and Woodworth and Schlosberg (1958). As we understand this theory, it suggests that emotional states should be considered as at one end of a continuum of activation which is defined in terms of degree of autonomic arousal and of electroencephalographic measures of activation. The results of the experiment described in this paper do, of course, suggest that such a formulation is not completely adequate. It is possible to have very high degrees of activation without a subject either appearing to be or describing himself as "emotional." Cognitive factors appear to be indispensable elements in any formulation of emotion.

SUMMARY

It is suggested that emotional states may be considered a function of a state of physiological arousal and of a cognition appropriate to this state of arousal. From this follows these propositions:

1. Given a state of physiological arousal for which an individual has no immediate explanation, he will label this state and describe his feelings in terms of the cognitions available to him. To the extent that cognitive factors are potent determiners of emotional states, it should be anticipated that precisely the same state of physiological arousal could be labeled "joy" or "fury" or "jealousy" or any of a great diversity of emotional labels depending on the cognitive aspects of the situation.

2. Given a state of physiological arousal for which an individual has a completely appropriate explanation, no evaluative needs will arise and the individual is unlikely to label his feelings in terms of the alternative cognitions available.

3. Given the same cognitive circumstances, the individual will react emotionally or describe his feelings as emotions only to the extent that he experiences a state of physiological arousal.

An experiment is described which, together with the results of other studies, supports these propositions.

REFERENCES

Ax, A. F. Physiological differentiation of emotional states. *Psychosom. Med.,* 1953, *15,* 435–442.

Cannon, W. B. *Bodily changes in pain, hunger, fear and rage.* (2nd ed.) New York: Appleton, 1929.

Cantril, H., & Hunt, W. A. Emotional effects produced by the injection of adrenalin. *Amer. J. Psychol.,* 1932, *44,* 300–307.

Festinger, L. A theory of social comparison processes. *Hum. Relat.,* 1954, *7,* 114–140.

Hunt, J. McV., Cole, M. W., & Reis, E. E. Situational cues distinguishing anger, fear, and sorrow. *Amer. J. Psychol.,* 1958, *71,* 136–151.

James, W. *The principles of psychology.* New York: Holt, 1890.

Landis, C., & Hunt, W. A. Adrenalin and emotion. *Psychol. Rev.,* 1932, *39,* 467–485.

Latané, B., & Schachter, S. Adrenalin and avoidance learning. *J. Comp. Physiol. Psychol.,* 1962, *65,* 369–372.

Lindsley, D. B. Emotion. In S. S. Stevens (Ed.), *Handbook of experimental psychology.* New York: Wiley, 1951. Pp. 473–516.

Marañon, G. Contribution à l'étude de l'action émotive de l'adrénaline. *Rev. Francaise Endocrinol.,* 1924, *2,* 301–325.

Nowlis, V., & Nowlis, H. H. The description and analysis of mood. *Ann. N. Y. Acad. Sci.,* 1956, *65,* 345–355.

Ruckmick, C. A. *The psychology of feeling and emotion.* New York: McGraw-Hill, 1936.

Schachter, J. Pain, fear, and anger in hypertensives and normotensives: A psychophysiologic study. *Psychosom. Med.,* 1957, *19,* 17–29.

Schachter, S. *The psychology of affiliation.* Stanford, CA: Stanford Univer. Press, 1959.

Schachter, S., & Wheeler, L. Epinephrine, chlorpromazine, and amusement. *J. Abnorm. Soc. Psychol.,* 1962, *65,* 121–128.

Singer, J. E. The effects of epinephrine, chlorpromazine and dibenzyline upon the fright responses of rats under stress and non-stress conditions. Unpublished doctoral dissertation, University of Minnesota, 1961.

Wolf, S., & Wolff, H. G. *Human gastric function.* New York: Oxford Univer. Press, 1947.

Woodworth, R. S., & Schlosberg, H. *Experimental psychology.* New York: Holt, 1958.

Wrightsman, L. S. Effects of waiting with others on changes in level of felt anxiety. *J. Abnorm. Soc. Psychol.,* 1960, *61,* 216–222.

ENDNOTES

1. This experiment is part of a program of research on cognitive and physiological determinants of emotional state which is being conducted at the Department of Social Psychology at Columbia University under PHS Research Grant M-2584 from the National Institute of Mental Health, United States Public Health Service. This experiment was conducted at the Laboratory for Research in Social Relations at the University of Minnesota.

   The authors wish to thank Jean Carlin and Ruth Hase, the physicians in the study, and Bibb Latané and Leonard Weller who were the paid participants.

2. Though our experiments are concerned exclusively with the physiological changes produced by the injection of adrenalin, which appear to be primarily the result of sympathetic excitation, the term physiological arousal is used in preference to the more specific "excitation of the sympathetic nervous system" because there are indications, to be discussed later, that this formulation is applicable to a variety of bodily states.

3. Translated copies of Marañon's (1924) paper may be obtained by writing to the senior author.

4. This suggestion is not new for several psychologists have suggested that situational factors should be considered the chief differentiators of the emotions. Hunt, Cole, and Reis (1958) probably make this point most explicitly in their study distinguishing among fear, anger, and sorrow in terms of situational characteristics.

5. In his critique of the James-Lange theory of emotion, Cannon (1929) also makes the point that sympathectomized animals and patients do seem to manifest emotional behavior. This criticism is, of course, as applicable to the above proposition as it was to the James-Lange formulation. We shall discuss the issues involved in later papers.

6. It was, of course, imperative that the sequence with the stooge begin before the subject felt his first symptoms for otherwise the subject would be virtually forced to interpret his feelings in terms of events preceding the stooge's entrance. Pretests had indicated that, for most subjects, epinephrine-caused symptoms began within 3–5 minutes after injection. A deliberate attempt was made then to bring in the stooge within 1 minute after the subject's injection.

CRITICAL THINKING QUESTIONS

1. In order to conduct the experiment, the researchers deceived the subjects. What ethical issues are involved in this type of research? The obvious deception was not telling the subjects the true nature of the experiment. Does the use of injections of a drug that had a physiological impact on the subjects prompt additional ethical considerations? Explain your answer.

2. This study examines the effects of just one drug, epinephrine, which has excitatory effects on people. Would you expect a similar pattern of results for other classes of drugs? Why or why not? Which ones might be interesting to study?

3. What might the implications of this study be for people who use drugs in a social setting? Would the feelings that they associate with using drugs be due to how others around them responded? Explain your answer. How could you test this possibility?

4. Do you think it is possible to change the emotion you are experiencing by changing the label of the emotion? For example, if you were afraid of public speaking, could you change your emotion from a negative one (fear) to a positive one (excitement) by changing the label given to your physiological arousal? Have you had any personal experience with something like this that may have occurred or a situation when you were aware of how other people influenced how you interpreted the situation? Explain your answer.

ADDITIONAL RELATED READINGS

Lazarus, R. S. (1984). On the primacy of cognition. *American Psychologist, 39,* 124–129.

Zajonc, R. B. (1984). On the primacy of affect. *American Psychologist, 39,* 117–123.

ARTICLE 9 _____

Have you ever heard about the breakup of a married couple and thought, "I'm not surprised; I didn't think it would last"? Or while observing a series of events unfold, have you ever known all along that things would turn out the way they did? If so, you may have experienced a very common social cognition effect know as *hindsight bias.*

Basically, hindsight bias is at work when someone erroneously believes that he or she knew all along what the outcome would be but confirms this belief only *after* the outcome is known. In short, the individual forgets or distorts what his or her beliefs were prior to learning the outcome. Part of this effect is due to selective remembering of evidence, in which people focus primarily on the evidence that is congruent with the actual outcomes and forget the inconsistent information. In a sense, we retroactively construct a series of causal links that explains the current outcome. What we may fail to realize, however, is that given a different outcome, we would be just as likely to explain it, as well.

In fact, hindsight bias may operate in a manner a bit more complex than explained above. For example, the tendency to use hindsight bias may be influenced by whether the outcome under question is positive or negative. Hindsight bias also may operate differently if the outcome is one we personally experience versus one that happened to someone else.

As it turns out, the tendency to use hindsight bias may have some serious implications. If we tend to reconstruct events retroactively (especially those with positive outcomes) so that we think that we know all along what the outcomes will be, might not we become overconfident in our presumed ability to predict future outcomes? Doing so could lead to making erroneous and potentially harmful choices in the future. The following article by Therese A. Louie, Mary T. Curren, and Katrin R. Harich examines some of the issues surrounding hindsight bias and specifically applies the concept to team decision making and outcomes.

"I Knew We Would Win"
Hindsight Bias for Favorable and Unfavorable Team Decision Outcomes

■ Therese A. Louie, Mary T. Curren, and Katrin R. Harich

This study examined hindsight bias for team decisions in a competitive setting in which groups attempted to outperform each other. It was anticipated that, because of self-serving mechanisms, individuals would show hindsight bias only when decision outcomes allowed them to take credit for their own team's success or to downgrade another team for being unsuccessful. MBA students playing a market simulation game made hindsight estimates regarding the likelihood that either their own or another team would perform well. Consistent with a self-serving interpretation, when decision outcomes were favorable individuals evaluating their own team, but not those evaluating another, showed hindsight bias. When outcomes were unfavorable individuals evaluating their own team did not show hindsight bias, but those evaluating another team did. Discussion focuses on implications of hindsight bias in team decision-making settings.

Reprinted from *Journal of Applied Psychology,* 2000, *85*(2), 264–272. Copyright © 2000 by the American Psychological Association. Reprinted with permission.

In the 1970s, the Washington Public Power Supply System (WPPSS), a consortium of public utilities, planned to build seven nuclear power plants to meet energy needs that were forecasted to grow by 7% per year (Baden, 1995). Up through the early 1980s more than 27,000 investors bought bonds supporting the project. During that time, however, higher energy prices prompted consumers to insulate water heaters and lower thermostats. As a result of these consumption changes and advances in technology, the demand for power grew by only 1–2%. Ultimately, just one of the seven nuclear power plants was completed, so in 1983 WPPSS defaulted on bonds worth $2.25 billion. Investors decided to sue. As a group they were involved in lawsuits that continued well into the 1990s. WPPSS claimed throughout the process that the default was unfortunate but not highly foreseeable. In contrast, investors claimed that WPPSS should have known that the demand for power would change such that there would no longer be a need for large-scale high-technology projects.

The different perspectives held by the two sides of the WPPSS fiasco bring to mind the question of how outcome information can bias the perception of what individuals would or should have known at the time that a decision was originally made. In particular, research indicates that hindsight distortion can influence post-outcome perceptions (Fischhoff, 1975). This bias occurs when outcomes seem more inevitable in hindsight than they did in foresight. Referred to as the "knew-it-all-along effect," hindsight bias occurs when individuals feel as if they would have predicted the outcome to events better than they actually did, or better than they actually would have had they been asked to make a forecast. The bias occurs when individuals are asked to recall original predictions (Fischhoff & Beyth, 1975) and even when individuals are specifically asked to ignore outcome information (Fischhoff, 1977).

In terms of legal strategy, it made sense for WPPSS to state that the default was not foreseeable and for investors to claim it was. Yet, because of mechanisms that influence hindsightful reasoning, it is also possible that each team to some degree truly believed their position. Although hindsight bias has been studied extensively, a review of research to date reveals no studies that have investigated whether or why com-

petitors show hindsight bias. Given the prevalence of team decision making, an understanding of factors that influence hindsight bias in such settings would presumably be of theoretical and practical interest. This research investigated the extent of bias that individuals show both for their own and for competing teams' decision outcomes.

BACKGROUND

Hindsight Bias

Hindsight distortion is a pervasive bias that has occurred in a variety of political, managerial, military, and health care settings (for a review, see Christensen-Szalanski & Willham, 1991, and Hawkins & Hastie, 1990). For example, Bukszar and Connolly (1988) asked research participants to read a managerial case that described a group's decision to expand a company. One set of participants was asked to make predictions regarding the likelihood that the decision would result in a favorable or an unfavorable outcome. The remaining participants read about the same event but were additionally told that either a favorable or an unfavorable outcome had actually occurred. These participants then made "postdictions": they estimated the a priori likelihood of occurrence of the two outcomes. As expected, participants who had received outcome information, relative to those who had not, assigned higher likelihoods of occurrence to the particular outcome they received.

Bukszar and Connolly (1988) used a between-subjects hindsight design wherein participants made either predictions or postdictions. Using a different approach, Fischhoff and Beyth (1975) tested hindsight bias with a within-subject design wherein participants were asked to make both types of estimates. When making postdictions, these participants were asked to remember their original predictions. In some respects the within-subject design is a more rigorous test of hindsight effects. It may be easier for individuals to recall closely their own predictions—and hence to show little or no bias—than it is for them to estimate what they think they would have predicted. Even with the more conservative within-subject task, Fischhoff and Beyth's (1975) research participants showed hindsight bias.

Although Bukszar and Connolly's (1988) work indicated that individuals show hindsight bias when observing a group's decision, the WPPSS example suggests the question of how individuals display the bias when evaluating their own group's decision. Uninvestigated in past work is how individuals show hindsight bias when they participate in, instead of observe, a group or team effort.

Team Members' Perspectives

When individuals are asked to make hindsight estimates for their own team's outcome, it might be reasoned that—similar to Bukszar and Connolly's (1988) participants—they would show the bias for favorable as well as unfavorable decision outcomes. Yet when making hindsight estimates for their own, instead of another, team's decision individuals have heightened personal relevance. Investigations of hindsight bias in more self-relevant settings suggest that individuals do not show the bias indiscriminately (Louie, 1999; Mark & Mellor, 1991). Instead, they show the bias selectively for favorable outcomes.

For example, Mark and Mellor (1991) used a naturally occurring situation to investigate how personal relevance influences hindsight bias. They asked three teams of individuals to make postdictions regarding the foreseeability of a layoff: laid-off workers, workers who kept their jobs through the layoffs, and community members. The first set of participants rated the layoff as less foreseeable than the second set, which in turn rated the layoff as less foreseeable than the third set. As the personal relevance of the layoff increased, hindsight bias decreased.

Mark and Mellor (1991) interpreted their results as consistent with the influence of the self-serving bias. Self-serving mechanisms prompt individuals to take credit for favorable outcomes and avoid blame for unfavorable outcomes (Bradley, 1978; Wortman, Costanzo, & Witt, 1973). Whereas the former may encourage hindsight effects (e.g., "I knew my decision would result in a favorable outcome"), the latter may dampen the bias (e.g., "The unfavorable decision outcome was not foreseeable and was not my fault"). The laid-off individuals may not have shown the bias because they wanted to avoid blame for an outcome that was unfavorable to them.

Another explanation for Mark and Mellor's (1991) findings is that the laid-off individuals were surprised at the outcome and that their astonishment prevented feelings of foreseeability. This interpretation is consistent with the findings of research investigating the influence of surprise (e.g., Hoch & Loewenstein, 1989; Ofir &Mazursky, 1997). However, to further support a self-serving interpretation, research efforts (Louie, 1999) found that (a) participants who received favorable outcomes displayed hindsight bias, but not when their inclination to take credit for success was suppressed, and (b) those who received unfavorable outcomes did not show hindsight effects and made more external than internal attributions for the outcome. These findings provided additional support that self-serving mechanisms can influence hindsight effects in addition to any reactions of surprise.

Curren, Folkes, and Steckel (1992) found that when individuals arrive together at a team decision, they show group-serving attributions that parallel the individual-level self-serving bias. Therefore, we proposed that individuals would show hindsight bias when their team decision outcomes were favorable, but not when the outcomes were unfavorable. It is worthwhile to note that some group research findings suggest a different pattern of hindsight effects. Schlenker and Miller (1977) found that individuals whose judgments were combined into a team decision distanced themselves from unfavorable team outcomes. In such settings, the distancing process may prompt individuals to show hindsight bias for unfavorable outcomes (e.g., "I am not really involved in the team, and I knew the outcome would be unfavorable"). Given the possibility of individual dissociation, it is worthwhile to examine whether team members show a pattern of hindsight bias similar to that shown by individual decision makers.

In summary, if individuals involved in team decision making feel more personal relevance than those who are not involved, and if heightened relevance triggers self-serving mechanisms, then team members may show hindsight bias when their decision outcomes are favorable but not when they are unfavorable. The latter finding would be consistent with the WPPSS officials' perspective that they could not have foreseen the bond default. Similar to Curren et al.'s (1992) work, these ideas are tested in this research using a naturally existing, personally relevant setting. Management students who were divided into 10 decision-making teams made predictions and postdictions for their performance on a graded class assignment.

Competing Team Members' Perspectives

The setting for this research provided an additional opportunity to explore how self-serving mechanisms influence hindsight bias. It is possible to examine how individuals react to other teams' decision outcomes in a competitive setting in which groups want to outperform one another. To illustrate, suppose that of the 10 teams mentioned above, the members of the first 5 teams were asked to make hindsight estimates for the performance outcome of the last 5 teams. Although the performance outcome of the last 5 teams would not be directly self-relevant to members of the first 5 teams, in a competitive setting other teams' outcomes would not be completely irrelevant or inconsequential. It is interesting to consider how hindsight bias would be displayed for other teams' outcomes given a game-type environment, as it presumably has implications in professional environments where resources and awards are allocated competitively.

There is reason to believe that in competitive settings, self-serving tendencies may have opposite effects when individuals evaluate another, rather than their own, team. Research findings suggest that individuals give others less credit for favorable outcomes, and more blame for unfavorable outcomes, than they do for themselves (for a review, see Taylor & Brown, 1988). In addition, Taylor and Koivumaki (1976) found that attributions regarding specified others can differ depending upon the role the others have in the life of the person making the attribution. For example, the researchers found that spouses and friends were more likely to be seen as causing positive behaviors than were strangers and acquaintances. Their research findings differ from those of other work wherein participants were asked to make attributions for an anonymous group (e.g., "most students," or "most people"); in the latter situation, attributions were generally neutral with regard to whether the other individuals caused favorable or unfavorable outcomes (Mirels, 1980).

If attributions for close others are similar to those for oneself, and if attributions for a group of anonymous others are neutral, it is reasonable to propose that attributions are quite dissimilar when the self–other relationship becomes not only more distant but oppositional. This might be especially so for situations similar to that used in this study, in which team performances were interdependent. Accordingly, individuals may exhibit hindsight bias when observing another team's unfavorable outcome (e.g., "I knew they would not do well") but not when witnessing another's favorable outcome (e.g., "I did not foresee that they would do so well"). Building on past work in which participants were unconcerned observers of another team's performance (e.g., Bukszar & Connolly, 1988), this research examined hindsight bias in settings in which team participants want themselves, but not others, to succeed.

Measuring Team Members' Hindsight Bias and Self-Serving Mechanisms

The main focus of this research was to examine how individuals show hindsight bias for team decision outcomes in a competitive and personally consequential setting. Another way that this work builds on hindsight bias studies in self-relevant settings is that the bias was examined using the stringent within-subject design. Mark and Mellor (1991) measured postdictions only, and Louie (1999) used a between-subjects design. The present study provides a strong test of self-serving effects on hindsight bias by asking individuals to make, then recollect, their predictions.

In this research it is desirable to include measures to assess whether the decision outcome information does indeed prompt self-serving mechanisms. It is difficult, however, to measure such processes with direct questions (e.g., "How are you affected by the outcome information?") because self-protecting mechanisms might allow participants to deny successfully any negative reactions. In achievement settings researchers have overcome this issue by using participants' evaluations of the research tasks as indirect measures of self-serving activity (for a review, see Taylor & Brown, 1988). For example, individuals have shown self-serving mechanisms by positively evaluating tasks that allowed them to dwell on favorable rather than unfavorable feedback.

Therefore, in this work the participants' reactions to the outcome information were assessed through their feelings about the task of making postdictions. If outcomes are favorable and participants are influenced by self-serving mechanisms, those reviewing their own team's decisions (who would react positively to their own success) should show more interest in making postdictions than those reviewing another team's decision. In contrast, when outcomes are unfavorable, participants reviewing their own rather than another's past decision should react more negatively to the task of making postdictions.

In summary, we hypothesized that when individuals received favorable outcome information they (a) would show hindsight bias for their own, but not for another, team's decision outcome and (b) would react more favorably to the task of making postdictions, when reviewing their own, rather than another, team. In contrast, when participants received unfavorable outcome information they (a) would show hindsight bias for another, but not their own, team's decision outcome and (b) would react more negatively to the task of making postdictions for their own rather than another team.

METHOD

Overview

As stated above, this study was conducted in a personally relevant setting wherein student teams' performances on a decision-making task affected their course grades. The context for this research was a marketing strategy computer simulation game called MARKSTRAT (Larreche & Gatignon, 1990). This game was deemed an appropriate context for this study because both academics and managers believe MARKSTRAT constitutes a realistic environment in which students can become actively involved in making managerial decisions (Kinnear & Klammer, 1987). Also, using this game, Curren et al. (1992) demonstrated that self-serving mechanisms (as measured with rating scales) are triggered in team decision-making settings. In MARKSTRAT, teams of students are assigned to one of five business firms. With the goal of strengthening their market position, the members of each firm meet together regularly to make a series of managerial decisions. As with real-world companies, a MARKSTRAT firm's performance depends on its own decisions and those of the

other firms. The players in this study received weekly feedback about their performance, such as their team's proportion of total dollar sales or market share.

Participants

Seventy-one MBA students, enrolled in a marketing course, participated in this study. They had an average of 2 years' work experience. As stated above, the students in each firm made managerial decisions jointly. In contrast, they responded to the research materials individually and were assured anonymity.

Procedure

Participants were told that the study was being conducted to explore the dynamics of managerial decision making. When the study questionnaires were distributed, the instructor was running separate MARKSTRAT simulation games, referred to as Game I and Game II, each with five teams or firms, A through E. For the study, the players were instructed to make hindsight estimates regarding a specific target firm's market-share performance. That is, at the start of the games, each participant was asked to review the first set of decisions made by those in the target firm he or she was assigned to evaluate. The participant was then asked to make predictions about the target firm's upcoming market-share performance.

One week after making predictions, and after the game administrator had run the market simulation, the participants were individually presented with the decision information that they reviewed earlier. This time, however, they also received updates regarding the target firm's actual performance. After being reminded that they had made predictions a week earlier, they then made postdictions (i.e., were asked to recall their preoutcome estimates) regarding the target firm's market share.

Independent Variables

Self and Other Team Evaluation Conditions The participants were divided into "self" and "other" team evaluation conditions. Players in the self-evaluation condition were asked to make estimates regarding the market share of their own firm. The remaining players were assigned to the other-evaluation condition.

These participants provided estimates for a firm participating in a MARKSTRAT game other than their own. For example, in the other-evaluation condition a participant in Game I, Firm A, made hindsight estimates for the team decision of the participants in Game II, Firm A.

It is important to note that each participant in the other-evaluation condition did not compete directly in the same MARKSTRAT game with participants in the team he or she evaluated. For example, those in Game I, Firm A did not evaluate those in Game I, Firm B. Informing individuals of firm decisions within the same game would have compromised the integrity of the assignment, as part of the task was for each team to anticipate how firms in the same game would behave. Showing a participant the decision of a firm in the same game would be like giving a football player an opposing team's playbook. However, all teams from both games were opponents in that their performance influenced their course grade. They were informed that the two teams that achieved the best performance in the class as a whole (not just in their particular game) received a grade of A for their game, the next two received an A–, and so on down to the worst two teams. In this manner, teams competed against each other not only in their respective games but also against every other team in the class. For this reason, all firms wanted to perform the best and did not want other firms to do well.

Favorable and Unfavorable Outcome Conditions
To test the influence of outcome information, firms were divided into those that received favorable and those that received unfavorable feedback. Outcome favorableness was measured by the direction in which the target firm's market share changed after the initial decisions were implemented. Because an objective of the game was for players to increase their firm's standing, players who evaluated target firms that had increases in market share were in the favorable-outcome condition, and those who evaluated firms that had decreases in market share were in the unfavorable-outcome condition.

Dependent Variables

Hindsight Estimates   Before receiving outcome information, participants predicted the likelihood that

the target firm's market share would increase, decrease, and stay the same. Participants were instructed that their estimates should sum to 100%.

A week after making predictions, the participants were informed of their target firm's actual market share performance (either that market share had increased or decreased, as no firm's share remained the same). They were reminded that they had previously made predictions about the outcomes and then were asked to recall to the best of their ability what they had predicted. The instructions emphasized that participants should ignore outcome information when making postdictions.

Interest in Postdiction Task   Two measures were used to provide evidence of participants' self-serving activity upon receiving outcome information. After making postdictions, participants were asked the extent to which they thought the postdiction questionnaire was interesting. They responded on a scale of 1 (*not at all interesting*) to 10 (*very interesting*). Then participants were instructed to explain why they felt the postdiction questions were or were not interesting. Thus, both close-ended and open-ended measures were used to find evidence of the self-serving bias.

RESULTS

Prediction and Postdiction Scores

Three participants did not complete the postdiction task and were eliminated from the analysis. Similar to the procedure used in other within-subject hindsight studies (Campbell & Tesser, 1983; Haslam & Jayasinghe, 1995; Wood, 1978) the remaining participants' likelihood estimates were combined so that each participant had one prediction and one postdiction score. We simplified the prediction estimates by calculating the net likelihood of an increase. The likelihood of a market share increase was multiplied by 1, the likelihood of a decrease was multiplied by −1, and the likelihood of market share staying the same was multiplied by 0. The resulting three numbers were summed to form each participant's prediction score. A participant who predicted that the target firm's market share had a 50% chance of increasing, a 30% chance of decreasing, and a 20% chance of staying the same had a prediction score of 20. The same calculations were made for the postdiction estimates. In this coding scheme, participants who were informed that their target firm's market share increased showed hindsight bias if the postdiction score exceeded the prediction score. In contrast, for unfavorable outcomes (i.e., reduced market share) a drop in the net likelihood of an increase from prediction to postdiction reflected hindsight bias.

The changes between the participants' predictions and postdictions were analyzed across evaluation conditions using a repeated measures analysis of variance, with firm membership as a factor in the model. Because outcome favorableness was based on the actual results of the market simulation game, it was not appropriate to use it as a factor, as this would have required random assignment to the outcome conditions. Therefore, the analysis was conducted first for those in the favorable-outcome condition, then separately for those in the unfavorable-outcome condition.

Favorable-Outcome Condition

Hindsight Findings The mean prediction and postdiction scores for the favorable- and unfavorable-outcome conditions are presented in Table 1. A favorable outcome is represented by an increase in market share. A repeated measures analysis of variance (ANOVA) revealed a significant within-subject main effect of prediction versus postdiction score that was qualified by a significant within-subject interaction of these estimates across the evaluation conditions, $F(1, 29) = 11.02$, $p < .01$, $\omega^2 = .19$. We anticipated that participants receiving favorable outcome information would show hindsight bias for their own, but not another, team's decision. As we expected, a within-subject test of the difference between prediction and postdiction scores revealed that self-evaluation participants showed the bias: their mean net postdiction score for an increase in market share exceeded their mean prediction score, $t(14) = 3.72$, $p < .01$, $d = 0.73$. In contrast, and also as we anticipated, other-evaluation condition participants did not show the bias, as their mean postdiction score for their target firm did not differ significantly from their prediction score, $t(17) = 0.29$, *ns, d* = 0.04.

There is further evidence that self-evaluation condition participants shifted their estimates according to the nature of the outcome information. As can be seen in Table 1, their mean prediction score did not differ significantly from that of other-evaluation participants, $t(31) = 1.52$, *ns, d* = 0.56. Yet the self-evaluation participants' mean postdiction score was significantly higher, $t(31) = 4.02$, $p < .01$, $d = 1.35$. In support of a hindsight effect, we found that after self-evaluation participants received favorable outcome information, they felt more strongly than did other-

TABLE 1 / Mean Hindsight Estimates

	Net Likelihood of an Increase	
Measure	Prediction	Postdiction
Favorable-outcome condition		
Self-evaluation (*n* = 15)[a]	16.00	39.33
	(33.34)	(30.81)
Other evaluation (*n* = 18)	−1.39	−0.28
	(28.48)	(27.89)
Unfavorable-outcome condition		
Self-evaluation (*n* = 17)	14.12	16.18
	(30.37)	(30.80)
Other evaluation (*n* = 18)[a]	0.00	−17.22
	(45.86)	(30.78)

Note: Numbers in parentheses are standard deviations.
[a]Means in this row differ at *p* < .05.

evaluation participants that they had previously predicted a favorable outcome.

Interest in Postdiction Questions   The mean ratings for the favorable-outcome participants' level of interest in the postdiction questions are presented in Table 2. The data are consistent with the view that, relative to other-evaluation participants, self-evaluation participants reacted more positively to the outcome information. As we anticipated, participants rated the task of making postdictions as more interesting when evaluating their own instead of another firm's decision, $t(31) = 2.52$, $p < .05$, $d = 0.82$.

We also analyzed the participants' open-ended remarks about their interest in the postdiction questions. The responses for the favorable- and unfavorable-outcome teams were shuffled randomly together and then analyzed by two independent coders. Both coders were undergraduates who were trained to categorize open-ended responses. They were not informed of the research hypotheses or the experimental conditions. After the coders counted the total number of thoughts for each participant, they coded the content of the comments. Most of the responses, as we had requested, were about the

TABLE 2 / Treatment Means for Reaction to Postdiction Task

	Evaluation Condition	
Measure	Self	Other
Favorable-outcome condition		
n	15	18
Interest rating[a]	6.13	4.28
	(2.10)	(2.37)
Total number of thoughts	0.53	0.72
	(0.92)	(1.02)
Positive comments about postdiction questionnaire	0.20	0.39
	(0.56)	(0.70)
Negative comments about postdiction questionnaire	0.13	0.28
	(0.35)	(0.46)
Miscellaneous comments	0.20	0.05
	(0.56)	(0.24)
Unfavorable-outcome condition		
n	17	18
Interest rating	5.00	5.56
	(1.73)	(2.03)
Total number of thoughts	1.35	0.72
	(1.32)	(0.96)
Positive comments about postdiction questionnaire	0.29	0.17
	(0.59)	(0.38)
Negative comments about postdiction questionnaire[a]	1.00	0.33
	(1.12)	(0.59)
Miscellaneous comments	0.06	0.22
	(0.24)	(0.43)

Note: Numbers in parentheses are standard deviations.
[a]Means in this row differ at $p < .05$.

postdiction questionnaire. These responses were separated into those that were positive about the materials (e.g., "This provides insight into the decision-making process"), and those that were negative (e.g., "This survey is given in conditions that make it relatively useless"). A third category was added to accommodate miscellaneous comments, that were irrelevant to the postdiction questionnaire (e.g., "R&D [research and development], sales, and research all have an impact on the team result"). Agreement between the coders was 81% with all discrepancies resolved through discussion.

Analysis of the favorable-outcome participants' open-ended responses across the self- and other-evaluation conditions revealed no significant differences in the total number of thoughts, $t(31) = 0.50$, *ns, d* = 0.19. We anticipated that compared with other-evaluation participants, self-evaluation participants would have more positive comments about the postdiction questions. However, the self-evaluation participants did not have a significantly higher mean number of positive comments, $t(31) = 0.72$, *ns, d* = 0.30. There were also no differences across evaluation conditions in the mean number of negative thoughts, $t(31) = 0.88$, *ns, d* = 0.37, or the mean number of miscellaneous thoughts, $t(31) = 0.82$, *ns, d* = 0.33.

In short, the self-evaluation participants had a higher rated level of interest in the postdiction task than did the other-evaluation participants, but an analysis of the open-ended responses revealed no greater number of positive comments. There is partial supporting evidence that the former participants' hindsight bias was based on their positive reaction to the outcome information.

Unfavorable Outcome Condition

Hindsight Findings For unfavorable-outcome-condition participants, hindsight bias was displayed if the mean postdiction score that market share will increase was lower than the mean prediction score. A repeated measures ANOVA revealed a significant within-subject interaction effect for the prediction and postdiction scores across evaluation conditions, $F(1, 31) = 4.90$, $p < .05$, $\omega^2 = .08$. As we anticipated, self-evaluation participants did not show hindsight distortion for their own team's unfavorable outcomes.

As can be seen by the means presented in Table 1, within-subject tests revealed that the self-evaluation participants' mean postdiction score was not significantly different from their mean prediction score, $t(16) = 0.23$, *ns, d* = 0.07. In contrast, and as we anticipated, the other-evaluation participants showed hindsight bias for another team's unfavorable outcome because their mean postdiction score was lower and significantly different from their mean prediction score, $t(17) = 2.34$, $p < .05$, *d* = 0.44.

Similar to the analysis for the favorable outcome team, an examination of the pattern of predictions and postdictions revealed that the differences between the self- and other-evaluation participants occurred after the presentation of outcome information. As can be seen in Table 1, the mean prediction scores do not differ significantly across the evaluation conditions, $t(33) = 0.71$, *ns, d* = 0.36. However, relative to the self-evaluation participants, the other-evaluation participants' mean postdiction score was significantly lower, $t(33) = 2.96$, $p < .01$, *d* = 1.08. In support of the notion of a hindsight effect, after receiving outcome information, other-evaluation participants felt more strongly than did self-evaluation participants that they had predicted unfavorable outcomes.

Interest in Postdiction Questions As can be seen in Table 2, and contrary to our expectations, the self-evaluation participants did not rate the experimental task as significantly less interesting than the other-evaluation participants after receiving unfavorable outcome information, $t(33) = 0.81$, *ns, d* = 0.30.

However, the participants' open-ended comments were consistent with the view that the self-evaluation participants reacted more negatively to the postdiction questions than the other-evaluation participants did. Although the total number of thoughts across the two evaluation conditions was not significantly different, $t(33) = 1.56$, *ns, d* = 0.55, self-evaluation participants provided a higher mean number of negative comments than did other-evaluation participants, $t(33) = 2.49$, $p < .05$, *d* = 0.75. There were no significant differences across self- and other-evaluation participants in the mean number of positive thoughts, $t(33) = 0.51$, *ns, d* = 0.24, or the mean number of miscellaneous thoughts, $t(33) = 1.54$, *ns, d* = 0.46. Whereas the favorable-outcome self-evaluation participants showed a more positive reaction to the postdiction task through the rating scale measure, the unfavorable-outcome self-evaluation participants showed a more negative reaction through open-ended comments.

Supplementary Hindsight Analysis

Although the hindsight findings are consistent with a self-serving interpretation, it is worthwhile to note potential limitations of the hindsight measure and to provide additional support for the findings. As in past work (e.g., Leary, 1981), the dependent variable was constructed as a net likelihood of an increase score because it standardized participants' likelihood estimates into a measure that represented the optimism (or lack thereof) they felt about their target firm. Yet this measure is potentially problematic because it is a difference score. For example, difference scores are less reliable than individual component scores when the latter are positively correlated (Peter, Churchill, & Brown, 1993). This particular issue is not a problem in this study because the participants' likelihood estimates for an increase and a decrease were negatively correlated ($r = -.73$), which enhances reliability (Peter et al., 1993, footnote 3). One might also say that because the hypothesized effects were found, credence is given to the validity of the measure. Nonetheless, it is worthwhile to examine the data in a manner that does not incur the errors caused by combining likelihood estimates.

We analyzed the data again using another representation of the dependent measure. One can examine predictions and postdictions by focusing on the outcome that meets the objective of the event of interest (e.g., Connolly & Bukszar, 1990; Schkade & Kilbourne, 1991). For this study, the relevant likelihood estimate would be the one that corresponds with the objective to increase market share. When we analyzed the data focusing on the likelihood of an increase estimate, the findings remained the same as when using the net likelihood of an increase score. For those who received favorable outcome information, participants in the self-evaluation condition showed a significant amount of hindsight bias in the difference between their predictions and postdictions ($M = 18.33$, $SD = 15.99$), $t(14) = 4.44$, $p < .01$, $d = 1.17$. Participants in the other-evaluation condition did not

($M = 1.11$, $SD = 12.43$), $t(17) = 0.38$, ns, $d = 0.07$. For those who received unfavorable outcome information, self-evaluation participants did not show a significant amount of hindsight bias ($M = -0.29$, $SD = 21.61$), $t(16) = -0.06$, ns, $d = 0.02$. The other-evaluation participants did show a significant amount of bias ($M = 10.56$, $SD = 19.17$), $t(17) = 2.34$, $p < .05$, $d = .54$.

To further explore the findings, the data were examined one final way using the original net likelihood of an increase score. Instead of investigating the results for the favorable- and unfavorable-outcome conditions separately, we pooled the data together and analyzed them with a regression. The participants were divided into two groups. A hindsight group was composed of participants who we anticipated would show a significant amount of bias (i.e., those in the self-evaluation/favorable-outcome and other-evaluation/unfavorable-outcome conditions). A no-hindsight group was composed of the participants who were not expected to show the bias (i.e., those in the self-evaluation/unfavorable-outcome and other-evaluation/favorable-outcome conditions). The differences between the prediction and postdiction scores were regressed on these dummy variables. As we expected, participants in the hindsight group showed a significant amount of hindsight bias; the estimated coefficient was 20.00, which was statistically significant ($p < .01$). Participants in the no-hindsight group did not show a significant amount of bias. The estimated coefficient for that group was -0.43 ($p > .90$). The difference between the two groups (i.e., 20.43) was significant ($p < .01$).

The hindsight results were consistent across three measurement approaches, and when the dependent variable was and was not measured as a difference score. (Complete details of the two supplementary analyses are available from the authors.) Together, the findings provide support for the anticipated effects.

DISCUSSION

Hindsight Bias in Team Decision-Making Settings

Taken together, the self- and other-evaluation findings strongly support the notion that self-serving mechanisms can influence hindsight bias when individuals evaluate team decision outcomes in personally relevant settings. First, consistent with past findings (Louie, 1999; Mark & Mellor, 1991) but applied to a team decision-making setting, the self-evaluation participants showed hindsight bias only when their outcomes were favorable. If the favorable-outcome participants had been asked to update their predictions based on outcome information, then it would have been appropriate for them to make postdictions that were influenced by outcome information. However, because they were asked not to revise but to recall their original predictions, and because their recollection was biased in the direction of outcome information, there is evidence of a systematic hindsight effect.

Second, this study investigated hindsight bias for other teams' decisions in a competitive setting. The interdependence of the teams' performances produced heightened relevance, which appears to have triggered self-serving mechanisms. This, in turn, prompted participants to show hindsight bias when other teams' outcomes were unfavorable but not when they were favorable. Unlike in past work—and as we expected for settings in which individuals want their own team, but not another's, to perform well—the patterns of hindsight bias for other-evaluation and for self-evaluation participants were opposites.

Finally, these findings were obtained using a conservative within-subject hindsight measure. Attesting to the strength of self-serving mechanisms, participants' recall of their predictions was influenced by outcome feedback in the pattern we anticipated.

The findings for the participants' interest in the task of making postdictions were not as consistent as we expected. The results prompt the question of why the interest ratings were significantly different, as we anticipated for the favorable but not the unfavorable outcome participants, and why the open-ended responses were significantly different, as we expected for unfavorable but not favorable outcomes. The answer may lie in the nature of positive and negative feedback for self-evaluation participants on personally relevant tasks. Research findings suggest that individuals strive to obtain a positive self-view, and hence are optimistic that they or their team will perform well (Taylor & Brown, 1988). When feedback is favorable, individuals may positively evaluate the tasks related to their performance but may not have many comments because the outcome matches their expectations.

In contrast, unfavorable feedback is unanticipated. Individuals are prompted to reconcile the discrepancy between what was expected and what actually occurred (Mandler, 1982). This may account for the higher number of negative comments from the unfavorable outcome participants in the self-evaluation rather than the other-evaluation condition. It is not clear why the former, relative to the latter, participants did not downgrade their rating of the task. However, it is possible that their required and continued participation in the game for their class assignment prevented them from expressing their discontent through a direct-ratings measure. In short, perhaps because of prior expectations and the anticipation of future performances, favorable and unfavorable outcome participants reacted differently to the interest measures.

Implications of Hindsight Bias in Team Decision-Making Settings

The findings help to explain why team members who receive unfavorable outcome feedback, such as the WPPSS officials, do not show hindsight bias. Alternatively, when outcomes are favorable, there are many implications when team members show the bias. Research suggests that hindsight distortion is linked to exaggerated confidence (e.g., Bodenhausen, 1990; Bukszar & Connolly, 1988) and to reduced predictive accuracy (Hoch & Loewenstein, 1989). Team members should beware of the hubris that can develop when favorable decision outcomes seem inevitable. One example of this is provided by Long-Term Capital Management, a group of prominent economists and stockbrokers who, some analysts would claim, became too self-assured that both past and future financial triumphs were inevitable (Glassman, 1998). Confident because of their past success, the group continued investing and borrowing heavily even when they were warned that collapsing economies around the world made their actions extremely risky. As a result, during the stock market turmoil of 1998 the company lost 90% of its investors' money. To prevent mistakes fueled by hindsight bias, teams would benefit from occasional audits conducted by an external party that does not have a personal stake in—and hence would not fall prey to self-serving mechanisms from—the favorable outcomes in question. An auditor who is aware of the tendency to take credit for success could attempt to keep teams grounded in reality.

Another idea is that team members could attempt to self-monitor. Although some researchers found that participants continued to show hindsight distortion even after being warned of its existence and asked to avoid it (Fischhoff, 1977; Pohl & Hell, 1996), other findings indicate that participants can indeed eliminate the bias if they are informed of personally relevant consequences to showing it. For example, Louie (1999) found that participants who received favorable decision outcomes showed the bias, but not when they were warned that it reduces predictive accuracy. Perhaps in the same manner, successful team members can be given a self-relevant incentive not to show the bias or can be warned of its future personal consequences.

Perhaps a more direct approach to reducing hindsight distortion is to make decreasing the bias a team objective. Stahlberg, Eller, Maass, and Frey (1995), although they did not study group decision making, investigated how individuals separately or in groups showed hindsight bias upon learning the outcomes to scientific studies or the answers to complex questions. The researchers found that individuals and groups show the same extent of hindsight bias with a between-subjects design and that groups show less bias when using the more conservative within-subject design. Hence, team members can formalize the desire to reduce or to stifle hindsight bias by collectively making predictions, which would decrease the magnitude of the bias (Stahlberg et al., 1995) and serve as a reality check that can be referred to when necessary. This process can be used for both an individual's own, as well as for another's, team decisions.

Hindsight bias for favorable outcomes can be dangerous not only to team members but also to those who want to be like them. The Long-Term Capital Management team included two Nobel laureates in economics and a former Federal Reserve Board vice chairman. With such pedigrees on the team, many of those who entrusted their funds were confident that success would continue and were therefore less concerned than usual with knowing the specifics of the company's dealings (O'Brien & Holson, 1998). Also, bank investment managers who admired the company partners and who carried out transactions for

them sought to imitate their strategy by making similar dealings for their own clients. Hence, those who aspire to be like a successful team should be careful, as they can be influenced by the team's biased perspective, as well as develop their own hindsight-based rationales. Should outcomes become highly unfavorable, the aspiring individuals can dissociate from the team and, like the WPPSS investors, become former allies turned legal foes.

When feedback is unfavorable, teams should be aware that even if they do not see the outcome as foreseeable, others, especially opponents, might. This perspective could be important in situations such as the WPPSS legal battle, in which team members must convince a judge that they did not have previous knowledge of potentially unfavorable outcomes. This point is also illustrated by the lawsuits faced by blood donation centers that collected and distributed blood in the early 1980s. During that time, thousands of individuals contracted HIV from contaminated blood-related products. Years later, some of those individuals or their families filed lawsuits, alleging that the centers did not do all they could to screen tainted blood (King, 1989). The donation centers responded by noting that the cause of AIDS was unknown until 1984 and that there was no antibody test available until 1985. This tragic example illustrates how important it can be to understand perceptions in hindsight; a crucial consideration in the cases was determining whether the donation centers should have known to be more careful with the blood products and should have warned blood recipients of the risk. An understanding of what causes hindsight effects could help teams in similar situations discern how their previous actions are perceived by others. (In the late 1980s, donation centers had won 57% of the cases against them; King, 1989.)

Although we hope that this work provides insight into hindsight bias for team decisions, it would be worthwhile to pursue research outside of a classroom setting to see whether the same pattern of hindsight bias emerges. In addition, this study is limited in that it measured hindsight bias for decisions at a competitive task that was new to the participants. Although research (e.g., Arkes, Wortmann, Saville, & Harkness, 1981) has suggested that even experienced professionals show hindsight bias, future research can explore the relationship between expertise and hindsight bias in personally relevant team settings. More generally, this study brings up the possibility that individual differences may play a role in hindsight bias. The Long-Term Capital Management example and the findings obtained in this work from experienced and bright MBA students suggest that achievement-oriented individuals (who have obtained past successes) may be more susceptible to hindsight effects. This possibility can be examined in future studies.

Finally, it is interesting to note that the founder of Long-Term Capital Management tried to warn his colleagues that market conditions were changing to their detriment. Yet his colleagues remained confident until the failure became too large for them to fix (Henriques, 1998). This suggests that team members might reinforce hindsight effects by reassuring each other of continued success. Researchers can investigate conditions under which people who show hindsight bias for favorable outcomes are more prone to overconfidence for team than for individual decisions. In sum, research can test the applicability of, as well as build on, this work in a variety of team decision-making settings.

REFERENCES

Arkes, H. R., Wortmann, R. L., Saville, P. D., & Harkness, A. R. (1981). Hindsight bias among physicians weighing the likelihood of diagnoses. *Journal of Applied Psychology, 66,* 252–254.

Baden, J. A. (1995, April 12). WHOOPS: An expensive, valuable history lesson. *Seattle Times,* p. B5.

Bodenhausen, G. V. (1990). Second-guessing the jury: Stereotypic and hindsight biases in perceptions of court cases. *Journal of Applied Social Psychology, 20,* 1112–1121.

Bradley, G. W. (1978). Self-serving biases in the attribution process: A reexamination of the fact or fiction question. *Journal of Personality and Social Psychology, 36,* 56–71.

Bukszar, E., & Connolly, T. (1988). Hindsight bias and strategic choice: Some problems in learning from experience. *Academy of Management Journal, 31,* 628–641.

Campbell, J. D., & Tesser, A. (1983). Motivational interpretations of hindsight bias: An individual difference analysis. *Journal of Personality, 51,* 605–620.

Christensen-Szalanski, J. J. J., & Willham, C. F. (1991). The hindsight bias: A meta-analysis. *Organizational Behavior and Human Decision Processes, 48,* 147–168.

Connolly, T., & Bukszar, E. W. (1990). Hindsight bias: Self-flattery or cognitive error? *Journal of Behavioral Decision Making, 3,* 205–211.

Curren, M. T., Folkes, V. S., & Steckel, J. H. (1992). Explanations for successful and unsuccessful marketing decisions: The decision maker's perspective. *Journal of Marketing, 56,* 18–31.

Fischhoff, B. (1975). Hindsight ≠ foresight: The effect of outcome knowledge on judgment under uncertainty. *Journal of Experimental Psychology: Human Perception and Performance, 1,* 288–299.

Fischhoff, B. (1977). Perceived informativeness of facts. *Journal of Experimental Psychology: Human Perception and Performance, 3,* 349–358.

Fischhoff, B., & Beyth, R. (1975). 'I knew it would happen'—Remembered probabilities of once-future things. *Organizational Behavior and Human Performance, 13,* 1–16.

Glassman, J. K. (1998, September 27). A simple strategy beats the 'experts.' *The Washington Post,* p. H01.

Haslam, N., & Jayasinghe, N. (1995). Negative affect and hindsight bias. *Journal of Behavioral Decision Making, 8,* 127–135.

Hawkins, S. A., & Hastie, R. (1990). Hindsight: Biased judgments of past events after the outcomes are known. *Psychological Bulletin, 107,* 311–327.

Henriques, D. B. (1998, September 27). Fault lines of risk appear as market hero stumbles. *New York Times,* p. 1.

Hoch, S. J., & Loewenstein, G. F. (1989). Outcome feedback: Hindsight and information. *Journal of Experimental Psychology: Learning, Memory, and Cognition, 15,* 605–619.

King, W. (1989, June 14). AIDS, blood and liability. *Seattle Times,* p. A1.

Kinnear, T. C., & Klammer, S. K. (1987). Management perspectives on MARKSTRAT: The GE experience and beyond. *Journal of Business Research, 15,* 491–502.

Larreche, J. C., & Gatignon, H. (1990). *MARKSTRAT2.* Redwood City, CA: Scientific Press.

Leary, Mark R. (1981). The distorted nature of hindsight. *Journal of Social Psychology, 115,* 25–29.

Louie, T. A. (1999). Decision makers' hindsight bias after receiving favorable and unfavorable feedback. *Journal of Applied Psychology, 84,* 29–41.

Mandler, G. (1982). The structure of value: Accounting for taste. In M. S. Clark & S. T. Fiske (Eds.), *Affect and cognition: The 17th Annual Carnegie Symposium* (pp. 3–36). Hillsdale, NJ: Erlbaum.

Mark, M. M., & Mellor, S. (1991). Effect of self-relevance of an event on hindsight bias: The foreseeability of a layoff. *Journal of Applied Psychology, 76*, 569–577.

Mirels, H. L. (1980). The avowal of responsibility for good and bad outcomes: The effects of generalized self-serving biases. *Personality and Social Psychology Bulletin, 6*, 299–306.

O'Brien, T. L., & Holson, L. M. (1998, October 23). A hedge fund's stars didn't tell and savvy financiers didn't ask. *New York Times*, p. 1.

Ofir, C., & Mazursky, D. (1997). Does a surprising outcome reinforce or reverse the hindsight bias? *Organizational Behavior and Human Decision Processes, 69*, 51–57.

Peter, J. P., Churchill, G. A., Jr., & Brown, T. J. (1993). Caution in the use of difference scores in consumer research. *Journal of Consumer Research, 19*, 655–662.

Pohl, R. F., & Hell, W. (1996). No reduction in hindsight bias after complete information and repeated testing. *Organizational Behavior and Human Decision Processes, 67*, 49–58.

Schkade, D. A, & Kilbourne, L. M. (1991). Expectation–outcome consistency and hindsight bias. *Organizational Behavior and Human Decision Processes, 49*, 105–123.

Schlenker, B. R., & Miller, R. S. (1977). Egocentrism in teams: Self-serving biases or logical information processing? *Journal of Personality and Social Psychology, 35*, 755–764.

Stahlberg, D., Eller, F., Maass, A., & Frey, D. (1995). We knew it all along: Hindsight bias in teams. *Organizational Behavior and Human Decision Processes, 63*, 46–58.

Taylor, S. E., & Brown, J. D. (1988). Illusion and well-being: A social psychological perspective on mental health. *Psychological Bulletin, 103*, 193–210.

Taylor, S. E., & Koivumaki, J. H. (1976). The perception of self and others: Acquaintanceship, affect, and actor-observer differences. *Journal of Personality and Social Psychology, 33*, 403–408.

Wood, G. (1978). The knew-it-all-along effect. *Journal of Experimental Psychology: Human Perception and Performance, 4*, 345–353.

Wortman, C. B., Costanzo, P. R., & Witt, T. R. (1973). Effect of anticipated performance on the attributions of causality to self and others. *Journal of Personality and Social Psychology, 27*, 372–381.

We thank Bridget Frances, Julie Ruth, Douglas MacLachlan, Richard Yalch, Shelley Taylor, Barbara Kahn, Mark Forehand, Brian Sternthal, S. Siddarth, and Richard Charles for their comments on previous versions of this article.

CRITICAL THINKING QUESTIONS

1. Describe a situation in which you have seen someone display hindsight bias.

2. What problems may result from a person's or group's tendency to use hindsight bias? For example, might an individual or group who is prone to hindsight bias also be overly (and perhaps falsely) confident in predicting future outcomes? Why or why not?

3. Using the information from the article, propose some techniques that individuals and groups could use to reduce their tendency toward hindsight bias. Explain why these techniques would work as well as any practical limitations in implementing them.

4. Near the end of the article, it is stated that "the findings obtained in this work from experienced and bright MBA students suggest that achievement-oriented individuals (who have obtained past successes) may be more susceptible to hindsight effects." Design a study to determine if achievement-oriented individuals with track records of success are, indeed, more susceptible to hindsight bias than other individuals.

5. Design a study to test hindsight bias in an election. Include the details of whom would be tested, when they would be tested, and what questions they would be asked. Also identify any variables that would need to be controlled in the study.

Chapter Four

ATTITUDES

THE STUDY OF attitudes is considered by many social psychologists to be the core issue in understanding human behavior. How we act in any given situation is the product of the attitudes that we have formed, which in turn are based on the experiences we have had.

Whether or not we believe that attitudes constitute the core of social psychology, the study of attitudes and attitude change has been prominent in social psychological research from the beginning. Part of this interest has been theoretically driven. How attitudes are formed and how they can be changed, as well as what factors make some attitudes so resistant to change, are but a few of the topics that theorists have studied. However, there is also a more pragmatic, applied reason for this interest in attitudes: Principles of attitude change and attitude measurement have a direct bearing on several major industries and even psychotherapy. For example, survey organizations and advertising agencies focus on attitudes, measuring what they are, how they change over time, as well as how best to change them. Likewise, a major goal of both therapy and health promotion might be viewed as modifying people's dysfunctional or health-endangering attitudes and behaviors. Theoretical research often has provided the foundation for the principles applied by clinicians, health professionals, and advertisers.

The readings in this chapter relate to various aspects of attitudes. Article 10, " Don't Even Think about It!" examines the issue of taboos as being a prime example of deeply held attitudes. How are taboos formed? Why are they maintained? How are they changed?

Article 11, "Cognitive Consequences of Forced Compliance," is a classic demonstration of a powerful theoretical model in social psychology known as *cognitive dissonance*. It is an excellent example of how common-sense predictions often are exactly opposite of what actually occurs.

Finally, Article 12, "Do Attitudes Affect Memory? Tests of the Congeniality Hypothesis," provides a contemporary examination of one aspect of cognitive dissonance theory. Specifically, the article addresses the question: Which type of information are we more likely to remember: information that is *consistent* with our own beliefs or information that is *inconsistent* with our beliefs? The answer to this question depends on several factors, all of which have important implications for how people are influenced (or not) by new information that is incongruent with their existing beliefs.

ARTICLE 10 _____

Obviously, attitudes are formed in a great variety of ways. Some are the result of direct experience. For instance, we meet someone from a certain country and, based on that limited experience, form an attitude (or stereotype) about people from that country. In other words, we generalize our experience to form an attitude. In many other cases, however, we do not experience the person, situation, or event directly but rather indirectly. These so-called *secondhand attitudes* are the result of information we received from someone else, such as our parents or friends. In fact, this kind of information is a major source of our beliefs.

The number of attitudes that people hold can be virtually limitless; however, some attitudes are held more strongly than others. The strength of these attitudes often can be seen most clearly by their absence. That is, what topics do we never discuss? What would we never admit, or what would we never do? In other words, what are our *taboos?* A taboo involves the three elements that comprise all attitudes: First, there is a *cognitive* or *belief* component, which is what we believe is or should be true. Additionally, there is an *affective* or *emotional* component to the taboo. We not only believe something to be true, we also feel very strongly about it. Just the idea of the taboo being violated may fill us with disgust. Finally, the taboo involves a *behavior tendency;* we strongly tend to avoid doing things that violate our taboo belief and affective components.

Many taboos are shared among people in a culture, while others are unique to individuals. Thus, most people in a given society tend to believe that it is acceptable to eat certain foods while other foods are off limits. Sometimes, taboos are more unique, such as beliefs that certain topics should never be mentioned to certain people. In all cases, taboos serve to set limits (sometimes, severe limits) on what we believe, feel, and do.

The following article by Michael Ventura examines the topic of taboos, including their origins and the impact that they have on our daily lives. After reading the article, you may agree with the author that we are not really as free as we would like to believe, despite the fact that freedom is a central concept in American culture.

Don't Even Think about It!

■ Michael Ventura

Taboos come in all sizes. Big taboos: when I was a kid in the Italian neighborhoods of Brooklyn, to insult someone's mother meant a brutal fight—the kind of fight no one interferes with until one of the combatants goes down and stays down. Little taboos: until the sixties, it was an insult to use someone's first name without asking or being offered permission. Personal taboos: Cyrano de Bergerac would not tolerate the mention of his enormous nose. Taboos peculiar to one city: in Brooklyn (again), when the Dodgers were still at Ebbets Field, if you rooted for the Yankees you kept it to yourself unless you wanted a brawl. Taboos, big or small, are always about having to respect somebody's (often irrational) boundary—or else.

There are taboos shared within one family: my father did not feel free to speak to us of his grandmother's suicide until his father died. Taboos within intellectual elites: try putting a serious metaphysical or spiritual slant on a "think-piece" (as we call them in the trade) written for the *New York Times,* the

Washington Post, or most big name magazines—it won't be printed. Taboos in the corporate and legal worlds: if you're male, you had best wear suits of somber colors, or you're not likely to be taken seriously; if you're female, you have to strike a very uneasy balance between the attractive and the prim, and even then you might not be taken seriously. Cultural taboos: in the Jim Crow days in the South, a black man who spoke with familiarity to a white woman might be beaten, driven out of town, or (as was not uncommon) lynched.

Unclassifiable taboos: in Afghanistan, as I write this, it is a sin—punishable by beatings and imprisonment—to fly a kite. Sexual taboos: there are few communities on this planet where two men can walk down a street holding hands without being harassed or even arrested; in Afghanistan (a great place for taboos these days) the Taliban would stone them to death. Gender taboos: how many American corporations (or institutions of any kind) promote women to power? National taboos: until the seventies, a divorced person could not run for major public office in America (it wasn't until 1981 that our first and only divorced president, Ronald Reagan, took office); today, no professed atheist would dare try for the presidency. And most readers of this article probably approve, as I do, of this comparatively recent taboo: even the most rabid bigot must avoid saying "nigger," "spic," or "kike" during, say, a job interview—and the most macho sexist must avoid words like "broad."

Notice that nearly all of our taboos, big and small, public and intimate, involve silence—keeping one's silence, or paying a price for not keeping it. Yet keeping silent has its own price: for then silence begins to fill the heart, until silence becomes the heart—a heart swelling with restraint until it bursts in frustration, anger, even madness.

The taboos hardest on the soul are those which fester in our intimacies—taboos known only to the people involved, taboos that can make us feel alone even with those to whom we're closest. One of the deep pains of marriage—one that also plagues brothers and sisters, parents and children, even close friends—is that as we grow more intimate, certain silences often become more necessary. We discover taboo areas, both in ourselves and in the other, that cannot be transgressed without paying an awful price.

If we speak of them, we may endanger the relationship; but if we do not speak, if we do not violate the taboo, the relationship may become static and tense, until the silence takes on a life of its own. Such silences are corrosive. They eat at the innards of intimacy until, often, the silence itself causes the very rupture or break-up that we've tried to avoid by keeping silent.

THE CANNIBAL IN US ALL

You may measure how many taboos constrict you, how many taboos you've surrendered to—at home, at parties, at work, with your lover or your family—by how much of yourself you must suppress. You may measure your life, in these realms, by what you cannot say, do, admit—cannot and must not, and for no better reason than that your actions or words would disrupt your established order. By this measure, most of us are living within as complex and strictured a system of taboos as the aborigines who gave us the word in the first place. You can see how fitting it is that the word "taboo" comes from a part of the world where cannibalism is said to be practiced to this day: the islands off eastern Australia—Polynesia, New Zealand, Melanesia. Until 1777, when Captain James Cook published an account of his first world voyage, Europe and colonial America had many taboos but no word that precisely meant taboo. Cook introduced this useful word to the West. Its instant popularity, quick assimilation into most European languages, and constant usage since, are testimony to how much of our lives the word describes. Before the word came to us, we'd ostracized, coerced, exiled, tormented, and murdered each other for myriad infractions (as we still do), but we never had a satisfying, precise word for our reasons.

We needed cannibals to give us a word to describe our behavior, so how "civilized" are we, really? We do things differently from those cannibals, on the surface, but is the nature of what we do all that different? We don't cook each other for ceremonial dinners, at least not physically (though therapists can testify that our ceremonial seasons, like Christmas and Thanksgiving, draw lots of business—something's cooking). But we stockpile weapons that can cook the entire world, and we organize our national priorities around their "necessity," and it's a national political taboo to seriously cut spending for those planet-cookers. If that's "progress," it's lost on me. In China it's taboo to be a Christian, in Israel it's taboo to be a Moslem, in Syria it's taboo to be a Jew, in much of the United States it's still taboo to be an atheist, while in American academia it's taboo to be deeply religious. Our headlines are full of this stuff. So it's hardly surprising that a cannibal's word still describes much of our behavior.

I'm not denying the necessity of every society to set limits and invent taboos (some rational, some not) simply in order to get on with the day—and to try to contain the constant, crazy, never-to-be-escaped longings that blossom in our sleep and distract or compel us while awake. Such longings are why even a comparatively tiny desert tribe like the ancient Hebrews needed commandments and laws against coveting each other's wives, stealing, killing, committing incest. That tribe hadn't seen violent, sexy movies, hadn't listened to rock 'n' roll, hadn't been bombarded with ads featuring half-naked models, and hadn't watched too much TV. They didn't need to. Like us, they had their hearts, desires, and dreams to instruct them how to be very, very naughty. The taboo underlying all others is that we must not live by the dictates of our irrational hearts—as though we haven't forgiven each other, or ourselves, for having hearts.

If there's a taboo against something, it's usually because a considerable number of people desire to do it. The very taboos that we employ to protect us from each other and ourselves, are a map of our secret natures. When you know a culture's taboos (or an individual's, or a family's) you know its secrets—you know what it really wants.

FAVORITE TABOOS

It's hard to keep a human being from his or her desire, taboo or not. We've always been very clever, very resourceful, when it comes to sneaking around our taboos. The Aztecs killed virgins and called it religion. The Europeans enslaved blacks and called it economics. Americans tease each other sexually and call it fashion.

If we can't kill and screw and steal and betray to our heart's desire, and, in general, violate every taboo in sight—well, we can at least watch other people do it. Or read about it. Or listen to it. As we have done, since ancient times, through every form of religion and entertainment. The appeal of taboos and our inability to escape our longing for transgression (whether or not we ourselves transgress) are why so many people who call themselves honest and law-abiding spend so much time with movies, operas, soaps, garish trials, novels, songs, Biblical tales, tribal myths, folk stories, and Shakespeare—virtually all of which, both the great and the trivial, are about those who dare to violate taboos. It's a little unsettling when you think about it: the very stuff we say we most object to is the fundamental material of what we call culture.

That's one reason that fundamentalists of all religions are so hostile to the arts. But fundamentalists partake of taboos in the sneakiest fashion of all. Senator Jesse Helms led the fight against the National Endowment for the Arts because he couldn't get the (vastly overrated) homosexual art of Robert Mapplethorpe or the most extreme performance artists out of his mind—he didn't and doesn't want to. He, like all fundamentalists, will vigorously oppose such art and all it stands for until he dies, because his very opposition gives him permission to concentrate on taboo acts. The Taliban of Afghanistan will ride around in jeeps toting guns, searching out any woman who dares show an inch of facial skin or wear white socks (Taliban boys consider white socks provocative), and when they find such a woman they'll jail and beat her—because their so-called righteousness gives them permission to obsess on their taboos. Pat Robertson and his ilk will fuss and rage about any moral "deviation," any taboo violation they can find, because that's the only way they can give themselves permission to entertain the taboos. They get to not have their taboo cake, yet eat it too.

We are all guilty of this to some extent. Why else have outlaws from Antigone to Robin Hood to Jesse James to John Gotti become folk heroes? Oedipus killed his father and slept with his mother, and we've been performing that play for 2500 years because he is the ultimate violator of our deepest taboos. Aristotle said we watch such plays for "catharsis," to purge our desires and fears in a moment of revelation. Baloney. Ideas like "catharsis" are an intellectual game, to glossy-up our sins. What's closer to the truth is that we need Oedipus to stand in for us. We can't have changed much in 2500 years, if we still keep him alive in our hearts to enact our darkest taboos for us. Clearly, the very survival of Oedipus as an instantly recognizable name tells us that we still want to kill our fathers and screw our mothers (or vice versa).

A COUNTRY OF BROKEN TABOOS

Taboos are a special paradox for Americans. However much we may long for tradition and order, our longings are subverted by the inescapable fact that our country was founded upon a break with tradition and a challenge to order—which is to say, the United States was founded upon the violation of taboos. Specifically, this country was founded upon the violation of Europe's most suffocating taboo: its feudal suppression (still enforced in 1776, when America declared its independence) of the voices of the common people. We were the first nation on earth to write into law that any human being has the right to say anything, and that even the government is (theoretically) not allowed to silence you.

At the time, Europe was a continent of state-enforced religions, where royalty's word was law and all other words could be crushed by law. (Again: taboo was a matter of enforced silence.) We were the first nation to postulate verbal freedom for everyone. All our other freedoms depend upon verbal freedom; no matter how badly and how often we've failed that ideal, it still remains our ideal.

Once we broke Europe's verbal taboos, it was only a matter of time before other traditional taboos fell too. As the writer Albert Murray has put it, Americans could not afford piety in their new homeland: "You can't be over respectful of established forms; you're trying to get through the wilderness of Kentucky." Thus, from the moment the Pilgrims landed, our famous puritanism faced an inherent contradiction. How could we domesticate the wilderness of this continent; how could peasants and rejects and "com-moners" form a strong and viable nation; how could we develop all the new social forms and technologies necessary to blend all the disparate peoples who came here—without violating those same Puritan taboos which are so ingrained, to this day, in our national character?

It can't be over-emphasized that America's fundamental stance against both the taboos of Europe and the taboos of our own Puritans, was our insistence upon freedom of speech. America led the attack against silence. And it is through that freedom, the freedom to break the silence, that we've destroyed so many other taboos. Especially during the last 40 years, we've broken the silence that surrounded ancient taboos of enormous significance. Incest, child abuse, wife-battering, homosexuality, and some (by no means all) forms of racial and gender oppression, are not merely spoken of, and spoken against, they're shouted about from the rooftops. Many breathe easier because of this inevitable result of free speech. In certain sections of our large cities, for the first time in modern history, gay people can live openly and without fear. The feminist movement has made previously forbidden or hidden behaviors both speakable and doable. The National Organization of Women can rail against the Promise Keepers all they want (and they have some good reasons), but when you get a million working-class guys crying and hugging in public, the stoic mask of the American male has definitely cracked. And I'm old enough to remember when it was shocking for women to speak about wanting a career. Now virtually all affluent young women are expected to want a career.

Fifty years ago, not one important world or national leader was black. Now there are more people of color in positions of influence than ever. Bad marriages can be dissolved without social stigma. Children born out of wedlock are not damned as "bastards" for something that wasn't their fault. And those of us who've experienced incest and abuse have finally found a voice, and through our voices we've achieved a certain amount of liberation from shame and pain.

These boons are rooted in our decidedly un-Puritan freedom of speech. But we left those Puritans behind a long time ago—for the breaking of silence is the fundamental political basis of our nation, and no taboo is safe when people have the right to speak.

KEEPER OF YOUR SILENCE

In the process, though, we've lost the sanctity of silence. We've lost the sense of dark but sacred power inherent in sex, in nature, even in crime. Perhaps that is the price of our new freedoms.

It's also true that by breaking the silence we've thrown ourselves into a state of confusion. The old taboos formed part of society's structure. Without them, that structure has undeniably weakened. We are faced with shoring up the weakened parts, inventing new ways of being together that have pattern and order—for we cannot live without some pattern and order—but aren't so restrictive. Without sexual taboos, for instance, what are the social boundaries between men and women? When are they breached? What is offensive? Nobody's sure. Everybody's making mistakes. This is so excruciating that many are nostalgic for some of the old taboos. But once a taboo is broken, then for good or ill it's very hard, perhaps impossible, to reinstate it.

But there is another, subtler confusion: yes, enormous taboos have fallen, but many taboos, equally important, remain. And, both as individuals and as a society, we're strained enough, confused enough, by the results of doing away with so many taboos in so short a time, that maybe we're not terribly eager for our remaining taboos to fall. We may sincerely desire that, but maybe we're tired, fed up, scared. Many people would rather our taboos remain intact for a couple of generations while we get our act together again, and perhaps they have a point. But the price of taboo remains what it's always been: silence and constriction.

What do we see, when we pass each other on the street, but many faces molded by the price paid for keeping the silences of the taboos that remain—spirits confined within their own, and their society's, silences? Even this brief essay on our public and intimate strictures is enough to demonstrate that we are still a primitive race, bounded by fear and prejudice, with taboos looming in every direction—no matter

how much we like to brag and/or bitch that modern life is liberating us from all the old boundaries. The word taboo still says much more about us than most prefer to admit.

What is the keeper of your silence? The answer to that question is your own guide to your personal taboos. How must you confine yourself in order to get through your day at the job, or to be acceptable in your social circle? The answer to that is your map of your society's taboos. What makes you most afraid to speak? What desire, what word, what possibility, freezes and fevers you at the same time, making any sincere communication out of the question? What makes you vanish into your secret? That's your taboo, baby. You're still in the room, maybe even still smiling, still talking, but not really—what's really happened is that you've vanished down some hole in yourself, and you'll stay there until you're sure the threat to your taboo is gone and it's safe to come out again. If, that is, you've ever come out in the first place. Some never have.

What utterance, what hint, what insinuation, can quiet a room of family or friends? What makes people change the subject? What makes those at a dinner party dismiss a remark as though it wasn't said, or dismiss a person as though he or she wasn't really there? We've all seen conversations suddenly go dead, and just as suddenly divert around a particular person or subject, leaving them behind in the dead space, because something has been said or implied that skirts a silently shared taboo. If that happens to you often, don't kid yourself that you're living in a "free" society. Because you're only as free as your freedom from taboos—not on some grand abstract level, but in your day-to-day life.

It is probably inherent in the human condition that there are no "last" taboos. Or perhaps it just feels that way because we have such a long way to go. But at least we can know where to look: right in front of our eyes, in the recesses of our speechlessness, in the depths of our silences. And there is nothing for it but to confront the keepers of our silence. Either that, or to submit to being lost, as most of us silently are, without admitting it to each other or to ourselves—lost in a maze of taboos.

In Search of the Last Taboo

There is no "last taboo," according to Michael Ventura. But there certainly are a lot of contenders, scattered like clues in a treasure hunt for the heart of our culture. Here, an assortment of last taboos "discovered" by the media in the past few years.

"What a great story: **Incest.** The last taboo!"—*Esquire,* on Kathryn Harrison's memoir *The Kiss*

"'The very word is a room-emptier,' Tina Brown wrote in her editor's note when, in 1991, Gail Sheehy broke the silence with a story in *Vanity* Fair. . . . **Menopause** may be the last taboo."
—*Fort Lauderdale Sun-Sentinel*

"The last taboo for women is not, as Gail Sheehy would have it, menopause, but **facial hair.**"
—*New York Times*

"At a time when this is the last taboo, Moreton depicts **erections.**"—*Sunday Telegraph,* describing sculptor Nicholas Moreton's work

"Virtually no representations of **faith** are seen on television, it's the last taboo."—*Columbus Dispatch*

"Anything with **sex with underage kids** is the last taboo."—*Toronto Star*

"The last taboo: an openly **homosexual** actor playing a **heterosexual** lead."—*Boston Globe*

"With sexual mores gone the way of Madonna, **picking up the tab** has become the last taboo for women."—*Philadelphia Inquirer*

"Most Americans, if they think about **class** at all (it may be our last taboo subject), would surely describe themselves as middle class regardless of a petty detail like income."—*Los Angeles Times Syndicate*

"The Last Taboo Is **Age:** Why Are We Afraid of It?"—headline in the *Philadelphia Inquirer*

"Smash the last taboo! [Timothy] Leary says he's planning the first . . . **interactive suicide.**"
—*Washington Post*

"**Money** is the last taboo."—*Calgary Herald*

"**Menstruation** may be the last taboo."—*Manchester Guardian Weekly*

"The real last taboo is that of **privacy and dignity.**"—*Montreal Gazette*

"And then there's **bisexuality,** the last taboo among lesbians."—*Los Angeles Times*

"I think **personal smells** are one of the last taboos."—*The Observer*

"Television's last taboo, long after f-words and pumping bottoms became commonplace, was the **full-frontal vomit.** Now, even that last shred of inhibition has gone, and every drama . . . [has] a character heaving his guts all over the camera."—*The (London) Mail*

"**Tanning.** The last taboo. If you're tan, then your IQ must be lower than the SPF of the sunscreen you'd be using if you had any brains."—*Los Angeles Times*

CRITICAL THINKING QUESTIONS

1. What do you believe are the five strongest and most universally held taboos in your culture? What would be the sanctions for someone who violated these taboos? Why do these taboos remain so strong, and what function may each serve? Explain your answers.

2. Discuss two beliefs or behaviors that have been considered taboo in your lifetime but are not any longer. When and why did each of these taboos disappear? Is there any particular reason each disappeared when it did rather than, say, 50 years before? Explain your answers.

3. Name two current taboos that you do not believe will be considered taboos 20 years from now. What will it take to eliminate each of these taboos? In your opinion, what are the effects of eliminating taboos? Discuss the positive versus negative effects.

4. Do you hold any personal taboos (as opposed to cultural taboos)? For example, are there certain topics that you cannot discuss or things that you cannot do with certain people yet can with others? Discuss what you believe are the origins, functions, and impacts of these personal taboos on you and on the people affected by them.

ARTICLE 11 _____

Suppose someone asked you to publicly say something that contradicted your privately held beliefs and then offered you either a small reward (say, $1) or a large reward ($20) for doing so. Under which of those conditions would you be most likely to actually change your privately held belief to bring it more into the realm of what you just said? If you guessed that would be most likely to happen in the $20 condition, you would have guessed wrong.

A major theory in social psychology is known as *cognitive dissonance.* Briefly stated, this theory says that people feel a tension when they are aware of an inconsistency either between two attitudes or between an attitude and a behavior. Moreover, the theory asserts that such tension produces some type of change to reduce the state of dissonance. The resulting outcome often is counterintuitive to what common sense would predict. The exact conditions under which cognitive dissonance operates and how it is reduced have been investigated in many experiments over the years.

The following article by Leon Festinger and James M. Carlsmith is *the* classic study on dissonance theory. The hypothesis being tested is a simple yet powerful and nonobvious one. Aside from the outcomes, of particular interest is the elaborate design of the experiment. While reading the article, put yourself in the shoes of the subjects and try to imagine how their thinking might account for the obtained results.

Cognitive Consequences of Forced Compliance

■ Leon Festinger and James M. Carlsmith

What happens to a person's private opinion if he is forced to do or say something contrary to that opinion? Only recently has there been any experimental work related to this question. Two studies reported by Janis and King (1954; 1956) clearly showed that, at least under some conditions, the private opinion changes so as to bring it into closer correspondence with the overt behavior the person was forced to perform. Specifically, they showed that if a person is forced to improvise a speech supporting a point of view with which he disagrees, his private opinion moves toward the position advocated in the speech. The observed opinion change is greater than for persons who only hear the speech or for persons who read a prepared speech with emphasis solely on elocution and manner of delivery. The authors of these two studies explain their results mainly in terms of mental rehearsal and thinking up new arguments. In this way,

they propose, the person who is forced to improvise a speech convinces himself. They present some evidence, which is not altogether conclusive, in support of this explanation. We will have more to say concerning this explanation in discussing the results of our experiment.

Kelman (1953) tried to pursue the matter further. He reasoned that if the person is induced to make an overt statement contrary to his private opinion by the offer of some reward, then the greater the reward offered, the greater should be the subsequent opinion change. His data, however, did not support this idea. He found, rather, that a large reward produced less subsequent opinion change than did a smaller reward. Actually, this finding by Kelman is consistent with the theory we will outline below but, for a number of reasons, is not conclusive. One of the major weaknesses of the data is that not all subjects in the

Reprinted from *Journal of Abnormal and Social Psychology*, 1959, *58*, 203–210.

experiment made an overt statement contrary to their private opinion in order to obtain the offered reward. What is more, as one might expect, the percentage of subjects who complied increased as the size of the offered reward increased. Thus, with self-selection of who did and who did not make the required overt statement and with varying percentages of subjects in the different conditions who did make the required statement, no interpretation of the data can be unequivocal.

Recently, Festinger (1957) proposed a theory concerning cognitive dissonance from which come a number of derivations about opinion change following forced compliance. Since these derivations are stated in detail by Festinger (1957, Ch. 4), we will here give only a brief outline of the reasoning.

Let us consider a person who privately holds opinion "X" but has, as a result of pressure brought to bear on him, publicly stated that he believes "not X."

1. This person has two cognitions which, psychologically, do not fit together: one of these is the knowledge that he believes "X," the other the knowledge that he has publicly stated that he believes "not X." If no factors other than his private opinion are considered, it would follow, at least in our culture, that if he believes "X" he would publicly state "X." Hence, his cognition of his private belief is dissonant with his cognition concerning his actual public statement.

2. Similarly, the knowledge that he has said "not X" is consonant with (does fit together with) those cognitive elements corresponding to the reasons, pressures, promises of rewards and/or threats of punishment which induced him to say "not X."

3. In evaluating the total magnitude of dissonance, one must take account of both dissonances and consonances. Let us think of the sum of all the dissonances involving some particular cognition as "D" and the sum of all the consonances as "C." Then we might think of the total magnitude of dissonance as being a function of "D" divided by "D" plus "C."

Let us then see what can be said about the total magnitude of dissonance in a person created by the knowledge that he said "not X" and really believes "X." With everything else held constant, this total magnitude of dissonance would decrease as the number and importance of the pressures which induced him to say "not X" increased. Thus, if the overt behavior was brought about by, say, offers of reward or threats of punishment, the magnitude of dissonance is maximal if these promised rewards or threatened punishments were just barely sufficient to induce the person to say "not X." From this point on, as the promised rewards or threatened punishment become larger, the magnitude of dissonance becomes smaller.

4. One way in which the dissonance can be reduced is for the person to change his private opinion so as to bring it into correspondence with what he has said. One would consequently expect to observe such opinion change after a person has been forced or induced to say something contrary to his private opinion. Furthermore, since the pressure to reduce dissonance will be a function of the magnitude of the dissonance, the observed opinion change should be greatest when the pressure used to elicit the overt behavior is just sufficient to do it.

The present experiment was designed to test this derivation under controlled, laboratory conditions. In the experiment we varied the amount of reward used to force persons to make a statement contrary to their private views. The prediction [from 3 and 4 above] is that the larger the reward given to the subject, the smaller will be the subsequent opinion change.

PROCEDURE

Seventy-one male students in the introductory psychology course at Stanford University were used in the experiment. In this course, students are required to spend a certain number of hours as subjects (Ss) in experiments. They choose among the available experiments by signing their names on a sheet posted on the bulletin board which states the nature of the experiment. The present experiment was listed as a two-hour experiment dealing with "Measures of Performance."

During the first week of the course, when the requirement of serving in experiments was announced and explained to the students, the instructor also told them about a study that the psychology department was conducting. He explained that, since they were required to serve in experiments, the department was conducting a study to evaluate these experiments in order to be able to improve them in the future. They were told that a sample of students would be interviewed after having served as *S*s. They were urged to cooperate in these interviews by being completely frank and honest. The importance of this announcement will become clear shortly. It enabled us to measure the opinions of our *S*s in a context not directly connected with our experiment and in which we could reasonably expect frank and honest expressions of opinion.

When the *S* arrived for the experiment on "Measures of Performance" he had to wait for a few minutes in the secretary's office. The experimenter (*E*) then came in, introduced himself to the *S* and, together, they walked into the laboratory room where the *E* said:

This experiment usually takes a little over an hour but, of course, we had to schedule it for two hours. Since we have that extra time, the introductory psychology people asked if they could interview some of our subjects. [Offhand and conversationally.] Did they announce that in class? I gather that they're interviewing some people who have been in experiments. I don't know much about it. Anyhow, they may want to interview you when you're through here.

With no further introduction or explanation the *S* was shown the first task, which involved putting 12 spools onto a tray, emptying the tray, refilling it with spools, and so on. He was told to use one hand and to work at his own speed. He did this for one-half hour. The *E* then removed the tray and spools and placed in front of the *S* a board containing 48 square pegs. His task was to turn each peg a quarter turn clockwise, then another quarter turn, and so on. He was told again to use one hand and to work at his own speed. The *S* worked at this task for another half hour.

While the *S* was working on these tasks, the *E* sat, with a stop watch in his hand, busily making notations on a sheet of paper. He did so in order to make it convincing that this was what the *E* was interested in and that these tasks, and how the *S* worked on them, was the total experiment. From our point of view the

experiment had hardly started. The hour which the *S* spent working on the repetitive, monotonous tasks was intended to provide, for each *S* uniformly, an experience about which he would have a somewhat negative opinion.

After the half hour on the second task was over, the *E* conspicuously set the stop watch back to zero, put it away, pushed his chair back, lit a cigarette, and said:

O.K. Well, that's all we have in the experiment itself. I'd like to explain what this has been all about so you'll have some idea of why you were doing this. [E pauses.] Well, the way the experiment is set up is this. There are actually two groups in the experiment. In one, the group you were in, we bring the subject in and give him essentially no introduction to the experiment. That is, all we tell him is what he needs to know in order to do the tasks, and he has no idea of what the experiment is all about, or what it's going to be like, or anything like that. But in the other group, we have a student that we've hired that works for us regularly, and what I do is take him into the next room where the subject is waiting—the same room you were waiting in before—and I introduce him as if he had just finished being a subject in the experiment. That is, I say: "This is so-and-so, who's just finished the experiment and I've asked him to tell you a little of what it's about before you start." The fellow who works for us then, in conversation with the next subject, makes these points: [The E then produced a sheet headed "For Group B" which had written on it: It was very enjoyable, I had a lot of fun, I enjoyed myself, it was very interesting, it was intriguing, it was exciting. The E showed this to the S and then proceeded with his false explanation of the purpose of the experiment.] Now, of course, we have this student do this, because if the experimenter does it, it doesn't look as realistic, and what we're interested in doing is comparing how these two groups do on the experiment—the one with this previous expectation about the experiment, and the other, like yourself, with essentially none.

Up to this point the procedure was identical for *S*s in all conditions. From this point on they diverged somewhat. Three conditions were run, Control, One Dollar, and Twenty Dollars, as follows:

Control Condition

The *E* continued:

Is that fairly clear? [Pause.] Look, that fellow [looks at watch] I was telling you about from the introductory psychology class said he would get here a couple of minutes from now. Would you mind waiting to see if he wants to talk to you? Fine. Why don't we go into the other room to wait? [The E left the S in the secretary's office for four minutes. He then returned and said:] O.K. Let's check and see if he does want to talk to you.

One and Twenty Dollar Conditions

The *E* continued:

Is that fairly clear how it is set up and what we're trying to do? [Pause.] Now, I also have a sort of strange thing to ask you. The thing is this. [Long pause, some confusion and uncertainty in the following, with a degree of embarrassment on the part of the E. The manner of the E contrasted strongly with the preceding unhesitant and assured false explanation of the experiment. The point was to make it seem to the S that this was the first time the E had done this and that he felt unsure of himself.] The fellow who normally does this for us couldn't do it today—he just phoned in, and something or other came up for him—so we've been looking around for someone that we could hire to do it for us. You see, we've got another subject waiting [looks at watch] who is supposed to be in that other condition. Now Professor _____, who is in charge of this experiment, suggested that perhaps we could take a chance on your doing it for us. I'll tell you what we had in mind: the thing is, if you could do it for us now, then of course you would know how to do it, and if something like this should ever come up again, that is, the regular fellow couldn't make it, and we had a subject scheduled, it would be very reassuring to us to know that we had somebody else we could call on who knew how to do it. So, if you would be willing to do this for us, we'd like to hire you to do it now and then be on call in the future, if something like this should ever happen again. We can pay you a dollar (twenty dollars) for doing this for us, that is, for

doing it now and then being on call. Do you think you could do that for us?

If the *S* hesitated, the *E* said things like, "It will only take a few minutes," "The regular person is pretty reliable; this is the first time he has missed," or "If we needed you we could phone you a day or two in advance; if you couldn't make it, of course, we wouldn't expect you to come." After the *S* agreed to do it, the *E* gave him the previously mentioned sheet of paper headed "For Group B" and asked him to read it through again. The *E* then paid the *S* one dollar (twenty dollars), made out a hand-written receipt form, and asked the *S* to sign it. He then said:

O.K., the way we'll do it is this. As I said, the next subject should be here by now. I think the next one is a girl. I'll take you into the next room and introduce you to her, saying that you've just finished the experiment and that we've asked you to tell her a little about it. And what we want you to do is just sit down and get into a conversation with her and try to get across the points on that sheet of paper. I'll leave you alone and come back after a couple of minutes. O.K.?

The *E* then took the *S* into the secretary's office where he had previously waited and where the next *S* was waiting. (The secretary had left the office.) He introduced the girl and the *S* to one another saying that the *S* had just finished the experiment and would tell her something about it. He then left saying he would return in a couple of minutes. The girl, an undergraduate hired for this role, said little until the *S* made some positive remarks about the experiment and then said that she was surprised because a friend of hers had taken the experiment the week before and had told her that it was boring and that she ought to try to get out of it. Most *S*s responded by saying something like "Oh, no, it's really very interesting. I'm sure you'll enjoy it." The girl listened quietly after this, accepting and agreeing to everything the *S* told her. The discussion between the *S* and the girl was recorded on a hidden tape recorder.

After two minutes the *E* returned, asked the girl to go into the experimental room, thanked the *S* for talking to the girl, wrote down his phone number to continue the fiction that we might call on him again in the future and then said: "Look, could we check and see if that fellow from introductory psychology wants to talk to you?"

From this point on, the procedure for all three conditions was once more identical. As the *E* and the *S* started to walk to the office where the interviewer was, the *E* said: "Thanks very much for working on those tasks for us. I hope you did enjoy it. Most of our subjects tell us afterward that they found it quite interesting. You get a chance to see how you react to the tasks and so forth." This short persuasive communication was made in all conditions in exactly the same way. The reason for doing it, theoretically, was to make it easier for anyone who wanted to persuade himself that the tasks had been, indeed, enjoyable.

When they arrived at the interviewer's office, the *E* asked the interviewer whether or not he wanted to talk to the *S*. The interviewer said yes, the *E* shook hands with the *S*, said good-bye, and left. The interviewer, of course, was always kept in complete ignorance of which condition the *S* was in. The interview consisted of four questions, on each of which the *S* was first encouraged to talk about the matter and was then asked to rate his opinion or reaction on an 11-point scale. The questions are as follows:

1. Were the tasks interesting and enjoyable? In what way? In what way were they not? Would you rate how you feel about them on a scale from −5 to +5 where −5 means they were extremely dull and boring, +5 means they were extremely interesting and enjoyable, and zero means they were neutral, neither interesting nor uninteresting.

2. Did the experiment give you an opportunity to learn about your own ability to perform these tasks? In what way? In what way not? Would you rate how you feel about this on a scale from 0 to 10 where 0 means you learned nothing and 10 means you learned a great deal.

3. From what you know about the experiment and the tasks involved in it, would you say the experiment was measuring anything important? That is, do you think the results may have scientific value? In what way? In what way not? Would you rate your opinion on this matter on a scale from 0 to 10 where 0 means the results have no scientific value or impor-

tance and 10 means they have a great deal of value and importance.

4. Would you have any desire to participate in another similar experiment? Why? Why not? Would you rate your desire to participate in a similar experiment again on a scale from −5 to +5, where −5 means you would definitely dislike to participate, +5 means you would definitely like to participate, and 0 means you have no particular feeling about it one way or the other.

As may be seen, the questions varied in how directly relevant they were to what the *S* had told the girl. This point will be discussed further in connection with the results.

At the close of the interview the *S* was asked what he thought the experiment was about and, following this, was asked directly whether or not he was suspicious of anything and, if so, what he was suspicious of. When the interview was over, the interviewer brought the *S* back to the experimental room where the *E* was waiting together with the girl who had posed as the waiting *S*. (In the control condition, of course, the girl was not there.) The true purpose of the experiment was then explained to the *S* in detail, and the reasons for each of the various steps in the experiment were explained carefully in relation to the true purpose. All experimental *S*s in both One Dollar and Twenty Dollar conditions were asked, after this explanation, to return the money they had been given. All *S*s, without exception, were quite willing to return the money.

The data from 11 of the 71 *S*s in the experiment had to be discarded for the following reasons:

1. Five *S*s (three in the One Dollar and two in the Twenty Dollar condition) indicated in the interview that they were suspicious about having been paid to tell the girl the experiment was fun and suspected that that was the real purpose of the experiment.

2. Two *S*s (both in the One Dollar condition) told the girl that they had been hired, that the experiment was really boring but they were supposed to say it was fun.

3. Three *S*s (one in the One Dollar and two in the Twenty Dollar condition) refused to take the money and refused to be hired.

4. One *S* (in the One Dollar condition), immediately after having talked to the girl, demanded her phone number saying he would call her and explain things, and also told the *E* he wanted to wait until she was finished so he could tell her about it.

These 11 *S*s were, of course, run through the total experiment anyhow and the experiment was explained to them afterwards. Their data, however, are not included in the analysis.

Summary of Design

There remain, for analysis, 20 *S*s in each of the three conditions. Let us review these briefly: 1. *Control condition.* These *S*s were treated identically in all respects to the *S*s in the experimental conditions, except that they were never asked to, and never did, tell the waiting girl that the experimental tasks were enjoyable and lots of fun. 2. *One Dollar condition.* These *S*s were hired for one dollar to tell a waiting *S* that tasks, which were really rather dull and boring, were interesting, enjoyable, and lots of fun. 3. *Twenty Dollar condition.* These *S*s were hired for twenty dollars to do the same thing.

RESULTS

The major results of the experiment are summarized in Table 1 which lists, separately for each of the three experimental conditions, the average rating which the *S*s gave at the end of each question on the interview. We will discuss each of the questions on the interview separately, because they were intended to measure different things. One other point before we proceed to examine the data. In all the comparisons, the Control condition should be regarded as a baseline from which to evaluate the results in the other two conditions. The Control condition gives us, essentially, the reactions of *S*s to the tasks and their opinions about the experiment as falsely explained to them, without the experimental introduction of dissonance. The data from the other conditions may be viewed, in a sense, as changes from this baseline.

TABLE 1 / Average Ratings on Interview Questions for Each Condition

Question on Interview	Experimental Condition		
	Control (*N* = 20)	One Dollar (*N* = 20)	Twenty Dollars (*N* = 20)
How enjoyable tasks were (rated from −5 to +5)	−.45	+1.35	−.05
How much they learned (rated from 0 to 10)	3.08	2.80	3.15
Scientific importance (rated from 0 to 10)	5.60	6.45	5.18
Participate in similar exp. (rated from −5 to +5)	−.62	+1.20	−.25

How Enjoyable the Tasks Were

The average ratings on this question, presented in the first row of figures in Table 1, are the results most important to the experiment. These results are the ones most directly relevant to the specific dissonance which was experimentally created. It will be recalled that the tasks were purposely arranged to be rather boring and monotonous. And, indeed, in the Control condition the average rating was −.45, somewhat on the negative side of the neutral point.

In the other two conditions, however, the *S*s told someone that these tasks were interesting and enjoyable. The resulting dissonance could, of course, most directly be reduced by persuading themselves that the tasks were, indeed, interesting and enjoyable. In the One Dollar condition, since the magnitude of dissonance was high, the pressure to reduce this dissonance would also be high. In this condition, the average rating was +1.35, considerably on the positive side and significantly different from the Control condition at the .02 level[1] (*t* = 2.48).

In the Twenty Dollar condition, where less dissonance was created experimentally because of the greater importance of the consonant relations, there is correspondingly less evidence of dissonance reduction. The average rating in this condition is only –.05, slightly and not significantly higher than the Control condition. The difference between the One Dollar and Twenty Dollar conditions is significant at the .03 level ($t = 2.22$). In short, when an S was induced, by offer of reward, to say something contrary to his private opinion, this private opinion tended to change so as to correspond more closely with what he had said. The greater the reward offered (beyond what was necessary to elicit the behavior) the smaller was the effect.

Desire to Participate in a Similar Experiment

The results from this question are shown in the last row of Table 1. This question is less directly related to the dissonance that was experimentally created for the Ss. Certainly, the more interesting and enjoyable they felt the tasks were, the greater would be their desire to participate in a similar experiment. But other factors would enter also. Hence, one would expect the results on this question to be very similar to the results on "how enjoyable the tasks were" but weaker. Actually, the results, as may be seen in the table, are in exactly the same direction, and the magnitude of the mean differences is fully as large as on the first question. The variability is greater, however, and the differences do not yield high levels of statistical significance. The difference between the One Dollar condition (+1.20) and the Control condition (–.62) is significant at the .08 level ($t = 1.78$). The difference between the One Dollar condition and the Twenty Dollar condition (–.25) reaches only the .15 level of significance ($t = 1.46$).

The Scientific Importance of the Experiment

This question was included because there was a chance that differences might emerge. There are, after all, other ways in which the experimentally created dissonance could be reduced. For example, one way would be for the S to magnify for himself the value of the reward he obtained. This, however, was unlikely in this experiment because money was used for the reward and it is undoubtedly difficult to convince

oneself that one dollar is more than it really is. There is another possible way, however. The Ss were given a very good reason, in addition to being paid, for saying what they did to the waiting girl. The Ss were told it was necessary for the experiment. The dissonance could, consequently, be reduced by magnifying the importance of this cognition. The more scientifically important they considered the experiment to be, the less was the total magnitude of dissonance. It is possible, then, that the results on this question, shown in the third row of figures in Table 1, might reflect dissonance reduction.

The results are weakly in line with what one would expect if the dissonance were somewhat reduced in this manner. The One Dollar condition is higher than the other two. The difference between the One and Twenty Dollar conditions reaches the .08 level of significance on a two-tailed test ($t = 1.79$). The difference between the One Dollar and Control conditions is not impressive at all ($t = 1.21$). The result that the Twenty Dollar condition is actually lower than the Control condition is undoubtedly a matter of chance ($t = 0.58$).

How Much They Learned from the Experiment

The results on this question are shown in the second row of figures in Table 1. The question was included because, as far as we could see, it had nothing to do with the dissonance that was experimentally created and could not be used for dissonance reduction. One would then expect no differences at all among the three conditions. We felt it was important to show that the effect was not a completely general one but was specific to the content of the dissonance which was created. As can be readily seen in Table 1, there are only negligible differences among conditions. The highest t value for any of these differences is only 0.48.

DISCUSSION OF A POSSIBLE ALTERNATIVE EXPLANATION

We mentioned in the introduction that Janis and King (1954; 1956) in explaining their findings, proposed an explanation in terms of the self-convincing effect of mental rehearsal and thinking up new arguments by the person who had to improvise a speech. Kelman (1953), in the previously mentioned study, in attempting to explain the unexpected finding that the persons who complied in the moderate reward condition changed their opinion more than in the high reward condition, also proposed the same kind of explanation. If the results of our experiment are to be taken as strong corroboration of the theory of cognitive dissonance, this possible alternative explanation must be dealt with.

Specifically, as applied to our results, this alternative explanation would maintain that perhaps, for some reason, the *S*s in the One Dollar condition worked harder at telling the waiting girl that the tasks were fun and enjoyable. That is, in the One Dollar condition they may have rehearsed it more mentally, thought up more ways of saying it, may have said it more convincingly, and so on. Why this might have been the case is, of course, not immediately apparent. One might expect that, in the Twenty Dollar condition, having been paid more, they would try to do a better job of it than in the One Dollar condition. But nevertheless, the possibility exists that the *S*s in the One Dollar condition may have improvised more.

Because of the desirability of investigating this possible alternative explanation, we recorded on a tape recorder the conversation between each *S* and the girl. These recordings were transcribed and then rated, by two independent raters, on five dimensions. The ratings were, of course done in ignorance of which condition each *S* was in. The reliabilities of these ratings, that is, the correlations between the two independent raters, ranged from .61 to .88, with an average reliability of .71. The five ratings were:

1. The content of what the *S* said *before* the girl made the remark that her friend told her it was boring. The stronger the *S*'s positive statements about the tasks, and the more ways in which he said they were interesting and enjoyable, the higher the rating.
2. The content of what the *S* said *after* the girl made the above-mentioned remark. This was rated in the same way as for the content before the remark.
3. A similar rating of the overall content of what the *S* said.

4. A rating of how persuasive and convincing the *S* was in what he said and the way in which he said it.
5. A rating of the amount of time in the discussion that the *S* spent discussing the tasks as opposed to going off into irrelevant things.

The mean ratings for the One Dollar and Twenty Dollar conditions, averaging the ratings of the two independent raters, are presented in Table 2. It is clear from examining the table that, in all cases, the Twenty Dollar condition is slightly higher. The differences are small, however, and only on the rating of "amount of time" does the difference between the two conditions even approach significance. We are certainly justified in concluding that the *S*s in the One Dollar condition did not improvise more nor act more convincingly. Hence, the alternative explanation discussed above cannot account for the findings.

SUMMARY

Recently, Festinger (1957) has proposed a theory concerning cognitive dissonance. Two derivations from this theory are tested here. These are:

TABLE 2 / Average Ratings of Discussion between Subject and Girl

	Condition		
Dimensions Rated	One Dollar	Twenty Dollars	Value of *t*
Content before remark by girl (rated from 0 to 5)	2.26	2.62	1.08
Content after remark by girl (rated from 0 to 5)	1.63	1.75	0.11
Over-all content (rated from 0 to 5)	1.89	2.19	1.08
Persuasiveness and conviction (rated from 0 to 10)	4.79	5.50	0.99
Time spent on topic (rated from 0 to 10)	6.74	8.19	1.80

1. If a person is induced to do or say something which is contrary to his private opinion, there will be a tendency for him to change his opinion so as to bring it into correspondence with what he has done or said.
2. The larger the pressure used to elicit the overt behavior (beyond the minimum needed to elicit it) the weaker will be the above-mentioned tendency.

A laboratory experiment was designed to test these derivations. Subjects were subjected to a boring experience and then paid to tell someone that the experience had been interesting and enjoyable. The amount of money paid the subject was varied. The private opinions of the subjects concerning the experiences were then determined.

The results strongly corroborate the theory that was tested.

REFERENCES

Festinger, L. *A theory of cognitive dissonance.* Evanston, Ill.: Row Peterson, 1957.

Janis, I. L., & King, B. T. The influence of role-playing on opinion change. *Journal of Abnormal and Social Psychology,* 1954, *49,* 211–218.

Kelman, H. Attitude change as a function of response restriction. *Human Relations,* 1953, *6,* 185–214.

King, B. T., & Janis, I. L. Comparison of the effectiveness of improvised versus non-improvised role-playing in producing opinion changes. *Human Relations,* 1956, *9,* 177–186.

ENDNOTE

1. All statistical tests referred to in this paper are two-tailed.

CRITICAL THINKING QUESTIONS

1. Using the concept of dissonance theory, select an attitude or belief that you might want to change and design a procedure that could be effective in producing change in the desired direction.
2. This study was cited in Article 2 as an example of some of the ethical issues in social psychological research. What do you see as the ethical issues present in this experiment? Do you see any alternative to deception in this type of study? Why or why not?
3. Based on personal experience, have you ever suspected that cognitive dissonance was operating in some change that came about in your own attitudes? Elaborate on how that may have occurred.
4. Festinger and Carlsmith discuss a possible alternative explanation for the obtained results. What is your position on this alternative explanation? Discuss any other possible explanations for the findings of the study.
5. Might cognitive dissonance be operating in many real-life situations? For example, consider the initiation process (known as *hazing*) used in some social groups, such as fraternities, or the procedures used in the military as part of basic training. How might cognitive dissonance be operating in these or other situations to account for the outcomes of the experience?

ADDITIONAL RELATED READINGS

Harmon-Jones, E. (2000). Cognitive dissonance and experienced negative affect: Evidence that dissonance increases experienced negative affect even in the absence of aversive consequences. *Personality & Social Psychology Bulletin, 26*(12), 1490–1501.

Miller, D. I., Verhoek-Miller, N., Giesen, J. M., & Wells-Parker, E. (2000). Some empirical evidence for ecological dissonance theory. *Psychological Reports, 86*(2), 415–420.

ARTICLE 12 _____

In the years since publication of Festinger and Carlsmith's classic study (Article 11), many experiments have been done to test dissonance theory and to elaborate on the conditions necessary for its operation. As it turns out, there are many different causes of dissonance. For example, dissonance may be aroused when an individual puts a great deal of effort into a given activity, as though he or she needs to justify expending so much effort to obtain a certain goal. This is sort of a "suffering leads to liking" effect. Dissonance will also likely be aroused when an individual has the freedom to choose whether to do (or not do) something. There is little reason to experience dissonance when you are forced to do something. You know why you did it: Someone *made* you do it. Finally, issues such as self-esteem may influence the arousal (and subsequent reduction) of cognitive dissonance. People with high levels of self-esteem may actually be *more* likely to engage in dissonance reduction than those with low levels of self-esteem when they see their behavior as inconsistent with their beliefs.

The central premise of cognitive dissonance theory is that people are motivated to avoid or reduce any tension produced by a perceived inconsistency between two attitudes or between an attitude and a behavior. So, what would happen when someone encounters a persuasive argument that is contrary to his or her own privately held beliefs? Dissonance theory suggests that this person will be motivated to reduce the internal tension generated by that perceived inconsistency, which can be accomplished in several ways. For example, he or she simply might not pay attention to the opposing viewpoint, distort the message to make it more consistent with his or her own beliefs, or avoid the message altogether.

The earliest research on what happens when people encounter dissonance generally found that they tend to remember the content of those messages that are consistent with their own beliefs much better than the content of those messages that are inconsistent with their beliefs. These findings support the prediction of dissonance theory that people will find a way of reducing the inconsistency. However, later studies often found the opposite result: The inconsistent messages were better remembered than the consistent massages.

So, which is it? Do we better remember messages that are congruent or incongruent with our own beliefs? The following article by Alice H. Eagly, Patrick Kulesa, Serena Chen, and Shelly Chaiken performs a *meta-analysis* (a term discussed in the article) on previously done studies and reports the findings of original data to shed further light on these processes.

Do Attitudes Affect Memory?
Tests of the Congeniality Hypothesis

■ Alice H. Eagly, Patrick Kulesa, Serena Chen, and Shelly Chaiken

Abstract

Social psychologists have usually hypothesized that attitudinal selectivity biases people's memory in favor of information that is congenial to their attitudes, because they are motivated to defend their attitudes against un- *congenial information. However, our meta-analysis found that such effects have been only inconsistently obtained. One reason for these inconsistencies is that the defense of attitudes against attacks does not necessarily*

Reprinted from *Current Directions in Psychological Science*, 2001, *10*(1), 5–9. Copyright © 2001 by American Psychological Society. Reprinted with permission of Blackwell Publishers.

entail avoiding the uncongenial information. As shown by our experiments, people often expose themselves to attitudinally uncongenial information, attend to it, scrutinize it carefully, encode it accurately, and remember it fairly well, even though they dislike the information and are not persuaded by it. Given sufficient motivation and capacity, people mount an active defense that enhances memory for the information.

Think about the last time you listened to a debate on a controversial issue. Which presentation was more memorable—the one by the person who agreed with your views or the one by the person who disagreed? Social psychologists have usually assumed that people remember information more easily if it is consistent with their attitudes. If this assumption is right, you would remember more of the points made by the person who had agreed with you. This question of whether attitudes bias memory (and cognitive processes more generally) in favor of attitudinally agreeable information has often been tested and is known in social psychology as the *congeniality hypothesis* (see Eagly & Chaiken, 1993, 1998).

The usual rationale for predicting better memory for information that is attitudinally congenial than for information that is not congenial is that people are motivated to defend their attitudes against material that challenges them. Researchers assumed that people do this by screening out uncongenial information at various stages of information processing: People might avoid exposing themselves to uncongenial information in the first place; if exposed to such information, they might not pay much attention to it, they might distort its meaning, and they might have difficulty storing and retrieving it. In short, it would be consistent with early theorists' assumption that people are motivated to avoid information that challenges their attitudes (e.g., Festinger, 1957) if research revealed that people perform relatively poorly in encoding and remembering information that counters their existing attitudes.

The idea that uncongenial information is less memorable than congenial information was supported by several early experiments. Especially well-known are the dramatic findings of Levine and Murphy's (1943) experiment in which 5 pro-Communists and 5 anti-Communists received messages that were favorable or unfavorable to the

Soviet Union. As the congeniality hypothesis predicts, the anti-Communists showed better memory than the pro-Communists for the anti-Soviet Union message, and the pro-Communists showed better memory than the anti-Communists for the pro-Soviet Union message.

Subsequent to this experiment, substantial research on attitude memory accumulated, and findings became far less clear. Many researchers produced null effects (e.g., Greenwald & Sakumura, 1967), or occasionally even reversals in which uncongenial information was more memorable than congenial information (e.g., Cacioppo & Petty, 1979). In some experiments, congenial information was remembered better than uncongenial information only under specific circumstances (e.g., Jones & Aneshansel, 1956). In general, evidence for the greater memorability of congenial information became weaker over the years, but the reasons for this erosion remained mysterious.

META-ANALYSIS OF RESEARCH ON MEMORY FOR ATTITUDE-RELEVANT INFORMATION

The apparent inconsistencies of these findings prompted us to undertake a meta-analysis of this research (Eagly, Chen, Chaiken, & Shaw-Barnes, 1999). Meta-analyses synthesize results of many studies by using quantitative methods, which provide a clearer view of a set of findings than traditional, informal methods of reviewing (see Johnson & Eagly, 2000). More specifically, the quantitative synthesis of research literatures allows the strength and direction of studies' results to be represented precisely and related to studies' attributes (e.g., aspects of their procedure) so that one can detect whether the effects that studies produced were moderated by these characteristics.

Our thorough search for experiments that provided strong tests of the congeniality hypothesis yielded 70 experiments. In order to represent the individual features of each experiment, we coded the experiments' attributes (e.g., how memory was assessed, whether memory was assessed immediately or after a delay). To quantify the outcome of each study's test of the congeniality hypothesis, we computed an effect size, which represented the difference in memory between the experimental conditions presenting congenial information and those presenting uncongenial information. For many studies, we also computed these congeniality effect sizes within particular levels of the manipulated independent variables (e.g., separate effect sizes for differing levels of involvement in the issue and for immediate and delayed administrations of the memory measures).

Following the classic design of Levine and Murphy (1943), the typical experiment presented participants with information on one or both sides of an issue, and the participants' attitudes were pro or con on the issue. The information provided usually pertained to a controversial social issue—such as racial integration in the 1950s, the war in Vietnam in the 1960s, and nuclear power, capital punishment, and abortion in later years. In the usual procedure, attitude was assessed in a session prior to the experimental session, and the attitude-relevant information was presented and memory was assessed during the experimental session. Some experiments included a delayed memory measure in a later session.

The overall congeniality effect in this literature indicated slightly better memory for congenial information than for uncongenial information. The mean effect size was 0.23, with a 95% confidence interval of 0.18 to 0.27, when expressed by a statistic called *d*. This statistic was calculated for each experiment by dividing the mean difference in memory between the congenial and uncongenial conditions by the standard deviation averaged across conditions. One way of interpreting this number is that, in the average study, memory for congenial information exceeded memory for uncongenial information by an amount that was approximately one quarter of the size of the study's standard deviation. More important, however, the findings differed considerably across experiments: In 60% of them, the direction of the results favored congenial information, and in 40%, the direction favored uncongenial information. Figure 1 displays a plot of the effect sizes.

Analysis of these effect sizes revealed a very strong tendency for the congeniality effect to have eroded over the years. Our analyses suggested that this erosion was likely due in large part to improvements in the assessment of memory. One such improvement was later researchers' routine compliance with the important methodological rule that the people coding

FIGURE 1 / Stem-and-Leaf Plot of Effect Sizes (representing whole studies) from Eagly, Chen, Chaiken, and Shaw-Barnes (1999). Each effect size is represented by a stem, which appears to the left of the vertical line, and a leaf, which appears to the right of the vertical line. The stem gives the value of the effect size to the nearest 10th, and the leaf gives the 100ths' place value. For example, 0.8|024 denotes three effect sizes: 0.80, 0.82, and 0.84; and 0.7|9 denotes one effect size of 0.79. When no leaf appears to the right of a stem (e.g., 0.9), no effect size beginning with that stem value was obtained. The study yielding an effect size of 8.74 was eliminated as an outlier and removed from all but the initial analyses.

Stem	Leaf
8.7	4
.	
.	
.	
2.2	0
2.1	
2.0	
1.9	
1.8	
1.7	2
1.6	
1.5	
1.4	
1.3	7
1.2	
1.1	
1.0	4
0.9	
0.8	024
0.7	9
0.6	379
0.5	0337
0.4	5566
0.3	25
0.2	2458
0.1	0024566
0.0	013389
−0.0	9998876333221
−0.1	87210
−0.2	92
−0.3	5
−0.4	61
−0.5	5
−0.6	
−0.7	
−0.8	2
−0.9	
−1.0	
−1.1	
−1.2	4

study participants' recall of message content be blind to participants' attitudes. Indeed, earlier studies (i.e., published prior to 1960) that did not indicate that coding was blind produced effect sizes that were larger than those of other recall studies. Also, the less controlled recognition measures of memory, which generally involved counting the number of items correctly recognized, produced larger effect sizes than the recognition measures that were controlled for potential guessing biases (i.e., the recognition sensitivity measures; see Shapiro, 1994). In general, the shift to more stringent procedures for assessing both recall and recognition removed some of the artifacts that likely contributed to the apparent congeniality effects seen in earlier studies.

Although the meta-analysis yielded evidence of several other moderators of the congeniality effect (see Eagly et al., 1999), its most striking outcome is its demonstration of the general weakness of the congeniality effect in experiments that used memory measures that are relatively unlikely to produce artifacts. Despite this outcome, we did not conclude that attitudes have little impact on memory. On the contrary, we questioned the basic idea that congenial information is typically more memorable than uncongenial information. We suspected that one flaw in the reasoning underlying this idea is the assumption that people inevitably avoid information that challenges their attitudes. It may be more likely that under many circumstances people expose themselves to such material, attend to it, scrutinize it carefully, encode it accurately, and thus remember it fairly well, even though they dislike the information and are not persuaded by it. We posited that, given sufficient motivation and capability, people are likely to mount an active defense that would enhance rather than reduce memory for counterattitudinal information. Supporting our reasoning, Edwards and Smith (1996) showed that attitudinally uncongenial statements were scrutinized for a longer time than congenial statements and elicited more thinking, especially thinking that refuted the uncongenial statements. Through active defense, uncongenial information could become memorable, yet pose little threat to existing attitudes, as long as it was successfully refuted. This tendency for thorough processing of counterattitudinal information to improve memory may equal any tendency

for proattitudinal information to be remembered well because of its superior fit with existing attitudes, its inherent pleasantness, and other advantages it may possess. We have tested these ideas in new research.

NEW RESEARCH ON MEMORY FOR ATTITUDE-RELEVANT INFORMATION

To maximally illuminate the findings of the meta-analysis, our new experiments used the modal experimental paradigm, which featured the classic Levine and Murphy (1943) design (see Eagly, Kulesa, Brannon, Shaw, & Hutson-Comeaux, 2000; Kulesa, 1999). We thus located participants with opposing attitudes on an important social issue by assessing attitudes in a pretest session. Two weeks later, participants with pro or con attitudes on the issue attended the main experimental session, which included an audiotaped message in which a speaker took a pro or con position on this issue; after the message, memory and other dependent variables were measured. One of the experiments included memory measures administered 2 weeks after the main session.

In these experiments, congenial and uncongenial information proved to be equally memorable. This null effect was obtained under a wide range of circumstances across the conditions of these experiments. Specifically, the effect was null regardless of whether (a) messages pertained to abortion, gays in the military, or the death penalty or presented information on both sides or only one side of the issue; (b) the memory assessment was recognition or recall or was timed to occur soon after the message or 2 weeks later; and (c) participants were or were not activists on the issue, had stronger or weaker attitudes, had more prior knowledge of uncongenial than congenial arguments, or did or did not have their attention constrained to the message. Yet memory proved to be responsive to many other variables. For example, regardless of a message's congeniality, memory was better if participants had stronger attitudes, were activists on the issue, had better verbal skills, and responded to memory measures soon after hearing the message.

Relevant to our hypothesis that people often actively defend their attitudes were findings suggesting that uncongenial messages elicited more careful and effortful processing than congenial messages.

Compared with recipients of a congenial message, recipients of an uncongenial message not only rated themselves as giving more thought and attention to the message, but also generated more thoughts that were relevant to the message or issue when asked to list the thoughts that had come to mind as they listened to the message. We categorized these thoughts in two ways: whether they supported or opposed the position the message took on the issue and whether they were global (i.e., very general statements, such as "I agree") or differentiated (i.e., statements containing references to arguments in the message, new arguments, or relevant personal experience). The uncongenial messages elicited many differentiated thoughts that opposed the messages—in other words, counterarguments. Global thoughts, which were generally less frequent than differentiated thoughts, were more commonly elicited by the congenial than the uncongenial messages, especially if these thoughts supported the message. Figure 2 summarizes the thought data from one of our experiments. Consistent with these findings, participants indicated much less approval of the message and the speaker

when the message was uncongenial than when it was congenial.

These findings show that our participants dealt with uncongenial information mainly by active and skeptical scrutiny of its content, whereas they dealt with congenial information with a greater emphasis on confirming its overall match to their attitudes. Our participants' memory could have been enhanced by their careful scrutiny of the information or by simpler processing involving their matching the information to their existing attitudes. Our results supported the idea that careful scrutiny, by producing differentiated thoughts that opposed the message, enhanced memory for the uncongenial messages. Specifically, we consistently obtained significant positive correlations between the number of such thoughts that participants listed in response to these messages and their memory for the arguments contained in the messages. Although measures of cognitive processing have related less consistently to memory for congenial messages, we have obtained some evidence that memory for congenial messages improves to the extent that participants react with global thoughts that support

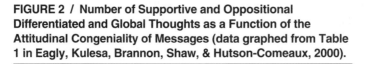

FIGURE 2 / Number of Supportive and Oppositional Differentiated and Global Thoughts as a Function of the Attitudinal Congeniality of Messages (data graphed from Table 1 in Eagly, Kulesa, Brannon, Shaw, & Hutson-Comeaux, 2000).

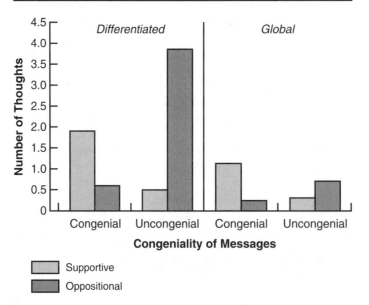

such messages (Kulesa, 1999). We suspect that arguments that are consistent with a person's attitudes are easily remembered, without more elaborate processing, because they fit readily into the structure of what the person already believes about the issue.

Our experiments also demonstrated that achieving good memory for uncongenial information does not necessarily make such information persuasive. On the contrary, in our experiment that presented messages on the highly contentious issue of abortion rights, better memory for uncongenial information was associated with reduced persuasion. To persuade people to accept a position that is highly divergent from their own attitudes, it is not necessarily helpful to capture their attention and induce them to pay close attention, because such attention may elicit active resistance to the persuasive goals of the message in the form of counterarguing. Because committed people defend their attitudes in this way, inducing them to change their attitudes may require an incremental approach whereby each exposure to uncongenial information produces only a small amount of change. The potential effectiveness of an incremental approach coheres with our finding of slight movement of participants' attitudes toward uncongenial messages—a shift that remained detectable even 2 weeks later.

CONCLUSION

Attitudes affect information processing, but they do so by processes that differ depending on whether information agrees or disagrees with recipients' attitudes. Attitude researchers failed to understand these effects for many decades because they persevered for so long with simple ideas about the processes that mediate memory and therefore with the prediction of better memory for congenial than uncongenial information. Especially neglected by earlier researchers were the implications of processes by which people actively confront attitudinally uncongenial information, in order to diminish its persuasive impact and thus protect their existing attitudes and beliefs.

The idea that defense of one's attitudes can involve active engagement of challenging information or more passive avoidance of it is in harmony with contemporary dual-process theories of social judgment,

which postulate more and less effortful modes of processing information (e.g., the heuristic-systematic model; see Chen & Chaiken, 1999; Eagly & Chaiken, 1993). These theories suggest that whether recipients of uncongenial messages adopt a cognitively demanding, active approach or an avoidant, passive approach to defending their attitudes would depend on their motivation and capacity to use the more effortful, active approach. Without motivation or capacity, the easier, passive route to defense would be likely, whereas in the presence of both motivation and capacity, the more effortful route of attacking uncongenial material would become more likely. Given the small overall congeniality effect size observed in the meta-analysis, it appears that in the typical study, both motivation and capacity likely were present, thus enabling an active defense that boosted memory for uncongenial information to the level attained for congenial information.

Despite its difficult history, research on memory for attitude-relevant information should thrive once more, now that some important conceptual hurdles have been surmounted. With increased understanding of the processes that mediate memory for congenial and uncongenial information, researchers have the power to control attitudes' effects on information processing. By establishing conditions that enhance or reduce the impact of these mediating processes, researchers should be able to produce better memory for congenial or uncongenial information, or equal memory for these two types of information. It will be important for researchers to consider variables that influence people's motivations and capabilities for processing attitude-relevant information, especially their motivation to defend their attitudes from counterattitudinal threats (see Chen & Chaiken, 1999).

Research on attitudinal selectivity in memory makes an important contribution to psychologists' broader understanding of memory and information processing. Because much of the information that people receive in daily life is relevant to one or more of their attitudes, memory for this information can be accurately predicted only by taking into account how the psychological processes that the information elicits depend on the attitudinal congeniality of the information. The active resistance processes that uncongenial information often elicits not only improve memory for the information but also enable people to avoid changing their attitudes.

RECOMMENDED READING

Eagly, A.H., & Chaiken, S. (1983). (See References)

Eagly, A.H., & Chaiken, S. (1998). (See References)

Eagly, A.H., Chen, S., Chaiken, S., & Shaw-Barnes, K. (1999). (See References)

Johnson, B.T., & Eagly, A.H. (2000). (See References)

REFERENCES

Cacioppo, J.T., & Petty, R.E. (1979). Effects of message repetition and position on cognitive response, recall, and persuasion. *Journal of Personality and Social Psychology, 37,* 97–109.

Chen, S., & Chaiken, S. (1999). The heuristicsystematic model in its broader context. In S. Chaiken & Y. Trope (Eds.), *Dual-process theories in social psychology* (pp. 73–96). New York: Guilford Press.

Eagly, A.H., & Chaiken, S. (1993). *The psychology of attitudes.* Fort Worth, TX: Harcourt, Brace, Jovanovich.

Eagly, A.H., & Chaiken, S. (1998). Attitude structure and function. In D.T. Gilbert, S.T. Fiske, & G. Lindzey (Eds.), *The handbook of social psychology* (4th ed., Vol. 1, pp. 269–322). New York: McGraw-Hill.

Eagly, A.H., Chen, S., Chaiken, S., & Shaw-Barnes, K. (1999). The impact of attitudes on memory: An affair to remember. *Psychological Bulletin, 125,* 64–89.

Eagly, A.H., Kulesa, P., Brannon, L.A., Shaw, K., & Hutson-Comeaux, S. (2000). Why counterattitudinal messages are as memorable as proattitudinal messages: The importance of active defense against attack. *Personality and Social Psychology Bulletin, 26,* 1392–1408.

Edwards, K., & Smith, E.E. (1996). A disconfirmation bias in the evaluation of arguments. *Journal of Personality and Social Psychology, 71,* 5–24.

Festinger, L. (1957). *A theory of cognitive dissonance.* Evanston, IL: Row, Peterson.

Greenwald, A.G., & Sakumura, J.S. (1967). Attitude and selective learning: Where are the phenomena of yesteryear? *Journal of Personality and Social Psychology, 7,* 387–397.

Johnson, B.T., & Eagly, A.H. (2000). Quantitative synthesis of social psychological research. In H.T. Reis & C.M. Judd (Eds.), *Handbook of research methods in social and personality psychology* (pp. 496–528). London: Cambridge University Press.

Jones, E.E., & Aneshansel, J. (1956). The learning and utilization of contravaluant material. *Journal of Abnormal and Social Psychology, 53,* 27–33.

Kulesa, P. (1999). *The effects of expectancies on cognitive processes mediating memory for attitude-relevant material.* Unpublished doctoral dissertation, Northwestern University, Evanston, IL.

Levine, J.M., & Murphy, G. (1943). The learning and forgetting ot controversial material. *Journal of Abnormal and Social Psychology, 38,* 507–517.

Shapiro, M.A. (1994). Signal detection measures of recognition memory. In A. Lang (Ed.), *Measuring psychological responses to media messages* (pp. 133–148). Hillsdale, NJ: Erlbaum.

CRITICAL THINKING QUESTIONS

1. Think of the last time you listened to a debate between two people (such as two political candidates) in which one of them expressed beliefs consistent with your own and the other expressed opposite beliefs. Whose arguments did you remember best? Were you persuaded at all by the opposite views? Did listening to differing viewpoints strengthen or weaken your originally held views? Discuss your experience in terms of the concepts discussed in the article.

2. Under what conditions would *active resistance* to persuasion most likely occur? Can people be made less resistant to persuasion? If so, how? If not, why?

3. According to the article, whether someone uses a passive or active defense when confronting uncongenial information depends, in part, on his or her motivation and capacity to defend personal attitudes using the more effortful, active approach. Apply this concept to everyday situations that may involve attempts to persuade other people.

4. Using the information contained in the article, design a study that would examine the impact of watching presidential debates on viewers' attitudes. Be sure to control for any potential sources of bias, such as using blind coding of the responses.

Chapter Five

SOCIAL IDENTITY
Self and Gender

THE MAJORITY OF readings that you will encounter in this book focus on what might be called *situational variables:* particular circumstances that elicit predictable patterns of behavior in people. But do all people respond the same way in identical situations? Of course not. We each bring to every situation a set of experiences and characteristics that may influence how we act. Certainly, each of us has had unique life experiences that may be influential; biological dispositions, perhaps present from birth, may also play a role in determining behavior. Another influential factor is the personality of the individual.

But what is *personality?* Many theories have been developed to try to explain what this concept means. Some are *global theories* of personality, which attempt a total comprehensive portrait of an individual (e.g., Freud's), while others are *microtheories,* focusing on narrower, more particular dimensions of personality. Certainly, one major part of personality is *social identity*—the part of personality that is our internalized representation of how we view ourselves as being part of our social world. Two major parts of social identity—the *self* and *gender identity*—are addressed in the readings in this chapter.

Article 13, "The Many Me's of the Self-Monitor," looks at the sense of self that each of us has and asks whether that is comprised of a single sense of self or perhaps a number of selves, depending on the situation.

Article 14, "The Measurement of Psychological Androgyny," is a classic article that challenges the common-sense wisdom that the most appropriate gender-typed behavior is for a male to be masculine and a female, feminine. Perhaps masculinity and femininity are not mutually exclusive ends of a continuum after all.

Finally, the contemporary reading found in Article 15, "Adolescents' Use of Tobacco, Health Locus of Control, and Self-Monitoring," revisits the concept of self-monitoring introduced in Article 13 and considers the role it may play in smoking behavior in teens. The article also examines how certain other self variables may play a role in that behavior. Given the serious health consequences of smoking, the implications of this research are of particular interest.

ARTICLE 13 _____

Think about who you are. Do you have a stable sense of self, of knowing what you feel, believe, and want? Or do you have many selves, depending on when and in what situation you try to answer this question?

Now think about your behavior. Do you act consistently across many different situations? Or does your behavior depend on the specific situation in which you find yourself?

These questions are indeed intriguing. At one extreme may be individuals who consistently act the same way in every situation, even when doing so might not be appropriate. At the other extreme are people who modify their behavior to fit each situation, showing little consistency across contexts. These are the two extremes on a continuum of what is known as *self-monitoring.*

Self-monitoring refers to the extent to which an individual is aware of and able to control the impressions that he or she conveys to others. A high self-monitoring individual is very attuned to the situation and modifies his or her behavior according to the demands of the context. A low self-monitoring individual tends to behave more in accordance with internal dispositions than with the demands of the situation.

What are the consequences of these two styles of behaving? Does a high self-monitoring person actually have many different selves, while a low self-monitoring person has but a single self? The relationship between self-monitoring and the sense of self is but one of the issues addressed in the following article by Mark Snyder.

The Many Me's of the Self-Monitor

■ Mark Snyder

The image of myself which I try to create in my own mind in order that I may love myself is very different from the image which I try to create in the minds of others in order that they may love me.   —W. H. Auden

The concept of the self is one of the oldest and most enduring in psychological considerations of human nature. We generally assume that people are fairly consistent and stable beings: that a person who is generous in one situation is also likely to be generous in other situations, that one who is honest is honest most of the time, that a person who takes a liberal stance today will favor the liberal viewpoint tomorrow.

It's not always so: each of us, it appears, may have not one but many selves. Moreover, much as we might like to believe that the self is an integral feature of personal identity, it appears that, to a greater extent, the self is a product of the individual's relationships with other people. Conventional wisdom to the contrary, there may be striking gaps and contradictions—as Auden suggests—between the public appearances and private realities of the self.

Psychologists refer to the strategies and techniques that people use to control the impressions they convey to others as "impression management." One of my own research interests has been to understand why some individuals are better at impression management than others. For it is clear that some people are particularly sensitive to the ways they express and present themselves in social situations—at parties, job interviews, professional meetings, in confrontations of all kinds where one might choose to create and maintain an appearance, with or without a specific purpose in mind. Indeed, I have found that such people have developed the ability to carefully monitor their own performances and to skillfully adjust their performances when signals from others tell them that they are not having the desired effect. I call such persons "high self-monitoring individuals," and I have developed a 25-item measure—the Self-Monitoring Scale—that has proved its ability to distinguish high self-monitoring individuals from low self-monitoring individuals (see box [p. 132]). Unlike the high self-monitoring individuals, low self-monitoring individuals are not so concerned about taking in such information; instead, they tend to express what they feel, rather than mold and tailor their behavior to fit the situation.

My work on self-monitoring and impression management grew out of a long-standing fascination with explorations of reality and illusion in literature and in the theater. I was struck by the contrast between the way things often appear to be and the reality that lurks beneath the surface—on the stage, in novels, and in people's actual lives. I wanted to know how this world of appearances in social relationships was built and maintained, as well as what its effects were on the individual personality. But I was also interested in exploring the older, more philosophical question of whether, beneath the various images of self that people project to others, there is a "real me." If we are all actors in many social situations, do we then retain in any sense an essential self, or are we really a variety of selves?

SKILLED IMPRESSION MANAGERS

There are striking and important differences in the extent to which people can and do control their self-presentation in social situations: some people engage in impression management more often—and with greater skill—than others. Professional actors, as well as many trial lawyers, are among the best at it. So are successful salespeople, confidence artists, and politicians. The onetime mayor of New York, Fiorello LaGuardia, was particularly skilled at adopting the expressive mannerisms of a variety of ethnic groups. In fact, he was so good at it that in watching silent films of his campaign speeches, it is easy to guess whose vote he was soliciting.

Of course, such highly skilled performances are the exception rather than the rule. And people differ in the extent to which they can and do exercise control over their self-presentations. It is high self-monitoring individuals among us who are particularly talented in this regard. When asked to describe high self-monitoring individuals, their friends say that they are good at learning which behavior is appropriate in social situations, have good self-control of their emotional expression, and can effectively use this ability to create the impression they want. They are particularly skilled at intentionally expressing and accurately communicating a wide variety of emotions both vocally and facially. As studies by Richard Lippa of California State University at Fullerton have shown, they are usually such polished actors that they can effectively adopt the mannerisms of a reserved, withdrawn, and introverted individual and then do an abrupt about-face and portray, just as convincingly, a friendly, outgoing, and extroverted personality.

High self-monitoring individuals are also quite likely to seek out information about appropriate patterns of self-presentation. They invest considerable effort in attempting to "read" and understand others. In an experiment I conducted with Tom Monson (then one of my graduate students), various cues were given to students involved in group discussions as to what was socially appropriate behavior in the situation. For example, some of them thought that their taped discussions would be played back to fellow students; in those circumstances, I assumed they would want their opinions to appear as autonomous as possible. Others believed that their discussions were completely private; there, I assumed they would be most concerned with maintaining harmony and agreement in the group. High self-monitoring individuals were keenly attentive to these differences; they conformed with the group when conformity was the most appropriate behavior and did not conform when they knew that the norms of the larger student audience would favor autonomy in the face of social pressure. Low self-monitoring individuals were virtually unaffected by the differences in social setting: presumably, their self-presentations were more accurate

Monitor Your Self

On the scale I have developed to measure self-monitoring, actors are usually high scorers, as are many obese people, who tend to be very sensitive about the way they appear to others. For much the same reason, politicians and trial lawyers would almost certainly be high scorers. Recent immigrants eager to assimilate, black freshmen in a predominantly white college, and military personnel stationed abroad are also likely to score high on the scale.

The Self-Monitoring Scale measures how concerned people are with the impression they are making on others, as well as their ability to control and modify their behavior to fit the situation. I believe that it defines a distinct domain of personality that is quite different from the traits probed by other standard scales.

Several studies show that skill at self-monitoring is not associated with exceptional intelligence or with a particular social class. Nor is it related, among other things, to being highly anxious or extremely self-conscious, to being an extrovert, or to having a strong need for approval. They may be somewhat power-oriented or Machiavellian, but high self-monitoring individuals do not necessarily have high scores on the "Mach" scale, a measure of Machiavellianism developed by Richard Christie of Columbia University. (Two items from the scale: "The best way to handle people is to tell them what they want" and "Anyone who completely trusts anyone else is asking for trouble.") The steely-eyes Machiavellians are more manipulative, detached, and amoral than high self-monitoring individuals.

The Self-Monitoring Scale describes a unique trait and has proved to be both statistically valid and reliable, in tests on various samples.

[Below] is a 10-item abbreviated version of the Self-Monitoring Scale that will give readers some idea of whether they are low or high self-monitoring individuals. If you would like to test your self-monitoring tendencies, follow the instructions and then consult the scoring key.

—M. S.

These statements concern personal reactions to a number of different situations. No two statements are exactly alike, so consider each statement carefully before answering. If a statement is true, or mostly true, as applied to you, circle the T. If a statement is false, or not usually true, as applied to you, circle the F.

1.	I find it hard to imitate the behavior of other people.	T	F
2.	I guess I put on a show to impress or entertain people.	T	F
3.	I would probably make a good actor.	T	F
4.	I sometimes appear to others to be experiencing deeper emotions than I actually am.	T	F
5.	In a group of people I am rarely the center of attention.	T	F
6.	In different situations and with different people, I often act like very different persons.	T	F
7.	I can only argue for ideas I already believe.	T	F
8.	In order to get along and be liked, I tend to be what people expect me to be rather than anything else.	T	F
9.	I may deceive people by being friendly when I really dislike them.	T	F
10.	I'm not always the person I appear to be.	T	F

SCORING: Give yourself one point for each of questions 1, 5 and 7 that you answered F. Give yourself one point for each of the remaining questions that you answered T. Add up your points. If you are a good judge of yourself and scored 7 or above, you are probably a high self-monitoring individual; 3 or below, you are probably a low self-monitoring individual.

reflections of their personal attitudes and dispositions. Thus, as we might have guessed, people who are most skilled in the arts of impression management are also most likely to practice it.

Although high self-monitoring individuals are well skilled in the arts of impression management, we should not automatically assume that they necessarily use these skills for deceptive or manipulative purposes. Indeed, in their relationships with friends and acquaintances, high self-monitoring individuals are eager to use their self-monitoring abilities to promote smooth social interactions.

We can find some clues to this motive in the way high self-monitoring individuals tend to react to, and cope with, unfamiliar and unstructured social settings. In a study done at the University of Wisconsin, psychologists William Ickes and Richard Barnes arranged for pairs of strangers to spend time together in a waiting room, ostensibly to wait for an experiment to begin. The researchers then recorded the verbal and nonverbal behavior of each pair over a five-minute period, using video and audio tapes. All possible pairings of same-sex undergraduates at high, moderate, and low levels of self-monitoring were represented. Researchers scrutinized the tapes for evidence of the impact of self-monitoring on spontaneous encounters between strangers.

In these meetings, as in so many other aspects of their lives, high self-monitoring individuals suffered little or no shyness. Soon after meeting the other person, they took an active and controlling role in the conversation. They were inclined to talk first and to initiate subsequent conversational sequences. They also felt, and were seen by their partners to have, a greater need to talk. Their partners also viewed them as having been the more directive member of the pair. It was as if high self-monitoring individuals were particularly concerned about managing their behavior in order to create, encourage, and maintain a smooth flow of conversation. Perhaps this quality may help self-monitoring people to emerge as leaders in groups, organizations, and institutions.

DETECTING IMPRESSION MANAGEMENT IN OTHERS

High self-monitoring individuals are also adept at detecting impression management in others. To demonstrate this finely tuned ability, three communications researchers at the University of Minnesota made use of videotaped excerpts from the television program "To Tell the Truth." On this program, one of the three guest contestants (all male in the excerpts chosen for the study) is the "real Mr. X." The other two who claim to be the real Mr. X are, of course, lying. Participants in the study watched each excerpt and then tried to identify the real Mr. X. High self-

---

William James on the Roles We Play

A man has as many social selves as there are individuals who recognize him and carry an image of him in their mind. . . . But as the individuals who carry the images form naturally into classes, we may practically say that he has as many different social selves as there are distinct *groups* of persons about whose opinions he cares. He generally shows a different side of himself to each of these different groups. Many a youth who is demure enough before his parents and teachers swears and swaggers like a pirate among his "tough" young friends. We do not show ourselves to our children as to our club companions, to our masters and employers as to our intimate friends. From this there results what practically is a division of the man into several selves; and this may be a discordant splitting, as where one is afraid to let one set of his acquaintances know him as he is elsewhere; or it may be a perfectly harmonious division of labor, as where one tender to his children is stern to the soldiers or prisoners under his command.

—William James
The Principles of Psychology, 1890

monitoring individuals were much more accurate than their low self-monitoring counterparts in correctly identifying the real Mr. X and in seeing through the deception of the other two contestants.

Not only are high self-monitoring individuals able to see beyond the masks of deception successfully but they are also keenly attentive to the actions of other people as clues to their underlying intentions. E. E. Jones and Roy Baumeister of Princeton University had college students watch a videotaped discussion between two men who either agreed or disagreed with each other. The observers were aware that one man (the target person) had been instructed either to gain the affection or to win the respect of the other. Low self-monitoring observers tended to accept behavior at face value. They found themselves attracted to the agreeable person, whether or not he was attempting to ingratiate himself with his discussion partner. In contrast, high self-monitoring observers were acutely sensitive to the motivational context within which the target person operated. They liked the target better if he was disagreeable when trying to ingratiate himself. But when he sought respect, they were more attracted to him if he chose to be agreeable. Jones and Baumeister suggest that high self-monitoring observers regarded agreeableness as too blatant a ploy in gaining affection and autonomy as an equally obvious route to respect. Perhaps the high self-monitoring individuals felt that they themselves would have acted with greater subtlety and finesse.

Even more intriguing is Jones's and Baumeister's speculation—and I share their view—that high self-monitoring individuals prefer to live in a stable, predictable social environment populated by people whose actions consistently and accurately reflect their true attitudes and feelings. In such a world, the consistency and predictability of the actions of others would be of great benefit to those who tailor and manage their own self-presentation in social situations. From this perspective, it becomes quite understandable that high self-monitoring individuals may be especially fond of those who avoid strategic posturing. Furthermore, they actually may prefer as friends those comparatively low in self-monitoring.

How can we know when strangers and casual acquaintances are engaged in self-monitoring? Are there some channels of expression and communication that are more revealing than others about a person's true, inner "self," even when he or she is practicing impression management?

Both scientific and everyday observers of human behavior have suggested that nonverbal behavior—facial expressions, tone of voice, and body movements—reveals meaningful information about a person's attitudes, feelings, and motives. Often, people who engage in self-monitoring for deceptive purposes are less skilled at controlling their body's expressive movements. Accordingly, the body may be a more revealing source of information than the face for detecting those who engage in self-monitoring and impression management.

More than one experiment shows how nonverbal behavior can betray the true attitude of those attempting impression management. Shirley Weitz of the New School for Social Research reasoned that on college campuses where there are strong normative pressures supporting a tolerant and liberal value system, all students would avoid saying anything that would indicate racial prejudice—whether or not their private attitudes supported such behavior. In fact, she found that among "liberal" white males at Harvard University, the most prejudiced students (as determined by behavioral measures of actual attempts to avoid interaction with blacks) bent over backwards to *verbally* express liking and friendship for a black in a simulated interracial encounter. However, their *nonverbal* behaviors gave them away. Although the prejudiced students made every effort to say kind and favorable things, they continued to do so in a cool and distant tone of voice. It was as if they knew the words but not the music: they knew *what* to say, but not *how* to say it.

Another way that prejudice can be revealed is in the physical distance people maintain between themselves and the target of their prejudice. To demonstrate this phenomenon, psychologist Stephen Morin arranged for college students to be interviewed about their attitudes toward homosexuality. Half the interviewers wore "Gay and Proud" buttons and mentioned their association with the Association of Gay Psychologists. The rest wore no buttons and simply mentioned that they were graduate students working on theses. Without the students' knowledge, the distance they placed their chairs from the interviewer was measured while the interviews were going on. The measure of social distance proved to be highly revealing. When the student and the interviewer were of the same sex, students tended to establish almost a foot more distance between themselves and the apparently gay interviewers. They placed their chairs an average of 32 inches away from apparently gay interviewers, but only 22 inches away from apparently nongay interviewers. Interestingly, most of the students expressed tolerant, and at times favorable, attitudes toward gay people in general. However, the distances they chose to put between themselves and the interviewers they thought gay betrayed underlying negative attitudes.

IMPRESSION MANAGERS' DILEMMAS

The well-developed skills of high self-monitoring individuals ought to give them the flexibility to cope quickly and effectively with a diversity of social roles. They can choose with skill and grace the self-presentation appropriate to each of a wide variety of social situations. But what happens when the impression manager must effectively present a true and honest image to other people?

Consider the case of a woman on trial for a crime that she did not commit. Her task on the witness stand is to carefully present herself so that everything she does and says communicates to the jurors clearly and unambiguously her true innocence, so that they will vote for her acquittal. Chances are good, however, that members of the jury are somewhat skeptical of the defendant's claims of innocence. After all, they might reason to themselves, the district attorney would not have brought this case to trial were the state's case against her not a convincing one.

The defendant must carefully manage her verbal and nonverbal behaviors so as to ensure that even a skeptical jury forms a true impression of her innocence. In particular, she must avoid the pitfalls of an image that suggests that "she doth protest her innocence too much and therefore must be guilty." To the extent that our defendant skillfully practices the art of impression management, she will succeed in presenting herself to the jurors as the honest person that she truly is.

It often can take as much work to present a truthful image as to present a deceptive one. In fact, in this case, just being honest may not be enough when facing skeptical jurors who may bend over backwards to interpret any and all of the defendant's behavior—nervousness, for example—as a sign of guilt.

The message from research on impression management is a clear one. Some people are quite flexible in their self-presentation. What effects do these shifts in public appearance have on the more private realities of self-concept? In some circumstances, we are persuaded by our own appearances: we become the persons we appear to be. This phenomenon is particularly likely to occur when the image we present wins the approval and favor of those around us.

In an experiment conducted at Duke University by psychologists E. E. Jones, Kenneth Gergen, and Keith Davis, participants who had been instructed to win the approval of an interviewer presented very flattering images of themselves. Half the participants (chosen at random) then received favorable reactions from their interviewers; the rest did not. All the participants later were asked to estimate how accurately and honestly their self-descriptions had mirrored their true personalities.

Those who had won the favor of their interviewers considered their self-presentations to have been the most honest of all. One interpretation of this finding is that those people were operating with rather pragmatic definitions of self-concept: that which produced the most positive results was considered to be an accurate reflection of the inner self.

The reactions of other people can make it all the more likely that we become what we claim to be. Other people may accept our self-presentations at face value; they may then treat us as if we really were the way we pretend to be. For example, if I act as if I like Chris, chances are Chris will like me. Chris will probably treat me in a variety of friendly ways. As a result of Chris's friendliness, I may come to like Chris, even though I did not in the first place. The result, in this case, may be beneficial to both parties. In other circumstances, however, the skilled impression manager may pay an emotional price.

High self-monitoring orientation may be purchased at the cost of having one's actions reflect and communicate very little about one's private attitudes, feelings, and dispositions. In fact, as I have seen time and again in my research with my former graduate students Beth Tanke and Bill Swann, correspondence between private attitudes and public behavior is often minimal for high self-monitoring individuals. Evidently, the words and deeds of high self-monitoring individuals may reveal precious little information about their true inner feelings and attitudes.

Yet, it is almost a canon of modern psychology that a person's ability to reveal a "true self" to intimates is essential to emotional health. Sidney Jourard, one of the first psychologists to hold that view, believed that only through self-disclosure could we achieve self-discovery and self-knowledge: "Through my self-disclosure, I let others know my soul. They can know it, really know it, only as I make it known. In fact, I am beginning to suspect that I can't even know *my own soul* except as I disclose it. I suspect that I will know myself 'for real' at the exact moment that I have succeeded in making it known through my disclosure to another person."

Only low self-monitoring individuals may be willing or able to live their lives according to Jourard's prescriptions. By contrast, high self-monitoring individuals seem to embody Erving Goffman's view of human nature. For him, the world of appearances appears to be all, and the "soul" is illusory. Goffman defines social interactions as a theatrical performance in which each individual acts out a "line." A line is a set of carefully chosen verbal and nonverbal acts that express one's self. Each of us, in Goffman's view, seems to be merely the sum of our various performances.

What does this imply for the sense of self and identity associated with low and high self-monitoring individuals?

I believe that high self-monitoring individuals and low self-monitoring individuals have very different ideas about what constitutes a self and that their notions are quite well-suited to how they live. High self-monitoring individuals regard themselves as rather flexible and adaptive people who tailor their social behavior shrewdly and pragmatically to fit appropriate conditions. They believe that a person is whoever he appears to be in any particular situation: "I am me, the me I am right now." This self-image fits well with the way high self-monitoring individuals present themselves to the world. It allows them to act in ways that are consistent with how they believe they should act.

By contrast, low self-monitoring individuals have a firmer, more single-minded idea of what a self should be. They value and strive for congruence between "who they are" and "what they do" and regard their actions as faithful reflections of how they feel and think. For them, a self is a single identity that must not be compromised for other people or in certain situations. Indeed, this view of the self parallels the low self-monitoring individual's consistent and stable self-presentation.

What is important in understanding oneself and others, then, is not the elusive question of whether there is a quintessential self, but rather, understanding how different people define those attributes of their behavior and experience that they regard as "me." Theory and research on self-monitoring have attempted to chart the processes by which beliefs about the self are actively translated into patterns of social behavior that reflect self-conceptions. From this perspective, the processes of self-monitoring are the processes of self—a system of operating rules that translate self-knowledge into social behavior.

CRITICAL THINKING QUESTIONS

1. Self-monitoring can be measured along a continuum. What are the advantages and disadvantages for someone who scores very high on this dimension (i.e., a high self-monitoring individual)? Very low (i.e., a low self-monitoring individual)?

2. How might high versus low self-monitoring individuals act differently in an intimate situation such as dating? Give examples to support your answer.

3. How do you think differences in self-monitoring develop? In other words, why might some people be attuned to external factors while others are not? In your opinion, what

level of self-monitoring might be best overall for healthy functioning? Explain your answers.

4. Article 11 dealt with the concept of cognitive dissonance. Based on your understanding of the concept, do you think that dissonance arousal in a given situation may affect the level of self-monitoring used by the person? How so?

ARTICLE 14 _____

Let's do a quick exercise. Make a list of words or adjectives that you would use to describe someone that you think of as being feminine. Make another list of masculine descriptors. Next, compare the lists. Does one set of characteristics seem better than the other or just different? Could it be that the different stereotypical characteristics associated with masculinity and femininity might each be important, depending on the situation?

Masculine characteristics are generally considered *instrumental*, meaning that they are useful in task- or goal-oriented situations. Feminine characteristics tend to be more *expressive*, meaning that they focus more on the affective concern of the welfare of others. Typically, American society socializes its members to believe that males should act masculine and females, feminine and that each gender should suppress the characteristics of its opposite.

The following classic article by Sandra L. Bem postulates that when males are only allowed to act masculine and females are only allowed to act feminine, each gender is, in a sense, limited in what it can do. Masculine males are thus good in situations that call for instrumental, get-the-job-done traits, whereas feminine females are good in settings where concern for the feelings of others is important. But what about the person of either gender who has both masculine *and* feminine characteristics? Might he or she not be more adaptive and flexible to a greater variety of human experiences? In short, might not this person be better adjusted than the more rigidly defined masculine males and feminine females? Besides attempting to answer these questions, Bem's article is also a good example of how an instrument designed to measure a dimension of behavior characteristics is developed.

The Measurement of Psychological Androgyny[1]

■ Sandra L. Bem

This article describes the development of a new sex-role inventory that treats masculinity and femininity as two independent dimensions, thereby making it possible to characterize a person as masculine, feminine, or "androgynous" as a function of the difference between his or her endorsement of masculine and feminine personality characteristics. Normative data are presented, as well as the results of various psychometric analyses. The major findings of conceptual interest are: (a) the dimensions of masculinity and femininity are empirically as well as logically independent; (b) the concept of psychological androgyny is a reliable one; and (c) highly sex-typed scores do not reflect a general tendency to respond in a socially desirable direction, but rather a specific tendency to describe oneself in accordance with sex-typed standards of desirable behavior for men and women.

Both in psychology and in society at large, masculinity and femininity have long been conceptualized as bipolar ends of a single continuum; accordingly, a person has had to be either masculine or feminine, but not both. This sex-role dichotomy has served to obscure two very plausible hypotheses: first, that many individuals might be "androgynous"; that is, they might be *both* masculine and feminine, *both* assertive and yielding, *both* instrumental and expressive—depending on the situational appropriateness of these various behaviors; and conversely, that strongly sex-

Reprinted from *Journal of Consulting and Clinical Psychology*, 1974, *42*, 155–162. Copyright © 1974 by the American Psychological Association. Reprinted by permission.

typed individuals might be seriously limited in the range of behaviors available to them as they move from situation to situation. According to both Kagan (1964) and Kohlberg (1966), the highly sex-typed individual is motivated to keep his behavior consistent with an internalized sex-role standard, a goal that he presumably accomplishes by suppressing any behavior that might be considered undesirable or inappropriate for his sex. Thus, whereas a narrowly masculine self-concept might inhibit behaviors that are stereotyped as feminine, and a narrowly feminine self-concept might inhibit behaviors that are stereotyped as masculine, a mixed, or androgynous, self-concept might allow an individual to freely engage in both "masculine" and "feminine" behaviors.

The current research program is seeking to explore these various hypotheses, as well as to provide construct validation for the concept of androgyny (Bem, 1974). Before the research could be initiated, however, it was first necessary to develop a new type of sex-role inventory, one that would not automatically build in an inverse relationship between masculinity and femininity. This article describes that inventory.

The Bem Sex-Role Inventory (BSRI) contains a number of features that distinguish it from other, commonly used, masculinity-femininity scales, for example, the Masculinity-Femininity scale of the California Psychological Inventory (Gough, 1957). First, it includes both a Masculinity scale and a Femininity scale, each of which contains 20 personality characteristics. These characteristics are listed in the first and second columns of Table 1, respectively. Second, because the BSRI was founded on a conception of the

sex-typed person as someone who has internalized society's sex-typed standards of desirable behavior for men and women, these personality characteristics were selected as masculine or feminine on the basis of sex-typed social desirability and not on the basis of differential endorsement by males and females as most other inventories have done. That is, a characteristic qualified as masculine if it was judged to be more desirable in American society for a man than for a woman, and it qualified as feminine if it was judged to be more desirable for a woman than for a man. Third, the BSRI characterizes a person as masculine, feminine, or androgynous as a function of the difference between his or her endorsement of masculine and feminine personality characteristics. A person is thus sex typed, whether masculine or feminine, to the extent that this difference score is high, the androgynous, to the extent that this difference score is low. Finally, the BSRI also includes a Social Desirability scale that is completely neutral with respect to sex. This scale now serves primarily to provide a neutral context for the Masculinity and Femininity scales, but it was utilized during the development of the BSRI to insure that the inventory would not simply be tapping a general tendency to endorse socially desirable traits. The 20 characteristics that make up this scale are listed in the third column of Table 1.

ITEM SELECTION

Both historically and cross-culturally, masculinity and femininity seem to have represented two complementary domains of *positive* traits and behaviors (Barry,

TABLE 1 / Sample of Items on the Masculinity, Femininity, and Social Desirability Scales of the BSRI

Masculine Items	Feminine Items	Neutral Items
Aggressive	Tender	Friendly
Competitive	Affectionate	Conscientious

Note: This table includes only a few samples of the items found in the BSRI. For the full list of items in each category, see the original source.

Bacon, & Child, 1957; Erikson, 1964; Parsons & Bales, 1955). In general, masculinity has been associated with an instrumental orientation, a cognitive focus on "getting the job done"; and femininity has been associated with an expressive orientation, an affective concern for the welfare of others.

Accordingly, as a preliminary to item selection for the Masculinity and Femininity scales, a list was compiled of approximately 200 personality characteristics that seemed to the author and several students to be both positive in value and either masculine or feminine in tone. This list served as the pool from which the masculine and feminine characteristics were ultimately chosen. As a preliminary to item selection for the Social Desirability scale, an additional list was compiled of 200 characteristics that seemed to be neither masculine nor feminine in tone. Of these "neutral" characteristics, half were positive in value and half were negative.

Because the BSRI was designed to measure the extent to which a person divorces himself from those characteristics that might be considered more "appropriate" for the opposite sex, the final items were selected for the Masculinity and Femininity scales if they were judged to be more desirable in American society for one sex than for the other. Specifically, judges were asked to utilize a 7-point scale, ranging from 1 ("Not at all desirable") to 7 ("Extremely desirable"), in order to rate the desirability in American society of each of the approximately 400 personality characteristics mentioned above. (E.g., "In American society, how desirable is it for a man to be truthful?" "In American society, how desirable is it for a woman to be sincere?") Each individual judge was asked to rate the desirability of all 400 personality characteristics either "for a man" or "for a woman." No judge was asked to rate both. The judges consisted of 40 Stanford undergraduates who filled out the questionnaire during the winter of 1972 and an additional 60 who did so the following summer. In both samples, half of the judges were male and half were female.

A personality characteristic qualified as masculine if it was independently judged by both males and females in both samples to be significantly more desirable for a man than for a woman ($p < .05$).[2] Similarly, a personality characteristic qualified as feminine if it was independently judged by both males and females

in both samples to be significantly more desirable for a woman than for a man ($p < .05$). Of those characteristics that satisfied these criteria, 20 were selected for the Masculinity scale and 20 were selected for the Femininity scale (see the first and second columns of Table 1, respectively).

A personality characteristic qualified as neutral with respect to sex and hence eligible for the Social Desirability scale (a) if it was independently judged by both males and females to be no more desirable for one sex than for the other ($t < 1.2$, $p > .2$) and (b) if male and female judges did not differ significantly in their overall desirability judgments of that trait ($t < 1.2$, $p > .2$). Of those items that satisfied these several criteria, 10 positive and 10 negative personality characteristics were selected for the BSRI Social Desirability scale in accordance with Edwards' (1964) finding that an item must be quite positive or quite negative in tone if it is to evoke a social desirability response set. (The 20 neutral characteristics are shown in the third column of Table 1.)

After all of the individual items had been selected, mean desirability scores were computed for the masculine, feminine, and neutral items for each of the 100 judges. As shown in Table 2, for both males and females, the mean desirability of the masculine and feminine items was significantly higher for the "appropriate" sex than for the "inappropriate" sex, whereas the mean desirability of the neutral items was no higher for one sex than for the other. These results are, of course, a direct consequence of the criteria used for item selection.

Table 3 separates out the desirability ratings of the masculine and feminine items for male and female judges rating their *own* sex. These own-sex ratings seem to best represent the desirability of these various items as perceived by men and women when they are asked to describe *themselves* on the inventory. That is, the left-hand column of Table 3 represents the phenomenology of male subjects taking the test and the right-hand column represents the phenomenology of female subjects taking the test. As can be seen in Table 3, not only are "sex-appropriate" characteristics more desirable for both males and females than "sex-inappropriate" characteristics, but the phenomenologies of male and female subjects are almost perfectly symmetric: that is, men and women are nearly equal

TABLE 2 / Mean Social Desirability Ratings of the Masculine, Feminine, and Neutral Items

Item	Male Judges			Female Judges		
	Masculine Item	Feminine Item	Neutral Item	Masculine Item	Feminine Item	Neutral Item
For a man	5.59	3.63	4.00	5.83	3.74	3.94
For a woman	2.90	5.61	4.08	3.46	5.55	3.98
Difference	2.69	1.98	.08	2.37	1.81	.04
t	14.41*	12.13*	.17	10.22*	8.28*	.09

*$p < .001$.

in their perceptions of the desirability of sex-appropriate characteristics, sex-inappropriate characteristics, and the difference between them ($t < 1$ in all three comparisons).

SCORING

The BSRI asks a person to indicate on a 7-point scale how well each of the 60 masculine, feminine, and neutral personality characteristics describes himself. The scale ranges from 1 ("Never or almost never true") to 7 ("Always or almost always true") and is labeled at each point. On the basis of his responses, each person receives three major scores: a Masculinity score, a Femininity score and, most important, an Androgyny score. In addition, a Social Desirability score can also be computed.

The Masculinity and Femininity scores indicate the extent to which a person endorses masculine and feminine personality characteristics as self-descriptive.

TABLE 3 / Mean Social Desirability Ratings of the Masculine and Feminine Items for One's Own Sex

Item	Male Judges for a Man	Female Judges for a Woman
Masculine	5.59	3.46
Feminine	3.63	5.55
Difference	1.96	2.09
t	11.94*	8.88*

*$p < .001$.

Masculinity equals the mean self-rating for all endorsed masculine items, and Femininity equals the mean self-rating for all endorsed feminine items. Both can range from 1 to 7. It will be recalled that these two scores are logically independent. That is, the structure of the test does not constrain them in any way, and they are free to vary independently.

The Androgyny score reflects the relative amounts of masculinity and femininity that the person includes in his or her self-description, and, as such, it best characterizes the nature of the person's total sex role. Specifically, the Androgyny score is defined as Student's t ratio for the difference between a person's masculine and feminine self-endorsement; that is, the Androgyny score is the difference between an individual's masculinity and femininity normalized with respect to the standard deviations of his or her masculinity and femininity scores. The use of a t ratio as the index of androgyny—rather than a simple difference score—has two conceptual advantages: first, it allows us to ask whether a person's endorsement of masculine attributes differs significantly from his or her endorsement of feminine attributes and, if it does ($|t| \geq 2.025$, $df = 38$, $p < .05$), to classify that person as significantly sex typed; and second, it allows us to compare different populations in terms of the percentage of significantly sex-typed individuals present within each.[3]

It should be noted that the greater the absolute value of the Androgyny score, the more the person is sex typed or sex reversed, with high positive scores indicating femininity and high negative scores indicating masculinity. A "masculine" sex role thus represents not only the endorsement of masculine attributes but the simultaneous rejection of feminine attributes. Similarly, a "feminine" sex role represents not only the endorsement of feminine attributes but the simultaneous rejection of masculine attributes. In contrast, the closer the Androgyny score is to zero, the more the person is androgynous. An "androgynous" sex role thus represents the equal endorsement of both masculine and feminine attributes.

The Social Desirability score indicates the extent to which a person describes himself in a socially desirable direction on items that are neutral with respect to sex. It is scored by reversing the self-endorsement ratings for the 10 undesirable items and then calculating the subject's mean endorsement score across all 20 neutral personality characteristics. The Social Desirability score can thus range from 1 to 7, with 1 indicating a strong tendency to describe oneself in a socially undesirable direction and 7 indicating a strong tendency to describe oneself in a socially desirable direction.

PSYCHOMETRIC ANALYSES

Subjects

During the winter and spring of 1973, the BSRI was administered to 444 male and 279 female students in introductory psychology at Stanford University. It was also administered to an additional 117 male and 77 female paid volunteers at Foothill Junior College. The data that these students provided represent the normative data for the BSRI, and, unless explicitly noted, they serve as the basis for all of the analyses that follow.

Internal Consistency

In order to estimate the internal consistency of the BSRI, coefficient alpha was computed separately for the Masculinity, Femininity and Social Desirability scores of the subjects in each of the two normative samples. (Nunnally, 1967). The results showed all three scores to be highly reliable, both in the Stanford sample (Masculinity a = .86; Femininity a = .80; Social Desirability a = .75) and in the Foothill sample (Masculinity a = .86; Femininity a = .82; Social Desirability a = .70). Because the reliability of the

Androgyny t ratio could not be calculated directly, coefficient alpha was computed for the highly correlated Androgyny difference score, Femininity-Masculinity, using the formula provided by Nunnally (1967) for linear combinations. The reliability of the Androgyny difference score was .85 for the Stanford sample and .86 for the Foothill sample.

Relationship between Masculinity and Femininity

As indicated earlier, the Masculinity and Femininity scores of the BSRI are logically independent. That is, the structure of the test does not constrain them in any way, and they are free to vary independently. The results from the two normative samples reveal them to be empirically independent as well (Stanford male $r = .11$, female $r = -.14$; Foothill male $r = -.02$, female $r = -.07$). This finding vindicates the decision to design an inventory that would not artifactually force a negative correlation between masculinity and femininity.

Social Desirability Response Set

It will be recalled that a person is sex typed on the BSRI to the extent that his or her Androgyny score reflects the greater endorsement of "sex-appropriate" characteristics than of "sex-inappropriate" characteristics. However, because of the fact that the masculine and feminine items are all relatively desirable, even for the "inappropriate" sex, it is important to verify that the Androgyny score is not simply tapping a social desirability response set.

Accordingly, product-moment correlations were computed between the Social Desirability score and the Masculinity, Femininity, and Androgyny scores for the Stanford and Foothill samples separately. They were also computed between the Social Desirability score and the absolute value of the Androgyny score. These correlations are displayed in Table 4. As expected, both Masculinity and Femininity were correlated with Social Desirability. In contrast, the near-zero correlations between Androgyny and Social Desirability confirm that the Androgyny score is not measuring a general tendency to respond in a socially desirable direction. Rather, it is measuring a very specific tendency to describe oneself in accordance

TABLE 4 / Correlation of Masculinity, Femininity, and Androgyny with Social Desirability

Sample	Masculinity with Social Desirability		Femininity with Social Desirability		Androgyny with Social Desirability		|Androgyny| with Social Desirability	
	Males	Females	Males	Females	Males	Females	Males	Females
Stanford	.42	.19	.28	.26	.12	.03	.08	−.10
Foothill	.23	.19	.15	.15	−.07	.06	−.12	−.09
Stanford and Foothill combined	.38	.19	.28	.22	.08	.04	.03	−.10

with sex-typed standards of desirable behavior for men and women.

Test-Retest Reliability

The BSRI was administered for a second time to 28 males and 28 females from the Stanford normative sample. The second administration took place approximately four weeks after the first. During this second administration, subjects were told that we were interested in how their responses on the test might vary over time, and they were explicitly instructed not to try to remember how they had responded previously. Product-moment correlations were computed between the first and second administrations for the Masculinity, Femininity, Androgyny, and Social Desirability scores. All four scores proved to be highly reliable over the four-week interval (Masculinity r = .90; Femininity r = .90; Androgyny r = .93; Social Desirability r = .89).

Correlations with Other Measures of Masculinity-Femininity

During the second administration of the BSRI, subjects were also asked to fill out the Masculinity-Femininity scales of the California Psychological Inventory and the Guilford-Zimmerman Temperament Survey, both of which have been utilized rather frequently in previous research on sex roles. Table 5 presents the correlations between these two scales and the Masculinity, Femininity, and Androgyny scales of the BSRI. As can be seen in the table, the Guilford-Zimmerman scale is not at all correlated with any of the three scales of the BSRI, whereas the California Psychological Inventory is moderately correlated with

all three. It is not clear why the BSRI should be more highly correlated with the CPI than with the Guilford-Zimmerman scale, but the fact that none of the correlations is particularly high indicates that the BSRI is measuring an aspect of sex roles which is not directly tapped by either of these two scales.

NORMS

Table 6 presents the mean Masculinity, Femininity, and Social Desirability scores separately by sex for both the Stanford and the Foothill normative samples. It also presents means for both the Androgyny *t* ratio and the Androgyny difference score. As can be seen in the table, males scored significantly higher than females on the Masculinity scale, and females scored significantly higher than males on the Femininity scale in both samples. On the two measures of androgyny, males scored on the masculine side of zero and females scored on the feminine side of

TABLE 5 / Correlation of the Masculinity-Femininity Scales of the California Psychological Inventory (CPI) and Guilford-Zimmerman Scale with the Masculinity, Femininity, and Androgyny Scales of the BSRI

Scale	CPI		Guilford-Zimmerman	
	Males	Females	Males	Females
BSRI Masculinity	−.42	−.25	.11	.15
BSRI Femininity	.27	.25	.04	−.06
BSRI Androgyny	.50	.30	−.04	−.06

Note: The CPI scale is keyed in the feminine direction, whereas the Guilford-Zimmerman scale is keyed in the masculine direction.

TABLE 6 / Sex Differences on the BSRI

Scale Score	Stanford University			Foothill Junior College		
	Males (n = 444)	Females (n = 279)	t	Males (n = 117)	Females (n = 77)	t
Masculinity						
M	4.97	4.57		4.96	4.55	
SD	.67	.69	7.62*	.71	.75	3.86*
Femininity						
M	4.44	5.01		4.62	5.08	
SD	.55	.52	13.88*	.64	.58	5.02*
Social Desirability						
M	4.91	5.08		4.88	4.89	
SD	.50	.50	4.40*	.50	.53	ns
Androgyny t Ratio						
M	−1.28	1.10		−.80	1.23	
SD	1.99	2.29	14.33*	2.23	2.42	5.98*
Androgyny Difference Score						
M	−0.53	.43		−.34	.53	
SD	.82	.93	14.28*	.97	.97	6.08*

*$p < .001$.

zero. This difference is significant in both samples and for both measures. On the Social Desirability scale, females scored significantly higher than males at Stanford but not at Foothill. It should be noted that the size of this sex difference is quite small, however, even in the Stanford sample.

Table 7 presents the percentage of subjects within each of the two normative samples who qualified as masculine, feminine, or androgynous as a function of the Androgyny *t* ratio. Subjects are classified as sex typed, whether masculine or feminine, if the androgyny *t* ratio reaches statistical significance ($|t| \geq 2.025$, $df = 38$, $p < .05$), and they are classified as androgynous if the absolute value of the *t* ratio is less than or equal to one. Table 7 also indicates the percentage of subjects who fall between these various cutoff points. It should be noted that these cut-off points are somewhat arbitrary and that other investigators should feel free to adjust them in accordance with the characteristics of their particular subject populations.

CONCLUDING COMMENT

It is hoped that the development of the BSRI will encourage investigators in the areas of sex differences and sex roles to question the traditional assumption that it is the sex-typed individual who typifies mental health and to begin focusing on the behavioral and societal consequences of more flexible sex-role self-concepts. In a society where rigid sex-role differentiation has already outlived its utility, perhaps the androgynous person will come to define a more human standard of psychological health.

REFERENCES

Barry, H., Bacon, M. K., & Child, I. L. A cross-cultural survey of some sex differences in socialization. *Journal of Abnormal and Social Psychology,* 1957, *55,* 327–332.

Bem, S. L. Sex-role adaptability: One consequence of psychological androgyny. *Journal of Personality and Social Psychology,* 1974, in press.

TABLE 7 / Percentage of Subjects in the Normative Samples Classified as Masculine, Feminine, or Androgynous

Item	Stanford University		Foothill Junior College	
	Males ($n = 444$)	Females ($n = 279$)	Males ($n = 117$)	Females ($n = 77$)
% feminine ($t \geq 2.025$)	6	34	9	40
% near feminine ($1 < t < 2.025$)	5	20	9	8
% androgynous ($-1 \leq t \leq +1$)	34	27	44	38
% near masculine ($-2.025 < t < -1$)	19	12	17	7
% masculine ($t \leq -2.025$)	36	8	22	8

Edwards, A. L. The measurement of human motives by means of personality scales. In D. Levine (Ed.), *Nebraska symposium on motivation: 1964.* Lincoln: University of Nebraska Press, 1964.

Erikson, E. H. Inner and outer space: Reflections on womanhood. In R. J. Lifton (Ed.), *The woman in America.* Boston: Houghton Mifflin, 1964.

Gough, H. G. *Manual for the California Psychological Inventory.* Palo Alto, Calif.: Consulting Psychologists Press, 1957.

Kagan, J. Acquisition and significance of sex-typing and sex-role identity. In M. L. Hoffman & L. W. Hoffman (Eds.), *Review of child development research.* Vol. 1. New York: Russell Sage Foundation, 1964.

Kohlberg, L. A cognitive-developmental analysis of children's sex-role concepts and attitudes. In E. E. Maccoby (Ed.), *The development of sex differences.* Stanford, Calif.: Stanford University Press, 1966.

Nunnally, J. C. *Psychometric theory.* New York: McGraw-Hill, 1967.

Parsons, T., & Bales, R. F. *Family, socialization, and interaction process.* New York: Free Press of Glencoe, 1955.

ENDNOTES

1. This research was supported by IROIMH 21735 from the National Institute of Mental Health. The author is grateful to Carol Korula, Karen Rook, Jenny Jacobs, and Odile van Embden for their help in analyzing the data.
2. All significance levels in this article are based on two-tailed t tests.
3. A Statistical Package for the Social Sciences (SPSS) computer program for calculating individual t ratios is available on request from the author. In the absence of computer facilities, one can utilize the simple Androgyny difference score, Femininity-Masculinity, as the index of androgyny. Empirically, the two indices are virtually identical ($r = .98$), and one can approximate the t-ratio value by multiplying the Androgyny difference score by 2.322. This conversion factor was derived empirically from our combined normative sample of 917 students at two different colleges.

CRITICAL THINKING QUESTIONS

1. Examine the sample items in Table 1 that are categorized as masculine, feminine, or neutral. Since this article was written in 1974, these items were selected almost three decades ago. Do you think that these items are still applicable today, or are some of them dated and perhaps even controversial? Have notions of masculinity and femininity changed over time? Explain.

2. The BSRI (Bem Self-Role Inventory) is a self-report instrument. Do you think the way someone describes his or her characteristics on paper is necessarily an accurate portrayal of the way he or she really acts? In what way? How could you test this possibility?

3. What do you think of the concept of *androgyny*? Would society be better off if more people were androgynous rather than being either masculine *or* feminine? Why or why not?

4. Based on the information in the article, describe specific situations where an androgynous individual might be better suited than either a masculine or feminine individual. In what, if any, situations would someone only capable of masculine behaviors be more appropriate? What about someone only capable of feminine behaviors? Explain your answers.

5. After reading the article, you should have a good grasp of the concept of androgyny. If you explained this concept to others, do you think that most people would agree that they would be better off if they were androgynous rather than either masculine or feminine? Why or why not?

ADDITIONAL RELATED READINGS

Auster, C. J., & Ohm, S. C. (2000). Masculinity and femininity in contemporary American society: A reevaluation using the Bem Sex-Role Inventory. *Sex Roles, 43*(7–8), 499–528.

Ward, C. A. (2000). Models and measurements of psychological androgyny: A cross-cultural extension of theory and research. *Sex Roles, 43*(7–8), 529–552.

ARTICLE 15 _____

We could argue that one of the major differences separating we humans from nonhumans is our ability to self-reflect. Indeed, we spend a tremendous amount of time and energy thinking about ourselves and who we are. And while we look at and evaluate many different aspects of ourselves, perhaps the most central is that of *self-concept*. Briefly stated, our self-concept is our organized set of beliefs and feelings about ourselves. It is the totality of who we are as we see it.

Think about that for a second. If someone asked you to tell who you are, how would you describe yourself? What qualities would you mention—and not mention? However you answer these questions will give you (and the other person) insight into your self-concept.

Even though self-concept is the centralized and organized set of images we have about ourselves, many other important aspects of the self also influence how we feel and how we act. For example, *self-esteem* is the affective evaluation we make about ourselves. That is, do we feel worthwhile, good, capable, and desirable—all characteristics of high self-esteem? Or do we not feel particularly good about ourselves—that we do not quite measure up to other people—as is the case with low self-esteem?

Yet another aspect of the self concerns the self-evaluation we make of our ability or competence to achieve a particular outcome. *Self-efficacy* refers to our confidence that we can achieve a particular task, such as getting a college degree, learning to fly an airplane, or being able to hold up under pressure. People with high self-efficacy are much more likely to achieve their goals than those with low self-efficacy, perhaps, in part, because having confidence in their ability to succeed allows high self-efficacy individuals to attempt the task in the first place.

Locus of control is another dimension of self-concept. In understanding our world, we can either believe that we exert control over what happens to us in life (i.e., an *internal* locus of control orientation), or, at the other extreme, we can believe that what happens is largely a matter of chance and not under our control (i.e., an *external* locus of control orientation). The degree of internal or external control we feel greatly influences not only how we interpret events but also the steps that we may take in trying to influence the outcomes.

Last, but certainly not least, is *self-monitoring*. This concept, discussed previously in Article 13, concerns how adaptable people are in responding to their external environment. Low self-monitors, for example, tend to act consistently across different situations, whereas high self-monitors are more apt to modify their behavior to suit the situation in which they find themselves.

Certainly, there are many other aspects of the self; the above-mentioned factors were discussed because they may have a particular impact on smoking behavior. The following article by Melanie Booth-Butterfield, Robert H. Anderson, and Steve Booth-Butterfield examines the association between these variables and the development of adolescent smoking. The implications of these findings for curbing teen smoking are of particular importance.

Adolescents' Use of Tobacco, Health Locus of Control, and Self-Monitoring

■ Melanie Booth-Butterfield, Robert H. Anderson, and Steve Booth-Butterfield

This study examined the association of the traits, health locus of control, and self-monitoring with adolescents' tobacco uptake. Participants were 112 rural adolescents (12 to 19 years old, M = 15.3). Of that sample, 33% used tobacco. Tobacco users were found to score lower on the dimension of Internality and higher on the dimension of Chance, as compared with nonusers of tobacco, indicating a more external Health Locus of Control. In addition, tobacco users were lower self-monitors than were nonusers. These results suggest that adolescents who use tobacco feel less in control of their lives in relation to nonusers, believe that chance plays a larger role in their health, and believe they may be unable to monitor and adapt their communication to achieve positive outcomes.

The decision to take up smoking is an individual one. Regardless of the myriad of external or situational factors, no one forces people to experiment with tobacco use. Even though contacts and interaction with smoking peers and family members are major predictors of eventual smoking uptake (e.g., Greenland, Johnson, Webber, & Berenson, 1997; Hunter, Croft, Vizelberg, & Berenson, 1987), the actual choice ultimately rests with the individual.

If the tobacco problem is examined from a different perspective, however, most adolescents do not become smokers. Figures from the 1990 California Tobacco Survey indicate that 73% of the junior high to high school group constituted "never-smokers" (Hu, Lin, & Keeler, 1998). However, since 1991, the proportion of teens smoking has consistently increased (Centers for Disease Control and Prevention, 1996), and this has occurred despite numerous federal programs, community interventions, and state and legislative efforts to reduce adolescent smoking rates. Thus, critical questions about the process of preventing smoking are (a) What is it about this subgroup of adolescents that influences their decision to use

tobacco? and (b) As communication social scientists, how can we best design messages or interventions to be more effective in preventing tobacco uptake?

PERSONALITY TRAITS AS INFLUENCING FACTORS

Our personality makeup predisposes us to numerous behaviors and has long been studied as a predictor of communicative actions. For example, Rancer and colleagues studied trait argumentativeness and verbal aggression (Rancer, 1998), McCroskey studied communication apprehension (McCroskey & Beatty, 1998), and predictors of deception effectiveness such as Machiavellianism were studied (Miller & Stiff, 1993). Although the question of whether those personality traits are inborn or developed early in life (e.g., Beatty, McCroskey, & Heisel, 1998; Chorpita & Barlow, 1998) is not central to this study, personality traits certainly influence our communication and the decisions we enact.

It is clear that simple knowledge of the dangers associated with tobacco use has little impact on adolescent tobacco uptake (Nutbeam, Mavaskil, Smith, Simpson, & Catford, 1992). Individual predispositions, however, show promise for understanding the decisions. Booth-Kewley and Vickers (1994) advocated increased attention to personality factors in the study of health patterns when they found conscientiousness and agreeableness to be intertwined with preventive actions and risky health behaviors. Even breast cancer has been linked with personality traits such as being out of touch with emotions (Bleiker, van der Ploeg, Hendriks, & Ader, 1996).

In the realm of tobacco use and communication traits, it has been noted that neurotic, depressed, low-conscientious, and socially alienated individuals are more likely to smoke as well as to make other

Reprinted from *Health Communication*, 2000, *12*(2), 137–148. Copyright © 2000 by Lawrence Erlbaum Associates, Inc. Reprinted with permission.

unproductive health decisions (Friedman et al., 1995; Gilbert & Gilbert, 1995; Patton et al., 1996; Spielberger, Foreyt, Reheiser, & Poston, 1998). It may be that such individuals do not feel in control of their world or their life. They may feel that it is futile to try to change outcomes and, hence, make "decisions" about tobacco use that exemplify a lack of fortitude to resist tobacco or low self-efficacy.

Bandura (1991) described self-efficacy as "beliefs about one's capabilities to mobilize the motivation, cognitive resources, and courses of action needed to meet given situational demands" (p. 229). Self-efficacy, or the confidence in your ability to shape your own situational outcomes, has been shown to be related to a wide range of health-related behaviors, from recovery from coronary problems to pain control to coping with stress (O'Leary, Schoor, Lorig, & Holman, 1988; Wortman, Panciera, Shusterman, & Hibscher, 1976). Bandura conceptualized self-efficacy as a situational response but one that can be built and enhanced through mastery experiences, positive modeling, influential messages, and so forth (Bandura, 1991; Norman & Bennett, 1996). For example, a social influence approach in Finland reduced smoking uptake by 22% (Vartiainen, Paavola, McAlister, & Puska, 1998). The crucial link with adolescents who smoke, however, is that they may be considerably less likely to have positive mastery experiences about achievement-oriented outcomes in their lives and subsequently less likely to develop health protective communication or attitudinal patterns.

It appears that tobacco-using adolescents are likely to feel less self-efficacious and more controlled externally rather than in control of their health-related outcomes. Low self-efficacy smokers have been shown to be less successful in their attempts to quit (Bandura, 1991). It is further reasonable that feeling mastery situationally regarding tobacco use should also be related to health locus of control (HLC); for example, internal locus of control individuals should feel more responsible for their tobacco behavior and less likely to blame health outcomes on external sources.

HEALTH LOCUS OF CONTROL

HLC is a subset of the larger concept of generalized locus of control. HLC represents people's perceptions of the controllability of health outcomes and whether responsibility for illnesses resides in their own behavior or outside influences. According to Wallston, Wallston, and DeVellis (1978), there are three distinct dimensions to the belief structure: (a) control of health is internally based, therefore making the individual responsible; (b) our health and health decisions are controlled by powerful others such as physicians and other high-status health care providers; and (c) health outcomes are due to chance and therefore entirely out of our control. These aspects have been shown to differentially predict health-related behaviors in that people with more internal HLC generally adhere more closely to health regimens, whereas more externally oriented individuals are less likely to engage in health-protective behaviors (e.g., Jessor, Turbin, & Costa, 1998; Newsom, Knapp, & Schulz, 1996).

For example, higher internal HLC (using various measures of that construct) has been shown to be associated with greater likelihood of engaging in preventive health behaviors, such as Pap screenings, breast exams, healthy diet, and wearing seat belts (Bundek, Marks, & Richardson, 1993). However, at least one study found evidence counter to this pattern.

In a study of Welsh smokers, Bennett, Norman, Moore, Murphy, and Tudor-Smith (1997) found that adult smokers actually had higher internality on the HLC scale. Yet they simultaneously evidenced higher scores for the Chance and Others dimensions. This seems contradictory in that it is difficult to understand how one could believe he or she controlled health while believing that chance and other people such as physicians controlled health outcomes. The authors speculated that this was an older, adult group who may have been in a form of denial. In contrast, an earlier study of young adolescent smokers in the United Kingdom did evidence the predicted locus of control effects using an alternate operationalization of HLC (Eiser, Eiser, Gammage, & Morgan, 1989).

Generalized internal locus of control has been found to correlate with conscientiousness ($r = .37$) and with subjective well-being or life satisfaction ($r = .42$; Morrison, 1997). In addition, higher conscientiousness is associated with lower rates of smoking and other risky behaviors (Friedman et al., 1995). Hence, HLC should be associated with predictable patterns related to adolescents' tobacco use.

Self-Monitoring   Much of a teenager's communication may be aimed at appropriately fitting in with peers. Part of the ability to adapt and fit in is the monitoring and adjustment of one's own communicative behavior to suit receiver expectations. This describes the personality trait of self-monitoring (Snyder, 1974).

Self-monitoring (Lennox & Wolfe, 1984; Snyder, 1974, 1979) is the degree to which people use social comparison information and attend to cues to guide their own communication and communicative adaptation. High self-monitors are quite aware of how others perceive them and alter their behavior and self-presentation to meet the needs of the situation. Low self-monitors tend to be less conscious of how others view them. They tend to be more consistent in their communication across situations, regardless of whether that communication is productive.

The relation between tobacco use among teens and self-monitoring is not clear. On one hand, tobacco-using adolescents might be predicted to score higher on self-monitoring if they use tobacco as a symbol of group membership or to project a mature image. Smokers achieve less and encounter more conflict in school (Hu et al., 1998), so self-monitoring may be associated with attempts to manipulate a "tough" adult image (Chassin, Presson, Sherman, & Edwards, 1992). If this is the case, then tobacco users should be higher self-monitors.

On the other hand, tobacco use may be associated with lower self-monitoring. These tobacco-using adolescents, who tend not to achieve as much (Hu et al., 1998), may lack the sociocommunicative skill to read communication cues and adjust to varying situations. They may be unable (or unwilling) to manipulate their external image and adapt their behavior, thus suggesting lower levels of self-monitoring. We examined the relations between personality traits, self-monitoring, HLC, and tobacco use.

HYPOTHESES

Based on this rationale, our research project was directed by three hypotheses (Hs) and a research question (RQ).

H1:   Tobacco users perceive less self-control over their health than do nonusers.

H2:   Tobacco users perceive more external control over their health from others than do nonusers.

H3:   Tobacco users perceive their health to be more controlled by chance factors than do nonusers.

RQ1:   What is the relation between smoking status and self-monitoring?

METHODS

This study was a part of a larger, multisite project investigating adolescent tobacco use funded by the Centers for Disease Control and Prevention. This investigation focused on empirical personality factors that appear to support and maintain tobacco use. All research groups were adolescents from public school systems.

Participants and Procedures

Participants were recruited with the cooperation of three public middle and high schools in the Appalachian region—a region with higher than national average tobacco use rates (West Virginia Department of Health and Human Resources, 1995). Participating schools were located in rural communities at a distance from the university to minimize over-representation of academic families. Students were informed of the study in advance and given consent forms to take home for parental signatures. Those students whose parents signed and returned consent forms were administered questionnaires, including HLC, self-monitoring, assessments of sex, and their tobacco-use status.[1] Tobacco use was defined, as is typical for adolescents, by asking the question, "Have you smoked cigarettes or used smokeless tobacco during the past 30 days?" (e.g., Biener, Aseltine, Cohen, & Anderka, 1998).

The final data set consisted of 112 adolescents (age range 12 to 19 years old), in which the mean age was 15.3 (*SD* = 2). Female participants constituted 42% of the sample, with 2 individuals not reporting their sex.

Measurement

The HLC measure is a shortened adaptation of the Multidimensional Health Locus of Control Questionnaire (Wallston et al., 1978). It assesses the strength of belief in each dimension (Internal, Other, Chance), using three items for each dimension with a 4-point response format. Internal reliabilities for the shortened version have ranged from .58 (Internal), .61 (Other), and .69 (Chance; Bennett et al., 1997) to .82, .82, and .72, respectively (Bundek et al., 1993).

The Revised Self-Monitoring Scale (Lennox & Wolfe, 1984) was employed rather than the Snyder (1974) version due to (a) problems with Snyder's factor structure discussed by Gabrenya and Arkin (1980) and Lennox and Wolfe (1984) and (b) the consistently low internal reliabilities obtained with Snyder's scale. This scale consists of 13 items employing a five-step format to describe the "truth" of the respondent's statement. The scale addresses how individuals "read" and react to situational presentational demands: for example, "I have the ability to control the way I come across to people, depending on the impression I want to give."

RESULTS

Descriptive and Preliminary Analyses

Of the 112 participants, 37 were current tobacco users and 75 were not. However, female participants were slightly more likely to be in the tobacco-using group. Of the adolescent smokers, 54.3% were female, whereas males constituted 45.7% of the smokers. Of the nonusers, 64% were male and 36% were female, $\chi^2(1, N = 112) = 3.3, p = .07.$[2] This pattern of male/female use is consistent with previous findings (e.g., Eiser et al., 1989). The means, standard deviations, and reliabilities for all scales are shown in Table 1. The Hs were tested with t tests adjusted for unequal cell sizes.

Analysis of Hypotheses and Research Question

H1 predicted that tobacco-using adolescents would be less likely to perceive internal control of their health, compared with nonusers. This was confirmed. The mean for smokers was 9.2 ($SD = 1.3$), and the nonsmoking mean was 10.5 ($SD = 1.5$), $t(110) = 4.25, p < .0001, d = .93$.

H2 stated that adolescent tobacco users would have greater belief that other people controlled their health than would nonusers. This H was not supported. The mean for tobacco users on the Other dimension of the HLC was 5.7 ($SD = 2.0$), compared with 6.3 ($SD = 1.6$) for nonusers, $t(110) = 1.55, p = .13, d = .33$.

H3 predicted that tobacco users would feel that their health was controlled by chance factors more than would nonusers, and this was confirmed. The mean Chance score for users was 6.9 ($SD = 1.9$), but the mean for nonusers was 5.8 ($SD = 1.5$), $t(110) = 3.3, p < .001, d = .65$.

The RQ examined the relation between trait self-monitoring and tobacco use status. Comparisons revealed that nonusing adolescents scored higher on self-monitoring than did their smoking counterparts, $t(110) = 2.3, p < .023, d = .45$. The mean Self-Monitoring score for tobacco users was 45.5 ($SD = 9.8$) and for nonusers was 48.9 ($SD = 5.7$).

Post hoc analysis indicated that nonsmoking students were somewhat more likely to participate in organized sports programs, although not significantly so. Sixteen of the 37 smokers participated in sports, whereas 43 of the 85 nonsmokers did so, $\chi^2(1, N = 112) = 1.97, p = .16, \phi = .133$. This finding is

TABLE 1 / Descriptive Statistics: Health Locus of Control (HLC) and Self-Monitoring

Scales	M	SD	Internal Reliability
HLC			
Internal	10.1	1.5	.60
Other	6.1	1.7	.57
Chance	6.2	1.8	.42
Self-monitoring	47.8	7.5	.79[a]
			.72[b]

Note: N = 112.
[a]Spearman-Brown.
[b]Alpha.

consistent with a recent study by Emmons, Wechsler, Dowdall, and Abraham (1998) that found that college students who smoked were significantly less likely to participate in sports programs.

To summarize, these results demonstrate that adolescent smokers are more externally oriented, believe their health is controlled more by chance factors, and are lower self-monitors than nonsmoking adolescents from the same schools.

DISCUSSION

This study of adolescents confirms some distressing information about their perceptions of their own ability to change health-related behaviors. To the extent that they feel controlled by external forces, they appear to be less likely to step up and take responsibility for "saying no" to tobacco or for quitting after they start smoking.

Compared with nonusing adolescents, the students who used tobacco were lower on internality and higher on their beliefs that chance or fate controlled their health outcomes. Thus, the tobacco-using students attributed more responsibility for their behavior to external forces, denying their own control of the situation. As one adolescent put it, "I look at it this way. You're going to die sometime. Why not be happy doing it?" Another evidenced a very external attitude when he said, "I think I wouldn't do it [use tobacco] if they *made* us quit. Like sign a Prom Promise or something."

The only dimension of HLC that did not follow the predicted pattern for tobacco users was control by "powerful others." In fact, the means were in the opposite direction (i.e., higher for nonusers), which may suggest that these nonsmoking adolescents are more compliant with authority figures. Other researchers (e.g., Norman & Bennett, 1996) have also found inconsistent patterns on the dimension of Powerful Others. For instance, Eiser et al. (1989) found that adolescents who have never smoked were higher in their beliefs in powerful others, which may have indicated a reliance on the credibility, knowledge, and curative abilities of health care providers.

The general pattern of externality revealed in this study undermines the independence and self-reliance that teens often say they desire in other areas, and the pattern may be a symptom of generalized low self-efficacy as well as external locus of control. Tobacco-using adolescents apparently do not believe they can avoid negative health consequences on their own, so it must be done for them. This is somewhat supported by recent studies on the use of external influences to lower teen smoking. Analysis of the enforcement of no-sell laws demonstrates that strict enforcement of laws against selling cigarettes to minors does work to lower smoking (DiFranza, Savageau, & Aisquith, 1996). Another externally imposed option that reduces teen smoking is raising tobacco taxes, such as those imposed in Massachusetts (Biener et al., 1998; Centers for Disease Control and Prevention, 1994).

Thus, when we examine tobacco prevention and cessation efforts, we are faced with two distinctly different options. Preventionists either can work to alter the adolescents' HLC to be more internal and therefore under the control of the adolescent or can apply external constraints that lower access to tobacco. If we look at the first option, Chorpita and Barlow (1998) contended that early childhood experiences and environments in which children are allowed no control, or ones in which they see individual control as random, contribute to development of external locus of control. Such long-term experiences could prove almost impossible to change, but because adolescents are young, they may be more malleable if sufficient prevention resources were devoted. To illustrate the investment necessary, the Vartiainen et al. (1998) study, which utilized social influence strategies to obtain smoking reductions at the 15-year follow-up, also incorporated intensive skill training, counseling, and extensive mass media messages. Flynn, Worden, and Secker-Walker (1994) contended that individual approaches are not sufficient to address smoking uptake, and therefore they advocated a strong mass media component to any intervention. Hence, one is tempted to speculate that external constraints, influences, and legislative efforts may be more cost-effective in preventing tobacco uptake, at least in the short term, because of the difficulty of significantly altering personality traits.

This research project also provides evidence that tobacco-using adolescents are lower on the trait of self-monitoring, suggesting a lack of flexibility or adaptability to changing communication demands.

Our data differ from the results of Sharp and Getz (1996), who found that although alcohol use was linked to impression management needs and self-monitoring, tobacco use was not. Our data suggest that adolescent tobacco users may be unaware of the perceptions others have of them, or if aware, are unable to modify their communication to produce positive outcomes. Nonusers, by comparison, are more aware of the image they are creating and apparently care more about the social appropriateness of that image. If interventions are to work, they may need to include components of communicative skills training to enhance the adolescents' capabilities. These adolescents may need to learn to recognize the communication that is necessary and then believe they can enact the behaviors in a given situation, achieving self-efficacy.

A limitation of this study is that the sample was within the Appalachian region. However, the general HLC findings are consistent with other studies both in the United States and abroad (e.g., Bennett, Moore, et al., 1997; Bundek et al., 1993; Eiser et al., 1989; Wallston et al., 1978). Further, our differences in HLC and self-monitoring were even found using the liberal definition of tobacco use that would include experimenters as well as more established smokers.

Of larger concern in this study is the low internal reliability of the HLC scales. These reliabilities are quite similar to those found by Bennett, Moore, et al. (1997) but lower than those found by Bundek et al. (1993) among elderly Hispanic women. However, it should be noted that in the latter study, in-home interviews were conducted with the respondents, and higher reliabilities than typically found for this measure were obtained using this method.

Nevertheless, the obtained internal reliabilities are lower than we would like. Such lower reliabilities may be due to the adolescent nature of this sample and their not fully formed ideas about their own health or, more likely, due to the fact that each HLC dimension contains only three items in this shortened version. Our results may suggest that the original, longer version would be preferable. That being said, low internal reliabilities of the locus of control dimensions should have weakened any results by increasing the error variance. Thus, the fact that we did obtain significant differences between tobacco-using and nonusing adolescents is notable.

The effect sizes for these research outcomes are gratifying. Effect sizes range from a low of .33 to a high of .93, indicating that the HLC and self-monitoring concepts are substantially linked with tobacco use status. This is especially important in light of the low scale reliabilities.

IMPLICATIONS

The prevention of adolescent tobacco uptake is the ultimate goal here. Although progress is being made in the form of Clean Air Acts and enforcement of laws banning the sale of tobacco to people under 18 years old, it is highly unlikely that tobacco itself will be outlawed. The option to smoke or not to smoke will remain with the individual. Thus, communication researchers need to address how to best influence adolescents not to become tobacco users.

The design of messages and intervention programs tailored to personality traits that have been identified as accompanying tobacco use may enhance their effectiveness (Booth-Kewley & Vickers, 1994). For example, Dillard, Plotnick, Godbold, Freimuth, and Edgar (1996) found that respondents who were higher on the personality trait of affective orientation responded more favorably to fear appeals. In the arena of tobacco use, however, little has been done to address focusing prevention messages on specific target groups. A recent study examined print and video tobacco prevention materials, finding that many materials were low involving, were not relevant to the intended audience, and often were written at a more advanced level than most readers could interpret (Booth-Butterfield, Meyer, Toborg, & Mande, 1998). There is a need to tailor messages and strategies to the intended target audience—in this instance, adolescents who tend to be external in their HLC and low on self-monitoring.

Such reasoning implies that negative appeals to changing one's image or adapting to social situations would be less productive when aimed at smoking teens. It also explains why positive image ads do have impact in attracting adolescents to smoke. They may feel that because they cannot achieve certain positively valenced impressions via their communicative skills, the use of tobacco can communicate for them.

Further, prevention messages centering around health problems, especially those with long-term consequences, are likely to have little impact (see also Norman & Bennett, 1996). If these adolescents have an external HLC, they may not believe they can avoid negative health outcomes on their own, despite hard facts to the contrary.

Therefore, to be most effective, it appears that tobacco prevention efforts will have to focus on immediate consequences and positive outcomes that high-risk adolescents actually believe they can achieve. Because of these adolescents' tendency to externalize causes of health behavior and their self-perception of an inability to monitor and adapt to situational demands, tobacco prevention efforts need to provide concrete, pragmatic support and communication guidance for these adolescents.

ACKNOWLEDGMENTS

This research project was supported by the Centers for Disease Control and Prevention Grant U48/ CCU310821.

REFERENCES

Bandura, A. (1991). Self-efficacy mechanism in physiological activation and health-promoting behavior. In J. Madden (Ed.), *Neurobiology of learning, emotion, and affect* (pp. 229–269). New York: Raven.

Beatty, M., McCroskey, J., & Heisel, A. (1998), Communication apprehension as temperamental expression: A communibiological paradigm. *Communication Monographs, 65,* 197–219).

Bennett, P., Moore, L., Norman, P., & Murphy, S. (1997). Health locus of control and value for health in smokers and nonsmokers. *Health Psychology, 16,* 179–182.

Bennett, P., Norman, P., Moore, L., Murphy, S., & Tudor-Smith, C. (1997). Health locus of control and value for health in smokers and nonsmokers. *Health Psychology, 16,* 179–182.

Biener, L., Aseltine, R., Cohen, B., & Anderka, M. (1998). Reactions of adult and teenage smokers to the Massachusetts tobacco tax. *American Journal of Public Health, 88,* 1389–1391.

Bleiker, V., van der Ploeg, H., Hendriks, J., & Ader, H.

(1996). Personality factors and breast cancer development: A prospective longitudinal study. *Journal of the National Cancer Institute, 88,* 1478–1482.

Booth-Butterfield, M., Meyer, M., Toborg, M., & Mande, M. (1998, November). *Content analysis of tobacco prevention materials in use in Appalachia.* Paper presented at the annual conference of the National Communication Association, New York.

Booth-Kewley, S., & Vickers, R. (1994). Associations between major domains of personality and health behavior. *Journal of Personality, 62,* 281–298.

Bundek, N., Marks., G., & Richardson, J. (1993). Role of health locus of control beliefs in cancer screening of elderly Hispanic women. *Health Psychology, 12,* 193–199.

Centers for Disease Control and Prevention. (1994). *Preventing tobacco use among young people: A report of the Surgeon General.* Atlanta, GA: USDHHS, Public Health Service, CDC, National Center for Chronic Disease Prevention & Health Promotion, Office of Smoking and Health.

Centers for Disease Control and Prevention. (1996). Youth risk behavior surveillance—United States, 1995. *Morbidity and Mortality Weekly Report Centers for Disease Control Surveillance Summary, 45.*

Chassin, L., Presson, C., Sherman, S., & Edwards, D. (1992). The natural history of cigarette smoking and young adult social roles. *Journal of Health and Social Behavior, 33,* 328–347.

Chorpita, B., & Barlow, D. (1998). The development of anxiety: The role of control in the early environment. *Psychological Bulletin, 124,* 3–21.

DiFranza, J., Savageau, J., & Aisquith, B. (1996). Youth access to tobacco: The effects of age, gender, vending machine locks, and "It's the Law" programs. *American Journal of Public Health, 86,* 221–224.

Dillard, J., Plotnick, C., Godbold, L., Freimuth, V., & Edgar, T. (1996). The multiple affective outcomes of AIDS PSAs: Fear appeals do more than scare people. *Communication Research, 23,* 44–72.

Eiser, J., Eiser, C., Gammage, P., & Morgan, M. (1989). Health locus of control and health beliefs in relation to adolescent smoking. *British Journal of Addiction, 84,* 1059–1065.

Emmons, K., Wechsler, H., Dowdall, G., & Abraham, M. (1998). Predictors of smoking among U.S. college students. *American Journal of Public Health, 88,* 104–107.

Flynn, B., Worden, J., & Secker-Walker, R. (1994). Mass media and school interventions for cigarette smoking prevention: Effects 2 years after completion. *American Journal of Public Health, 44,* 1148–1150.

Friedman, H., Tucker, J., Schwartz, J., Martin, L., Tomlinson-Keasey, C., Wingard, D., & Criqui, M. (1995). Childhood conscientiousness and longevity: Health behaviors and cause of death. *Journal of Personality and Social Psychology, 68,* 696–703.

Gabrenya, A., & Arkin, R. (1980). Factor structure and factor correlates of the Self-Monitoring scale. *Personality and Social Psychology Bulletin, 6,* 13–22.

Gilbert, D., & Gilbert, B. (1995). Personality, psychopathology, and nicotine response as mediators of the genetics of smoking. *Behavior Genetics, 25,* 131–147.

Greenland, K., Johnson, C., Webber, L., & Beronson, G. (1997). Cigarette smoking attitudes and first use among third- through sixth-grader students: The Bogalusa Heart Study, *American Journal of Public Health, 87,* 1345–1348.

Hu, T., Lin, Z., & Keeler, T. (1998), Teenage smoking, attempts to quit, and school performance. *American Journal of Public Health, 88,* 940–943.

Hunter, S., Croft, J., Vizelberg, I., & Berenson, G. (1987). Psychosocial influences on cigarette smoking among youth in a southern community: The Bogalusa Heart Study. *Morbidity and Mortality Weekly Report* (Suppl.), 17S–23S.

Jessor, R., Turbin, M., & Costa, F. (1998). Protective factors in adolescent health behavior. *Journal of Personality and Social Psychology, 75,* 788–800.

Lennox, R., & Wolfe, R. (1984). Revision of the self-monitoring scale. *Journal of Personality and Social Psychology, 46,* 1349–1364.

McCroskey, J., & Beatty, M. (1998). Communication apprehension. In J. McCroskey, J. Daly, M. Martin, & M. Beatty (Eds.), *Communication and personality: Trait perspectives* (pp. 215–231). Cresskill, NJ: Hampton.

Miller, G., & Stiff, J. (1993). *Deceptive communication.* Newbury Park, CA: Sage.

Morrison, K. (1997). Personality correlates of the 5-factor model for a sample of business owners/managers: Associations with scores on self-monitoring, Type A behavior, locus of control, and subjective well-being. *Psychology Reports, 80,* 255–272.

Newsom, J., Knapp, J., & Schulz, R. (1996). Longitudinal analysis of specific domains of internal control and depressive symptoms in patients with recurrent cancer. *Health Psychology, 15,* 323–331.

Norman, P., & Bennett, P. (1996). Health locus of control. In M. Conner & P. Norman (Eds.), *Predicting health behavior: Research and practice with social cognition models* (pp. 62–94). Buckingham, England: Open University Press.

Nutbeam, D., Mavaskil, P., Smith, C., Simpson, J., &

Catford, J. (1992). Evaluation of two school smoking educational programmes under normal classroom conditions. *British Medical Journal, 306,* 102–107.

O'Leary, A., Schoor, S., Long, K., & Holman, H. (1988). A cognitive-behavioral treatment for rheumatoid arthritis. *Health Psychology, 7,* 527–544.

Patton, G., Hibbert, M., Rosier, M., Carlin, J., Caust, J., & Bowes, G. (1996). *American Journal of Public Health, 86,* 225–230.

Rancer, A. (1998). Argumentativeness. In J. McCroskey, J. Daly, M. Martin, & M. Beatty (Eds.), *Communication and personality: Trait perspectives* (pp. 149–170). Cresskill, NJ: Hampton.

Sharp, M., & Getz, J. G. (1996). Substance use as impression management. *Personality and Social Psychology Bulletin, 22,* 60–67.

Snyder, M. (1974). Self-monitoring of expressive behavior. *Journal of Personality and Social Psychology, 30,* 526–537.

Snyder, M. (1979). Self monitoring processes. In L. Berkowitz (Ed.), *Advances in experimental social psychology* (Vol. 12, pp. 85–128). New York: Academic.

Spielberger, C., Foreyt, J., Reheiser, E., & Poston, W. (1998). Motivational, emotional and personality characteristics of smokeless tobacco users compared with cigarette smokers. *Personality and Individual Differences, 25,* 821–932.

Vartiainen, E., Paavola, M., McAlister, A., & Puska, P. (1998). Fifteen-year follow-up of smoking prevention effects in the North Karelia youth project. *American Journal of Public Health, 88,* 81–85.

Wallston, K., Wallston, B., & DeVeltis, R. (1978). Development of the multidimensional health locus of control (MHLOC) scales. *Health Education Monographs, 6,* 160–170.

West Virginia Department of Health and Human Resources, Bureau for Public Health, Office of Epidemiology and Health Promotion. (1995). *Health risks: The Appalachian lifestyle.* Charleston: West Virginia Department of Health and Human Services.

Wortman, C., Panciera, L., Shusterman, L., & Hibscher, J. (1976). Attributions of causality and reactions to uncontrollable outcomes. *Journal of Experimental and Social Psychology, 12,* 301–316.

ENDNOTES

1. We recognize that these selection procedures may result in a not fully representative sample of adolescent tobacco users (see also Jessor et al., 1998). For a variety of reasons, parents of tobacco-using students may be less likely to return parental forms, or

tobacco-using students may be less likely to complete the forms and take them home for signatures. However, this is the system of human participant protection within which we work, and we must realize that our sample may not include some of the most entrenched tobacco users.

2. This effect is actually stronger than indicated by this analysis because smokeless tobacco users were included and only boys reported using smokeless tobacco.

CRITICAL THINKING QUESTIONS

1. Read Endnote 1. Assuming that there may be differences between the individuals who did and did not agree to participate in the study, how might the latter group differ from the former group? What information might you use to bolster your speculation?

2. The article states that "one is tempted to speculate that external constraints, influences, and legislative efforts may be more cost-effective in preventing tobacco uptake, at least in the short term, because of the difficulty of significantly altering personality traits." Do you agree or disagree with this statement? Defend your position.

3. "There is a need to tailor messages and strategies to the intended target audience—in this instance, adolescents who tend to be external in their HCL (*health locus of control*) and low on self-monitoring." Using this quote from the article as a guide, design a specific campaign to curb teen smoking that focuses on locus of control and self-monitoring factors.

4. Do you think that the variables associated with adolescent smoking identified in the article are also associated with other health-related adolescent issues, such as underage drinking and illicit drug use? Why or why not?

5. What early life experiences may predispose someone to develop an external health locus of control and low self-monitoring tendencies? Could specific early intervention strategies minimize the likelihood of developing these tendencies? Explain your answers.

Chapter Six

PREJUDICE
AND DISCRIMINATION

PREJUDICE. THINK OF the implications of that word. It is so negative that even people who are highly prejudiced often are reluctant to use that term to describe themselves. Instead, prejudiced people may say that their opinions about members of certain groups are accurate and well founded, perhaps even that these groups deserve disdain.

Although the words *prejudice* and *discrimination* are often used interchangeably, they actually refer to two different things. *Prejudice* is an attitude, a set of beliefs about a member of a group based just on membership in that group. *Discrimination,* on the other hand, is a behavior, the differential treatment of a person based on membership in a particular group. You do not need to look far for the results of prejudiced attitudes and discriminatory behaviors: History is full of suffering that has been inflicted on people due solely to their membership in particular groups.

During the last several decades of the twentieth century, many great strides were made in the area of social justice. Overt discrimination against various groups was outlawed and, in many cases, was reduced significantly. Consider the overtly stated opinions of people that you hear from day to day. The amount of racism, for example, is less noticeable than it would have been only 20 or 30 years ago.

So, does this mean that the level of prejudiced thinking has, indeed, decreased over time? Not necessarily. It may be that people just *express* these prejudices more subtlety than they did in the past. In fact, prejudiced thinking may be rooted in how our minds process information. Article 16, "Where Bias Begins: The Truth about Stereotypes," examines how prejudicial thinking may be automatically activated, even in overtly unprejudiced persons.

Article 17, "Attitudes vs. Actions," deals with the consistency between people's attitudes and behaviors, or, more specifically, the consistency between prejudice and discrimination. Do we always act in accordance with our prejudiced attitudes? Or do we sometimes contradict what we say we believe? This classic article was one of the first to address the issue of whether prejudice and discrimination necessarily occur together.

Finally, Article 18 presents a recent theoretical explanation for prejudice in a unique context. While much prejudice is acquired from negative beliefs being passed on from one generation to the next (so-called old-fashioned racism), this article adds to that explanation another factor: namely, prejudice stemming from the perceived failure to live up to certain treasured and traditional cultural values. For example, some groups may be the target of prejudice because they supposedly do not demonstrate the same work ethic embraced by the majority. What is unique about this article is that the focus on the targets of prejudice is not on what usually is studied—racial, ethnic, or religious prejudice—but instead on another highly stigmatized group: fat people.

ARTICLE 16 _____

Just about anyone, by virtue of membership in a particular group, can be a target of prejudice and discrimination. The standard scenario is that a person is prejudged and reacted to not as an individual but as a member of some group, such that the presumed general characteristics of the group are automatically attributed to the individual. This process is known as *stereotyping*.

Stereotyping is an everyday fact of life. Although we may hope that we judge every person as an individual, the cognitive strategies we use to make sense of our would, as discussed in Chapter 3, suggest otherwise. In particular, when confronted with a member of an identifiable group, we may rely on a stereotype as a sort of decision-making shortcut, rather than consider the person on his or her own merits. How we feel about the person and how we treat him or her will be based on the stereotype, not the individual. As such, stereotypes frequently underlie prejudiced attitudes and discriminatory behaviors.

Are people less prejudiced today than in the past? In attempting to answer this question, it may be useful to distinguish between the various ways in which prejudice can be expressed. At one extreme are legalized forms of discrimination, such as the so-called Jim Crow laws of the past, which institutionalized discrimination against African Americans, and current laws that restrict women from combat roles in the U.S. military. At the other extreme are subtle types of differential treatment, such as how people are addressed and even how much eye contact they receive. While subtle, these types of behaviors may have a huge impact on the people against whom they are directed. Furthermore, while it is relatively easy to control what we say (e.g., not making racist remarks), it is much more difficult to control the nonverbal cues that may betray our underlying feelings (e.g., moving away from someone).

The following article by Annie Murphy Paul examines research indicating that the stereotypes underlying prejudice may operate automatically, which means they are not used only by people who are overtly bigoted. In fact, even people who do not consider themselves prejudiced and who may go to great lengths not to be biased may automatically activate these stereotypes when interacting with members of various groups. Doing so, in turn, may impact their treatment of sterotyped individuals, perhaps without their awareness.

Where Bias Begins
The Truth about Stereotypes

■ Annie Murphy Paul

Mahzarin Banaji doesn't fit anybody's idea of a racist. A psychology professor at Yale University, she studies stereotypes for a living. And as a woman and a member of a minority ethnic group, she has felt firsthand the sting of discrimination. Yet when she took one of her own tests of unconscious bias, "I showed very strong prejudice," she says. "It was truly a disconcerting experience." And an illuminating one. When Banaji was in graduate school in the early 1980s, theories about stereotypes were concerned only with their explicit expression: outright and unabashed racism, sexism, anti-Semitism. But in the years since, a new approach to stereotypes has shattered that simple notion. The bias Banaji and her colleagues are studying is something far more subtle, and more insidious: what's known as automatic or implicit stereotyping, which, they find, we do all the time without knowing it. Though out-and-out bigotry may be on the decline, says Banaji, "if anything, stereotyping is a bigger problem than we ever imagined."

Previously, researchers who studied stereotyping had simply asked people to record their feelings about minority groups and had used their answers as an index of their attitudes. Psychologists now understand that these conscious replies are only half the story. How progressive a person seems to be on the surface bears little or no relation to how prejudiced he or she is on an unconscious level—so that a bleeding-heart liberal might harbor just as many biases as a neo-Nazi skinhead.

As surprising as these findings are, they confirmed the hunches of many students of human behavior. "Twenty years ago, we hypothesized that there were people who said they were not prejudiced but who really did have unconscious negative stereotypes and beliefs," says psychologist Jack Dovidio, Ph.D., of Colgate University. "It was like theorizing about the existence of a virus, and then one day seeing it under a microscope."

The test that exposed Banaji's hidden biases—and that this writer took as well, with equally dismaying results—is typical of the ones used by automatic stereotype researchers. It presents the subject with a series of positive or negative adjectives, each paired with a characteristically "white" or "black" name. As the name and word appear together on a computer screen, the person taking the test presses a key, indicating whether the word is good or bad. Meanwhile, the computer records the speed of each response.

A glance at subjects' response times reveals a startling phenomenon: Most people who participate in the experiment—even some African-Americans—respond more quickly when a positive word is paired with a white name or a negative word with a black name. Because our minds are more accustomed to making these associations, says Banaji, they process them more rapidly. Though the words and names

aren't subliminal, they are presented so quickly that a subject's ability to make deliberate choices is diminished—allowing his or her underlying assumptions to show through. The same technique can be used to measure stereotypes about many different social groups, such as homosexuals, women, and the elderly.

THE UNCONSCIOUS COMES INTO FOCUS

From these tiny differences in reaction speed—a matter of a few hundred milliseconds—the study of automatic stereotyping was born. Its immediate ancestor was the cognitive revolution of the 1970s, an explosion of psychological research into the way people think. After decades dominated by the study of observable behavior, scientists wanted a closer look at the more mysterious operation of the human brain. And the development of computers—which enabled scientists to display information very quickly and to measure minute discrepancies in reaction time—permitted a peek into the unconscious.

At the same time, the study of cognition was also illuminating the nature of stereotypes themselves. Research done after World War II—mostly by European émigrés struggling to understand how the Holocaust had happened—concluded that stereotypes were used only by a particular type of person: rigid, repressed, authoritarian. Borrowing from the psychoanalytic perspective then in vogue, these theorists suggested that biased behavior emerged out of internal conflicts caused by inadequate parenting.

The cognitive approach refused to let the rest of us off the hook. It made the simple but profound point that we all use categories—of people, places, things—to make sense of the world around us. "Our ability to categorize and evaluate is an important part of human intelligence," says Banaji. "Without it, we couldn't survive." But stereotypes are too much of a good thing. In the course of stereotyping, a useful category—say, women—becomes freighted with additional associations, usually negative. "Stereotypes are categories that have gone too far," says John Bargh, Ph.D., of New York University. "When we use stereotypes, we take in the gender, the age, the color of the skin of the person before us, and our minds respond with messages that say hostile, stupid, slow, weak.

Those qualities aren't out there in the environment. They don't reflect reality."

Bargh thinks that stereotypes may emerge from what social psychologists call in-group/out-group dynamics. Humans, like other species, need to feel that they are part of a group, and as villages, clans, and other traditional groupings have broken down, our identities have attached themselves to more ambiguous classifications, such as race and class. We want to feel good about the group we belong to—and one way of doing so is to denigrate all those who aren't in it. And while we tend to see members of our own group as individuals, we view those in out-groups as an undifferentiated—stereotyped—mass. The categories we use have changed, but it seems that stereotyping itself is bred in the bone.

Though a small minority of scientists argues that stereotypes are usually accurate and can be relied upon without reservations, most disagree—and vehemently. "Even if there is a kernel of truth in the stereotype, you're still applying a generalization about a group to an individual, which is always incorrect," says Bargh. Accuracy aside, some believe that the use of stereotypes is simply unjust. "In a democratic society, people should be judged as individuals and not as members of a group," Banaji argues. "Stereotyping flies in the face of that ideal."

PREDISPOSED TO PREJUDICE

The problem, as Banaji's own research shows, is that people can't seem to help it. A recent experiment provides a good illustration. Banaji and her colleague, Anthony Greenwald, Ph.D., showed people a list of names—some famous, some not. The next day, the subjects returned to the lab and were shown a second list, which mixed names from the first list with new ones. Asked to identify which were famous, they picked out the Margaret Meads and the Miles Davises—but they also chose some of the names on the first list, which retained a lingering familiarity that they mistook for fame. (Psychologists call this the "famous overnight-effect.") By a margin of two-to-one, these suddenly "famous" people were male.

Participants weren't aware that they were preferring male names to female names, Banaji stresses. They were simply drawing on an unconscious stereo-

type of men as more important and influential than women. Something similar happened when she showed subjects a list of people who might be criminals: without knowing they were doing so, participants picked out an overwhelming number of African-American names. Banaji calls this kind of stereotyping *implicit,* because people know they are making a judgment—but just aren't aware of the basis upon which they are making it.

Even further below awareness is something that psychologists call automatic processing, in which stereotypes are triggered by the slightest interaction or encounter. An experiment conducted by Bargh required a group of white participants to perform a tedious computer task. While performing the task, some of the participants were subliminally exposed to pictures of African-Americans with neutral expressions. When the subjects were then asked to do the task over again, the ones who had been exposed to the faces reacted with more hostility to the request—because, Bargh believes, they were responding in kind to the hostility which is part of the African-American stereotype. Bargh calls this the "immediate hostile reaction," which he believes can have a real effect on race relations. When African-Americans accurately perceive the hostile expressions that their white counterparts are unaware of, they may respond with hostility of their own—thereby perpetuating the stereotype.

Of course, we aren't completely under the sway of our unconscious. Scientists think that the automatic activation of a stereotype is immediately followed by a conscious check on unacceptable thoughts—at least in people who think that they are not prejudiced. This internal censor successfully restrains overtly biased responses. But there's still the danger of leakage, which often shows up in non-verbal behavior: our expressions, our stance, how far away we stand, how much eye contact we make.

The gap between what we say and what we do can lead African-Americans and whites to come away with very different impressions of the same encounter, says Jack Dovidio. "If I'm a white person talking to an African-American, I'm probably monitoring my conscious beliefs very carefully and making sure everything I say agrees with all the positive things I want to express," he says. "And I usually believe I'm pretty successful because I hear the right words coming out of my mouth." The listener who is paying attention to non-verbal behavior, however, may be getting quite the opposite message. An African-American student of Dovidio's recently told him that when she was growing up, her mother had taught her to observe how white people moved to gauge their true feelings toward blacks. "Her mother was a very astute amateur psychologist—and about 20 years ahead of me," he remarks.

WHERE DOES BIAS BEGIN?

So where exactly do these stealth stereotypes come from? Though automatic-stereotype researchers often refer to the unconscious, they don't mean the Freudian notion of a seething mass of thoughts and desires, only some of which are deemed presentable enough to be admitted to the conscious mind. In fact, the cognitive model holds that information flows in exactly the opposite direction: connections made often enough in the conscious mind eventually become unconscious. Says Bargh: "If conscious choice and decision making are not needed, they go away. Ideas recede from consciousness into the unconscious over time."

Much of what enters our consciousness, of course, comes from the culture around us. And like the culture, it seems that our minds are split on the subjects of race, gender, class, sexual orientation. "We not only mirror the ambivalence we see in society, but also mirror it in precisely the same way," says Dovidio. Our society talks out loud about justice, equality, and egalitarianism, and most Americans accept these values as their own. At the same time, such equality exists only as an ideal, and that fact is not lost on our unconscious. Images of women as sex objects, footage of African-American criminals on the six o'clock news—"this is knowledge we cannot escape," explains Banaji. "We didn't choose to know it, but it still affects our behavior."

We learn the subtext of our culture's messages early. By five years of age, says Margo Monteith, Ph.D., many children have definite and entrenched stereotypes about blacks, women, and other social groups. Adds Monteith, professor of psychology at the University of Kentucky: "Children don't have a choice about accepting or rejecting these conceptions, since they're acquired well before they have the cogni-

tive abilities or experiences to form their own beliefs." And no matter how progressive the parents, they must compete with all the forces that would promote and perpetuate these stereotypes: peer pressure, mass media, the actual balance of power in society. In fact, prejudice may be as much a result as a cause of this imbalance. We create stereotypes—African-Americans are lazy, women are emotional—to explain why things are the way they are. As Dovidio notes, "Stereotypes don't have to be true to serve a purpose.

WHY CAN'T WE ALL GET ALONG?

The idea of unconscious bias does clear up some nettlesome contradictions. "It accounts for a lot of people's ambivalence toward others who are different, a lot of their inconsistencies in behavior," says Dovidio. "It helps explain how good people can do bad things." But it also prompts some uncomfortable realizations. Because our conscious and unconscious beliefs may be very different—and because behavior often follows the lead of the latter—"good intentions aren't enough," as John Bargh puts it. In fact, he believes that they count for very little. "I don't think free will exists," he says, bluntly—because what feels like the exercise of free will may be only the application of unconscious assumptions.

Not only may we be unable to control our biased responses, we may not even be aware that we have them. "We have to rely on our memories and our awareness of what we're doing to have a connection to reality," says Bargh. "But when it comes to automatic processing, those cues can be deceptive." Likewise, we can't always be sure how biased others are. "We all have this belief that the important thing about prejudice is the external expression of it," says Banaji. "That's going to be hard to give up."

One thing is certain: We can't claim that we've eradicated prejudice just because its outright expression has waned. What's more, the strategies that were so effective in reducing that sort of bias won't work on unconscious beliefs. "What this research is saying is that we are going to have to change dramatically the way we think we can influence people's behaviors," says Banaji. "It would be naive to think that exhortation is enough." Exhortation, education, political protest—all of these hammer away at our conscious beliefs while leaving the bedrock below untouched. Banaji notes, however, that one traditional remedy for discrimination—affirmative action—may still be effective since it bypasses our unconsciously compromised judgment.

But some stereotype researchers think that the solution to automatic stereotyping lies in the process itself. Through practice, they say, people can weaken the mental links that connect minorities to negative stereotypes and strengthen the ones that connect them to positive conscious beliefs. Margo Monteith explains how it might work. "Suppose you're at a party and someone tells a racist joke—and you laugh," she says. "Then you realize that you shouldn't have laughed at the joke. You feel guilty and become focused on your thought processes. Also, all sorts of cues become associated with laughing at the racist joke: the person who told the joke, the act of telling jokes, being at a party, drinking." The next time you encounter these cues, "a warning signal of sorts should go off—'wait, didn't you mess up in this situation before?'—and your responses will be slowed and executed with greater restraint."

That slight pause in the processing of a stereotype gives conscious, unprejudiced beliefs a chance to take over. With time, the tendency to prevent automatic stereotyping may itself become automatic. Monteith's research suggests that, given enough motivation, people may be able to teach themselves to inhibit prejudice so well that even their tests of implicit bias come clean.

The success of this process of "de-automatization" comes with a few caveats, however. First, even its proponents concede that it works only for people disturbed by the discrepancy between their conscious and unconscious beliefs, since unapologetic racists or sexists have no motivation to change. Second, some studies have shown that attempts to suppress stereotypes may actually cause them to return later, stronger than ever. And finally, the results that Monteith and other researchers have achieved in the laboratory may not stick in the real world, where people must struggle to maintain their commitment to equality under less-than-ideal conditions.

Challenging though that task might be, it is not as daunting as the alternative researchers suggest: changing society itself. Bargh, who likens de-automatization to closing the barn door once the horses have escaped, says that "it's clear that the way to get rid of stereotypes is by the roots, by where they come from in the first place." The study of culture may someday tell us where the seeds of prejudice originated; for now, the study of the unconscious shows us just how deeply they're planted.

CRITICAL THINKING QUESTIONS

1. What role does the media play in reinforcing, creating, or changing stereotypes? Give specific examples to bolster your premise.

2. Based on the information in this article, how would you answer someone who claims that he or she is not in the least bit prejudiced?

3. After reading this article, how optimistic or pessimistic are you that prejudice can be eliminated from society? Specifically, can people overcome stereotypical thinking? Give examples to support your position.

4. If you were a parent and wanted to minimize the formation of stereotypical thinking in your children, what would you do? Despite your good intentions, what might limit your ability to accomplish this? Explain your answers.

5. Based on your own observations, has the overall level of prejudice in the United States decreased over the years? Or has the level remained the same, but how and where prejudice is expressed have changed? Give examples to support your position.

6. Many studies on prejudice involve asking subjects about their attitudes toward particular groups. What do the findings of this article suggest about the validity of such self-reporting techniques? What may be a more accurate way of assessing prejudiced attitudes? Explain your proposal.

ARTICLE 17 _____

As mentioned in the introduction to this chapter, the terms *prejudice* and *discrimination* often are used interchangeably, but, in fact, they refer to two different concepts. Prejudice is an *attitude,* whereby a particular person is judged based solely on his or her membership in a particular group. Discrimination refers to the *behavior* of treating people differently based upon their membership in a group.

While the two terms do, indeed, refer to different things, do they occur together in the real world? It stands to reason that if you have negative beliefs about a particular group of people, then you would act in a negative fashion toward them. Or does it? Are we always consistent in our attitudes and behaviors?

Sometimes there is a strong consistency between what people say about their beliefs and how they act. For example, surveys are usually accurate in predicting outcomes of elections based upon asking people about their attitudes toward the candidates. In other cases, such consistency simply does not exist.

"Attitudes vs. Actions" is a classic work in the field that addresses the issue of attitude-behavior consistency. Before LaPiere's publication of this study in 1934, attitude research on prejudice involved asking respondents to give hypothetical responses to hypothetical situations (e.g., Would you serve a person of a given race at your restaurant?). LaPiere measured the number of times that a Chinese couple was actually refused lodging or food and then followed up with a questionnaire to the same establishments six months later, asking if they would serve Chinese persons. In doing so, LaPiere claimed to demonstrate the lack of consistency between what people say and what they actually do. Even though the study does have some methodological flaws, it is a good example of pioneering research in the field. It also provides an interesting microcosm of prejudice and discrimination issues that existed in the United States over a half-century ago.

Attitudes vs. Actions

■ Richard T. LaPiere

By definition, a social attitude is a behaviour pattern, anticipatory set or tendency, predisposition to specific adjustment to designated social situations, or, more simply, a conditioned response to social stimuli.[1] Terminological usage differs, but students who have concerned themselves with attitudes apparently agree that they are acquired out of social experience and provide the individual organism with some degree of preparation to adjust, in a well-defined way, to certain types of social situations if and when these situations arise. It would seem, therefore, that the totality of the social attitudes of a single individual would include all his socially acquired personality which is involved in the making of adjustments to other human beings.

But by derivation social attitudes are seldom more than a verbal response to a symbolic situation. For the conventional method of measuring social attitudes is to ask questions (usually in writing) which demand a verbal adjustment to an entirely symbolic situation. Because it is easy, cheap, and mechanical, the attitudinal questionnaire is rapidly becoming a major method of sociological and socio-psychological investigation.

Reprinted from *Social Forces,* Vol. 13, 1934. "Attitudes vs. Actions" by Richard T. LaPiere. Copyright © The University of North Carolina Press.

Note: Some of the language used and views presented are indicative of the time in which the article was written. The reader should consider the article in that context.

The technique is simple. Thus from a hundred or a thousand responses to the question "Would you get up to give an Armenian woman your seat in a street-car?" the investigator derives the "attitude" of non-Armenian males toward Armenian females. Now the question may be constructed with elaborate skill and hidden with consummate cunning in a maze of supplementary or even irrelevant questions yet all that has been obtained is a symbolic response to a symbolic situation. The words "Armenian woman" do not constitute an Armenian woman of flesh and blood, who might be tall or squat, fat or thin, old or young, well or poorly dressed—who might, in fact, be a goddess or just another old and dirty hag. And the questionnaire response, whether it be "yes" or "no," is but a verbal reaction and this does not involve rising from the seat or stolidly avoiding the hurt eyes of the hypothetical woman and the derogatory stares of other street-car occupants. Yet, ignoring these limitations, the diligent investigator will jump briskly from his factual evidence to the unwarranted conclusion that he has measured the "anticipatory behavior patterns" of non-Armenian males toward Armenian females encountered on street cars. Usually he does not stop here, but proceeds to deduce certain general conclusions regarding the social relationships between Armenians and non-Armenians. Most of us have applied the questionnaire technique with greater caution, but not I fear with any greater certainty of success.

Some years ago I endeavored to obtain comparative data on the degree of French and English antipathy towards dark-skinned peoples.[2] The informal questionnaire technique was used, but, although the responses so obtained were exceedingly consistent, I supplemented them with what I then considered an index to overt behavior. The hypothesis as then stated *seemed* entirely logical. "Whatever our attitude on the validity of 'verbalization' may be, it must be recognized that any study of attitudes through direct questioning is open to serious objection, both because of the limitations of the sampling method and because in classifying attitudes the inaccuracy of human judgment is an inevitable variable. In this study, however, there is corroborating evidence on these attitudes in the policies adopted by hotel proprietors. Nothing could be used as a more accurate index of color prejudice than the admission or non-admission of colored people to hotels. For the proprietor must reflect the group attitude in his policy regardless of his own feelings in the matter. Since he determines what the group attitude is towards Negroes through the expression of that attitude in overt behavior and over a long period of actual experience, the results will be exceptionally free from those disturbing factors which inevitably affect the effort to study attitudes by direct questioning."

But at that time I overlooked the fact that what I was obtaining from the hotel proprietors was still a "verbalized" reaction to a symbolic situation. The response to a Negro's request for lodgings might have been an excellent index of the attitude of hotel patrons towards living in the same hotel as a Negro. Yet to ask the proprietor "Do you permit members of the Negro race to stay here?" does not, it appears, measure his potential response to an actual Negro.

All measurement of attitudes by the questionnaire technique proceeds on the assumption that there is a mechanical relationship between symbolic and non-symbolic behavior. It is simple enough to prove that there is no *necessary* correlation between speech and action, between response to words and to the realities they symbolize. A parrot can be taught to swear, a child to sing "Frankie and Johnny" in the Mae West manner. The words will have no meaning to either child or parrot. But to prove that there is no *necessary* relationship does not prove that such a relationship may not exist. There need be no relationship between what the hotel proprietor says he will do and what he actually does when confronted with a colored patron. Yet there may be. Certainly we are justified in assuming that the verbal response of the hotel proprietor would be more likely to indicate what he would actually do than would the verbal response of people whose personal feelings are less subordinated to economic expediency. However, the following study indicates that the reliability of even such responses is very small indeed.

Beginning in 1930 and continuing for two years thereafter, I had the good fortune to travel rather extensively with a young Chinese student and his wife.[3] Both were personable, charming, and quick to win the admiration and respect of those they had the opportunity to become intimate with. But they were foreign-born Chinese, a fact that could not be disguised. Knowing the general "attitude" of Americans towards the Chinese as indicated by the "social distance" studies which have been made, it was with considerable trepidation that I first approached a hotel clerk in their company. Perhaps the clerk's eyebrows lifted slightly, but he accommodated us without a show of hesitation. And this in the "best" hotel in a small town noted for its narrow and bigoted "attitude" towards Orientals. Two months later I passed that way again, phoned the hotel and asked if they would accommodate "an important Chinese gentleman." The reply was an unequivocal "No." That aroused my curiosity and led to this study.

In something like ten thousand miles of motor travel, twice across the United States, up and down the Pacific Coast, we met definite rejection from those asked to serve us just once. We were received at 66 hotels, auto camps, and "Tourist Homes," refused at one. We were served in 184 restaurants and cafes scattered throughout the country and treated with what I judged to be more than ordinary consideration in 72 of them. Accurate and detailed records were kept of all these instances. An effort, necessarily subjective, was made to evaluate the overt response of hotel clerks, bell boys, elevator operators, and waitresses to the presence of my Chinese friends. The factors entering into the situations were varied as far and as often as possible. Control was not, of course, as exacting as that required by laboratory experimentation. But it was as rigid as is humanly possible in human situations. For example, I did not take the "test" subjects into my confidence fearing that their behavior might become self-conscious and thus abnormally affect the response of others towards them. Whenever possible I let my Chinese friend negotiate for accommodations (while I concerned myself with the car or luggage) or sent them into a restaurant ahead of me. In this way I attempted to "factor" myself out. We sometimes patronized high-class establishments after a hard and dusty day on the road and stopped at inferior auto camps when in our most presentable condition.

In the end I was forced to conclude that those factors which most influenced the behavior of others towards the Chinese had nothing at all to do with race. Quality and condition of clothing, appearance of baggage (by which, it seems, hotel clerks are prone to base their quick evaluations), cleanliness and neatness were far more significant for person to person reaction in the situations I was studying than skin pigmentation, straight black hair, slanting eyes, and flat noses. And yet an air of self-confidence might entirely offset the "unfavorable" impression made by dusty clothes and the usual disorder to appearance consequent upon some hundred miles of motor travel. A supercilious desk clerk in a hotel of noble aspirations could not refuse his master's hospitality to people who appeared to take their request as a perfectly normal and conventional thing, though they might look like tin-can tourists and two of them belong to the racial category "Oriental." On the other hand, I became rather adept at approaching hotel clerks with that peculiar crab-wise manner which is so effective in provoking a somewhat scornful disregard. And then a bland smile would serve to reverse the entire situation. Indeed, it appeared that a genial smile was the most effective password to acceptance. My Chinese friends were skillful smilers, which may account, in part, for the fact that we received but one rebuff in all our experience. Finally, I was impressed with the fact that even where some tension developed due to the strangeness for the Chinese it would evaporate immediately when they spoke in unaccented English.

The one instance in which we were refused accommodations is worth recording here. The place was a small California town, a rather inferior auto-camp into which we drove in a very dilapidated car plied with camp equipment. It was early evening, the light so dim that the proprietor found it somewhat difficult to decide the genus *voyageur* to which we belonged. I left the car and spoke to him. He hesitated, wavered, said he was not sure that he had two cabins, meanwhile edging towards our car. The realization that the two occupants were Orientals turned the balance or, more likely, gave him the excuse he was looking for. "No," he said, "I don't take Japs!" In a more pretentious establishment we secured accommodations, and with an extra flourish of hospitality.

To offset this one flat refusal were the many instances in which the physical peculiarities of the Chinese served to heighten curiosity. With few exceptions this curiosity was considerately hidden behind an exceptional interest in serving us. Of course, outside of the Pacific Coast region, New York, and Chicago, the

Chinese physiognomy attracts attention. It is different, hence noticeable. But the principal effect this curiosity has upon the behavior of those who cater to the traveler's needs is to make them more attentive, more responsive, more reliable. A Chinese companion is to be recommended to the white traveling in his native land. Strange features when combined with "human" speech and action seems, at times, to heighten sympathetic response, perhaps on the same principle that makes us uncommonly sympathetic toward the dog that has a "human" expression in his face.

What I am trying to say is that in only one out of 251 instances in which we purchased goods or services necessitating intimate human relationships did the fact that my companions were Chinese adversely affect us. Factors entirely unassociated with race were, in the main, the determinant of significant variations in our reception. It would appear reasonable to conclude that the "attitude" of the American people, as reflected in the behavior of those who are for pecuniary reasons presumably most sensitive to the antipathies of their white clientele, is anything but negative towards the Chinese. In terms of "social distance" we might conclude that native Caucasians are not averse to residing in the same hotels, auto-camps, and "Tourist Homes" as Chinese and will with complacency accept the presence of Chinese at an adjoining table in restaurant or cafe. It does not follow that there is revealed a distinctly "positive" attitude towards the Chinese, that whites prefer the Chinese to other whites. But the facts as gathered certainly preclude the conclusion that there is an intense prejudice towards the Chinese.

Yet the existence of this prejudice, very intense, is proven by a conventional "attitude" study. To provide a comparison of symbolic reaction to symbolic social situations with actual reaction to real social situations, I "questionnaired" the establishments which we patronized during the two year period. Six months were permitted to lapse between the time I obtained the overt reaction and the symbolic. It was hoped that the effects of the actual experience with Chinese guests, adverse or otherwise, would have faded during the intervening time. To the hotel or restaurant a questionnaire was mailed with an accompanying letter purporting to be a special and personal plea for re-

sponse. The questionnaires all asked the same question, "Will you accept members of the Chinese race as guests in your establishment?" Two types of questionnaire were used. In one this question was inserted among similar queries concerning Germans, French, Japanese, Russians, Armenians, Jews, Negroes, Italians, and Indians. In the other the pertinent question was unencumbered. With persistence, completed replies were obtained from 128 of the establishments we had visited; 81 restaurants and cafes and 47 hotels, auto-camps, and "Tourist Homes." In response to the relevant question 92 per cent of the former and 91 per cent of the latter replied "No." The remainder replied "Uncertain; depend upon circumstances." From the woman proprietor of a small auto-camp I received the only "Yes," accompanied by a chatty letter describing the nice visit she had had with a Chinese gentleman and his sweet wife during the previous summer.

A rather unflattering interpretation might be put upon the fact that those establishments who had provided for our needs so graciously were, some months later, verbally antagonistic towards hypothetical Chinese. To factor this experience out responses were secured from 32 hotels and 96 restaurants located in approximately the same regions, but uninfluenced by this particular experience with Oriental clients. In this, as in the former case, both types of questionnaires were used. The results indicate that neither the type of questionnaire nor the fact of previous experience had important bearing upon the symbolic response to symbolic social situations.

It is impossible to make direct comparison between the reactions secured through questionnaires and from actual experience. On the basis of the above data it would appear foolhardy for a Chinese to attempt to travel in the United States. And yet, as I have shown, actual experience indicates that the American people, as represented by the personnel of hotels, restaurants, etc., are not at all averse to fraternizing with Chinese within the limitations which apply to social relationships between Americans themselves. The evaluations which follow are undoubtedly subject to the criticism which any human judgment must withstand. But the fact is that, although they began their travels in this country with considerable trepidations, my Chinese friends soon lost all fear that they might receive a rebuff. At first somewhat timid and

**TABLE 1 / Distribution of Results from Questionnaire Study of Establishment "Policy"
Regarding Acceptance of Chinese as Guests**
  Replies are to the question: "Will you accept members of the Chinese race as guests
in your establishment?"

	Hotels, Etc. Visited		Hotels, Etc. Not Visited		Restaurants, Etc. Visited		Restaurants, Etc. Not Visited	
Total	47		32		81		96	
	1*	2*	1	2	1	2	1	2
Number replying	22	25	20	12	43	38	51	45
No	20	23	19	11	40	35	37	41
Undecided: depend upon circumstances	1	2	1	1	3	3	4	3
Yes	1	0	0	0	0	0	0	1

*Column (1) indicates in each case those responses to questionnaires which concerned Chinese only. The figures in
column (2) are from the questionnaires in which the above was inserted among questions regarding Germans, French,
Japanese, etc.

considerably dependent upon me for guidance and support, they came in time to feel fully self-reliant and would approach new social situations without the slightest hesitation.

The conventional questionnaire undoubtedly has significant value for the measurement of "political attitudes." The presidential polls conducted by the *Literary Digest* have proven that. But a "political attitude" is exactly what the questionnaire can be justly held to measure; a verbal response to a symbolic situation. Few citizens are ever faced with the necessity of adjusting themselves to the presence of the political leaders whom, periodically, they must vote for—or against. Especially is this true with regard to the president, and it is in relation to political attitudes towards presidential candidates that we have our best evidence. But while the questionnaire may indicate what the voter will do when he goes to vote, it does not and cannot reveal what he will do when he meets Candidate Jones on the street, in his office, at his club, on the golf course, or wherever two men may meet and adjust in some way one to the other.

The questionnaire is probably our only means of determining "religious attitudes." An honest answer to the question "Do you believe in God?" reveals all there is to be measured. "God" is a symbol; "belief" a verbal expression. So here, too, the questionnaire is efficacious. But if we would know the emotional responsiveness of a person to the spoken or written word "God" some other method of investigation must be used. And if we would know the extent to which that responsiveness restrains his behavior it is to his behavior that we must look, not to his questionnaire response. Ethical precepts are, I judge, something more than verbal professions. There would seem little to be gained from asking a man if his religious faith prevents him from committing sin. Of course it does—on paper. But "moral attitudes" must have a significance in the adjustment to actual situations or they are not worth the studying. Sitting at my desk in California I can predict with a high degree of certainty what an "average" business man in an average Mid-Western city will reply to the question "Would you engage in sexual intercourse with a prostitute in a Paris brothel?" Yet no one, least of all the man himself, can predict what he would actually do should he by some misfortune find himself face to face with the situation in question. His moral "attitudes" are no doubt already stamped into his personality. But just what those habits are which will be invoked to provide him with some sort of adjustment to this situation is quite indeterminate.

TABLE 2 / Distribution of Results Obtained from Actual Experience in the Situation Symbolized in the Questionnaire Study

Conditions	Hotels, Etc.		Restaurants, Etc.	
	Accompanied by investigator	Chinese not so accompanied at inception of situation*	Accompanied by investigator	Chinese not so accompanied at inception of situation
Total	*55*	*12*	*165*	*19*
Reception very much better than investigator would expect to have received had he been alone, but under otherwise similar circumstances	6	19	63	9
Reception different only to extent of heightened curiosity, such as investigator might have incurred were he alone but dressed in manner unconventional to region yet not incongruous	3	22	76	6
Reception "normal"	2	9	21	3
Reception perceptibly hesitant and not to be explained on other than "racial" grounds	1	3	4	1
Reception definitely, though temporarily, embarrassing	0	1	1	0
Not accepted	0	1	0	0

*When the investigator was not present at the inception of the situation the judgments were based upon what transpired after he joined the Chinese. Since intimately acquainted with them it is probable that errors in judgment were no more frequent under these conditions than when he was able to witness the inception as well as results of the situation.

It is highly probable that when the "Southern Gentleman" says he will not permit Negroes to reside in his neighborhood we have a verbal response to a symbolic situation which reflects the "attitudes" which would become operative in an actual situation. But there is no need to ask such a question of the true "Southern Gentleman." We knew it all the time. I am inclined to think that in most instances where the questionnaire does reveal non-symbolic attitudes the case is much the same. It is only when we cannot easily observe what people do in certain types of situations that the questionnaire is resorted to. But it is just here that the danger in the questionnaire technique arises. If Mr. A adjusts himself to Mr. B in a specified way we can deduce from his behavior that he has a certain "attitude" towards Mr. B and, perhaps, all of Mr. B's class. But if no such overt adjustment is made it is impossible to discover what A's adjustment would be should the situation arise. A questionnaire will reveal what Mr. A writes or says when confronted with a certain combination of words. But not what he will do when he meets Mr. B. Mr. B is a great deal more than a series of words. He is a man and he acts. His action is not necessarily what Mr. A "imagines" it will be when he reacts verbally to the symbol "Mr. B."

No doubt a considerable part of the data which the social scientist deals with can be obtained by the questionnaire method. The census reports are based upon verbal questionnaires and I do not doubt their basic integrity. If we wish to know how many children a man has, his income, the size of his home, his age, and the condition of his parents, we can reasonably ask him. These things he has frequently and conventionally converted into verbal responses. He is competent to report upon them, and will do so accurately, unless indeed he wishes to do otherwise. A careful investigator could no doubt even find out by verbal means whether the man fights with his wife (frequently, infrequently, or not at all), though the neighbors would be a more reliable source. But we should not expect to obtain by the questionnaire method his "anticipatory set or tendency" to action should his wife pack up and go home to Mother, should Elder Son get into trouble with the neighbor's daughter, the President assume the status of a dictator, the Japanese take over the rest of China, or a Chinese gentleman come to pay a social call.

Only a verbal reaction to an entirely symbolic situation can be secured by the questionnaire. It may indicate what the responder would actually do when confronted with the situation symbolized in the question, but there is no assurance that it will. And so to call the response a reflection of a "social attitude" is to entirely disregard the definition commonly given for the phrase "attitude." If social attitudes are to be conceptualized as partially integrated habit sets which will become operative under specific circumstances and lead to a particular pattern of adjustment they must, in the main, be derived from a study of humans behaving in actual social situations. They must not be imputed on the basis of questionnaire data.

The questionnaire is cheap, easy, and mechanical. The study of human behavior is time consuming, intellectually fatiguing, and depends for its success upon the ability of the investigator. The former method gives quantitative results, the latter mainly qualitative. Quantitative measurements arc quantitatively accurate; qualitative evaluations are always subject to the errors of human judgment. Yet it would seem far more worth while to make a shrewd guess regarding that which is essential than to accurately measure that which is likely to prove quite irrelevant.

NOTES

1. See Daniel D. Droba, "Topical Summaries of Current Literature," *The American Journal of Sociology,* 1934, p. 513.

2. "Race Prejudice: France and England," *Social Forces,* September 1928, pp. 102–111.

3. The results of this study have been withheld until the present time out of consideration for their feelings.

CRITICAL THINKING QUESTIONS

1. A central thesis of the LaPiere article was that the method of directly asking people about their attitudes has certain limitations in terms of accuracy and consistency. What are these limitations? How could they be overcome, other than in the ways suggested by the author?

2. LaPiere maintained that there is little consistency between responses to attitude surveys and actual behavior. If that is the case, then what is the value (if any) of the multitude of attitude surveys that are regularly administered in the United States? Support your position.

3. Did the study involve any ethical issues? For example, what do you think about the fact that the author did not tell his Chinese friends that they were part of a study he was conducting? Are there any other ethical considerations? Explain your answers.

4. The article ended by making a distinction between *quantitative results,* such as those obtained by questionnaires, and *qualitative results,* such as those obtained by the author in his visits to the establishments. LaPiere obviously favors qualitative methods, arguing that although they are prone to errors of human judgment, such methods are preferred because it is better to "make a shrewd guess regarding what is essential than to accurately measure that which is likely quite irrelevant." Are the results of attitude questionnaires "likely quite irrelevant"? Why or why not?

5. If you were to conduct the study, what methodological improvements would you make to reduce the subjectivity of the measures?

6. A major conclusion of the study was that responses to hypothetical questions do not necessarily predict actual behavior. Is this evidence for a lack of consistency between attitudes and behavior? In answering this, think of the specific methodology that was employed. Was there anything wrong with it, given the conclusions that were drawn? What methodology could be used to more directly assess the consistency between attitudes and behavior? Explain your answers.

7. LaPiere made the observation that factors such as clothing, cleanliness, and smiles were more important in determining whether the couple was served than was skin color. Design a study that would experimentally test this observation.

ADDITIONAL RELATED READINGS

Brewer, M. B. (1999). The psychology of prejudice: Ingroup love or outgroup hate? *Journal of Social Issues, 55*(3), 429–444.

Fiske, S. T. (2000). Stereotyping, prejudice, and discrimination at the seam between the centuries: Evolution, culture, mind, and brain. *European Journal of Social Psychology, 30*(3), 299–322.

ARTICLE 18 _____

Why are people prejudiced? Any social psychology text will list a number of reasons that account for prejudiced attitudes and discriminatory behaviors. For example, social learning approaches will focus on the attitudes a person learns in his or her environment, particularly at home, to account for prejudice. The realistic group conflict approach will focus on the competition between groups for scarce resources as a cause of prejudice. Yet other approaches will try to identify a personality type that might be related to prejudice—for instance, the authoritarian personality.

A recent theoretical explanation for racial prejudice focuses on something known as *symbolic racism*. According to this approach, racial prejudice is a combination of old-fashioned racism (i.e., negative beliefs passed down from one generation to the next) and the belief that the target of the prejudice does not live up to traditional, and treasured, cultural values. An example of the latter might be the perceived failure of a certain group to live up to the Protestant work ethic, which stresses hard work, self-reliance, and self-discipline. The individuals within this group are held personally responsible for not living up to these standards.

Although the vast majority of research on prejudice has focused on racial and ethnic prejudice, other studies have investigated whether the same processes involved in racial prejudice, for example, also operate in prejudice against other stigmatized groups. The following article by Christian S. Crandall, Silvana D'Anello, Nuray Sakalli, Eleana Lazarus, Grazyna Wieczorkowska, and N. T. Feather examines prejudice against fat people in several nations. The authors propose and test an *Attribution-Value model of prejudice,* which maintains that people develop prejudice toward groups who have some negative characteristics for which they are held personally responsible. Moreover, what are considered negative characteristics vary from one culture to another, as does the tendency to hold people personally responsible for such characteristics. Although this article focuses specifically on prejudice toward fat people, the model presented may be applicable to various types of prejudice in different cultures.

An Attribution-Value Model of Prejudice
Anti-Fat Attitudes in Six Nations

■ Christian S. Crandall, Silvana D'Anello, Nuray Sakalli, Eleana Lazarus,
Grazyna Wieczorkowska, and N. T. Feather

The authors propose an Attribution-Value model of prejudice, which hypothesizes that people are prejudiced against groups that they feel have some negative attribute for which they are held responsible. The structure of prejudice against fat people was compared in six nations: Australia, India, Poland, Turkey, the United States of America, and Venezuela. Both a negative cultural value for fatness and a tendency to hold people responsible predicts anti-fat prejudice. Most important, a multiplicative hypothesis was supported—people with both a negative value for fatness and a tendency to hold people responsible were more anti-fat than could be predicted from cultural value and attributions alone. These effects were more pronounced in individualist cultures. The

Reprinted from C. S. Crandall et al., *Personality and Social Psychology Bulletin, 27*(1), pp. 30–37, copyright © 2001 by Sage Publications, Ltd. Reprinted by permission of Sage Publications, Inc.

authors develop the Attribution-Value model of prejudice that can apply to prejudice of many sorts across many cultures.

Antipathy toward outgroups is common across cultures, time, languages, and national boundaries. No culture, race, ethnic group, or gender has a monopoly on prejudice, and much can be learned about prejudice from studying processes not limited by culture or social group.

The majority of research in American psychology on prejudice has focused on race (the anti-Black affect of Whites) and gender (attitudes toward women). This research has been fruitful but the trend toward studying prejudice toward other groups (homosexuals, physical illess, regional groups) has the salutory effect of broadening our conceptions of prejudice and gaining perspective on aspects of prejudice that may be idiosyncratic to a group, time, or culture.

The manner in which prejudice appears at any given time or place can differ widely. To investigate the factors that lead to prejudice, we study the beliefs, values, and geography of one particular prejudice—prejudice against fat people. A theme of research on anti-fat antipathy is that beliefs about the social world promote prejudice (Crandall, 1994). One reliable finding is that the attribution of controllability for fatness leads to rejection (Weiner, Perry, & Magnusson, 1988). Our research suggests that an individual's beliefs about the controllability of fatness are linked to other more fundamental beliefs about the nature of the social world—what we have called a social ideology. Crandall (1994) found that anti-fat prejudice was closely linked to belief in the just world, political conservatism, authoritarianism, belief in the Protestant Ethic, and the belief that poverty is controllable. Crandall and Biernat (1990) found that anti-fat prejudice was correlated with authoritarianism, politics, racism, and support for capital punishment and traditional marriages.

Thus, we argue that attributions of controllability stem from underlying beliefs about causality in the physical and social world and are intricately related to social ideologies. A person who believes that people get what they deserve, and have acted in such a way as to cause what they get, should be treated in accordance with the value of their outcome (Lerner, 1980).

People with successes should be treated as heroes and people with negative characteristics such as fatness should be punished, avoided, and stigmatized—in short, they deserve anger and prejudice (Feather, 1996). This pattern of belief has broad implications for how we behave toward others (see also Feather, 1985; Skitka & Tetlock, 1993; Zucker & Weiner, 1993).

A GENERAL MODEL OF PREJUDICE

We propose a simple model of prejudice that is likely to have broad applicability to feelings of prejudice toward many groups. This model comes from the perspective gained from research on anti-fat prejudice. We suggest that a significant amount of the affective component of attitudes and prejudice toward groups is based on two interrelated factors: attributions of controllability and cultural value.

A significant portion of prejudice is based on attributions for the stereotypical attributes of the groups. Although one may hold fat people responsible for their weight, it is difficult to imagine that prejudice comes from blaming African Americans for their skin color or anyone for their gender. Instead, we hypothesize that this prejudice derives from holding group members responsible for negative stereotypic behaviors, such as believing that Hispanic Americans are responsible for their relative unemployment, American Southerners responsible for the American history of slavery, and so on. Judging individuals responsible for their stereotypic attributes can lead to prejudice against them.

Because prejudice is conceptualized as negative affect directed toward members of a social group, prejudice does not come from holding members responsible for all of the stereotype, only the negative attributes. The second factor of prejudice is a negative cultural value for an attribute that characterizes the social group. For prejudice to develop, members of a group must be believed to have some important negative characteristic, such as a physical handicap, aggression, low intelligence, laziness, and so on. It is only necessary that the group stereotypically has some important negative characteristic to qualify for prejudicial rejection from social life; all members need not exactly fit this stereotype. Individuals are excused from prejudice individually.

CROSS-CULTURAL APPROACHES TO ATTRIBUTION

Individualism and Collectivism   Previous research on both attributions and values suggests that the structure and function of the model might be very different across cultures. One important dimension of culture is individualism/collectivism (Triandis, 1996); a wide variety of studies have shown that social psychological processes can operate differently in countries that differ on this dimension (Hofstede, 1980; Markus & Kitayama, 1991; Triandis et al., 1993). Triandis (1994) defines individualism as

> *a social pattern that consists of loosely-linked individuals who view themselves as independent of collectives; are primarily motivated by their own preferences, needs, rights, and the contracts that they have established with others; give priority to their personal goals over the goals of others; and emphasize rational analyses of the advantages and disadvantages to associating with others. (p. 2)*

By contrast, collectivism is

> *a social pattern consisting of closely linked individuals who see themselves as part of one or more collectives (family, co-workers, tribe, nation); are primarily motivated by the norms of and duties imposed by these collectives; are willing to give priority to the goals of these collectives over their own personal goals; and emphasize their connectedness to members of these collectives. (Triandis, 1994, p. 2)*

Culture, Attributions, and Prejudice   In an initial test of the Attribution-Value model of prejudice, Crandall and Martinez (1996) compared attributions and anti-fat prejudice in the United States (quite high in individualism) and Mexico (quite low in individualism). In the United States, attributions were a key factor in the rejection of fat people, and attributions and prejudice were closely connected to a range of ideological beliefs about justice, politics, and poverty. In Mexico, attributions were not closely connected to prejudice or ideology. A sociocultural context of individualism may be a necessary condition for responsi-

bility and its ideological counterparts to play a role in prejudice. As predicted, Mexicans reported less anti-fat prejudice than did Americans. However, Crandall and Martinez (1996) were not able to test the Attribution-Value model because the groups differed in both attributions and cultural value. Attributions of control were not only lower in Mexico but also were less relevant to prejudice. In addition, the negative cultural value of fatness was significantly greater in the United States than in Mexico.

ANTI-FAT PREJUDICE IN SIX NATIONS

This article represents a test of a hypothesis put forward in Crandall (1994) and Crandall and Martinez (1996). We suggest that prejudice of many sorts is dependent on two factors: attributions of responsibility and a negative cultural value for some important stereotypical trait. To feel the affective punch of prejudice toward a group member, the perceiver must find something objectionable about the group and its members and they must hold the group and its members responsible for this objectionable state of affairs.

In the current study, we begin to test the Attribution-Value model of prejudice by applying it to anti-fat prejudice. We measured ideology, attributions, a negative cultural value for fatness, and anti-fat prejudice in Australia, India, Poland, Turkey, the United States, and Venezuela. In measuring a wide range of countries, we hope to find respondents who range from negative through neutral to positive values for corpulence and from low to high in attributions of controllability for fatness. The sample of countries in this study included three that rank low in individualism in Hofstede's (1980) analysis of 50 nations—India (21st), Turkey (28th), and Venezuela (50th)—and two that rank high—the United States (1st) and Australia (2nd). Poland was not included in Hofstede's research but we relied on other sources, including Triandis et al. (1993), which suggests that Poland is more similar to the United States than any other country in their analysis; we classified Poland as an individualist country.

Hypothesis 1: We predict that, across all samples, (a) attributions of controllability and (b) a negative value toward fatness will separately predict anti-fat prejudice.

Hypothesis 2: The simultaneous presence of an attribution of control and negative cultural value (represented by a multiplicative interaction of negative value and attribution) will predict anti-fat prejudice, over and above the additive effect of value and control.

Hypothesis 3: If individualism moderates the power of person attributions and their connection to responsibility and blame, then we can expect the Attribution × Value term to be a more powerful predictor in the individualist than the collectivist countries.

METHOD

Participants

Participants were 970 (538 women and 432 men) respondents from six nations. An English questionnaire was used in Australia, the United States, and India; translations were used in Poland, Venezuela, and Turkey. We followed the methods for translation and back-translation outlined in Lonner and Berry (1986), excepting Poland, where time constraints interfered. A subsequent back-translation in the United States supported the Polish translation's accuracy.

Nearly all participants were students. From Australia, the sample was 171 undergraduates from a psychology class at Flinders University. From India, the sample included 188 English-speaking participants from southern India, composed of 47 high school students, 80 technical college students, 30 university students, and 31 participants who were family and friends of the student participants. From Poland, the sample included 202 university undergraduates from the University of Warsaw. From Turkey, the sample was 200 undergraduates from the University of Ankara. From the United States, the sample of 111 included 58 students from a psychology class at the University of Kansas and 53 shoppers at a retail factory outlet mall. From Venezuela, the sample included 98 students from the University of the Andes and the Polytechnic University of Barquisimeto. (All statistical analyses were performed looking for

subsample variation; subsample effects did not substantially affect any hypothesis test.)

Questionnaire

The questionnaire had four basic sections: anti-fat prejudice, cultural value of fatness, attributions of controllability, and demographics. Anti-fat prejudice was measured by the Anti-Fat Attitudes scale (AFA) (Crandall, 1994). This instrument has 13 items (scales 0 to 9 on Likert-type response scales), comprising three subscales: Dislike measures prejudice against fat people (e.g., "I really don't like fat people much"), Willpower measures judgments of responsibility for being fat (e.g., "Some people are fat because they have no willpower"), and Fear of Fat measures personal concern with weight (e.g., "I worry about becoming fat"). Reliability and validity data for these scales are presented in Crandall (1994), and their cross-cultural value has been demonstrated in Crandall and Martinez (1996). The Dislike scale is the primary measure of anti-fat prejudice in this research; across all samples, $\alpha = .81$.

The cultural value of fat was measured by a series of seven items developed expressly for this questionnaire. Each item was rated on a 0 to 9 Likert scale, $\alpha = .71$; examples include the following: "In our culture, being fat is considered a bad thing" and "In our culture, being thin is an important part of being attractive." Higher scores correspond with a more negative value for fatness. Attributions were measured both with the three-item Willpower scale ($\alpha = .66$) and five items that measured people's tendency to make controllable attributions, adapted from previous research (Control, see Crandall & Martinez, 1996). Questions about poverty, grades, welfare, AIDS, and wealth were answered on a 1 to 7 semantic differential; an example of these items is "To what extent do you believe that poverty is caused by factors that poor people can control or factors outside of poor people's control?" The ends of the scale were labeled "Poor people can control it" or "Outside of poor people's control" ($\alpha = .53$). Because both of these scales measure tendency to make controllable attributions (they differ only in specificity), the Willpower scale and Control were combined into an attribution index ($\alpha = .71$).

Demographic information was gathered from all participants, including gender, height, age, and weight. To measure the degree of fatness (weight independent of height), the body mass index (BMI) was calculated. BMI, calculated as weight/height squared, is highly correlated with weight, is not correlated with height, and is a good measure of fatness (see Kraemer, Berkowitz, & Hammer, 1990).

RESULTS

The overall pattern of means and standard deviation of the basic variables can be found in Table 1. Although they are interesting, our primary hypotheses are not based in mean differences but rather patterns of correlations. Subtle differences in translations can affect mean levels of agreement across languages but they will preserve order within samples.

Hypothesis 1: Prejudice, Attributions, and Value

To test Hypothesis 1, we correlated Dislike with negative cultural value and the attribution index. Dislike was significantly correlated with both the attribution index ($r = .35$, $N = 930$, $p < .001$) and negative cultural value ($r = .18$, $N = 934$, $p < .001$). These results support Hypothesis 1; anti-fat prejudice is correlated with negative value for fatness and the judgment of responsibility for one's weight.

Hypothesis 2: Six Nations and the Attribution-Value Hypothesis

We hypothesized that people who both make attributions of controllability and devalue fatness will be most likely to express anti-fat prejudice. To test the multiplicative hypothesis—that simultaneous negative value and attributions of control lead to prejudice—we performed a hierarchical multiple regression. In the first step, we regressed prejudice (Dislike) on the attribution index, cultural value, BMI, and gender (0 = male, 1 = female). In the second step, we added an Attribution × Value interaction. In both steps, we used centered predictor variables (see Aiken & West, 1991). We first tested the multiplicative hypothesis on a global basis across all six nations; the

TABLE 1 / Means of Basic Variables by Country

Country	Age	Body Mass Index[a]	Anti-Fat Attitudes (AFA) Subscales			Control	Cultural Value	Fat Is OK	Sample Size	
			Dislike	Fear	Will-power				Males	Females
Australia	22.0	23.1	1.49	4.96	4.26	4.35	6.04	3.13	53	117
	(6.5)	(3.4)	(1.2)	(2.6)	(1.9)	(0.69)	(1.2)	(1.5)		
India	22.4	21.0	2.49	4.45	5.05	4.40	4.91	3.88	100	82
	(6.9)	(3.5)	(1.8)	(2.7)	(1.9)	(0.84)	(1.4)	(1.9)		
Poland	37.2	23.7	2.12	5.15	5.27	4.65	6.92	2.89	52	50
	(18.9)	(3.8)	(1.9)	(2.9)	(2.1)	(0.95)	(1.2)	(2.0)		
Turkey	29.8	22.9	2.09	3.82	5.17	4.82	5.32	2.86	94	97
	(9.9)	(2.8)	(1.8)	(1.8)	(1.9)	(0.90)	(1.4)	(2.0)		
United States	27.7	23.4	2.09	5.11	5.10	4.55	6.77	2.59	47	61
	(10.4)	(2.8)	(1.6)	(2.8)	(2.1)	(0.87)	(1.1)	(1.4)		
Venezuela	20.6	22.8	2.03	4.80	5.30	4.83	5.26	2.22	30	65
	(2.7)	(2.9)	(1.8)	(2.3)	(1.9)	(0.87)	(1.4)	(1.4)		
r[b]	.33	.28	.18	.18	.18	.18	.52	.24		

Note: Standard deviations appear in parentheses.
[a]BMI is adjusted for sex.
[b]All rs are significant at $p < .05$.

increase in R^2 provides a direct test of the multiplicative hypothesis. The results of the regression can be seen in Table 2.

For the entire sample, in Step 1, the attribution index and the cultural value for fatness independently predicted greater Dislike; the multiple R for the regression that does not include the multiplicative term was .39, $F4, 863) = 38.59, p < .0001$. In Step 2, the multiplicative Attribution x Value term was added, with a multiple R of .40 and $F5, 862) = 32.14, p < .0001$. To test for the increased explanatory value of the multiplicative term, we calculated the F for the increase in R^2; this increase was significant, $F_{inc}(1, 862) = 5.11, p < .02$. Over and above the direct effect of attributions of controllability and a negative perceived cultural value, the simultaneous high presence of both terms predicted prejudice. These results support Hypothesis 2.

Hypothesis 3: The Role of Individualism/Collectivism

To test for differences based on culture, we repeated the hierarchical multiple regressions separately for the individualist and collectivist countries; the results are also displayed in Table 2. In the first step, both regression equations were very similar to the overall results.

The results diverged at Step 2; in individualist countries, the Attribution × Value term added to the prediction of anti-fat prejudice, $F_{inc}(1, 436) = 8.74, p < .005$, but for collectivist countries, this term added little to the prediction of prejudice, $F_{inc}(1, 420) = 1.42, ns$. To test this difference, we calculated a hierarchical multiple regression of the model represented in Table 2 but added an interaction for Cultural Orientation (collective vs. individual) × Attribution × Value term. This three-way interaction ($(\beta) = .24$) significantly increased variance explained, with $F_{inc}(1, 854) = 4.07, p < .05$. Hypothesis 2 appeared to receive support using the whole sample, but it is clear that the multiplicative term added little predictive value in the collectivist nations. This result instead supports Hypothesis 3; individualism moderates the power of person attributions for prejudice.

To further test Hypothesis 3, we correlated Dislike with Willpower and Negative Cultural Value by cultural orientation. Making a control attribution for fatness was associated with a more negative evaluation of fat people, but the attribution was somewhat more related to rejection in the individualist countries ($r = .40$) than in the collectivist countries ($r = .28$), $Z =$

TABLE 2 / Hierarchical Regression as Test of the Attribution-Value Model: Overall and by Culture

Predictor	Overall Sample		Individualist Countries		Collectivist Countries	
	β	ρ	β	ρ	β	ρ
Step 1						
Attribution index	0.50	<.005	0.50	<.005	0.41	<.005
Cultural value	0.14	<.005	0.30	<.005	0.12	<.05
Body mass index	−0.01	ns	0.03	ns	−0.03	ns
Gender	−0.31	<.005	−0.24	<.09	−0.37	<.025
Multiple R	.39	<.0001	.49	<.0001	.33	<.0001
F(df)	38.59	(4,863)	33.95	(4,437)	12.61	(4,421)
Step 2						
Attibution value	0.07	<.025	0.13	<.005	0.06	ns
Multiple R	.40	<.0001	.50	<.0001	.33	<.0001
F(df)	32.14	(4,862)	29.42	(4,436)	10.40	(4,420)

Note: $n = 442$ for individualist countries, $n = 426$ for collectivist countries. For individualist countries, $F_{Increase}(1, 436) = 8.74, p < .005$; for collectivist countries, $F_{Increase}(1, 420) = 1.42$ *ns*. For difference between individualist and collectivist countries on Attribution-Value term, $F(1, 854) = 4.65, p < .05$.

2.22, $p < .05$. More important, prejudice against fat people was more closely associated with cultural value in the individualist countries ($r = .35$) than in the collectivist countries ($r = .16$), $Z = 2.98$, $p < .005$.

Summary of Analyses

Attributions of control and perceptions of cultural value both predict prejudice in cultural groups. These data generally support an attribution and value model for the collectivist and individualist cultures. An Attribution × Value model was strongly supported for the individualist cultures but not the collectivist cultures.

DISCUSSION

Attributions and value predicted prejudice across the samples and in both cultural orientations. The simultaneous presence of both attribution of responsibility and negative cultural value significantly increased prediction of prejudice over and above the additive effect of the two; subsequent analyses showed that this effect appeared primarily in the individualist countries. The Attribution-Value model received good support in this study and shows some promise as a model for prejudice, and fat prejudice in particular.

Values and Prejudice

The Attribution-Value model of prejudice explicitly states that prejudice toward a person will only occur to the extent that that person has some negatively valued characteristic. This differs from, say, most current theories of racism, which tend to presuppose the negative value for the target as a function of their group membership.

Some theories of prejudice are explicit about negative values toward the group as a whole. For example, Social Identity Theory (Tajfel & Turner, 1979) explicitly focuses on the value of an ingroup for self-esteem and points to how ingroup preference and discriminatory behavior follows from group categorization. However, the Attribution-Value model focuses on the value of perceived group characteristics (e.g., their aggressiveness, laziness, cleanliness, clannishness). In this model, prejudice comes from believing that individual group members generally tend to

embody some scorned or odious trait or behavior and that this behavior is freely chosen.

One theory of prejudice that does specify values directly is Rokeach's (1960) belief-congruence model of prejudice that focused on similarity of beliefs and values. In Rokeach's model, one's own value system serves as a standard against which all others (both individuals and groups) are judged. Our model differs from Rokeach's in several important ways. The first is our emphasis on control and responsibility; this is not an element of Rokeach's theory. The second is that, for Rokeach, values are an individual difference variable, whereas in the Attribution-Value model we tend to focus on values that are generally shared (e.g., "In our culture, being fat is considered a bad thing"). The most important way our model differs from Rokeach's (1960) is that if a person has a belief or personal value that may culturally be defined as negative, in Rokeach's model, when that person's values and beliefs are congruent with the perceiver's, then the perceiver should tend to like and be attracted to the person. However, in our model, the self has no special status and prejudice against the self is a distinct possibility. If a heavyweight person hates fatness and believes people to be personally responsible for their weight, then we predict that they will have self-focused prejudice and will exhibit this self-prejudice with shame, guilt, depression, and low self-esteem. Several authors have found exactly this sort of result (Crandall & Biernat, 1990; Crocker, Cornwell, & Major, 1993; Quinn & Crocker, 1999).

Attributions and Prejudice

These results are consistent with a wide variety of data that attributions of controllability for negative life events lead to a hostile, angry, unhelpful, and generally unsympathetic response. We suggest that these attributions are a cause of prejudice in domains including obesity, abortion, poverty, alcoholism, AIDS, divorce, unemployment, posttraumatic stress disorder, failure at school, crime, depression, and so on (see Weiner, 1995).

Attributions may cause prejudice but there is also evidence that people make attributions of internal controllability toward members of groups against whom they are already prejudiced (Hewstone, 1990).

The current data are consistent with Heider's (1958) view that attributions can serve the purpose of creating or preserving an effectively consistent perception of people.

Attributions × Value

The simultaneous presence of negative cultural value and attributions of controllability added explanatory power to attributions and value taken separately; this effect was limited to the individualist countries. This interaction hypothesis is usually a difficult kind of hypothesis to find in linear models and provides compelling support for the model.

One important issue that requires some discussion is the question of why the Attribution-Value term significantly adds to prediction only in the individualist samples. Among individualist cultures, impression formation is based on the perception that a relatively autonomous human makes personal choices, achieves individually set goals, and who and what one is comes as the result of self-determined actions (Triandis et al., 1993).

According to Heider (1958), attributions of controllability are perceptions of unit relationship between a person and an action or outcome. Entities "form a unit when they are perceived as belonging together" (Heider, 1958, p. 176) and "attribution = balance with a causal unit" (Heider, 1988, p. 44). When a perceiver believes people are fat "because they have no will power" or "it's their own fault," the perceiver sees the fatness and the person in unit relationship—as a single thing. Because people are motivated to have effectively consistent perceptions (e.g., "good is connected only with good; bad only with bad") (Heider, 1988, p. 85), when fat is bad, ipso facto a fat person is bad. Weight becomes an outward symbol of inner value.

Heider's (1958) book is a classic that promoted a wide range of useful and generative theories. But it is a highly individualistic account for layperson perception. The perception of unit relationship between a person and their weight, that is, whether fatness reveals a person's essence, in collectivist countries is not based on attributions of controllability or judgments of responsibility; prejudice is significantly less likely to be related to attributions of controllability.

What would take the central place of attributions among collectivist countries? Several lines of evidence converge in suggesting that group membership is more central to the self in collectivist countries (Markus & Kitayama, 1991). If group membership as a heavyweight or lightweight person matters more to prejudice in collectivist countries than individualist ones, then the correlation between group membership and prejudice should be more negative in collectivist countries. To test this idea, we calculated the correlation between Dislike and BMI separately for individualist and collectivist nations; outgroup prejudice/ingroup bias would be manifested by a negative correlation between BMI and Dislike.

Among the individualist nations, we replicated Crandall's (1994) United States findings exactly, finding a slight and nonsignificant positive correlation ($r = .07$, $n = 461$, *ns*). By contrast, the collectivist nations showed a slight reversal of this effect ($r = -.07$, $n = 464$, *ns*). Although the difference between these two correlations cannot be described as impressive, it can be described as statistically significant ($Z = 3.01$, $p < .005$). This provides rather modest support for the idea that group membership as a lightweight person leads to more outgroup, anti-fat prejudice.

In the individualist sample, we argue that our participants were very well prepared, even eager, to make a correspondent inference about fatness and a person's value. In an individualist, self-controlled, and self-determined world, outcomes reveal character and justice is reliably served because outcomes are under an individual's self-control. A unit relationship is rapidly and easily perceived between a person's moral character and their fatness.

This unit relationship argument is supported by the pattern of correlations between prejudice (Dislike), attributions, and values. Although the cultural value index is correlated modestly with Dislike among collectivist countries ($r = .16$), it was correlated much more substantially among individualist countries ($r = .35$). In the individualist countries, where blame is much more taken for granted, thinking "fat is bad" is very close to thinking "fat people are bad." In collectivist countries, a close connection between the outcome and the person is not so boldly perceived and, as a result, there is not such a solid connection between cultural value and prejudice.

Overall, we expect that cultural value for a trait/behavior/stigma should be more highly correlated with prejudice toward people with that characteristic in individualist cultures than in collectivist cultures because people in the individualist cultures will reliably perceive a unit relationship, simply reflecting their worldview. Blaming the victim is a cultural phenomenon.

Attribution-Value Model and Ideology

The Attribution-Value model is an ideological theory of prejudice. Ideology is a network of interrelated beliefs and values that "not only enshrine ideas and explanations but entail evaluation and affect" (Brown, 1973, p. 13). The negative evaluation of fatness, along with the explanation of its cause that leads to a perception of unit relationship, leads to an affectively consistent negative attitude toward fat people.

For prejudice to exist, according to this model, there is no need to have realistic conflict, a history of competition, or even any contact with members of a group toward which one is prejudiced. Neither is there a need to categorize one's self and others as ingroup or outgroup members or to posit a motive for self-esteem to create prejudice or discrimination. By contrast to these models, the ideological Attribution-Value model of prejudice hypothesizes that prejudice can come from perceptual processes based on beliefs about causality and personal and cultural values for traits, characteristics, and stereotypic attributes about members of groups.

Deservingness

An alternative conceptual model, consistent with this research, is Feather's (1996) model of deservingness. An outcome is seen as deserved when the person is seen as responsible for the action that leads to the outcome and when the value of the outcome matches the value of the action. Deservingness, then, is a central variable in determining the attitudes toward the target. In the context of our data, when fatness is a negative outcome that follows negatively valued behavior (greed and sloth) and the behavior is perceived to be intentional and under personal control, fat people seem deserving of ill treatment and rejection.

Stereotyping and Prejudice

As we argued in the introduction, prejudice toward a group can arise when a group has, stereotypically, some negative characteristic and is judged responsible for this characteristic. Here we are proposing a causal link from stereotypes to prejudice by way of responsibility (unit relationship). In this way, no contact is needed to generate prejudice toward a group of people. Communication of the stereotype will suffice to create prejudice to the extent that stereotypic beliefs coexist with judgments of responsibility for the negative stereotypic attribute. In addition, meeting counterstereotypic exemplars should not reduce overall prejudice for the same reasons that it does not reduce overall stereotyping (see von Hippel, Sekaquaptewa, & Vargas, 1997, for a review).

In addition, the Attribution-Value model of prejudice is consistent with the notion that prejudice can be quite flexible. If cultural values change, due to social, economic, or historical forces (e.g., beauty norms), then prejudices should change along with the norms. Cultural values are relatively malleable and, in the presence of realistic conflict between groups, the value of a trait stereotypic of a group can change (Haslam, Turner, Oakes, & McGarty, 1992).

Correlations, Convenience Samples, and Other Caveats

This is a correlation study, which attempts to test a particular causal theory. As a result, the results reported must be considered tentative support for the Attribution-Value model. We did not manipulate causal attributions; prior research has shown that when experimentally led to believe that fat was not controllable (Crandall, 1994), fat prejudice was reduced—but there is no reason not to believe the reverse would not also be true, that is, if fat prejudice were reduced, attributions would become more charitable. In this case, attributions and judgments of cultural value might serve as justifications for prejudice rather than as causes of it. We cannot rule out this possibility. However, such a causal ordering would not explain why the simultaneous presence of both would predict prejudice better than the direct effects of one or the other.

The samples we have used here are primarily students in their late teens, in addition to a number of adults. We made little effort to ensure that these samples were representative of the countries and cultures from which they originate. To the extent that our original intent was to ensure inclusion of people representing the range of attributions and values, this limit is of little concern. However, one must hold tentative any conclusions based on these samples as representative of their countries or cultures—although the data fit cultural theory quite well, the inferences one makes from these particular participants must be qualified by the age, education, and nonrandom selection of the respondents.

SUMMARY

The Attribution-Value model is a general model of prejudice, although we apply it here only to anti-fat prejudice. We look forward to applying the model to attitudes toward homosexuality across cultures, sexism and achievement, and a variety of other contexts.

The model proved a good fit to anti-fat prejudice in individualist cultures but the results were not as compelling in the collectivist countries. The causes of prejudice in collectivist cultures do not appear to be based so highly on individual responsibility.

The Attribution-Value model of prejudice argues that, at least among individualist cultures and people, the tendency to make judgments of responsibility will increase prejudice of many kinds. As a result, the Attribution-Value model speaks to the longstanding problem of whether social psychology should have general theories of prejudice or specific theories of prejudices (e.g., racism, sexism, homophobia, anti-Semitism, etc.). We argue that the study of prejudice will be enhanced by unifying and simplifying the field of prejudice, by positing a common model that can underlie and cause some prejudices, and by specifying a process that can enhance and exacerbate prejudices developed through other means.

REFERENCES

Aiken, L. S., & West, S. G. (1991). *Multiple regression: Testing and interpreting interactions.* Thousand Oaks, CA: Sage.

Brown, L. B. (1973). *Ideology.* Harmondsworth, UK: Penguin.

Crandall, C. S. (1994). Prejudice against fat people: Ideology and self-interest. *Journal of Personality and Social Psychology, 66,* 882–894.

Crandall, C. S., & Biernat, M. R. (1990). The ideology of anti-fat attitudes. *Journal of Applied Social Psychology, 20,* 227–243.

Crandall, C. S., & Martinez, R. (1996). Culture, ideology, and anti-fat attitudes. *Personality and Social Psychology Bulletin, 22,* 1165–1176.

Crocker, J., Cornwell, B., & Major, B. (1993). The affective consequences of attributional ambiguity: The case of overweight women. *Journal of Personality and Social Psychology, 64,* 60–70.

Feather, N. T. (1985). Attitudes, values, and attributions: Explanations of unemployment. *Journal of Personality and Social Psychology, 48,* 876–889.

Feather, N. T. (1996). Reactions to penalties for an offense in relation to authoritarianism, values, perceived responsibility, perceived seriousness, and deservingness. *Journal of Personality and Social Psychology, 71,* 571–587.

Haslam, S. A., Turner, J. C., Oakes, P. J., & McGarty, C. (1992). Context-dependent variation in social stereotyping. *European Journal of Social Psychology, 22,* 3–20.

Heider, F. (1958). *The psychology of interpersonal relations.* New York: John Wiley.

Heider, F. (1988). Balance theory: Vol. 4. In M. Benesh-Weiner (Ed.), *The notebooks of Fritz Heider.* Munich, Germany: Psycologie Verlags Union.

Hewstone, M. (1990). The "ultimate attribution error"? A review of the literature on intergroup causal attribution. *European Journal of Social Psychology, 20,* 311–335.

Hofstede, G. (1980). *Cultural consequences: Individual differences in work-related values.* Beverly Hills, CA: Sage.

Kraemer, H. C., Berkowitz, R. I., & Hammer, L. D. (1990). Methodological difficulties in studies of obesity: I. Measurement issues. *Annals of Behavioral Medicine, 12,* 119–124.

Lerner, M. J. (1980). *Belief in the just world: A fundamental delusion.* New York: Plenum.

Lonner, W. J., & Berry, J. W. (Eds.). (1986). *Field methods in cross-cultural research* (Vol. 8). Beverly Hills, CA: Sage.

Markus, H. R., & Kitayama, S. (1991). Culture and the self: Implications for cognition, emotion, and motivation. *Psychological Review, 98,* 224–253.

Quinn, D. M., & Crocker, J. (1999). When ideology hurts: Effects of belief in the Protestant ethic and feeling overweight on the psychological well-being of women. *Journal of Personality and Social Psychology,* p. 77.

Rokeach, M. (1960). *The open and closed mind.* New York: Basic Books.

Skitka, L. J., & Tetlock, P. E. (1993). Providing public assistance: Cognitive and motivational processes underlying liberal and conservative policy preferences. *Journal of Personality and Social Psychology, 65,* 1205–1223.

Tajfel, H., & Turner, J. (1979). An integrative theory of intergroup conflict. In R. Austin & S. Worchel (Eds.), *Social psychology of intergroup relations* (pp. 33–47). Chicago: Nelson-Hall.

Triandis, H. C. (1994). *Culture and social behavior.* New York: McGraw-Hill.

Triandis, H. C. (1996). The psychological measurement of cultural syndrome. *American Psychologist, 51,* 407–415.

Triandis, H. C., Betancourt, H., Iwao, S., Leung, I. C., Salazar, J. M., Setiadi, B., Sinha, J. B. P., Touzard, H.,

& Zaleski, Z. (1993). An etic-emic analysis of individualism and collectivism. *Journal of Cross-Cultural Psychology, 24,* 366–383.

von Hippel, W., Sekaquaptewa, D., Vargas, P (1997). Linguistic intergroup bias as an implicit indicator of prejudice. *Journal of Experimental Social Psychology, 33,* 490–509.

Weiner, B. (1995). *Judgments of responsibility.* New York: Guilford.

Weiner, B., Perry, R. P., & Magnusson, J. (1988). An attributional analysis of reactions to stigmas. *Journal of Personality and Social Psychology, 55,* 738–748.

Zucker, G. S., & Weiner, B. (1993). Conservatism and perceptions of poverty: An attributional analysis. *Journal of Applied Social Psychology, 23,* 925–943.

CRITICAL THINKING QUESTIONS

1. Identify a group in your culture that is stigmatized with negative prejudice. Using the Attribution-Value model of prejudice discussed in the article, first identify the specific negative attributes given to this group. Next, identify which of these attributes can be ascribed to personal responsibility (i.e., characteristics that are under control of the group members). Discuss your findings in terms of the Attribution-Value model of prejudice.

2. The authors state that "attributions of controllability for negative life events lead to a hostile, angry, unhelpful, and generally unsympathetic response." Discuss how these attributions may underlie prejudice toward individuals experiencing poverty, AIDS, drug abuse, divorce, and unemployment.

3. The article distinguishes between cultures that value individualism versus collectivism. Identify an individual from a culture with a different orientation than your own (i.e., if you are from an individualism culture, talk to someone from a collectivism culture), and discuss with him or her your views regarding prejudice toward fat people. How are your views alike? How are they different?

4. Some people would suggest that it is more sociably acceptable today to express negative attitudes toward fat people than it is to express negative attitudes toward people of racial and ethnic groups. Do you agree? Why or why not? In addition to fat people, what other groups may experience negative attitudes overtly expressed toward them in socially acceptable ways?

5. From your understanding of the Attribution-Value model of prejudice, how can prejudiced attitudes be changed? Would this model suggest a different approach than, say, trying to reduce "old-fashioned prejudice" (discussed in the introduction to the article)? Explain your answers.

Chapter Seven

INTERPERSONAL ATTRACTION

Do "BIRDS OF A FEATHER flock together," or do "Opposites attract"? Both of these folk wisdoms, as contradictory as they are, attempt to answer an age-old question: To whom are we attracted and why?

The research on *interpersonal attraction* has gone in various directions in an attempt to answer this question. *Attraction* here is defined not in the narrow sense of romantic attraction but as attraction to anyone with whom we may associate—a friend, a co-worker, or even a child. Many factors have been identified as important determinants of interpersonal attraction, but perhaps the most widely investigated factor (and the one with the most distressing findings) is that of *physical attractiveness.* Study after study seems to demonstrate that how someone looks is a major determinant of how he or she is viewed and treated by other people.

"The Biology of Beauty," Article 19, discusses the serious influence that physical attractiveness has on our judgments of other people and how our preferences may be biologically rooted in our evolutionary past. So even though many of us may feel that "Beauty is in the eye of the beholder," whom we find attractive and how we react to them may be hardwired into our brains. Moreover, these preferences may transcend cultural biases. Undoubtedly, we may feel reluctant to admit that looks play such an important role in our lives. After all, we should not judge people by superficial characteristics like appearance. Nonetheless, a large body of research suggests that we do exactly that.

Our judgment of physical attractiveness is not just limited to selecting potential partners, however. It may also influence what other characteristics we ascribe to people based solely on their looks. Article 20, "What Is Beautiful Is Good," is a classic demonstration of how positive stereotypes are associated with physical attractiveness. Given the pervasiveness of this physical attractiveness effect, it has real implications for how we deal with and judge others in our daily lives.

Finally, Article 21, "Physical and Psychological Correlates of Appearance Orientation," provides a contemporary example of the role that physical attractiveness may play in behavior and personality. Specifically, the article examines the personality variables that may be associated with women's tendency to *self-objectify*—that is, to view themselves as objects and hence place considerable emphasis on their appearance. This tendency to spend a lot of time and energy on appearance may, in turn, influence the development of other aspects of the self. This final article rounds out this chapter on the varied and far-reaching impact of physical attractiveness on people's behaviors.

ARTICLE 19 _____

Physical attractiveness is perhaps the most widely researched topic in the area of interpersonal attraction. Part of this interest may be due to the importance of physical appearance in interpersonal interactions. When we meet a new person, physical appearance is the first thing we notice. Although perceptions of attractiveness are, to some extent, a matter of individual taste, some cultural stereotypes also define what constitutes attractiveness. Thus, another reason that attractiveness is so heavily investigated may be that it is relatively easy to get subjects to agree on what it means. Beauty is not just in the eye of the beholder, in other words.

Although attractiveness is something that can be readily observed about a person, most people would agree that it should not be used to make judgments about him or her. Indeed, most people would strongly protest the suggestion that how they see a person's values, skills, personality, or attributes may be influenced by what that person looks like. Yet a large body of literature developed over the years suggests that this indeed is the case. For example, research suggests that attractive people are rated more highly on a number of valued attributes; this is perhaps best summarized as the "What is beautiful is good" stereotype. Other studies have demonstrated that attractiveness may influence outcomes in serious situations. For example, attractive defendants are generally less likely to be convicted, and when they are convicted, they are more likely to receive lighter sentences than their less attractive counterparts.

The following article by Geoffrey Cowley discusses not only *what* we find attractive but also *why*. Rooted in evolutionary psychology, the article suggests that preferences regarding human beauty may be rooted in our biological past. Viewed in this light, our preferences for what we find beautiful may not be arbitrary or even culture specific but may have universal underpinnings.

The Biology of Beauty

■ Geoffrey Cowley

When it comes to choosing a mate, a female penguin knows better than to fall for the first creep who pulls up and honks. She holds out for the fittest suitor available—which in Antarctica means one chubby enough to spend several weeks sitting on newly hatched eggs without starving to death. The Asian jungle bird *Gallus gallus* is just as choosy. Males in that species sport gaily colored head combs and feathers, which lose their luster if the bird is invaded by parasites. By favoring males with bright ornaments, a hen improves her odds of securing a mate (and bearing offspring) with strong resistance to disease. For female scorpion flies, beauty is less about size or color than about symmetry. Females favor suitors who have well-matched wings—and with good reason. Studies show they're the most adept at killing prey and at defending their catch from competitors. There's no reason to think that any of these creatures understands its motivations, but there's a clear pattern to their preferences. "Throughout the animal world," says University of New Mexico ecologist Randy Thornhill, "attractiveness certifies biological quality."

Is our corner of the animal world different? That looks count in human affairs is beyond dispute. Studies have shown that people considered attractive fare better with parents and teachers, make more friends and more money, and have better sex with more (and more beautiful) partners. Every year, 400,000 Americans, including 48,000 men, flock to cosmetic surgeons. In other lands, people bedeck themselves with scars, lip plugs or bright feathers. "Every culture is a 'beauty culture,'" says Nancy Etcoff, a neuroscientist who is studying human attraction at the MIT Media Lab and writing a book on the subject. "I defy anyone to point to a society, any time in history or any place in the world, that wasn't preoccupied with beauty." The high-minded may dismiss our preening and ogling as distractions from things that matter, but the stakes can be enormous. "Judging beauty involves looking at another person," says University of Texas psychologist Devendra Singh, "and figuring out whether you want your children to carry that person's genes."

It's widely assumed that ideals of beauty vary from era to era and from culture to culture. But a harvest of new research is confounding that idea. Studies have established that people everywhere—regardless of race, class or age—share a sense of what's attractive. And though no one knows just how our minds translate the sight of a face or a body into rapture, new studies suggest that we judge each other by rules we're not even aware of. We may consciously admire Kate Moss's legs or Arnold's biceps, but we're also viscerally attuned to small variations in the size and symmetry of facial bones and the placement of weight on the body.

This isn't to say that our preferences are purely innate—or that beauty is all that matters in life. Most of us manage to find jobs, attract mates and bear offspring despite our physical imperfections. Nor should anyone assume that the new beauty research justifies the biases it illuminates. Our beautylust is often better suited to the Stone Age than to the Information Age; the qualities we find alluring may be powerful emblems of health, fertility and resistance to disease, but they say nothing about people's moral worth. The human weakness for what Thornhill calls "biological quality" causes no end of pain and injustice. Unfortunately, that doesn't make it any less real.

No one suggests that points of attraction never vary. Rolls of fat can signal high status in a poor society or low status in a rich one, and lip plugs go over better in the Kalahari than they do in Kansas. But local fashions seem to rest on a bedrock of shared preferences. You don't have to be Italian to find Michelangelo's David better looking than, say, Alfonse D'Amato. When British researchers asked women from England, China and India to rate pictures of Greek men, the women responded as if working from the same crib sheet. And when researchers at the University of Louisville showed a diverse collection of faces to whites, Asians and Latinos from 13 countries, the subjects' ethnic background scarcely affected their preferences.

To a skeptic, those findings suggest only that Western movies and magazines have overrun the world. But scientists have found at least one group that hasn't been exposed to this bias. In a series of groundbreaking experiments, psychologist Judith Langlois of the University of Texas, Austin, has shown that even infants share a sense of what's attractive. In the late '80s, Langlois started placing 3- and 6-month-old babies in front of a screen and showing them pairs of facial photographs. Each pair included one considered attractive by adult judges and one considered unattractive. In the first study, she found that the infants gazed significantly longer at "attractive" white female faces than at "unattractive" ones. Since then, she has repeated the drill using white male faces, black female faces, even the faces of other babies, and the same pattern always emerges. "These kids don't read Vogue or watch TV," Langlois says. "They haven't been touched by the media. Yet they make the same judgments as adults."

What, then, is beauty made of? What are the innate rules we follow in sizing each other up? We're obviously wired to find robust health a prettier sight than infirmity. "All animals are attracted to other animals that are healthy, that are clean by their standards and that show signs of competence," says Rutgers University anthropologist Helen Fisher. As far as anyone knows, there isn't a village on earth where skin lesions, head lice and rotting teeth count as beauty aids. But the rules get subtler than that. Like scorpion flies, we love symmetry. And though we generally favor average features over unusual ones, the people we find extremely beautiful share certain exceptional qualities.

When Randy Thornhill started measuring the wings of Japanese scorpion flies six years ago, he wasn't much concerned with the orgasms and infidelities of college students. But sometimes one thing leads to another. Biologists have long used bilateral symmetry—the extent to which a creature's right and left sides match—to gauge what's known as developmental stability. Given ideal growing conditions, paired features such as wings, ears, eyes and feet would come out matching perfectly. But pollution, disease and other hazards can disrupt development. As a result, the least resilient individuals tend to be the most lopsided. In chronicling the scorpion flies' daily struggles, Thornhill found that the bugs with the most symmetrical wings fared best in the competition for food and mates. To his amazement, females preferred symmetrical males even when they were hidden from view; evidently, their smells are more attractive. And when researchers started noting similar trends in other species, Thornhill turned his attention to our own.

Working with psychologist Steven Gangestad, he set about measuring the body symmetry of hundreds of college-age men and women. By adding up right-left disparities in seven measurements—the breadth of the feet, ankles, hands, wrists and elbows, as well as the breadth and length of the ears—the researchers scored each subject's overall body asymmetry. Then they had the person fill out a confidential questionnaire covering everything from temperament to sexual behavior, and set about looking for connections. They weren't disappointed. In a 1994 study, they found that the most symmetrical males had started having sex three to four years earlier than their most lopsided brethren. For both men and women, greater symmetry predicted a larger number of past sex partners.

That was just the beginning. From what they knew about other species, Thornhill and Gangestad predicted that women would be more sexually responsive to symmetrical men, and that men would exploit that advantage. To date, their findings support both suspicions. Last year they surveyed 86 couples and found that women with highly symmetrical partners were more than twice as likely to climax during intercourse (an event that may foster conception by ushering sperm into the uterus) than those with low-symmetry partners. And in separate surveys, Gangestad and Thornhill have found that, compared with regular Joes, extremely symmetrical men are less attentive to their partners and more likely to cheat on them. Women showed no such tendency.

It's hard to imagine that we even notice the differences between people's elbows, let alone stake our love lives on them. No one carries calipers into a singles bar. So why do these measurements predict so much? Because, says Thornhill, people with symmetrical elbows tend to have "a whole suite of attractive features." His findings suggest that besides having attractive (and symmetrical) faces, men with symmetrical bodies are typically larger, more muscular and more athletic than their peers, and more dominant in personality. In a forthcoming study, researchers at the University of Michigan find evidence that facial symmetry is also associated with health. In analyzing diaries kept by 100 students over a two-month period, they found that the least symmetrical had the most physical complaints, from insomnia to nasal congestion, and reported more anger, jealousy and withdrawal. In light of all Thornhill and Gangestad's findings, you can hardly blame them.

If we did go courting with calipers, symmetry isn't all we would measure. As we study each other in the street, the office or the gym, our beauty radars pick up a range of signals. Oddly enough, one of the qualities shared by attractive people is their averageness. Researchers discovered more than a century ago that if they superimposed photographs of several faces, the resulting composite was usually better looking than any of the images that went into it. Scientists can now average faces digitally, and it's still one of the surest ways to make them more attractive. From an evolutionary perspective, a preference for extreme normality makes sense. As Langlois has written, "Individuals with average population characteristics should be less likely to carry harmful genetic mutations."

So far, so good. But here's the catch: while we may find average faces attractive, the faces we find most beautiful are not average. As New Mexico State University psychologist Victor Johnston has shown, they're extreme. To track people's preferences, Johnston uses a computer program called FacePrints. Turn it on, and it generates 30 facial images, all male or all female, which you rate on a 1–9 beauty scale.

The program then "breeds" the top-rated face with one of the others to create two digital offspring, which replace the lowest-rated faces in the pool. By rating round after round of new faces, you create an ever more beautiful population. The game ends when you award some visage a perfect 10. (If you have access to the World Wide Web, you can take part in a collective face-breeding experiment by visiting http://www.psych.nmsu.edu/~vic/faceprints/.)

For Johnston, the real fun starts after the judging is finished. By collecting people's ideal faces and comparing them to average faces, he can measure the distance between fantasy and reality. As a rule, he finds that an ideal female has a higher forehead than an average one, as well as fuller lips, a shorter jaw and a smaller chin and nose. Indeed, the ideal 25-year-old woman, as configured by participants in a 1993 study, had a 14-year-old's abundant lips and an 11-year-old's delicate jaw. Because her lower face was so small, she also had relatively prominent eyes and cheekbones.

The participants in that study were all college kids from New Mexico, but researchers have since shown that British and Japanese students express the same bias. And if there are lingering doubts about the depth of that bias, Johnston's latest findings should dispel them. In a forthcoming study, he reports that male volunteers not only consciously prefer women with small lower faces but show marked rises in brain activity when looking at pictures of them. And though Johnston has yet to publish specs on the ideal male, his unpublished findings suggest that a big jaw, a strong chin and an imposing brow are as prized in a man's face as their opposites are in a woman's.

Few of us ever develop the heart-melting proportions of a FacePrints fantasy. And if it's any consolation, beauty is not an all-or-nothing proposition. Madonna became a sex symbol despite her strong nose, and Melanie Griffith's strong jaw hasn't kept her out of the movies. Still, special things have a way of happening to people who approximate the ideal. We pay them huge fees to stand on windblown bluffs and stare into the distance. And past studies have found that square-jawed males not only start having sex earlier than their peers but attain higher rank in the military.

FIGURE 1 / Facial Fantasies. As a rule, average faces are more attractive than unusual ones. But when people are asked to develop ideal faces on a computer, they tend to exaggerate certain qualities.

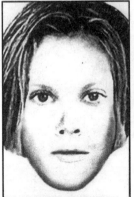 

Average Proportions
This computer-generated face has the dimensions typical of Caucasian 20-year-olds.

Ideal Proportions
Most visions of the perfect female face have small jaws and abnormally lush lips.

Source: Victor Johnston, New Mexico State University. Used with permission.

None of this surprises evolutionary psychologists. They note that the facial features we obsess over are precisely the ones that diverge in males and females during puberty, as floods of sex hormones wash us into adulthood. And they reason that hormonal abundance would have been a good clue to mate value in the hunter-gatherer world where our preferences evolved. The tiny jaw that men favor in women is essentially a monument to estrogen—and, obliquely, to fertility. No one claims that jaws reveal a woman's odds of getting pregnant. But like breasts, they imply that she could.

Likewise, the heavy lower face that women favor in men is a visible record of the surge in androgens (testosterone and other male sex hormones) that turns small boys into 200-pound spear-throwers. An oversized jaw is biologically expensive, for the androgens required to produce it tend to compromise the immune system. But from a female's perspective, that should make jaw size all the more revealing. Evolutionists think of androgen-based features as "honest advertisements" of disease resistance. If a male can afford them without falling sick, the thinking goes, he must have a superior immune system in the first place.

No one has tracked the immune responses of men with different jawlines to see if these predictions bear out (Thornhill has proposed a study that would involve comparing volunteers' responses to a vaccine). Nor is it clear whether penis size figures into these equations. Despite what everyone thinks he knows on the subject, scientists haven't determined that women have consistent preferences one way or the other.

Our faces are our signatures, but when it comes to raw sex appeal, a nice chin is no match for a perfectly sculpted torso—especially from a man's perspective. Studies from around the world have found that while both sexes value appearance, men place more stock in it than women. And if there are social reasons for that imbalance, there are also biological ones. Just about any male over 14 can produce sperm, but a woman's ability to bear children depends on her age and hormone levels. Female fertility declines by two thirds between the ages of 20 and 44, and it's spent by 54. So while both sexes may eyeball potential partners, says Donald Symons, an anthropologist at the University of California in Santa Barbara, "a larger proportion of a woman's mate value can be detected from visual cues." Mounting evidence suggests there is no better cue than the relative contours of her waist and hips.

Before puberty and after menopause, females have essentially the same waistlines as males. But during puberty, while boys are amassing the bone and muscle of paleolithic hunters, a typical girl gains nearly 35 pounds of so-called reproductive fat around the hips and thighs. Those pounds contain roughly the 80,000 calories needed to sustain a pregnancy, and the curves they create provide a gauge of reproductive potential. "You have to get very close to see the details of a woman's face," says Devendra Singh, the University of Texas psychologist. "But you can see the shape of her body from 500 feet, and it says more about mate value."

Almost anything that interferes with fertility— obesity, malnutrition, pregnancy, meno-pause— changes a woman's shape. Healthy, fertile women typically have waist-hip ratios of .6 to .8, meaning their waists are 60 to 80 percent the size of their hips,

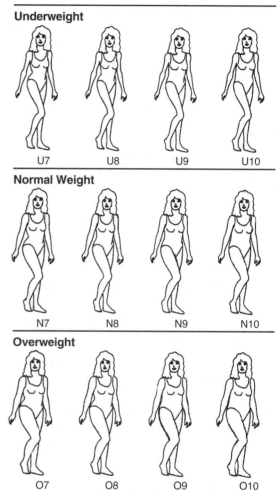

FIGURE 2 / Body Language. When men are asked to rank figures with various weights and waist-hip ratios (0.7 to 1.0), they favor a pronounced hourglass shape. The highest-ranked figures are N7, N8 and U7 (in that order). The lowest ranked is O10.

Underweight

U7   U8   U9   U10

Normal Weight

N7   N8   N9   N10

Overweight

O7   O8   O9   O10

The Order Chosen: (1) N7, (2) N8, (3) U7, (4) U8, (5) N9, (6) N10, (7) O7, (8) U9, (9) O8, (10) U10, (11) O9, (12) O10.

Source: Devendra Singh, University of Texas at Austin. Used with permission.

whatever their actual weight. To take one familiar example, a 36-25-36 figure would have a WHR of .7. Many women outside this range are healthy and capable of having children, of course. But as researchers in the Netherlands discovered in a 1993 study, even a slight increase in waist size relative to hip size can signal reproductive problems. Among 500 women who were attempting in vitro fertilization, the odds of conceiving during any given cycle declined by 30 percent with every 10 percent increase in WHR. In other words, a woman with a WHR of .9 was nearly a third less likely to get pregnant than one with a WHR of .8, regardless of her age or weight. From an evolutionary perspective, it's hard to imagine men not responding to such a revealing signal. And as Singh has shown repeatedly, they do.

Defining a universal standard of body beauty once seemed a fool's dream; common sense said that if spindly Twiggy and Rubens's girthy Three Graces could all excite admiration, then nearly anyone could. But if our ideals of size change from one time and place to the next, our taste in shapes is amazingly stable. A low waist-hip ratio is one of the few features that a long, lean Barbie doll shares with a plump, primitive fertility icon. And Singh's findings suggest the fashion won't change any time soon. In one study, he compiled the measurements of Playboy centerfolds and Miss America winners from 1923 to 1990. Their bodies got measurably leaner over the decades, yet their waist-hip ratios stayed within the narrow range of .68 to .72. (Even Twiggy was no tube; at the peak of her fame in the 1960s, the British model had a WHR of .73.)

The same pattern holds when Singh generates line drawings of different female figures and asks male volunteers to rank them for attractiveness, sexiness, health and fertility. He has surveyed men of various backgrounds, nationalities and ages. And whether the judges are 8-year-olds or 85-year-olds, their runaway favorite is a figure of average weight with a .7 WHR. Small wonder that when women were liberated from corsets and bustles, they took up girdles, wide belts and other waist-reducing contraptions. Last year alone, American women's outlays for shape-enhancing garments topped a half-billion dollars.

To some critics, the search for a biology of beauty looks like a thinly veiled political program. "It's the fantasy life of American men being translated into genetics," says poet and social critic Katha Pollitt. "You can look at any feature of modern life and make up a story about why it's genetic." In truth, says Northwestern University anthropologist Micaela di Leonardo, attraction is a complicated social phenomenon, not just a hard-wired response. If attraction were governed by the dictates of baby-making, she says, the men of ancient Greece wouldn't have found young boys so alluring, and gay couples wouldn't crowd modern sidewalks. "People make decisions about sexual and marital partners inside complex networks of friends and relatives," she says. "Human beings cannot be reduced to DNA packets."

Homosexuality is hard to explain as a biological adaptation. So is stamp collecting. But no one claims that human beings are mindless automatons, blindly striving to replicate our genes. We pursue countless passions that have no direct bearing on survival. If we're sometimes attracted to people who can't help us reproduce, that doesn't mean human preferences lack any coherent design. A radio used as a doorstop is still a radio. The beauty mavens' mission—and that of evolutionary psychology in general—is not to explain everything people do but to unmask our biases and make sense of them. "Our minds have evolved to generate pleasurable experiences in response to some things while ignoring other things," says Johnston. "That's why sugar tastes sweet, and that's why we find some people more attractive than others."

The new beauty research does have troubling implications. First, it suggests that we're designed to care about looks, even though looks aren't earned and reveal nothing about character. As writer Ken Siman observes in his new book, "The Beauty Trip," "the kind [of beauty] that inspires awe, lust, and increased jeans sales cannot be evenly distributed. In a society where everything is supposed to be within reach, this is painful to face." From acne to birth defects, we wear our imperfections as thorns, for we know the world sees them and takes note.

A second implication is that sexual stereotypes are not strictly artificial. At some level, it seems, women are designed to favor dominant males over meek ones, and men are designed to value women for youthful qualities that time quickly steals. Given the slow pace of evolutionary change, our innate preferences aren't likely to fade in the foreseeable future. And if they exist for what were once good biological reasons, that doesn't make them any less nettlesome. "Men often forgo their health, their safety, their spare time and their family life in order to get rank," says Helen Fisher, the Rutgers anthropologist, "because unconsciously, they know that rank wins women." And all too often, those who can trade cynically on their rank do.

But do we have to indulge every appetite that natural selection has preserved in us? Of course not. "I don't know any scientist who seriously thinks you can look to nature for moral guidance," says Thornhill. Even the fashion magazines would provide a better compass.

With Karen Springen

CRITICAL THINKING QUESTIONS

1. Critically examine the explanations given by evolutionary psychology to explain people's beauty preferences. Are the arguments valid? As one critic notes in the article, "You can look at any feature of modern life and make up a story about why it's genetic." Defend your position.

2. The introduction to this article noted that people's beauty preferences may extend beyond simple mate selection and also be associated with hiring preferences, the likelihood of being convicted of a crime, and so on. What, if any, are the inherent risks involved whenever biological explanations are used to explain human behavior?

3. Why do you think the vast majority of the studies reported in the article concern *female* beauty? Why isn't the same amount of research being done on *male* attractiveness?

4. Based on your own experiences, is there a prejudice favoring attractive people? Provide evidence to support your point. Do you feel the effects of attractiveness are really as pervasive as suggested by the article? Why or why not? If being attractive has this great an impact, could this form of prejudice be reduced or eliminated or is it inevitable? Explain your answer.

ARTICLE 20 _____

It may seem obvious that looks matter when it comes to dating and mate selection. While many people would argue that physical attractiveness is not the only thing that they look for in a potential partner, few would argue that they are oblivious to appearance. Furthermore, according to Article 19—which considered how people's beauty preferences might have biological roots—there is fairly strong agreement as to what features people find attractive.

So, what is life like for people who happen to have the features that others find attractive? Are their lives significantly different from those of individuals who do not possess such good looks? Furthermore, do looks have any impact on people's lives outside the areas of dating and mating popularity? For example, compared to a less attractive counterpart, will an attractive person more likely be successful in the work world? Be a better parent? Be a happier person overall? The following classic article by Karen Dion, Ellen Berscheid, and Elaine Walster was one of the first studies to investigate the "What is beautiful is good" effect. As indicated in the article, attractiveness may convey a great many benefits to those people who possess it.

What Is Beautiful Is Good[1]

■ Karen Dion, Ellen Berscheid, and Elaine Walster

A person's physical appearance, along with his sexual identity, is the personal characteristic that is most obvious and accessible to others in social interaction. The present experiment was designed to determine whether physically attractive stimulus persons, both male and female, are (a) assumed to possess more socially desirable personality traits than physically unattractive stimulus persons and (b) expected to lead better lives (e.g., be more competent husbands and wives, be more successful occupationally, etc.) than unattractive stimulus persons. Sex of Subject × Sex of Stimulus Person interactions along these dimensions also were investigated. The present results indicate a "what is beautiful is good" stereotype along the physical attractiveness dimension with no Sex of Judge × Sex of Stimulus interaction. The implications of such a stereotype on self-concept development and the course of social interaction are discussed.

A person's physical appearance, along with his sexual identity, is the personal characteristic most obvious and accessible to others in social interaction. It is perhaps for this reason that folk psychology has always contained a multitude of theorems which ostensibly permit the forecast of a person's character and personality simply from knowledge of his outward appearance. The line of deduction advanced by most physiognomic theories is simply that "What is beautiful is good . . . [Sappho, Fragments, No. 101]," and that "Physical beauty is the sign of an interior beauty, a spiritual and moral beauty . . . [Schiller, 1882]."

Several processes may operate to make the soothsayers' prophecies more logical and accurate than would appear at first glance. First, it is possible that a correlation between inward character and appearance exists because certain personality traits influence one's appearance. For example, a calm, relaxed person may develop fewer lines and wrinkles than a tense, irritable person. Second, cultural stereotypes about the kinds of personalities appropriate for beautiful or ugly people may mold the personalities of these individuals. If casual acquaintances invariably assume that attractive individuals are more sincere, noble, and honest than unattractive persons, then attractive individuals should be habitually regarded with more respect than unattractive persons. Many have noted that one's self-concept develops from observing what oth-

Reprinted from *Journal of Personality and Social Psychology*, 1972, *24*, 285–290. Copyright © 1972 by the American Psychological Association. Reprinted with permission.

ers think about oneself. Thus, if the physically attractive person is consistently treated as a virtuous person, he may become one.

The above considerations pose several questions: (*a*) Do individuals in fact have stereotyped notions of the personality traits possessed by individuals of varying attractiveness? (*b*) To what extent are these stereotypes accurate? (*c*) What is the cause of the correlation between beauty and personality if, in fact, such a correlation exists?

Some observers, of course, deny that such stereotyping exists, and thus render Questions *b* and *c* irrelevant. Chief among these are rehabilitation workers (cf. Wright, 1960) whose clients possess facial and other physical disabilities. These researchers, however, may have a vested interest in believing that physical beauty is a relatively unimportant determinant of the opportunities an individual has available to him.

Perhaps more interestingly, it has been asserted that other researchers also have had a vested interest in retaining the belief that beauty is a peripheral characteristic. Aronson (1969), for example, has suggested that the fear that investigation might prove this assumption wrong has generally caused this to be a taboo area for social psychologists:

> As an aside, I might mention that physical attractiveness is rarely investigated as an antecedent of liking—even though a casual observation (even by us experimental social psychologists) would indicate that we seem to react differently to beautiful women than to homely women. It is difficult to be certain why the effects of physical beauty have not been studied more systematically. It may be that, at some levels, we would hate to find evidence indicating that beautiful women are better liked than homely women—somehow this seems undemocratic. In a democracy we like to feel that with hard work and a good deal of motivation, a person can accomplish almost anything. But, alas (most of us believe), hard work cannot make an ugly woman beautiful. Because of this suspicion perhaps most social psychologists implicitly prefer to believe that beauty is indeed only skin deep—and avoid the investigation of its social impact for fear they might learn otherwise [p. 160].

The present study was an attempt to determine if a physical attractiveness stereotype exists and, if so, to investigate the content of the stereotype along several dimensions. Specifically, it was designed to investigate (*a*) whether physically attractive stimulus persons, both male and female, are assumed to possess more *socially desirable personality traits* than unattractive persons and (*b*) whether they are expected to *lead better lives* than unattractive individuals. With respect to the latter, we wished to determine if physically attractive persons are generally expected to be better husbands and wives, better parents, and more successful socially and occupationally than less attractive persons.

Because it seemed possible that jealousy might attenuate these effects (if one is jealous of another, he may be reluctant to accord the other the status that he feels the other deserves), and since subjects might be expected to be more jealous of attractive stimulus persons of the same sex than of the opposite sex, we examined the Sex of Subject × Sex of Stimulus Person interactions along the dimensions described above.

METHOD

Subjects

Sixty students, 30 males and 30 females, who were enrolled in an introductory course in psychology at the University of Minnesota participated in this experiment. Each had agreed to participate in return for experimental points to be added to their final exam grade.

Procedure

When the subjects arrived at the designated rooms, they were introduced to the experiment as a study of accuracy in person perception. The experimenter stated that while psychological studies have shown that people do form detailed impressions of others on the basis of a very few cues, the variables determining the extent to which these early impressions are generally accurate have not yet been completely identified. The subjects were told that the purpose of the present study was to compare person perception accuracy of untrained college students with two other groups who had been trained in various interpersonal perception techniques, specifically graduate students in clinical psychology and clinical psychologists. The experimenter noted his belief that person perception accuracy is a general ability varying among people. Therefore, according to the experimenter, college students who are high on this ability may be as accurate as some professional clinicians when making first-impression judgments based on noninterview material.

The subjects were told that standard sets of photographs would be used as the basis for personality inferences. The individuals depicted in the photographs were said to be part of a group of college students currently enrolled at other universities who were participating in a longitudinal study of personality development scheduled to continue into adulthood. It would be possible, therefore, to assess the accuracy of each subject's judgments against information currently available on the stimulus persons and also against forthcoming information.

Stimulus materials. Following the introduction, each subject was given three envelopes. Each envelope contained one photo of a stimulus person of approximately the subject's own age. One of the three envelopes that the subject received contained a photograph of a physically attractive stimulus person; another contained a photograph of a person of average attractiveness; and the final envelope contained a photograph of a relatively unattractive stimulus person.[2] Half of our subjects received three pictures of girls; the remainder received pictures of boys.

To increase the generalizability of our findings and to insure that the general dimension of attractiveness was the characteristic responded to (rather than unique characteristics such as hair color, etc.), 12 different sets of three pictures each were prepared. Each subject received and rated only 1 set. Which 1 of the 12 sets of pictures the subject received, the order in which each of the three envelopes in the set were presented, and the ratings made of the person depicted, were all randomly determined.

Dependent variables. The subjects were requested to record their judgments of the three stimulus persons in several booklets.[3] The first page of each booklet cautioned the subjects that this study was an investigation of accuracy of person perception and that we were not interested in the subjects' tact, po-

liteness, or other factors usually important in social situations. It was stressed that it was important for the subject to rate the stimulus persons frankly.

The booklets tapped impressions of the stimulus person along several dimensions. First, the subjects were asked to open the first envelope and then to rate the person depicted on 27 different *personality traits* (which were arranged in random order).[4] The subjects' ratings were made on 6-point scales, the ends of which were labeled by polar opposites (i.e., exciting–dull). When these ratings had been computed, the subject was asked to open the second envelope, make ratings, and then open the third envelope.

In a subsequent booklet, the subjects were asked to assess the stimulus persons on five additional personality traits.[5] These ratings were made on a slightly different scale. The subjects were asked to indicate which stimulus person possessed the "most" and "least" of a given trait. The stimulus person thought to best represent a positive trait was assigned a score of 3; the stimulus person thought to possess an intermediate amount of the trait was assigned a score of 2; and the stimulus person thought to least represent the trait was assigned a score of 1.

In a previous experiment (see Endnote 3), a subset of items was selected to comprise an index of the *social desirability* of the personality traits assigned to the stimulus person. The subjects' ratings of each stimulus person on the appropriate items were simply summed to determine the extent to which the subject perceived each stimulus person as socially desirable.

In order to assess whether or not attractive persons are expected to lead happier and more successful lives than unattractive persons, the subjects were asked to estimate which of the stimulus persons would be most likely, and which least likely, to have a number of different life experiences. The subjects were reminded again that their estimates would eventually be checked for accuracy as the lives of the various stimulus persons evolved. The subjects' estimates of the stimulus person's probable life experiences formed indexes of the stimulus person's future happiness in four areas: (*a*) marital happiness (Which stimulus person is most likely to ever be divorced?); (*b*) parental happiness (Which stimulus person is most likely to be a good parent?); (*c*) social and professional happiness (Which stimulus person is most likely to experience deep personal fulfillment?); and (*d*) total happiness (sum of Indexes *a, b,* and *c*).

A fifth index, an occupational success index, was also obtained for each stimulus person. The subjects were asked to indicate which of the three stimulus persons would be most likely to engage in 30 different occupations. (The order in which the occupations were presented and the estimates made was randomized.) The 30 occupations had been chosen such that three status levels of 10 different general occupations were represented, three examples of which follow: Army sergeant (low status); Army captain (average status); Army colonel (high status). Each time a high-status occupation was foreseen for a stimulus person, the stimulus person was assigned a score of 3; when a moderate status occupation was foreseen, the stimulus person was assigned a score of 2; when a low-status occupation was foreseen, a score of 1 was assigned. The average status of occupations that a subject ascribed to a stimulus person constituted the score for that stimulus person in the occupational status index.

RESULTS AND DISCUSSION

Manipulation Check

It is clear that our manipulation of the relative attractiveness of the stimulus persons depicted was effective. The six unattractive stimulus persons were seen as less attractive than the average stimulus persons, who, in turn, were seen as less attractive than the six attractive stimulus persons. The stimulus persons' mean rankings on the attractiveness dimension were 1.12, 2.02, and 2.87, respectively. These differences were statistically significant ($F = 939.32$).[6]

Test of Hypotheses

It will be recalled that it was predicted that the subjects would attribute more socially desirable personality traits to attractive individuals than to average or unattractive individuals. It also was anticipated that jealousy might attenuate these effects. Since the subjects might be expected to be more jealous of stimulus persons of the same sex than of the opposite sex, we blocked both on sex of subject and sex of stimulus person. If jealousy attenuated the predicted main effect, a significant Sex of Subject × Sex of Stimulus Person interaction should be secured in addition to the main effect.

All tests for detection of linear trend and interaction were conducted via a multivariate analysis of variance. (This procedure is outlined in Hays, 1963.)

The means relevant to the hypothesis that attractive individuals will be perceived to possess more socially desirable personalities than others are reported in Table 1. Analyses reveal that attractive individuals were indeed judged to be more socially desirable than are unattractive ($F = 29.61$) persons. The Sex of Subject × Sex of Stimulus Person interac-

TABLE 1 / Traits Attributed to Various Stimulus Others

Trait Ascription[a]	Unattractive Stimulus Person	Average Stimulus Person	Attractive Stimulus Person
Social desirability of the stimulus person's personality	56.31	62.42	65.39
Occupational status of the stimulus person	1.70	2.02	2.25
Marital competence of the stimulus person	.37	.71	1.70
Parental competence of the stimulus person	3.91	4.55	3.54
Social and professional happiness of the stimulus person	5.28	6.34	6.37
Total happiness of the stimulus person	8.83	11.60	11.60
Likelihood of marriage	1.52	1.82	2.17

[a]The higher the number, the more socially desirable, the more prestigious an occupation, etc., the stimulus person is expected to possess.

tion was insignificant (interaction $F = .00$). Whether the rater was of the same or the opposite sex as the stimulus person, attractive stimulus persons were judged as more socially desirable.[7]

Furthermore, it was also hypothesized that the subjects would assume that attractive stimulus persons are likely to secure more prestigious jobs than those of lesser attractiveness, as well as experiencing happier marriages, being better parents, and enjoying more fulfilling social and occupational lives.

The means relevant to these predictions concerning the estimated future life experiences of individuals of varying degrees of physical attractiveness are also depicted in Table 1. As shown in the table, there was strong support for all of the preceding hypotheses save one. Attractive men and women were expected to attain more prestigious occupations than were those of lesser attractiveness ($F = 42.30$), and this expectation was expressed equally by raters of the same or the opposite sex as the stimulus person (interaction $F = .25$).

The subjects also assumed that attractive individuals would be more competent spouses and have happier marriages than those of lesser attractiveness ($F = 62.54$). (It might be noted that there is some evidence that this may be a correct perception. Kirkpatrick and Cotton (1951), reported that "well-adjusted" wives were more physically attractive than "badly adjusted" wives. "Adjustment," however, was assessed by friends' perceptions, which may have been affected by the stereotype evident here.)

According to the means reported in Table 1, it is clear that attractive individuals were not expected to be better parents ($F = 1.47$). In fact, attractive persons were rated somewhat lower than any other group of stimulus persons as potential parents, although no statistically significant differences were apparent.

As predicted, attractive stimulus persons were assumed to have better prospects for happy social and professional lives ($F = 21.97$). All in all, the attractive stimulus persons were expected to have more total happiness in their lives than those of lesser attractiveness ($F = 24.20$).

The preceding results did not appear to be attenuated by a jealousy effect (Sex of Subject × Stimulus Person interaction Fs = .01, .07, .21, and .05, respectively).

The subjects were also asked to estimate the likelihood that the various stimulus persons would marry early or marry at all. Responses were combined into a single index. It is evident that the subjects assumed that the attractive stimulus persons were more likely to find an acceptable partner than those of lesser attractiveness ($F = 35.84$). Attractive individuals were expected to marry earlier and to be less likely to remain single. Once again, these conclusions were reached by all subjects, regardless of whether they were of the same or opposite sex of the stimulus person (interaction $F = .01$).

The results suggest that a physical attractiveness stereotype exists and that its content is perfectly compatible with the "What is beautiful is good" thesis. Not only are physically attractive persons assumed to possess more socially desirable personalities than those of lesser attractiveness, but it is presumed that their lives will be happier and more successful.

The results also suggest that the physical attractiveness variable may have a number of implications for a variety of aspects of social interaction and influence. For example, it is clear that physically attractive individuals may have even more advantages in the dating market than has previously been assumed. In addition to an aesthetic advantage in marrying a beautiful spouse (cf. Josselin de Jong, 1952), potential marriage partners may also assume that the beautiful attract all of the world's material benefits and happiness. Thus, the lure of an attractive marriage partner should be strong indeed.

We do not know, of course, how well this stereotype stands up against contradictory information. Nor do we know the extent to which it determines the pattern of social interaction that develops with a person of a particular attractiveness level. Nevertheless, it would be odd if people did not behave toward others in accordance with this stereotype. Such behavior has been previously noted anecdotally. Monahan (1941) has observed that

Even social workers accustomed to dealing with all types often find it difficult to think of a normal, pretty girl as being guilty of a crime. Most people, for some inexplicable reason, think of crime in terms of abnormality in appearance, and I must say that beautiful women are not often convicted [p. 103].

A host of other familiar social psychological dependent variables also should be affected in predictable ways.

In the above connection, it might be noted that if standards of physical attractiveness vary widely, knowledge of the content of the physical attractiveness stereotype would be of limited usefulness in predicting its effect on social interaction and the development of the self-concept. The present study was not designed to investigate the degree of variance in perceived beauty. (The physical attractiveness ratings of the stimulus materials were made by college students of a similar background to those who participated in this study.) Preliminary evidence (Cross & Cross, 1971) suggests that such differences in perceived beauty may not be as severe as some observers have suggested.

REFERENCES

Aronson, E. Some antecedents of interpersonal attraction. In W. J. Arnold & D. Levine (Eds.), *Nebraska Symposium on Motivation*, 1969, *17*, 143–177.

Cross, J. F., & Cross, J. Age, sex, race, and the perception of facial beauty. *Developmental Psychology*, 1971, *5*, 433–439.

Hays, W. L. *Statistics for psychologists*. New York: Holt, Rinehart & Winston, 1963.

Josselin de Jong, J. P. B. *Lévi-Strauss' theory on kinship and marriage*. Leiden, Holland: Brill, 1952.

Kirkpatrick, C., & Cotton, J. Physical attractiveness, age, and marital adjustment. *American Sociological Review*, 1951, *16*, 81–86.

Monahan, F. *Women in crime*. New York: Ives Washburn, 1941.

Schiller, J. C. F. *Essays, esthetical and philosophical, including the dissertation on the "Connexions between the animal and the spiritual in man."* London: Bell, 1882.

Wright, B. A. *Physical disability—A psychological approach*. New York: Harper & Row, 1960.

ENDNOTES

1. This research was financed in part by National Institute of Mental Health Grants MH 16729 to Berscheid and MH 16661 to Walster.

2. The physical attractiveness rating of each of the pictures was determined in a preliminary study. One hundred Minnesota undergraduates rated 50 yearbook pictures of persons of the opposite sex with respect to physical attractiveness. The criteria for choosing the 12 pictures to be used experimentally were (*a*) high-interrater agreement as to the physical attractiveness of the stimulus (the average interrater correlation for all of the pictures was .70); and (*b*) pictures chosen to represent the very attractive category and very unattractive category were not at the extreme ends of attractiveness.

3. A detailed report of the items included in these booklets is available. Order Document No. 01972 from the National Auxiliary Publication Service of the American Society for Information Science, c/o CCM Information Services, Inc., 909 3rd Avenue, New York, New York 10022. Remit in advance $5.00 for photocopies or $2.00 for microfiche and make checks payable to: Research and Microfilm Publications, Inc.

4. The subjects were asked how altruistic, conventional, self-assertive, exciting, stable, emotional, dependent, safe, interesting, genuine, sensitive, outgoing, sexually permissive, sincere, warm, sociable, competitive, obvious, kind, modest, strong, serious, sexually warm, simple, poised, bold, and sophisticated each stimulus person was.

5. The subjects rated stimulus persons on the following traits: friendliness, enthusiasm, physical attractiveness, social poise, and trustworthiness.

6. Throughout this report, $df = 1/55$.

7. Before running the preliminary experiment to determine the identity of traits usually associated with a socially desirable person (see Endnote 3), we had assumed that an exciting date, a nurturant person, and a person of good character would be perceived as quite different personality types. Conceptually, for example, we expected that an exciting date would be seen to require a person who was unpredictable, challenging, etc., while a nurturant person would be seen to be predictable and unthreatening. It became clear, however, that these distinctions were not ones which made sense to the subjects. There was almost total overlap between the traits chosen as representative of an exciting date, of a nurturant person, and a person of good or ethical character. All were strongly correlated with social desirability. Thus, attractive stimulus persons are assumed to be more exciting dates ($F = 39.97$), more nurturant individuals ($F = 13.96$), and to have better character ($F = 19.57$) than persons of lesser attractiveness.

CRITICAL THINKING QUESTIONS

1. The study used college students, presumably most of them ages 18 to 22. Do you think that the age of the subjects might influence the results? Why or why not? Design a study to test this possibility.

2. The study used photographs as stimulus materials. Do you think that the "What is beautiful is good" effect also would occur in face-to-face encounters? Or might the

judgments made in person somehow be different than those made by looking at photographs? How could you test this possibility?

3. The study indicated that physically attractive people are perceived as having more socially desirable traits and are expected to be more successful in life than their less attractive counterparts. Do you think that attractive people *actually* are more desirable and more successful in life? Why or why not? How could this question be tested?

4. Relate the results of this study to the information presented in Article 19. How would an evolutionary psychologist explain the results of the present study?

ADDITIONAL RELATED READINGS

McCall, M. (1999). Physical attractiveness, mood, and the decision to card for the purchase of alcohol: Evidence for a mood-management hypothesis. *Journal of Applied Social Psychology, 29*(6), 1172–1190.

Watkins, L. M., & Johnson, L. (2000). Screening job applicants: The impact of physical attractiveness and application quality. *International Journal of Selection & Assessment, 8*(2), 76–84.

ARTICLE 21 _____

Both of the preceding articles looked at the important role that physical attractiveness plays in interpersonal attraction. Article 19 focused not only on what we find physically attractive but also why we may hold these values, attributing biological preferences to our evolutionary roots. Article 20 demonstrated that we place great importance on physical attractiveness in deciding whom we want to date and that we associate all sorts of positive and desirable characteristics with people we find attractive. This "What is beautiful is good" effect may bestow significant benefits on people deemed physically attractive in a given society.

One consequence of this importance that society places on physical attractiveness is that people who are attractive may come to spend a great deal of time and energy focusing on that single quality. Since both time and energy are finite, the more time and energy spent focusing on appearance, the less time and energy available to devote to other aspects of the self. Typically, society places a greater emphasis on the value of female physical attractiveness than that of males. Consequently, the tendency to view onself as an object may be more pronounced in females.

Previous research has indicated that self-objectification has a number of negative consequences for women. For example, women who view themselves as objects are more likely to have eating disorders and body shame. The following article by Caroline Davis, Michelle Dionne, and Barbara Shuster extends previous research on this topic by examining both the physical and personality correlates of self-objectification. In other words, given that not all women of the same level of attractiveness will demonstrate the same level of self-objectification, what personality factors may be involved? Namely, why do some women self-objectify at a higher level than others?

Physical and Psychological Correlates of Appearance Orientation

■ Caroline Davis, Michelle Dionne, and Barbara Shuster

ABSTRACT

Objectification theory posits that the sexualization of women in our culture socializes them to "self-objectify"— that is, to place considerable emphasis on their appearance and to have diminished confidence in competence-related activities. Recent studies have found that self-objectification is associated with a number of negative consequences for women such as symptoms of disordered eating, body shame, and poor math performance. The present study is the first to consider both physical and personality correlates of self-objectification.

In a sample of young women, we investigated, using multiple regression procedures, whether certain physical and personality traits would predict the variance in a measure of appearance orientation. We found that narcissistic and neurotic traits were positively related to the dependent variable, and that women who had higher facial-attractiveness ratings were also more appearance focused, but only if they had low perfectionism scores. Results are discussed in the context of expectancy effects on personality development.

Reprinted from *Personality and Individual Differences, 30,* C. Davis, M. Dionne, & B. Shuster, "Physical and psychological correlates of appearance orientation," pp. 21–30. Copyright © 2001, with permission from Elsevier Science.

1. INTRODUCTION

There is abundant evidence that the visual and evaluative scrutiny of the female body is a fundamental feature of male heterosexuality (Buss, 1994; Mazur, 1986). It is also clear that this behaviour contributes, in large part, to the tendency for women, more than men, to be viewed and treated as sexual objects in our culture (see Fredrickson & Roberts, 1997). There is less agreement, however, on the reasons for this sex-biased behaviour. One popular viewpoint is that because certain physical characteristics of the female advertise her health and fertility—that is, her ability to bear live children—these have evolved as the preeminent influences in mate selection for the male. Consequently they are the features that he has learned to regard as sexually and aesthetically pleasing (Barber, 1995; Buss, 1994).

It has become very clear that social benefits—beyond those related to reproduction—accrue to individuals who are physically attractive. Not only is it believed that physically attractive individuals possess more desirable personal traits, such as greater warmth, intelligence, and dominance, but they are offered assistance more readily, secure better jobs, and generally wield more influence than their less attractive counterparts (see Berscheid & Walster, 1974; Feingold, 1992 for reviews). Moreover, these effects appear to be more salient for women because attractive women consistently receive higher ratings than men (by both male and female judges) on a number of desirable qualities such as sociability, good character, and mental health (Feingold, 1998).

In recent years, some have moved beyond providing explanations for the sexualization of women to studies that have examined the psychological consequences of this behaviour for women. An appealing theoretical framework within which to consider these issues has been presented by Fredrickson and Roberts (1997). They have proposed that sexualization serves to socialize women, from an early age, to *self-objectify.* That is, because of the manner in which women are regarded in our society, they learn to see themselves primarily as objects designed for visual inspection and assessment. The result is a heightened focus on grooming and other image-enhancing behaviours, and a diminution in their confidence in activities other than those related to appearance. We see this attitude both reflected in, and promoted by, the media. For example, it was found that articles offering "self-improvement" suggestions in female teen magazines focused almost entirely on self-beautification rather than non-appearance factors such as identity development (Evans, Rutberg, Sather, & Turner, 1991). There is also a deeply entrenched and popular belief that competence and attractiveness in women are inversely related—a fact that is aptly demonstrated by a recent study. A female job applicant was rated by judges as significantly more capable, and assigned a higher starting salary, when she was depicted without cosmetics than when she was depicted wearing cosmetics (Kyle & Mahler, 1996).

A basic tenet of objectification theory is that there is considerable variability in the degree to which women self-objectify. Consequently self-objectification has been conceptualized as a relatively stable individual difference trait. To date, research has focused on the psychological and experiential *consequences* of sexual objectification. For example, in studies of college-aged women, self-objectification was positively and significantly related to heightened body shame and to symptoms of disordered eating (Fredrickson, Roberts, Noll, Quinn, & Twenge, 1998; Noll & Fredrickson, 1998). It was also related to diminished math performance in women but not men—a finding which was consistent with the authors' prediction that self-objectification consumes considerable mental and emotional resources (Fredrickson et al., 1998). Fredrickson and her colleagues acknowledge that many elements will influence the degree to which individuals self-objectify, but no systematic research has yet been done to identify any of these factors. The purpose of the present study was to examine this issue in a preliminary way by investigating whether certain physical and personality characteristics account for the variability in women's focus on their appearance. Previous research has indicated that appearance orientation is positively correlated with body surveillance—that is, viewing one's body as an outside observer (McKinley & Hyde, 1996). Although correlational research cannot establish causality, the discovery of associations among factors is an important first step.

As physical attractiveness is a highly admired attribute, we can assume that beautiful women experience more evaluative gazing and greater sexualization than less attractive women. We reasoned, therefore, that they would also be more prone to self-objectification than their less attractive counterparts. Certain core personality factors are also likely to contribute to the tendency to self-objectify. In this study, we have focused on three particular personality constructs because of their aetiological significance in related body-image research.

Numerous studies have found that neuroticism [N] (a biologically-based and higher-order personality trait) is the single strongest psychological correlate of poor body image, low self-esteem, and general negative affectivity (see Claridge & Davis, 2000, submitted for a review). Research evidence indicates that high N participants react more strongly to a wide variety of arousing or stressful stimuli and return to baseline states more slowly than low N participants (Eysenck & Eysenck, 1991). Because neuroticism reflects worry, anxiousness, and emotional sensitivity, we hypothesized that individuals with this temperamental predisposition would also be more vulnerable to the sexualization process than their more stable counterparts and, therefore, more likely to self-objectify.

Although earlier measurements of perfectionism viewed it as a unitary trait, recent theorists have shown that perfectionism is most appropriately examined as a multidimensional construct that includes both self-imposed expectations of perfection and success, as well as those imposed by those around us. Research has also indicated that high perfectionism is a central feature of many psychological disturbances, including depression and eating-related disorders (Bastiani, Rao, Weltzin, & Kaye, 1995; Blatt, 1995; Slade, 1982). These findings mesh with evidence that perfectionism correlates positively with weight preoccupation and body dissatisfaction among young women in the general population (Hewitt, Flett, & Ediger, 1995; Minarik & Ahrens, 1996). We propose that women who are goal directed and who set high personal standards are also more likely to conform to social expectations. In our image-conscious culture, they are therefore more likely to internalize a concern with their physical appearance than those who are less perfectionistic. Women for whom many, rather than few, roles (the "superwoman") were important for

their sense of self-worth, reported a greater number of eating disorder symptoms (Timko, Striegel-Moore, Silberstein, & Rodin, 1987).

Finally, women's attentiveness to their appearance has often been viewed as a demonstration of their vain and narcissistic self-interest. However, some have pointed out that because of the advantages of being physically attractive, the use of appearance-enhancing behaviours are actually highly adaptive coping strategies employed by women to improve their economic and social prospects (see Fredrickson & Roberts, 1997). Because of the potential relevance of these issues, narcissistic personality characteristics were also examined in the statistical analysis.

2. METHOD

2.1. Participants

One hundred and two White women were recruited from the campus of a large Canadian university by posters requesting volunteers to take part in a "short psychology study". Their mean age was 21.46 years (SD = 3.49), and their mean Body Mass Index (weight [kg]/height [m^2]) was 213.23 (SD = 4.89).

2.2. Measures

Appearance Orientation was assessed by the 12-item Appearance Orientation subscale of the *Multidimensional Body-Self Relations Questionnaire* (Cash, 1994). High scorers place greater importance on how they look, and they engage in more grooming behaviours to manage their appearance. This scale is similar to the *Self-Objectification Questionnaire* (Fredrickson et al., 1998) as it reflects the degree of concern respondents have with their appearance without including an evaluative component of how they appraise their appearance.

Facial Attractiveness was operationally defined as the mean of 8 judges' (4 females between the ages of 23–31 years, and 4 males between the ages of 24–30 years) ratings of Polaroid photographs taken of each participant. Ratings were given on a scale of 0–10, to the nearest 0.5. With the participant facing the camera, two photographs were taken at a fixed distance of 3 feet from the camera—a distance that provided a head and shoulders image. For one picture, the participant was asked to smile, and for the other she was asked not to smile. In each photo, a black gown with a high neckline was worn in order to remove the possible influence of clothing and jewellery on the judges' ratings.

The judges were told that they should examine all the photographs before beginning their ratings in order to become familiar with the quality of Polaroid photographs. They were instructed to use the value "5" to rate a face that they considered "average" (i.e., not attractive or unattractive), and to use that as the standard from which to move up or down the scale when they assigned a rating to each pair of photographs. They were also told to assume that facial attractiveness, like most other physical variables, would be more or less normally distributed, and so they would expect to find many more observations in the middle range than ones at either extreme.

Narcissism was assessed by *The Narcissistic Personality Inventory* [NPI] (Raskin & Hall, 1979). This is a 40-item, forced choice questionnaire whose items are based on the diagnostic criteria, as defined by DSM-III, for Narcissistic Personality Disorder. A factor analysis of the NPI (Raskin & Terry, 1988) identified seven factors: authority, exhibitionism, superiority, vanity, exploitiveness, entitlement, and self-sufficiency. The reliability and validity of the NPI has been established in clinical (e.g., Priftera & Ryan, 1984) and non-clinical samples (Emmons, 1984; 1987; Raskin & Hall, 1981). Although there are a number of scales that have been developed to assess narcissism, this is the most commonly used, particularly in non-clinical research. Because some of the subscales have relatively few items, and because they tend to be moderately to highly intercorrelated, our analyses will employ, as is often done, the total NPI score (e.g., Davis, Claridge, & Brewer, 1996; Eyring & Sobelman, 1996; Smalley & Stake, 1996).

Neuroticism was assessed by the 24-item neuroticism-stability (N) scale of the *Eysenck Personality Questionnaire-Revised* (Eysenck & Eysenck, 1991). This is a measure of emotional lability or reactivity and the degree to which individuals are nervous, easily made anxious, and preoccupied by things that might go wrong.

Perfectionism was assessed by the 45-item *Multidimensional Perfectionism Scale [MPS]* (Hewitt & Flett, 1989). This questionnaire comprises three low to moderately correlated subscales. The items of the *Self-Oriented [SOP]* subscale reflect self-imposed expectations of perfection. whereas *Other-Oriented [OOP]*, and *Socially-Prescribed [SPP]* perfectionism subscales reflect the perception that expectations of perfection are being imposed on oneself by external forces—either other individuals or society in general.

2.3. Procedure

When participants were recruited for the study, they were not aware that they would be asked to have their photographs taken. After arriving at the laboratory and giving written informed consent, each participant completed the questionnaire package, had her height and weight measured, and was paid a small sum for her participation. At this point, the experimenter mentioned that a separate study was being conducted in our laboratory and that the researchers were attempting to collect a large number of photographed faces in order to study "impression formation." Each participant was invited to take part and to have her picture taken. She was also offered an additional small stipend. Of the eligible participants who completed the first study, only three declined to take part in the second study. This paradigm gave us confidence that the questionnaire responses were not biased by the knowledge that each participant was going to have her photograph taken.

3. RESULTS

Table 1 lists the means and standard deviations for all variables used in the analyses. For the personality variables, these are very similar to statistics published in other studies with comparable samples (e.g., *Appearance Orientation*: Cash, 1994; *Narcissism*: Davis, Claridge, & Cerullo, 1997a; Raskin & Terry, 1988; *Neuroticism*: Eysenck & Eysenck, 1991; *Perfectionism*: Hewitt, Flett & Ediger, 1995; Hobden & Pliner, 1995).

A multiple regression analysis was used to test the combined contribution of narcissism, neuroticism,

TABLE 1 / Means and Standard Deviations of All Variables Used in the Analyses

Variable	Mean	Standard Deviation
Appearance Orientation	3.60	0.56
Facial Attractiveness	5.00	1.11
Narcissism	15.36	7.25
Neuroticism	14.88	5.09
Self-Oriented Perfectionism	73.63	15.18
Other-Oriented Perfectionism	59.00	12.77
Socially-Prescribed Perfectionism	55.11	15.28

perfectionism, and objective ratings of facial attractiveness on appearance orientation by entering these together as independent variables in the model. As indicated by the consistently low values obtained for the variance inflation factor, multicollinearity among the independent variables was not a problem in this analysis.

Results indicated that neuroticism and narcissism predicted the criterion variable, in the positive direction, after accounting for all other variables in the model. However, contrary to expectation, none of the perfectionism subscales, nor facial attractiveness, related to appearance orientation. A summary of these results is presented in Table 2.

At this point we decided to explore the possibility that facial attractiveness interacted with one of the personality variables in predicting appearance orientation. To test this, we entered in the regression model,

together with the main-effect variables, an interaction term for facial attractiveness and each of the personality variables. We found a statistically significant interaction of facial attractiveness and self-oriented perfectionism. Narcissism and neuroticism also remained as signifcant main effects.[1] Table 3 presents a summary of this regression model including only the significant main effects and the significant interaction term.

A plot of the facial attractiveness × self-oriented perfectionism interaction can be seen in Figure 1. Here the four regression lines illustrate the relationship between self-oriented perfectionism and appearance orientation, at different levels of attractiveness. It can be seen that appearance orientation increases as attractiveness ratings increase—that is, as hypothesized, attractive women report being more focused on their physical appearance than do their less attractive counterparts. However, this relationship only obtains at low to moderate levels of perfectionism. As self-oriented perfectionism increases, the relationship between attractiveness and appearance orientation is systematically eroded so that at relatively high levels of perfectionism differences in attractiveness do not influence appearance orientation.

According to the procedures recommended by Aiken and West (1991), *post hoc* probing of the perfectionism × facial attractiveness interaction was carried out by simple slope analysis. It was found that at the levels of attractiveness illustrated in Figure 1, the slopes defining the relationship between perfectionism and

TABLE 2 / Multiple Regression Analysis with *Appearance Orientation* as the Dependent Variable Showing the Full Model Main Effects

Variable	Parameter Est.	SE	$t(H_0)$	p	VIF
Intercept	2.47	0.40			
Facial Attractiveness	0.06	0.05	1.29	0.1989	1.08
Neuroticism	0.04	0.01	2.84	0.0056	1.44
Narcissism	0.03	0.01	3.14	0.0023	1.28
Self-Oriented Perfectionism	−0.005	0.004	−1.02	0.3116	1.56
Socially-Prescribed Perfectionism	−0.002	0.004	−0.35	0.7300	1.55
Other-Oriented Perfectionism	0.005	0.005	1.03	0.3082	1.38

$R^2 = 0.17$

TABLE 3 / Multiple Regression Analysis, with *Appearance Orientation* as the Dependent Variable, Showing Only the Significant Main Effects and Interaction Terms in the Model

Variable	Parameter Est.	SE	$t(H_0)$	p
Intercept	−1.90	1.32		
Facial Attractiveness	1.004	0.27	3.72	0.0003
Neuroticism	0.03	0.01	2.92	0.0044
Narcissism	0.03	0.01	3.41	0.0009
Self-Oriented Perfectionism	0.06	0.02	3.24	0.0016
Self-Oriented Perfectionism × Facial Attractiveness	−0.01	0.003	−3.51	0.0007
$R^2 = 0.26$				

appearance orientation (holding the other independent variables constant) were significantly different from zero ($p < 0.05$).

Finally, Table 4 presents a matrix of all pairwise simple correlations among the variables used in the above analyses. There is very little intercorrelation among the variables except for the expected low to moderate relationships among the perfectionism subscales. It is noteworthy, however, that physical attractiveness was not correlated with any of the personality variables. Of additional interest is the observation that neuroticism was negatively correlated with narcissism.

4. DISCUSSION

We predicted that a proportion of the variance in appearance orientation would be explained by a linear function of both physical and psychological characteristics. With respect to the former, our results indicated, as hypothesised, that women with attractive faces place greater emphasis on their appearance than do their less attractive counterparts, but only at relatively low levels of self-oriented perfectionism (SOP). As described earlier, objectification theory provides one explanatory mechanism for understanding the relationship between attractiveness and focus on appearance. Women who are attractive are more likely to be the subject of visual scrutiny and evaluation and, therefore, are more likely to self-objectify.

A regression plot of the attractiveness × SOP interaction (see Figure 1) has indicated that as SOP scores increase, the influence of attractiveness on the dependent variable operates in opposite directions. Very attractive women become less focused on appearance as SOP increases, whereas unattractive women become more focused. The latter association seems logical, the former is more difficult to explain. One possibility is that because high SOP women tend to set high standards in most aspects of their lives, those who are also beautiful can afford to place a lower priority on their appearance (and perhaps more on non-appearance pursuits) than can high SOP women who are less attractive.

FIGURE 1 / Fitted Appearance Orientation as a Function of Facial Attractiveness and Self-Oriented Perfectionism

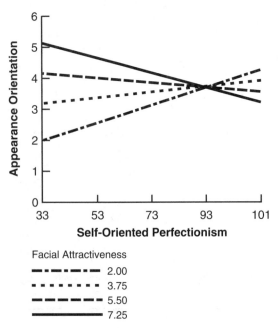

Facial Attractiveness

— ·— ·— · 2.00
· · · · · · · 3.75
— — — — 5.50
———— 7.25

TABLE 4 / A Matrix of Pairwise Correlation Coefficients among Variables[a]

	AO	FA	NAR	N	SOP	OOP	SPP
AO		0.16	0.27*	0.16	0.05	0.17	0.06
FA			0.21	−0.13	0.09	0.12	−0.12
NAR				−0.31*	0.18	0.28*	−0.03
N					0.19	0.02	0.46*
SOP						0.48*	0.46*
OOP							0.25
SPP							

[a]AO = Appearance Orientation; FA = Facial Attractiveness; NAR = Narcissism; N = Neuroticism; SOP = Self-Oriented Perfectionism; OOP= Other-Oriented Perfectionism; SPP = Socially-Prescribed Perfectionism
*= < 0.01.

Another interesting finding in our study was that narcissism was positively related to appearance orientation, independent of the other variables in the model. Two matters deserve consideration here. The first concerns the definition and measurement of narcissism. It has recently been argued that narcissism is best conceptualized as a continuum of self-functioning with the healthier aspects of the construct anchoring one pole and the more pathological aspects, the other (Watson, Hickman & Morris, 1996). As operationalizations of narcissism move from the maladaptive end to the more adjusted end they are more likely to predict good self-esteem and lower personal shame. In the present study, narcissism was assessed by the NPI. Since the development of this scale, considerable evidence has demonstrated that its items tend to reflect the more adaptive aspects of narcissism because it correlates positively with a number of traits that are indicative of good psychological functioning such as body satisfaction and good self-esteem (see Davis, Claridge, & Cerullo, 1997b; Watson et al., 1996). Based on this association it appears that high appearance orientation is related to psychological characteristics associated with good adjustment.

On the other hand, and in accord with the tenets of objectification theory, Miller (1992) has pointed out other important aspects of narcissism. He has explained that there are many sources of self-affirmation available to all of us; these range along a continuum from those that risk almost no interpersonal vulnerability to those that require a great deal of interpersonal vulnerability. At the low risk end of this dimension are activities related to the physical self (e.g., appearance-related activities). As these require little if any interpersonal interaction, they tend to be overused in self-esteem regulation by the narcissist. Although these pursuits may have *short-term* benefits, they are likely to be maladaptive in the long term *and* if taken to excess because, in the process, individuals tend to neglect the development of competence in other sources of self-fulfilment such as work, hobbies, family, and friendships which are potentially more lasting. This point is especially relevant to the argument presented by Fredrickson and her colleagues that self-objectification consumes valuable energy and resources that could be directed to other pursuits in a person's life, and a more balanced lifestyle (Fredrickson & Roberts, 1997).

Finally, and not unexpectedly, neuroticism was positively related to appearance orientation, which supports evidence that emotionally reactive women are more likely to perceive and respond to social cues than those with low levels of this trait. In this context, the deleterious psychological consequences of self-objectification (see Fredrickson et al., 1998; Noll & Fredrickson, 2000, in press) appear to be exacerbated in high N women.

In conclusion, this study has identified certain factors that may affect why some women more than others attach great importance to their appearance and assiduously engage in behaviours to enhance their physical selves. Fredrickson and her colleagues have demonstrated that, in general, this trait is higher among women than among men, and they have argued that this occurs largely because of the pervasive manner in which women's bodies are observed, evaluated, and potentially sexualized in our culture. Our data have shown that both narcissistic and neurotic traits are positively related to appearance orientation. In addition, physically attractive women are more prone to focus on their appearance than those who are less attractive, but only when they exhibit low to moderate levels of self-oriented perfectionism. Despite the correlational nature of this study—and therefore our inability to establish firmly the direction of causality—it is nevertheless reasonable to assume that core personality factors and physical characteristics can influence the development of traits, such as self-objectification, that are essentially learned. However, future research in this area would benefit from studying these issues longitudinally and from a developmental perspective.

ACKNOWLEDGEMENTS

This study was supported by grants to the first author from the Social Sciences and Humanities Research Council of Canada (410-97-1149), and from the Faculty of Arts, York University, Toronto, Canada.

REFERENCES

Aiken, L. S. & West, S. G. (1991). *Multiple regression: testing and interpreting interactions.* Newbury Park, CA: Sage Publications.

Barber, N. (1995). The evolutionary psychology of physical attractiveness: Sexual selection and human morphology. *Ethology and Sociobiology, 16,* 395–424.

Bastiani, A. M., Rao, R., Weltzin, T., & Kaye, W. H. (1995). Perfectionism in anorexia nervosa. *International Journal of Eating Disorders, 17,* 147–152.

Berscheid, E., & Walster, E. (1974). Physical attractiveness. In L. Berkowitz, *Advances in experimental social psychology Vol. 7* (pp. 157–215). San Diego: Academic Press.

Blatt, S. J. (1995). The destructiveness of perfectionism. *American Psychologist, 50,* 1003–1020.

Buss, D. M. *The evolution of desire.* New York: Basic.

Cash, T. F. (1994). *The multidimensional body-self relations questionnaire.* Unpublished test manual, Old Dominion University, Norfolk, VA.

Claridge, G., & Davis, C. (2000). What's the use of N? (submitted)

Davis, C., Claridge, G., & Brewer, H. (1996). The two faces of narcissism: Personality dynamics of body esteem. *Journal of Social and Clinical Psychology, 15,* 153–166.

Davis, C., Claridge, G., & Cerullo, D. (1997a). Personality factors and weight preoccupation: A continuum approach to the association between eating disorders and personality disorders. *Journal of Psychiatric Research, 31,* 467–480.

Davis, C., Claridge, G., & Cerullo, D. (1997b). Reflections on narcissism: conflicts about body-image perceptions in women. *Personality and Individual Differences, 22,* 309–316.

Emmons, R. A. (1984). Factor analysis and construct validity of the Narcissistic Personality Inventory. *Journal of Personality Assessment, 48,* 291–300.

Emmons, R. A. (1987). Narcissism: Theory and measurement. *Journal of Personality and Social Psychology, 52,* 11–17.

Evans, E. D., Rutberg, J., Sather, C., & Turner, C. (1991). Content analysis of contemporary teen magazines for adolescent females. *Youth and Society, 23,* 99–120.

Eyring, W. E. III, & Sobelman, S. (1996). Narcissism and birth order. *Psychological Reports, 78,* 403–406.

Eysenck, H. J. & Eysenck, S. B. G. (1991). *Manual of the Eysenck Personality Scales.* London: Hodder & Stoughton.

Feingold, A. (1992). Good-looking people are not what we think. *Psychological Bulletin, 111,* 304–341.

Feingold, A. (1998). Gender stereotyping for sociability, dominance, character, and mental health: A meta-analysis of findings from the bogus stranger paradigm. *Genetic, Social, and General Psychology Monographs, 124,* 253–270.

Fredrickson, B. L., & Roberts, T.-A. (1997). Objectification theory: Toward understanding women's lived experiences and mental health risks. *Psychology of Women Quarterly, 21,* 173–206.

Fredrickson, B. L., Roberts, T.-A., Noll, S. M., Quinn, D. M., & Twenge, J. M. (1998). That swimsuit becomes you. Sex differences in self-objectification, restrained eating and math performance. *Journal of Personality and Social, 75,* 269–284.

Hewitt, P. L., & Flett, G. L. (1989). The Multidimensional Perfectionism Scale: Development and validation. *Canadian Psychology, 30,* 339.

Hewitt, P. L., Flett, G. L., & Ediger, E. (1995). Perfectionism traits and perfectionistic self-presentation in eating disordered attitudes, characteristics, and symptoms. *International Journal of Eating Disorders, 4,* 317–326.

Hobden, K., & Pliner, P. (1995). Self-handicapping and dimensions of perfectionism: Self-presentation vs self-protection. *Journal of Research in Personality, 29,* 461–474.

Kyle, D. J., & Mahler, H. I. M. (1996). The effects of hair color and cosmetic use on perceptions of a female's ability. *Psychology of Women Quarterly, 20,* 447–455.

Mazur, A. (1986). US trends in feminine beauty and overadaptation. *The Journal of Sex Research, 22,* 281–303.

McKinley, N. M., & Hyde, J. S. (1996). The objectified body consciousness scale: Development and validation. *Psychology of Women Quarterly, 20,* 181–215.

Miller, I. J. (19921). Interpersonal vulnerability and narcissism: A conceptual continuum for understanding and treating narcissistic psychopathology. *Psychotherapy, 29,* 216–224.

Minarik, M. L., & Ahrens, A. H. (1996). Relations of eating behaviour and symptoms of depression and anxiety to the dimensions of perfectionism among undergraduate women. *Cognitive Therapy and Research, 20,* 155–169.

Noll, S. M., & Fredrickson, B. L. (1998). A mediational model linking self-objectification, body shame, and disordered eating. *Psychology of Women Quarterly, 22,* 623–636.

Priftera, A., & Ryan, J. J. (1984). Validation of the Narcissistic Personality Inventory (NPI) in a psychiatric sample. *Journal of Clinical Psychology, 40,* 140–142.

Raskin, R., & Hall, C. S. (1979). A narcissistic personality inventory. *Psychological Reports, 45,* 590.

Raskin, R., & Hall, C. S. (1981). The Narcissistic Personality Inventory: Alternate form reliability and further evidence of construct validity. *Journal of Personality Assessment, 45,* 159–162.

Raskin, R., & Terry, H. (1988). A prinicipal-components analysis of the Narcissistic Personality Inventory and further evidence of its construct validity. *Journal of Personality and Social Psychology, 54,* 890–902.

Slade, P. (1982). Towards a functional analysis of anorexia nervosa and bulimia nervosa. *British Journal of Clinical Psychology, 21,* 167–179.

Smalley, R. L., & Stake, J. E. (1996). Evaluating sources of ego-threatening feedback: Self-esteem and narcissism effects. *Journal of Research in Personality, 30,* 483–495.

Timko, C., Striegel-Moore, R. H., Silberstein, L. R., & Rodin, J. (1987). Femininity/masculinity and disordered eating in women: How are they related? *International Journal of Eating Disorders, 6,* 701–712.

Watson, P. J., Hickman, S. E., & Morris, R. J. (1996). Self-reported narcissism and shame: Testing the defensive self-esteem and continuum hypotheses. *Personality and Individual Differences, 21,* 253–259.

ENDNOTE

1. Given that body size might also play a role in influencing appearance orientation, the model was refit including Body Mass Index [weight (kg)/height(m²)], derived from measured height and weight, as an additional independent variable. It was not a significant predictor, nor did its presence in the model change the size or significance of the parameter estimates for the other independent variables or the interaction term.

CRITICAL THINKING QUESTIONS

1. The article states that "the visual and evaluative scrutiny of the female body is a fundamental feature of male heterosexuality." Do you agree? Why or why not? Use other sources of information on physical attractiveness to develop your answer.

2. Do homosexual males place as strong an emphasis on the physical attractiveness of other males as do heterosexual males on females? Why or why not? Relate your answer to the information you gathered to answer Question 1. Then design a study to test your theories.

3. The authors suggest that a longitudinal study is needed to investigate this topic. What could a longitudinal study determine that the present study could not? What advantages would that knowledge create? Design such a longitudinal study.

4. Given the weight that society places on female physical attractiveness, what can be done to help very young women from developing some of the problems discussed in the article? Suggest some interventions that might be made on their behalf.

Chapter Eight

CLOSE RELATIONSHIPS
Friendship, Love, and Sexuality

OF ALL THE interactions that occur between human beings, perhaps none is more capable of producing such intense feelings as love. If we look at how often love is portrayed in the popular media, we get the definite impression that it is a major concern, almost a preoccupation, of most people. However, if we look at the literature in social psychology, we might get a very different impression. Until recently, the topic of love was largely ignored in the research literature.

A specific subject of interest to many people is the failure of love and the dissolution of relationships. Anyone who has been through a divorce or has witnessed its effects on someone close to them knows that the ending of a marriage is usually an extremely painful ordeal. Yet in spite of the pain involved in splitting up, nearly half of all marriages end up in divorce. What goes wrong? More importantly, what can be done earlier in a relationship to decrease the likelihood of divorce later on? Article 22, "Will Your Marriage Last?" presents the results of recent research that studied couples throughout the relationship cycle. Unlike most self-help books on how to make a marriage last, this article presents data, not just the opinion of the author.

After meeting someone who catches your attention, and then deciding that you would like to get to know him or her better, comes a big step: asking the person out. So you take the chance and ask for a date. Which response to your request would increase your liking of the recipient of your request the most: The person enthusiastically accepts your offer, or the person first plays "hard to get" and then later accepts your invitation? Much folk wisdom would suggest the value of not appearing too eager. But does that hard-to-get strategy actually work? Article 23, "Playing Hard to Get," is an amusing classic article that addresses this dating dilemma.

Most studies of physical attractiveness look at the role this factor plays in the initial stages of a relationship. Article 24, "Perception of Physical Attractiveness throughout Loving Relationships," is unique in that it examines how the perceived physical attractiveness of our partners changes over time. Perhaps these changes have implications for other aspects of satisfaction in relationships, as well.

ARTICLE 22 _____

The high divorce rate in the United States is of social concern to a large number of Americans. Current statistics indicate that nearly half of all marriages will end in divorce. And while the number of divorces has decreased slightly in the last few years, it still remains around the 50% mark. Whether the high rates of divorce seen over the last few decades will remain the same, increase, or decrease remains to be seen. Nonetheless, the prevalence of divorce is certainly characteristic of contemporary U.S. society.

In spite of the 50/50 odds that a marriage will not last, nearly 95% of the adult U.S. population will marry at least once in their lifetimes. Marriage obviously holds a strong attraction for most people. Even among those who divorce, many will remarry, further pointing to the importance that most people place on the institution of marriage. It probably is a rare couple who marry with the thought that they will divorce. Indeed, most people take to heart the wedding vows of "For better or worse, in sickness and in health, until death do us part," believing that the dire divorce statistics apply to other couples, not them.

So, what is known about how to make a marriage work? Is it a matter of learning to communicate? Having to work hard on the relationship? Learning to compromise? Go to any self-help section of a bookstore, and you will find scores of publications on how to make your marriage last. But how much of this advice is grounded in research, and how much is simply the opinion of the author? Sadly, many, if not most, of these books present one person's opnion, which is usually based on his or her own experiences with marriage or his or her work as a therapist counseling distressed couples.

What's wrong with that, especially the opinions of a therapist in the marriage-counseling field? For one thing, therapists usually see couples when they are quite distressed and perhaps already headed toward divorce. But what about the people in happy marriages who never see the inside of a therapist's office? What is known about those couples and how they make their marriages work?

Until recently, not a lot of research has been conducted on why people divorce. While much is known about the demographic factors associated with divorce (e.g., early age of marriage, premarital pregnancy, living together before marriage, etc.), the factors that may be present early on in a relationship—and that may predict divorce—are not as well understood. Even the available data on why couples divorce have limited value because, like the therapists, they reflect the experiences of couples who have been married a number of years, not those at the beginning of the relationship.

The following article by Aviva Patz discusses recent studies that differ from previous work in that they followed couples from their courtship stage though the various cycles of marriage. What distinguishes couples who eventually divorce from those who remain married may surprise you.

Will Your Marriage Last?

■ Aviva Patz

What if I told you that there is a man in America who can predict, from the outset, whether or not your marriage will last? He doesn't need to hear you arguing; he doesn't need to know what you argue about. He doesn't even care whether you argue at all.

I was dubious, too, but I was curious enough to attend a lecture on the subject at the most recent American Psychological Association convention in Boston. Ted Huston, Ph.D., a professor of human ecology and psychology at the University of Texas at Austin, was showcasing the results of a long-term study of married couples that pierces the heart of social psychological science: the ability to forecast whether a husband and wife, two years after taking their vows, will stay together and whether they will be happy.

My press pass notwithstanding, I went to the seminar for reasons of my own. Fresh out of college I had gotten married—and burned. Some part of me was still reeling from three years of waking up angry every morning, not wanting to go home after work, feeling lonely even as my then husband sat beside me. I went because I have recently remarried and just celebrated my one-year anniversary. Needless to say, I'd like to make this one work. So I scribbled furiously in my notebook, drinking in the graphs and charts—for psychology, for husbands and wives everywhere, but mostly for myself.

Huston, a pioneer in the psychology of relationships, launched the Processes of Adaptation in Intimate Relationships (the "PAIR Project") in 1981, in which he followed 168 couples—drawn from marriage license records in four counties in a rural and working-class area of Pennsylvania—from their wedding day through 13 years of marriage.

Through multiple interviews, Huston looked at the way partners related to one another during courtship, as newlyweds and through the early years of marriage. Were they "gaga?" Comfortable? Unsure? He measured their positive and negative feelings for each other and observed how those feelings changed over time. Are newlyweds who hug and kiss more likely than other couples to have a happy marriage, he wondered, or are they particularly susceptible to divorce if their romance dissipates? Are newlyweds who bicker destined to part ways?

Since one in two marriages ends in divorce in this country, there ought to be tons of research explaining why. But the existing literature provides only pieces of the larger puzzle.

Past research has led social scientists to believe that newlyweds begin their life together in romantic bliss, and can then be brought down by their inability to navigate the issues that inevitably crop up during the marriage. When Benjamin Karny and Thomas Bradbury did a comprehensive review of the literature in 1995, they confirmed studies such as those of John Gottman and Neil Jacobson, maintaining that the best predictors of divorce are interactive difficulties, such as frequent expressions of antagonism, lack of respect for each other's ideas and similar interpersonal issues.

But most of this research was done on couples who had been married a number of years, with many of them already well on their way to divorce. It came as no surprise, then, that researchers thought their hostility toward one another predicted the further demise of the relationship.

Huston's study was unique in that it looked at couples much earlier, when they were courting and during the initial years of marriage, thus providing the first complete picture of the earliest stages of distress. Its four main findings were quite surprising.

First, contrary to popular belief, Huston found that many newlyweds are far from blissfully in love. Second, couples whose marriages begin in romantic bliss are particularly divorce-prone because such intensity is too hard to maintain. Believe it or not, marriages that start out with less "Hollywood

Reprinted from *Psychology Today*, 2000 (January/February), *33*(1), 58–65. Reprinted with permission from *Psychology Today* magazine. Copyright © 2000 (Sussex Publishers, Inc.).

romance" usually have more promising futures. Accordingly, and this is the third major finding, spouses in lasting but lackluster marriages are not prone to divorce, as one might suspect; their marriages are less fulfilling to begin with, so there is no erosion of a Western-style romantic ideal. Lastly, and perhaps most importantly, it is the loss of love and affection, not the emergence of interpersonal issues, that sends couples journeying toward divorce.

By the end of Huston's study in 1994, the couples looked a lot like the rest of America, falling into four groups. They were either married and happy; married and unhappy; divorced early, within seven years; or divorced later, after seven years—and each category showed a distinct pattern.

Those who remained happily married were very "in love" and affectionate as newlyweds. They showed less ambivalence, expressed negative feelings less often and viewed their mate more positively than other couples. Most importantly, these feelings remained stable over time. By contrast, although many couples who divorced later were very affectionate as newlyweds, they gradually became less loving, more negative, and more critical of their spouse.

Indeed, Huston found that how well spouses got along as newlyweds affected their future, but the major distinguishing factor between those who divorced and those who remained married was the amount of change in the relationship over its first two years.

"The first two years are key—that's when the risk of divorce is particularly high," he says. "And the changes that take place during this time tell us a lot about where the marriage is headed."

What surprised Huston most was the nature of the changes that led to divorce: The experiences of the 56 participating couples who divorced showed that loss of initial levels of love and affection, rather than conflict, was the most salient predictor of distress and divorce. This loss sends the relationship into a downward spiral, leading to increased bickering and fighting, and to the collapse of the union.

"This ought to change the way we think about the early roots of what goes wrong in marriage," Huston said. "The dominant approach has been to work with couples to resolve conflict, but it should focus on preserving the positive feelings. That's a very important take-home lesson."

"Huston's research fills an important gap in the literature by suggesting that there is more to a successful relationship than simply managing conflict," said Harry Reis, Ph.D., of the University of Rochester, a leading social psychologist.

"My own research speaks to 'loss of intimacy,' in the sense that when people first become close they feel a tremendous sense of validation from each other, like their partner is the only other person on earth who sees things as they do. That feeling sometimes fades, and when it does, it can take a heavy toll on the marriage."

Social science has a name for that fading dynamic—"disillusionment": Lovers initially put their best foot forward, ignoring each other's—and the relationship's—shortcomings. But after they tie the knot, hidden aspects of their personalities emerge, and idealized images give way to more realistic ones. This can lead to disappointment, loss of love and, ultimately, distress and divorce.

WHEN MARRIAGE FAILS

The story of Peter and Suzie, participants in the PAIR Project, shows classic disillusionment. When they met, Suzie was 24, a new waitress at the golf course where Peter, then 26, played. He was "awed" by her beauty. After a month the two considered themselves an exclusive couple. Peter said Suzie "wasn't an airhead; she seemed kind of smart, and she's pretty." Suzie said Peter "cared a lot about me as a person, and was willing to overlook things."

By the time they strolled down the aisle on Valentine's Day in 1981, Peter and Suzie had dated only nine months, experiencing many ups and downs along the way.

Huston says couples are most vulnerable to disillusionment when their courtship is brief. In a whirlwind romance, it's easy to paint an unrealistically rosy picture of the relationship, one that cannot be sustained.

Sure enough, reality soon set in for Peter and Suzie. Within two years, Suzie was less satisfied with almost every aspect of their marriage. She expressed less affection for Peter and felt her love decline continuously. She considered him to have "contrary"

Bliss or Bust?
Take the Marriage Quiz

—Created for *Psychology Today* by Ted Huston, Ph.D., Shanna Smith, Sylvia Niehuis, Christopher Rasmussen and Paul Miller

Circle the answer that best describes your level of agreement with each of the following statements:

Part 1 Our Relationship As Newlyweds

1. **As newlyweds, we were constantly touching, kissing, pledging our love or doing sweet things for one another.**
   Strongly disagree (1 pt.)   Disagree (2 pts.)
   Agree (3 pts.)   Strongly agree (4 pts.)

2. **As newlyweds, how often did you express criticism, anger, annoyance, impatience or dissatisfaction to one another?**
   Often (1 pt.)   Sometimes (2 pts.)
   Rarely (3 pts.)   Almost never (4 pts.)

3. **As newlyweds, my partner and I felt we belonged together; we were extremely close and deeply in love.**
   Disagree (1 pt.)   Mildly agree (2 pts.)
   Agree (3 pts.)   Strongly agree (4 pts.)

4. **As a newlywed, I think one or both of us were confused about our feelings toward each other, or worried that we were not right for each other.**
   Strongly agree (1 pt.)   Agree (2 pts.)
   Disagree (3 pts.)   Strongly disagree (4 pts.)

Part 2 Our Relationship By Our Second Anniversary

1. **By our second anniversary, we were disappointed that we touched, kissed, pledged our love or did sweet things for one another less often than we had as newlyweds.**
   Strongly disagree (1 pt.)   Disagree (2 pts.)
   Agree (3 pts.)   Strongly agree (4 pts.)

2. **By our second anniversary, we expressed criticism, anger, annoyance, impatience or** dissatisfaction a lot more than we had as newlyweds.
   Strongly disagree (1 pt.)   Disagree (2 pts.)
   Agree (3 pts.)   Strongly agree (4 pts.)

3. **By our second anniversary, we felt much less belonging and closeness with one another than we had before.**
   Disagree (1 pt.)   Mildly agree (2 pts.)
   Agree (3 pts.)   Strongly agree (4 pts.)

4. **By our second anniversary, I felt much more confused or worried about the relationship than I did as a newlywed.**
   Strongly disagree (1 pt.)   Disagree (2 pts.)
   Agree (3 pts.)   Strongly agree (4 pts.)

Scoring: Add up the points that correspond to your answers in Part 1. If you scored between 4 and 8, place yourself in Group "A." If you scored between 9 and 16, place yourself in Group "B." Now add up the points that correspond to your answers in Part 2. If you scored between 4 and 8, place yourself in Group "C." If you scored between 9 and 16, place yourself in Group "D."

Your Results: Find the type of marriage first by considering your score in part 1 (either A or B) in combination with your score in part 2 (either C or D): If you scored A + C, read "'Mixed Blessings"; If you scored A + D, read "Disengaging Duo"; If you scored B + C, read "A Fine Romance"; If you scored B + D, read "Disaffected Lovers."

Disaffected Lovers

The contrast between the giddiness you felt as newlyweds and how you felt later may cause disenchantment. While you and your spouse are still affectionate and in love, there are clouds behind the silver lining. You may bicker and disagree, which, combined with a loss of affection and love in your relationship, could give rise to the first serious doubts about your future together.

Food for Thought: Your relationship may be at risk for eventual divorce. But the pattern of decline early on does not have to continue. Ask yourself: Did we set ourselves up for disappointment with an overly romantic view of marriage? Did we assume it would require little effort to sustain? Did we take each other for granted? Did our disappointment lead to frustration and anger? Will continued bickering erode the love we have left?

A Fine Romance

You have a highly affectionate, loving and harmonious marriage. It may have lost a touch of its initial glow as the mundane realities of marriage have demanded more of your time. But you feel a certain sense of security in the marriage: The relationship's gifts you unwrapped as newlyweds continue to delight.

Food for Thought: You have the makings of a happy, stable marriage. The cohesive partnership you have maintained bodes well for its future. You will not always be happy—all marriages go through rough periods. But your ability to sustain a healthy marriage over the critical first two years suggests that you and your partner operate together like a thermostat in a home—when it's chilly, you identify the source of the draft and eliminate it, and when it's hot, you find ways to circulate cool air.

Mixed Blessings

Your marriage is less enchanting and filled with more conflict and ambivalence than Western society's romantic ideal, but it has changed little over its first two years, losing only a modicum of "good feeling." It seems to coast along, showing few signs that it will deteriorate further or become deeply distressed.

Food for Thought: This relationship may not be the romance you envisioned, but it just might serve you well. Many people in such relationships are content, finding their marriage a reassuringly stable foundation that allows them to devote their attention to career, children or other pursuits. Other people in these relationships are slightly dissatisfied, but stay married because the rewards outweigh the drawbacks. A few people may eventually leave such marriages in search of a "fine romance."

Disengaging Duo

You and your mate are not overly affectionate and frequently express displeasure with one another. In contrast to those in a marriage of "mixed blessings," the love you once felt diminished soon after the wedding, and you became more ambivalent about the relationship. You may already have a sense that your relationship is on shaky ground.

Food for Thought: Your relationship may be in immediate trouble. You may have married hoping that problems in the relationship would go away after the wedding, but they didn't. Ask yourself: Did I see our problems coming while we were dating? Did I think they would dissolve with marriage? What kinds of changes would I need to see in my partner in order to be happy? How likely are they to occur? How bad would things have to get before the marriage would no longer be worthwhile?

Note: This quiz is reproduced with permission of Ted Huston, University of Texas.

traits, such as jealousy and possessiveness, and resented his propensity to find fault with her.

Peter, for his part, was disappointed that his wife did not become the flawless parent and homemaker he had envisioned.

Another danger sign for relationships is a courtship filled with drama and driven by external circumstances. For this pair, events related to Peter's jealousy propelled the relationship forward. He was the force behind their destroying letters and pictures from former lovers. It was a phone call between Suzie and an old flame that prompted him to bring up the idea of marriage in the first place. And it was a fit of jealousy—over Suzie's claiming to go shopping and then coming home suspiciously late—that convinced Peter he was ready to marry.

Theirs was a recipe for disaster: A short courtship, driven largely by Peter's jealousy, enabled the pair to ignore flaws in the relationship and in each other, setting them up for disappointment. That disappointment eroded their love and affection, which soured their perception of each other's personalities, creating feelings of ambivalence.

Ten years after saying "I do," the disaffected lovers were in the midst of divorce. When Suzie filed the papers, she cited as the primary reason a gradual loss of love.

The parallels between Peter and Suzie's failed marriage and my own are striking: My courtship with my first husband was short, also about nine months. Like Peter, I had shallow criteria: This guy was cool; he had long hair, wore a leather jacket, played guitar and adored the same obscure band that I did.

When it came time to build a life together, however, we were clearly mismatched. I wanted a traditional family with children; he would have been happy living on a hippie commune. In college, when we wanted to move in together, we thought our parents would be more approving if we got engaged first. So we did, even though we weren't completely sold on the idea of marriage.

The road to divorce was paved early, by the end of the first year: I had said I wanted us to spend more time together; he accused me of trying to keep him from his hobbies, and told me, in so many words, to "get a life." Well I did, and, two years later, he wasn't in it.

WHEN MARRIAGE SUCCEEDS

While the disillusionment model best describes those who divorce, Huston found that another model suits those who stay married, whether or not they are happy: The "enduring dynamics model," in which partners establish patterns of behavior early and maintain them over time, highlights stability in the relationship—the feature that distinguishes those who remain together from those who eventually split up.

The major difference between the unhappily married couples and their happy counterparts is simply that they have a lower level of satisfaction across the board. Yet, oddly enough, this relative unhappiness by itself does not doom the marriage. "We have a whole group of people who are stable in unhappy marriages and not necessarily dissatisfied," Huston said. "It's just a different model of marriage. It's not that they're happy about their marriage, it's just that the discontent doesn't spill over and spoil the rest of their lives."

And while all married couples eventually lose a bit of that honeymoon euphoria, Huston notes, those who remain married don't consider this a crushing blow, but rather a natural transition from "romantic relationship" to "working partnership." And when conflict does arise, they diffuse it with various constructive coping mechanisms.

Nancy and John, participants in Huston's study, are a shining example of happy, healthy balance. They met in February 1978 and were immediately attracted to each other. John said Nancy was "fun to be with" and he "could take her anywhere." Nancy said John always complimented her and liked to do things she enjoyed, things "other guys wouldn't do."

During their courtship, they spent a lot of time together, going to dances at their high school and hanging out with friends. They became comfortable with each other and began to openly disclose their opinions and feelings, realizing they had a lot in common and really enjoyed each other's company.

John paid many surprise visits to Nancy and bought her a number of gifts. Toward the end of the summer, John gave Nancy a charm necklace with a "genuine diamond." She recalls his saying: "This isn't your ring, honey, but you're going to get one." And she did. The two married on Jan. 17, 1981, nearly three years after they began dating.

The prognosis for this relationship is good. Nancy and John have a "fine romance"—a solid foundation of love and affection, built on honesty and intimacy. A three-year courtship enabled them to paint realistic portraits of one another, lessening the chances of a rude awakening after marriage.

In 1994, when they were last interviewed, Nancy and John were highly satisfied with their marriage.

They were very compatible, disagreeing only about politics. Both felt they strongly benefited from the marriage and said they had no desire to leave.

When the seminar ends, I can't get to a pay phone fast enough. After two rings, the phone is answered. He's there, of course. Dependable. Predictable. That's one of the things that first set my husband apart. At the close of one date, he'd lock in the next. "Can I see you tomorrow for lunch?" "Will you have dinner with me next week?"

Unlike the fantasy-quality of my first marriage, I felt a deep sense of comfort and companionship with him, and did not harbor outrageous expectations. We exchanged vows three and a half years later, in August 1998.

There at the convention center, I try to tell my husband about Huston's study, about the critical first few years, about "enduring dynamics." It all comes out in a jumble.

"You're saying we have a good marriage, that we're not going to get divorced?" he asks.

"Yes," I say breathlessly, relieved of the burden of explanation.

"Well I'm glad to hear that," he says, "but I wasn't really worried."

Sometimes I wonder: Knowing what I know now, could I have saved my first marriage? Probably not. Huston's research suggests that the harbingers of disaster were present even before my wedding day.

And he blames our culture. Unlike many other world cultures, he says, Western society makes marriage the key adult relationship, which puts a lot of pressure on people to marry. "People feel they have to find a way to get there and one way is to force it, even if it only works for the time being," he says.

Our culture is also to blame, Huston says, for perpetuating the myth of storybook romance, which is more likely to doom a marriage than strengthen it. He has few kind words for Hollywood, which brings us unrealistic, unsustainable passion.

So if your new romance starts to resemble a movie script, try to remember: The audience never sees what happens after the credits roll.

READ MORE ABOUT IT

Men Love Dies: The Process of Marital Disaffection, Karen Kayser, Ph.D. (Guildford Press, 1993)

Fighting For Your Marriage: Positive Steps For Preventing Divorce and Preserving A Lasting Love, H. Markman, S. Stanley and S. Blumberg (Jossey-Bass, 1994)

CRITICAL THINKING QUESTIONS

1. Who were the subjects in the Huston PAIR Project? Can the findings from this group of people be generalized to all groups of people? Why or why not?

2. Do an informal survey of people to find out what they think is the most important factor in a successful relationship. Chances are, "good communication" will most often be cited. How does this factor (or whatever factor your survey finds most important) relate to the information contained in the article? Discuss.

3. List five things that you learned from this article that may decrease the chance of your getting divorced. Which of these factors would be the easiest to change or control? Which would be the most difficult? Explain your answers.

4. How are love and marriage portrayed in the movies? Identify specific films, and discuss each in terms of whether it portrays a realistic or storybook view of love and marriage. What, if any, problems are associated with the general media portrayals of love and marriage?

5. According to the article, "Western society makes marriage the key adult relationship, which puts a lot of pressure on people to marry." Do you agree or disagree with this statement? Have you ever felt or observed pressure on people to marry? Does this societal pressure to marry contribute in any way to the high divorce rate? Discuss your answers.

ARTICLE 23 _____

Wanting to love and be loved is perhaps the most profound and universal human longing. As personal experience teaches us, love is not only a highly desired and sought after state but it also may actually be necessary for our very well-being. Yet exactly what love means and how it is expressed and felt may be something that differs in each of us.

Let's back up a step. Before talking about a deep and profound love for another person, what about the initial stages that may precede it? In other words, what factors are involved in the initial attraction to another potential romantic partner? People vary considerably in what they find attractive and desirable in another person, but there are common dimensions that seem to be fairly universal—the importance of physical attractiveness and certain personality traits such as intelligence, for instance.

Suppose that you have just met someone who has caught your attention. You are interested enough that you want to ask the person out on a date. Whether you are the iniator or the recipient of the request, a date often creates a set of mixed feelings. On one hand, the potential pleasure that one can have in a successful relationship is highly desirable. On the other hand, most people do not like rejection, and any such beginning also carries with it the possibility of an end.

All right, so he finally asks her out. (Although females certainly initiate dates, research still shows that males typically take this first step in U.S. culture.) How does she respond to his request? Obviously, she can say no. If she says yes, however, there are many ways that it can be said. Which do you think would be most favorably received by the man—someone who enthusiastically and without hesitation says "Yes. I thought you'd never ask" or someone who plays hard to get, ultimately accepting the invitation but only after some hesitation or convincing?

Folk advice going back thousands of years states that playing hard to get might be the way to proceed. As this classic article by Elaine Hatfield, G. William Walster, Jane Piliavin, and Lynn Schmidt indicates, however, that might not be the best advice to follow.

"Playing Hard to Get"
Understanding an Elusive Phenomenon
■ Elaine Hatfield, G. William Walster, Jane Piliavin, and Lynn Schmidt

According to folklore, the woman who is hard to get is a more desirable catch than the woman who is too eager for an alliance. Five experiments were conducted to demonstrate that individuals value hard-to-get dates more than easy-to-get ones. All five experiments failed. In Experiment VI, we finally gained an understanding of this elusive phenomenon. We proposed that two components contribute to a woman's desirability: (a) how hard the woman is for the subject to get and (b) how hard she is for other men to get. We predicted that the selectively hard-to-get woman (i.e., a woman who is easy for the subject to get but hard for all other men to get) would be preferred to either a uniformly hard-to-get woman, a uniformly easy-to-get woman, or a woman about which the subject has no information. This hypothesis received strong support. The reason for the popularity of the*

Reprinted from *Journal of Personality and Social Psychology*, 1973, *26,* 113–121. Copyright © 1973 by the American Psychological Association. Reprinted by permission.

selective woman was evident. Men ascribe to her all of the assets of uniformly hard-to-get and the uniformly easy-to-get women and none of their liabilities.

According to folklore, the woman who is hard to get is a more desirable catch than is the woman who is overly eager for alliance. Socrates, Ovid, Terence, the *Kama Sutra,* and Dear Abby all agree that the person whose affection is easily won is unlikely to inspire passion in another. Ovid, for example, argued:

> *Fool, if you feel no need to guard your girl for her own sake, see that you guard her for mine, so I may want her the more. Easy things nobody wants, but what is forbidden is tempting. . . . Anyone who can love the wife of an indolent cuckold, I should suppose, would steal buckets of sand from the shore. (pp. 65–66)*

When we first began our investigation, we accepted cultural lore. We assumed that men would prefer a hard-to-get woman. Thus, we began our research by interviewing college men as to why they preferred hard-to-get women. Predictably, the men responded to experimenter demands. They explained that they preferred hard-to-get women because the elusive woman is almost inevitably a valuable woman. They pointed out that a woman can only afford to be "choosy" if she is popular—and a woman is popular for some reason. When a woman is hard to get, it is usually a tip-off that she is especially pretty, has a good personality, is sexy, etc. Men also were intrigued by the challenge that the elusive woman offered. One can spend a great deal of time fantasizing about what it would be like to date such a woman. Since the hard-to-get woman's desirability is well recognized, a man can gain prestige if he is seen with her.

An easy-to-get woman, on the other hand, spells trouble. She is probably desperate for a date. She is probably the kind of woman who will make too many demands on a person; she might want to get serious right away. Even worse, she might have a "disease."

In brief, nearly all interviewees agreed with our hypothesis that a hard-to-get woman is a valuable woman, and they could supply abundant justification for their prejudice. A few isolated men refused to cooperate. These dissenters noted that an elusive woman is not always more desirable than an available woman. Sometimes the hard-to-get woman is not only hard to get—she is *impossible* to get, because she is misanthropic and cold. Sometimes a woman is easy to get because she is a friendly, outgoing woman who boosts one's ego and insures that dates are "no hassle." We ignored the testimony of these deviant types.

We then conducted five experiments designed to demonstrate that an individual values a hard-to-get date more highly than an easy-to-get date. All five experiments failed.

THEORETICAL RATIONALE

Let us first review the theoretical rationale underlying these experiments.

In Walster, Walster, and Berscheid (1971) we argued that if playing hard to get does increase one's desirability, several psychological theories could account for this phenomenon:

1. Dissonance theory predicts that if a person must expend great energy to attain a goal, one is unusually appreciative of the goal (see Aronson and Mills, 1959; Gerard and Mathewson, 1966; Zimbardo, 1965). The hard-to-get date requires a suitor to expend more effort in her pursuit than he would normally expend. One way for the suitor to justify such unusual effort is by aggrandizing her.

2. According to learning theory, an elusive person should have two distinct advantages: (*a*) Frustration may increase drive—by waiting until the suitor has achieved a high sexual drive state, heightening his drive level by introducing momentary frustration, and then finally rewarding him, the hard-to-get woman can maximize the impact of the sexual reward she provides (see Kimball, 1961, for evidence that frustration does energize behavior and does increase the impact of appropriate rewards). (*b*) Elusiveness and value may be associated—individuals may have discovered through frequent experience that there is more competition for socially desirable dates than for undesirable partners. Thus, being "hard to get" comes to be associated with "value." As a consequence, the conditional stimulus (CS) of being hard to get generates a fractional antedating goal response and a fractional goal response, which leads to the conditioned response of liking.

3. In an extension of Schachterian theory, Walster (1971) argued that two components are necessary

before an individual can experience passionate love; (*a*) He must be physiologically aroused; and (*b*) the setting must make it appropriate for him to conclude that his aroused feelings are due to love. On both counts, the person who plays hard to get might be expected to generate unusual passion. Frustration should increase the suitor's physiological arousal, and the association of "elusiveness" with "value" should increase the probability that the suitor will label his reaction to the other as "love."

From the preceding discussion, it is evident that several conceptually distinct variables may account for the hard-to-get phenomenon. In spite of the fact that we can suggest a plethora of reasons as to why the playing hard-to-get strategy might be an effective strategy, all five studies failed to provide any support for the contention that an elusive woman is a desirable woman. Two experiments failed to demonstrate that outside observers perceive a hard-to-get individual as especially "valuable." Three experiments failed to demonstrate that a suitor perceives a hard-to-get date as especially valuable.

Walster, Walster, and Berscheid (1971) conducted two experiments to test the hypothesis that teenagers would deduce that a hard-to-get boy or girl was more socially desirable than was a teenager whose affection could be easily obtained. In these experiments high school juniors and seniors were told that we were interested in finding out what kind of first impression various teenagers made on others. They were shown pictures and biographies of a couple. They were told how romantically interested the stimulus person (a boy or girl) was in his partner after they had met only four times. The stimulus person was said to have liked the partner "extremely much," to have provided no information to us, or to have liked the partner "not particularly much." The teenagers were then asked how socially desirable both teenagers seemed (i.e., how likable, how physically attractive, etc.). Walster, Walster, and Berscheid, of course, predicted that the more romantic interest the stimulus person expressed in a slight acquaintance, the less socially desirable that stimulus person would appear to an outside observer. The results were diametrically opposed to those predicted. The more romantic interest the stimulus person expressed in an acquaintance, the *more* socially

desirable teenagers judged him to be. Restraint does not appear to buy respect. Instead, it appears that "All the world *does* love a lover."

Lyons, Walster, and Walster (1971) conducted a field study and a laboratory experiment in an attempt to demonstrate that men prefer a date who plays hard to get. Both experiments were conducted in the context of a computer matching service. Experiment III was a field experiment. Women who signed up for the computer matching program were contacted and hired as experimenters. They were then given precise instructions as to how to respond when their computer match called them for a date. Half of the time they were told to pause and think for 3 seconds before accepting the date. (These women were labeled "hard to get.") Half of the time they were told to accept the date immediately. (These women are labeled "easy to get.") The data indicated that elusiveness had no impact on the man's liking for his computer date.

Experiment IV was a laboratory experiment. In this experiment, Lyons et al. hypothesized that the knowledge that a woman is elusive gives one indirect evidence that she is socially desirable. Such indirect evidence should have the biggest impact when a man has no way of acquiring *direct* evidence about a coed's value or when he has little confidence in his own ability to assess value. When direct evidence is available, and the man possesses supreme confidence in his ability to make correct judgments, information about a woman's elusiveness should have little impact on a man's reaction to her. Lyons et al. thus predicted that when men lacked direct evidence as to a woman's desirability, a man's self-esteem and the woman's elusiveness should interact in determining his respect and liking for her. Lyons et al. measured males' self-esteem via Rosenberg's (1965) measure of self-esteem, Rosenfeld's (1964) measure of fear of rejection, and Berger's (1952) measure of self-acceptance.

The dating counselor then told subjects that the computer had assigned them a date. They were asked to telephone her from the office phone, invite her out, and then report their first impression of her. Presumably the pair would then go out on a date and eventually give us further information about how successful our computer matching techniques had been. Actually, all men were assigned a confederate as a date.

Half of the time the woman played hard to get. When the man asked her out she replied:

Mmm [slight pause] No, I've got a date then. It seems like I signed up for that Date Match thing a long time ago and I've met more people since then—I'm really pretty busy all this week.

She paused again. If the subject suggested another time, the confederate hesitated only slightly, then accepted. If he did not suggest another time, the confederate would take the initiative of suggesting: "How about some time next week—or just meeting for coffee in the Union some afternoon?" And again, she accepted the next invitation. Half of the time, in the easy-to-get condition, the confederate eagerly accepted the man's offer of a date.

Lyons et al. predicted that since men in this blind date setting lacked direct evidence as to a woman's desirability, low-self-esteem men should be more receptive to the hard-to-get woman than were high-self-esteem men. Although Lyons et al.'s manipulation checks indicate that their manipulations were successful and their self-esteem measure was reliable, their hypothesis was not confirmed. Elusiveness had no impact on liking, regardless of subject's self-esteem level.

Did we give up our hypothesis? Heavens no. After all, it had only been disconfirmed four times.

By Experiment V, we had decided that perhaps the hard-to-get hypothesis must be tested in a sexual setting. After all, the first theorist who advised a woman to play hard to get was Socrates; his pupil was Theodota, a prostitute. He advised:

They will appreciate your favors most highly if you wait till they ask for them. The sweetest meats, you see, if served before they are wanted seem sour, and to those who had enough they are positively nauseating; but even poor fare is very welcome when offered to a hungry man. [Theodota inquired] And how can I make them hungry for my fare? [Socrates' reply] Why, in the first place, you must not offer it to them when they have had enough—but prompt them by behaving as a model of Propriety, by a show of reluctance to yield, and by holding back until they are as keen as can be; and then the same gifts are much more to the

recipient than when they're offered before they are desired. (see Xenophon, p. 48)

Walster, Walster, and Lambert (1971) thus proposed that a prostitute who states that she is selective in her choice of customers will be held in higher regard than will be the prostitute who admits that she is completely unselective in her choice of partners.

In this experiment, a prostitute served as the experimenter. When the customer arrived, she mixed a drink for him; then she delivered the experimental manipulation. Half of the time, in the hard-to-get condition, she stated, "Just because I see you this time it doesn't mean that you can have my phone number or see me again. I'm going to start school soon, so I won't have much time, so I'll only be able to see the people that I like the best." Half of the time, in the easy-to-get condition, she did not communicate this information. From this point on, the prostitute and the customer interacted in conventional ways.

The client's liking for the prostitute was determined in two ways: First, the prostitute estimated how much the client had seemed to like her. (Questions asked were, for example, How much did he seem to like you? Did he make arrangements to return? How much did he pay you?) Second, the experimenter recorded how many times within the next 30 days the client arranged to have sexual relations with her.

Once again we failed to confirm the hard-to-get hypothesis. If anything, those clients who were told that the prostitute did not take just anyone were *less* likely to call back and liked the prostitute less than did other clients.

At this point, we ruefully decided that we had been on the wrong track. We decided that perhaps all those practitioners who advise women to play hard to get are wrong. Or perhaps it is only under very special circumstances that it will benefit one to play hard to get.

Thus, we began again. We reinterviewed students—this time with an open mind. This time we asked men to tell us about the advantages *and* disadvantages of hard-to-get and easy-to-get women. This time replies were more informative. According to reports, choosing between a hard-to-get woman and an easy-to-get woman was like choosing between Scylla and Charybdis—each woman was uniquely desirable and uniquely frightening.

Although the elusive woman was likely to be a popular prestige date, she presented certain problems. Since she was not particularly enthusiastic about you, she might stand you up or humiliate you in front of your friends. She was likely to be unfriendly, cold, and to possess inflexible standards.

The easy-to-get woman was certain to boost one's ego and to make a date a relaxing, enjoyable experience, but . . . Unfortunately, dating an easy woman was a risky business. Such a woman might be easy to get, but hard to get rid of. She might "get serious." Perhaps she would be so oversexed or overaffectionate in public that she would embarrass you. Your buddies might snicker when they saw you together. After all, they would know perfectly well why you were dating *her.*

The interlocking assets and difficulties envisioned when they attempted to decide which was better—a hard-to-get or an easy-to-get woman—gave us a clue as to why our previous experiments had not worked out. The assets and liabilities of the elusive and the easy dates had evidently generally balanced out. On the average, then, both types of women tended to be equally well liked. When a slight difference in liking did appear, it favored the easy-to-get woman.

It finally impinged on us that there are *two* components that are important determinants of how much a man likes a woman: (*a*) How hard or easy she is for him to get, and (*b*) how hard or easy she is for *other men* to get. So long as we were examining the desirability of women who were hard or easy for everyone to get, things balanced out. The minute we examined other possible configurations, it became evident that there is one type of woman who can transcend the limitations of the uniformly hard-to-get or the uniformly easy-to-get woman. If a woman has a reputation for being hard to get, but for some reason she is easy for the subject to get, she should be maximally appealing. Dating such a woman should insure one of great prestige; she is, after all, hard to get. Yet, since she is exceedingly available to the subject, the dating situation should be a relaxed, rewarding experience. Such a *selectively* hard-to-get woman possesses the assets of both the easy-to-get and the hard-to-get women, while avoiding all of their liabilities.

Thus, in Experiment VI, we hypothesized that a selectively hard-to-get woman (i.e., a woman who is easy for the subject to get but very hard for any other man to get) will be especially liked by her date. Women who are hard for everyone—including the subject—to get, or who are easy for everyone to get—or control women, about whom the subject had no information—will be liked a lesser amount.

METHOD

Subjects were 71 male summer students at the University of Wisconsin. They were recruited for a dating research project. This project was ostensibly designed to determine whether computer matching techniques are in fact more effective than is random matching. All participants were invited to come into the dating center in order to choose a date from a set of five potential dates.

When the subject arrived at the computer match office, he was handed folders containing background information on five women. Some of these women had supposedly been "randomly" matched with him; others had been "computer matched" with him. (He was not told which women were which.)

In reality, all five folders contained information about fictitious women. The first item in the folder was a "background questionnaire" on which the woman had presumably described herself. This questionnaire was similar to one the subject had completed when signing up for the match program. We attempted to make the five women's descriptions different enough to be believable, yet similar enough to minimize variance. Therefore, the way the five women described themselves was systematically varied. They claimed to be 18 or 19 years old; freshmen or sophomores; from a Wisconsin city, ranging in size from over 500,000 to under 50,000; 5 feet 2 inches to 5 feet 4 inches tall; Protestant, Catholic, Jewish or had no preference; graduated in the upper 10 to 50 percent of their high school class; and Caucasians who did not object to being matched with a person of another race. The women claimed to vary on a political spectrum from "left of center" through "moderate" to "near right of center"; to place little or no importance on politics and religion; and to like recent popular movies. Each woman listed four or five activities she liked to do on a first date (i.e., go to a movie, talk in a quiet place, etc.).

In addition to the background questionnaire, three of the five folders contained five "date selection forms." The experimenter explained that some of the women had already been able to come in, examine the background information of their matches, and indicate their first impression of them. Two of the subject's matches had not yet come in. Three of the women had already come in and evaluated the subject along with her four other matches. These women would have five date selection forms in their folders. The subject was shown the forms, which consisted of a scale ranging from "definitely do *not* want to date" (–10) to "definitely want to date" (+10). A check appeared on each scale. Presumably the check indicated how much the woman had liked a given date. (At this point, the subject was told his identification number. Since all dates were identified by numbers on the forms, this identification number enabled him to ascertain how each date had evaluated both him and her four other matches.)

The date selection forms allowed us to manipulate the elusiveness of the woman. One woman appeared to be uniformly hard to get. She indicated that though she was willing to date any of the men assigned to her, she was not enthusiastic about any of them. She rated all five of her date choices from +1 to +2, including the subject (who was rated 1.75).

One woman appeared to be uniformly easy to get. She indicated that she was enthusiastic about dating all five of the men assigned to her. She rated her desire to date all five of her date choices +7 to +9. This included the subject, who was rated 8.

One woman appeared to be easy for the subject to get but hard for anyone else to get (i.e., the selectively hard-to-get woman). She indicated minimal enthusiasm for four of her date choices, rating them from +2 to +3, and extreme enthusiasm (+8) for the subject.

Two women had no date selection forms in their folders (i.e., no information women).

Naturally, each woman appeared in each of the five conditions.

The experimenter asked the man to consider the folders, complete a "first impression questionnaire" for each woman, and then decide which *one* of the women he wished to date. (The subject's rating of the dates constitute our verbal measure of liking; his choice in a date constitutes our behavioral measure of liking.)

The experimenter explained that she was conducting a study of first impressions in conjunction with the dating research project. The study, she continued, was designed to learn more about how good people are at forming first impressions of others on the basis of rather limited information. She explained that filling out the forms would probably make it easier for the man to decide which one of the five women he wished to date.

The first impression questionnaire consisted of three sections:

Liking for Various Dates   Two questions assessed subjects' liking for each woman: "If you went out with this girl, how well do you think you would get along?"—with possible responses ranging from "get along extremely well" (5) to "not get along at all" (1)—and "What was your overall impression of the girl?"—with possible responses ranging from "extremely favorable" (7) to "extremely unfavorable" (1). Scores on these two questions were summed to form an index of expressed liking. This index enables us to compare subjects' liking for each of the women.

Assets and Liabilities Ascribed to Various Dates   We predicted that subjects would prefer the selective woman, because they would expect her to possess the good qualities of both the uniformly hard-to-get and the uniformly easy-to-get woman, while avoiding the bad qualities of both her rivals. Thus, the second section was designed to determine the extent to which subjects imputed good and bad qualities to the various dates.

This section was comprised of 10 pairs of polar opposites. Subjects were asked to rate how friendly–unfriendly, cold–warm, attractive–unattractive, easy-going–rigid, exciting–boring, shy–outgoing, fun-loving–dull, popular–unpopular, aggressive–passive, selective–nonselective each woman was. Ratings were made on a 7-point scale. The more desirable the trait ascribed to a woman, the higher the score she was given.

Liabilities Attributed to Easy-to-Get Women   The third scale was designed to assess the extent to which subjects attributed selected negative attributes to each woman. The third scale consisted of six statements:

> She would more than likely do something to embarrass me in public.
> She probably would demand too much attention and affection from me.
> She seems like the type who would be too dependent on me.
> She might turn out to be too sexually promiscuous.
> She probably would make me feel uneasy when I'm with her in a group.
> She seems like the type who doesn't distinguish between the boys she dates. I probably would be "just another date."

Subjects were asked whether they anticipated any of the above difficulties in their relationship with each woman. They indicated their misgivings on a scale ranging from "certainly true of her" (1) to "certainly not true of her" (7).

The experimenter suggested that the subject carefully examine both the background questionnaires and the date selection forms of all potential dates in order to decide whom he wanted to date. Then she left the subject. (The experimenter was, of course, unaware of what date was in what folder.)

The experimenter did not return until the subject had completed the first impression questionnaires. Then she asked him which woman he had decided to date.

After his choice had been made, the experimenter questioned him as to what factors influenced his choice. Frequently men who chose the selectively easy-to-get woman said that "She chose me, and that made me feel really good" or "She seemed more selective than the others." The uniformly easy-to-get woman was often rejected by subjects who complained "She must be awfully hard up for a date—she really would take anyone." The uniformly hard-to-get woman was once described as a "challenge" but more often rejected as being "snotty" or "too picky."

At the end of the session, the experimenter debriefed the subject and then gave him the names of five actual dates who had been matched with him.

RESULTS

We predicted that the selectively hard-to-get woman (easy for me but hard for everyone else to get) would be liked more than women who were uniformly hard to get, uniformly easy to get, or neutral (the no information women). We had no prediction as to whether or not her three rivals would differ in attractiveness. The results strongly support our hypothesis.

Dating Choices

When we examine the men's choices in dates, we see that the selective woman is far more popular than any of her rivals. (See Table 1.) We conducted a chi-square test to determine whether or not men's choices in dates were randomly distributed. They were not ($\chi^2 = 69.5$, $df = 4$, $p < .001$). Nearly all subjects preferred to date the selective woman. When we compare the frequency with which her four rivals (combined) are chosen, we see that the selective woman does get far more than her share of dates ($\chi^2 = 68.03$, $df = 1$, $p < .001$).

We also conducted an analysis to determine whether or not the women who are uniformly hard to get, uniformly easy to get, or whose popularity is unknown, differed in popularity. We see that they did not ($\chi^2 = 2.86$, $df = 3$).

TABLE 1 / Men's Choices in a Date

Item	Selectively Hard to Get	Uniformly Hard to Get	Uniformly Easy to Get	No Information for No. 1	No Information for No. 2
Number of men choosing to date each woman	42	6	5	11	7

Liking for the Various Dates

Two questions tapped the men's romantic liking for the various dates: (*a*) "If you went out with this woman, how well do you think you'd get along?"; and (*b*) "What was your overall impression of the woman?" Scores on these two indexes were summed to form an index of liking. Possible scores ranged from 2 to 12.

A contrast was then set up to test our hypothesis that the selective woman will be preferred to her rivals. The contrast that tests this hypothesis is of the form Γ_1 = 4μ (selectively hard to get) – 1 (uniformly hard to get) – 2μ (neutral). We tested the hypothesis Γ_1 = 0 against the alternative hypothesis $\Gamma_1 \neq 0$. An explanation of this basically simple procedure may be found in Hays (1963). If our hypothesis is true, the preceding contrast should be large. If our hypothesis is false, the resulting contrast should not differ significantly from 0. The data again provide strong support for the hypothesis that the selective woman is better liked than her rivals (F = 23.92, *df* = 1/70, p < .001).

Additional Data Snooping

We also conducted a second set of contrasts to determine whether the rivals (i.e., the uniformly hard-to-get woman, the uniformly easy-to-get woman, and the control woman) were differentially liked. Using the procedure presented by Morrison (1967) in chapter 4, the data indicate that the rivals are differentially liked (F = 4.43, *df* = 2/69). As Table 2 indicates, the uniformly hard-to-get woman seems to be liked slightly less than the easy-to-get or control woman.

In any attempt to explore data, one must account for the fact that observing the data permits the researcher to capitalize on chance. Thus, one must use simultaneous testing methods so as not to spuriously inflate the probability of attaining statistical significance. In the present situation, we are interested in comparing the means of a number of dependent measures, namely the liking for the different women in the dating situation. To perform post hoc multiple comparisons in this situation, one can use a transformation of Hotelling's t^2 statistic, which is distributed as *F*. The procedure is directly analogous to Scheffé's multiple-comparison procedure for independent groups, except where one compares means of a number of dependent measures.

To make it abundantly clear that the main result is that the discriminating woman is better liked than each of the other rivals, we performed an additional post hoc analysis, pitting each of the rivals separately

TABLE 2 / Men's Reactions to Various Dates

Item	Type of Date			
	Selectively Hard to Get	Uniformly Hard to Get	Uniformly Easy to Get	No Information
Men's liking for dates	9.41[a]	7.90	8.53	8.58
Evaluation of women's assets and liabilities				
Selective[b]	5.23	4.39	2.85	4.30
Popular[b]	4.83	4.58	4.65	4.83
Friendly[c]	5.58	5.07	5.52	5.37
Warm[c]	5.15	4.51	4.99	4.79
Easy Going[c]	4.83	4.42	4.82	4.61
Problems expected in dating	5.23[d]	4.86	4.77	4.99

[a]The higher the number, the more liking the man is expressing for the date.
[b]Traits we expected to be ascribed to the selectively hard-to-get and the uniformly hard-to-get dates.
[c]Traits we expected to be ascribed to the selectively hard-to-get and the uniformly easy-to-get dates.
[d]The higher the number the *fewer* the problems the subject anticipates in dating.

against the discriminating woman. In these analyses, we see that the selective woman is better liked than the woman who is uniformly easy to get ($F = 3.99$, $df = 3/68$), than the woman who is uniformly hard to get ($F = 9.47$, $df = 3/68$), and finally, than the control women ($F = 4.93$, $df = 3/68$).

Thus, it is clear that although there are slight differences in the way rivals are liked, these differences are small, relative to the overwhelming attractiveness of the selective woman.

Assets and Liabilities Attributed to Dates

We can now attempt to ascertain *why* the selective woman is more popular than her rivals. Earlier, we argued that the selectively hard-to-get woman should occupy a unique position; she should be assumed to possess all of the virtues of her rivals, but none of their flaws.

The virtues and flaws that the subject ascribed to each woman were tapped by the polar–opposite scale. Subjects evaluated each woman on 10 characteristics.

We expected that subjects would associate two assets with a uniformly hard-to-get woman: Such a woman should be perceived to be both "selective" and "popular." Unfortunately, such a woman should also be assumed to possess three liabilities—she should be perceived to be "unfriendly," "cold," and "rigid." Subjects should ascribe exactly the opposite virtues and liabilities to the easy-to-get woman: Such a woman should possess the assets of "friendliness," "warmth," and "flexibility," and the liabilities of "unpopularity" and "lack of selectivity." The selective woman was expected to possess only assets: She should be perceived to be as "selective" and "popular" as the uniformly elusive woman, and as "friendly," "warm," and "easy-going" as the uniformly easy woman. A contrast was set up to test this specific hypothesis. (Once again, see Hays for the procedure.) This contrast indicates that our hypothesis is confirmed ($F = 62.43$, $df = 1/70$). The selective woman is rated most like the uniformly hard-to-get woman on the first two positive characteristics and most like the uniformly easy-to-get woman on the last three characteristics.

For the reader's interest, the subjects' ratings of all five women's assets and liabilities are presented in Table 2.

Comparing the Selective and the Easy Women

Scale 3 was designed to assess whether or not subjects anticipated fewer problems when they envisioned dating the selective woman than when they envisioned dating the uniformly easy-to-get woman. On the basis of pretest interviews, we compiled a list of many of the concerns men had about easy women (e.g., "She would more than likely do something to embarrass me in public.").

We, of course, predicted that subjects would experience more problems when contemplating dating the uniformly easy woman than when contemplating dating a woman who was easy for *them* to get, but hard for anyone else to get (i.e., the selective woman).

Men were asked to say whether or not they envisioned each of the difficulties were they to date each of the women. Possible replies varied from 1 (certainly true of her) to 7 (certainly not true of her). The subjects' evaluations of each woman were summed to form an index of anticipated difficulties. Possible scores ranged from 6 to 42.

A contrast was set up to determine whether the selective woman engendered less concern than the uniformly easy-to-get woman. The data indicate that she does ($F = 17.50$, $df = 1/70$). If the reader is interested in comparing concern engendered by each woman, these data are available in Table 2.

The data provide clear support for our hypotheses: The selective woman is strongly preferred to any of her rivals. The reason for her popularity is evident. Men ascribe to her all of the assets of the uniformly hard-to-get and the uniformly easy-to-get women, and none of their liabilities.

Thus, after five futile attempts to understand the "hard-to-get" phenomenon, it appears that we have finally gained an understanding of this process. It appears that a woman can intensify her desirability if she acquires a reputation for being hard-to-get and then, by her behavior, makes it clear to a selected romantic partner that she is attracted to him.

In retrospect, especially in view of the strongly supportive data, the logic underlying our predictions sounds compelling. In fact, after examining our data, a colleague who had helped design the five ill-fated experiments noted that, "That is exactly what I would have predicted" (given his economic view of man).

Unfortunately, we are all better at postdiction than prediction.

REFERENCES

Aronson, E., and Mills, J. The effect of severity of initiation on liking for a group. *Journal of Abnormal and Social Psychology,* 1959, 67, 31–36.

Berger, E. M. The relation between expressed acceptance of self and expressed acceptance of others. *Journal of Abnormal and Social Psychology,* 1952, 47, 778–782.

Gerard, H. B. and Mathewson, G. C. The effects of severity of initiation and liking for a group: A replication. *Journal of Experimental Social Psychology,* 1966, 2, 278–287.

Hays, W. L. *Statistics for psychologists.* New York: Holt, Rinehart, 1963.

Kimball, G. A. *Hilgard and Marquis' conditioning and learning.* New York: Appleton-Century-Crofts, 1961.

Lyons, J., Walster, and Walster, G. W. Playing hard-to-get: An elusive phenomenon University of Wisconsin, Madison: Author, 1971. (Mimeo)

Morrison, D. F. *Multivariate statistical methods.* New York: McGraw-Hill, 1967.

Ovid. *The art of love.* Bloomington: University of Indiana Press, 1963.

Rosenberg, M. *Society and the adolescent self image.* Princeton, N.J.: Princeton University Press, 1965.

Rosenfeld, H. M. Social choice conceived as a level of aspiration. *Journal of Abnormal and Social Psychology,* 1964, 68, 491–499.

Walster, E. Passionate love. In B. I. Murstein (Ed.), *Theories of attraction and love.* New York: Springer, 1971.

Walster, E., Walster, G. W., and Berscheid, E. The efficacy of playing hard-to-get. *Journal of Experimental Education,* 1971, 39, 73–77.

Walster, G. W., and Lambert, P. Playing hard-to-get: A field study. University of Wisconsin, Madison: Author, 1971. (Mimeo)

Xenophon. *Memorabilia.* London: Heinemann, 1923.

Zimbardo, P. G. The effect of effort and improvisation on self persuasion produced by role-playing. *Journal of Experimental Social Psychology,* 1965, 1, 103–120.

This research was supported in part by National Science Foundation Grants GS 2932 and GS 30822X and in part by National Institute for Mental Health Grant MH 16661.

CRITICAL THINKING QUESTIONS

1. Nonsignificant results are difficult to interpret in research. For example, if a woman playing hard to get is not viewed differently from one playing "easy," is there really no difference? Why or why not? Or is it possible that the experimental manipulation (how playing hard to get or easy were varied in the study) was not strong enough to produce an effect? Discuss this possibility by examining how playing hard to get was manipulated in the first five experiments reported in this article.

2. Are ethical issues involved in any of the studies? In particular, what are your views of Study 5, which involved the services of a prostitute?

3. This study ultimately determined that selectively hard-to-get women were most preferred by the men. Do you think the reverse is true—that women most prefer selectively hard-to-get men? Why or why not?

4. Do you think that the results of this study could be generalized to the sexual arena (i.e., when it comes to sex, a selectively hard-to-get woman would be preferred over either a hard-to-get or easy-to-get woman)? Explain.

ADDITIONAL RELATED READINGS

Cole, T. (2001). Lying to the one you love. *Journal of Social and Personal Relationships,* *18*(1), 107–129.

Kramer, D., & Moore, M. (2001). Family myths in romantic fiction. *Psychological Reports,* *88,* 29–41.

ARTICLE 24

The three articles in Chapter Seven all related to the impact of physical attractiveness on human interactions. In its own way, each article demonstrated how physical attractiveness carries enormous weight in how we evaluate and treat our fellow human beings. While most of us would argue (and rightfully so) that this should *not* be the case, in fact, it is.

Almost all of the literature on physical attractiveness examines its role in the initial stages of a relationship. Thus, the subjects in these studies are either strangers meeting for the first time or people just beginning or considering a romantic relationship with one another. It stands to reason that looks may play a role in the initial stages of a relationship, but how about in an established, long-term relationship? For example, over the years, do people come to view their partners as less physically attractive, or do they see their partners as more attractive or at least the same? The following article by Carlos Yela and Jose Luis Sangrador examines this unexplored question.

Perception of Physical Attractiveness throughout Loving Relationships

■ Carlos Yela and Jose Luis Sangrador

ABSTRACT

We try to verify various hypotheses about the importance of physical attractiveness (PA) in loving relationships, based on known psycho-social processes. We select a representative sample of the Spanish population (n = 1949) and evaluate the PA subjectively perceived by subjects in themselves and in their partners. This evaluation is carried out using self-report techniques, measuring PA both at the present moment and retrospectively at the start of the relationship. The results suggest that we tend to form loving relationships with people perceived as similar in attractiveness to ourselves (matching hypothesis). We also tend to perceive our partner, in a biased way, as a little more attractive than ourselves. Furthermore, with the passing of time, the effects that would tend to diminish the perceived PA of our partner (habituation, differential reinforcements value, etc.) seem to be counterbalanced by others which tend to increase it (familiarity, cognitive dissonance, etc).

INTRODUCTION

Whilst little recognized (by people in general) as an important factor in people's choice of partner (Hadjistavropoulos & Genest 1994), social psychology has made clear the important role played by physical attractiveness (PA henceforth) in our social cognition (e.g. Metee and Aronson 1974; Sangrador 1993), behaviors (e.g. Griffitt 1979), and interpersonal relationships (especially in loving relationships; e.g. Cook and Wilson 1979).

In a recent study (Sangrador and Yela 2000), and in line with the consequences of the well-known "halo effect" (Dion et al. 1972; Feingold 1992), we showed the influence of the PA of the loved one on the desire to initiate a relationship with them, the manner of falling in love, the intensity of feelings of love, idealization of the other, and even satisfaction with the relationship (see also Yela 2000a). In the current study, our aim is to investigate the possible relation-

Reprinted from *Current Research in Social Psychology,* February 16, 2001, *6*(5), pp. 57–75. Reprinted with permission of Carlos Yela.

ship between the PA of both partners in a couple, and the course that each one's PA takes throughout the duration of the relationship. To our knowledge, empirical studies of this precise point are very scarce (f.ex. Margolin and White 1987; Zajonc 1987).

At the same time, it is important to stress certain refinements which characterize the present study and differentiate it from common studies in this area:

First of all, the dimension of PA has more often been investigated in studies of attraction than of love. Thus, for example, the effect of PA in first interactions, or in the formation of an impression of the other is studied (from the classic studies of Byrne 1971 to more recent studies by Chen et al. 1997). Research dealing with the role of PA in loving behavior however, as in the present investigation, are few and far between.

Secondly, a significant proportion of research has endeavored to operationalize the variable PA in an "objective" manner (for example by means of an "objective" evaluation—in reality inter-subjective—of PA by a panel of "judges"). In the present investigation however, PA is, strictly speaking, "perceived" PA (PPA henceforth), perceived by the interviewee both in themselves and in their partner, and so it may be independent of both partners' "objective" PA, if such thing could exist.

Thirdly, while the majority of the literature in this area normally speaks of PA restricted to the PA of one person, and in general a stranger, we have considered the interviewee's PA for him or herself (PPAS henceforth), as well as the interviewee's PPA off his or her partner (PPAO henceforth, the "O" representing the "other"). Furthermore, we have considered these dimensions both at the present moment and at the start of the relationship (in this last case indicated by a [lower-case] "o," for origin). This allows very subtle analysis from diverse perspectives.

Lastly, while the immense majority of empirical studies are carried out with samples of students (or in any case with non-representative samples), our data have been collected from a representative sample of the Spanish population (see also Barrón et al. 1999).

HYPOTHESES

In the current study, we aim to verify what is often referred to in classic positivist language as a confirma-

tory hypothesis, a critical hypothesis, and an exploratory hypothesis, based on different processes and classical theoretical viewpoints in social psychology:

Confirmatory Hypothesis

The well-known matching hypothesis predicts that (even though we desire people with the highest possible PA) our partners are in fact people with a PA similar to our own (see, for example, Murstein 1972, and some controversial papers: Kalick and Hamilton 1986; Aron 1988). We attempt to verify, on a non-student and non-US representative sample, a subjective version of this hypothesis: that *we perceive our partner to be about as attractive as we perceive ourselves to be.*

So on one hand, we tend to feel attracted to, and to desire people with a higher PA. This is the case across a range of diverse cultures, regardless of differences in aesthetic criteria (Wilson and Nias 1976; Cook and McHenry 1978; Feingold 1990, 1992; Buss 1994, 1998; Sangrador and Yela 2000). But on the other hand, at the same time it is true that our partners tend to be people similar to ourselves in terms of PA. This is known as the matching hypothesis, although it has been repeatedly verified (Murstein 1972; Huston and Levinger 1978; Feingold 1990; Wong et al. 1991, etc.). This has been explained, within exchange theory, using the concepts of a balance between costs and rewards, and a search for equity (Walster et al. 1978; Critelli and Waid 1980). In this context, PA is a powerful personal reinforcement (by means of socialization in the relationship "beautiful-good"; Sangrador 1993) and a powerful social reinforcement, due to the high importance socially attached to this characteristic, even though it is not often acknowledged. A partner much more attractive than oneself could involve a series of additional costs and additional effort in both starting and maintaining the relationship. Similarly, a much less attractive partner involves a high cost (or a deficit in rewards, at least in physical appearance), for which reason either the partner is not chosen, or else is chosen at the cost of an increase in the PPAO, as suggested by the cognitive dissonance perspective (Festinger 1957). Furthermore, similarity in general has been proved as one of the main factors in the courtship, mate preference and mate selection processes (since Reiss 1960; Byrne, 1971; Lewis 1972).

Critical Hypothesis

If the effects of habituation and of relative value of reinforcements (Skinner 1953; Aronson and Linder 1965; Frijda 1988) *prevail, then the PPAO will decay with time, but if the effects of familiarity and cognitive dissonance prevail* (Festinger 1957; Aronson and Mills 1959; Zajonc 1968) *then the PPAO will be increased throughout the relationship.*

As is well-known, one of the most important factors relative to all psycho-social processes, and perhaps in particular to the one that interests us (i.e., the loving relationship), is the passing of time (in fact, for that reason we speak of processes instead of structures). It seems evident that we do not feel (nor think, nor perceive) the same feeling for a stranger who we are suddenly attracted to, as we do for a new lover who we are getting to know, or for a person with whom we have shared the last, say, ten thousand days (and the last ten thousand nights, one could cynically add). It should be noted in any case, that to affirm that one doesn't feel the same does not imply any value judgement about whether one feels more or less, or if they are better or worse feelings. How does that passing of time affect in our specific example the perception of the partner's PA?

On one hand, given that repeated exposure to a stimulus tends to reduce the intensity of the elicited response (according to the well-known law of habituation; Skinner 1953), we might suppose that living together with the passing of time can diminish the response of physical attraction that our partner provokes. In a similar way, according to the gain-loss theory (Aronson and Linder 1965), the subjective value of reinforcements is not measured in absolute terms but rather is relative to our reinforcement history. In this way, the power of reinforcement of our partner's physical attractiveness would tend to reduce in intensity as we get used to him or her. Finally, according to the change of emotions law, and the comparative feeling law (Frijda 1988), which indicate that the hedonic value of a stimulus depends on the baseline and on the change in the situation, more than on the stimulus or situation itself, we could make an

identical prediction: the perception of the partner's PA will tend to decrease with time.

There are many other processes however, that would imply the opposite. For example, the effects of familiarity and mere exposure (Zajonc 1968) explain the attraction that we experience toward stimuli that are well-known (familiar), and even the attraction raised by the mere exposure to a stimulus (without positive hedonic value). In this way, on many occasions we find people physically more attractive as we get to know them (and, therefore, expose ourselves to them and make them familiar) than we do just after meeting them. Something similar could happen within the couple. And on the other hand, as a corollary of cognitive dissonance theory (Festinger 1957), it is known that we tend to value more a posteriori, that which it is supposed to have been a personal and free choice, and which requires of us an effort to obtain and/or to maintain (Aronson and Mills 1959). If we value PA (and we do so greatly, as we have shown in a separate study; Sangrador and Yela 2000) and we perceive that our partner (who we have chosen freely and who requires of us an effort "x" to maintain) no longer seems as attractive as before, a state of cognitive dissonance is produced, which will tend to be reduced, by either reducing the value assigned to PA (something easy to do verbally but not so easy internally, given the socialization process and opposing social pressure), or by convincing ourselves that he/she continues to seem as attractive as on the first day (or even more).

While recognizing that other contingencies exist which can affect the perception of the partner's PA over time (possible negligence in care for physical appearance with time, an eventual "objective" increase in physical attractiveness, etc.), we will try to establish which of the aforementioned processes is more likely to predominate according the empirical fluctuation of PPAO.

Exploratory Hypothesis: If the matching effect is verified, *will that similarity of perceived PA remain throughout the relationship, or will it decay with the passing of time?*

Will the matching effect prevail or will biased information processing prevail, so that the partner is perceived as more and more attractive than oneself? Can both effects be compatible, so that the PA perceived in the partner and in oneself will be relatively similar throughout the relationship, while always superior that perceived in the partner to that attributed to oneself? If it is the case, it could be that both the matching effect and certain cognitive processes (cognitive dissonance, social desirability, reestablishment of equity, etc.) intervene when formulating the perception of our partner's PA, and our own PA, throughout the relationship.

We will try to find answers to these questions in the third part of the study.

METHOD

This study falls within the framework of a larger investigation into loving behavior conducted by means of individual interviews with a representative sample of the Spanish population. Here we refer only to those methodological aspects related to the testing of the aforementioned hypotheses.

Participants

The sample was composed of 1,949 individuals of both sexes, between 18 and 64 years of age, residents in towns with a population of over 2,000 inhabitants throughout Spanish territory. The sampling procedure was multi-stage, stratified by conglomerates, with selection of the primary units (towns) and the secondary units (sections) carried out in a random proportional manner, and of the last units (individuals) by random means considering sex and age quotas, so that the definitive sample is highly representative of the Spanish population (sampling error ± 2.23, with a level of confidence of 95.5%).

Variables and Measurement Technique

Four basic variables of PA have been used, each of them assessed by means of the interviewee's own self-report, with an item range 0 (minimum PA) to 10 (maximum PA). Two of the variables refer to the perceived PA (PPA) for the interviewee in his/her partner or "other" (PPAO), both at the beginning of the relationship and at the present moment. The other two refer to the perceived PA by the interviewee

in him or herself (PPAS), both at the beginning of the relationship and at the present moment. Naturally, the questions about the beginning of the relationship are of retrospective character, with all the limitations that this implies (basically referred to the possibility of perceiving the past biased by the present situation: in our case, the possibility to perceive PPAOo biased by the PPAO tending to adjust them, and even biased by the present level of satisfaction with the partner and with the relationship).

Therefore, the four basic variables are configured as follows:

- PPA of the other, at the origin (PPAOo): perceived PA in the other at the beginning of the relationship.
- Current PPA of the other (PPAO): perceived PA at the present time in the other.
- Own PPA at the origin (PPASo): PA perceived by the subject in him/herself at the beginning of the relationship.
- Current own PPA (PPAS): PA perceived by the interviewee in him or herself at the present time.

For the first three variables data has only been obtained from the interviewees with partners (involved in a loving relationship) at the moment in which the interview was carried out. For the last variable data has been obtained from all subjects, both those with partners and those without. Obviously, we have only taken into account the PPAS data from subjects with partners when carrying out the comparative analyses between the PA of both members of a couple.

Lastly, we introduced two further variables operating with the four basic variables:

- PPAOo-PPAO: the difference between the PA perceived in the other at the outset of the relationship and the current perceived PA.
- PPAO-PPAS: the difference between the PA perceived in one's partner and in oneself, at the present time.

In addition, information was gathered about the variable "duration of the relationship" and "cohabitation" (whether the couple lives together or not), by asking the subjects directly.

Procedure and Analysis Technique

Each interview was carried out individually in the interviewee's own home, and anonymity was guaranteed to all subjects. Interviewees were selected according to the sampling procedure detailed above. Once the responses had been coded, different types of data analysis were carried out; in the current study descriptive statistics, linear correlations, variance analysis, difference of averages and regression analysis are included. The statistical package used was SPSS 9.0 for Windows.

RESULTS AND DISCUSSION

Confirmatory Hypothesis: The Matching Effect

The first part of the hypothesis, that we love people with higher PA, is not really tested in this study, but it has been repeatedly verified (e.g. Wilson and Nias 1976; Cook and McHenry 1978; or more recently Buss 1998). In a recent study we verified that PPAO was the characteristic most valued in the partner (out of a long and varied fist of characteristics) for short-term relationships, and that it also had an important effect in long-term relationships: on falling in love, the intensity of loving feelings, idealization and personal satisfaction with the relationship (Sangrador and Yela 2000).

Let us see now if our hypothesis (i.e., in spite of the above, we tend to form relationships with people of a similar PA to our own, or more exactly, with people of a similar PPA to our own perceived one) is verified. If this were not true, we could expect a random distribution of PA so that the correlation between partners PA was not significantly different from zero.

Pearson's correlation coefficient between PPASo and PPAOo is .43 (p < .000; n = 1078). This is the appropriate index to verify the matching hypothesis, since in this case we are not so much interested in the correlation between current values (that is also relatively high and significant; r = .39; p < .000; n = 1251), as in the correlation between values at the origin of the relationship. The fact that the correlation obtained is significantly different from 0 indicates the confirmation of the hypothesis. The fact that it is different from 1 indicates that the correspondence is not perfect, absolute and certain; but, as is almost

universally the case in psychology, a trend. That is to say, it is not that we always form relationships with people of PA exactly the same as our own, but rather that we tend to form relationships with people of a similar PA to our own, or at least who we perceive as similarly attractive to ourselves.

In any case, and while it is necessary to note that in this case the difference between averages is not the best statistic (because it can hide intra-couple differences and compensate them with inter-couple differences of similar magnitude and opposed direction). We should also point out that we obtained a significant difference between the average value of the perceived PA in the other and in the self at the start of the relationship, the values obtained being PPAOo = 8.55 (SD = 1.71) and PPASo = 7.41 (SD = 2.09) (p < .000; n = 1078). This seems to indicate that, at the start of the relationship, besides the matching effect, a favorable perceptual bias tends to take place towards the partner with respect to the perception of PA; a bias that may be explained on different ways, for example in terms of enhancing self-esteem, or (as it was suggested by a reviewer) simply as normative modesty.

Critical Hypothesis: PPAO and the Passing of Time

Initially the value of the linear correlation between the PA perceived in the partner and the duration of the relationship is not significantly different from 0 (r PPAO-duration of the relationship = .06 ns). This indicates that on average, there is no linear uniform change in PA over time, neither an increase, nor a decrease. It could be that the relationship between PPAO and the passing of time is not linear, but rather fluctuates as a function of the passing of time in a certain way. To check this possibility, we established certain bands for the variable, duration of the relationship, and plotted the curve for PPAO bearing in mind the averages of the variable PPAO in each one of the time bands. In Figure 1 we can see this fluctuation.

The graph raises diverse questions, although we should note that the magnitude of the fluctuations is remarkably low (in fact, an ANOVA shows significant differences only between the lowest point (7.89) and highest point (8.22) of the graph, although this depends on the selected bands). In our opinion, the

FIGURE 1

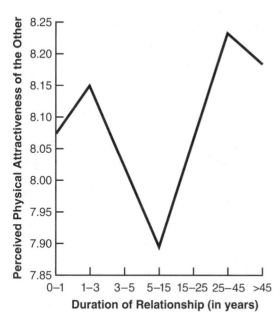

during advanced stages of the relationship. We know that perception of the PA is not based exclusively on physical factors (Sangrador 1993). So it is possible that in older people PA becomes increasingly related to fundamentally psychological components, and less to specifically physical components (this distinction should be understood without the implication of any kind of ontogenetic dualism). This could attenuate the decline in the PPAO or even increase the PPAO, as a result of greater intimacy and commitment, characteristic of the late stages of loving relationships (of those relationships which survive, which are those that compose the sample) (Yela 1998). In any case, this latter explanation is perfectly compatible with the proposals in our hypothesis. (As always, there is another possible explanation. Perhaps this dip-increase pattern could be related to marital satisfaction rates and divorce trends. Dissatisfying marriages are more likely to end by 5–15 years, so that the later time periods include a higher percentage of satisfying relationships. The earlier periods may include couples on their way to divorce, who perceive their partners as being less attractive.)

Finally, the small decrease that is observed in the last part of the graph suggests that the tension between those opposed forces continues to operate but no one force definitively overcomes the other.

Given the results obtained we could suggest that at first the effects of habituation prevail but later on they are compensated by those of familiarity and dissonance.

And if we keep in mind the average initial value of PPAOo (8.55), those two successive periods of habituation and familiarity-dissonance appear even more clearly. If we consider the value of PPAOo (retrospectively evaluated) we note that PPAO decays with time, but slightly, and in any case far less than we would expect if the forces of habituation acted alone. And if we only consider the fluctuation of PPAO from the average value of the first time band (the relationships between 1 day and 1 year of duration), then we cannot even affirm that the PPAO decays with the passing of time, but rather stays stable on average, although it fluctuates in the way that we have commented.

We wonder then, how the difference perceived between the partner's PA would fluctuate between the

pertinent point here is that we can appreciate different stages in the fluctuation of PPAO that could correspond to the preponderance of some bi-psycho-social or other processes.

Thus, the initial increase corresponds to the falling in love phase (see Yela 1998). After this, at a certain point (which varies for different individuals and couples, and perhaps between cultures) the PPAO begins to decay, as a result of the passionate components of love (Sternberg 1986, 1988; Fisher 1992; Yela 1996, 1998, 2000b). The processes mentioned in our hypothesis probably intervene here: habituation and the relative value of reinforcements (Skinner 1953; Aronson and Linder 1965; Frijda 1988 etc.).

There is however, also a point (which in our study is located in the uncertain interval between 5 and 15 years, and which should also show clear interpersonal variability), where these processes begin to be compensated by others of an opposed nature, and the PPAO increases again. The processes in question probably include those processes proposed in our hypothesis, namely the effects of familiarity and cognitive dissonance (Festinger 1957; Aronson and Mills 1959; Zajonc 1968), although another explanation could be offered for the moderate increase in PPAO beginning of the relationship and the current moment. In this case the correlation obtained is significant, although quite low: r (PPAOo − PPAO) − duration = .13 (p < .000; n = 1131).

This indicates that on average for the sample, the more time passes the greater the difference between how the partner is perceived physically and how they were perceived at the beginning of the relationship (or strictly speaking, how they say now that they perceived themselves then). This means that with time, either the partner's PA at the outset of the relationship is idealized, or the perceived PA diminishes (or both things), albeit slightly.

Lastly, we try to discover the fluctuation of that difference (PPAOo − PPAO, that is to say, the fall in PPAO from the start of the relationship to the current moment) this time in function not of the passing of time, but of a variable that normally co-varies with it: living together as a couple. Variance analysis gives the [results shown in Table 1].

As we can see, the decrease in the PA perceived in the partner from the beginning of the relationship to the present time is greater for those who live together than for those who do not. This would lean towards the explanation offered by the habituation process. The reduction observed in the PPAO should not be attributed so much to the mere passing of time itself, but to the fact that this usually implies a continuous exposure to the partner (since the vast majority—83%—of the couples live together). The fact that the differences are not bigger could be explained by the action of the aforementioned opposing mechanisms (principally familiarity and dissonance).

Exploratory Hypothesis:
Relationship between PPAO and PPAS throughout the Loving Relationship

Again, the data gathered does not allow us to clarify this relationship definitively. Rather it seems as if, as in the previous case, that both processes (matching and cognitive biases) play a part.

As in the confirmatory hypothesis about matching, the differences in averages do not interest us (this could hide the intra-couple variability, which is what affirms matching) but rather the correlations between PPA in oneself and one's partner.

Firstly, if the correlation between the PA perceived in the partner and the self at the start of the relationship, was of .43 (p < .000), as we saw above, the same correlation referring to the course of the relationship (not to the outset) is: r PPAO − PPAS = .39 (p < .000; n = 1251), which suggests that the matching effect tends to last over time.

On the other hand, the difference between PPAO and PPAS neither increases nor diminishes systematically throughout the relationship, at least on average: r (PPAO less PPAS) − duration of relationship = −.02 (n.s.).

At the same time however, we can appreciate that the PA attributed to oneself, at least on average, is always significantly smaller (around 1 or 1.5 points out of 10) than the PA attributed to the partner. In the verification of the matching hypothesis we show this for the beginning of the relationship. The same effect can be observed for relationships in progress, PPAO being = 8.04 (SD = 1.79) and PPAS − 6.49 (SD = 2.10), also a significant difference (p < .000; n =

TABLE 1 / PPAOo − PPAO (PA of the other at the origin less current PA of the other)

They live together all the time.	0.55		
They live together sporadically.	0.12	F = 4.72	p < .000
They do not live together.	−0.07		

1251). Such a result suggests the influence of the aforementioned perceptual biases (relative over-valuation of the PA of the other).

Finally, let us see what is the correlation between the PA perceived in oneself and in the partner (that is to say, matching) at the different temporal points that we have defined in the variable, duration of the relationship (taking p < .000) [see Table 2].

The results suggest that the matching hypothesis is verified both at the outset of the relationship (that is to say, at the time of forming a relationship with the partner) and later, from a certain point time (in our study, starting at around 5 years) until the end of the relationship. However, there is one period where a systematic and significant relationship doesn't seem to exist between the perception of PA in oneself and in the partner: between the beginning of the relationship and more or less, 5 years. This is perhaps not so surprising if we bear in mind that those years are in fact those that the specialized literature has denominated the falling in love and passionate love phase (Yela 1998; 2000b). In this phase one of the most relevant processes is certainly idealization of the partner, which includes the idealization of the PA. If during this period the PPAO is high, it is plausible to assume that it will become more different from the PA attributed to oneself. On the other hand, with the diminishing of passionate factors (among them idealization), PPAO will descend (as can also be observed at the outset in Figure 1), tending towards the PPAS and strengthening the relationship between them.

Finally, if the correlation stays high until the end and, as we have observed, PPAO tends to increase in late stages of the relationship (Figure 2), this should mean that the PPAS does likewise. In fact this is exactly what happens.

As we can see, the course of PPAS is relatively similar to that of PPAO. The later, and in principle surprising phase of growth could be attributed to any combination of a number of factors of a very diverse nature. Firstly an attempt (be it primarily conscious or unconscious) to maintain equity by means of matching, secondly an attempt to protect self-esteem (now that physical appearance in fact begins to deteriorate gradually), thirdly a conception of PA which focuses on psychological rather than specific, exclusively physical aspects (as we suggest above). Finally, a hypothetically smaller capacity for critical analysis in the sub-sample whose relationship has lasted more than 25 years, who are different in that they have a lower cultural level (lower critical analysis which could lead them to directly assign themselves the maximum PA score, as in fact is the case in more than 40% of these sub-groups).

All things considered, given the results, it seems that throughout the relationship the matching effect cohabits with the relative over-valuation of our partner's PA.

TABLE 2

r PPAOo-PPASo	0.43
r PPAO-PPAS (for t < 1 year)	0.21 (n.s.)
r PPAO-PPAS (for t = 1 to 3 years)	0.26 (n.s.)
r PPAO-PPAS (for t = 3 to 5 years)	0.13 (n.s.)
r PPAO-PPAS (for t = 5 to 15 years)	0.40
r PPAO-PPAS (for t = 15 to 25 years)	0.42
r PPAO-PPAS (for t = 25 to 45 years)	0.43
r PPAO-PPAS (for t > 45 years)	0.46

FIGURE 2

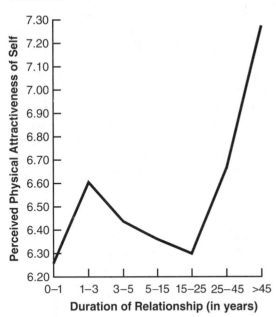

Therefore, from the results obtained we could conclude:

- as predicted by the matching hypothesis, (Spanish) people tend to form loving relationships with people who they perceive as similarly attractive to themselves.
- that in spite of this, people tend to perceive their partner in a biased way as a little more attractive than themselves.
- that the two previous effects last, in general terms, throughout the couple's relationship.
- and that throughout the loving relationship, it seems that the effects that cause PA perceived in the partner to fall (for example, habituation and relative value of reinforcements), are attenuated and counteracted by those that increase it (for example familiarity and cognitive dissonance).

Nevertheless and before concluding, we should remind ourselves of the methodological limitations that, as with all empirical studies, limit our capacity to generalize from the results:

Firstly, we should remember that whenever the passing of time is an important variable in a study, the ideal situation would be to have a longitudinal design, instead of transverse as in our case: to see each couple's evolution over time, instead of comparing different couples at different moments in time, albeit on average. Secondly, the use of the self-report technique, whilst allowing us to evaluate beliefs, attitudes and feelings difficult to access using observation, always leaves us open to biases in the answers (just to mention one of them, one of the reviewers wondered whether matching hypothesis could be debt to a tendency for people who rate themselves high in PA to rate all others high in PA as well. It could be). And finally, the retrospective nature of the perception of PA at the beginning of the relationship also calls for caution when interpreting the results (as Machado wrote: "In man neither *tomorrow* nor *yesterday* is written").

Secondly, we are aware about some potential sex differences in the way men and women perceive PA throughout loving relationship. We take them into account on our next project that is already in preparation.

Nevertheless, and given that we have just highlighted the methodological limitations, it is also fair to say that the use of a representative sample of the Spanish population, besides being extraordinarily uncommon in social psychology (and in psychology in general), leaves considerable room for generalization from the obtained results. What is truly important is that these results could be replicated and confirmed in later studies. This would signify a substantial step forward in the clarification of the paradox surrounding the decisive importance which something so seemingly frivolous as PA has on something that we do not dare to consider frivolous (i.e., love and relationships between couples) (Sangrador and Yela 2000).

REFERENCES

Aron, A. (1988). "The matching hypothesis reconsidered again: comment on Kalick and Hamilton." *Journal of Personality and Social Psychology,* 54:441–446.

Aronson, E. and D. Linder (1965). "Gain and loss of esteem as determinants of interpersonal attractiveness." *Journal of Experimental Social Psychology,* 1:156–171.

Aronson, E. and J. Mills (1959). "The effect of severity of initiation on liking for a group." *Journal of Abnormal and Social Psychology,* 59:177–181.

Barron, A., D. Martinez-Inigo, P. D. E. Paul, and C. Yela (1999). "Romantic beliefs and myths in Spain." *The Spanish Journal of Psychology,* 2(1):64–73.

Buss, D. M. (1994). *The Evolution of Desire: Strategies on human mating.* New York: Basic Books.

Buss, D. M. (1998). "The psychology of human mate selection." In C. B. Crawford et al. (eds.): *Handbook of Evolutionary Psychology: Ideas, issues and applications.* pp. 405–429. Mahwah, NJ: LEA.

Byrne, D. (1971). *The attraction paradigm.* New York: Academic Press.

Chen, N. Y., D. R. Shaffer, and C. Wu (1997). "On physical attractiveness stereotyping in Taiwan: A revised sociocultural perspective." *Journal of Social Psychology,* 137(1):117–124.

Critelli, J. W. and L. R. Waid (1980). "Physical attractiveness, romantic love and equity restoration in dating relationships." *Journal of Personality Assessment,* 44.

Cook, M. and R. McHenry (1978). *Sexual attraction.* Oxford: Pergamon Press.

Cook, M. and G. Wilson (Eds.) (1979). *Love & Attraction.* Oxford: Pergamon Press.

Dion, K. K., E. Berscheid, and E. Walster (1972). "What is beautiful is good." *Journal of Personality & Social Psychology,* 24(3):285–290.

Feingold, A. (1990). "Gender differences in effects of physical attractiveness on romantic attraction." *Journal of Personality and Social Psychology,* 59(5):981–993.

Feingold, A. (1992). "Good-looking people are not what we think." *Psychological Bulletin,* 111(2):304–341.

Festinger, L. (1957). "A Theory of Cognitive Dissonance." California: Stanford Univ. Press.

Fisher, H. (1992). *The Anatomy of Love.* New York: W. W. Norton.

Frijda, N. H. (1988). "The laws of emotion." *American Psychologist,* 43(5):349–358.

Griffitt, W. (1979). "Sexual stimulation and sociosexual behaviors." In M. Cook & G. Wilson (Eds.): *Love & Attraction.* Oxford: Pergamon Press.

Hadjistavropoulos, T. and M. Genest (1994). "The underestimation of the role of physical attractiveness in dating preferences: Ignorance or taboo?" *Canadian Journal of Behavioural Science,* 26(2):298–318.

Huston, T. L. and G. Levinger (1978). "Interpersonal attraction and relationships." *Annual Review of Psychology,* 29:115–156.

Kalick, S. M. and T. E. Hamilton (1986). "The matching hypothesis re-examined." *Journal of Personality and Social Psychology,* 51:673–682.

Lewis, R. A. (1972). "A developmental framework for the analysis of premarital dyadic formation." *Family Process,* 11: 17–48

Mettee, D. R. and E. Aronson (1974). "Affective reactions to appraisal from others." In T. L. Huston (Ed.): *Foundations on Interpersonal Attraction.* New York: Academic Press.

Murstein, B. I. (1972). "Physical attractiveness and marital choice." *Journal of Personality and Social Psychology,* 22:8–12.

Reiss, I. L. (1960). "Toward a sociology of the heterosexual love relationships." *Marriage and Family Living,* 22:139–145.

Sangrador, J. L. (1993). "Consideraciones psicosociales sobre el amor romántico [Psychosocial considerations about romantic love]." *Psicothema,* 5:181–196.

Sangrador, J. L. and C. Yela (2000). "What is beautiful is loved: Physical attractiveness in love relationships on a representative sample." *Social Behavior and Personality,* 28(3):207–218.

Skinner, B. F. (1953). *Science and human behavior.* New York: Macmillan.

Sternberg, R. J. (1986). "A triangular theory of love." *Psychological Review,* 93(2):119–135.

Sternberg, R. J. (1988). *The triangle of love: Intimacy, Passion and Commitment.* New York: Basic Books.

Walster, E., G. W. Walster, and E. Berscheid (1978). *Equity: Theory and Research.* Boston: Allyn & Bacon.

Wilson, G. and D. Nias (1976). *Love's mysteries.* Glasgow: W. Collins Sons.

Wong, F. Y., D. R. McCreary, C. C. Bowden, and S. M. Jenner (1991). "The matching hypothesis: Factors influencing dating preferences." *Psychology: A Journal of Human Behavior,* 28(34):27–31.

Yela, C. (1996). "Componentes básicos del amor: algunas matizaciones al modelo de R. J. Sternberg [Basic components of love: some refinements to the model of R. J. Sternberg]." *Revista de Psicología Social,* 11(2):185–201.

Yela, C. (1998). "Temporal course of the basic components of love throughout relationships." *Psychology in Spain,* 2(1):76–78

Yela, C. (2000a). "Predictors of and factors related to loving and sexual satisfaction for men and women." *European Review of Applied Psychology,* 50(1):235–242.

Yela, C. (2000b). *El amor desde la Psicología Social: ni tan libres ni tan racionales* [Love from Social Psychology: nor so free neither so rational]. Madrid: Pirámide.

Zajonc, R. B. (1968). "Attitudinal effects of mere exposure." *Journal of Personality and Social Psychology,* 9:1–29.

Zajonc, R. B. (1987). "Convergence in the physical appearance of spouses." *Motivation and Emotion,* 11:333–346.

ACKNOWLEDGEMENTS

This paper is part of a bigger research project funded by the "Comisión Interministerial de Ciencia y Tecnología" (PB 91-0360), carried out by: Ana Barrón, David Martínez-Iñigo, Pilar de Paúl, Jose Luis Sangrador and Carlos Yela, and supervised by Florencio Jiménez Burillo (in alphabetical order).

CRITICAL THINKING QUESTIONS

1. The study employed a sample of subjects who were asked to recall their evaluations of the partner's physical attractiveness at the beginning of the relationship—however long ago that may have been. Explain the possible limitations of this methodology. Design a longitudinal study that would measure the role in physical attractiveness across the span of a relationship. What would be the limitations of that methodology?

2. A large number of studies in psychology tend to use American college students. This study employed a representative sample of the Spanish population. Which of these two sets of subjects would yield the best information with the most practical implications for the American population as a whole? For human beings as a whole? Explain your answers.

3. The study indicates that "each interview was carried out individually in the interviewee's own home, and that anonymity was guaranteed to all subjects." How might this methodology have influenced the results?

4. Review Figure 1. Do you agree with the authors' explanation as to why the perceived physical attractiveness of the partner rises at first, then decreases to a low at the 5- to 15-year mark, and then increases again to an even higher rate than that at the initial stages of the relationship? Why or why not? What alternate interpretations are feasible?

Chapter Nine

SOCIAL INFLUENCE

SOCIAL INFLUENCE IS the process of inducing change in other people. Sometimes social change results from direct orders to do something, such as when a military officer gives an order to a subordinate. When this happens, we call it *obedience*. Basic to situations involving obedience is some sort of power, either real or imagined, that the person giving the orders has over the person obeying him or her.

Not all social influence is due to direct orders from people in positions of authority. Instead, we may simply ask that a person do something for us. *Compliance* is when a person does something just because he or she was asked to, not because the requestor had any type of power over him or her.

Finally, social influence also operates in a very subtle way when people follow *norms,* or generally expected ways of behaving in certain situations. For example, when you are in an elevator, what do you do? Most likely, you face forward and stare at the numbers. *Conformity* occurs in many situations where norms exist for proper behavior. In a sense, conformity is the lifeblood of a society, for without conformity to rules, society could not exist.

The articles selected for this chapter primarily deal with obedience and compliance, although issues of conformity also can be found. Article 25, "The Education of a Torturer," gives a chilling account of what types of social influence go into the transformation of a normal human being into someone capable of inflicting the most hideous punishment and pain on someone else. As the article notes, the transformation is not due just to obedience to authority but also to compliance to requests and conformity to the norms of the torturer subculture.

Article 26, a classic work on obedience to authority, is perhaps one of the most widely known studies in the field of social psychology. "Behavioral Study of Obedience" seeks to demonstrate experimentally that the average person could be induced to harm another person simply by being ordered to do so by someone in a position of authority. The large number of people who fully obeyed orders is surprising.

Article 27, "Doing What the Mob Do: Priming Effects on Conformity," examines at least one of the factors that may influence conforming behavior. Building upon the methodology of a classic experiment on conformity (i.e., the Asch line-judgment study), this article also demonstrates how research concepts are continually refined over the years.

ARTICLE 25 _____

When people read about a horrendous act that has been committed, they naturally think that the person who committed it is somehow deranged or inhuman. Sometimes that is indeed the case, as when a psychotic commits an act under orders he or she has supposedly received during hallucinations. Personal pathology and mental illness are certainly involved in many of the hideous acts that people commit. But are personality or psychological factors always the cause of such behavior? Is it possible that an otherwise normal individual may commit an abnormal, sick act not because there is something wrong with him or her but because of the situation he or she might be in?

History is full of examples of normal people who have committed abnormal acts. For example, warfare has often induced otherwise normal, nonviolent people not only to kill but also to commit atrocities. Yet the suggestion that somehow anyone placed in the same situation may act the same way is repugnant. It might be a lot more personally comforting to believe that people who do bad things are somehow different from us. We, after all, are good and certainly incapable of being mass murderers. Only other people who are either sick or are somehow overly conforming could do such things. In other words, we tend to attribute others' acts to their disposition—that is, some personality or other enduring trait causes them to act that way.

In this article, Janice T. Gibson and Mika Haritos-Fatouros present both field and experimental research to suggest that perhaps it is not so much individual characteristics (disposition) that result in people performing terrible acts but rather the situation that produces the behavior. The authors review the step-by-step process of taking a normal person who does not enjoy hurting other people and transforming him into a torturer. Similar steps of inducing obedience found in other studies also are presented. If you strongly believe that a torturer is somehow different from other people, this article may make you think again.

The Education of a Torturer

■ Janice T. Gibson and Mika Haritos-Fatouros

Torture—for whatever purpose and in whatever name—requires a torturer, an individual responsible for planning and causing pain to others. "A man's hands are shackled behind him, his eyes blindfolded," wrote Argentine journalist Jacobo Timerman about his torture by Argentine army extremists. "No one says a word. Blows are showered . . . [He is] stripped, doused with water, tied . . . And the application of electric shocks begins. It's impossible to shout—you howl." The governments of at least 90 countries use similar methods to torture people all over the world, Amnesty International reports.

What kind of person can behave so monstrously to another human being? A sadist or a sexual deviant? Someone with an authoritarian upbringing or who was abused by parents? A disturbed personality affected somehow by hereditary characteristics?

On the contrary, the Nazis who tortured and killed millions during World War II "weren't sadists or killers by nature," Hannah Arendt reported in her book *Eichmann in Jerusalem.* Many studies of Nazi behavior concluded that monstrous acts, despite their horrors, were often simply a matter of faithful bureaucrats slavishly following orders.

Reprinted from *Psychology Today,* 1986 (November), *20,* 50–58. Reprinted with permission from *Psychology Today* magazine. Copyright © 1986 (Sussex Publishers, Inc.).

In a 1976 study, University of Florida psychologist Molly Harrower asked 15 Rorschach experts to examine ink-blot test reports from Adolph Eichmann, Rudolf Hess, Hermann Goering and five other Nazi war criminals, made just before their trials at Nuremberg. She also sent the specialists Rorschach reports from eight Americans, some with well-adjusted personalities and some who were severely disturbed, without revealing the individuals' identities. The experts were unable to distinguish the Nazis from the Americans and judged an equal number of both to be well-adjusted. The horror that emerges is the likelihood that torturers are not freaks; they are ordinary people.

Obedience to what we call the "authority of violence" often plays an important role in pushing ordinary people to commit cruel, violent and even fatal acts. During wartime, for example, soldiers will follow orders to kill unarmed civilians. Here, we will look at the way obedience and other factors combine to produce willing torturers.

Twenty-five years ago, the late psychologist Stanley Milgram demonstrated convincingly that people unlikely to be cruel in everyday life will administer pain if they are told to by someone in authority. In a famous experiment, Milgram had men wearing laboratory coats direct average American adults to inflict a series of electric shocks on other people. No real shocks were given and the "victims" were acting, but the people didn't know this. They were told that the purpose of the study was to measure the effects of punishment on learning. Obediently, 65 percent of them used what they thought were dangerously high levels of shocks when the experimenter told them to. While they were less likely to administer these supposed shocks as they were moved closer to their victims, almost one-third of them continued to shock when they were close enough to touch.

This readiness to torture is not limited to Americans. Following Milgram's lead, other researchers found that people of all ages from a wide range of countries were willing to shock others even when they had nothing to gain by complying with the command or nothing to lose by refusing it. So long as someone else, an authority figure, was responsible for the final outcome of the experiment, almost no one absolutely refused to administer shocks. Each study

also found, as Milgram had, that some people would give shocks even when the decision was left up to them.

Milgram proposed that the reasons people obey or disobey authority fall into three categories. The first is personal history family or school backgrounds that encourage obedience or defiance. The second, which he called "binding," is made up of ongoing experiences that make people feel comfortable when they obey authority. Strain, the third category, consists of bad feelings from unpleasant experiences connected with obedience. Milgram argued that when the binding factors are more powerful than the strain of cooperating, people will do as they are told. When the strain is greater, they are more likely to disobey.

This may explain short-term obedience in the laboratory, but it doesn't explain prolonged patterns of torture during wartime or under some political regimes. Repeatedly, torturers in Argentina and elsewhere performed acts that most of us consider repugnant, and in time this should have placed enough strain on them to prevent their obedience. It didn't. Nor does Milgram's theory explain undirected cruel or violent acts, which occur even when no authority orders them. For this, we have developed a more comprehensive learning model; for torture, we discovered, can be taught (see "Teaching to Torment," this article).

We studied the procedures used to train Greek military police as torturers during that country's military regime from 1967 through 1974. We examined the official testimonies of 21 former soldiers in the ESA (Army Police Corps) given at their 1975 criminal trials in Athens; in addition, Haritos-Fatouros conducted in-depth interviews with 16 of them after their trials. In many cases, these men had been convicted and had completed prison sentences. They were all leading normal lives when interviewed. One was a university graduate, five were graduates of higher technical institutes, nine had completed at least their second year of high school and only one had no more than a primary school education.

All of these men had been drafted, first into regular military service and then into specialized units that required servicemen to torture prisoners. We found no record of delinquent or disturbed behavior before their military service. However, we did find several features of the soldiers' training that helped to turn them into willing and able torturers.

The initial screening for torturers was primarily based on physical strength and "appropriate" political beliefs, which simply meant that the recruits and their families were anticommunists. This ensured that the men had hostile attitudes toward potential victims from the very beginning.

Once they were actually serving as military police, the men were also screened for other attributes. According to former torturer Michaelis Petrou, "The most important criterion was that you had to keep your mouth shut. Second, you had to show aggression. Third, you had to be intelligent and strong. Fourth, you had to be 'their man,' which meant that you would report on the others serving with you, that [the officers] could trust you and that you would follow their orders blindly."

Binding the recruits to the authority of ESA began in basic training, with physically brutal initiation rites. Recruits themselves were cursed, punched, kicked and flogged. They were forced to run until they collapsed and prevented from relieving themselves for long stretches of time. They were required to swear allegiance to a symbol of authority used by the regime (a poster of a soldier superimposed on a large phoenix rising from its own ashes), and they had to promise on their knees to obey their commander-in-chief and the military revolution.

While being harassed and beaten by their officers, servicemen were repeatedly told how fortunate they were to have joined the ESA, the strongest and most important support of the regime. They were told that an ESA serviceman's action is never questioned: "You can even flog a major." In-group language helped the men to develop elitist attitudes. Servicemen used

---

Teaching to Torment

There are several ways to teach people to do the unthinkable, and we have developed a model to explain how they are used. We have also found that college fraternities, although they are far removed from the grim world of torture and violent combat, use similar methods for initiating new members, to ensure their faithfulness to the fraternity's rules and values. However, this unthinking loyalty can sometimes lead to dangerous actions: Over the past 10 years, there have been countless injuries during fraternity initiations and 39 deaths. These training techniques are designed to instill unquestioning obedience in people, but they can easily be a guide for an intensive course in torture.

1. Screening to find the best prospects: normal, well-adjusted people with the physical, intellectual and, in some cases, political attributes necessary for the task.
2. Techniques to increase binding among these prospects:

- Initiation rites to isolate people from society and introduce them to a new social order, with different rules and values.
- Elitist attitudes and "in-group" language, which highlight the differences between the group and the rest of society.

3. Techniques to reduce the strain of obedience:
- Blaming and dehumanizing the victims, so it is less disturbing to harm them.
- Harassment, the constant physical and psychological intimidation that prevents logical thinking and promotes the instinctive responses needed for acts of inhuman cruelty.
- Rewards for obedience and punishments for not cooperating.
- Social modeling by watching other group members commit violent acts and then receive rewards.
- Systematic desensitization to repugnant acts by gradual exposure to them, so they appear routine and normal despite conflicts with previous moral standards.

nicknames for one another and, later, they used them for victims and for the different methods of torture. "Tea party" meant the beating of a prisoner by a group of military police using their fists, and "tea party with toast" meant more severe group beatings using clubs. Gradually, the recruits came to speak of all people who were not in their group, parents and families included, as belonging to the "outside world."

The strain of obedience on the recruits was reduced in several ways. During basic training, they were given daily "national ethical education" lectures that included indoctrination against communism and enemies of the state. During more advanced training, the recruits were constantly reminded that the prisoners were "worms," and that they had to "crush" them. One man reported that when he was torturing prisoners later, he caught himself repeating phrases like "bloody communists!" that he had heard in the lectures.

The military police used a carrot-and-stick method to further diminish the recruits' uneasiness about torture. There were many rewards, such as relaxed military rules after training was completed, and torturers often weren't punished for leaving camp without permission. They were allowed to wear civilian clothes, to keep their hair long and to drive military police cars for their personal use. Torturers were frequently given a leave of absence after they forced a confession from a prisoner. They had many economic benefits as well, including free bus rides and restaurant meals and job placement when military service was over. These were the carrots.

The sticks consisted of the constant harassment, threats and punishment for disobedience. The men were threatened and intimidated, first by their trainers, then later by senior servicemen. "An officer used to tell us that if a warder helps a prisoner, he will take the prisoner's place and the whole platoon will flog him," one man recalled. Soldiers spied on one another, and even the most successful torturers said that they were constantly afraid.

"You will learn to love pain," one officer promised a recruit. Sensitivity to torture was blunted in several steps. First, the men had to endure it themselves, as if torture were a normal act. The beatings and other torments inflicted on them continued and became worse. Next, the servicemen chosen for the Persecu-

tion Section, the unit that tortured political prisoners, were brought into contact with the prisoners by carrying food to their cells. The new men watched veteran soldiers torture prisoners, while they stood guard. Occasionally, the veterans would order them to give the prisoners "some blows."

At the next step, the men were required to participate in group beatings. Later, they were told to use a variety of torture methods on the prisoners. The final step, the appointment to prison warder or chief torturer, was announced suddenly by the commander-in-chief, leaving the men no time to reflect on their new duties.

The Greek example illustrates how the ability to torture can be taught. Training that increases binding and reduces strain can cause decent people to commit acts, often over long periods of time, that otherwise would be unthinkable for them. Similar techniques can be found in military training all over the world, when the intent is to teach soldiers to kill or perform some other repellent act. We conducted extensive interviews with soldiers and ex-soldiers in the U.S. Marines and the Green Berets, and we found that all the steps in our training model were part and parcel of elite American military training. Soldiers are screened for intellectual and physical ability, achievement and mental health. Binding begins in basic training, with initiation rites that isolate trainees from society, introduce them to new rules and values and leave them little time for clear thinking after exhausting physical exercise and scant sleep. Harassment plays an important role, and soldiers are severely punished for disobedience, with demerits, verbal abuse, hours of calisthenics and loss of eating, sleeping and other privileges.

Military training gradually desensitizes soldiers to violence and reduces the strain normally created by repugnant acts. Their revulsion is diminished by screaming chants and songs about violence and killing during marches and runs. The enemy is given derogatory names and portrayed as less than human; this makes it easier to kill them. Completing the toughest possible training and being rewarded by "making it" in an elite corps bring the soldiers confidence and pride, and those who accomplish this feel they can do anything. "Although I tried to avoid killing, I learned to have confidence in myself and was never afraid," said a former Green Beret who served in Vietnam. "It was part of the job. . . . Anyone who goes through that kind of training could do it."

The effectiveness of these techniques, as several researchers have shown, is not limited to the army. History teacher Ronald Jones started what he called the Third Wave movement as a classroom experiment to show his high school students how people might have become Nazis in World War II. Jones began the Third Wave demonstration by requiring students to stand at attention in a unique new posture and follow strict new rules. He required students to stand beside their desks when asking or answering questions and to begin each statement by saying, "Mr. Jones." The students obeyed. He then required them to shout slogans, "Strength through discipline!" and "Strength through community!" Jones created a salute for class members that he called the Third Wave: the right hand raised to the shoulder with fingers curled. The salute had no meaning, but it served as a symbol of group belonging and a way of isolating members from outsiders.

The organization expanded quickly from 20 original members to 100. The teacher issued membership cards and assigned students to report members who didn't comply with the new rules. Dutifully, 20 students pointed accusing fingers at their classmates.

Then Jones announced that the Third Wave was a "nationwide movement to find students willing to fight for political change," and he organized a rally, which drew a crowd of 200 students. At the rally, after getting students to salute and shout slogans on command, Jones explained the true reasons behind the Third Wave demonstration. Like the Nazis before them, Jones pointed out, "You bargained your freedom for the comfort of discipline."

The students, at an age when group belonging was very important to them, made good candidates for training. Jones didn't teach his students to commit atrocities, and the Third Wave lasted for only five days; in that time, however, Jones created an obedient group that resembled in many ways the Nazi youth groups of World War II (see "The Third Wave: Nazism in a High School," *Psychology Today,* July 1976).

Psychologists Craig Haney, W. Curtis Banks and Philip Zimbardo went even further in a remarkable simulation of prison life done at Stanford University.

With no special training and in only six days' time, they changed typical university students into controlling, abusive guards and servile prisoners.

The students who agreed to participate were chosen randomly to be guards or prisoners. The mock guards were given uniforms and nightsticks and told to act as guards. Prisoners were treated as dangerous criminals: Local police rounded them up, fingerprinted and booked them and brought them to a simulated cell block in the basement of the university psychology department. Uniformed guards made them remove their clothing, deloused them, gave them prison uniforms and put them in cells.

The two groups of students, originally found to be very similar in most respects, showed striking changes within one week. Prisoners became passive, dependent and helpless. In contrast, guards expressed feelings of power, status and group belonging. They were aggressive and abusive within the prison, insulting and bullying the prisoners. Some guards reported later that they had enjoyed their power, while others said they had not thought they were capable of behaving as they had. They were surprised and dismayed at what they had done: "It was degrading. . . . To me, those things are sick. But they [the prisoners] did everything I said. They abused each other because I requested them to. No one questioned my authority at all."

The guards' behavior was similar in two important ways to that of the Greek torturers. First, they dehumanized their victims. Second, like the torturers, the guards were abusive only when they were within the prison walls. They could act reasonably outside the prisons because the two prison influences of binding and reduced strain were absent.

All these changes at Stanford occurred with no special training, but the techniques we have outlined were still present. Even without training, the student guards "knew" from television and movies that they were supposed to punish prisoners; they "knew" they were supposed to feel superior; and they "knew" they were supposed to blame their victims. Their own behavior and that of their peers gradually numbed their sensitivity to what they were doing, and they were rewarded by the power they had over their prisoners.

There is no evidence that such short-term experiments produce lasting effects. None were reported from either the Third Wave demonstration or the Stanford University simulation. The Stanford study, however, was cut short when depression, crying and psychosomatic illnesses began to appear among the students. And studies of Vietnam veterans have revealed that committing abhorrent acts, even under the extreme conditions of war, can lead to long-term problems. In one study of 130 Vietnam veterans who came to a therapist for help, almost 30 percent of them were concerned about violent acts they had committed while in the service. The veterans reported feelings of anxiety, guilt, depression and an inability to carry on intimate relationships. In a similar fashion, after the fall of the Greek dictatorship in 1974, former torturers began to report nightmares, irritability and episodes of depression.

"Torturing became a job," said former Greek torturer Petrou. "If the officers ordered you to beat, you beat. If they ordered you to stop, you stopped. You never thought you could do otherwise." His comments bear a disturbing resemblance to the feelings expressed by a Stanford guard: "When I was doing it, I didn't feel regret. . . . I didn't feel guilt. Only afterwards, when I began to reflect . . . did it begin to dawn on me that this was a part of me I hadn't known before."

We do not believe that torture came naturally to any of these young men. Haritos-Fatouros found no evidence of sadistic, abusive or authoritarian behaviors in the Greek soldiers' histories prior to their training. This, together with our study of Marine training and the Stanford and Third Wave studies, leads to the conclusion that torturers have normal personalities. Any of us, in a similar situation, might be capable of the same cruelty. One probably cannot train a deranged sadist to be an effective torturer or killer. He must be in complete control of himself while on the job.

CRITICAL THINKING QUESTIONS

1. What are the real implications of the studies summarized in the article? Could anyone, including you, be induced to do the same things if you were put into the same situations? Do personality and perhaps free will really have nothing to do with whether you choose to obey the orders? Or is free choice not really possible in such situations? Support your answers.

2. If inhuman behaviors can be induced by the techniques used to get torturers to do their deeds, does that mean that people should not be held responsible for the things they do? Would a defense of "I was conditioned to do it" absolve an individual of personal responsibility for his or her actions? Explain your responses.

3. The article seemed to suggest that it is fairly easy to get people to do some terrible things under the right set of conditions. How could you prevent such effects? For example, would forewarning people about possible recrimination lessen the likelihood that they would be influenced by the process?

ARTICLE 26 _____

Stanley Milgram's article "Behavioral Study of Obedience" was one of his first describing a series of studies investigating the conditions that produce obedience to authority. This study, as well as Milgram's subsequent research, is truly classic. In fact, if you asked someone who has had only minimal exposure to the field of social psychology about landmark research, this study would perhaps come to mind.

Part of the widespread interest in Milgram's work is due to the implications it has. Basically, Milgram took a group of male volunteers from various backgrounds and ages and induced them to perform acts that appeared to harm another person. Nearly two-thirds of the subjects were fully obedient, continuing to give shocks even though it was apparent that they were harming the victim. Does that mean that just about anyone could be made to do the same? More importantly, while reading the article, keep in mind the actual situation confronting the subjects: What would have happened to them if they had refused to obey? Would the effect demonstrated by Milgram be greater for real-life situations, where there might be punishments for failing to obey?

Besides the implications of the research, Milgram's work on obedience also has attracted considerable interest over the years because of the ethical issues raised. When reading the article, try to put yourself in the shoes of the subjects: How would you feel if you volunteered for a study on learning and instead walked out of the experiment an hour later with the realization that you were willing to harm someone just because an authority figure told you to do so? Think about the ethical issues involved in the study, including the issue of debriefing subjects following an experiment.

Behavioral Study of Obedience

■ Stanley Milgram

This chapter describes a procedure for the study of destructive obedience in the laboratory. It consists of ordering a naive S to administer increasingly more severe punishment to a victim in the context of a learning experiment. Punishment is administered by means of a shock generator with thirty graded switches ranging from Slight Shock to Danger: Severe Shock. The victim is a confederate of the E. The primary dependent variable is the maximum shock the S is willing to administer before he refuses to continue further. Twenty-six Ss obeyed the experimental commands fully, and administered the highest shock on the generator. Fourteen Ss broke off the experiment at some point after the victim protested and refused to provide further answers. The procedure created extreme levels of nervous tension in some Ss. Profuse

sweating, trembling and stuttering were typical expressions of this emotional disturbance. One unexpected sign of tension—yet to be explained—was the regular occurrence of nervous laughter, which in some Ss developed into uncontrollable seizures. The variety of interesting behavioral dynamics observed in the experiment, the reality of the situation for the S, and the possibility of parametric variation within the framework of the procedure, point to the fruitfulness of further study.

Obedience is as basic an element in the structure of social life as one can point to. Some system of authority is a requirement of all communal living, and it is only the man dwelling in isolation who is not forced to respond, through defiance or submission, to the

Reprinted from *Journal of Abnormal and Social Psychology,* 1963, *67,* 371–378. Copyright renewed 1991 by Alexandra Milgram. All rights reserved. Reprinted by permission.

commands of others. Obedience, as a determinant of behavior, is of particular relevance to our time. It has been reliably established that from 1933–1945 millions of innocent persons were systematically slaughtered on command. Gas chambers were built, death camps were guarded, daily quotas of corpses were produced with the same efficiency as the manufacture of appliances. These inhumane policies may have originated in the mind of a single person, but they could only be carried out on a massive scale if a very large number of persons obeyed orders.

Obedience is the psychological mechanism that links individual action to political purpose. It is the dispositional cement that binds men to systems of authority. Facts of recent history and observation in daily life suggest that for many persons obedience may be a deeply ingrained behavior tendency, indeed, a prepotent impulse overriding training in ethics, sympathy, and moral conduct. C. P. Snow (1961) points to its importance when he writes:

> When you think of the long and gloomy history of man, you will find more hideous crimes have been committed in the name of obedience than have ever been committed in the name of rebellion. If you doubt that, read William Shirer's "Rise and Fall of the Third Reich." The German Officer Corps were brought up in the most rigorous code of obedience . . . in the name of obedience they were party to, and assisted in, the most wicked large scale actions in the history of the world. (p. 24)

While the particular form of obedience dealt with in the present study has its antecedents in these episodes, it must not be thought all obedience entails acts of aggression against others. Obedience serves numerous productive functions. Indeed, the very life of society is predicated on its existence. Obedience may be ennobling and educative and refer to acts of charity and kindness, as well as to destruction.

GENERAL PROCEDURE

A procedure was devised which seems useful as a tool for studying obedience (Milgram, 1961). It consists of ordering a naive subject to administer electric shock to a victim. A simulated shock generator is used, with 30 clearly marked voltage levels that range from 15 to 450 volts. The instrument bears verbal designations that range from Slight Shock to Danger: Severe Shock. The responses of the victim, who is a trained confederate of the experimenter, are standardized. The orders to administer shocks are given to the naive subject in the context of a "learning experiment" ostensibly set up to study the effects of punishment on memory. As the experiment proceeds the naive subject is commanded to administer increasingly more intense shocks to the victim, even to the point of reaching the level marked Danger: Severe Shock. Internal resistances become stronger, and at a certain point the subject refuses to go on with the experiment. Behavior prior to this rupture is considered "obedience," in that the subject complies with the commands of the experimenter. The point of rupture is the act of disobedience. A quantitative value is assigned to the subject's performance based on the maximum intensity shock he is willing to administer before he refuses to participate further. Thus for any particular subject and for any particular experimental condition the degree of obedience may be specified with a numerical value. The crux of the study is to systematically vary the factors believed to alter the degree of obedience to the experimental commands.

The technique allows important variables to be manipulated at several points in the experiment. One may vary aspects of the source of command, content and form of command, instrumentalities for its execution, target object, general social setting, etc. The problem, therefore, is not one of designing increasingly more numerous experimental conditions, but of selecting those that best illuminate the process of obedience from the sociopsychological standpoint.

RELATED STUDIES

The inquiry bears an important relation to philosophic analyses of obedience and authority (Arendt, 1958; Friedrich, 1958; Weber, 1947), an early experimental study of obedience by Frank (1944), studies in "authoritarianism" (Adorno, Frenkel-Brunswik, Levinson, and Sanford, 1950; Rokeach, 1961), and a recent series of analytic and empirical studies in social power (Cartwright, 1959). It owes much to the long concern with *suggestion* in social psychology, both in its normal forms (e.g., Binet, 1900) and in its clinical manifestations (Charcot, 1881). But it derives, in the first instance, from direct observation of a social fact; the individual who is commanded by a legitimate authority ordinarily obeys. Obedience comes easily and often. It is a ubiquitous and indispensable feature of social life.

METHOD

Subjects

The subjects were 40 males between the ages of 20 and 50, drawn from New Haven and the surrounding communities. Subjects were obtained by a newspaper advertisement and direct mail solicitation. Those who responded to the appeal believed they were to participate in a study of memory and learning at Yale University. A wide range of occupations is represented in the sample. Typical subjects were postal clerks, high school teachers, salesmen, engineers, and laborers. Subjects ranged in educational level from one who had not finished elementary school, to those who had doctorate and other professional degrees. They were paid $4.50 for their participation in the experiment. However, subjects were told that payment was simply for coming to the laboratory, and that the money was theirs no matter what happened after they arrived. Table 1 shows the proportion of age and occupational types assigned to the experimental condition.

Personnel and Locale

The experiment was conducted on the grounds of Yale University in the elegant interaction laboratory. (This detail is relevant to the perceived legitimacy of the experiment. In further variations, the experiment

was dissociated from the university, with consequences for performance.) The role of experimenter was played by a 31-year-old high school teacher of biology. His manner was impassive, and his appearance somewhat stern throughout the experiment. He was dressed in a gray technician's coat. The victim was played by a 47-year-old accountant, trained for the role; he was of Irish-American stock, whom most observers found mild-mannered and likable.

Procedure

One naive subject and one victim (an accomplice) performed in each experiment. A pretext had to be devised that would justify the administration of electric shock by the naive subject. This was effectively accomplished by the cover story. After a general introduction on the presumed relation between punishment and learning, subjects were told:

> But actually, we know very little *about the effect of punishment on learning, because almost no truly scientific studies have been made of it in human beings.*
>
> *For instance, we don't know how* much *punishment is best for learning—and we don't know how much difference it makes as to who is giving the punishment, whether an adult learns best from a younger or an older person than himself—or many things of that sort.*
>
> *So in this study we are bringing together a number of adults of different occupations and ages. And we're asking some of them to be teachers and some of them to be learners.*
>
> *We want to find out just what effect different people have on each other as teachers and learners,*

TABLE 1 / Distribution of Age and Occupational Types in the Experiment

Occupations	20–29 Years *n*	30–39 Years *n*	40–50 Years *n*	Percentage of Total (Occupations)
Workers, skilled and unskilled	4	5	6	37.5
Sales, business, and white-collar	3	6	7	40.0
Professional	1	5	3	22.5
Percentage of total (age	20	40	40	

Note: Total *n* = 40.

and also what effect punishment will have on learning in this situation.

Therefore, I'm going to ask one of you to be the teacher here tonight and the other one to be the learner.

Does either of you have a preference?

Subjects then drew slips of paper from a hat to determine who would be the teacher and who would be the learner in the experiment. The drawing was rigged so that the naive subject was always the teacher and the accomplice always the learner. (Both slips contained the word "Teacher.") Immediately after the drawing the teacher and learner were taken to an adjacent room and the learner was strapped into an "electric chair" apparatus.

The experimenter explained that the straps were to prevent excessive movement while the learner was being shocked. The effect was to make it impossible for him to escape from the situation. An electrode was attached to the learner's wrist, and electrode paste was applied "to avoid blisters and burns." Subjects were told that the electrode was attached to the shock generator in the adjoining room.

In order to improve credibility the experimenter declared, in response to a question by the learner: "Although the shocks can be extremely painful, they cause no permanent tissue damage."

Learning Task   The lesson administered by the subject was a paired-associate learning task. The subject read a series of word pairs to the learner, and then read the first word of the pair along with four terms. The learner was to indicate which of the four terms had originally been paired with the first word. He communicated his answer by pressing one of four switches in front of him, which in turn lit up one of four numbered quadrants in an answer-box located atop the shock generator.

Shock Generator   The instrument panel consists of 30 lever switches set in a horizontal line. Each switch is clearly labeled with a voltage designation that ranges from 15 to 450 volts. There is a 15-volt increment from one switch to the next going from left to right. In addition, the following verbal designations are clearly indicated for groups of four

switches going from left to right: Slight Shock, Moderate Shock, Strong Shock, Very Strong Shock, Intense Shock, Extreme Intensity Shock, Danger: Severe Shock. (Two switches after this last designation are simply marked XXX.)

Upon depressing a switch: a pilot light corresponding to each switch is illuminated in bright red; an electric buzzing is heard; an electric blue light, labeled "voltage energizer," flashes; the dial on the voltage meter swings to the right; various relay clicks are sounded.

The upper left-hand corner of the generator is labeled Shock Generator, Type ZLB, Dyson Instrument Company, Waltham, Mass. Output 15 Volts–450 Volts.

Details of the instrument were carefully handled to insure an appearance of authenticity. The panel was engraved by precision industrial engravers, and all components were of high quality. No subject in the experiment suspected that the instrument was merely a simulated shock generator.[1]

Sample Shock   Each naive subject is given a sample shock on the shock generator, prior to beginning his run as teacher. This shock is always 45 volts, and is applied by pressing the third switch of the generator. The shock is applied to the wrist of the naive subject, and has its source in a 45-volt battery wired into the generator. This further convinces the subject of the authenticity of the generator.

Shock Instructions   The subject is told to administer a shock to the learner each time he gives a wrong response. Moreover—and this is the key command—the subject is instructed to "move one lever higher on the shock generator each time the learner flashes a wrong answer." He is also instructed to announce the voltage level before administering a shock. This serves to continually remind subjects of the increasing intensity of shocks administered to the learner.

Preliminary and Regular Run   Pretests revealed that the procedure of reading words and administering shocks requires some practice before it can be handled smoothly. Therefore, immediately preceding the regular run, the teacher is given a preliminary series of 10 words to read to the learner. There are 3 neutral words in the practice series (i.e., words that the learner answers correctly), so that shocks are administered for 7 of the words, with the maximum shock at 105 volts (moderate shock). Almost all subjects master the procedure by the time the preliminary run is over.

Subjects are then presented with a second list, and are told that the procedure is the same as for the first list; the experimenter adds, however:

> *When you get to the bottom of the list, repeat it over again, and continue giving shocks, until the learner has learned all the pairs correctly.*

The experimenter instructs the subject to

> *start from 15 volts and increase the shock level one step each time the learner gives a wrong answer.*

Feedback from the Victim   In all conditions the learner gives a predetermined set of responses to the word pair test, based on a schedule of approximately three wrong answers to one correct answer. In the present experimental condition no vocal response or other sign of protest is heard from the learner until Shock Level 300 is reached. When the 300-volt shock is administered, the learner pounds on the wall of the room in which he is bound to the electric chair. The pounding can be heard by the subject. From this point on, the learner's answers no longer appear on the four-way panel.

At this juncture, subjects ordinarily turn to the experimenter for guidance. The experimenter instructs the subject to treat the absence of a response as a wrong answer, and to shock the subject according to the usual schedule. He advises the subjects to allow 5–10 seconds before considering no response as a wrong answer, and to increase the shock level one step each time the learner fails to respond correctly. The learner's pounding is repeated after the 315-volt shock is administered; afterwards he is not heard from, nor do his answers reappear on the four-way signal box.

Experimenter Feedback   At various points in the experiment the subject may turn to the experimenter for advice on whether he should continue to administer shocks. Or he may indicate that he does not wish to go on. It was important to standardize the experimenter's responses to these inquiries and reactions.

If the subject indicated his unwillingness to go on, the experimenter responded with a sequence of "prods," using as many as necessary to bring the subject into line.

> *Prod 1: Please continue* or *Please go on.*
> *Prod 2: The experiment requires that you continue.*
> *Prod 3: It is absolutely essential that you continue.*
> *Prod 4: You have no other choice, you* must *go on.*

The prods were always made in sequence: Only if Prod 1 had been unsuccessful, could Prod 2 be used. If the subject refused to obey the experimenter after Prod 4, the experiment was terminated. The experimenter's tone of voice was at all times firm, but not impolite. The sequence was begun anew on each occasion that the subject balked or showed reluctance to follow orders.

Special Prods   If the subject asked if the learner was liable to suffer permanent physical injury, the experimenter said:

> *Although the shocks may be painful, there is no permanent tissue damage, so please go on. [Followed by Prods 2, 3, and 4 if necessary.]*

If the subject said that the learner did not want to go on, the experimenter replied:

> *Whether the learner likes it or not, you must go on until he has learned all the word pairs correctly. So please go on. [Followed by Prods 2, 3, and 4 if necessary.]*

Dependent Measures

The primary dependent measure for any subject is the maximum shock he administers before he refuses to go any further. In principle this may vary from 0 (for a subject who refuses to administer even the first shock) to 30 (for a subject who administers the highest shock on the generator). A subject who breaks off the experiment at any point prior to administering the thirtieth shock level is termed a *defiant* subject. One who complies with experimental commands fully, and proceeds to administer all shock levels commanded, is termed an *obedient* subject.

Further Records   With few exceptions, experimental sessions were recorded on magnetic tape. Occasional photographs were taken through one-way mirrors. Notes were kept on any unusual behavior occurring during the course of the experiments. On occasion, additional observers were directed to write objective descriptions of the subjects' behavior. The latency and duration of shocks were measured by accurate timing devices.

Interview and Dehoax Following the experiment, subjects were interviewed; open-ended questions, projective measures, and attitude scales were employed. After the interview, procedures were undertaken to assure that the subject would leave the laboratory in a state of well being. A friendly reconciliation was arranged between the subject and the victim, and an effort was made to reduce any tensions that arose as a result of the experiment.

RESULTS

Preliminary Notions

Before giving an account of the experimental results, it is instructive to consider how persons predict others will perform when commanded to administer powerful shocks to another person. Fourteen Yale seniors, all psychology majors, were provided with a detailed description of the experimental situation. They were asked to reflect carefully on it, and to predict the behavior of 100 hypothetical subjects. More specifically, they were instructed to plot the distribution of obedience of "100 Americans of diverse occupations, and ranging in age from 20 to 50 years," who were placed in the experimental situation.

There was considerable agreement among the respondents on the expected behavior of hypothetical subjects. All respondents predicted that only an insignificant minority would go through to the end of the shock series. (The estimates ranged from 0 to 3 percent; i.e., the most "pessimistic" member of the class predicted that of 100 persons, 3 would continue through to the most potent shock available on the shock generator—450 volts.) The class mean was 1.2 percent. The question was also posed informally to colleagues of the author, and the most general feeling was that few if any subjects would go beyond the designation Very Strong Shock.

Result of Experiment 1

Subjects Accept Situation With few exceptions subjects were convinced of the reality of the experimental situation, that they were administering shocks to another person, and the most potent shocks were extremely painful. In the post-experimental interview subjects were asked: "How painful to the learner were the last few shocks that you administered to him?" Subjects were instructed to indicate their answers on a printed 14-point scale ranging from "Not at all painful" to "Extremely painful." The modal response was 14 (Extremely painful) with the mean at 13.42.

Signs of Extreme Tension Many subjects showed signs of nervousness in the experimental situation, and especially upon administering the more powerful shocks. In a large number of cases the degree of tension reached extremes that are rarely seen in sociopsychological laboratory studies. Subjects were observed to sweat, tremble, stutter, bite their lips, groan, and dig their fingernails into their flesh. These were characteristic rather than exceptional responses to the experiment.

One sign of tension was the regular occurrence of nervous laughing fits. Fourteen of the 40 subjects showed definite signs of nervous laughter and smiling. The laughter seemed entirely out of place, even bizarre. Full-blown, uncontrollable seizures were observed for 3 subjects. On one occasion we observed a seizure so violently convulsive that it was necessary to call a halt to the experiment. The subject, a 46-year-old encyclopedia salesman, was seriously embarrassed by his untoward and uncontrollable behavior. In the post-experimental interviews subjects took pains to point out that they were not sadistic types, and that the laughter did not mean they enjoyed shocking the victim.

Distribution of Scores It had been conjectured that persons would not, in general, agree to administer shocks beyond the level designated as Very Strong Shock. The distribution of maximum shocks for this experiment is shown in Table 2. The obtained distribution of scores deviates radically from the prediction.

Upon command of the experimenter, each of the 40 subjects went beyond the expected breakoff point.

TABLE 2 / Distribution of Breakoff Points

Verbal Designation and Voltage Indication	Number of Subjects for Whom This Was Maximum Shock
Slight Shock	
15	
30	0
45	0
60	0
Moderate Shock	
75	0
90	0
105	0
120	0
Strong Shock	
135	0
150	0
165	0
180	0
Very Strong Shock	
195	0
210	0
225	0
240	0
Intense Shock	
255	0
270	0
285	0
300	5
Extreme Intensity Shock	
315	4
330	2
345	1
360	1
Danger: Severe Shock	
375	1
390	0
405	0
420	0
XXX	
435	0
450	26

No subject stopped prior to administering Shock Level 20. (At this level—300 volts—the victim kicks on the wall and no longer provides answers to the teacher's multiple-choice questions.)

Of the 40 subjects, 5 refused to obey the experimental commands beyond the 300-volt level. Four more subjects administered one further shock, and then refused to go on. Two broke off at the 330-volt level, and 1 each at 345, 360, and 375 volts. Thus a total of 14 subjects defied the experimenter. It is instructive to reprint their remarks at the point of defiance, as transcribed from the tape recordings:

> *[0124] I think he's trying to communicate, he's knocking . . . Well it's not fair to shock the guy . . . these are terrific volts. I don't think this is very humane . . . Oh, I can't go on with this; no, this isn't right. It's a hell of an experiment. The guy is suffering in there. No, I don't want to go on. This is crazy. [Subject refused to administer more shocks.]*
>
> *[0123] He's hanging in there. I'm gonna chicken out. I'd like to continue, but I can't do that to a man . . . I'm sorry I can't do that to a man. I'll hurt his heart. You take your check . . . No really, I couldn't do it.*

These subjects were frequently in a highly agitated and even angered state. Sometimes, verbal protest was at a minimum, and the subject simply got up from his chair in front of the shock generator, and indicated that he wished to leave the laboratory.

Of the 40 subjects, 26 obeyed the orders of the experimenter to the end, proceeding to punish the victim until they reached the most potent shock available on the shock generator. At that point, the experimenter called a halt to the session. (The maximum shock is labeled 450 volts, and is two steps beyond the designation: Danger: Severe Shock.) Although obedient subjects continued to administer shocks, they often did so under extreme stress. Some expressed reluctance to administer shocks beyond the 300-volt level, and displayed fears similar to those who defied the experimenter; yet they obeyed.

After the maximum shocks had been delivered, and the experimenter called a halt to the proceedings, many obedient subjects heaved sighs of relief, mopped their brows, rubbed their fingers over their eyes, or nervously fumbled cigarettes. Some shook their heads, apparently in regret. Some subjects had remained calm throughout the experiment, and displayed only minimal signs of tension from beginning to end.

DISCUSSION

The experiment yielded two findings that were surprising. The first finding concerns the sheer strength of obedient tendencies manifested in this situation. Subjects have learned from childhood that it is a fundamental breach of moral conduct to hurt another person against his will. Yet, 26 subjects abandon this tenet in following the instructions of an authority who has no special powers to enforce his commands. To disobey would bring no material loss to the subject; no punishment would ensue. It is clear from the remarks and outward behavior of many participants that in punishing the victim they are often acting against their own values. Subjects often expressed deep disapproval of shocking a man in the face of his objections, and others denounced it as stupid and senseless. Yet the majority complied with the experimental commands. This outcome was surprising from two perspectives: first, from the standpoint of predictions made in the questionnaire described earlier. (Here, however, it is possible that the remoteness of the respondents from the actual situation, and the difficulty of conveying to them the concrete details of the experiment, could account for the serious underestimation of obedience.)

But the results were also unexpected to persons who observed the experiment in progress, through one-way mirrors. Observers often uttered expressions of disbelief upon seeing a subject administer more powerful shocks to the victim. These persons had a full acquaintance with the details of the situation, and yet systematically underestimated the amount of obedience that subjects would display.

The second unanticipated effect was the extraordinary tension generated by the procedures. One might suppose that a subject would simply break off or continue as his conscience dictated. Yet, this is very far from what happened. There were striking reactions of tension and emotional strain. One observer related:

I observed a mature and initially poised businessman enter the laboratory smiling and confident. Within 20 minutes he was reduced to a twitching, stuttering wreck, who was rapidly approaching a point of nervous collapse. He constantly pulled on his earlobe, and twisted his hands. At one point he pushed his fist into his forehead and muttered: "Oh God, let's stop it." And yet he continued to respond to every word of the experimenter and obeyed to the end.

Any understanding of the phenomenon of obedience must rest on an analysis of the particular conditions in which it occurs. The following features of the experiment go some distance in explaining the high amount of obedience observed in the situation.

1. The experiment is sponsored by and takes place on the grounds of an institution of unimpeachable reputation, Yale University. It may be reasonably presumed that the personnel are competent and reputable. The importance of this background authority is now being studied by conducting a series of experiments outside of New Haven, and without any visible ties to the university.

2. The experiment is, on the face of it, designed to attain a worthy purpose—advancement of knowledge about learning and memory. Obedience occurs not as an end in itself, but as an instrumental element in a situation that the subject construes as significant, and meaningful. He may not be able to see its full significance, but he may properly assume that the experimenter does.

3. The subject perceives that the victim has voluntarily submitted to the authority system of the experimenter. He is not (at first) an unwilling captive impressed for involuntary service. He has taken the trouble to come to the laboratory presumably to aid the experimental research. That he later becomes an involuntary subject does not alter the fact that, initially, he consented to participate without qualification. Thus he has in some degree incurred an obligation toward the experimenter.

4. The subject, too, has entered the experiment voluntarily, and perceives himself under obligation to aid the experimenter. He has made a commitment, and to disrupt the experiment is a repudiation of this initial promise of aid.

5. Certain features of the procedure strengthen the subject's sense of obligation to the experimenter.

For one, he has been paid for coming to the laboratory. In part this is canceled out by the experimenter's statement that:

Of course, as in all experiments, the money is yours simply for coming to the laboratory. From this point on, no matter what happens, the money is yours.[2]

6. From the subject's standpoint, the fact that he is the teacher and the other man the learner is purely a chance consequence (it is determined by drawing lots) and he, the subject, ran the same risk as the other man in being assigned the role of learner. Since the assignment of positions in the experiment was achieved by fair means, the learner is deprived of any basis of complaint on this count. (A similar situation obtains in Army units, in which—in the absence of volunteers—a particularly dangerous mission may be assigned by drawing lots, and the unlucky soldier is expected to bear his misfortune with sportsmanship.)

7. There is, at best, ambiguity with regard to the prerogatives of a psychologist and the corresponding rights of his subject. There is a vagueness of expectation concerning what a psychologist may require of his subject, and when he is overstepping acceptable limits. Moreover, the experiment occurs in a closed setting, and thus provides no opportunity for the subject to remove these ambiguities by discussion with others. There are few standards that seem directly applicable to the situation, which is a novel one for most subjects.

8. The subjects are assured that the shocks administered to the subject are "painful but not dangerous." Thus they assume that the discomfort caused the victim is momentary, while the scientific gains resulting from the experiment are enduring.

9. Through Shock Level 20 the victim continues to provide answers on the signal box. The subject may construe this as a sign that the victim is still willing to "play the game." It is only after Shock Level 20 that the victim repudiates the rules completely, refusing to answer further.

These features help to explain the high amount of obedience obtained in this experiment. Many of the arguments raised need not remain matters of speculation, but can be reduced to testable propositions to be confirmed or disproved by further experiments.[3]

The following features of the experiment concern the nature of the conflict which the subject faces.

10. The subject is placed in a position in which he must respond to the competing demands of two persons: the experimenter and the victim. The conflict must be resolved by meeting the demands of one or the other; satisfaction of the victim and the experimenter are mutually exclusive. Moreover, the resolution must take the form of a highly visible action, that of continuing to shock the victim or breaking off the experiment. Thus the subject is forced into a public conflict that does not permit any completely satisfactory solution.

11. While the demands of the experimenter carry the weight of scientific authority, the demands of the victim spring from his personal experience of pain and suffering. The two claims need not be regarded as equally pressing and legitimate. The experimenter seeks an abstract scientific datum; the victim cries out for relief from physical suffering caused by the subject's actions.

12. The experiment gives the subject little time for reflection. The conflict comes on rapidly. It is only minutes after the subject has been seated before the shock generator that the victim begins his protests. Moreover, the subject perceives that he has gone through but two-thirds of the shock levels at the time the subject's first protests are heard. Thus he understands that the conflict will have a persistent aspect to it, and may well become more intense as increasingly more powerful shocks are required. The rapidity with which the conflict descends on the subject, and his realization that it is predictably recurrent may well be sources of tension to him.

13. At a more general level, the conflict stems from the opposition of two deeply ingrained behavior dispositions: first, the disposition not to harm other people, and second, the tendency to obey those whom we perceive to be legitimate authorities.

REFERENCES

Adorno, T., Frenkel-Brunswik, Else, Levinson, D. J., and Sanford, R. N. *The authoritarian personality.* New York: Harper, 1950.

Arendt, H. What was authority? In C. J Friedrich (ed.), *Authority.* Cambridge: Harvard Univer. Press, 1958. Pp. 81–112.

Binet, A. *La suggestibilité.* Paris: Schleicher, 1900.

Buss, A. H. *The psychology of aggression.* New York: Wiley, 1961.

Cartwright, S. (ed.) *Studies in social power.* Ann Arbor: University of Michigan Institute for Social Research, 1959.

Charcot, J. M. *Oeuvres complètes.* Paris: Bureaux du Progrès Médical, 1881.

Frank, J. D. Experimental studies of personal pressure and resistance. *J. Gen. Psychol.* 1944, *30*, 23–64.

Freidrich, C. J. (ed.) *Authority.* Cambridge: Harvard Univer. Press, 1958.

Milgram, S. Dynamics of obedience. Washington: National Science Foundation, 25 January 1961. (Mimeo).

Milgram, S. Some conditions of obedience and disobedience to authority. *Hum. Relat.,* 1965, *18,* 57–76.

Rokeach, M. Authority, authoritarianism, and conformity. In I. A. Berg and B. M. Bass (eds.), *Conformity and deviation.* New York: Harper, 1961. Pp. 230–257.

Snow, C. P. Either-or. *Progressive,* 1961 (Feb.) 24.

Weber, M. *The theory of social and economic organization.* Oxford: Oxford Univer. Press, 1947.

ENDNOTES

1. A related technique, making use of a shock generator, was reported by Buss (1961) for the study of aggression in the laboratory. Despite the considerable similarity in technical detail in the experimental procedures, each investigator proceeded in ignorance of the other's work. Milgram provided plans and photographs of his shock generator, experimental procedure, and first results in a report to the National Science Foundation in January 1961. This report received only limited circulation. Buss reported his procedure six months later, but to a wider audience. Subsequently, technical information and reports were exchanged. The present article was first received in the editor's office on December 27, 1961; it was resubmitted with deletions on July 27, 1962.

2. Forty-three subjects, undergraduates at Yale University, were run in the experiment without payment. The results are very similar to those obtained with paid subjects.

3. A series of recently completed experiments employing the obedience paradigm is reported in Milgram (1965).

This research was supported by a grant (NSF G-17916) from the National Science Foundation. Exploratory studies conducted in 1960 were supported by a grant from the Higgins Fund at Yale University. The research assistance of Alan E. Elms and Jon Wayland is gratefully acknowledged.

CRITICAL THINKING QUESTIONS

1. What are the ethical implications of this study? In particular, are you satisfied that no lasting harm was done to the participants? Would the debriefing at the end of the experiment be sufficient to eliminate any long-term problems from participation in the study? What about short-term effects? Many of the subjects obviously suffered during the experiment. Was the infliction of this distress on the subjects justified? Support your answers. (*Note:* For a good discussion of the ethics of the study, see the Baumrind and Milgram articles cited on the next page.)

2. What are the implications of this study for people accused of committing atrocities? Suppose that the results of this study had been known when the Nazi war criminals were put on trial in Nuremberg. Could the information have been used in their defense? Do the results remove some of the personal responsibility that people have for their actions? Explain your answers.

3. Subjects were paid a nominal amount for participation in the study. They were told that the money was theirs to keep simply because they showed up, regardless of what happened after they arrived. Do you think that this payment was partly responsible for the findings? Why or why not? Do you think that paying someone, no matter how small the amount, somehow changes the dynamics of the situation? Explain.

ADDITIONAL RELATED READINGS

Baumrind, D. (1964). Some thoughts on ethics of research after reading Milgram's "Behavioral study of obedience." *American Psychologist, 19,* 421–423.

Blass, T. (Ed.). (2000). *Obedience to authority: Current perspectives on the Milgram paradigm.* Mahwah, NJ: Lawrence Erlbaum Associates.

Milgram, S. (1964). Issues in the study of obedience: A reply to Baumrind. *American Psychologist, 19,* 848–852.

ARTICLE 27

Conformity is a fact of life yet a behavior toward which we have decidedly ambivalent feelings. On the one hand, none of us like to think of ourselves as *conformist*. For most people, this word has a fairly negative connotation, suggesting people who mindlessly go along with the group rather than thinking for themselves. Even people who see themselves as nonconformist (such as in how they dress) often are just conforming to an alternative set of norms. Perhaps the best example of this is the teenager who dyes his hair blue because he wants to be "different in a conforming sort of way."

On the other hand, conformity is the very background of culture. How could we drive our cars, engage in social interactions, or do just about anything involving other people if we did not conform to what was expected of us in those situations? Without some level of conformity, total chaos would result. Even when we feel independent in the decisions we make, in fact, our choice is not *whether* to conform but rather which norms to conform to.

So, why is conformity such a vital part of the human experience? At a very basic level, it helps to promote survival of the group. After all, people are fundamentally social creatures, and without conformity, the daily interactions that make life possible would be impossible. But people conform for other reasons, as well. One such reason may be to obtain information about an otherwise ambiguous situation. For example, if you wanted to know the distance between Washington, DC, and New York City, you could look it up in a book. That information is a *fact*: an agreed upon, accepted piece of knowledge. As such, you need only to consult the proper source to find it.

But how much of social life is about readily determinable facts? Not much. Most of the situations and questions we face are not factual but rather matters of belief, custom, or opinion. Whom should I vote for? What is the right thing to do? What is the best way to live my life? The answers to questions such as these often come from other people. Thus, another reason we conform is because other people often are able to provide us with clues for how to behave, especially when the situation is otherwise ambiguous and we are unsure of what is expected of us.

People also conform to be accepted. If you have ever deviated from the norms or beliefs of a group to which you belong, you already know the intensely uncomfortable experience of being rejected or pressured by others in the group. To be accepted by the group, we must go along with them. Thus, we sometimes conform just to be accepted and to fit into a particular group.

One of the earliest influential studies on conformity was conducted by Soloman Asch in the 1950s. In his famous *line-judgment study*, groups of subjects were presented with a line as a stimulus and asked to select which of three other lines were the same length as the stimulus line. Preceding the judgment of the group, a number of experimental confederates would give incorrect answers. The majority of subjects went along with an obviously incorrect group answer at least once. Overall, subjects expressed agreement with the wrong group responses 37% of the time.

The following article by Louise Pendry and Rachael Carrick uses an Asch-like paradigm to investigate the mechanisms behind conforming behaviors. This study is a good example of how the original findings of classic studies, such as that of Asch, are continually refined to better determine the underlying factors behind such behaviors.

Doing What the Mob Do
Priming Effects on Conformity

■ Louise Pendry and Rachael Carrick

ABSTRACT

This study considered whether participants' tendency to conform to a group norm could be influenced by priming them with categories associated with either conformity or anarchy. Participants were primed with one of two categories: "accountant prime," "punk prime" (plus a baseline "no prime"). They then participated in a variant of the Asch (1951) conformity paradigm. Results indicated that "punk"-primed participants conformed significantly less than did "accountant"-primed participants, with the mean for the "no-prime" condition lying in between the two. "Accountant"-primed participants conformed to the group norm more than did the "no-prime" participants. In addition, the performance of "punk"-primed participants was comparable to that of participants who performed the judgment task in isolation ("solo" condition). This indicates that conformity pressures did not affect estimates for "punk"-primed participants. Implications of these findings are discussed.

> *"It's always best on these occasions to do what the mob do." "But suppose there are two mobs?" suggested Mr Snodgrass. "Shout with the largest," replied Mr Pickwick.*
>
> (Charles Dickens, 1837/1977, p. 239)

When pondering over the socially acceptable thing to do, Mr Pickwick was fervent in his belief that it was safest to "do what the mob do." A century after Dickens' observations on group behavior, Solomon Asch (1951) demonstrated this conformity effect in his now-classical series of studies on perceptions of line length. Naive participants in his studies conformed to the obviously errant group norm in 37% of their responses. In the years that followed, researchers have established a number of reasons why conformity occurs (e.g. Asch, 1956; Bond & Smith, 1996; Crutchfield, 1955; Deutsch & Gerard, 1955; Eagly &

Carli, 1981; Gerard, Wilhelmy, & Connolly, 1989; Insko, Smith, Alicke, Wade, & Taylor, 1985). The present article contributes to this debate by considering whether the tendency to conform can be influenced by priming participants with categories associated with either anarchic or conformist behavior.

WHY WE OFTEN DO WHAT THE MOB DO

Acquiescence with the prevailing group belief or behavior can be determined by a number of factors. Informational social influence, or the desire to know what is right, is one such factor. This need for clarification in social settings can happen for many reasons. We look to others to determine how to behave in situations which are new or alien to us, or in some way ambiguous, in times of crisis, or when we feel another person has more expertise in a situation (Bickman, 1974; Deutsch & Gerard, 1955; Kelley, 1955; Sherif, 1935; Thomas, 1928). Sometimes we resist informational social influence, for example if we believe its source to be illegitimate or biased (Cantril, 1940). On the whole, though, informational social influence seems to play a significant role in conformity effects.

The second major reason why we may conform is because we need to be accepted: that is, normative social influence (Deutsch & Gerard, 1955; Kelley, 1955). Social groups evolve certain expectations about how group members should behave, and as a group member it is often easier to go along with such beliefs to avoid ridicule, punishment or ostracism (Miller & Anderson, 1979). We are social beings and in general, we crave social companionship and acceptance. This need pervades many social settings and can exert a strong effect upon our behavioral

Reprinted from L. Pendre and R. Carrick, *European Journal of Social Psychology*, 2001, *31*(1), 83–92. Copyright © 2001 John Wiley & Sons, Ltd. Reproduced by permission of John Wiley & Sons, Limited.

responses. People are liable to conform to normative social influence for a number of reasons (for a review see Hogg & Vaughan, 1998).

Thus, it seems we are influenced by others either because we depend upon them for information that disambiguates reality and hence establishes subjective validity, or because we seek social approval and acceptance. This distinction has been termed a *dual process dependency model* of social influence, and there are some who would challenge it as the optimum explanation for conformity (Abrams & Hogg, 1990; Hogg & Turner, 1987; Turner, 1991). Such Social Identity Theorists believe that classical explanations of conformity give too little weight to the role of group belongingness. Instead, they advance a separate process, *referent informational influence,* that operates via the process of *self-categorisation.* Stated simply, within a group, individuals categorise themselves and others as members of the same social group. They then strive to find relevant group norms to set the standards for appropriate behavior. This norm works to minimise within group differences and maximise ingroup/outgroup differences. Via self-categorisation, then, similarities between own behavior and that prescribed by the group norm are highlighted. Since group members construct (and internalise) a similar group norm, self-categorisation produces intragroup convergence and uniformity: that is, the typical conformity effect (Hogg & Turner, 1987).

THE PRESENT STUDY

In sum, while explanations for conformity vary, it is a fairly robust experimental phenomenon. The present article considers the conformity issue from a different angle. Recent research in the domain of perception and social behavior has reliably demonstrated that, in certain domains at least, it is possible to influence social behavior via the process of priming (e.g. Bargh, Chen, & Burrows, 1996; Bargh, Gollwitzer, & Barndollar, unpublished manuscript; Dijksterhuis & van Knippenberg, 1998). For example, Bargh *et al.* (1996, Study 2) have shown that priming participants with the stereotype of an older person (using a scrambled sentence completion task, cf. Srull & Wyer, 1979) caused them to leave the experimental corridor at a slower walking pace. Subliminally prim-

ing participants with the African-American stereotype (Study 3) resulted in more aggressive facial expressions and hostile behavior being shown toward an experimenter when equipment malfunctioned.

Priming can be achieved in a number of ways. It can, for example, be brought about via the use of a social category (e.g. instructions to write about the day in the life of a professor: see Dijksterhuis & van Knippenberg, 1998). In this case, priming is thought to activate a certain stereotype (e.g. professor) and this activation renders the contents of the stereotype (e.g. wise) accessible (Blair & Banaji, 1996; Devine, 1989; Dijksterhuis & van Knippenberg, 1996; Dovidio, Evans, & Tyler, 1986; Macrae, Stangor, & Milne, 1994). Priming effects on social behaviour can also be achieved via the use of trait primes as opposed to social categories (e.g. helping: see Macrae & Johnston, 1999).

The observed effect has been termed "automatic social behavior" because participants appear to engage in the prime-induced behavior without any conscious awareness of the link. Bargh *et al.* (1996) hypothesise that automatic social behavior findings such as those outlined above may have important implications for a range of simple and more complex social behaviors. In the present study, accordingly, we revisit the Asch conformity paradigm to investigate whether conformist/non-conformist behaviors can be successfully induced via priming techniques. Recent research by Epley and Gilovich (1999) has also considered this issue. They utilised a scrambled sentence-priming procedure and a conformity paradigm whereby participants had to provide feedback on a study in a group situation. Nonconformity involved their having to give negative, as opposed to positive, feedback. Results suggested that the conformity prime produced stronger effects than did the non-conformity prime.

The present study complements this research in several ways. First, by utilising a different priming procedure and conformity paradigm we can consider the extent to which the obtained effects generalise. Second, we include certain *post-hoc* tests that attempt to shed additional light upon the reasons for the obtained findings. Our pre-testing revealed that a category strongly associated with non-conformity was that of punks; whereas for conformity, a popular group was that of accountants. We expected that priming participants with the punk category would lead to less conforming behavior, in line with the activated behavior associated with punks (i.e. anarchy). On the other hand, we expected that participants primed with the accountant category would conform more.

METHOD

Participants and Design

Forty-eight male and female undergraduates aged between eighteen and twenty-one years participated in the main study on a voluntary basis. The study had a single factor (experimental condition: accountant prime or punk prime or no prime or solo) between-participants design. None of the participants had any background in psychology.

Stimulus Materials and Procedure

To obtain the prime materials, 12 participants were asked to list as many groups as they could that they considered to be either conformist or non-conformist. From this, 12 groups were generated and given to a further 10 participants who rated the extent to which the groups were considered conformist or non-conformist (on 7-point scales anchored 1 *not at all conformist* to 7 *very conformist*). On the basis of this pilot study, punks and accountants were selected as the non-conformist and conformist primes to be used in the study proper (respective *M*s: 2.3 versus 5.4).

We used a variant of the Asch paradigm to test our predictions. More recent research (e.g. Bond & Smith, 1996; Lalancette & Standing, 1990; Larsen, 1990; Nicholson, Cole, & Rocklin, 1985; Perrin & Spencer, 1981) has suggested that conformity in Asch-type studies may be decreasing. We therefore decided to use a more ambiguous aural discrimination task in which participants had to count a large number of randomly made sounds and subsequently report their estimates in a group setting (Wolosin, Sherman, & Cann, 1975). For the aural discrimination stimuli, a tape comprising 100 random sounds was recorded using an electric guitar passed through an amplifier in order to make beep-like sounds. The same note was played each time and the exact posi-

tioning was pre-conscribed by writing it down in tablature beforehand. Pre-testing established that estimating the exact number of sounds was difficult enough that individuals could not be entirely sure of their estimate, but not so hard that they could not estimate within six or seven sounds of the actual number.

Participants signed up for an experiment in aural discrimination. Upon arrival at the laboratory, they were greeted by the experimenter. Participants in either of the prime conditions were asked if they would mind participating in an extra task prior to the aural discrimination task. The rationale for this was that another experimenter was about to run a study and wanted some of the stimulus materials checking for clarity and focus. Depending upon experimental condition, participants were then given a photograph of either an accountant or a punk and instructed to study it carefully for a few moments. The accountant photo depicted a man with neat appearance, wearing a suit, with short hair, and glasses. The punk photo showed a young man with spiky hair, and torn clothing covered in graffiti. Whilst the target in the punk photo was unambiguously a punk rocker, the target in the accountant photo could have been an accountant, but could equally have been a member of any of a number of white-collar occupational groups. To ensure the target group category was activated in each condition, brief biographical information about the target was embedded within each photograph: either "Norman, who is an accountant" or "Norman, who is a punk rocker." This text was legible, but slightly distorted due to the colour of the background picture. Participants were asked whether they could clearly make out both the target and the written information and if possible to read out the words (all participants were able to do so). The experimenter noted their responses, thanked them for their help, and then told them that they would now participate in the study proper.

Participants in the prime conditions were then told that they were the last participant for that particular session, and that the four people waiting in the room had already looked at the photo. The "no prime" participants were told just that they were the last participants for the session, and that the others were already waiting in the room. In fact the four people (two male and two female) were experimental confederates. The participant was directed to sit in the seat furthest from the experimenter. At this point the tape was switched on, and the beeps played to the group, who were instructed to try to keep a mental tally of the number of beeps they heard, as they would be asked to reproduce their estimate later. Afterwards, the experimenter first asked each of the confederates to say aloud their estimate of how many sounds they had heard. All confederates were trained to give predetermined responses ranging from 120 to 125. The experimenter repeated each estimate, and recorded it on a sheet. The participant was then asked to give his or her estimate, which was also recorded. A further 12 participants also completed the aural discrimination task on their own (i.e. the "solo" condition). This condition provided the baseline condition against which the degree of group conformity could be measured. All participants were fully debriefed upon completion of the aural discrimination task. None of them detected a link between the two studies and indeed none had even heard of the conformity paradigm.

RESULTS AND DISCUSSION

Aural Estimates

The confederates' mean estimate was 123 beeps, but the actual number on the tape recording was 100 beeps. Thus, a mean estimate closer to the actual number could be taken as evidence of non-conformity with the group mean; whereas a mean estimate closer to the confederates' estimate might be indicative of conformity with the group mean. The primary dependent variable was participants' estimate of the number of beeps they had heard. These estimates were submitted to a single factor (experimental condition: accountant or punk or none or solo) between-participants analysis of variance. This revealed a significant effect of experimental condition, $F(3, 44) = 9.97$, $p < 0.0001$ (see Table 1).

Post hoc *t*-tests revealed that estimates given by participants in the "punk" and "accountant" prime conditions differed significantly ($t(22) = 5.23$, $p < 0.0005$), with "punk"-primed participants conforming less than did "accountant"-primed participants.

TABLE 1 / Mean Aural Estimates as a Function of Experimental Condition

	Accountant	Punk	No Prime	Solo
Estimates	113.67	103.83	109.75	103.58

Moreover, the "accountant"-primed participants conformed to the group norm more than did the "no-prime" participants ($t(22) = 1.82$, $p < 0.05$). Estimates for the "punk" prime and "solo" conditions did not differ from each other.

These results provide support for the experimental predictions. Participants primed with "punk" conformed significantly less with the group norm than did participants in the "accountant" or "no-prime" conditions. Moreover, "punk"-primed participants' mean estimates did not differ significantly from those in the "solo" group. This suggests that the "punk" prime was strong enough to lead participants to give responses uncontaminated by prevailing group pressures. Furthermore, in comparison with the "no-prime" condition, "accountant"-primed participants demonstrated increased conformity with the group norm. Thus the data provide fairly good support for our hypotheses, in terms of priming effects upon conformity.[1]

However, one criticism that has been raised about priming effects of this kind is that the data could be indicative of semantic priming as opposed to category priming *per se* (e.g. Greenwald & Banaji, 1995; Hamilton & Sherman, 1994; Lepore & Brown, 1997). In the present study, then, our effects might not be due to the activation of anarchy versus conformity-related constructs. Rather, the negative semantic associations of the punk prime could have cued anti-social behavior. To evaluate this alternative explanation, an additional *post-hoc* test was conducted. Ten independent participants drawn from the same participant population were asked to rate a series of different social groups (including punks and accountants) for how positive or negative they felt each was (on 7-point scales anchored 1 *very negative* to 7 *very positive*). Results indicated that the means for both target groups fell close to the mid-point of the scale and did not differ significantly from each other ($t < 1$, *ns*). Among this population (young students), then, it appears that accountants and punks are viewed as equivalent in terms of valence, and neither strongly negative nor positive. This result suggests that a valence interpretation of the present data is not applicable.

It is noteworthy that the "punk" prime produced slightly stronger effects than did the "accountant" prime. Priming effects are usually strongest when the link between category and behavior are unambiguous (Bargh *et al.,* 1996; Carver & Scheier, 1981; Prinz, 1990). One possibility, then, is that the weaker effects of the "accountant" prime are indicative of a weaker strength of association between the category "accountant" and the behavior "conformity." The attribute "non-conformist," on the other hand, may assume more weight in the punk stereotype in comparison to other characteristics and hence the link between category and behavior could be stronger. This finding would tie in with related research by Dijksterhuis and van Knippenberg (1998). They found that priming the "professor" category made people perform better on a general knowledge task while priming "soccer hooligan" made people perform worse. However, the effects of the professor prime were stronger than those of the soccer hooligan. They reasoned that intelligence is probably more central to (or more strongly associated with) the "professor" stereotype than stupidity is to the "soccer hooligan" stereotype. If the association of a trait with a stereotype is weak, then, evidence suggests that the effects of priming will be similarly weak compared to a stereotype with a stronger association.

To investigate this possibility, an additional pilot study was conducted. Ten independent participants were given a subsample taken from the list of groups used in the earlier pilot study and asked to list all the attributes they felt were associated with each group. Within this list were the two target groups. Attributes provided for each group were then scored for the number of times each was mentioned by various participants. The attributes mentioned most often for accountants were those related to their inherent dullness and materialistic tendencies. Whilst conformity was arguably implicit in some of the lists (in the attributes "straight" and "normal," for example) it was not provided explicitly by any of the participants. For punks, however, non-conformist behavior (e.g. "anar-

chic," "rebellious" or "anti-establishment") was mentioned on six occasions. It seems plausible to suggest, then, that non-conformity may be a stronger behavioral component in the punk stereotype than is conformity in the accountant stereotype.

Additionally, it should be noted that we used photographs to prime participants with the selected target groups. Whilst the physical appearance of the punk needed no clarification, the image of the target person used to convey an accountant was arguably more ambiguous. The biographical information provided may have helped ensure the category was activated in both conditions, as we had anticipated, but it might in addition have amplified the degree of activation for "punk"-primed participants.

Recent research by Epley and Gilovich (1999), utilising a different priming procedure and conformity paradigm from our own, found a different asymmetry in the effects of conformity and non-conformity primes. Specifically, effects were stronger for participants primed with conformity than for those primed for non-conformity. Epley and Gilovich (1999) offer several explanations for their findings. First, they suggest, it could be because it is easier to conform than to rebel. Second, because their confederates modeled conformity and not dissent, participants in the conformity conditions may have been doubly primed (by both the priming phase and the confederates' behavior). Third, priming non-conformity may simultaneously prime conformity and thus weaken effects. How can we reconcile these seemingly disparate effects?

We suspect that the answer lies in the marked methodological differences between the present research and that of Epley and Gilovich (1999). The skinhead prime, as noted, probably evoked strong links with non-conformity. Our data and *post-hoc* tests all point to the fact that our priming manipulation was stronger for the skinhead than for the accountant prime. Although we cannot be certain, it seems plausible that the skinhead photograph acted as a more powerful non-conformity prime than would a comparable semantic prime. Also, in the Epley and Gilovich (1999) study, the conformity paradigm differed from our own in several key respects. First, the confederates modeled conformity and not dissent whereas in our study, the confederates modeled dissent. One could argue, then, that our paradigm invited dissent rather than conformity, and that participants in the "punk"-primed conditions may have been doubly primed, leading to automatic mimicry (see Chartrand & Bargh, 1999). This might have exacerbated the effect of the punk prime and diminished the effect of the accountant prime. Second, non-conformity in the Epley and Gilovich (1999) study involved participants telling the experimenter that the tasks were dull, which they may have felt uncomfortable about doing. In our study, non-conformity was demonstrated by participants providing more accurate estimates of the number of beeps, which was probably a less anxiety-provoking task. In sum, we feel our findings, alongside those of Epley and Gilovich (1999) generate a number of interesting avenues that may merit future research.

Explanations for the Obtained Effects

Recent explanations of priming effects on automatic social behavior propose that the activation of a particular mental representation triggers the activation of corresponding behavioral mechanisms (e.g. Bargh, 1994). This type of explanation has been advanced for priming effects on behaviors such as hostility, walking speed, or performance on an intelligence task (Bargh *et al.*, 1996; Dijksterhuis & van Knippenberg, 1997). In these situations, participants are typically alone or with one other person. In the present study, however, participants' behavior takes place in the presence of several others. This may be an important difference. In ambiguous situations such as the one in which our participants found themselves, it is considered usual to search for the correct way to behave by locating and imitating a suitable reference point, if one is available (Deutsch & Gerard, 1955; Kelley, 1955). Participants could certainly look to others in the group to guide their own behavior (as per traditional conformity explanations). Alternatively, they might be guided by their prior priming experience. People often rely on stereotypes that have been activated recently (Higgins, Rholes, & Jones, 1977; Srull & Wyer, 1979, 1986; Wyer & Srull, 1980, 1981). Having engaged in the first stage of the study, participants enter the conformity setting with a readily accessible prime to guide their behavior. We suggest, then, that explanations for

priming effects upon social behavior may differ depending upon the context (i.e. alone or in a group) in which the behavior takes place. Future research might consider this point.

Bargh (1997) has recently proposed a model whereby several systems are responsible for turning environmental information into action, including a motivational system and a perceptual system. If we consider first the motivational system, there are two kinds of motivational explanations (see Dijksterhuis & van Knippenberg, 1998). The first would explain the present findings by assuming less motivation among "punk"-primed participants in a more general sense. We have no reason to believe this to be the case. The second explanation is that low motivation is part of the "punk" stereotype, and this is activated by the "punk" prime. Although this latter explanation is motivational, it is clearly also perceptual. Dijksterhuis and van Knippenberg (1998) have suggested that this explanation might be applicable in their intelligence-related paradigm if one believes that low motivation is part of the "soccer hooligan" stereotype. If we return to the pilot test mentioned above, the same argument seems less plausible as an explanation for the performance of the "punk"-primed participants. No participants mentioned concepts associated with low motivation when asked to list attributes associated with the punk stereotype. We therefore have no reason to believe that this second motivational explanation is applicable to the present data set.

Perceptual explanations of priming may be tied to the relationship between magnitude of priming and magnitude of effect (Bargh *et al.*, 1996; Carver & Scheier, 1981; Dijksterhuis & van Knippenberg, 1998; Prinz, 1990). Dijksterhuis and van Knippenberg's (1998, Studies 2 and 3) earlier findings that prolonged priming (9 minutes as opposed to 2) led to stronger behavioral effects provide some support for this viewpoint. Our own data do not really speak directly to this issue. Recall, however, that the priming phase in our study was quite short (one minute), and yet the observed effects were fairly strong. It is possible, then, that the perceptual explanation may therefore be less suited to the present data than is the motivational account.[2]

Finally, the priming manipulations employed in this study might have interfered with traditional conformity processes. For example, acquiescence with the prevailing group norm because of a desire to be right (i.e. informational social influence) may have been exacerbated for "accountant"-primed participants (Deutsch & Gerard, 1955). Equally, the "punk" prime might have caused participants to feel less bound by normative desires to be accepted (via conforming behavior; Kelley, 1955). It could also be that self-categorisation processes (e.g. Abrams & Hogg, 1990) could be impeded by the priming experience. Priming participants with "punk" may have interfered with the establishment and internalisation of the appropriate group norm (i.e. conformity) and facilitated behavior at odds with this norm (i.e. nonconformity). Conversely, the "accountant" prime may have facilitated the group norm establishment process.

CONCLUSIONS

Whilst at present the mechanisms for the observed effects are not entirely clear, it seems that the usual processes considered to underlie traditional conformity effects may be somewhat malleable. They may be processes that can be facilitated or diminished by prior circumstances encouraging deviation from or adherence to a desire to conform. The present study therefore contributes to our understanding of conformity processes by considering the role of certain pre-conditions (e.g. category priming) that may influence conformity effects, and highlights a number of important avenues for future research in this domain.

ACKNOWLEDGEMENTS

This research was facilitated by a University Research Fund awarded to the first author.

REFERENCES

Abrams D, Hogg MA. 1990. Social identification, self-categorization, and social influence. *European Review of Social Psychology* 1: 195–228.

Asch SE. 1951. Effects of group pressure on the modification and distortion of judgment. In *Groups, Leadership, and Men,* Guetzow H. (ed.). Carnegie Press: Pittsburgh, PA.

Asch SE. 1956. Studies of independence and conformity: 1. A minority of one against a unanimous majority. *Psychological Monographs* 70: (9).

Bargh JA. 1994. The four horsemen of automaticity: Awareness, intention, efficiency and control in social cognition. In *The Handbook of Social Cognition* (Vol. 2), Wyer, RS Jr, Srull TK (eds). Erlbaum: Hillsdale, NJ; 1–40.

Bargh JA. 1997. The automaticity of everyday life. In *Advances in Social Cognition* (Vol. 10), Wyer, RS Jr (ed.), Erlbaum: Mahwah, NJ; 1–61.

Bargh JA, Chen M, Burrows L. 1996. Automaticity of social behavior: Direct effects of trait construct and stereotype activation on action. *Journal of Personality and Social Psychology* 71: 230–244.

Bickman L. 1974. The social power of a uniform. *Journal of Applied Social Psychology* 4: 47–61.

Blair I, Banaji M. 1996. Automatic and controlled processes in stereotype priming. *Journal of Personality and Social Psychology* 70: 1142–1163.

Bond MH, Smith PB. 1996. Culture and conformity: A meta-analysis of the Asch line judgment task. *Psychological Bulletin* 119: 111–137.

Cantril H. 1940. America faces the war: A study in public opinion. *Public Opinion Quarterly* 4: 387–407.

Carver CS, Scheier MF. 1981. *Attention and Self-regulation: A control-theory approach to human behavior.* Springer-Verlag: New York.

Chartrand TL, Bargh JA. 1999. The chameleon effect: The perception-behavior link and social interaction. *Journal of Personality and Social Psychology* 76: 893–910.

Crutchfield RS. 1955. Conformity and character. *American Psychologist* 10: 191–198.

Deutsch M, Gerard HB. 1955. A study of normative and informational social influences upon individual judgment. *Journal of Abnormal and Social Psychology* 51: 629–636.

Devine PG. 1989. Stereotypes and prejudice: Their automatic and controlled components. *Journal of Personality and Social Psychology* 56: 680–690.

Dickens C. 1977. *The Pickwick Papers,* Penguin: Harmondsworth.

Dijksterhuis A, van Knippenberg A. 1996. The knife that cuts both ways: Facilitated and inhibited access to traits as a result of stereotype activation. *Journal of Experimental Social Psychology* 32: 271–288.

Dijksterhuis A, van Knippenberg A. 1998. The relation between perception and behavior, or how to win a game of Trivial Pursuit. *Journal of Personality and Social Psychology* 74: 865–877.

Dovidio JF, Evans N, Tyler RB. 1986. Racial stereotypes:

The contents of their cognitive representations. *Journal of Experimental Social Psychology* **56**: 5–18.

Eagly AH, Carli LL. 1981. Sex of researchers and sex-typed communications as determinants of sex differences in influenceability: A meta-analysis of social influence studies. *Psychological Bulletin* **90**: 1–20.

Epley N, Gilovich T. 1999. Just going along: Non-conscious priming and conformity to social pressure. *Journal of Experimental Social Psychology* **35**: 578–589.

Gerard HB, Wilhelmy RA, Connolly ES. 1968. Conformity and group size. *Journal of Personality and Social Psychology* **8**: 79–82.

Greenwald AG, Banaji MR. 1995. Implicit Social Cognition: Attitudes, self-esteem and stereotypes. *Psychological Review* **102**: 4–27.

Hamilton DL, Sherman JW. 1994. Stereotypes. In *Handbook of Social Cognition* (Vol. 2), Wyer RS Jr, Srull TK (eds). Erlbaum: Hillsdale, NJ; 1–68.

Higgins ET, Rholes WS, Jones CR. 1977. Category accessibility and impression formation. *Journal of Experimental Social Psychology* **13**: 141–154.

Hogg MA, Turner JC. 1987. Social identity and conformity: A theory of referent informational influence. In *Current Issues in European Social Psychology* (Vol. 2), Doise W, Moscovici S (eds), Cambridge University Press: Cambridge; 139–182.

Hogg MA, Vaughan GM. 1998. *Social Psychology*. Prentice Hall: London.

Insko CA, Smith RH, Alicke MD, Wade J, Taylor S. 1985. Conformity and group size: The concern with being right and the concern with being liked. *Personality and Social Psychology Bulletin* **11**: 41–50.

Kelley HH. 1955. The two functions of reference groups. In *Readings in Social Psychology* (2nd edn), Swanson GE, Newcomb TM, Hartley EL (eds). Holt: New York; 410–414.

Lalancette M-F, Standing LG. 1990. Asch fails again. *Social Behavior and Personality* **18**: 7–12.

Larsen KS. 1990. The Asch conformity experiment: Replication and transhistorical comparisons. *Journal of Social Behavior and Personality* **5**: 163–168.

Lepore L, Brown R. 1997. Category and stereotype activation: Is prejudice inevitable? *Journal of Personality and Social Psychology* **72**: 275–287.

Macrae CN, Johnston LJ. 1999. Help, I need somebody: Automatic action and inaction. *Social Cognition* **16**: 400–417.

Macrae CN, Stangor C, Milne AB. 1994. Activating social stereotypes: A functional analysis. *Journal of Experimental Social Psychology* **30**: 370–389.

Miller CE, Anderson PD. 1979. Group decision rules and the rejection of deviates. *Social Psychology Quarterly* **42**: 354–363.

Nicholson N, Cole SG, Rocklin T. 1985. Conformity in the Asch situation: A comparison between contemporary British and U.S. university students. *British Journal of Social Psychology* **24**: 59–63.

Perrin S, Spencer C. 1981. Independence or conformity in the Asch paradigm as a reflection of cultural or situational factors. *British Journal of Social Psychology* **20**: 205–209.

Prinz W. 1990. A common coding approach to perception and action. In *Relationships between Perception and Action*, Neumann O, Prinz W. (eds). Springer-Verlag: Berlin; 167–201.

Sherif M. 1935. A study of some social factors in perception. *Archives of Psychology* **27**: 1–60.

Srull TK, Wyer RS Jr. 1979. The role of category accessibility in the interpretation of information about persons. *Journal of Personality and Social Psychology* **37**: 1660–1672.

Srull TK, Wyer RS Jr. 1986. The role of chronic and temporary goals in social information processing. in *Handbook of Motivation and Cognition: Foundations of social behavior*, Sorrentino RM, Higgins ET (eds). Guilford Press: New York; 503–549.

Thomas W. 1928. *The Child in America*, Alfred A. Knop: New York.

Turner JC. 1991. *Social Influence*. Brooks Cole: Pacific Grove, CA.

Wolosin RJ, Sherman SJ, Cann A. 1975. Predictions of own and others' conformity. *Journal of Personality* **43**: 357–378.

Wyer RS Jr, Srull TK. 1980. The processing of social stimulus information: A conceptual integration. In *Person Memory: The cognitive basis of social perception*, Hastie R, Ostrom TM, Ebbesen EB, Wyer RS, Hamilton D, Carlston DE (eds). Erlbaum: Hillsdale, NJ; 227–300.

Wyer RS Jr, Srull TK. 1981. Category accessibility: Some theoretical and empirical issues concerning the processing of social stimulus information. In *Social Cognition: The Ontario Symposium* (Vol. 1). Higgins ET, Herman CP, Zanna MP (eds). Erlbaum: Hillsdale, NJ; 161–198.

ENDNOTES

1. As pointed out by one of our reviewers, we need to exercise caution when discussing our findings in the context of automatic

social behavior. Whilst it is true that participants did not perceive a link between the priming phase and the conformity phase of the study, we still have no direct evidence that the obtained conformity effects occurred in the absence of awareness. Throughout the article, therefore, we use the term "priming effects upon conformity" rather than saying our findings are evidence of automatic social behavior.

2. However, more recently, Dijksterhuis (personal communication) reports that the success of even short-lasting subliminal priming manipulations makes this interpretation less valid. Given this recent observation, it would appear that the short duration of our own priming phase does not really speak to the perceptual versus motivational issue. We thank Ap Dijksterhuis for pointing this out to us.

CRITICAL THINKING QUESTIONS

1. The article notes that conformity in Asch-type experiments has decreased over time. Why do you think this is the case? Could this trend be age specific (i.e., that younger people are less conforming than older people), or does it indicate a general change in attitudes toward conformity? Defend your position.

2. This study dealt with priming as a precondition influencing conformity. What other possible preconditions may influence conforming behavior? Design a study to test one of these possible preconditions.

3. This study involved conformity to rather trivial judgments: the number of sounds that were heard. Would the same effect be obtained if the judgments had more significant consequences, such as deciding whether a certain medical procedure should be used or determining the guilt or innocence of someone on trial? Why or why not?

4. Do you think the incidence of conformity varies from one culture to the next? Find research studies that have examined this question, and report their findings.

Chapter Ten

PROSOCIAL BEHAVIOR

H ELP. IT IS something that we all need at some time in our lives, and hopefully, it is something that we all give to others. Dramatic examples of helping or failing to help are not hard to find in the mass media. Consider the various published accounts of people needing help yet receiving none versus those of people who risk their own lives to help strangers.

Why do people help or not help? Is helpfulness a personality trait, so that some people are simply helpful individuals who give assistance in a variety of settings? Or does it have more to do with the specific situation, so that a person who helps in one situation is not necessarily more likely to help in another? Or perhaps these two factors somehow interact with one another, so that people with a certain type of personality in a certain type of situation are more likely to help than others.

Article 28, "Why Don't Moral People Act Morally? Motivational Considerations," examines the question of moral motivation in explaining why people act the way they do. The article not only attributes the failure to act morally to not having been properly socialized or to the situational forces operating at the moment; it also explores the underlying motivations people may have for acting morally in the first place.

Article 29, "From Jerusalem to Jericho," is a classic example of a study that examines both situational and personality factors as influences on helping behavior. It turns out that both factors may be operating, with situational factors determining whether people will offer help in the first place and dispositional factors determining the character of the helping response.

Article 30, "Bystander Attitudes toward Victims of Violence: Who's Worth Helping?" further examines some of the factors that may influence people's decisions to intervene or not intervene when witnessing violence directed toward a child, a woman, or a dog. These factors include who or what needs help and the characteristics of the witnesses to such violence.

ARTICLE 28 _____

If asked whether they consider themselves moral and decent individuals, most people would likely say yes. With the exception of those individuals who blatantly consider only their own self-interests, most people seem to want to do the right thing. Even those individuals who are blatantly selfish often justify their behavior in moral terms. Thus, the person who kills does so for a higher cause, and the person who steals has needs that are more important than those of the victim.

Reflect for a moment on your own life. Do you always act consistently with your moral principles, or have you done things that you knew were not the right things to do? If you are like most people, you do not always act with total moral integrity. The fact is, most of us violate our own moral codes. But why?

Two general theoretical explanations may help account for this tendency. First, perhaps we did not know or were not sure of what was the right thing to do at the moment. This is a *developmental* perspective, one that explains moral failings as the result of not having learned the correct moral principles—or at least not having learned them well enough to make them salient at the proper time. The other explanation is a *situational* perspective, whereby moral lapses are attributed to external influences that constrain our otherwise tendency to act morally. Thus, external pressures—such as being in a hurry or wanting to fit in with a certain group—may result in people not acting in accord with their moral principles.

The following article by C. Daniel Batson and Elizabeth R. Thompson addresses the very important question of why moral people do not always act morally. The authors begin with the developmental and situational perspectives just described and then expand on other explanations of this fairly common moral dilemma.

Why Don't Moral People Act Morally?
Motivational Considerations

■ C. Daniel Batson and Elizabeth R. Thompson

Abstract

Failure of moral people to act morally is usually attributed to either learning deficits or situational pressures. We believe that it is also important to consider the nature of moral motivation. Is the goal actually to be moral (moral integrity) or only to appear moral while, if possible, avoiding the cost of being moral (moral hypocrisy)? Do people initially intend to be moral, only to surrender this goal when the costs of being moral become clear (overpowered integrity)? We have found evidence of both moral hypocrisy and overpowered integrity. Each can lead ostensibly moral people to act immorally. These findings raise important questions for future research on the role of moral principles as guides to behavior.

Moral people often fail to act morally. One of the most important lessons to be learned from the tragically common atrocities of the past century—the endless procession of religious wars, mass killings, ethnic cleansings, terrorist bombings, and corporate coverups of product dangers—is that horrendous deeds are not done only by monsters. People who sincerely value morality can act in ways that seem to

Reprinted from *Current Directions in Psychological Science*, 2001, *10*(2), 54–57. Copyright © 2001 by American Psychological Society. Reprinted with permission of Blackwell Publishers.

show a blatant disregard for the moral principles held dear. How is this possible?

Answers by psychologists tend to be of two types. Those who approach the problem from a developmental perspective are likely to blame a learning deficit: The moral principles must not have been learned well enough or in the right way. Those who approach the problem from a social-influence perspective are likely to blame situational pressures: Orders from a higher authority (Milgram, 1974) and pressure to conform (Asch, 1956) can lead one to set aside or disengage moral standards (Bandura, 1999).

There is truth in each of these explanations of moral failure. Yet neither, nor the two combined, is the whole truth. Even people who have well-internalized moral principles, and who are in relatively low-pressure situations, can fail to act morally. To understand how, one needs to consider the nature of moral motivation.

MORAL HYPOCRISY

It is often assumed that moral individuals want to be moral, to display *moral integrity*. But our research suggests that at least some individuals want to appear moral while, if possible, avoiding the cost of actually being moral. We call this motive *moral hypocrisy*.

To examine the nature of moral motivation, we have used a simple—but real—moral dilemma. The dilemma involves having research participants assign themselves and another participant (actually fictitious) to different tasks. One task is clearly more desirable; it has positive consequences (the chance to earn raffle tickets). The other task has neutral consequences (no chance to earn raffle tickets) and is described as rather dull and boring. Participants are told that the other participant will not know that they were allowed to assign the tasks; the other participant will think the assignment was made by chance.

Most research participants faced with this simple situation assign themselves the positive-consequences task (70% to 80%, depending on the specific study), even though in retrospect very few (less than 10%) say that this was the moral thing to do. Their actions fail to fit their moral principles (Batson, Kobrynowicz, Dinnerstein, Kampf, & Wilson, 1997).

Adding a Salient Moral Standard . . . and a Coin

Other participants have been confronted with a slightly more complex situation. The written instructions that inform them of the opportunity to assign the tasks include a sentence designed to make the moral standard of fairness salient: "Most participants feel that giving both people an equal chance—by, for example, flipping a coin—is the fairest way to assign themselves and the other participant to the tasks." A coin is provided for participants to flip if they wish. Under these conditions, virtually all participants say in retrospect that either assigning the other participant the positive-consequences task or using a fair method such as the coin flip is the most moral thing to do. Yet only about half choose to flip the coin.

Of those who choose not to flip, most (80% to 90%, depending on the specific study) assign themselves to the positive-consequences task. More interesting and revealing, the same is true of those who flip the coin; most (85% to 90%) assign themselves the positive consequences. In study after study, the proportion who assign themselves the positive-consequences task after flipping the coin has been significantly greater than the 50% that would be expected by chance. This was true even in a study in which the coin was labeled "SELF to POS" on one side and "OTHER to POS" on the other side. Clearly, some participants who flip the coin do not abide by the outcome. To appear fair by flipping the coin, yet still serve self-interest by ignoring the coin and assigning oneself the positive-consequences task, seems to be evidence of moral hypocrisy. Ironically, this hypocrisy pattern was especially strong among persons scoring high on a self-report measure of moral responsibility (Batson et al., 1997; Batson, Thompson, Seuferling, Whitney, & Strongman, 1999).

. . . And a Mirror

Other participants face an even more complex situation. After being provided the fairness standard and coin to flip, they assign the tasks while sitting in front of a mirror. The mirror is used to increase self-awareness and, thereby, pressure to reduce discrepancy between the moral standard of fairness and the task assignment (Wicklund 1975). In a study that presented participants with this situation, exactly half of those who chose to flip the coin assigned themselves to the positive-consequences task. Apparently, having to face head-on the discrepancy between their avowed moral standard (be fair) and their standard-violating behavior (unfairly ignoring the result of the coin flip) was too much. In front of the mirror, those who wish to appear moral must be moral (Batson et al., 1999).

Taken together, the results of these studies seem to provide considerable evidence of moral hypocrisy. They conform precisely to the pattern we would expect if the goal of at least some research participants is to appear moral yet, if possible, avoid the cost of being moral. To the extent that moral hypocrisy is their motive, it is hardly surprising that ostensibly moral people fail to act morally. Any situational ambiguity that allows them to feign morality yet still serve self-interest—such as we provide by allowing participants to flip the coin—will undermine moral action if their motive is moral hypocrisy.

OVERPOWERED INTEGRITY

Before concluding that the world is full of moral hypocrites, it is important to consider a quite different motivational explanation for the failure of participants in our studies to act morally. Perhaps at least some of those who flip the coin do so with a genuine intent to assign the tasks fairly. Their initial motive is to be moral (moral integrity). But when they discover that the flip has gone against them and their intent to be moral will cost them the positive-consequences task, conflict arises. Self-interest overpowers integrity, with the result that they appear moral by flipping the coin, yet still serve self-interest. The general idea of overpowered integrity is, then, that a person's motivation to be truly moral may be overpowered by stronger self-interested motives when being moral entails personal cost (as it often does). In the words of the oft-quoted biblical phrase, "The spirit is willing, but the flesh is weak" (Matthew 26: 41).

Empirically Differentiating Moral Hypocrisy and Overpowered Integrity

How might one know which motivational process is operating, moral hypocrisy or overpowered integrity?

The key difference between the two is the actor's intent when initially faced with a moral dilemma. In the former process, the initial motive is to appear moral yet avoid the cost of being moral; in the latter, the initial motive is to be moral. One factor that should clarify which of these motives is operating when people initially face a moral dilemma is whether they want to maintain control over the outcome of an apparently moral way to resolve the dilemma.

In our task-assignment paradigm, research participants motivated by moral hypocrisy, who intend to give themselves the positive consequences yet also appear moral, should be reluctant to let someone else flip the coin. If a coin is to be flipped, it is important that they be the ones to do so because only then can they rig the outcome. In contrast, participants initially motivated to be moral, who genuinely want to assign the tasks fairly, should have no need to maintain control of the flip. It should make no difference who flips the coin; any fair-minded person will do.

Following this logic, we gave participants an additional decision option: They could allow the task assignment to be determined by the experimenter flipping a coin. Of participants who were faced with this situation (no mirror present) and used a coin flip, 80% chose to have the assignment determined by the experimenter's flip rather than their own. This pattern suggested that many participants' initial motive was moral integrity, not moral hypocrisy (Batson, Tsang, & Thompson, 2000).

Two further studies provided evidence that this integrity could be overpowered. In these studies, we increased the cost of being moral. Instead of being neutral, consequences of the less desirable task were negative. Participants were told that every incorrect response on the negative-consequences task would be punished with a mild but uncomfortable electric shock. Faced with the prospect of receiving shocks, only one fourth of the participants were willing to let the experimenter's flip determine the task assignment. Another fourth flipped the coin themselves; of these, 91% assigned themselves the positive consequences task, indicating once again a biased coin flip. Almost all of the remaining one half showed clear signs of overpowered integrity. They gave up any pretense of morality and assigned themselves the positive-consequences task without even feigning fairness. They were also quite ready, in retrospect, to admit that the way they assigned the tasks was not morally right.

Cost-Based Justification for Setting Morality Aside

How did these last participants deal with the clear discrepancy between their moral standards and their action? Comments made during debriefing suggest that many considered the relatively high personal cost introduced by the prospect of receiving electric shocks to be sufficient justification for not acting on their principles.

A cost-based justification for setting aside moral principles may seem quite understandable. After all, it is no surprise that participants do not want to receive electric shocks. But a cost-based justification carries ironic and chilling implications. Just think: If personal cost is sufficient to justify setting aside moral principles, then one can set aside morality when deciding whether to stand by or intervene as the perpetrators of hate crimes pursue their victims. One can set aside morality when considering one's own position of wealth while others are in poverty. One can set aside morality when considering whether to recycle newspaper or plastic containers or whether to contribute one's fair share to public television. Yet is it not in precisely such situations that moral principles are supposed to do their most important work as guides to behavior?

If, as is often assumed, the social role of morality is to keep individuals from placing their own interests ahead of the parallel interests of others, then cost-based justification poses a serious problem. A principle that says, "Do not give your own interests priority . . . unless there is personal cost," is tantamount to having no real principle at all. It turns morality into a luxury item—something one might love to have but, given the cost, is content to do without.

CONCLUSION

We have considered the interplay of three different motives: First is self-interest. If the self has no clear stake in a situation, then moral principles are not needed to restrain partiality. Second is moral integ-

rity, motivation to be moral as an end in itself. Third is moral hypocrisy, motivation to appear moral while, if possible, avoiding the cost of actually being moral. We have suggested two motivational explanations for the failure of ostensibly moral people to act morally: moral hypocrisy and overpowered integrity. The latter is the product of a conflict between self-interest and moral integrity: A person sincerely intends to act morally, but once the costs of being moral become clear, this initial intent is overpowered by self-interest. Our research indicates that both moral hypocrisy and overpowered integrity exist, and that each can lead moral people to act immorally. Moreover, our research indicates that the problem is not simply one of inconsistency between attitude and behavior—between saying and doing—produced by failure to think about relevant behavioral standards. Making relevant moral standards salient (e.g., by suggesting that a coin toss would be the fairest way to assign tasks) did little to increase moral behavior. The moral lapses we have observed are, we believe, best understood motivationally.

We have only begun to understand the nature of moral motivation. There are persistent and perplexing questions still to be answered. For example, what socialization experiences stimulate moral integrity and hypocrisy, respectively? To what degree do parents preach the former but teach the latter? How might one structure social environments so that even those individuals motivated by moral hypocrisy or vulnerable to overpowered integrity might be led to act morally? Answers to such intriguing—and challenging—questions may help society avoid the atrocities of the past century in the next.

RECOMMENDED READING

Bandura, A. (1999). (See References)

Batson, C.D., Kobrynowicz, D., Dinnerstein, J.L., Kampf, H.C., & Wilson, A.D. (1997). (See References)

Batson, C.D., Thompson, E.R., Seuferling, G., Whitney, H., & Strongman, J. (1999). (See References)

Bersoff, D.M. (1999). Why good people sometimes do bad things: Motivated reasoning and unethical behavior. *Personality and Social Psychology Bulletin, 25,* 28–39.

Todorov, T. (1996). *Facing the extreme: Moral life in the concentration camps* (A. Denner & A. Pollak, Trans.). New York: Henry Holt.

REFERENCES

Asch, S. (1956). Studies of independence and conformity: A minority of one against a unanimous majority. *Psychological Monographs, 70*(Whole No. 416).

Bandura, A. (1999). Moral disengagement in the perpetration of inhumanities. *Personality and Social Psychology Review, 3,* 193–209.

Batson, C.D., Kobrynowicz, D., Dinnerstein, J.L, Kampf, H.C., & Wilson, A.D. (1997). In a very different voice: Unmasking moral hypocrisy. *Journal of Personality and Social Psychology, 72,* 1335–1348.

Batson, C.D., Thompson, E.R., Seuferling, G., Whitney, H., & Strongman, J. (1999). Moral hypocrisy: Appearing moral to oneself without being so. *Journal of Personality and Social Psychology, 77,* 525–537.

Batson, C.D., Tsang, J., & Thompson, E.R. (2000). *Weakness of will: Counting the cost of being moral.* Unpublished manuscript, University of Kansas, Lawrence.

Milgram, S. (1974). *Obedience to authority: An experimental view.* New York: Harper & Row.

Wicklund, R.A. (1975). Objective self-awareness., In L. Berkowitz (Ed.), *Advances in experimental and social psychology* (Vol. 8, pp. 233–275). New York: Academic Press.

CRITICAL THINKING QUESTIONS

1. On a personal level, reflect on when you have engaged in *moral hypocrisy.* Have you ever experienced *overpowered integrity?* In retrospect, why did you not act in accord with your moral values? Did you learn anything from that experience that would make you less likely to act the same way in a similar situation in the future? Explain your answers.

2. Based on the concepts discussed in the article, what could a parent do to help develop a strong sense of moral integrity in his or her children? Explain your suggestions.

3. Find examples of moral hypocrisy in the public domain—that is, situations in which a public figure, such as a politician or member of the clergy, has espoused certain moral values yet acted inconsistently with them. Do these public moral lapses affect the moral behavior of other people? Discuss.

4. Respond to the question from the article: "How might one structure social environments so that even those individuals motivated by moral hypocrisy might be led to act morally?"

ARTICLE 29 _____

Many variables can potentially influence whether an individual will help someone in need. One such factor, moral motivation, was discussed in the previous article. But what other factors may influence prosocial behavior?

Broadly speaking, two types of determinants can be considered. The first concerns *situational* factors: What circumstances surrounding the specific situation may affect helping behavior? The second variable concerns *dispositions:* To what extent are decisions to help due to relatively permanent personality factors? In other words, are some people more likely to help than others because of their unique personality makeup? Or does the situation, rather than personality, influence helping?

In "From Jerusalem to Jericho," John M. Darley and C. Daniel Batson examine both situational and dispositional variables in an experiment modeled after a biblical parable. Specifically, the study looks at helping as influenced by situational variables—whether the subjects were in a hurry and what they were thinking at the time—and dispositional variables—the religious orientations of the subjects. This classic article is interesting not only because of the methodology used but also because of the important implications of the results.

"From Jerusalem to Jericho"
A Study of Situational and Dispositional Variables in Helping Behavior

■ John M. Darley and C. Daniel Batson

The influence of several situational and personality variables on helping behavior was examined in an emergency situation suggested by the parable of the Good Samaritan. People going between two buildings encountered a shabbily dressed person slumped by the side of the road. Subjects in a hurry to reach their destination were more likely to pass by without stopping. Some subjects were going to give a short talk on the parable of the Good Samaritan, others on a nonhelping relevant topic; this made no significant difference in the likelihood of their giving the victim help. Religious personality variables did not predict whether an individual would help the victim or not. However, if a subject did stop to offer help, the character of the helping response was related to his type of religiosity.

Helping other people in distress is, among other things, an ethical act. That is, it is in act governed by

ethical norms and precepts taught to children at home, in school, and in church. From Freudian and other personality theories, one would expect individual differences in internalization of these standards that would lead to differences between individuals in the likelihood with which they would help others. But recent research on bystander intervention in emergency situations (Bickman, 1969; Darley & Latané, 1968; Korte, 1969; but see also Schwartz & Clausen, 1970) has had bad luck in finding personality determinants of helping behavior. Although personality variables that one might expect to correlate with helping behavior have been measured (Machiavellianism, authoritarianism, social desirability, alienation, and social responsibility), these were not predictive of helping. Nor was this due to a generalized lack of predictability in the helping situation examined, since variations in the experimental situation, such as the

Reprinted from *Journal of Personality and Social Psychology*, 1973, *27*, 100–108. Copyright © 1973 by the American Psychological Association. Reprinted by permission.

availability of other people who might also help, produced marked changes in rates of helping behavior. These findings are reminiscent of Hartshorne and May's (1928) discovery that resistance to temptation, another ethically relevant act, did not seem to be a fixed characteristic of an individual. That is, a person who was likely to be honest in one situation was not particularly likely to be honest in the next (but see also Burton, 1963).

The rather disappointing correlation between the social psychologist's traditional set of personality variables and helping behavior in emergency situations suggests the need for a fresh perspective on possible predictors of helping and possible situations in which to test them. Therefore, for inspiration, we turned to the Bible, to what is perhaps the classical helping story in the Judeo-Christian tradition, the parable of the Good Samaritan. The parable proved of value in suggesting both personality and situational variables relevant to helping.

"And who is my neighbor?" Jesus replied, "A man was going down from Jerusalem to Jericho, and he fell among robbers, who stopped him and beat him, and departed, leaving him half dead. Now by chance a priest was going down the road; and when he saw him he passed by on the other side. So likewise a Levite, when he came to the place and saw him, passed by on the other side. But a Samaritan, as he journeyed, came to where he was; and when he saw him, he had compassion, and went to him and bound his wounds, pouring on oil and wine; then he set him on his own beast and brought him to an inn, and took care of him. And the next day he took out two dennarii and gave them to the innkeeper, saying, "Take care of him; and whatever more you spend, I will repay you when I come back." Which of these three, do you think, proved neighbor to him who fell among the robbers? He said, "The one who showed mercy on him." And Jesus said to him, "Go and do likewise." (Luke 10: 29–37 RSV)

To psychologists who reflect on the parable, it seems to suggest situational and personality differences between the nonhelpful priest and Levite and the helpful Samaritan. What might each have been thinking and doing when he came upon the robbery

victim on that desolate road? What sort of persons were they?

One can speculate on differences in thought. Both the priest and the Levite were religious functionaries who could be expected to have their minds occupied with religious matters. The priest's role in religious activities is obvious. The Levite's role, although less obvious, is equally important: The Levites were necessary participants in temple ceremonies. Much less can be said with any confidence about what the Samaritan might have been thinking, but, in contrast to the others, it was most likely not of a religious nature, for Samaritans were religious outcasts.

Not only was the Samaritan most likely thinking about more mundane matters than the priest and Levite, but, because he was socially less important, it seems likely that he was operating on a quite different time schedule. One can imagine the priest and Levite, prominent public figures, hurrying along with little black books full of meetings and appointments, glancing furtively at their sundials. In contrast, the Samaritan would likely have far fewer and less important people counting on him to be at a particular place at a particular time, and therefore might be expected to be in less of a hurry than the prominent priest or Levite.

In addition to these situational variables, one finds personality factors suggested as well. Central among these, and apparently basic to the point that Jesus was trying to make, is a distinction between types of religiosity. Both the priest and Levite are extremely "religious." But it seems to be precisely their type of religiosity that the parable challenges. At issue is the motivation for one's religion and ethical behavior. Jesus seems to feel that the religious leaders of his time, though certainly respected and upstanding citizens, may be "virtuous" for what it will get them, both in terms of the admiration of their fellowmen and in the eyes of God. New Testament scholar R. W. Funk (1966) noted that the Samaritan is at the other end of the spectrum:

The Samaritan does not love with side glances at God. The need of neighbor alone is made self-evident, and the Samaritan responds without other motivation. (pp. 218–219)

That is, the Samaritan is interpreted as responding spontaneously to the situation, not as being preoccupied with the abstract ethical or organizational do's and don'ts of religion as the priest and Levite would seem to be. This is not to say that the Samaritan is portrayed as irreligious. A major intent of the parable would seem to be to present the Samaritan as a religious and ethical example, but at the same time to contrast his type of religiosity with the more common conception of religiosity that the priest and Levite represent.

To summarize the variables suggested as affecting helping behavior by the parable, the situational variables include the content of one's thinking and the amount of hurry in one's journey. The major dispositional variable seems to be differing types of religiosity. Certainly these variables do not exhaust the list that could be elicited from the parable, but they do suggest several research hypotheses.

Hypothesis 1 The parable implies that people who encounter a situation possibly calling for a helping response while thinking religious and ethical thoughts will be no more likely to offer aid than persons thinking about something else. Such a hypothesis seems to run counter to a theory that focuses on norms as determining helping behavior because a normative account would predict that the increased salience of helping norms produced by thinking about religious and ethical examples would increase helping behavior.

Hypothesis 2 Persons encountering a possible helping situation when they are in a hurry will be less likely to offer aid than persons not in a hurry.

Hypothesis 3 Concerning types of religiosity, persons who are religious in a Samaritan-like fashion will help more frequently than those religious in a priest or Levite fashion.

Obviously, this last hypothesis is hardly operationalized as stated. Prior research by one of the investigators on types of religiosity (Batson, 1971), however, led us to differentiate three distinct ways of being religious: (a) for what it will gain one (cf. Freud, 1927, and perhaps the priest and Levite), (b) for its own intrinsic value (cf. Allport & Ross, 1967), and (c) as a response to and quest for meaning in one's everyday life (cf. Batson, 1971). Both of the latter conceptions would be proposed by their exponents as related to the

more Samaritanlike "true" religiosity. Therefore, depending on the theorist one follows, the third hypothesis may be stated like this: People (a) who are religious for intrinsic reasons (Allport & Ross, 1967) or (b) whose religion emerges out of questioning the meaning of their everyday lives (Batson, 1971) will be more likely to stop to offer help to the victim.

The parable of the Good Samaritan also suggested how we would measure people's helping behavior—their response to a stranger slumped by the side of one's path. The victim should appear somewhat ambiguous—dressed, possibly in need of help, but also possibly drunk or even potentially dangerous.

Further, the parable suggests a means by which the incident could be perceived as a real one rather than part of a psychological experiment in which one's behavior was under surveillance and might be shaped by demand characteristics (Orne, 1962), evaluation apprehension (Rosenberg, 1965), or other potentially artifactual determinants of helping behavior. The victim should be encountered not in the experimental context but on the road between various tasks.

METHOD

In order to examine the influence of these variables on helping behavior, seminary students were asked to participate in a study on religious education and vocations. In the first testing session, personality questionnaires concerning types of religiosity were administered. In a second individual session, the subject began experimental procedures in one building and was asked to report to another building for later procedures. While in transit, the subject passed a slumped "victim" planted in an alleyway. The dependent variable was whether and how the subject helped the victim. The independent variables were the degree to which the subject was told to hurry in reaching the other building and the talk he was to give when he arrived there. Some subjects were to give a talk on the jobs in which seminary students would be most effective, others, on the parable of the Good Samaritan.

Subjects

The subjects for the questionnaire administration were 67 students at Princeton Theological Seminary.

Forty-seven of them, those who could be reached by telephone, were scheduled for the experiment. Of the 47, 7 subjects' data were not included in the analyses—3 because of contamination of the experimental procedures during their testing and 4 due to suspicion of the experimental situation. Each subject was paid $1 for the questionnaire session and $1.50 for the experimental session.

Personality Measures

Detailed discussion of the personality scales used may be found elsewhere (Batson, 1971), so the present discussion will be brief. The general personality construct under examination was religiosity. Various conceptions of religiosity have been offered in recent years based on different psychometric scales. The conception seeming to generate the most interest is the Allport and Ross (1967) distinction between "intrinsic" versus "extrinsic" religiosity (cf. also Allen & Spilka, 1967, on "committed" versus "consensual" religion). This bipolar conception of religiosity has been questioned by Brown (1964) and Batson (1971), who suggested three-dimensional analyses instead. Therefore, in the present research, types of religiosity were measured with three instruments which together provided six separate scales; (a) a *doctrinal orthodoxy* (D-O) scale patterned after that used by Glock and Stark (1966), scaling agreement with classic doctrines of Protestant theology; (b) the Allport-Ross *extrinsic* (AR-E) scale, measuring the use of religion as a means to an end rather than as an end in itself; (c) the Allport-Ross *intrinsic* (AR-I) scale, measuring the use of religion as an end in itself; (d) the *extrinsic external* scale of Batson's Religious Life Inventory (RELI-EE), designed to measure the influence of significant others and situations in generating one's religiosity; (e) the *extrinsic internal* scale of the Religious Life Inventory (RELI-EI), designed to measure the degree of "driveness" in one's religiosity; and (f) the *intrinsic* scale of the Religious Life Inventory (RELI-I), designed to measure the degree to which one's religiosity involves a questioning of the meaning of life arising out of one's interactions with his social environment. The order of presentation of the scales in the questionnaire was RELI, AR, D-O.

Consistent with prior research (Batson, 1971), a principal-component analysis of the total scale scores

and individual items for the 67 seminarians produced a theoretically meaningful, orthogonally rotated three-component structure with the following loadings:

Religion as means received a single very high loading from AR-E (.903) and therefore was defined by Allport and Ross's (1967) conception of this scale as measuring religiosity as a means to other ends. This component also received moderate negative loadings from D-O (–.400) and AR-I (–.372) and a moderate positive loading from RELI-EE (.301).

Religion as an end received high loadings from RELI-EI (.874), RELI-EE (.725), AR-I (.768), and D-O (.704). Given this configuration, and again following Allport and Ross's conceptualization, this component seemed to involve religiosity as an end in itself with some intrinsic value.

Religion as quest received a single very high loading from RELI-I (.945) and a moderate loading from RELI-EE (.75). Following Batson, this component was conceived to involve religiosity emerging out of an individual's search for meaning in his personal and social world.

The three religious personality scales examined in the experimental research were constructed through the use of complete-estimation factor score coefficients from these three components.

Scheduling of Experimental Study

Since the incident requiring a helping response was staged outdoors, the entire experimental study was run in 3 days, December 14–16, 1970, between 10 A.M. and 4 P.M. A tight schedule was used in an attempt to maintain reasonably consistent weather and light conditions. Temperature fluctuation according to the *New York Times* for the 3 days during these hours was not more than 5 degrees Fahrenheit. No rain or snow fell, although the third day was cloudy, whereas the first two were sunny. Within days the subjects were randomly assigned to experimental conditions.[1]

Procedure

When a subject appeared for the experiment, an assistant (who was blind with respect to the personality scores) asked him to read a brief statement which explained that he was participating in a study of the vocational careers of seminary students. After developing the rationale for the study, the statement read:

What we have called you in for today is to provide us with some additional material which will give us a clearer picture of how you think than does the questionnaire material we have gathered thus far. Questionnaires are helpful, but tend to be somewhat oversimplified. Therefore, we would like to record a 3–5 minute talk you give based on the following passage. . . .

Variable 1: Message   In the task-relevant condition the passage read,

With increasing frequency the question is being asked: What jobs or professions do seminary students subsequently enjoy most, and in what jobs are they most effective? The answer to this question used to be so obvious that the question was not even asked. Seminary students were being trained for the ministry, and since both society at large and the seminary student himself had a relatively clear understanding of what made a "good" minister, there was no need even to raise the question of for what other jobs seminary experience seems to be an asset. Today, however, neither society nor many seminaries have a very clearly defined conception of what a "good" minister is or of what sorts of jobs and professions are the best context in which to minister. Many seminary students, apparently genuinely concerned with "ministering," seem to feel that it is impossible to minister in the professional clergy. Other students, no less concerned, find the clergy the most viable profession for ministry. But are there other jobs and/or professions for which seminary experience is an asset? And, indeed, how much of an asset is it for the professional ministry? Or, even more broadly, can one minister through an "establishment" job at all?

In the helping-relevant condition, the subject was given the parable of the Good Samaritan exactly as printed earlier in this article. Next, regardless of condition, all subjects were told,

You can say whatever you wish based on the passage. Because we are interested in how you think on your

feet, you will not be allowed to use notes in giving the talk. Do you understand what you are to do? If not, the assistant will be glad to answer questions.

After a few minutes the assistant returned, asked if there were any questions, and then said:

Since they're rather tight on space in this building, we're using a free office in the building next door for recording the talks. Let me show you how to get there [draws and explains map on 3 × 5 card]. This is where Professor Steiner's laboratory is. If you go in this door [points at map], there's a secretary right here, and she'll direct you to the office we're using for recording. Another of Professor Steiner's assistants will set you up for recording your talk. Is the map clear?

Variable 2: Hurry   In the high-hurry condition the assistant then looked at his watch and said, "Oh, you're late. They were expecting you a few minutes ago. We'd better get moving. The assistant should be waiting for you so you'd better hurry. It shouldn't take but just a minute." In the intermediate-hurry condition he said, "The assistant is ready for you, so please go right over." In the low-hurry condition, he said, "It'll be a few minutes before they're ready for you, but you might as well head on over. If you have to wait over there, it shouldn't be long."

The Incident   When the subject passed through the alley, the victim was sitting slumped in a doorway, head down, eyes closed, not moving. As the subject went by, the victim coughed twice and groaned, keeping his head down. If the subject stopped and asked if something was wrong or offered to help, the victim, startled and somewhat groggy, said, "Oh, thank you [cough]. . . . No, it's all right. [Pause] I've got this respiratory condition [cough]. . . . The doctor's given me these pills to take, and I just took one. . . . If I just sit and rest for a few minutes I'll be O.K. . . . Thanks very much for stopping though [smiles weakly]." If the subject persisted, insisting on taking the victim inside the building, the victim allowed him to do so and thanked him.

Helping Ratings   The victim rated each subject on a scale of helping behavior as follows:

0 = failed to notice the victim as possibly in need at all; 1 = perceived the victim as possibly in need but did not offer aid; 2 = did not stop but helped indirectly (e.g., by telling Steiner's assistant about the victim); 3 = stopped and asked if victim needed help; 4 = after stopping, insisted on taking the victim inside and then left him.

The victim was blind to the personality scale scores and experimental conditions of all subjects. At the suggestion of the victim, another category was added to the rating scales, based on his observations of the pilot subjects' behavior:

5 = after stopping, refused to leave the victim (after 3–5 minutes) and/or insisted on taking him somewhere outside experimental context (e.g., for coffee or to the infirmary).

(In some cases it was necessary to distinguish Category 0 from Category 1 by the postexperimental questionnaire and Category 2 from Category 1 on the report of the experimental assistant.)

This 6-point scale of helping behavior and a description of the victim were given to a panel of 10 judges (unacquainted with the research) who were asked to rank order the (unnumbered) categories in terms of "the amount of helping behavior displayed toward the person in the doorway." Of the 10, 1 judge reversed the order of Categories 0 and 1. Otherwise there was complete agreement with the ranking implied in the presentation of the scale above.

The Speech After passing through the alley and entering the door marked on the map, the subject entered a secretary's office. She introduced him to the assistant who gave the subject time to prepare and privately record his talk.

Helping Behavior Questionnaire After recording the talk, the subject was sent to another experimenter, who administered "an exploratory questionnaire on personal and social ethics." The questionnaire contained several initial questions about the interrelationship between social and personal ethics, and then asked three key questions: (a) "When was the last time you saw a person who seemed to be in need of help?" (b) "When was the last time you stopped to help someone in need?" (c) "Have you had experience helping persons in need? If so, outline briefly." These

data were collected as a check on the victim's ratings of whether subjects who did not stop perceived the situation in the alley as one possibly involving need or not.

When he returned, the experimenter reviewed the subject's questionnaire, and, if no mention was made of the situation in the alley, probed for reactions to it and then phased into an elaborate debriefing and discussion session.

Debriefing

In the debriefing, the subject was told the exact nature of the study, including the deception involved, and the reasons for the deception were explained. The subject's reactions to the victim and to the study in general were discussed. The role of situational determinants of helping behavior was explained in relation to this particular incident and to other experiences of the subject. All subjects seemed readily to understand the necessity for the deception, and none indicated any resentment of it. After debriefing, the subject was thanked for his time and paid, then he left.

RESULTS AND DISCUSSION

Overall Helping Behavior

The average amount of help that a subject offered the victim, by condition, is shown in Table 1. The unequal-N analysis of variance indicates that while the hurry variable was significantly ($F = 3.56$, $df = 2.34$, $p < .05$) related to helping behavior, the message variable was not. Subjects in a hurry were likely to offer less help than were subjects not in a hurry. Whether the subject was going to give a speech on the parable of the Good Samaritan or not did not significantly affect his helping behavior on this analysis.

Other studies have focused on the question of whether a person initiates helping action or not, rather than on scaled kinds of helping. The data from the present study can also be analyzed on the following terms: Of the 40 subjects, 16 (40%) offered some form of direct or indirect aid to the victim (Coding Categories 2–5), 24 (60%) did not (Coding Categories 0 and 1). The percentages of subjects who offered aid by situational variable were, for low hurry, 63% offered help, intermediate hurry 45%, and high hurry 10%, for helping-relevant message 53%, task-relevant message 29%. With regard to this more general question of whether help was offered or not, an unequal-N analysis of variance (arc sine transformation of percentages of helpers, with low- and intermediate-hurry conditions pooled) indicated that again only the hurry main effect was significantly ($F = 5.22$, $p < .05$) related to helping behavior; the subjects in a hurry were more likely to pass by the victim than were those in less of a hurry.

Reviewing the predictions in the light of these results, the second hypothesis, that the degree of hurry a person is in determines his helping behavior, was supported. The prediction involved in the first hypothesis concerning the message content was based on the parable. The parable itself seemed to suggest that thinking pious thoughts would not increase helping. Another and conflicting prediction might be produced by a norm salience theory. Thinking about the parable should make norms for helping salient and therefore produce more helping. The data, as hypothesized, are more congruent with the prediction drawn from the parable. A person going to speak on the parable of the Good Samaritan is not significantly more likely to stop to help a person by the side of the road than is a person going to talk about possible occupations for seminary graduates.

Since both situational hypotheses are confirmed, it is tempting to stop the analysis of these variables at this point. However, multiple regression analysis procedures were also used to analyze the relationship of all of the independent variables of the study and the helping behavior. In addition to often being more statistically powerful due to the use of more data information, multiple regression analysis has an advantage over analysis of variance in that it allows for a comparison of the relative effect of the various independent variables in accounting for variance in the dependent variable. Also, multiple regression analysis can compare the effects of continuous as well as nominal independent variables on both continuous and nominal dependent variables (through the use of point biserial correlations, *rpb*) and shows considerable robustness to violation of normality assumptions (Cohen, 1965, 1968). Table 2 reports the results of the multiple regression analysis using both help versus no help and the graded helping scale as dependent measures. In this table the overall equation Fs show the F value of the entire regression equation as a particular row variable enters the equation. Individual variable Fs were computed with all five independent variables in the equation. Although the two situational variables, hurry and message condition, correlated more highly with the dependent measure than any of the religious dispositional variables, only hurry was a significant predictor of whether one will help or not (column 1) or of the overall amount of help given (column 2). These results corroborate the findings of the analysis of variance.[2]

Notice also that neither form of the third hypothesis, that types of religiosity will predict helping, received support from these data. No correlation between the various measures of religiosity and any form of the dependent measure ever came near statistical significance, even though the multiple regression analysis procedure is a powerful and not particularly conservative statistical test.

TABLE 1 / Means and Analysis of Variance of Graded Helping Responses

	M			
	Hurry			Sum-
Message	Low	Medium	High	mary
Helping relevant	3.800	2.000	1.000	2.263
Task relevant	1.667	1.667	.500	1.333
Summary	3.000	1.818	.700	

Analysis of Variance				
Source	SS	df	MS	F
Message (A)	7.766	1	7.766	2.65
Hurry (B)	20.884	2	10.442	3.50*
A x B	5.237	2	2.619	.89
Error	99.633	34	2.930	

Note: $N = 40$.
*$p < .05$.

TABLE 2 / Stepwise Multiple Regression Analysis

	Help vs. No Help					Graded Helping			
	Individual Variable		Overall Equation			Individual Variable		Variable Equation	
Step	r^a	*F*	*R*	*F*	Step	*r*	*F*	*R*	*F*
1. Hurry[b]	−.37	4.537*	.37	5.884*	1. Hurry	−.42	6.665*	.42	8.196**
2. Message[c]	.25	1.495	.41	3.834*	2. Message	.25	1.719	.46	5.083*
3. Religion as quest	−.03	.081	.42	2.521	3. Religion as quest	−.16	1.297	.50	3.897*
4. Religion as means	−.03	.003	.42	1.838*	4. Religion as means	−.08	.018	.50	2.848*
5. Religion as end	.06	.000	.42	1.430	5. Religion as end	−.07	.001	.50	2.213

Note: $N = 40$. Helping is the dependent variable. $df = 1/34$.
[a]Individual variable correlation coefficient is a point biserial where appropriate.
[b]Variables are listed in order of entry into stepwise regression equations.
[c]Helping-relevant message is positive.
*$p < .05$.
**$p < .01$.

Personality Difference among Subjects Who Helped

To further investigate the possible influence of personality variables, analyses were carried out using only the data from subjects who offered some kind of help to the victim. Surprisingly (since the number of these subjects was small, only 16) when this was done, one religiosity variable seemed to be significantly related to the kind of helping behavior offered. (The situational variables had no significant effect.) Subjects high on the religion as quest dimension appear likely, when they stop for the victim, to offer help of a more tentative or incomplete nature than are subjects scoring low on this dimension ($r = -.53, p < .05$).

This result seemed unsettling for the thinking behind either form of Hypothesis 3. Not only do the data suggest that the Allport-Ross-based conception of religion as *end* does not predict the degree of helping, but the religion as quest component is a significant predictor of offering less help. This latter result seems counterintuitive and out of keeping with previous research (Batson, 1971), which found that this type of religiosity correlated positively with other socially valued characteristics. Further data analysis, however, seemed to suggest a different interpretation of this result.

It will be remembered that one helping coding category was added at the suggestion of the victim after his observation of pilot subjects. The correlation of religious personality variables with helping behavior dichotomized between the added category (1) and all of the others (0) was examined. The correlation between religion as quest and this dichotomous helping scale was essentially unchanged ($rpb = -.54, p < .05$). Thus, the previously found correlation between the helping scale and religion as quest seems to reflect the tendency of those who score low on the quest dimension to offer help in the added helping category.

What does help in this added category represent? Within the context of the experiment, it represented an embarrassment. The victim's response to persistent offers of help was to assure the helper he was all right, had taken his medicine, just needed to rest for a minute or so, and, if ultimately necessary, to request the helper to leave. But the *super* helpers in this added category often would not leave until the final appeal was repeated several times by the victim (who was growing increasingly panicky at the possibility of the arrival of the next subject). Since it usually involved the subject's attempting to carry through a preset plan (e.g., taking the subject for a cup of coffee or revealing to him the strength to be found in Christ), and did not allow information from the victim to change that plan, we originally labeled this kind of helping as rigid—an interpretation supported by its increased likelihood among highly doctrinal orthodox subjects ($r = .63$, $p < .01$). It also seemed to have an inappropriate character. If this more extreme form of helping behavior is indeed effectively less helpful, then the second form of Hypothesis 3 does seem to gain support.

But perhaps it is the experimenters rather than the super helpers who are doing the inappropriate thing; perhaps the best characterization of this kind of helping is as different rather than as inappropriate. This kind of helper seems quickly to place a particular interpretation on the situation, and the helping response seems to follow naturally from this interpretation. All that can safely be said is that one style of helping that emerged in this experiment was directed toward the presumed underlying needs of the victim and was little modified by the victim's comments about his own needs. In contrast, another style was more tentative and seemed more responsive to the victim's statements of his need.

The former kind of helping was likely to be displayed by subjects who expressed strong doctrinal orthodoxy. Conversely, this fixed kind of helping was unlikely among subjects high on the religion as quest dimension. These latter subjects, who conceived their religion as involving an ongoing search for meaning in their personal and social world, seemed more responsive to the victim's immediate needs and more open to the victim's definitions of his own needs.

CONCLUSION AND IMPLICATIONS

A person not in a hurry may stop and offer help to a person in distress. A person in a hurry is likely to keep going. Ironically, he is likely to keep going even if he is hurrying to speak on the parable of the Good Samaritan, thus inadvertently confirming the point of the parable. (Indeed, on several occasions, a seminary student going to give his talk on the parable of the Good Samaritan literally stepped over the victim as he hurried on his way!)

Although the degree to which a person was in a hurry had a clearly significant effect on his likelihood of offering the victim help, whether he was going to give a sermon on the parable or on possible vocational roles of ministers did not. This lack of effect of sermon topic raises certain difficulties for an explanation of helping behavior involving helping norms and their salience. It is hard to think of a context in which norms concerning helping those in distress are more salient than for a person thinking about the Good Samaritan, and yet it did not significantly increase helping behavior. The results were in the direction suggested by the norm salience hypothesis, but they were not significant. The most accurate conclusion seems to be that salience of helping norms is a less strong determinant of helping behavior in the present situation than many, including the present authors, would expect.

Thinking about the Good Samaritan did not increase helping behavior, but being in a hurry decreased it. It is difficult not to conclude from this that the frequently cited explanation that ethics becomes a luxury as the speed of our daily lives increases is at least an accurate description. The picture that this explanation conveys is of a person seeing another, consciously noting his distress, and consciously choosing to leave him in distress. But perhaps this is not entirely accurate, for, when a person is in a hurry, something seems to happen that is akin to Tolman's (1948) concept of the "narrowing of the cognitive map." Our seminarians in a hurry noticed the victim in that in the postexperiment interview almost all mentioned him as, on reflection, possibly in need of help. But it seems that they often had not worked this out when they were near the victim. Either the interpretation of their visual picture as a person in distress or the empathic reactions usually associated with that interpretation had been deferred because they were hurrying. According to the reflections of some of the subjects, it would be inaccurate to say that they realized the victim's possible distress, then chose to ignore it; instead, because of the time pressures, they did not perceive the scene in the alley as an occasion for an ethical decision.

For other subjects it seems more accurate to conclude that they decided not to stop. They appeared aroused and anxious after the encounter in the alley. For these subjects, what were the elements of the choice that they were making? Why were the seminarians hurrying? Because the experimenter, *whom the subject was helping* was depending on him to get to a particular place quickly. In other words, he was in conflict between stopping to help the victim and continuing on his way to help the experimenter. And this is often true of people in a hurry; they hurry because somebody depends on their being somewhere. Conflict, rather than callousness, can explain their failure to stop.

Finally, as in other studies, personality variables were not useful in predicting whether a person helped or not. But in this study, unlike many previous ones, considerable variations were possible in the kinds of help given, and these variations did relate to personality measures—specifically to religiosity of the quest sort. The clear light of hindsight suggests that the dimension of kinds of helping would have been the appropriate place to look for personality differences all along; *whether* a person helps or not is an instant decision likely to be situationally controlled. How a person helps involves a more complex and considered number of decisions, including the time and scope to permit personality characteristics to shape them.

REFERENCES

Allen, R. O., & Spilka, B. Committed and consensual religion. A specification of religion-prejudice relationships. *Journal for the Scientific Study of Religion,* 1967, *6,* 191–206.

Allport, G. W., & Ross, J. M. Personal religious orientation and prejudice. *Journal of Personality and Social Psychology,* 1967, *5,* 432–443.

Batson, C. D. Creativity and religious development: Toward a structural-functional psychology of religion Unpublished doctoral dissertation, Princeton Theological Seminary, 1971.

Bickman, L. B. The effect of the presence of others on bystander intervention in an emergency. Unpublished doctoral dissertation, City College of the City University of New York, 1969.

Brown, L. B. Classifications of religious orientation. *Journal for the Scientific Study of Religion,* 1964, *4,* 91–99.

Burton, R. V. The generality of honesty reconsidered. *Psychological Review,* 1963, *70,* 481–499.

Cohen, J. Multiple regression as a general data-analytic system. *Psychological Bulletin,* 1968, *70,* 426–443.

Cohen, J. Some statistical issues in psychological research. In B. B. Wolman (Ed.), *Handbook of clinical psychology.* New York: McGraw-Hill, 1965.

Darley, J. M., & Latané, B. Bystander intervention in emergencies: Diffusion of responsibility. *Journal of Personality and Social Psychology,* 1968, *8,* 377–383.

Freud, S. *The future of an illusion.* New York: Liveright, 1953.

Funk, R. W. *Language, hermeneutic, and word of God.* New York: Harper & Row, 1966.

Glock, C. Y., & Stark, R. *Christian beliefs and anti-Semitism.* New York: Harper & Row, 1966.

Hartshorne, H., & May, M. A. *Studies in the nature of character.* Vol. 1. *Studies in deceit.* New York: Macmillan, 1928.

Korte, C. Group effects on help-giving in an emergency. *Proceedings of the 77th Annual Convention of the American Psychological Association,* 1969, *4,* 383–384. (Summary)

Orne, M. T. On the social psychology of the psychological experiment: With particular reference to demand characteristics and their implications. *American Psychologist,* 1962, *17,* 776–783.

Rosenberg, M. J. When dissonance fails: On eliminating evaluation apprehension from attitude measurement. *Journal of Personality and Social Psychology,* 1965, *1,* 28–42.

Schwartz, S. H., & Clausen, G. T. Responsibility, norms, and helping in an emergency. *Journal of Personality and Social Psychology,* 1970, *16,* 299–310.

Tolman, E. C. Cognitive maps in rats and men. *Psychological Review,* 1948, *55,* 189–208.

ENDNOTES

1. An error was made in randomizing that increased the number of subjects in the intermediate-hurry conditions. This worked against the prediction that was most highly confirmed (the hurry prediction) and made no difference to the message variable tests.

2. To check the legitimacy of the use of both analysis of variance and multiple regression analysis, parametric analyses, on this ordinal data, Kendall rank correlation coefficients were calculated between the helping scale and the five independent variables. As expected t approximated the correlation quite closely in each case and was significant for hurry only (hurry τ −.38, $p < .001$).

For assistance in conducting this research thanks are due Robert Wells, Beverly Fisher, Mike Shafto, Peter Sheras, Richard Detweiler, and Karen Glasser. The research was funded by National Science Foundation Grant GS-2293.

CRITICAL THINKING QUESTIONS

1. Being prompted to think of the parable of the Good Samaritan did not increase the subjects' helping behavior in this study, but being in a hurry actually decreased it. Suppose that you are in the business of soliciting money for a worthy purpose. What strategies could you use to maximize the money you receive, based on the implications of this study? Explain.

2. *Rush hour,* as the name implies, describes a time of day when people are in a hurry to get to or from work. Do you think that people would be less likely to help someone in need during rush hour than at other times of the day? What about on weekends? Design a study to test this possibility, being sure to address any ethical issues that may be involved.

3. Reading about the Good Samaritan had no impact on subsequent helping behavior. Do you think that reading an article such as this one would change people's helping behavior? Why or why not? Specifically, now that you know that being in a hurry will decrease the likelihood of your giving help, do you think that this awareness will make you more likely to give help in the future, even if you are in a hurry? Why or why not? If simply telling someone about the Good Samaritan was not enough to improve people's helping behavior, what might be more effective?

ADDITIONAL RELATED READINGS

Bar-On, D. (2001). The bystander in relation to the victim and the perpetrator: Today and during the Holocaust. *Social Justice Research, 14*(2), 125–148.

Batson, C. D., Eidelman, S. H., Higley, S. L., and Russel, S. A. (2001). "And who is my neighbor?" II: Quest religion as a source of universal compassion. *Journal for the Scientific Study of Religion, 40*(1), 39–50.

ARTICLE 30

Have you ever witnessed a child being abused in public—perhaps slapped or violently shaken? If so, did you do anything to intervene, either directly by trying to stop the abuse or indirectly by getting help? What was going on inside you that may have influenced your decision to act or not to act?

Now, consider these questions: Have you ever seen a man physically abuse a woman in public? How about a man abusing a pet, such as a dog? Would your decision on whether or how to intervene hinge on whom or what was being abused? What other factors might influence your decision? For example, would the size of the abuser make a difference? Would your own size play a role in deciding to help?

The following article by Mary R. Laner, Mary H. Benin, and Nicole A. Ventrone builds upon the research literature on bystander intervention in cases of observed violence. It examines the question of whether the type of victim—a woman, a child, or a dog—makes a difference in bystanders' decisions to help along with what bystander characteristics may influence decisions to help. This article is closely related to the two other articles in this chapter: Article 28 considered why moral people often fail to act morally, and Article 29 examined certain situational factors that influence actual helping behavior. This article expands on the often complex set of factors that may influence people's decisions to help or not help in emergency situations.

Bystander Attitudes toward Victims of Violence
Who's Worth Helping?

■ Mary R. Laner, Mary H. Benin, and Nicole A. Ventrone

Most studies examining bystanders' reactions to a violent attack have used an experimental or hypothetical situation involving a single victim. This study compares the intention to intervene on behalf of three hypothetical victims: a woman, a child, and a dog. Using a sample of over 700 college students, we found that there was not a significant difference in intention to intervene by type of victim. However, there was a significant interaction between the sex of the bystander and the type of victim, such that women are most likely to intervene on behalf of children, while men are most likely to intervene to aid a woman. We found that people who perceived themselves to be stronger, more aggressive, and more sympathetic than others are most likely to intend to intervene.

The study of bystander behavior in cases of observed violence began in earnest almost four decades ago after the infamous Genovese case of 1964. That case raised questions about "the faith people might have that a neighbor or a stranger would recognize one's plight, would appreciate one's agony, and would be willing to render aid" (Sheleff 1978:203). Kitty Genovese was assaulted and murdered within sight and/or hearing of at least 38 persons, none of whom assisted her either directly by trying to stop the assailant or indirectly by calling the police, despite her screams and cries for help over a period of about 40 minutes. After the case came to public attention, a number of scholars conducted studies in an effort to understand bystanders' behavior, their motives for involvement or noninvolvement, and how bystanders resolve various dilemmas such as danger and inconvenience on the one hand, and guilt or feelings of powerlessness on the other. The present study adds to the bystander literature by examining whether some victims of violent attacks are more likely to be helped by a bystander than others.

Using a large sample, we asked respondents about their attitudes toward helping any of three victims of violence—a child, a woman, or a dog. We present in this article a review of the relevant theoretical and empirical literature, and then provide our rationale for having chosen certain bystander and situational characteristics for investigation. In asking about attitudes, we follow the reasoning of Feld and Robinson (1998) who state:

> We do not assume that each respondent's report of how s/he would behave directly corresponds to how s/he would actually behave in real situations, but we do assume that variation in subjects' reports in response to variations in the experimental conditions reveals general tendencies of how their behavior would vary in response to similar variations in real situations. (p. 280)[1]

THEORETICAL BACKGROUND

Smithson, Amato, and Pearce (1983) have reviewed the theoretical perspectives that have been applied to the study of helping behavior. The broad approaches include learning theory, equity theory, attribution theory, cognitive development theory, and the sociobiological perspective. Specifically related to bystander intervention in emergency situations, middle-range approaches have been applied, the best known of which is Latane and Darley's (1970) decision making model,[2] based on reinforcement theory (see also Piliavin, Rodin, and Piliavin 1969; Kidd 1979; Clarkson 1987). Darley and Latane (1970) held that helping someone in distress arouses empathetic feelings in the observer; attempts to relieve the victim's suffering reduce the observer's own distress. These researchers also note that there are basic norms for helping persons in distress. For those who have internalized the norm, not helping subjects the

bystander to guilt feelings (punishment) for failing to act.

Most studies of helping behavior have attempted to locate predictors such as demographic variables or personal characteristics. "Two of the most appealing clusters of studies with both theoretical development and empirical support revolve around the concepts of personal norms and empathy" (Smithson, Amato, and Pearce 1983:14; See also Rushton 1980). Others have added such factors as the dependency or deservingness of the victim as theoretically important (Howard and Crano 1974). In sum the favored approach involves social psychological factors—the situation, the bystander's perception of it, and the bystander's competence—rather than larger social factors.

RESEARCH ON BYSTANDER BEHAVIOR[3]

Many studies of bystander behavior have used college student samples and employed laboratory or field experiment designs to examine student behavior in simulated emergencies where actual involvement and risk are minimal (Huston et al. 1981). More recently, survey techniques have uncovered considerable amounts of helping behavior (Rabow et al. 1990). In these questionnaire surveys of small convenience samples, college students are asked about their attitudes toward violence in a variety of circumstances (Feld and Robinson 1998). One study (Davis 1991) asked 50 persons who had actually intervened or who had witnessed interventions for their recollections, but interview-based research in this area is rare.

Latane and Darley's studies raised strong doubts about the utility of either social norms or personal characteristics as being important in predicting bystander intervention in emergencies (although some scholars have focused on personality, network, and biological factors; See Amato 1990; Dovidio 1984). Most norms, they held, were too vague and general, and characteristics were poor predictors. Rather, the situation itself, they contended would override values, norms, and dispositions.[4] In subsequent investigations, a large number of situational variables were studied including the ambiguity of the situation, the cost involved in the intervention, the severity of the victim's distress, the victim's level of dependency, the style of the request for help, the degree of threat in the situation, and the physical attractiveness of the victim, among other factors. However, according to a review of research findings, factors such as race, intelligence, and social class have not yielded consistent results, but the bystander's competence has been consistently relevant (Midlarsky, 1968).

Huston et al. (1981) found that interveners in several kinds of dangerous events had more exposure to crime, both in personal experience and in witnessing others' victimization. They were also taller, heavier, better trained to cope with emergencies (e.g., significantly more life-saving, medical and/or police training) and were more likely to see themselves as physically strong, aggressive, emotional, and principled. Thus, they were not motivated to intervene by strong humanitarian purposes but rather acted out of a sense of capability. Geis and Huston (1983) also found that those attributes were more strongly related to intervening than were rewards. Finally, Ofshe and Christman (1986) argued that it was not internalized rules but rather one's behavioral skills, activated by situational cues, that were related to intervening. Situational cues, they suggested, are neither available to verbalization nor to introspection. These scholars applied their theory of bystander intervention to selected studies as well as to other bodies of research. As Sheleff (1978:25) points out, "While the concept of altruism does conjure up the idea of sacrificing behavior, it involves sacrifice within the framework of one's competence."

With regard to bystanders, a large number of studies have found no differences between men and women in rates of helping, but a few have found differences. The probable explanation lies in the nature of the help required in the situation. Active, doing, spontaneous, and anonymous acts are more likely to be carried out by men than by women. Women are more likely to help than men (as a small number of studies have found) when helping is more planned, formal, personal, and less likely to involve direct intervention.

VICTIMS OF VIOLENCE IN BYSTANDER INTERVENTION STUDIES

Women are much more likely to receive help from strangers than are men (Howard and Crano 1974).

Male aggression toward female victims is seen as less acceptable, more injurious, and more criminal than female aggression toward male victims (Bethke and DeJoy 1993). However, women as targets have not been compared with other targets such as children—a consideration that the present study addresses.

Approval for physical punishment of children is widespread. In the face of such approval, what does a bystander do when rules for intervention are not formalized, and it is difficult to judge whether the punishment is normal or deviant? Davis' (1991) study, mentioned earlier, provides descriptions of intervention events that had occurred anywhere from earlier the same day to 12 years before. These were all cases of children being abused in a public setting. However, his sample consisted primarily of women who were parents. Would men or nonparents take the same considerable risks as Davis' sample recalled? Christy and Voight (1994), using college students and faculty members as respondents to a questionnaire, examined decisions to intervene in the case of a child being abused in public. They located factors related to decisions that included bystander, victim, and abuser characteristics as well as situational factors. However, since there was no comparison with any other target or victim, it is not known whether the same factors would apply across the board or are unique to the case of child victims.

We know of no studies that examine victimization of a dog. Most Americans, however, have pets and in the majority of cases, that pet is a dog (U.S. Bureau of the Census 1997). We can assume, then, that there would be empathy for an abused dog, and that the helping norm would apply in the case of this nonhuman victim of abuse. The present study includes, for comparative purposes, a dog, a child, and a woman—all victims of violence taking place in a public setting. Our inclusion of the dog as victim follows Flynn's (2000) contention that we should not neglect violence toward animals since, he argues, it "is a serious antisocial behavior . . . [and] is related to interpersonal violence" (2000:87), among other negative connotations.

The Good Samaritan law (ARS 32-1471) in the state where this study was conducted indicates that anyone rendering emergency care in a public place is not liable for any civil or other damages that might occur, either as a result of the intervention or of a failure to act. (The only exception is for gross negligence in the event of rendering care.) Thus, these laws do not compel intervention and for practical purposes, exempt interveners from liability.

METHODS

It has been shown that feelings of "we-ness" with a victim influence a bystander's arousal level and the perceived costs and rewards for intervention. "Helping is most likely when a bystander's arousal is high, and perceived costs are low and rewards high for helping" (Brigham 1986:177; see also Masser & Brown 1996). In this study, we are interested in the relative likelihood of helping any of three target victims. We held constant the level of bystander arousal by presenting respondents with vignettes that differed only by the identification of the victim.[5] All other conditions remained the same. Our vignette for the child victim was as follows:

> *The scene: You are in a parking lot and there in front of you is an approximately 140–150 pound man kicking, yelling at, and hitting an approximately 6-year old child. The child is crying and seems to be in pain. You can't tell whether the man is the father or not. The child is not putting up a defense. There is no one else around. What do you think you would do?*

The man's size was 180–190 pounds for half of the questionnaires. The victim was alternatively a woman and "an approximately 40 pound dog." The statement that "You can't tell whether the man is the *father* or not" was changed to "husband" and "owner" for the woman and dog respectively. The statement that the victim is crying was changed to whimpering for the dog. Otherwise, the vignette remained the same.

A series of questions asked respondents how likely they are to intervene on behalf of the victim. *Intervene* is our primary dependent variable and is measured on a 1–4 scale, where 4 = very likely to intervene.

Our first independent variable is the *victim*. The three victims were a 6-year old child, a 40-pound dog, and a woman. We also measured the physical characteristics of the respondent. These are the respondent's sex, *age* (measured in years), *height* (measured on a 1 [≤ 5'2"] to 8 [≥ 6'3"] scale); and *weight* (measured on a 1 [< 100 pounds] to 9 [≥ 205 pounds] scale). We also asked about *life experiences* that might affect the

respondent's likelihood of intervening. We asked if respondents had personally *witnessed* or *been a victim* of a serious crime (or if a *family member* had been such a victim) and if the respondent had ever *broken up a fight* between persons he or she knew. We asked if the respondent had training in *self-defense* or *life-saving* since these are potentially relevant to intervention. These variables were measured on dichotomous scales, with 0 = no experience (training), 1 = experience (training).

Following Huston et al. (1981), we also asked respondents to assess themselves relative to others regarding whether they were *stronger,* more *aggressive, principled, religious, sympathetic,* or *emotional* than other people. These variables were measured on a 1–5 scale with 1 = strongly disagree and 5 = strongly agree (with having the trait). We also varied the size of the perpetrator. In half of the vignettes he was a 140–150 pound man, while in the other half he was 180–190 pounds.

We were interested in the impact that the relationship between the abuser and victim would have on intention to intervene. To measure the impact that knowledge would have, we added a statement to the vignette in which the abuser's relationship to the victim (as father, husband, or dog owner) is established. Respondents were asked "What do you think you would do, now that you know that the child (woman, dog) is the man's child (wife, dog)?" Respondents are again asked how likely they would be to intervene on a four point scale. *Knowledge* is the difference between the likelihood of intervening before and after they learn that the victim is related to the abuser.

We obtained our data from college students during class from several different sociology classes that are taken by both majors and nonmajors, such as Introduction to Sociology, Social Problems, and Adolescence. The enrollment of the classes totaled 795; 711 students were in class and completed and returned the questionnaires. Respondents in each class were randomly given one of six scenarios (child, dog, or woman victim with a large or medium-sized perpetrator). Our sample was typical of college students: Sex is evenly divided (females = 51%). Although our respondents ranged in age from 17–54, 96% were 30 years old or under. Sixty percent of our students were upperclassmen, typical of this university which has a large number of transfers from local community colleges. The students were fairly evenly split between social science, business, and other majors (39%, 37%, and 24%, respectively).

The variables included for study are based on our review of the relevant literature, as are the following hypotheses:

H1 Children will be most likely to be helped; then women, then dogs.

H2 Sex of respondents will not affect the intention to intervene.

H3 Physical characteristics of respondents will affect the likelihood of intervention. Specifically, taller, heavier, and younger respondents will be more likely to intend to intervene than shorter, lighter, and older respondents.

H4 Previous experiences of respondents with crime, fighting, and intervening will increase the perceived likelihood of intervention. Specifically, people who have been a victim or whose family member has been a victim of a crime, those who have witnessed crime or fights between parents, have experience breaking up fights, or have had training in self-defense or life-saving will be more likely to intend to intervene than those who have not had those experiences.

H5 Self-perceptions of respondents that they are stronger, more aggressive, principled, sympathetic, religious, and emotional than the others will be more likely to intend to intervene.

H6 Size of the abuser will affect the likelihood of intervention. Respondents will be more likely to intend to intervene with mid-sized rather than with larger abusers.

H7 Knowledge that the abuser is related to the victim will affect the likelihood of intervention. If respondents know that the abuser and victim are related (or the abuser is the owner in the case of the dog) respondents will be less likely to intend to intervene.

The first hypothesis is derived from Howard and Crano's (1974) contention about differences in dependency and deservingness of victims. The second hypothesis derives from Latane and Darley's (1970) contention that personal characteristics such as the sex of the bystander are relatively unimportant. Our third hypothesis rests on Midlarsky's (1968) contention

that the bystander's competence is an important consideration. We chose his or her size, strength, and age as the characteristics relevant to the bystander's perception of his or her intervention capability or competence. Hypothesis four also derives from Midlarsky (1968) in that previous experience with crime, with fighting, and with intervention comprise a relevant part of the bystander's assessment of his or her intervention capabilities, or perception of the situation. The fifth hypothesis is based partly on Midlarsky's (1968) notion that aggressiveness and strength form part of the bystander's perception of the situation (i.e., response capability), and partly on Smithson et al. (1983) and Rushton (1980) who argue that personal norms such as seeing one's self as principled, sympathetic, religious, and emotional affect one's decisions about intervention. Midlarsky's (1968) theory forms the basis for our sixth and seventh hypothesis—specifically, that the size of the abuser and knowledge of the abuser's relationship with the victim are particulars of the situation that make a difference in intervention decisions.

RESULTS

Table 1 gives the means for the continuous variables and percentages for the dichotomous variables included in this study. Most of the respondents felt that they were somewhat likely to intervene. The average student was 22 years old, approximately 5'8" tall, and weighed around 145. Most students felt that they were more principled and sympathetic than others and a bit stronger; they felt that they were slightly more aggressive and religious than others. The vast majority had been involved in breaking up a fight between people that they knew, while a minority had been a victim or had a family member be a victim of a crime. Most had not had self-defense or life-saving training.

Our first hypothesis was that respondents would be most likely to perceive that they would intervene for children, and least likely to perceive that they would intervene for dogs. Our one way analysis of variance showed no significant difference in the likelihood of intervention by the type of victim.[6] Although children had the highest mean (3.34), the means for women (3.26) and dogs (3.16) were not significantly

TABLE 1 / Descriptive Statistics

Ordinal and Continuous Variables			
	Mean	Standard Deviation	N
Intention to intervene (4 = very likely, 1 = very unlikely)	3.25	.85	711
Age	21.97	4.32	705
Weight (9 point scale [4 = 130–144, 5 = 145–159])	4.90	2.10	709
Height (8 point scale [4 = 5'7"–5'8", 5 = 5'9"–5'10"])	4.22	1.96	710
Strong[a] (5 point scale [1 = strongly disagree, 5 = strongly agree)	3.59	.54	704
Aggressive[a] (5 point scale [1 = strongly disagree, 5 = strongly agree])	3.30	1.05	706
Principled[a] (5 point scale [1 = strongly disagree, 5 = strongly agree])	4.21	.71	697
Sympathetic[a] (5 point scale [1 = strongly disagree, 5 = strongly agree])	4.23	.75	705
Emotional[a] (5 point scale [1 = strongly disagree, 5 = strongly agree])	3.79	.94	702
Religious[a] (5 point scale [1 = strongly disagree, 5 = strongly agree])	3.20	1.21	705

Nominal Variables		
	Percent	N
Sex (female)	51.2	709
Witnessed a crime in the past ten years (yes)	38.0	707
Been a victim of a crime in the past ten years (yes)	20.9	708
Family member has been a victim of a crime in the past ten years (yes)	29.9	708
Been involved in breaking up a fight between people Respondent knows (yes)	73.5	705
Had self-defense training (yes)	21.1	710
Had life-saving training (yes)	35.4	710

[a]The preface to the question was "Compared to others I am . . ."

lower. Thus, our college sample reports a strong likelihood of intervening on behalf of any victim, and the support is not significantly lower for dogs than for children or women.

Our second hypothesis was that male and female respondents would not differ in reporting an intention to intervene. A *t*-test indicated a small but significantly higher perception of intervention by men (3.37) than women (3.14). Although this is not consistent with our hypothesis or with the prior literature, the *t*-test does not control for the size of the respondent.

We used multiple regression to test the effects of sex of the respondent and type of victim controlling for the height, weight, and age of the respondent. As the results in Table 2, Model 1 demonstrate, there is a significant interaction between the type of victim and the sex of the respondent in predicting the intention to intervene. Female respondents are significantly

more likely than male respondents to perceive that they would intervene on behalf of a child. Figure 1 shows the estimated marginal means of intervention by the sex of respondent and the type of victim, controlling for the height, weight, and age of the respondent. Men are most likely to intervene on behalf of women, while women are most likely to intervene on behalf of children, and not any more likely to intervene for women victims than they are for dogs. Several interpretations of this result are possible. Perhaps the simplest explanation is that women perceive that they are more powerful than children, but are not able to handle an attacker any better than the woman in the vignette. Men's greater likelihood to intervene for women than children may reflect a clearer normative role for them as a defender of women than children when both are strangers.

Hypothesis three suggested that taller, heavier, and younger respondents would be more likely to say that

TABLE 2 / Regression Coefficients (unstandardized) for Four Models Predicting Perceived Likelihood of Intervention

	Model 1[a]	Model 2[b]	Model 3[c]	Model 4[d]
Intercept	3.097**	2.933**	1.327**	1.487**
Age	.002			
Height	−.049*			−.029
Weight	.074**			.038
Sex (F)	−.332**			−.339**
Child	−.182	.086	.108	−.146
Dog	−.245*	−.119	−.092	−.226*
Sex Child*	.469**			.425**
Sex Dog*	.260			.204
Witness		.058		
Been victim		.077		
Family victim		.049		
Break fight		.322**		.219**
Self-defense		.138		
Life save		.042		
Strong			.118**	.088*
Aggressive			.159**	.152**
Principled			.091	
Sympathetic			.191**	.214**
Emotional			−.027	
Religious			−.038	
	$R^2 = .054$	$R^2 = .058$	$R^2 = .116$	$R^2 = .164$
	$N = 704$	$N = 704$	$N = 691$	$N = 699$

*$p < .05$, **$p < .01$

[a]Physical characteristics, type of victim, sex of respondent, and interactions between type of victim and sex of respondent
[b]Life experiences, controlling for type of victim
[c]Self-assessments, controlling for type of victim
[d]Best predictors of models containing physical characteristics, life experiences, and self-assessments

they would intervene. As Table 2, Model 1 shows, weight ($p < .01$) and height ($p < .05$), but not age have significant effects on intervention intention. Controlling for age, gender, and height, heavier respondents report a greater likelihood of intervention. However, for a given weight, age, and sex, it is the shorter respondents who are more likely to perceive that they would intervene. This could simply be that at a given weight, the shorter respondents have a stockier build, and they may perceive themselves to be stronger than the taller respondents. Stockier respondents may feel more confident in their ability to handle a potentially physical confrontation.

The age of the respondent was not significantly related to the perceived likelihood of intervening.

However, we have limited variation in age in our college sample (95% of our sample is under 30 years of age). Age is much more likely to be a factor when a representative number of middle age and older adults are included.

Hypothesis four concerns the relevant life experiences of respondents. We had hypothesized that several types of exposure to violence and crime would significantly affect intervention expectations. However, as is shown in Model 2 of Table 2, having witnessed or been a victim of crime, and having had a family member be a victim were not statistically significant. The only life experience that was relevant to whether respondents believed that they would intervene is whether they had experience in breaking up

FIGURE 1 / Estimated Marginal Means for Intention to Intervene by Victim and Sex of Respondent Controlling for Respondent's Age, Height, and Weight

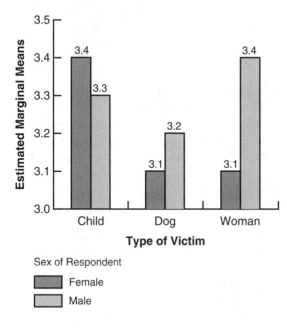

Sex of Respondent

- Female
- Male

fights. Experience as a victim or witness to crime and training in self-defense and life-saving were not important, controlling for experience in breaking up fights and type of victim.

Hypothesis five concerns the self-assessments of the respondents regarding physical and character traits. The results for Model 3 of Table 2 show that respondents who thought that—relative to others—they were stronger, more aggressive, and sympathetic were more likely to perceive themselves as intervening on behalf of a victim than respondents who didn't identify with these characteristics. Being more religious, principled, or emotional did not affect the perception of respondents that they would intervene. Since all of the perception variables are on the same scale, the difference in the magnitude of the coefficients reveals that perception of self as more aggressive and sympathetic predicted intention to intervene better than perception of self as stronger than others.

Hypothesis six concerns the size of the perpetrator. We hypothesized that respondents would be more willing to intervene when the man was medium-sized.

A *t*-test for intervention by size of perpetrator showed no significant difference. However, it seems possible that the size of the perpetrator may be more important once the size of the respondent is controlled. Thus, we included sex, height, and weight of respondent and type of victim into a model which included size of perpetrator to predict intervention. In this more elaborate model, size of perpetrator again failed to achieve significance.

We gathered all the significant predictors concerning the respondent from Models 1 through 3 into a final model, Model 4 of Table 2. This allows us to see whether physical characteristics, life experiences, or self-assessments are the most important predictors of intention to intervene. When combined, the physical characteristics of height and weight become insignificant, although the perception of self as aggressive remains significant. Perception of self as strong is only marginally significant, while perception of self as sympathetic remains highly important. The type of victim by sex of respondent interaction remains significant and the pattern is still consistent with Figure 1. Women are significantly more likely to intervene on behalf of children than men are. The experience of breaking up fights remains a powerful predictor. Thus, the combination of characteristics of respondents that is most likely to lead to intervention is aggressiveness, sympathy, and experience breaking up fights. Additionally, men are most likely to help women, while women are most likely to help children. The combination of factors in Model 4 explains 16% of the variation on intention to intervene.

The last hypothesis is that if respondents know that the victim and abuser are related (abuser is the owner in the case of the dog), they will have a lower intention to intervene than if they are not sure of the relationship between them. A paired *t*-test between the respondent's intention to intervene before and after knowledge of the abuser-victim relationship did not reveal a significant difference. However, it seems quite likely that the impact of knowledge could differ by the sex of the respondent, the type of victim, or the combination of the two. We regressed the difference between the intention to intervene before and after knowledge of the abuser-victim relationship on sex of respondent, type of victim, and the interaction between them. The interaction was significant and the

FIGURE 2 / Change in Marginal Means in Intention to Intervene Knowing That the Abuser and Victim Are Family (owner for dogs)

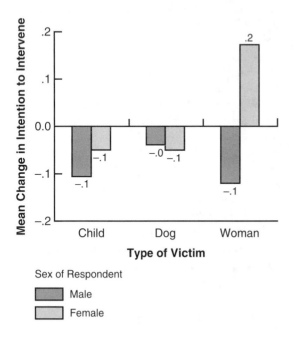

pattern is displayed in Figure 2. For male respondents, knowledge reduced the likelihood of intervention a small amount for all victims; for female respondents, knowledge reduced the likelihood of intervention for children and dogs, but increased the likelihood for women. One plausible interpretation is that women feel less fearful for themselves when intervening between a husband and wife than between a male abuser and a woman with whom his relationship is not known. Female respondents may fear that they could easily become a second victim in the latter case.

DISCUSSION

Our primary goal was to add to the bystander intervention literature by examining the differences in respondents' willingness to give aid to three different victims: a woman, a child, and a dog. We had hypothesized that people would be most willing to intervene on behalf of children since children are less able than adult women to defend themselves against an adult

male attacker. We assumed that the dog would have the least support for intervention because of the greater value placed on human than animal life. However, although the means for perceived intervention were in the expected direction (children highest, then women, then dogs), the closeness of the means (and lack of significance for the differences) was surprising. Several explanations are possible. One interpretation is that intent to intervene has more to do with the bystander than it does the victim. In other words, in a situation in which a person or a dog is being attacked, people who have the appropriate capacity and beliefs will report an intention to intervene, regardless of the victim. Another interpretation is that the norms regarding intervention are similar across victims. Bystanders must weigh the abusers' right to privacy against the victims' right for protection. Perhaps the point at which the abuser loses the right to privacy depends more upon the abuser's actions than the type of victim. The abuser's actions were identical in our scenarios.

An important finding is that the gender of the bystander interacts with the type of victim to predict intention to intervene. Men and women were equally likely to report an intention to intervene, but women were most likely to help children, while men were most likely to help women. As mentioned earlier, women's greater intention to help children rather than other women may reflect these respondents' perceptions that they would not be any better able to handle the attacker than the other woman, but do feel more powerful than children. This interpretation is strengthened by the finding that women are more likely to intervene on behalf of other women if they know that the abuser and victim are husband and wife. Female respondents may feel concerned for their own safety if they believe the abuser is attacking a woman who is not his wife.

The fact that men have a greater intention to intervene on behalf of women than children may reflect that men have an unclear role as protectors of other people's children. Our male college students probably have had limited contact with young children, as they are unlikely to be fathers at their age and young men are unlikely to work in day care centers or as babysitters. Perhaps this greater intention to help young women is simply a reflection of clearer norms about the appropriateness of male intervention on behalf of women than children when both are unknown to the man.

Huston et al. (1981) found that several measures of life skills (life saving, first aid, medical and police training), physical stature, and self-attributions of physical strength and aggressiveness were related to intention to intervene. However, those researchers used *t*-tests and other univariate analysis techniques and did not determine which factors were most relevant, controlling for others. In our final regression equation, we combined the best predictors from physical size, life experiences, and self-assessments of physical and personality traits, and found that controlling for other factors, perceptions of self as strong and aggressive were statistically significant while actual size was not. Experience breaking up fights was the only life experience that was an important predictor of intention to intervene, controlling for other factors. We found that people who rated themselves as more sympathetic than others were also significantly more likely to say that they would intervene on behalf of a victim. Thus, it is not simply factors related to competence of the bystander (experience breaking up fights, being stronger and more aggressive than others) which leads bystanders to intervene, but also being sympathetic to others.

Our interpretation that intent to intervene has more to do with the bystander than with the victim is consistent with Midlarsky's (1968) contention that intervention rests in part on the bystander's perception of the situation and on the bystander's competence. We also speculate that the norms regarding intervention may be similar across victims, which is consistent with Darley and Latane's (1970) argument that basic norms call for helping, and that not helping produces guilt feelings in bystanders. Moreover, we found that men and women evidently have different views of the "deservingness" of various victims, consistent with Howard and Crano's (1974) argument. Our finding that perceptions of the situation (including perceptions of one's capabilities) are more important than actual capabilities such as size of the bystander, reminds us of W. I. Thomas' famous dictum that what one perceives to be real *is* real in its consequences. Finally, bystanders' past experience in breaking up fights as an important predictor of intention to

intervene is congruent with Midlarsky's (1968) reminder of the three basic relevant components of that decision: the situation, the bystander's perception of it, and especially, the bystander's competence.

Our results must be interpreted with caution. First, we measured intention to intervene and did not observe actual intervention. Thus, we can only assume that the factors related to intention to intervene would be related to actual intervention. Second, our respondents were college students in a large public university and therefore our findings should not be generalized beyond a similar population. Our contribution to the literature is that we have compared intention to intervene across three types of victims and we have examined how the sex of the respondent interacts with the type of victim to impact the likelihood that she or he would intervene. By using multivariate statistical techniques we have been able to determine that controlling for other factors, respondents are most likely to believe that they would intervene if they perceive that they are stronger, more aggressive, and more sympathetic than others and if they have had experience breaking up fights. Further, men believe that they would be most likely to intervene on behalf of women, while women believe that they would be most likely to help children.

Using experimental designs of simulated emergency situations, researchers would be able to see whether the patterns of intention to intervene found in this study are repeated. Specifically, it would be useful to determine whether overall there is no difference in rates of intervention when the victim is a woman, child, or dog. Further, it would help our understanding of gender roles to determine whether women and men display different rates of intervention depending on whether the victim is a woman or child. Since our sample consisted of college students, it would also be useful to repeat this study with a more general population to determine whether intentions to intervene follow the same patterns among older adults and less well-educated adults.

REFERENCES

Amato, Paul R. 1990. "Personality and Social Network Involvement as Predictors of Helping Behavior in Everyday Life." *Social Psychology Quarterly* 53:31–43.

Berkowitz, Leonard. 1972. "Social Norms, Feelings, and Other Factors Affecting Helping and Altruism." In *Advances in Experimental Social Psychology,* p. 68 edited by L. Berkowitz. New York: Academic Press.

Bethke, T. M. and D. M. DeJoy. 1993. "An Experimental Study of Factors Influencing the Acceptability of Dating Violence." *Journal of Interpersonal Violence* 8:36–51.

Bickman, Leonard and Helen Hellwig. 1979. "Bystander Reporting of a Crime: The Impact of Incentives." *Criminology* 17:283–300.

Brigham, John C. 1986. *Social Psychology.* Boston: Little Brown.

Christy, Cathryn A. and Harrison Voight. 1994. "Bystander Responses to Public Episodes of Child Abuse." *Journal of Applied Social Psychology* 24:824–847.

Clark, Russell D. and Larry E. Word. 1972. "Why Don't Bystanders Help? Because of Ambiguity?" *Journal of Personality and Social Psychology* 24:392–400.

Clarkson, Petruska. 1987. "The Bystander Role." *Transactional Analysis Journal* 17:82–87.

Darley, John M. and Bibb Latane. 1968. "Norms and Normative Behavior: Field Studies of Social Interdependence." In *Altruism and Helping Behavior,* pp. 83–101 edited by L. Berkowitz. New York: Academic Press.

Davis, Phillip W. 1991. "Stranger Intervention into Child Punishment in Public Places." *Social Problems* 38:227–246.

Dovidio, John F. 1984. "Helping Behavior and Altruism: An Empirical and Conceptual Overview." *Advances in Experimental Social Psychology* 17:361–427.

Feld, Scott L. 1977. "The Rationality of Social Action, Applied to the Consequence of Group Size for Helping Behavior." *Sociological Review* 24:79–96.

Feld, Scott L. and Dawn Robinson. 1998. "Secondary Bystander Effects on Intimate Violence: When Norms of Restraint Reduce Deterrence." *Journal of Social and Personal Relationships* 15:277–285.

Flynn, Clifton P. 2000. "Why Family Professionals Can No Longer Ignore Violence Toward Animals." *Family Relations* 49:87–95.

Geis, Gilbert and Ted L. Huston. 1983. "Bystander Intervention into Crime: Public Policy Considerations." *Policy Studies Journal* 11:398–408.

Geis, Gilbert, Ted L. Huston, and Richard Wright. 1976. "Compensating Good Samaritans." *Crime Prevention Review* 5:28–35.

Howard, William and William D. Crano. 1974. "Effects of Sex, Conversation, Location, and Size of Observer Group on Bystander Intervention in a High Risk Situation." *Sociometry* 37:491–507.

Huston, Ted L. and Chuck Korte. 1976. "The Responsive Bystander: Why He Helps." In *Moral Development and Behavior: Theory, Research, and Social Issues,* pp. 269–283 edited by T. Likona. New York: Holt, Rinehart, and Winston.

Huston, Ted L., Mary Ruggiero, Ross Conner, and Gilbert Geis. 1981. "Bystander Intervention Into Crime: A Study Based on Naturally Occurring Episodes." *Social Psychology Quarterly* 14:14–23.

Kidd, Robert F. 1979. "Crime Reporting: Toward a Social Psychological Model." *Criminology* 17:380–394.

Latane, Bibb and John M. Darley. 1970. *The Unresponsive Bystander. Why Doesn't He Help?* Englewood Cliffs, NJ: Prentice-Hall.

Lerner, Melvin J. 1966. "'The Desire for Justice and Reactions to Victims." In *Altruism and Helping Behavior,* pp. 205–229 edited by L. Berkowitz. New York: Academic Press.

Masser, Barbara and Rupert Brown. 1996. "When Would You Do It? An Investigation into the Effects of Retaliation, Seriousness of Malpractice, and Occupation on Willingness to Blow the Whistle." *Journal of Community and Applied Social Psychiatry* 6:127–130.

Midlarsky, Elizabeth. 1968. "'Aiding Responses: An Analysis and Review." *Merrill-Palmer Quarterly* 14:229–260.

Ofshe, Richard and Kenneth Christman. 1986. "A Two-Process Theory of Social Behavior." In *Rationality and Collective Belief,* edited by Gerald M. Platt. Norwood, NJ: Ablex Publishing Company.

Piliavin, Irving M., Judith Rodin, and Jane A. Piliavin. 1969. "Good Samaritanism: An Underground Phenomenon?" *Journal of Personality and Social Psychology* 13:289–299.

Rabow, Jerome, Michael Newcomb, Martin Monto, and Anthony Hernandez. 1990. "Altruism in Drunk Driving Situations: Personal and Situational Factors in Intervention." *Social Psychology Quarterly* 59:199–213.

Rushton, J. P. 1980. *Altruism, Socialization, and Society.* Englewood Cliffs, NJ: Prentice-Hall.

Ryan, William. 1972. *Blaming the Victim.* New York: Vintage.

Schwartz, Shalom H. 1977. "Normative Influences in Altruism." In *Advances in Experimental Social Psychology,* pp. 222–280 edited by L. Berkowitz. New York: Academic Press.

Sheleff, Leon S. 1978. *The Bystander: Behavior, Law, Ethics.* Lexington, MA: D. C. Heath.

Smithson, Michael, Paul R. Amato, and Philip Pearce. 1983. *Dimensions of Helping Behavior.* New York: Pergamon Press.

Ungar, Sheldon. 1979. "The Effects of Effort and Stigma on Helping." *Journal of Social Psychology* 107:23–28.

U.S. Bureau of the Census. 1997. *Statistical Abstract of the United States 1977* (117th ed.). Washington, DC.

ENDNOTES

1. In a field experiment testing the impact of incentives on the likelihood of bystanders reporting a crime (finding that incentives were ineffective), Bickman and Helwig (1979) compared experimental results with preincident survey results and report that the only factor relating consistently to actual reporting behavior was attitude or "intention to report" a witnessed crime.

2. In that model, intervention depends on the bystander noticing the event, recognizing it as a serious situation calling for a response, deciding whether or not he or she has any personal responsibility in the situation, has the capacity to identify an effective form of intervention, and has the capability to undertake that intervention (Latane and Darley, 1970).

3. We do not review in detail the many studies that have focused on variations in the size of the bystander "group" and its effects (Latane and Darley 1970; Howard and Crano 1974; Darley and Latane 1968; Feld 1977).

4. However, Latane and Darley's work has been challenged by Huston and Korte (1976) who contend that bystander response may be more complex than Latane and Darley suggested (see also Geis, Huston, and Wright 1976). They argued that intervention may be not just a product of altruism but based on a desire to foment trouble or to mete out immediate punishment to the harm-doer. Intervening bystanders may also be risk takers for whom "violence and the potential of violence, is something with which they are on familiar and rather amiable terms . . . it is often primary anger toward the offender rather than concern for the victim which induces intervention" (Geis et al. 1976). Still, as Sheleff (1978) points out, "research has indicated a fairly widespread willingness to help, especially where there is no ambiguity as to the need of the victim, and minimal inconvenience as to the nature of the required intervention" (p. 19; See also Clark and Word 1972). Other scholars who disagree with Latane and Darley about the place of altruism in bystander motivation are Berkowitz 1972, Lerner 1966, and Schwartz 1977. Lerner, for instance, argues that belief in a just world leads to concern for the victim but that instances of apparently undeserved suffering threaten that belief. The bystander then has two alternatives: Aiding the victim or deciding that the victim deserves the suffering (which reduces the desire to give aid). Note the conjunction of this view with Ryan's (1972) discussion of victim-blaming.

5. We know of only one other study that examined responses to different victims. Ungar (1979) assessed the likelihood of intervention when a victim was stigmatized (wearing an eyepatch but not disabled) and when the same victim was not wearing an eyepatch.

6. Since our sample was not random, statistical significance tests are not appropriate for the purpose of inference to the population at large. However, we use and report them as a heuristic device to decide which differences are large enough to merit further attention.

CRITICAL THINKING QUESTIONS

1. This article examined *intentions* to help, not actual helping behavior. Do you think that people's stated intentions of behavior are predictive of how they actually do behave? Why or why not? Discuss the assumption stated in the article: "We do not assume that each respondent's report of how s/he would behave directly corresponds to how s/he would actually behave in real situations, but we do assume that variation on subjects' reports in response to variations in the experimental conditions reveals general tendencies of how their behavior would vary in response to similar variations in real situations."

2. Design a study to test the findings reported in this article, but use actual measures of helping behavior. What ethical concerns would need to be addressed in conducting such a study?

3. Besides those variables investigated in this study, what other factors may impact people's intentions to help? Explain why you think they may influence helping behavior.

4. In all of the conditions in this study, the abuser was a man. Do you think that it would make a difference if the abuser were a woman? Why or why not?

5. Have you personally witnessed any type of abuse in public? If so, what did you do about it and why? If you personally have not witnessed abuse, find someone who has and ask him or her the same questions. How do your experiences or those of another person relate to the findings presented in this article?

Chapter Eleven

AGGRESSION

Pick up a copy of today's newspaper. How much of it concerns acts of violence, whether from war, terrorism, homicide, or domestic violence? Aggression seems to be a fairly common part of modern life.

Now think about your own experiences. Chances are, you have not directly experienced a murder or assault. But what other types of aggressive behavior have you witnessed? Have you seen verbal aggression, where the intention was to hurt another person's feelings? Have you experienced cruelty in one form or another, where pain was experienced, even though no blood was shed?

Must aggression be part of life? Is it simply human nature and consequently something that cannot be changed? Or is it possible that the amount of aggression in the world could be reduced, if not actually eliminated?

Article 31, "Bad Girls," reports on an alarming trend in the last few years in which rates of female aggression are increasing dramatically—in some cases, nearly equaling those of males. This article suggests that it may no longer be warranted to think of aggression as a male tendency.

In contrast, Article 32, "Transmission of Aggression through Imitation of Aggressive Models," represents one of the earliest studies demonstrating that aggression is learned and in particular that the violence portrayed on television may contribute to aggressiveness in children. Since many behavioral patterns, such as aggression, may be learned in childhood, knowledge about what contributes to aggression can be used to help reduce those very behaviors.

Finally, Article 33 examines the role of the environment in provoking aggression. "Heat and Violence" examines the mounting evidence that high temperature may be a causative factor in aggression. In addition to examining the role of temperature in humanmade environments, such as inside buildings, the article also presents evidence that even a small rise in the outside temperature—such as a 2° rise in the earth's temperature due to global warming—may cause major increases in aggression and violence.

ARTICLE 31 _____

What causes aggression? Psychologists have asked that question for nearly a century now. In their search for an answer, several theoretical perspectives have emerged.

One such perspective holds that aggression is an innate tendency, something toward which people are biologically predisposed. This view, espoused by theorists such as Sigmund Freud, maintains that people periodically need to discharge a natural buildup of aggressive energy. Thus, human aggressiveness may be a normal and perhaps unavoidable fact of life.

A second view suggests that aggression is a drive to harm someone elicited by some external stimulus. In other words, certain external conditions, such as frustration, produce a tendency for people to want to harm or injure others.

Other theories of aggression maintain that aggressive behavior is purely the product of social learning. People are aggressive because they have *learned* how to be aggressive, perhaps by watching other people act in such a fashion.

If aggressive behavior is somehow a biological predisposition, we might expect a universal manifestation of its occurrence. For example, if males are naturally more aggressive than females, then this pattern should be relatively constant in varying cultures around the world. Furthermore, we might expect that the rates of aggression for males and females in a given culture would likewise be fairly constant, with males consistently acting more aggressively than females across different points in time.

Common-sense observations, as well as attention to media reports, certainly confirm the fact that men are more aggressive than women. Or are they? Perhaps male aggression is more likely to be noticed and reported than female aggression. Or maybe males are more likely to be punished than females who commit the same acts. The following article by Barry Yeoman presents strong evidence that the rates of female violence may be much higher than most people think. Moreover, the incidence of female aggression may be increasing at rates far exceeding those of males.

Bad Girls

■ Barry Yeoman

Sante Kimes doesn't exactly match the popular image of the career outlaw. A low-rent Elizabeth Taylor look-alike, the 64-year-old widow is partial to gaudy jewelry, thick perfume and towering black wigs, and to rid herself of her wattles, she got lipo-sculpture at a California clinic.

But beneath the big hair is a criminal whose rap sheet dates back almost four decades. In the mid-'80s, Kimes went to prison for enslaving a platoon of teen-age maids from Mexico City. The women were forced to work 18-hour days without weekend breaks, and Kimes kept them in line by beating them with coat hangers and throwing them into searing showers. When one young woman declined to strip for an inspection, according to court records and news reports, Kimes attacked her with a hot iron.

Then came the apparent murders, for which Kimes is a principal suspect. A banker vanished after a dinner appointment with her. A family friend was pulled out of a dumpster, a bullet in his head, after

Reprinted from *Psychology Today,* 1999 (November/December), *32*(6), 54–57, 71. Reprinted with permission from *Psychology Today* magazine. Copyright © 2001 (Sussex Publishers, Inc.).

expressing his reservations about a real-estate scam involving Kimes and her husband. And last summer, New Yorkers were shocked by the disappearance of 82-year-old Irene Silverman, a diminutive former ballerina who was the landlady of Kimes' son. The Kimeses were allegedly trying to defraud Silverman out of her $4 million mansion—and then the retired dancer turned up missing. Kimes claims she's innocent.

What makes this gruesome crime spree hard to grasp is that Kimes, a former pinup model, doesn't fit any of our ruffian archetypes: the L.A. gang member, the Mafia hit man, the young street punk. She's now at an age when many women are described as grandmotherly. Most significantly, she's a woman. "Woman is the creator and fosterer of life; man has been the mechanizer and destroyer of life," anthropologist Ashley Montagu once said. "Women love the human race; men are on the whole hostile to it."

But our cultural assumptions may be off the mark. Witness the proliferation of female perpetrators like Kimes making headlines. The tabloids had a field day with Lorena Bobbitt, who amputated the penis of her sleeping husband. She in turn was eclipsed by Susan Smith, who drowned her two sons in a South Carolina lake. More recently came the murder last May of former Saturday Night Live actor Phil Hartman by his wife Brynn, who then turned around and shot herself.

The increase in female violence over the past century has been dramatic. When Auburn University sociologist Penelope Hanke, Ph.D., reviewed records from an Alabama prison from 1929 to 1985, she discovered that 95% of the cases where women murdered strangers occurred after 1970, along with 60% of slayings of friends and relatives. In another study of 460 female murderers, Illinois State University's Ralph Weisheit, Ph.D., Distinguished Professor of criminal justice, found that women were becoming more stereotypically male in their reasons for murdering. He revealed that robbery-murders accounted for 42% of the cases in 1983, compared to 18% in 1940. And even though males commit the vast majority of street violence, females seem to be catching up. "In 10 or 20 years, those statistics should be equal," predicts Coramae Ritchey Mann, Ph.D., professor emerita of criminal justice at Indiana University.

The recent surge in crime among women illustrates that in spite of their stereotype as gentle nurturers, women have the natural capacity to be as violent as men, according to a growing number of experts. The difference, behavioral studies suggest, is that women need greater incentives to express that violence. Social changes over the years—especially the movement toward gender equality—have provided several.

Freda Adler, Ph.D., Distinguished Professor of criminal justice at Rutgers University, calls this the "liberation hypothesis." As the tightly constructed sex roles of previous years start to weaken, she says, women simply have more and more opportunities to break the law. "Women are more involved in what's going on in the world than they were a generation ago," she says. "You can't embezzle if you're not near funds. You can't get involved in a fight at the bar if you're not allowed in the bar."

VIOLENCE AT HOME

The most revolutionary discoveries about women and aggression involve violence toward loved ones. A preponderance of evidence shows that women can be just as ferocious as men. The most famous of these studies comes from Murray Straus, Ph.D., the founder and co-director of the University of New Hampshire's Family Research Laboratory. His National Family Violence Surveys, conducted in 1975 and 1985 with a total of 8,145 married and cohabiting couples, showed that 12.4% of women have assaulted their spouses, compared to 12.2% of men. When it comes to severe assaults, the numbers were 4.6% for women and 5% for men.

A 1999 study by the British Home Office, a government agency in the United Kingdom, found that 4.2% of men—the exact same figure as for women—had been assaulted by a partner in the previous year.

The patterns go back before marriage. Irene Frieze, Ph.D., remembers seeing studies that showed women to be more prone to violence in dating situations. "I didn't believe it," recalls Frieze, a professor of psychology and women's studies at the University of Pittsburgh. "I said, 'This can't be true. I'm going to do my own study.'" Sure enough, of the college students she

---

Really Bad Girls
The violence that made headlines

For Love or Money

From 1896 to 1908, Belle Gunness killed between 16 and 49 people, including her step-daughter, hired hands, lovers and husbands. When her homestead mysteriously burned in 1908, officials unearthed the bodies of 10 men and two women. Gunness escaped.

Sinister Sisters

"Sister Amy" Gilligan charged new patients $1,000 upon entry into the Archer Home for Elderly and Indigent Persons in Windsor, Connecticut, and then promptly dispatched them with arsenic, often tricking them into leaving her their insurance money. Arrested in 1916, Gilligan may have killed as many as 40 people in her care.

Angel Makers

Between 1911 and 1929, the Hungarian towns of Nagyrev and Tiszakurt saw the deaths of more than 100 people at the hands of women, led by village midwife Susanna Fazekas. She would boil flypaper and distribute the resulting poison to the women. Thirty-four women were put on trial; 18 went to prison; eight were executed. Fazekas killed herself with poison.

Brutal Brothel

For 10 years, sisters Delfine and Maria Gonzales ran a brothel on a ranch in central Mexico, torturing girls who resisted and killing those who fell ill, tried to run away or lost their looks. When police raided the ranch in 1964, the bodies of some 80 women were found buried, along with countless babies and 11 male migrant workers.

Smother Love

Over 13 years, Marybeth Tining killed nine of her own children while authorities held that the deaths were natural. "I smothered them each with a pillow," she said later, "because I'm not a good mother." In 1987, she was sentenced to 20 years to life, her husband still believing she was innocent.

Angel of Death

Waltraud Wagner used lethal injections, strangulation or drowning to kill between 49 and 300 elderly patients in an Austrian hospital in the mid-1980s. Wagner's motive, as one of her three conspirators put it: "The ones who got on my nerves were dispatched directly to a free bed with the good Lord." All four were sent to prison.

—*Sarah Blustain*

---

surveyed, 58% of women had assaulted their dates, compared to 55% of men.

When Frieze brought up her findings in her classes, the students weren't surprised. "One woman said, 'Well, it makes me feel strong and powerful when I hit my boyfriend.' They feel safe—that they can get away with this behavior—because the men have this moral code and they'll never strike back." The men, Frieze adds, don't take the violence seriously, because little of it causes serious injuries.

Straus admits that when it comes to the most brutal domestic assaults, the domain is still men's—they commit six times the number women do. "If by violence, you mean 'who's injured?,' then it's an overwhelmingly male crime," he says. That's why there's no great demand for battered men's shelters, and why a disproportionate number of wife beatings get reported to the police.

"You can't just equate numbers," says Ruth Brandwein, Ph.D., a social policy professor at the

State University of New York at Stony Brook. "Women who engage in violence are often already in violent relationships. They are living under such unbearable tension that it gives them some control over when they're going to be abused."

VIOLENCE ON THE STREET

Except for high profile lawbreakers like Aileen Wuornos, the Florida prostitute who robbed and killed at least seven of her johns, most of the crime news involves male perpetrators. If a woman is involved, she's generally considered an accomplice to a man. When Bonnie and Clyde were killed in the 1930s, the *New York Times* headline read, "Barrow and woman slain in Louisiana trap!" Even Karla Faye Tucker, executed in Texas last year for a pickax slaying, was working in concert with her boyfriend.

According to the FBI's Uniform Crime Report, women made up only 15% of all those arrested for violent crimes in 1996, but the gap is closing. The statistics show that arrests of women for violent crimes increased 90% between 1985 and 1994, compared to 43% for men. The numbers hold up across many specific crimes: aggravated assault, other assault, and sex offenses other than rape and prostitution. Only in the case of murder did men widen their lead: a 13% rise for men compared to a 4% drop for women.

Indiana University's Mann believes that crime statistics are only now starting to catch up with reality. "Women are just as violent as men, and were often just getting away with the violence," she says.

"Now, with equal rights, the justice system is looking at females differently," explains Mann. "Whereas before they were excused or overlooked, now they are being apprehended."

A criminal defense lawyer admitted, "If she hasn't committed murder and she has children at home, she walks." A judge confided, "It's difficult to send a mature woman to prison. I keep thinking, 'Hey! She is somebody's mother!'"

Frank Julian, J.D., a professor of legal studies at Murray State University in Kentucky, cites a Florida-based study showing that men were 23% more likely to be imprisoned than women who committed the same crime, partly because of the sentencing recommendations of the probation officers. "Women offenders were often viewed as suffering from psychological or emotional problems, or as victims of family problems, bad marriages or dependent relationships," Julian writes. "Men were more likely to have their cases judged in view of the seriousness of the offense committed, employment history and prior record."

IS VIOLENCE IN THE GENES?

In the 1960s, famed psychologist Albert Bandura conducted a series of experiments in which children watched adult models hitting inflatable Bobo dolls. The children were then offered the opportunity to imitate the behavior. Under normal circumstances, the boys knocked down the dolls far more often than the girls did. But when the models got rewarded for knocking down the Bobos, the children's behavior, changed—the boys and girls became almost equally aggressive.

That seems to suggest that males are innately more violent than females—but that women will resort to aggression when given an incentive. Which makes sense to Brenda Shook, Ph.D., a biological psychologist at Union Institute in Sacramento. "Females of all species will go to great lengths, including violence, to protect the young," says Shook. But among humans, the primary responsibility for defending the family—and thus preserving the family genes—went to the male.

But both biological and cultural theories of women's innate capacity for violence hinge on one major trigger. Says Freda Adler: "We're talking about socialization." And for time immemorial, males have been conditioned to be aggressive. Boys got G.I. Joes; girls got Barbies. Men were sent off to war; women bandaged their wounds.

But American girls have always gotten mixed messages. Our culture rewards a certain type of violence in women. "It is the height of femininity to slap a man's face," says Murray Straus. "It's drilled into them."

The groundwork for female violence, it seems, has been there all along. But what may have been a subtler message in a more genteel society has become a clearer directive. The media increasingly promote female violence: Weapon-wielding women are becoming commonplace in everything from Hollywood movies to Saturday morning cartoons.

Women also absorb the cultural norms aimed at everyone, and "this is a violent country," says Coramae Ritchey Mann. "There's no reason this wouldn't have rubbed off on them."

READ MORE ABOUT IT

When She Was Bad: Violent Women and the Myth of Innocence, Patricia Pearson (Viking, 1997).

Abused Men: The Hidden Side of Domestic Violence, Philip W. Cook (Praeger, 1997).

CRITICAL THINKING QUESTIONS

1. Interview someone who has worked or volunteered in a women's shelter. How does his or her report of the role of female aggression in domestic relationships confirm or differ from the information presented in the article?

2. Are "role models" of violent females more prevalent in the media today than they were 20 years ago? To test your hypothesis, sample four or five contemporary films as well as some released two decades ago.

3. Discuss the so-called liberation hypothesis discussed in the article. Develop your own list of reasons that may account for the increase in female aggression in recent years.

4. The article notes that women who commit the same aggressive acts as men may be less likely to be sentenced. What factors other than the actual crime may influence sentencing decisions? Explain your answers.

5. Survey your friends or fellow students regarding the use of aggression by males and females in dating relationships. Do you find results similar to those reported in the article? Explain.

ARTICLE 32 _____

Think of the amount of time that a typical child spends in front of the television. Do you think that what that child sees on "the tube" influences his or her behavior to a great extent? Or is television more neutral—just entertainment with no lasting effects?

A major concern of parents and social psychologists alike is the impact of one particular aspect of television on children's subsequent behavior: aggression. If you have not done so in a long time, sit down and watch the Saturday morning cartoons or other programs shown after school or in the early evening, when children are most likely to be watching. How many of these programs involve some sort of violence? What are these shows teaching children, not only in terms of behaviors but also in terms of values?

The following article by Albert Bandura, Dorothea Ross, and Sheila A. Ross was one of the earliest studies to examine the impact of televised aggression on the behavior of children. In the more than 30 years since its publication, numerous other experiments have been conducted on the same topic. Article 31 provided some of the more recent evidence for the connection between children's viewing television violence and subsequently displaying aggressive behavior. Many additional studies also strongly suggest that viewing televised aggression has a direct impact on the aggressive behavior of its viewers. The research by Bandura and his colleagues helped initiate this important line of research.

Transmission of Aggression through Imitation of Aggressive Models[1]

■ Albert Bandura, Dorothea Ross, and Sheila A. Ross[2]

A previous study, designed to account for the phenomenon of identification in terms of incidental learning, demonstrated that children readily imitated behavior exhibited by an adult model in the presence of the model (Bandura & Huston, 1961). A series of experiments by Blake (1958) and others (Grosser, Polansky, & Lippitt, 1951; Rosenblith, 1959; Schachter & Hall, 1952) have likewise shown that mere observation of responses of a model has a facilitating effect on subjects' reactions in the immediate social influence setting.

While these studies provide convincing evidence for the influence and control exerted on others by the behavior of a model, a more crucial test of imitative learning involves the generalization of imitative response patterns to new settings in which the model is absent.

In the experiment reported in this paper, children were exposed to aggressive and nonaggressive adult models and were then tested for amount of imitative learning in a new situation in the absence of the model. According to the prediction, subjects exposed to aggressive models would reproduce aggressive acts resembling those of their models and would differ in this respect both from subjects who observed nonaggressive models and from who had no prior exposure to any models. This hypothesis assumed that subjects had learned imitative habits as a result of prior reinforcement, and these tendencies would generalize to some extent to adult experimenters (Miller & Dollard, 1941).

It was further predicted that observation of subdued nonaggressive models would have a generalized inhibiting effect on the subjects' subsequent behavior,

Reprinted from *Journal of Abnormal and Social Psychology*, 1961, *63*, 575–583.

and this effect would be reflected in a difference between the nonaggressive and the control groups, with subjects in the latter group displaying significantly more aggression.

Hypotheses were also advanced concerning the influence of the sex of model and sex of subjects on imitation. Fauls and Smith (1956) have shown that preschool children perceive their parents as having distinct preferences regarding sex appropriate modes of behavior for their children. Their findings, as well as informal observation, suggest that parents reward imitation of sex appropriate behavior and discourage or punish sex inappropriate imitative responses, e.g., a male child is unlikely to receive much reward for performing female appropriate activities, such as cooking, or for adopting other aspects of the maternal role, but these same behaviors are typically welcomed if performed by females. As a result of differing reinforcement histories, tendencies to imitate male and female models thus acquire differential habit strength. One would expect, on this basis, subjects to imitate the behavior of a same-sex model to a greater degree than a model of the opposite sex.

Since aggression, however, is a highly masculine-typed behavior, boys should be more predisposed than girls toward imitating aggression, the difference being most marked for subjects exposed to the male aggressive model.

METHOD

Subjects

The subjects were 36 boys and 36 girls enrolled in the Stanford University Nursery School. They ranged in age from 37 to 69 months, with a mean age of 52 months.

Two adults, a male and a female, served in the role of model, and one female experimenter conducted the study for all 72 children.

Experimental Design

Subjects were divided into eight experimental groups of six subjects each and a control group consisting of 24 subjects. Half the experimental subjects were exposed to aggressive models and half were exposed to models that were subdued and nonaggressive in their behavior. These groups were further subdivided into male and female subjects. Half the subjects in the aggressive and nonaggressive conditions observed same-sex models, while the remaining subjects in each group viewed models of the opposite sex. The control group had no prior exposure to the adult models and was tested only in the generalization situation.

It seemed reasonable to expect that the subjects' level of aggressiveness would be positively related to the readiness with which they imitated aggressive modes of behavior. Therefore, in order to increase the precision of treatment comparisons, subjects in the experimental and control groups were matched individually on the basis of ratings of their aggressive behavior in social interactions in the nursery school.

The subjects were rated on four five-point rating scales by the experimenter and a nursery school teacher, both of whom were well acquainted with the children. These scales measured the extent to which subjects displayed physical aggression, verbal aggression, aggression toward inanimate objects, and aggressive inhibition. The latter scale, which dealt with the subjects' tendency to inhibit aggressive reactions in the face of high instigation, provided a measure of aggression anxiety.

Fifty-one subjects were rated independently by both judges so as to permit an assessment of interrater agreement. The reliability of the composite aggression score, estimated by means of the Pearson product-moment correlation, was .89.

The composite score was obtained by summing the ratings on the four aggression scales; on the basis of these scores, subjects were arranged in triplets and assigned at random to one of two treatment conditions or to the control group.

Experimental Conditions

In the first step in the procedure subjects were brought individually by the experimenter to the experimental room and the model who was in the hallway outside the room was invited by the experimenter to come and join in the game. The experimenter then escorted the subject to one corner of the room, which was structured as the subject's play area. After seating the child at a small table, the experimenter demonstrated how the subject could design pictures with potato prints and picture stickers provided. The potato prints included a variety of geometrical forms; the stickers were attractive multicolor pictures of animals, flowers, and western figures to be pasted on a pastoral scene. These activities were selected since they had been established, by previous studies in the nursery school, as having high interest value for the children.

After having settled the subject in his corner, the experimenter escorted the model to the opposite corner of the room which contained a small table and chair, a tinker toy set, a mallet, and a 5-foot inflated Bobo doll. The experimenter explained that these were the materials provided for the model to play with and, after the model was seated, the experimenter left the experimental room.

With subjects in the *nonaggressive condition,* the model assembled the tinker toys in a quiet subdued manner totally ignoring the Bobo doll.

In contrast, with subjects in the *aggressive condition,* the model began by assembling the tinker toys but after approximately a minute had elapsed, the model turned to the Bobo doll and spent the remainder of the period aggressing toward it.

Imitative learning can be clearly demonstrated if a model performs sufficiently novel patterns of responses which are unlikely to occur independently of the observation of the behavior of a model and if a subject reproduces these behaviors in substantially identical form. For this reason, in addition to punching the Bobo doll, a response that is likely to be performed by children independently of a demonstration, the model exhibited distinctive aggressive acts which were to be scored as imitative responses. The model laid Bobo on its side, sat on it and punched it repeatedly in the nose. The model then raised the Bobo doll, picked up the mallet and struck the doll on the head. Following the mallet aggression, the model tossed the doll up in the air aggressively and kicked it about the room. This sequence of physically aggressive acts was repeated approximately three times, interspersed with verbally aggressive responses such as "Sock him in the nose . . . ," "Hit him down . . . ," "Throw him in the air . . . ," "Kick him . . . ," "Pow . . . ," and two nonaggressive comments, "He keeps coming back for more" and "He sure is a tough fella."

Thus in the exposure situation, subjects were provided with a diverting task which occupied their attention while at the same time insured observation of the model's behavior in the absence of any instructions to observe or to learn the responses in question. Since subjects could not perform the model's aggressive behavior, any learning that occurred was purely on an observational or covert basis.

At the end of 10 minutes, the experimenter entered the room, informed the subject that he would now go to another game room, and bid the model goodbye.

AGGRESSION AROUSAL

Subjects were tested for the amount of imitative learning in a different experimental room that was set off from the main nursery school building. The two experimental situations were thus clearly differentiated; in fact, many subjects were under the impression that they were no longer on the nursery school grounds.

Prior to the test for imitation, however, all subjects, experimental and control, were subjected to mild aggression arousal to insure that they were under some degree of instigation to aggression. The arousal experience was included for two main reasons. In the first place, observation of aggressive behavior exhibited by others tends to reduce the probability of aggression on the part of the observer (Rosenbaum & deCharms, 1960). Consequently, subjects in the aggressive condition, in relation both to the nonaggressive and control groups, would be under weaker instigation following exposure to the models. Second, if subjects in the nonaggressive condition expressed little aggression in the face of appropriate instigation, the presence of an inhibitory process would seem to be indicated.

Following the exposure experience, therefore, the experimenter brought the subject to an anteroom that contained these relatively attractive toys: a fire engine, a locomotive, a jet fighter plane, a cable car, a colorful spinning top, and a doll set complete with wardrobe, doll carriage, and baby crib. The experimenter explained that the toys were for the subject to play with but, as soon as the subject became sufficiently involved with the play material (usually in about 2 minutes), the experimenter remarked that these were her very best toys, that she did not let just anyone play with them, and that she had decided to reserve these toys for the other children. However, the subject could play with any of the toys that were in the next room. The experimenter and the subject then entered the adjoining experimental room.

It was necessary for the experimenter to remain in the room during the experimental session; otherwise a number of the children would either refuse to remain alone or would leave before the termination of the session. However, in order to minimize any influence her presence might have on the subject's behavior, the experimenter remained as inconspicuous as possible by busying herself with paper work at a desk in the far corner of the room and avoiding any interaction with the child.

Test for Delayed Imitation

The experimental room contained a variety of toys including some that could be used in imitative or nonimitative aggression, and others that tended to elicit predominantly nonaggressive forms of behavior. The aggressive toys included a 3-foot Bobo doll, a mallet and peg board, two dart guns, and a tether ball with a face painted on it which hung from the ceiling. The nonaggressive toys, on the other hand, included a tea set, crayons and coloring paper, a ball, two dolls, three bears, cars and trucks, and plastic farm animals.

In order to eliminate any variation in behavior due to mere placement of the toys in the room, the play material was arranged in a fixed order for each of the sessions.

The subject spent 20 minutes in this experimental room during which time his behavior was rated in terms of predetermined response categories by judges who observed the session through a one-way mirror in an adjoining observation room. The 20-minute session was divided into 5-second intervals by means of an electric interval timer, thus yielding a total number of 240 response units for each subject.

The male model scored the experimental sessions for all 72 children. Except for the cases in which he served as model, he did not have knowledge of the subjects' group assignments. In order to provide an estimate of interscorer agreement, the performances of half the subjects were also scored independently by a second observer. Thus one or the other of the two observers usually had no knowledge of the conditions to which the subjects were assigned. Since, however, all but two of the subjects in the aggressive condition performed the models' novel aggressive responses while subjects in the other conditions only rarely exhibited such reactions, subjects who were exposed to the aggressive models could be readily identified through their distinctive behavior.

The responses scored involved highly specific concrete classes of behavior and yielded high interscorer reliabilities, the product-moment coefficients being in the .90s.

Response Measures

Three measures of imitation were obtained:

Imitation of physical aggression: This category included acts of striking the Bobo doll with the mallet, sitting on the doll and punching it in the nose, kicking the doll, and tossing it in the air.

Imitative verbal aggression: Subject repeats the phrases, "Sock him," "Hit him down," "Kick him," "Throw him in the air," or "Pow."

Imitative nonaggressive verbal responses: Subject repeats, "He keeps coming back for more," or "He sure is a tough fella."

During the pretest, a number of the subjects imitated the essential components of the model's behavior but did not perform the complete act, or they directed the imitative aggressive response to some object other than the Bobo doll. Two responses of this type were therefore scored and were interpreted as partially imitative behavior.

Mallet aggression: Subject strikes objects other than the Bobo doll aggressively with the mallet.

Sits on the Bobo doll: Subject lays the Bobo doll on its side and sits on it, but does not aggress toward it.

The following additional nonimitative aggressive responses were scored:

Punched Bobo doll: Subject strikes, slaps, or pushes the doll aggressively.

Nonimitative physical and verbal aggression: This category included physically aggressive acts directed toward objects other than the Bobo doll and any hostile remarks except for those in the verbal imitation category; e.g., "Shoot the Bobo," "Cut him," "Stupid ball," "Knock over people," "Horses fighting, biting."

Aggressive gun play: Subject shoots darts or aims the guns and fires imaginary shots at objects in the room.

Ratings were also made of the number of behavior units in which subjects played nonaggressively or sat quietly and did not play with any of the material at all.

RESULT

Complete Imitation of Models' Behavior

Subjects in the aggression condition reproduced a good deal of physical and verbal aggressive behavior resembling that of the models, and their mean scores differed markedly from those of subjects in the nonaggressive and control groups who exhibited virtually no imitative aggression (see Table 1).

Since there were only a few scores for subjects in the nonaggressive and control conditions (approximately 70% of the subjects had zero scores), and the assumption of homogeneity of variance could not be made, the Friedman two-way analysis of variance by ranks was employed to test the significance of the obtained differences.

The prediction that exposure of subjects to aggressive models increases the probability of aggressive behavior is clearly confirmed (see Table 2). The main effect of treatment conditions is highly significant both for physical and verbal imitative aggression. Comparison of pairs of scores by the sign test shows that the obtained over-all differences were due almost entirely to the aggression displayed by subjects who had been exposed to the aggressive models. Their scores were significantly higher than those of either the nonaggressive or control groups, which did not differ from each other (Table 2).

Imitation was not confined to the model's aggressive responses. Approximately one-third of the subjects in the aggressive condition also repeated the model's nonaggressive verbal responses while none of the subjects in either the nonaggressive or control groups made such remarks. This difference, tested by means of the Cochran Q test, was significant well beyond the .001 level (Table 2).

Partial Imitation of Models' Behavior

Differences in the predicted direction were also obtained on the two measures of partial imitation.

Analysis of variance of scores based on the subjects' use of the mallet aggressively toward objects other than the Bobo doll reveals that treatment conditions are a statistically significant course of variation (Table 2). In addition, individual sign tests show that both the aggressive and the control groups, relative to subjects in the nonaggressive condition, produced significantly more mallet aggression, the difference being particularly marked with regard to female subjects. Girls who observed nonaggressive models performed a mean number of 0.5 mallet aggression responses as compared to mean values of 18.0 and 13.1 for girls in the aggressive and control groups, respectively.

Although subjects who observed aggressive models performed more mallet aggression ($M = 20.0$) than their controls ($M = 13. 3$), the difference was not statistically significant.

With respect to the partially imitative response of sitting on the Bobo doll, the over-all group differences were significant beyond the .01 level (Table 2). Comparison of pairs of scores by the sign test procedure reveals that subjects in the aggressive group reproduced this aspect of the models' behavior to a greater extent than did the nonaggressive ($p = .018$) or the control ($p = .059$) subjects. The latter two groups, on the other hand, did not differ from each other.

Nonimitative Aggression

Analyses of variance of the remaining aggression measures (Table 2) show that treatment conditions did not influence the extent to which subjects engaged in aggressive gun play or punched the Bobo doll. The effect of conditions is highly significant ($\chi^2 r = 8.96$, $p < .02$), however, in the case of the subjects' expression of nominative physical and verbal aggression. Further comparison of treatment pairs reveals that the main

TABLE 1 / Mean Aggression Scores for Experimental and Control Subjects

| | Experimental Groups | | | | |
| | Aggressive | | Nonaggressive | | |
Response Category	F Model	M Model	F Model	M Model	Control Groups
Imitative physical aggression					
Female subjects	5.5	7.2	2.5	0.0	1.2
Male subjects	12.4	25.8	0.2	1.5	2.0
Imitative verbal aggression					
Female subjects	13.7	2.0	0.3	0.0	0.7
Male subjects	4.3	12.7	1.1	0.0	1.7
Mallet aggression					
Female subjects	17.2	18.7	0.5	0.5	13.1
Male subjects	15.5	28.8	18.7	6.7	13.5
Punches Bobo doll					
Female subjects	6.3	16.5	5.8	4.3	11.7
Male subjects	18.9	11.9	15.6	14.8	15.7
Nonimitative aggression					
Female subjects	21.3	8.4	7.2	1.4	6.1
Male subjects	16.2	36.7	26.1	22.3	24.6
Aggressive gun play					
Female subjects	1.8	4.5	2.6	2.5	3.7
Male subjects	7.3	15.9	8.9	16.7	14.3

source of the over-all difference was the aggressive and nonaggressive groups which differed significantly from each other (Table 2), with subjects exposed to the aggressive models displaying the greater amount of aggression.

Influence of Sex of Model and Sex of Subjects on Imitation

The hypothesis that boys are more prone than girls to imitate aggression exhibited by a model was only partially confirmed. t tests computed for subjects in the aggressive condition reveal that boys reproduced more imitative physical aggression than girls ($t = 2.50$, $p < .01$). The groups do not differ, however, in their imitation of verbal aggression.

The use of nonparametric tests, necessitated by the extremely skewed distributions of scores for subjects in the nonaggressive and control conditions, preclude

an over-all test of the influence of sex of model per se, and of the various interactions between the main effects. Inspection of the means presented in Table 1 for subjects in the aggression condition, however, clearly suggests the possibility of a Sex × Model interaction. This interaction effect is much more consistent and pronounced for the male model than for the female model. Male subjects, for example, exhibited more physical ($t = 2.07$, $p < .05$) and verbal imitative aggression ($t = 2.51$, $p < .05$), more nonimitative aggression ($t = 3.15$, $p < .025$), and engaged in significantly more aggressive gun play ($t = 2.12$, $p < .05$) following exposure to the aggressive male model than the female subjects. In contrast, girls exposed to the female model performed considerably more imitative verbal aggression and more nonimitative aggression than did the boys (Table 1). The variances, however, were equally large and with only a small N in each cell the mean differences did not reach statistical significance.

TABLE 2 / Significance of the Differences between Experimental and Control Groups in the Expression of Aggressive

Response Category	χ^2_r	Q	P	Comparison of Pairs of Treatment Conditions		
				Aggressive vs. Nonaggressive p	Aggressive vs. Control p	Nonaggressive vs. Control p
Imitative responses						
Physical aggression	27.17		< .001	< .001	< .001	.09
Verbal aggression	9.17		< .02	.004	.048	.09
Nonaggressive verbal responses		17.50	< .001	.004	.004	ns
Partial imitation						
Mallet aggression	11.06		< .01	.026	ns	.005
Sits on Bobo		13.44	< .01	.018	.059	ns
Nonimitative aggression						
Punches Bobo doll	2.87		ns			
Physical and verbal	8.96		< .02	.026	ns	ns
Aggressive gun play	2.75		ns			

Note: ns = nonsignificant.

Data for the nonaggressive and control subjects provide additional suggestive evidence that the behavior of the male model exerted a greater influence than the female model on the subjects' behavior in the generalization situation.

It will be recalled that, except for the greater amount of mallet aggression exhibited by the control subjects, no significant differences were obtained between the nonaggressive and control groups. The data indicate, however, that the absence of significant differences between these two groups was due primarily to the fact that subjects exposed to the nonaggressive female model did not differ from the controls on any of the measures of aggression. With respect to the male model, on the other hand, the differences between the groups are striking. Comparison of the sets of scores by means of the sign test reveals that, in relation to the control group, subjects exposed to the nonaggressive male model performed significantly less imitative physical aggression ($p = .06$), less imitative verbal aggression ($p = .002$), less mallet aggression ($p = .003$), less nonimitative physical and verbal aggression ($p = .03$) and they were less inclined to punch the Bobo doll ($p = .07$).

While the comparison of subgroups, when some of the over-all tests do not reach statistical significance, is likely to capitalize on chance differences, nevertheless the consistency of the findings adds support to the interpretation in terms of influence by the model.

Nonaggressive Behavior

With the exception of expected sex differences, Lindquist (1956) Type III analyses of variance of the nonaggressive response scores yielded few significant differences.

Female subjects spent more time than boys playing with dolls ($p < .001$), with the tea set ($p < .001$), and coloring ($p < .05$). The boys, on the other hand, devoted significantly more time than the girls to exploratory play with the guns ($p < .01$). No sex differences were found in respect to the subjects' use of the other stimulus objects, i.e., farm animals, cars, or tether ball.

Treatment conditions did produce significant differences on two measures of nonaggressive behavior that are worth mentioning. Subjects in the nonaggressive condition engaged in significantly more nonaggressive play with dolls than either subjects in the aggressive group ($t = 2.67$, $p < .02$), or in the control group ($t = 2.57$, $p < .02$).

Even more noteworthy is the finding that subjects who observed nonaggressive models spent more than twice as much time as subjects in aggressive condition ($t = 3.07$, $p < .01$) in simply sitting quietly without handling any of the play material.

DISCUSSION

Much current research on social learning is focused on the shaping of new behavior through rewarding and punishing consequences. Unless responses are emitted, however, they cannot be influenced. The results of this study provide strong evidence that observation of cues produced by the behavior of others is one effective means of eliciting certain forms of responses for which the original probability is very low or zero. Indeed, social imitation may hasten or short-cut the acquisition of new behaviors without the necessity of reinforcing successive approximations as suggested by Skinner (1953).

Thus subjects given an opportunity to observe aggressive models later reproduced a good deal of physical and verbal aggression (as well as nonaggressive responses) substantially identical with that of the model. In contrast, subjects who were exposed to nonaggressive models and those who had no previous exposure to any models only rarely performed such responses.

To the extent that observation of adult models displaying aggression communicates permissiveness for aggressive behavior, such exposure may serve to weaken inhibitory responses and thereby to increase the probability of aggressive reactions to subsequent frustrations. The fact, however, that subjects expressed their aggression in ways that clearly resembled the novel patterns exhibited by the models provides striking evidence for the occurrence of learning by imitation.

In the procedure employed by Miller and Dollard (1941) for establishing imitative behavior, adult or peer models performed discrimination responses following which they were consistently rewarded, and the subjects were similarly reinforced whenever they matched the leaders' choice responses. While these experiments have been widely accepted as demonstrations of learning by means of imitation, in fact, they simply involve a special case of discrimination learning in which the behavior of others serves as discriminative stimuli for responses that are already part of the subject's repertoire. Auditory or visual environmental cues could easily have been substituted for the social stimuli to facilitate the discrimination learning. In contrast, the process of imitation studied in the present experiment differed in several important respects from the one investigated by Miller and Dollard in that subjects learned to combine fractional responses into relatively complex novel patterns solely by observing the performance of social models without any opportunity to perform the models' behavior in the exposure setting, and without any reinforcers delivered either to the models or to the observers.

An adequate theory of the mechanisms underlying imitative learning is lacking. The explanations that have been offered (Logan, Olmsted, Rosner, Schwartz, & Stevens, 1955; Maccoby, 1959) assume that the imitator performs the model's responses covertly. If it can be assumed additionally that rewards and punishments are self-administered in conjunction with the covert responses, the process of imitative learning could be accounted for in terms of the same principles that govern instrumental trial-and-error learning. In the early stages of the developmental process, however, the range of component responses in the organism's repertoire is probably increased through a process of classical conditioning (Bandura & Huston, 1961; Mowrer, 1950).

The data provide some evidence that the male model influenced the subjects' behavior outside the exposure setting to a greater extent than was true for the female model. In the analyses of the Sex × Model interactions, for example, only the comparisons involving the male model yielded significant differences. Similarly, subjects exposed to the nonaggressive male model performed less aggressive behavior than the controls, whereas comparisons involving the female model were consistently nonsignificant.

In a study of learning by imitation, Rosenblith (1959) has likewise found male experimenters more effective than females in influencing children's behavior. Rosenblith advanced the tentative explanation that the school setting may involve some social deprivation in respect to adult males which, in turn, enhances the male's reward value.

The trends in the data yielded by the present study suggest an alternative explanation. In the case of a highly masculine-typed behavior such as physical aggression, there is a tendency for both male and female subjects to imitate the male model to a greater degree than the female model. On the other hand, in the case of verbal aggression, which is less clearly sex linked, the greatest amount of imitation occurs in relation to the same-sex model. These trends together with the finding that boys in relation to girls are in general more imitative of physical aggression but do not differ in imitation of verbal aggression, suggest that subjects may be differentially affected by the sex of the model but that predictions must take into account the degree to which the behavior in question is sex-typed.

The preceding discussion has assumed that maleness-femaleness rather than some other personal characteristics of the particular models involved, is the significant variable—an assumption that cannot be tested directly with the data at hand. It was clearly evident, however, particularly from boys' spontaneous remarks about the display of aggression by the female model, that some subjects at least were responding in terms of a sex discrimination and their prior learning about what is sex appropriate behavior (e.g., "Who is that lady? That's not the way for a lady to behave. Ladies are supposed to act like ladies. . . ." "You should have seen what that girl did in there. She was just acting like a man. I never saw a girl act like that before. She was punching and fighting but not swearing."). Aggression by the male model, on the other hand, was more likely to be seen as appropriate and approved by both the boys ("Al's a good socker, he beat up Bobo. I want to sock like Al.") and the girls ("That man is a strong fighter, he punched and punched and he could hit Bobo right down to the floor and if Bobo got up he said, 'Punch your nose.' He's a good fighter like Daddy.").

The finding that subjects exposed to the quiet models were more inhibited and unresponsive than subjects in the aggressive condition, together with the obtained difference on the aggression measures, suggests that exposure to inhibited models not only decreases the probability of occurrence of aggressive behavior but also generally restricts the range of behavior emitted by the subjects.

"Identification with aggressor" (Freud, 1946) or "defensive identification" (Mowrer, 1950), whereby a person presumably transforms himself from object to agent of aggression by adopting the attributes of an aggressive threatening model so as to allay anxiety, is widely accepted as an explanation of the imitative learning of aggression.

The development of aggressive modes of response by children of aggressively punitive adults, however, may simply reflect object displacement without involving any such mechanism of defensive identification. In studies of child training antecedents of aggressively antisocial adolescents (Bandura & Walters, 1959) and of young hyperaggressive boys (Bandura, 1960), the parents were found to be nonpermissive and punitive of aggression directed toward themselves. On the other hand, they actively encouraged and reinforced their sons' aggression toward persons outside the home. This pattern of differential reinforcement of aggressive behavior served to inhibit the boys' aggression toward the original instigators and fostered the displacement of aggression toward objects and situations eliciting much weaker inhibitory responses.

Moreover, the findings from an earlier study (Bandura & Huston, 1961), in which children imitated to an equal degree aggression exhibited by a nurturant and a nonnurturant model, together with the results of the present experiment in which subjects readily imitated aggressive models who were more or less neutral figures suggest that mere observation of aggression, regardless of the quality of the model-subject relationship, is a sufficient condition for producing imitative aggression in children. A comparative study of the subjects' imitation of aggressive models who are feared, who are liked and esteemed, or who are essentially neutral figures would throw some light on whether or not a more parsimonious theory than the one involved in "identification with the aggressor" can explain the modeling process.

SUMMARY

Twenty-four preschool children were assigned to each of three conditions. One experimental group observed aggressive adult models; a second observed inhibited nonaggressive models; while subjects in a control group had no prior exposure to the models. Half the subjects in the experimental conditions observed same-sex models and half viewed models of the opposite sex. Subjects were then tested for the amount of imitative as well as nonimitative aggression performed in a new situation in the absence of the models.

Comparison of the subjects' behavior in the generalization situation revealed that subjects exposed to aggressive models reproduced a good deal of aggression resembling that of the models, and that their mean scores differed markedly from those of subjects in the nonaggressive and control groups. Subjects in the aggressive condition also exhibited significantly more partially imitative and nonimitative aggressive behavior and were generally less inhibited in their behavior than subjects in the nonaggressive condition.

Imitation was found to be differentially influenced by the sex of the model with boys showing more aggression than girls following exposure to the male model, the difference being particularly marked on highly masculine-typed behavior.

Subjects who observed the nonaggressive models, especially the subdued male model, were generally less aggressive than their controls.

The implications of the findings based on this experiment and related studies for the psychoanalytic theory of identification with the aggressor were discussed.

REFERENCES

Bandura, A. Relationship of family patterns to child behavior disorders. Progress Report, 1960, Stanford University, Project No. M-1734, United States Public Health Service.

Bandura, A., & Huston, Aletha C. Identification as a process of incidental learning. *J. abnorm. soc. Psychol.*, 1961, *63*, 311–318.

Bandura, A., & Walters, R. H. *Adolescent aggression.* New York: Ronald, 1959.

Blake, R. R. The other person in the situation. In R. Tagiuri & L. Petrullo (Eds.), *Person perception and interpersonal behavior.* Stanford, Calif.: Stanford Univer. Press, 1958. Pp. 229–242.

Fauls, Lydia B., & Smith, W. D. Sex-role learning of five-year olds. *J. genet. Psychol.*, 1956, *89*, 105–117.

Freud, Anna. *The ego and the mechanisms of defense.* New York: International Univer. Press, 1946.

Grosser, D., Polansky, N., & Lippitt, R. A laboratory study of behavior contagion. *Hum. Relat.*, 1951, *4*, 115–142.

Lindquist, E. F. *Design and analysis of experiments.* Boston: Houghton Mifflin, 1956.

Logan, F., Olmsted, O. L., Rosner, B. S., Schwartz, R. D., & Stevens, C. M. *Behavior theory and social science.* New Haven: Yale Univer. Press, 1955.

Maccoby, Eleanor E. Role-taking in childhood and its consequences for social learning. *Child Develpm.*, 1959, *30*, 239–252.

Miller, N. E., & Dollard, J. *Social learning and imitation.* New Haven: Yale Univer. Press, 1941.

Mowrer, O. H. (Ed.) Identification: A link between learning theory and psychotherapy In, *Learning theory and personality dynamics.* New York: Ronald, 1950. Pp. 69–94.

Rosenbaum, M. E., & deCharms, R. Direct and vicarious reduction of hostility. *J. abnorm. soc. Psychol.*, 1960, *60*, 105–111.

Rosenblith, Judy F. Learning by imitation in kindergarten children. *Child Develpm.*, 1959, *30*, 69–80.

Schachter, S., & Hall, R. Group-derived restraints and audience persuasion. *Hum. Relat.*, 1952, *5*, 397–406.

Skinner, B. F. *Science and human behavior.* New York: Macmillan, 1953.

ENDNOTES

1. This investigation was supported by Research Grant M-4398 from the National Institute of Health, United States Public Health Service.

2. The authors wish to express their appreciation to Edith Dowley, Director, and Patricia Rowe, Head Teacher, Stanford University Nursery School for their assistance throughout this study.

CRITICAL THINKING QUESTIONS

1. Notice that the children's anger was aroused prior to their being placed in the situation where their aggression would be measured. Why was this done? What might have resulted had their anger not been aroused beforehand? Were there different effects,

depending on whether the children experienced prior anger arousal? If so, then what are the implications for generalizing the results of this study to how violent television affects its young viewers? Explain your answers.

2. This study reported that the gender of the actor made a difference in how much physical aggression was imitated. It also mentioned that some of the children simply found it inappropriate for a female actor to act aggressively. Some 40 years have passed since publication of this study. Do you think children today would still see physical aggression by a female as inappropriate? Support your answer.

3. Analyze the content of television shows directed toward children (including cartoons) for aggression, examining the type of aggression (physical versus verbal) and the gender of the aggressive character. Relate the findings to question 2, above.

4. Examine research conducted over the last three decades that documents the impact of televised aggression on children's behavior. Given these findings, what should be done? Should laws be passed to regulate the amount of violence shown on television? Or should this form of censorship be avoided? Explain. What other alternatives might exist to reverse or prevent the potential harm of observing violence on television?

ADDITIONAL RELATED READINGS

Krcmar, M., and Cooke, M. C. (2001). Children's moral reasoning and their perceptions of television violence. *Journal of Communication, 51*(2), 300–316.

Scharrer, E. (2001). Men, muscles, and machismo: The relationship between television violence exposure and aggression and hostility in the presence of hypermasculinity. *Media Psychology, 3*(2), 159–188.

ARTICLE 33 _____

An important area of research on aggression concerns its causes. Three general classes of theories have emerged: The first class, which can be called *instinct theories,* explains aggression as somehow rooted in biology. Thus, aggression stems from internally generated forces and is something that human beings are genetically programmed to do. A second type of theory, called *drive reduction,* essentially explains aggression as arising from forces outside the individual; for instance, experiencing frustration may produce readiness to engage in aggressive behavior. *Social learning* is the third theoretical explanation of aggression. Basically, this approach maintains that aggression, like many other behaviors, is learned. It is not instinctive nor is it simply a reaction to a specific external event. Rather, like other complex social behaviors, aggression is learned.

Each of these theoretical views attributes aggression to a different cause. It follows, then, that whichever theoretical explanation you adopt will influence how optimistic you are about the possible control of aggression. For example, if you believe that aggression is innate, a biological predisposition of sorts, then there is not much that can be done about it. It is simply human nature to be aggressive. However, if you believe that aggression is learned, then it is not inevitable that people be aggressive. After all, if aggressive behaviors can be learned, then nonaggressive behaviors can be learned, as well. And if aggression arises from forces outside the individual, then aggression can be reduced to the extent that one can control those outside forces.

One set of factors that has been considerably investigated over the years for its possible impact on aggressive behavior is *environmental influences.* In particular, it has long been noted that excessive heat seems to be associated with increases in aggression. Statistics confirm the fact that violent crimes are more likely to occur in hotter temperatures, but the reason for this phenomenon is not necessarily obvious. Do hot temperatures simply make people feel miserable and thus more prone to acting out their discomfort through aggressive acts? Or are people who live in hotter climates somehow different from people who live in colder climates? What else could account for the heat/aggression association other than heat per se?

The following article by Craig A. Anderson examines the heat hypothesis not by conducting a study on the question but by using a method known as *triangulation,* whereby multiple perspectives are used to examine differing explanations of the heat effect. The impacts of trends discussed in this article—such as global warming and our ability to better regulate indoor temperatures—are worthy of attention.

Heat and Violence

■ Craig A. Anderson[1]

Abstract

The heat hypothesis states that hot temperatures can increase aggressive motives and behaviors. Although alternative explanations occasionally account for some portion of the observed increases in aggression when temperatures are high, none are sufficient to account for most such heat effects. Hot temperatures increase aggression by

Reprinted from *Current Directions in Psychological Science,* 2001, *10*(1), 33–38. Copyright © 2001 by the American Psychological Society. Reprinted with permission of Blackwell Science Ltd.

directly increasing feelings of hostility and indirectly increasing aggressive thoughts. Results show that global warming trends may well increase violent-crime rates. Better climate controls in many institutional settings (e.g., prisons, schools, the workplace) may reduce aggression-related problems in those settings.

> I pray thee, good Mercutio, let's retire;
> The day is hot, the Capulets abroad,
> And, if we meet, we shall not 'scape a brawl,
> For now, these hot days, is the mad blood stirring.
> —William Shakespeare,
> *Romeo and Juliet, Act 3,* Scene 1

Does excessive heat increase violence? Social commentators have long noted effects of weather on human behavior and have used heat-related imagery in their works (e.g., Cicero, 106–32 B.C.; Siouxsie and the Banshees, in their song "92°," 1986). Empirical methods were first applied to this theory in the middle 1700s. Montesquieu (1748/1989) noted that "you will find in the northern climates peoples who have few vices, enough virtues, and much sincerity and frankness. As you move toward the countries of the south, you will believe you have moved away from morality itself: the liveliest passions will increase crime . . ." (p. 234). In the late 1800s and early 1900s, a number of European and North American scholars found that rates of violent crime increased during the hottest times of the year, and were higher in regions with hotter climates (Anderson, 1989). Perhaps Shakespeare was right.

The *heat hypothesis* states that hot temperatures increase aggressive motivation and (under some conditions) aggressive behavior. The *heat effect* is the observation of higher rates of aggression by people who are hot relative to people who are cooler. Methodological difficulties and the lack of modern statistical analyses in early studies made causal statements risky, but causal issues are crucial. For example, more assaults occur during the summer months than during other months, but this could be a spurious artifact of differences in the daily activities people perform at different times of the year. Perhaps people are outside more during the summer, increasing the opportunity for conflicts. Routine activities associated with summer may increase assault rates, and heat-induced discomfort may play no direct causal role in this increase. Such mediated, or indirect, heat effects are important in their own right, of course.

MODERN STUDIES OF THE HEAT HYPOTHESIS

Modern studies (i.e., post-1950) address these methodological issues in several ways. The research can be classed into three broad categories: (a) field studies, all of which focus on some form of aggression; (b) laboratory studies with a focus on aggression; and (c) laboratory studies with a focus on aggression-related variables, such as hostile feelings, beliefs, and arousal.

The results can be characterized with four summary statements. First, periodic claims that observed heat effects result solely from artifactual processes have, to date, proven false. Second, the ongoing search for conditions under which excessive heat may cause a decline in aggression has largely failed. Third, there has been a growing realization that other aggression-related processes sometimes obscure, exaggerate, or modify the heat effect. Fourth, a simple version of the heat hypothesis (e.g., Berkowitz, 1993)—that people get cranky when uncomfortable—has proven surprisingly robust to all challenges. In short, excessive heat appears to cause increases in aggression in many settings.

In investigating the relation between heat and aggression, my students and I have relied on a well-worn philosophical approach know as triangulation. This involves examining competing explanations of the heat effect from multiple perspectives. Because the weaknesses of one particular methodology differ from those of other methodologies, an explanation of observed heat effects that works across different methodologies is less likely to be invalid than explanations that work only for one or two methods. For example, changes in routine activities may be able to explain summer increases in violent crime, but cannot account for the finding that baseball pitchers are more likely to hit batters with a pitched ball on hot days than on cool days (Reifman, Larrick, & Fein, 1991). The parsimonious explanation is that heat-induced discomfort increases aggressive inclinations on the baseball field and in other naturalistic settings.

Field Studies of Heat and Aggressive Behavior

Field studies may be categorized according to whether they compare aggression rates (usually violent-crime rates) across geographic regions that are similar in many respects but differ in climate, or whether they compare aggression rates in one geographic region but across time periods that differ in temperature.

Studies Comparing Geographic Regions Data consistently show that violent-crime rates are higher in the South than in other regions of the United States. Similar patterns appeared in the older European studies (Anderson, 1989).

The heat hypothesis is only one of several explanations of the U.S. version of the hot-region effect. One alternative explanation is that, for some reason, a culture of violence (e.g., Nisbett, 1993) developed in the U.S. South, and that this cultural difference has been passed on to present-day inhabitants. Reasons given for this cultural development differ among scholars; analyses of who settled the South, the institution of slavery, and the effects of being a frontier or a herding economy have all been offered. Nonetheless, claims that Southern culture accounts for the observed high violent-crime rate in hotter regions of the United States are contradicted by recent analyses of violent-crime rates in 260 U.S. cities (Anderson, Anderson, Dorr, DeNeve, & Flanagan, 2000). Latent variable statistical techniques were used to estimate the effect of temperature on violent-crime rate, while statistically controlling for the Southernness, population size, and socioeconomic status of the cities. This same analysis estimated the effect of Southernness on violent-crime rate, while statistically controlling for the temperature, population size, and socioeconomic status of the cities. As shown by the positive path coefficient for the link between temperature and violent crime in Figure 1 (.43), temperature was significantly and positively related to violent-crime rate. That is, hotter cities were more violent than cooler cities even after city-to-city differences in Southernness, population size, and socioeconomic status were statistically controlled. However, the path coefficient for the link between Southernness and violent crime (.14) was not reliably different from zero (no effect), casting further doubt on the claim that a Southern

culture of violence is the sole or primary cause of higher violent-crime rates in hotter U.S. cities.

Studies Comparing Time Periods Field studies comparing aggression rates in hotter versus cooler time periods also support the heat hypothesis. For example, there are about 2.6% more murders and assaults in the United States during the summer than other seasons of the year; hot summers produce a bigger increase in violence than cooler summers; and violence rates are higher in hotter years than in cooler years even when various statistical controls are used (Anderson et al., 2000). Other time-period studies provide consistent results. Aggression—as measured by assault rates, spontaneous riots, spouse batterings, and batters being hit by pitched baseballs—is higher during hotter days, months, seasons, and years.

FIGURE 1 / Latent Variable Model of Effects of Temperature and Southernness on Violent Crime, Controlling for Population and Socioeconomic Status (SES). Positive path coefficients (e.g., the .43 above the line connecting "Temperature" to "Violent Crime") indicate a positive relation between the variables linked by that path. Negative path coefficients would indicate a negative relation between the linked variables. A path coefficient of zero would indicate that the two variables are totally unrelated. Solid lines linking two variables indicate that the associated path coefficient is reliably different from zero (i.e., is statistically significant). The dashed line indicates that the link between the two variables is not reliably different from zero. Adapted from Anderson, Anderson, Dorr, DeNeve, and Flanagan (2000).

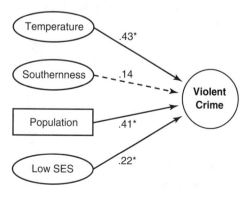

Several studies have examined the heat hypothesis with time periods even shorter than days. Some have found increases in assaults, rapes, and domestic violence at hotter temperatures (Anderson et al., 2000). Studies that have measured temperature at the exact time that aggressive behaviors occurred have also yielded the standard heat effect. Kenrick and MacFarlane's (1984) classic study in Phoenix, Arizona, found that aggressive horn honking increased at hotter temperatures, but only for drivers without air-conditioned cars. More recently, Vrij, van der Steen, and Koppelaar (1994) conducted a field experiment in which Dutch police officers performed in a simulated burglary scenario under hot or comfortable conditions. Hot officers reported more aggressive and threatening impressions of the suspect, and were more likely to draw their weapon and shoot the suspect (with laser training weapons), relative to officers in the cool condition.

Summary of Field Studies   Field studies consistently find positive associations between uncomfortable heat and aggression. Most field studies are correlational, so causal interpretation must be tempered by the possibility that unknown extraneous variables caused a spurious relation between heat and aggression. However, the two major challenges to the heat hypothesis—changes in routine activities and Southern culture—do not fare well from a broad perspective. Each can account for a few findings, but neither can account for the broad array of heat effects. The consistency of findings across many settings and methods provides strong support for the causal version of the heat hypothesis, even from correlational studies. Furthermore, the few experimental and quasi-experimental field studies lend considerable support to the causal interpretation.

Laboratory Studies and Aggressive Behavior

Mixed Results   Lab studies of the heat hypothesis have yielded somewhat mixed results. The negative-affect escape model (Anderson, 1989; Anderson et al., 2000; Baron & Bell, 1976) postulates that excessive heat increases aggression when the total amount of negative affect a person experiences is in the low to moderate range (the fight response), but that excessive

heat decreases aggression when total negative affect gets too high (the flight response). In other words, if other aspects of a particular situation (such as being insulted) also produce negative affect, then further increases in negative affect caused by hot temperature should (according to this model) lead to escape behavior instead of aggressive behavior. In brief, hot temperatures should produce a decline in aggression in situations that have other negative-affect-producing factors present. A meta-analysis (i.e., an analysis combining results across all relevant studies) yielded some support for the standard heat effect (hot temperatures increased aggression) in lab settings that had few extraneous negative-affect-producing factors present. However, there was little support for the predicted decrease in aggression when extraneous negative-affect-producing factors were present (Anderson et al., 2000). Many early lab studies, especially those that used kerosene heaters, suffered from potential suspicion problems. That is, some participants in those studies may have become suspicious about the "true" purpose of the study, and may therefore have behaved in an artificial way. Boyanowsky (1999) recently discussed other methodological problems with early lab studies and provided experimental evidence that when people's attention is not focused on temperature (as in most naturalistic settings), hot temperatures increase aggression even when additional negative-affect-producing factors (such as being insulted) are present.

One recent experiment using more subtle ways to manipulate temperature than kerosene heaters succeeded in creating conditions that yielded both heat-induced increases and decreases in aggression. Two factors were involved: an ambiguous provocation, followed by multiple opportunities to retaliate. Under these conditions, my colleagues and I found an initial heat-induced increase in aggressive retaliation, followed by a decrease (Anderson et al., 2000). One explanation of this pattern involves two separate processes. The initial outburst of aggression may have been the result of heat-induced increases in aggressive inclinations (via hostile affect and cognition). The later decrease may have been the result of a social justice norm; hot participants may have decided that the initial retaliation was sufficient. Of course, in most natural settings, the initial outburst will itself provoke an aggressive response from the victim, initiating an escalating cycle of retaliatory aggression.

Summary of Laboratory Studies of Aggressive Behavior   In affectively neutral and positive circumstances, hot temperatures cause increases in aggression. Recent lab studies show that even in affectively negative circumstances, heat causes increases in initial retaliatory aggression.

Laboratory Studies and Aggression-Related Variables

Heat effects on affective, cognitive, and arousal variables have proven quite consistent. Exposure to hot temperatures increases heart rate, endorsement of aggressive attitudes and beliefs, and feelings of hostility, all the while decreasing feelings of arousal and comfort. The heat-induced increase in endorsement of aggressive attitudes and beliefs looks, at first glance, like a cognitive priming effect, automatically increasing the accessibility of aggressive thoughts. However, hot temperatures do not automatically prime aggressive thoughts, at least not in the same way that viewing pictures of guns does (Anderson, Anderson, & Deuser, 1996). Thus, the effects of heat on attitudes and beliefs are indirect, most likely mediated by more direct effects of heat on hostile affect. Uncomfortably warm temperatures also produce biases in the interpretation of observed social interactions. Specifically, heat seems to increase the likelihood that ambiguous social interactions will be interpreted as having aggressive components (Anderson et al., 2000). Finally, heat stress decreases performance on many cognitive tasks.

PSYCHOLOGICAL PROCESSES UNDERLYING THE HEAT EFFECT

Numerous fascinating psychological processes might be involved in the typical effect of high temperatures on aggression and violence. The simplest and most powerful ones all revolve around the "crankiness" notion. Being uncomfortable colors the way people see things. Minor insults may be perceived as major ones, inviting (even demanding) retaliation. This notion is compatible with several well-established theories in social psychology, including Berko-

witz's (1984) cognitive neo-association theory and Zillmann's (1983) excitation transfer theory. Our own General Affective Aggression Model (GAAM; e.g., Anderson et al., 2000) explicitly incorporates the key aspects of these earlier models, including the crankiness notion.

GAAM also includes social interaction processes that play a key role in the genesis of violent behavior. Specifically, GAAM highlights the fact that any social interaction involves at least two people. Furthermore, aggression can come about through fairly automatic processes (i.e., impulsively) as well as through careful planning. My colleagues and I believe that most heat-induced increases in aggression, including the most violent behaviors, result from distortion of the social interaction process in a hostile direction. Heat-induced discomfort makes people cranky. It increases hostile affect (e.g., feelings of anger), which in turn primes aggressive thoughts, attitudes, preparatory behaviors (e.g., fist clenching), and behavioral scripts (such as "retaliation" scripts). A minor provocation can quickly escalate, especially if both participants are affectively and cognitively primed for hostility by their heightened level of discomfort. A mild insult is more likely to provoke a severe insult in response when people are hot than when they are more comfortable. This may lead to further increases in the aggressiveness of responses and counterresponses. An accidental bump in a hot and crowded bar can lead to the trading of insults, punches, and (eventually) bullets.

NEW RESEARCH DIRECTIONS

Many of the basic pieces of this puzzle have been found, but several are still missing. Though research on the heat hypothesis has been carried out for many years, my colleagues and I believe that the hardest work lies ahead and that the missing pieces are likely to be found in future laboratory studies. Additional work is needed to answer the following key questions.

1. Does excessive heat bias perceptions in ongoing social interactions?
2. Do people in hot conditions—and who are therefore physiologically aroused (i.e., have an increased heart rate) but psychologically unaroused (i.e., feel

lethargic)—misattribute some of their heat-based arousal to minor provoking social events?

3. Do the cognitive effects of heat stress interfere with normal mechanisms for inhibiting aggression?

4. How do escape motives influence the heat effect? The negative-affect escape model specifies that escape motives should play a major role. It predicts that under some circumstances, increases in heat-induced discomfort will increase the desire to escape more than the desire to retaliate, and therefore will reduce aggression if escape is incompatible with aggression. However, no research has explicitly pitted escape motives against aggressive motives.

5. Do social justice processes underlie the finding that excessive heat can at first increase and later decrease aggression?

CURRENT IMPLICATIONS

A broad view of the research—triangulation—suggests that in many settings hot temperatures cause increases in aggression. There are conditions that limit the generality of this conclusion, but the overall pattern of data is impressive and convincing.

The implications of this general conclusion are many. Consider the finding that hot years produce increases in violent-crime rates. If this heat effect is truly caused by heat-induced increases in aggressive motivation, then increased violence can be added to the list of negative social consequences of global warming. Figure 2 illustrates just how much of an increase can be expected, based on several estimates of the true relation between temperature and U.S. murder and assault rates, at several estimated levels of

FIGURE 2 / Estimated Effect of Global Warming on Murders and Assaults in the United States. The graph shows the estimated increase in the murder-assault rate and in the number of murders and assaults (for a population of 270 million) based on three estimates of the relation between temperature and violence. From Anderson, Anderson, Dorr, DeNeve, and Flanagan (2000).

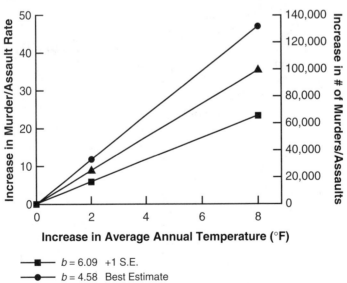

global warming. For example, using the best estimate of how much the violent-crime rate will increase for each 1°F increase in temperature (i.e., 4.58), we see that a 2°F increase in average temperature predicts an increase of about 9 more murders or assaults per 100,000 people, or more than 24,000 additional murders and assaults per year in a population of 270 million.

There are numerous institutional settings in which aggression is a problem and in which temperature can be controlled. Schools, prisons, and a wide variety of workplaces are good targets for intervention. Research on the effects of better climate control in such settings might well show that the additional costs are outweighed by the benefits—better learning, lower incarceration costs, less property damage, and increased productivity.

RECOMMENDED READING

Anderson, C.A., Anderson, K.B., Dorr, N., DeNeve, K.M., & Flanagan, M. (2000). (See References)
Berkowitz, L. (1993). (See References)
Geen, R.G. (1990). *Human aggression.* Pacific Grove, CA: Brooks Cole.
Reifman, A.S., Larrick, R.P., & Fein, S. (1991). (See References)

REFERENCES

Anderson, C.A. (1989). Temperature and aggression: Ubiquitous effects of heat on occurrence of human violence. *Psychological Bulletin, 106,* 74–96.
Anderson, C.A., Anderson, K.B., & Deuser, W.E. (1996). Examining an affective aggression framework: Weapon and temperature effects on aggressive thoughts, affect, and attitudes. *Personality and Social Psychology Bulletin, 22,* 366–376.
Anderson, C.A., Anderson, K.B., Dorr, N., DeNeve, K.M., & Flanagan, M. (2000). Temperature and aggression. In M. Zanna (Ed.), *Advances in experimental social psychology* (Vol. 32, pp. 63–133). New York: Academic Press.
Baron, R.A., & Bell, P.A. (1976). Aggression and heat: The influence of ambient temperature, negative affect, and a cooling drink on physical aggression. *Journal of Personality and Social Psychology, 33,* 245–255.
Berkowitz, L. (1984). Some effects of thoughts on anti- and prosocial influences of media events: A cognitive-neoassociation analysis. *Psychological Bulletin, 95,* 410–427.
Berkowitz, L. (1993). *Aggression: Its causes, consequences, and control.* New York: McGraw Hill.
Boyanowsky, E. (1999). Violence and aggression in the heat of passion and in cold blood. *International Journal of Law and Psychiatry, 22,* 257–271.
Kenrick, D.T., & MacFarlane, S.W. (1984). Ambient temperature and horn-honking: A field study of the heat/aggression relationship. *Environment and Behavior, 18,* 179–191.
Montesquieu, C. (1989). *The spirit of the laws* (A. Cohler, B. Miller, & H. Stone, Trans.). New York: Cambridge University Press. (Original work published 1748)
Nisbett, R.E. (1993). Violence and U.S. regional culture. *American Psychologist, 48,* 441–449.
Reifman, A.S., Larrick, R.P., & Fein, S. (1991). Temper and temperature on the diamond: The heat-aggression relationship in major league baseball. *Personality and Social Psychology Bulletin, 17,* 580–585.
Vrij, A., van der Steen, J., & Koppelaar, L. (1994). Aggression of police officers as a function of temperature: An experiment with the Fire Arms Training System. *Journal of Community and Applied Social Psychology, 4,* 365–370.
Zillmann, D. (1983). Arousal and aggression. In R. Geen & E. Donnerstein (Eds.), *Aggression: Theoretical and empirical reviews, Vol. 1. Theoretical and methodological issues* (pp. 75–101). New York: Academic Press.

Acknowledgements—I thank Kathryn Anderson, Brad Bushman, and Kristina DeNeve for their helpful comments on this article.

CRITICAL THINKING QUESTIONS

1. The article documents the numerous studies that find a causal link between high temperatures and increased aggression. But does this increase apply to *all* types of aggression or only some forms? For example, what about domestic violence and the "cabin fever" effect during the winter months? Does being confined inside for long periods of time increase violence toward others in the same setting? Investigate the existing literature on this question, or design a nonexperimental study to investigate it yourself.

2. The article notes five sets of questions for which additional work is needed to produce answers. Take one of the questions and design an experiment to investigate it.

3. Design a study to experimentally investigate the relationship between heat and aggression, but do not use any of the methodologies already discussed in the article.

4. The article notes that "Baseball pitchers are more likely to hit batters with a pitched ball on hot days than on cool days." What else might explain this finding, other than the discomfort of the heat inducing increased aggressive tendencies on the part of the pitcher?

5. Examine your own assumptions about aggression. Do you believe that it is part of human nature (i.e., genetically or biologically determined), due to forces outside the individual (e.g., heat), or due to learning and experience (e.g., family or cultural background)? How do these personally held assumptions influence your view of the purpose of punishing criminals, in general, and the issue of capital punishment, in particular? Explain your answers.

Chapter Twelve

GROUPS AND INDIVIDUAL BEHAVIOR

How MUCH OF your life is spent interacting with people in some sort of group? If we use the simple definition of a *group* as "two or more individuals that have some unifying relationship," then most likely a significant amount of your time is spent in groups, whether informal (such as two friends trying to decide what to do on a Saturday night) or formal (a work group deciding on a course of action).

Research on group behavior has gone in many directions. The three articles selected for this chapter focus on some of the most commonly investigated topics. Article 34, "Groupthink," examines a set of circumstances found in certain types of groups that may lead them to make very poor decisions, even when they may be composed of very competent individuals. Since the conditions that may contribute to groupthink are not uncommon, the implications of the article for developing more effective groups are clearly important.

Article 35, "The Effect of Threat upon Interpersonal Bargaining," is a classic work. Think of these two possible situations: In the first situation, Party 1 has the potential to inflict harm on Party 2, but Party 2 cannot reciprocate. In the second situation, both parties have equal threat potential; that is, if Party 1 inflicts harm, Party 2 can reciprocate. Which situation would yield the best outcomes for *both* parties? As the article demonstrates, the answer is not what you might think.

Article 36 returns to the concept of groupthink by experimentally investigating how two variables associated with this phenomenon—namely, having a directive leader and group members predisposed to conform—affects group processes and outcomes. "Testing the Groupthink Model: Effects of Promotional Leadership and Conformity Predisposition" provides a laboratory test of the groupthink model that uses measures of the full range of the symptoms of groupthink, decision quality, and symptoms of a poor decision—something that has not been done in prior laboratory experiments.

ARTICLE 34 _____

Let us suppose that you are in a position of authority. As such, you are called on to make some very important decisions. You want to make the best possible decisions, so you turn to other people for input. You assemble the best possible set of advisors—people distinguished by their abilities and knowledge. Before making a final decision, you meet with them to discuss the options.

Following such a procedure would seem to ensure that the decision you make will be a good one. After all, with your expert resources, how can you go wrong?

Actually, it is not very hard to imagine that the above procedure could go wrong. Working in a group, even when that group is composed of very competent individuals, does not guarantee quality decision making. To the contrary, as the following article by Irving L. Janis explains, groups may actually make some very poor decisions. The concept of *groupthink,* a term coined by Janis, explains how and why some groups come to make poor decisions, not only failing to recognize that these are poor decisions but actually convincing themselves more and more that these are good decisions. Considering the number of decisions that are made in groups, the process of groupthink, as well as the suggestions for how it can be minimized, are important indeed.

Groupthink

■ Irving L. Janis

The idea of "groupthink" occurred to me while reading Arthur M. Schlesinger's chapters on the Bay of Pigs in *A Thousand Days.* At first I was puzzled: How could bright men like John F. Kennedy and his advisers be taken in by such a stupid, patchwork plan as the one presented to them by the C.I.A. representatives? I began wondering if some psychological contagion of complacency might have interfered with their mental alertness.

I kept thinking about this notion until one day I found myself talking about it in a seminar I was conducting at Yale on the psychology of small groups. I suggested that the poor decision-making performance of those high officials might be akin to the lapses in judgment of ordinary citizens who become more concerned with retaining the approval of the fellow members of their work group than with coming up with good solutions to the tasks at hand.

When I re-read Schlesinger's account I was struck by many further observations that fit into exactly the pattern of concurrence-seeking that has impressed me

in my research on other face-to-face groups when a "we" feeling of solidarity is running high. I concluded that a group process was subtly at work in Kennedy's team which prevented the members from debating the real issues posed by the C.I.A.'s plan and from carefully appraising its serious risks.

By now I was sufficiently fascinated by what I called the "groupthink" hypothesis to start looking into similar historic fiascoes. I selected for intensive analysis three that were made during the administrations of three other American presidents: Franklin D. Roosevelt (failure to be prepared for Pearl Harbor), Harry S. Truman (the invasion of North Korea) and Lyndon B. Johnson (escalation of the Vietnam war). Each decision was a group product, issuing from a series of meetings held by a small and cohesive group of government officials and advisers. In each case I found the same kind of detrimental group process that was at work in the Bay of Pigs decision.

In my earlier research with ordinary citizens I had been impressed by the effects—both unfavorable and favorable—of the social pressures that develop in cohesive groups: in infantry platoons, air crews, therapy groups, seminars and self-study or encounter groups. Members tend to evolve informal objectives to preserve friendly intra-group relations, and this becomes part of the hidden agenda at their meetings. When conducting research on groups of heavy smokers, for example, at a clinic established to help people stop smoking, I noticed a seemingly irrational tendency for the members to exert pressure on each other to increase their smoking as the time for the final meeting approached. This appeared to be a collusive effort to display mutual dependence and resistance to the termination of the sessions.

Sometimes, even long before the final separation, pressures toward uniformity subverted the fundamental purpose. At the second meeting of one group of smokers, consisting of 12 middle-class American men and women, two of the most dominant members took the position that heavy smoking was an almost incurable addiction. Most of the others soon agreed that nobody could be expected to cut down drastically. One man took issue with this consensus, arguing that he had stopped smoking since joining the group and that everyone else could do the same. His declaration was followed by an angry discussion. Most of the others ganged up against the man who was deviating from the consensus.

At the next meeting the deviant announced that he had made an important decision. "When I joined," he said, "I agreed to follow the two main rules required by the clinic—to make a conscientious effort to stop smoking, and to attend every meeting. But I have learned that you can only follow one of the rules, not both. I will continue to attend every meeting but I have gone back to smoking two packs a day and I won't make any effort to stop again until after the last meeting." Whereupon the other members applauded, welcoming him back to the fold.

No one mentioned that the whole point of the meetings was to help each person to cut down as rapidly as possible. As a psychological consultant to the group, I tried to call this to the members' attention and so did my collaborator, Dr. Michael Kahn. But the members ignored our comments and reiterated their consensus that heavy smoking was an addiction from which no one would be cured except by cutting down gradually over a long period of time.

This episode—an extreme form of groupthink—was only one manifestation of a general pattern that the group displayed. At every meeting the members were amiable, reasserted their warm feelings of solidarity and sought concurrence on every important topic, with no reappearance of the unpleasant bickering that would spoil the cozy atmosphere. This tendency could be maintained, however, only at the expense of ignoring realistic challenges—like those posed by the psychologists.

The term "groupthink" is of the same order as the words in the "newspeak" vocabulary that George Orwell uses in *1984*—a vocabulary with terms such as "doublethink" and "crimethink." By putting "groupthink" with those Orwellian words, I realize that it takes on an invidious connotation. This is intentional: groupthink refers to a deterioration of mental efficiency, reality testing and moral judgment that results from in-group pressures.

When I investigated the Bay of Pigs invasion and other fiascoes, I found that there were at least six major defects in decision-making which contributed to failures to solve problems adequately.

First, the group's discussions were limited to a few alternatives (often only two) without a survey of the full range of alternatives. Second, the members failed to re-examine their initial decision from the standpoint of non-obvious drawbacks that had not been originally considered. Third, they neglected courses of action initially evaluated as unsatisfactory; they almost never discussed whether they had overlooked any nonobvious gains.

Fourth, members made little or no attempt to obtain information from experts who could supply sound estimates of losses and gains to be expected from alternative courses. Fifth, selective bias was shown in the way the members reacted to information and judgments from experts, the media and outside critics; they were only interested in facts and opinions that supported their preferred policy. Finally, they spent little time deliberating how the policy might be hindered by bureaucratic inertia, sabotaged by political opponents or derailed by the accidents that happen to the best of well-laid plans. Consequently, they failed to work out contingency plans to cope with foreseeable setbacks that could endanger their success.

I was surprised by the extent to which the groups involved in these fiascoes adhered to group norms and pressures toward uniformity, even when their policy was working badly and had unintended consequences that disturbed the conscience of the members. Members consider loyalty to the group the highest form of morality. That loyalty requires each member to avoid raising controversial issues, questioning weak arguments or calling a halt to soft-headed thinking.

Paradoxically, soft-headed groups are likely to be extremely hard-hearted toward out-groups and enemies. In dealing with a rival nation, policy-makers constituting an amiable group find it relatively easy to authorize dehumanizing solutions such as large-scale bombings. An affable group of government officials is unlikely to pursue the difficult issues that arise when alternatives to a harsh military solution come up for discussion. Nor are they inclined to raise ethical issues that imply that this "fine group of ours, with its humanitarianism and its high-minded principles, could adopt a course that is inhumane and immoral."

The greater the threat to the self-esteem of the members of a cohesive group, the greater will be their inclination to resort to concurrence-seeking at the expense of critical thinking. Symptoms of groupthink will therefore be found most often when a decision poses a moral dilemma, especially if the most advantageous course requires the policy-makers to violate their own standards of humanitarian behavior. Each member is likely to become more dependent than ever on the in-group for maintaining his self-image as a decent human being and will therefore be more strongly motivated to maintain group unity by striving for concurrence.

Although it is risky to make huge inferential leaps from theory to practice, we should not be inhibited from drawing tentative inferences from these fiascoes. Perhaps the worst mistakes can be prevented if we take steps to avoid the circumstances in which groupthink is most likely to flourish. But all the prescriptive hypotheses that follow must be validated by systematic research before they can be applied with any confidence.

The leader of a policy-forming group should, for example, assign the role of critical evaluator to each member, encouraging the group to give high priority to airing objections and doubts. He should also be impartial at the outset, instead of stating his own preferences and expectations. He should limit his briefings to unbiased statements about the scope of the problem and the limitations of available resources.

The organization should routinely establish several independent planning and evaluation groups to work on the same policy question, each carrying out its deliberations under a different leader.

One or more qualified colleagues within the organization who are not core members of the policy-making group should be invited to each meeting and encouraged to challenge the views of the core members.

At every meeting, at least one member should be assigned the role of devil's advocate, to function like a good lawyer in challenging the testimony of those who advocate the majority position.

Whenever the policy issue involves relations with a rival nation, a sizable block of time should be spent surveying all warning signals from the rivals and constructing alternative scenarios.

After reaching a preliminary consensus the policy-making group should hold a "second chance" meeting at which all the members are expected to express their residual doubts and to rethink the entire issue. They might take as their model a statement made by Alfred P. Sloan, a former chairman of General Motors, at a meeting of policy-makers:

"Gentlemen, I take it we are all in complete agreement on the decision here. Then I propose we postpone further discussion until our next meeting to give ourselves time to develop disagreement and perhaps gain some understanding of what the decision is all about."

It might not be a bad idea for the second-chance meeting to take place in a relaxed atmosphere far from the executive suite, perhaps over drinks. According to a report by Herodotus dating from about 450 B.C., whenever the ancient Persians made a decision following sober deliberations, they would always reconsider the matter under the influence of wine. Tacitus claimed that during Roman times the Germans also had a custom of arriving at each decision twice—once sober, once drunk.

Some institutionalized form of allowing second thoughts to be freely expressed might be remarkably effective for breaking down a false sense of unanimity and related illusions, without endangering anyone's reputation or liver.

PEARL HARBOR: GENIALITY AND SECURITY

On the night of Dec. 6, 1941—just 12 hours before the Japanese struck—Admiral Husband E. Kimmel (Commander in Chief of the Pacific Fleet) attended a dinner party given by his old crony, Rear Admiral H. Fairfax Leary, and his wife. Other members of the in-group of naval commanders and their wives were also present. Seated next to Admiral Kimmel was Fanny Halsey, wife of Admiral Halsey, who had left Hawaii to take his task force to the Far East. Mrs. Halsey said that she was certain the Japanese were going to attack. "She was a brilliant woman," according to Captain Joel Bunkley, who described the party, "but everybody thought she was crazy."

Admiral Leary, at a naval inquiry in 1944, summarized the complacency at that dinner party and at the daily conferences held by Admiral Kimmel during the preceding weeks. When asked whether any thought had been given to the possibility of a surprise attack by the Japanese, he said, "We all felt that the contingency was remote . . . and the feeling strongly existed that the Fleet would have adequate warning of any chance of an air attack." The same attitude was epitomized in testimony given by Captain J. B. Earle, chief of staff, Fourteenth Naval District. "Somehow or other," he said, "we always felt that 'it couldn't happen here.'"

From the consistent testimony given by Admiral Kimmel's advisers, they all acted on the basis of an "unwarranted feeling of immunity from attack," though they had been given a series of impressive warnings that they should be prepared for war with Japan.

Most illuminating of the norm-setting behavior that contributed to the complacency of Kimmel's in-group is a brief exchange between Admiral Kimmel and Lieutenant Commander Layton. Perturbed by the loss of radio contact with the Japanese aircraft carriers, Admiral Kimmel asked Layton on Dec. 1, 1941, to check with the Far East Command for additional information. The next day, discussing the lost carriers again with Layton, remarked jokingly: "What, you don't know where the carriers are? Do you mean to say that they could be rounding Diamond Head [at Honolulu] and you wouldn't know it?" Layton said he hoped they would be sighted well before that.

This exchange implies an "atmosphere of geniality and security." Having relegated the Japanese threat to the category of laughing matters, the admiral was making it clear that he would be inclined to laugh derisively at anyone who thought otherwise. "I did not at any time suggest," Layton later acknowledged at a Congressional hearing, "that the Japanese carriers were under radio silence approaching Oahu. I wish I had."

But the admiral's foolish little joke may have induced Layton to remain silent about any vague, lingering doubts he may have had. Either man would risk the scornful laughter of the other—whether expressed to his face or behind his back—if he were to express second thoughts such as, "Seriously, though, shouldn't we do something about the slight possibility that those carriers might *really* be headed this way?" Because this ominous inference was never drawn, not a single reconnaissance plane was sent out to the north of the Hawaiian Islands, allowing the Japanese to win the incredible gamble they were taking in trying to send their aircraft carriers within bombing distance of Pearl Harbor without being detected.

That joking exchange was merely the visible part of a huge iceberg of solid faith in Pearl Harbor's invulnerability. If a few warm advocates of preparedness had been within the Navy group, steamed up by the accumulating warning signals, they might have been able to melt it. But they would certainly have had a cold reception. To urge a full alert would have required presenting unwelcome arguments that countered the myth of Pearl Harbor's impregnability. Anyone who was tempted to do so knew that he would be deviating from the group norm: the others were likely to consider him "crazy," just as the in-group regarded Mrs. Halsey at the dinner party on the eve of the disaster when she announced her deviant opinion that the Japanese would attack.

ESCALATION IN VIETNAM: HOW COULD IT HAPPEN?

A highly revealing episode occurred soon after Robert McNamara told a Senate committee some impressive facts about the ineffectiveness of the bombings. President Johnson made a number of bitter comments about McNamara's statement. "That military genius,

McNamara, has gone dovish on me," he complained to one Senator. To someone in his White House staff he spoke even more heatedly, accusing McNamara of playing into the hands of the enemy. He drew the analogy of "a man trying to sell his house while one of his sons went to the prospective buyer to point out that there were leaks in the basement."

This strongly suggests that Johnson regarded his in-group of policy advisers as a family and its leading dissident member as an irresponsible son who was sabotaging the family's interest. Underlying this revealing imagery are two implicit assumptions that epitomize groupthink: We are a good group, so any deceitful acts that we perpetrate are fully justified. Anyone who is unwilling to distort the truth to help us is disloyal.

This is only one of the many examples of how groupthink was manifested in Johnson's inner circle.

A PERFECT FIASCO: THE BAY OF PIGS

Why did President Kennedy's main advisers, whom he had selected as core members of his team, fail to pursue the issues sufficiently to discover the shaky ground on which the faulty assumptions of the Cuban invasion plan rested? Why didn't they pose a barrage of penetrating and embarrassing questions to the representatives of the C.I.A. and the Joint Chiefs of Staff? Why were they taken in by the incomplete and inconsistent answers they were given in response to the relatively few critical questions they raised?

Schlesinger says that "for all the utter irrationality with which retrospect endowed the project, it had a certain queer logic at the time as it emerged from the bowels of government." Why? What was the source of the "queer logic" with which the plan was endowed? If the available accounts describe the deliberations accurately, many typical symptoms of groupthink can be discerned among the members of the Kennedy team: an illusion of invulnerability, a collective effort to rationalize their decision, an unquestioned belief in the group's inherent morality, a stereotyped view of enemy leaders as too evil to warrant genuine attempts to negotiate, and the emergence of self-appointed mind-guards.

Robert Kennedy, for example, who had been constantly informed about the Cuban invasion plan, asked Schlesinger privately why he was opposed. The President's brother listened coldly and then said: "You may be right or you may be wrong, but the President has made his mind up. Don't push it any further. Now is the time for everyone to help him all they can."

Here is a symptom of groupthink, displayed by a highly intelligent man whose ethical code committed him to freedom of dissent.

Robert Kennedy was functioning in a self-appointed role that I call being a "mind-guard." Just as a bodyguard protects the President and other high officials from physical harm, a mindguard protects them from thoughts that might damage their confidence in the soundness of the policies which they are about to launch.

CRITICAL THINKING QUESTIONS

1. How common is groupthink? Do you think that the conditions that give rise to groupthink are relatively rare or relatively common? Explain your answers. Cite additional examples of decisions that may have been influenced by groupthink.
2. Have you ever been involved in a group that experienced some sort of groupthink process? Describe the situation, and discuss the process in terms of groupthink.
3. If groupthink is common, then it would be useful if people were made aware of how it works. Should the conditions of groupthink, as well as how it can be prevented, be taught to leaders and potential leaders? How could this be accomplished?
4. The article gave some suggestions as to how groupthink could be prevented or at least minimized. Would all leaders be equally open to following these suggestions? Or might individual characteristics influence how open various leaders might be? How so?

ARTICLE 35 _____

Whenever two or more individuals act as a group, a central part of the interaction may involve trying to reach some agreement about an issue or activity. When the group consists of individuals or nations, reaching agreement is often a major concern.

Bargaining is one form that such negotiations take. The bargaining may be about something small and be informal in style, such as a couple deciding on which movie to see, or it may be major and formal, such as two nations trying to reach an agreement on nuclear arms control. In either case, central to the bargaining is the belief by both parties that reaching a mutually agreed upon solution will possibly benefit both of them.

Two broad approaches to bargaining are cooperation and competition. In a *competitive* situation, individuals or groups view the situation in "win-lose" terms: I want to win, and it most likely will be at your expense. In a *cooperative* arrangement, the situation is more likely to be viewed as a "win-win" opportunity: We can both get something good out of this; neither one has to lose. Other things being equal, a cooperative strategy is more likely to ensure a good outcome for all concerned. But is that the strategy most likely to be used? Or do individuals and groups tend to use competitive strategies instead, even if it might not ultimately be in their best interest to do so?

The following classic contribution by Morton Deutsch and Robert M. Krauss examines the effect of threat on interpersonal bargaining. One major finding of the study is that the presence of threat, as well as whether only one or both parties are capable of threat, has a major impact on the outcome of the bargaining situation. Common sense might suggest that if my opponent has some threat that he or she can use against me, then I would be better off having the same level of threat to use against him or her, rather than having no threat to retaliate with. The findings of the study do not confirm this expectation, however, and may suggest a rethinking of the use of threat and power in real-world negotiations.

The Effect of Threat
upon Interpersonal Bargaining

■ Morton Deutsch and Robert M. Krauss

A bargain is defined in *Webster's Unabridged Dictionary* as "an agreement between parties settling what each shall give and receive in a transaction between them"; it is further specified that a bargain is "an agreement or compact viewed as advantageous or the reverse." When the term "agreement" is broadened to include tacit, informal agreements as well as explicit agreements, it is evident that bargains and the processes involved in arriving at bargains ("bargaining") are pervasive characteristics of social life.

The definition of bargain fits under sociological definitions of the term "social norm." In this light, the experimental study of the bargaining process and of bargaining outcomes provides a means for the laboratory study of the development of certain types of social norms. But unlike many other types of social situations, bargaining situations have certain distinctive features that make it relevant to consider the conditions that determine whether or not a social norm will develop as well as those that determine the

Reprinted from *Journal of Personality and Social Psychology,* 1960, *61,* 181–189.

nature of the social norm if it develops. Bargaining situations highlight the possibility that, even where cooperation would be mutually advantageous, shared purposes may not develop, agreement may not be reached, and interaction may be regulated antagonistically rather than normatively.

The essential features of a bargaining situation exist when:

1. Both parties perceive that there is the possibility of reaching an agreement in which each party would be better off, or no worse off, than if no agreement were reached.
2. Both parties perceive that there is more than one such agreement that could be reached.
3. Both parties perceive each other to have conflicting preferences or opposed interests with regard to the different agreements that might be reached.

Everyday examples of bargaining include such situations as: the buyer-seller relationship when the price is not fixed, the husband and wife who want to spend an evening out together but have conflicting preferences about where to go, union-management negotiations, drivers who meet at an intersection when there is no clear right of way, disarmament negotiations.

In terms of our prior conceptualization of cooperation and competition (Deutsch, 1949) bargaining is thus a situation in which the participants have mixed motives toward one another: on the one hand, each has interest in cooperating so that they reach an agreement; on the other hand, they have competitive interests concerning the nature of the agreement they reach. In effect, to reach agreement the cooperative interest of the bargainers must be strong enough to overcome their competitive interests. However, agreement is not only contingent upon the *motivational* balances of cooperative to competitive interests but also upon the situational and *cognitive* factors which facilitate or hinder the recognition or invention of a bargaining agreement that reduces the opposition of interest and enhances the mutuality of interest.[1]

These considerations lead to the formulation of two general, closely related propositions about the likelihood that a bargaining agreement will be reached.

1. Bargainers are more likely to reach an agreement, the stronger are their cooperative interests in comparison with their competitive interests.
2. Bargainers are more likely to reach an agreement, the more resources they have available for recognizing or inventing potential bargaining agreements and for communicating to one another once a potential agreement has been recognized or invented.

From these two basic propositions and additional hypotheses concerning conditions that determine the strengths of the cooperative and competitive interests and the amount of available resources, we believe it is possible to explain the ease or difficulty of arriving at a bargaining agreement. We shall not present a full statement of these hypotheses here but turn instead to a description of an experiment that relates to Proposition 1.

The experiment was concerned with the effect of the availability of threat upon bargaining in a two-person experimental bargaining game.[2] Threat is defined as the expression of an intention to do something detrimental to the interests of another. Our experiment was guided by two assumptions about threat:

1. If there is a conflict of interest and one person is able to threaten the other, he will tend to use the threat in an attempt to force the other person to yield. This tendency should be stronger, the more irreconcilable the conflict is perceived to be.
2. If a person uses threat in an attempt to intimidate another, the threatened person (if he considers himself to be of equal or superior status) would feel hostility toward the threatener and tend to respond with counterthreat and/or increased resistance to yielding. We qualify this assumption by stating that the tendency to resist should be greater, the greater the perceived probability and magnitude of detriment to the other and the less the perceived probability and magnitude of detriment to the potential resister from the anticipated resistance to yielding.

The second assumption is based upon the view that when resistance is not seen to be suicidal or useless, to allow oneself to be intimidated, particularly by someone who does not have the right to expect deferential behavior, is to suffer a loss of social face and, hence, of self-esteem: and that the culturally defined way of maintaining self-esteem in the face of attempted intimidation is to engage in a contest for supremacy vis-à-vis the power to intimidate or, minimally, to resist intimidation. Thus, in effect, the use of threat (and if it is available to be used, there will be a tendency to use it) should strengthen the competitive interests of the bargainers in relationship to one another by introducing or enhancing the competitive struggle for self-esteem. Hence, from Proposition 1, it follows that the availability of a means of threat should make it more difficult for the bargainers to reach agreement (providing that the threatened person has some means of resisting the threat). The preceding statement is relevant to the comparison of both of our experimental conditions of threat, bilateral and unilateral (described below), with our experimental condition of nonthreat. We hypothesize that a bargaining agreement is more likely to be achieved when neither party can threaten the other, than when one or both parties can threaten the other.

Consider now the situations of bilateral threat and unilateral threat. For several reasons, a situation of bilateral threat is probably less conducive to agreement than is a condition of unilateral threat. First, the sheer likelihood that a threat will be made is greater when two people rather than one have the means of making the threat. Secondly, once a threat is made in the bilateral case it is likely to evoke counterthreat. Withdrawal of threat in the face of counterthreat probably involves more loss of face (for reasons analogous to those discussed in relation to yielding to intimidation) than does withdrawal of threat in the face of resistance to threat. Finally, in the unilateral case, although the person without the threat potential can resist and not yield to the threat, his position vis-à-vis the other is not so strong as the position of the threatened person in the bilateral case. In the unilateral case, the threatened person may have a worse outcome than the other whether he resists or yields; while in the bilateral case, the threatened person is sure to have a worse outcome if he yields but he may insure that he does not have a worse outcome if he does not yield.

METHOD

Procedure

Subjects (*S*s) were asked to imagine that they were in charge of a trucking company, carrying merchandise over a road to a destination. For each trip completed they made $.60, minus their operating expenses. Operating expenses were calculated at the rate of one cent per second. So, for example, if it took 37 seconds to complete a particular trip, the player's profit would be $.60 – $.37 or a net profit of $.23 for that particular trip.

Each *S* was assigned a name, Acme or Bolt. As the "road map" (see Figure 1) indicates, both players start from separate points and go to separate destinations. At one point their paths cross. This is the section of road labeled "one lane road," which is only one lane wide, so that two trucks, heading in opposite directions, could not pass each other. If one backs up the other can go forward, or both can back up, or both can sit there head-on without moving.

There is another way for each *S* to reach the destination on the map, labeled the "alternate route." The two players' paths do not cross on this route, but the alternative is 56% longer than the main route. *S*s were told that they could expect to lose at least $.10 each time they used the alternate route.

At either end of the one-lane section there is a gate that is under the control of the player to whose starting point it is closest. By closing the gate, one player can prevent the other from traveling over that section of the main route. The use of the gate provides the threat potential in this game. In the bilateral threat potential condition (Two Gates) both players had gates under their control. In a second condition of unilateral threat (One Gate) Acme had control of a gate but Bolt did not. In a third condition (No Gates) neither player controlled a gate.

*S*s played the game seated in separate booths placed so that they could not see each other but could see the experimenter (*E*). Each *S* had a "control panel" mounted on a 12" x 18" x 12" sloping-front cabinet (see Figure 2). The apparatus consisted essentially of a reversible impulse computer that was pulsed by a recycling timer. When the *S* wanted to move her truck forward she threw a key that closed a circuit pulsing the "add" coil of the impulse counter mounted on her

FIGURE 1 / Subject's Road Map

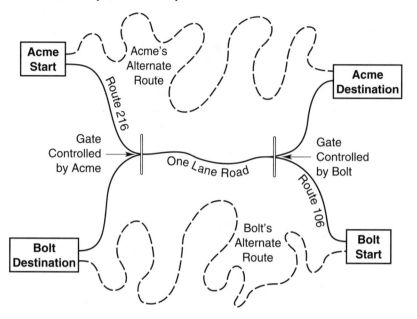

FIGURE 2 / Subject's Control Panel

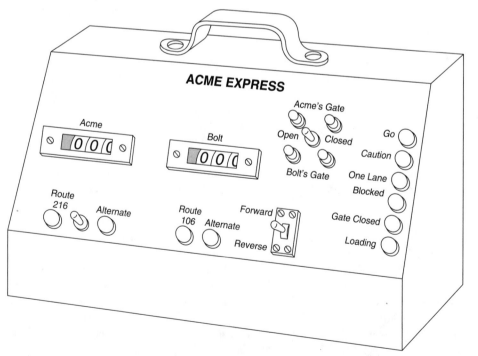

control panel. As the counter cumulated, *S* was able to determine her "position" by relating the number on her counter to reference numbers that had been written in on her road map. Similarly, when she wished to reverse, she would throw a switch that activated the "subtract" coil of her counter, thus subtracting from the total on the counter each time the timer cycled.

S's counter was connected in parallel to counters on the other *S*'s panel and on *E*'s panel. Thus each player had two counters on her panel, one representing her own position and the other representing the other player's. Provision was made in construction of the apparatus to permit cutting the other player's counter out of the circuit, so that each *S* knew only the position of her own truck. This was done in the present experiment. Experiments now in progress are studying the effects of knowledge of the other person's position and other aspects of interpersonal communication upon the bargaining process.

The only time one player definitely knew the other player's position was when they had met head-on on the one-way section of road. This was indicated by a traffic light mounted on the panel. When this light was on, neither player could move forward unless the other moved back. The gates were controlled by toggle switches and panel-mounted indicator lights showed, for both *S*s, whether each gate was open or closed.

The following "rules of the game" were stated to the *S*s:

1. A player who started out on one route and wished to switch to the other route could only do so after first reversing and going back to the start position. Direct transfer from one route to the other was not permitted except at the start position.
2. In the conditions where *S*s had gates, they were permitted to close the gates no matter where they were on the main route, so long as they were on the main route (i.e., they were not permitted to close the gate while on the alternate route or after having reached their destinations). However, *S*s were permitted to open their gates at any point in the game.

*S*s were taken through a number of practice exercises to familiarize them with the game. In the first trial they were made to meet head-on on the one-lane path; Acme was then told to back up until she was just off the one-lane path and Bolt was told to go forward. After Bolt had gone through the one-lane path, Acme was told to go forward. Each continued going forward until each arrived at her destination. The second practice trial was the same as the first except that Bolt rather than Acme backed up after meeting head-on. In the next practice trial, one of the players was made to wait just before the one-way path while the other traversed it and then was allowed to continue. In the next practice trial, one player was made to take the alternate route and the other was made to take the main route. Finally, in the bilateral and unilateral threat conditions the use of the gate was illustrated (by having the player get on the main route, close the gate, and then go back and take the alternate route). The *S*s were told explicitly, with emphasis, that they did *not* have to use the gate. Before each trial in the game the gate or gates were in the open position.

The instructions stressed an individualistic motivation orientation. *S*s were told to try to earn as much money for themselves as possible and to have no interest in whether the other player made money or lost money. They were given $4.00 in poker chips to represent their working capital and told that after each trial they would be given "money" if they made a profit or that "money" would be taken from them if they lost (i.e., took more than 60 seconds to complete their trip). The profit or loss of each *S* was announced so that both *S*s could hear the announcement after each trial. Each pair of *S*s played a total of 20 trials; on all trials, they started off together. In other words each trial presented a repetition of the same bargaining problem. In cases where *S*s lost their working capital before the 20 trials were completed, additional chips were given them. *S*s were aware that their monetary winnings and losses were to be imaginary and that no money would change hands as a result of the experiment.

Subjects

Sixteen pairs of *S*s were used in each of the three experimental conditions. The *S*s were female clerical and supervisory personnel of the New Jersey Bell Telephone Company who volunteered to participate during their working day.[3] Their ages ranged from 20 to 39, with a mean of 26.2. All were naive to the purpose of the experiment. By staggering the arrival times and choosing girls from different locations, we were able to insure that the *S*s did not know with whom they were playing.

Data Recorded

Several types of data were collected. We obtained a record of the profit or loss of each *S* on each trial. We also obtained a detailed recording of the actions taken by each *S* during the course of a trial. For this purpose, we used an Esterline-Angus model AW Operations Recorder which enabled us to obtain a "log" of each move each *S* made during the game (e.g., whether and when she took the main or alternate route; when she went forward, backward, or remained still; when she closed and opened the gate; when she arrived at her destination).

RESULTS[4]

The best single measure of the difficulty experienced by the bargainers in reaching an agreement is the sum of each pair's profits (or losses) on a given trial. The higher the sum of the payoffs to the two players on a given trial, the less time it took them to arrive at a procedure for sharing the one-lane path of the main route. (It was, of course, possible for one or both of the players to decide to take the alternate route so as to avoid a protracted stalemate during the process of bargaining. This, however, always results in at least a $.20 smaller joint payoff if only one player took the alternate route, than an optimally arrived at agreement concerning the use of the one-way path.) Figure 3 presents the medians of the summed payoffs (i.e., Acme's plus Bolt's) for all pairs in each of the three experimental conditions over the 20 trials.[5] These striking results indicate that agreement was least difficult to arrive at in the no threat condition, was more difficult to arrive at in the unilateral threat condition, and exceedingly difficult or impossible to arrive at in the bilateral threat condition (see also Table 1).

Examination of Figure 3 suggests that learning occurred during the 20 trials: the summed payoffs for pairs of *S*s tend to improve as the number of trials increases. This suggestion is confirmed by an analysis of variance of the slopes for the summed payoffs[6] over

the 20 trials for each of the 16 pairs in each of the 3 experimental treatments. The results of this analysis indicate that the slopes are significantly greater than zero for the unilateral threat ($p < .01$) and the no threat ($p < .02$) conditions; for the bilateral threat condition, the slope does not reach statistical significance ($.10 < p < .20$). The data indicate that the pairs in the no threat condition started off at a fairly high level but, even so, showed some improvement over the 20 trials; the pairs in the unilateral threat condition started off low and, having considerable opportunity for improvement, used their opportunity; the pairs in the bilateral threat condition, on the other hand, did not benefit markedly from repeated trials.

Figure 4 compares Acme's median profit in the three experimental conditions over the 20 trials; while Figure 5 compares Bolt's profit in the three conditions. (In the unilateral threat condition, it was Acme who controlled a gate and Bolt who did not.) Bolt's as well as Acme's outcome is somewhat better in the no threat condition than in the unilateral threat condition; Acme's, as well as Bolt's, outcome is clearly worst in the bilateral threat condition (see Table 1 also). However, Figure 6 reveals that Acme does somewhat better than Bolt in the unilateral condition. Thus, if threat-potential exists within a bargaining relationship it is better to possess it oneself than to have the other party possess it. However, it is even better for neither party to possess it. Moreover, Figure 5 shows that Bolt is better off not having than having a gate

FIGURE 3 / Median Joint Payoff (Acme + Bolt) over Trials

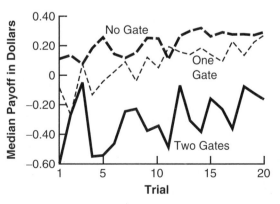

TABLE 1 / Mean Payoffs Summated over the Twenty Trials

	Means			Statistical Comparisons: p values[a]			
Variable	(1) No Threat	(2) Unilateral Threat	(3) Bilateral Threat	Overall	(1) vs. (2)	(1) vs. (3)	(2) vs. (3)
Summed Payoffs (Acme + Bolt)	203.31	−405.88	−875.12	.01	.01	.01	.05
Acme's Payoff	122.44	−118.56	−406.56	.01	.10	.01	.05
Bolt's Payoff	80.88	−287.31	−468.56	.01	.01	.01	.20
Absolute Differences in Payoff							
(A − B)	125.94	294.75	315.25	.05	.05	.01	*ns*

[a]Evaluation of the significance of overall variation between conditions is based on an *F* test with 2 and 45 *df*.
Comparisons between treatments are based on a two-tailed *t* test.

even when Acme has a gate: Bolt tends to do better in the unilateral threat condition than in the bilateral threat condition.

The size of the absolute discrepancy between the payoffs of the two players in each pair provides a measure of the confusion or difficulty in predicting what the other player was going to do. Thus, a large absolute discrepancy might indicate that after one player had gone through the one-way path and left it open, the other player continued to wait; or it might indicate that one player continued to wait at a closed gate hoping the other player would open it quickly but the other player did not; etc. Figure 7 indicates that the discrepancy between players in the no threat condition is initially small and remains small for the

20 trials. For the players in both the bilateral and unilateral threat conditions, the discrepancy is initially relatively larger; but it decreases more noticeably in the unilateral threat condition by the tenth trial and, therefore, is consistently smaller than in the bilateral condition.

By way of concrete illustration, we present a synopsis of the game for one pair in each of three experimental treatments.

No Threat Condition

Trial 1   The players met in the center of the one-way section. After some back-and-forth movement Bolt reversed to the end of the one-way section, allow-

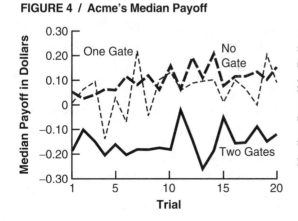

FIGURE 4 / Acme's Median Payoff

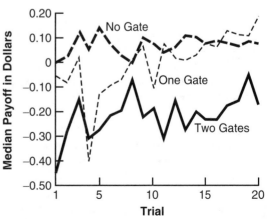

FIGURE 5 / Bolt's Median Payoff

FIGURE 6 / Acme's and Bolt's Median Payoffs in Unilateral Threat Condition

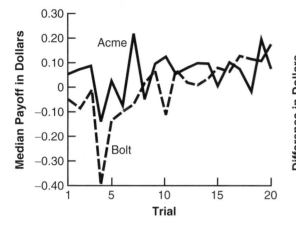

FIGURE 7 / Median Absolute Differences in Payoff

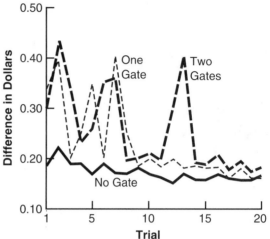

ing Acme to pass through, and then proceeded forward herself.

Trial 2   They again met at the center of the one-way path. This time, after moving back and forth deadlocked for some time, Bolt reversed to "start" and took the alternate route to her destination, thus leaving Acme free to go through on the main route.

Trial 3   The players again met at the center of the one-way path. This time, however, Acme reversed to the beginning of the path, allowing Bolt to go through to her destination. Then Acme was able to proceed forward on the main route.

Trial 5   Both players elected to take the alternate route to their destinations.

Trial 7   Both players took the main route and met in the center. They waited, deadlocked, for a considerable time. Then Acme reversed to the end of the one-way path allowing Bolt to go through, then proceeded through to her destination.

Trials 10–20   Acme and Bolt fall into a pattern of alternating who is to go first on the one-way section. There is no deviation from this pattern.

The only other pattern that emerges in this condition is one in which one player dominates the other.

That is, one player consistently goes first on the one-way section and the other player consistently yields.

Unilateral Threat Condition

Trial 1   Both players took the main route and met in the center of it. Acme immediately closed the gate, reversed to "start," and took the alternate route to her destination. Bolt waited for a few seconds, at the closed gate, then reversed and took the alternate route.

Trial 2   Both players took the main route and met in the center. After moving back and forth deadlocked for about 15 seconds, Bolt reversed to the beginning of the one-way path, allowed Acme to pass, and then proceeded forward to her destination.

Trial 3   Both players started out on the main route, meeting in the center. After moving back and forth deadlocked for a while, Acme closed her gate, reversed to "start," and took the alternate route. Bolt, meanwhile, waited at the closed gate. When Acme arrived at her destination she opened the gate, and Bolt went through to complete her trip.

Trial 5   Both players took the main route, meeting at the center of the one-way section. Acme immediately closed her gate, reversed, and took the alternate route. Bolt waited at the gate for about 10 seconds, then reversed and took the alternate route to her destination.

Trial 10   Both players took the main route and met in the center. Acme closed her gate, reversed, and took the alternate route. Bolt remained waiting at the closed gate. After Acme arrived at her destination, she opened the gate and Bolt completed her trip.

Trial 15   Acme took the main route to her destination and Bolt took the alternate route.

Trials 17–20   Both players took the main route and met in the center. Bolt waited a few seconds, then reversed to the end of the one-way section allowing Acme to go through. Then Bolt proceeded forward to her destination.

Other typical patterns that developed in this experimental condition included an alternating pattern similar to that described in the no threat condition, a dominating pattern in which Bolt would select the alternate route leaving Acme free to use the main route unobstructed, and a pattern in which Acme would close her gate and then take the alternate route, also forcing Bolt to take the alternate route.

Bilateral Threat Condition

Trial 1   Acme took the main route and Bolt took the alternate route.

Trial 2   Both players took the main route and met head-on. Bolt closed her gate. Acme waited a few seconds, then closed her gate, reversed to "start," then went forward again to the closed gate. Acme reversed and took the alternate route. Bolt again reversed, then started on the alternate route. Acme opened her gate and Bolt reversed to "start" and went to her destination on the main route.

Trial 3   Acme took the alternate route to her destination. Bolt took the main route and closed her gate before entering the one-way section.

Trial 5   Both players took the main route and met head-on. After about 10 seconds spent backing up

and going forward, Acme closed her gate, reversed, and took the alternate route. After waiting a few seconds, Bolt did the same.

Trials 8–10   Both players started out on the main route, immediately closed their gates, reversed to "start," and took the alternate route to their destinations.

Trial 15   Both players started out on the main route and met head-on. After some jockeying for position, Acme closed her gate, reversed, and took the alternate route to her destination. After waiting at the gate for a few seconds, Bolt reversed to "start" and took the alternate route to her destination.

Trials 19–20   Both players started out on the main route, immediately closed their gates, reversed to "start," and took the alternate routes to their destinations.

Other patterns that emerged in the bilateral threat condition included alternating first use of the one-way section, one player's dominating the other on first use of the one-way section, and another dominating pattern in which one player consistently took the main route while the other consistently took the alternate route.

DISCUSSION

From our view of bargaining as a situation in which both cooperative and competitive tendencies are present and acting upon the individual, it is relevant to inquire as to the conditions under which a stable agreement of any form develops. However, implicit in most economic models of bargaining (e.g., Stone, 1958; Zeuthen, 1930) is the assumption that the cooperative interests of the bargainers are sufficiently strong to insure that some form of mutually satisfactory agreement will be reached. For this reason, such models have focused upon the form of the agreement reached by the bargainers. Siegel and Fouraker (1960) report a series of bargaining experiments quite different in structure from ours in which only one of many pairs of *Ss* were unable to reach agreement. Siegel and Fouraker explain this rather startling result as follows:

Apparently the disruptive forces which lead to the rupture of some negotiations were at least partially controlled in our sessions. . . .

Some negotiations collapse when one party becomes incensed at the other, and henceforth strives to maximize his opponent's displeasure rather than his own satisfaction. . . . Since it is difficult to transmit insults by means of quantitative bids, such disequilibrating behavior was not induced in the present studies. If subjects were allowed more latitude in their communications and interactions, the possibility of an affront offense-punitive behavior sequence might be increased (p. 100).

In our experimental bargaining situation, the availability of threat clearly made it more difficult for bargainers to reach a mutually profitable agreement. These results, we believe, reflect psychological tendencies that are not confined to our bargaining situation: the tendency to use threat (if the means for threatening is available) in an attempt to force the other person to yield, when the other is seen as obstructing one's path; the tendency to respond with counterthreat or increased resistance to attempts at intimidation. How general are these tendencies? What conditions are likely to elicit them? Answers to these questions are necessary before our results can be generalized to other situations.

Dollard, Doob, Miller, Mowrer, and Sears (1939) have cited a variety of evidence to support the view that aggression (i.e., the use of threat) is a common reaction to a person who is seen as the agent of frustration. There seems to be little reason to doubt that the use of threat is a frequent reaction to interpersonal impasses. However, everyday observation indicates that threat does not inevitably occur when there is an interpersonal impasse. We would speculate that it is most likely to occur: when the threatener has no positive interest in the other person's welfare (he is either egocentrically or competitively related to the other); when the threatener believes that the other has no positive interest in his welfare; and when the threatener anticipates either that his threat will be effective or, if ineffective, will not worsen his situation because he expects the worst to happen if he does not use his threat. We suggest that these conditions were operative in our experiment; Ss were either egocentrically or competitively oriented to one another[7] and they felt that they would not be worse off by the use of threat.

Everyday observation suggests that the tendency to respond with counterthreat or increased resistance to attempts at intimidation is also a common occurrence. We believe that introducing threat into a bargaining situation affects the meaning of yielding. Although we have no data to support this interpretation directly, we will attempt to justify it on the basis of some additional assumptions.

Goffman (1955) has pointed out the pervasive significance of "face" in the maintenance of the social order. In this view, self-esteem is a socially validated system that grows out of the acceptance by others of the claim for deference, prestige, and recognition that a person presents in his behavior toward others. Since the rejection of such a claim would be perceived (by the recipient) as directed against his self-esteem, he must react against it rather than accept it in order to maintain the integrity of his self-esteem system.

One may view the behavior of our Ss as an attempt to make claims upon the other, an attempt to develop a set of shared expectations as to what each was entitled to. Why then did the Ss' reactions differ so markedly as a function of the availability of threat? The explanation lies, we believe, in the cultural interpretation of yielding (to a peer or subordinate) under duress, as compared to giving in without duress. The former, we believe, is perceived as a negatively valued form of behavior, with negative implications for the self-image of the person who so behaves. At least partly, this is so because the locus of causality is perceived to be outside the person's voluntary control. No such evaluation, however, need be placed on the behavior of one who "gives in" in a situation where no threat or duress is a factor. Rather, we should expect the culturally defined evaluation of such a person's behavior to be one of "reasonableness" or "maturity," because the source of the individual's behavior is perceived to lie within his own control.

Our discussion so far has suggested that the psychological factors which operate in our experimental bargaining situation are to be found in many real-life bargaining situations. However, it is well to recognize some unique features of our experimental game. First, the bargainers had no opportunity to communicate verbally with one another. Prior research on the role of communication in trust (Deutsch, 1958, 1960; Loomis, 1959) suggests that the opportunity for communication would have made reaching an agreement easier for individualistically-oriented bargainers. This same research (Deutsch, 1960) indicates, however, that communication may not be effective between competitively oriented bargainers. This possibility was expressed spontaneously by a number of our *S*s in a post-game interview.

Another characteristic of our bargaining game is that the passage of time, without coming to an agreement, is costly to the players. There are, of course, bargaining situations in which lack of agreement may simply preserve the *status quo* without any worsening of the bargainers' respective situations. This is the case in the typical bilateral monopoly case, where the buyer and seller are unable to agree upon a price (e.g., see Siegel & Fouraker, 1960). In other sorts of bargaining situations, however, (e.g., labor-management negotiations during a strike, international negotiations during an expensive cold war) the passage of time may play an important role. In our experiment, we received the impression that the meaning of time changed as time passed without the bargainers reaching an agreement. Initially, the passage of time seemed to place the players under pressure to come to an agreement before their costs mounted sufficiently to destroy their profit. With the continued passage of time, however, their mounting losses strengthened their resolution not to yield to the other player. They comment: "I've lost so much, I'll be damned if I give in now. At least I'll have the satisfaction of doing better than she does." The mounting losses and continued deadlock seemed to change the game from a mixed motive into a predominantly competitive situation.

It is, of course, hazardous to generalize from a laboratory experiment to the complex problems of the real world. But our experiment and the theoretical ideas underlying it can perhaps serve to emphasize some notions which, otherwise, have an intrinsic plausibility. In brief, these are that there is more safety in cooperative than in competitive coexistence, that it

is dangerous for bargainers to have weapons, and that it is possibly even more dangerous for a bargainer to have the capacity to retaliate in kind than not to have this capacity when the other bargainer has a weapon. This last statement assumes that the one who yields has more of his values preserved by accepting the agreement preferred by the other than by extended conflict. Of course, in some bargaining situations in the real world, the loss incurred by yielding may exceed the losses due to extended conflict.

SUMMARY

The nature of bargaining situations was discussed. Two general propositions about the conditions affecting the likelihood of a bargaining agreement were presented. The effects of the availability of threat upon interpersonal bargaining were investigated experimentally in a two-person bargaining game. Three experimental conditions were employed: no threat (neither player could threaten the other), unilateral threat (only one of the players had a means of threat available to her), and bilateral threat (both players could threaten each other). The results indicated that the difficulty in reaching an agreement and the amount of (imaginary) money lost, individually as well as collectively, was greatest in the bilateral and next greatest in the unilateral threat condition. Only in the no threat condition did the players make an overall profit. In the unilateral threat condition, the player with the threat capability did better than the player without the threat capability. However, comparing the bilateral and unilateral threat conditions, the results also indicate that when facing a player who had threat capability one was better off *not* having than having the capacity to retaliate in kind.

REFERENCES

Deutsch, M. A theory of cooperation and competition. *Hum. Relat.,* 1949, *2,* 129–152.

Deutsch, M. Trust and suspicion. *J. conflict Resolut.,* 1958, *2,* 265–279.

Deutsch, M. The effect of motivational orientation upon trust and suspicion. *Hum. Relat.,* 1960, *13,* 123–140.

Dollard, J., Doob, L. W., Miller, N. E., Mowrer, O. H., & Sears, R. H. *Frustration and aggression.* New Haven: Yale Univer. Press, 1939.

Goffman, E. On face-work, *Psychiatry,* 1955, *18,* 213–231.

Loomis, J. L. Communication, the development of trust and cooperative behavior. *Hum. Relat.,* 1959, *12,* 305–315.

Schelling, T. C. Bargaining, communication and limited war. *J. conflict Resolut.,* 1957, *1,* 19–38.

Schelling, T. C. The strategy of conflict: Prospectus for the reorientation of game theory. *J. conflict Resolut.,* 1958, *2,* 203–264.

Siegel, S., & Fouraker, L. E. *Bargaining and group decision making.* New York: McGraw-Hill, 1960.

Stone, J. J. An experiment in bargaining games. *Econometrica,* 1958, *26,* 286–296.

Zeuthen, F. *Problems of monopoly and economic warfare.* London: Routledge, 1930.

NOTES

1. Schelling in a series of stimulating papers on bargaining (1957, 1958) has also stressed the "mixed motive" character of bargaining situations and has analyzed some of the cognitive factors which determine agreements.

2. The game was conceived and originated by M. Deutsch; R. M. Krauss designed and constructed the apparatus employed in the experiment.

3. We are indebted to the New Jersey Bell Telephone Company for their cooperation in providing *Ss* and facilities for the experiment.

4. We are indebted to M. J. R. Healy for suggestions concerning the statistical analysis of our data.

5. Medians are used in graphic presentation of our results because the wide variability of means makes inspection cumbersome.

6. A logarithmic transformation of the summed payoffs on each trial for each pair was made before computing the slopes for a given pair.

7. A post-experimental questionnaire indicated that, in all three experimental conditions, the *Ss* were most strongly motivated to win money, next most strongly motivated to do better than the other player, next most motivated to "have fun," and were very little or not at all motivated to help the other player.

CRITICAL THINKING QUESTIONS

1. For many years, the mutually assured destruction (MAD) policy defined U.S. nuclear strategy. That is, nuclear war was to be prevented by the threat of assured destruction of the aggressor nation. What might be the implications of this study for the nuclear policies of nations?

2. The best performance in this study was obtained in the no-threat condition; the unilateral threat condition, in turn, produced better results than the bilateral threat condition, which did the worst. To what extent are these findings generalizable to other situations? In some situations, might it be best to have bilateral threat instead of unilateral threat? What variables might be important in determining when each would be preferred? Explain.

3. In an area such as international relations, how can the existence of threat be reduced? What role may communication play in the process?

ADDITIONAL RELATED READINGS

Boles, T. L., Cross, R. T. A., and Murnighan, J. K. (2000). Deception and retribution in repeated ultimatum bargaining. *Organizational Behavior and Human Decision Processes, 83*(2), 235–259.

Kray, L. J., Thompson, L., and Galinsky, A. (2001). Battle of the sexes: Gender stereotype confirmation and reactance in negotiations. *Journal of Personality and Social Psychology, 80*(6), 942–958.

ARTICLE 36 _____

Article 34 in this chapter presented the concept known as *groupthink*. Since Irving L. Janis proposed this hypothesis nearly 30 years ago, he and others have continued to refine understanding of the antecedent conditions, symptoms, and consequences of groupthink. Since its introduction, groupthink has been widely studied and broadly incorporated into the literature and knowledge base, not only in the field of social psychology but also in areas such as management and organizational behavior.

Many of the published studies about groupthink have consisted of analyses of historical events. For example, the ill-fated decision to launch the space shuttle *Challenger* and the Watergate fiasco are but two of the real-life decision-making processes that have been scrutinized according to the groupthink model. While these studies provide interesting *post hoc* analyses of groupthink experiences, relatively few *experimental* studies have tested the groupthink hypotheses. This is particularly surprising, given the strong appeal of Janis's concept.

The following article by Noni Richardson Ahlfinger and James K. Esser reports the findings of experimental tests of two hypotheses derived from groupthink theory. One is that groups whose leaders promote their own views are likely to experience groupthink, and the other is that groups made up of members who are predisposed to conform are more likely to experience groupthink. This article expands the empirical evidence for the viability of the groupthink concept.

Testing the Groupthink Model
Effects of Promotional Leadership and Conformity Predisposition
■ Noni Richardson Ahlfinger and James K. Esser

Two hypotheses derived from groupthink theory were tested in a laboratory study which included measures of the full range of symptoms of groupthink, symptoms of a poor decision process, and decision quality. The hypothesis that groups whose leaders promoted their own preferred solutions would be more likely to fall victim to groupthink than groups with nonpromotional leaders received partial support. Groups with promotional leaders produced more symptoms of groupthink, discussed fewer facts, and reached a decision more quickly than groups with nonpromotional leaders. The hypothesis that groups composed of members who were predisposed to conform would be more likely to fall victim to groupthink than groups whose members were not predisposed to conform received no support. It is suggested that groupthink research is hampered by measurement problems.

An important issue in the study of groups concerns the determinants of poor versus good decision making. One influential theory of group decision making is Janis's (1972, 1982) groupthink theory. *Groupthink theory* (Janis, 1982; Janis & Mann, 1977) specifies several factors (antecedents of groupthink) which, in combination, facilitate the poor decision making called *groupthink*. These antecedents include high group cohesiveness, a stressful situation, and a variety of structural or administrative factors such as

Reprinted from *Social Behavior and Personality,* 2001, *29*(1), 31–41. Copyright © 2001, Select Press. Reprinted with permission of Society for Personality Research.

insulation of the group, promotional leadership, lack of methodical decision-making procedures, and lack of variety among members' values and perspectives. The present study uses the framework of groupthink theory to investigate the influence of two factors on group decision making: (1) promotional leadership, an antecedent included by Janis, and (2) group members' conformity predisposition, a personality factor not considered by Janis.

The term *groupthink* refers to a premature striving by group members for unanimous agreement on a course of action. Groupthink is undesirable because it cuts off necessary consideration of the pros and cons of the various decision options. Groupthink is identifiable by eight symptoms which represent different ways that group members attempt to avoid, or reduce, the anxiety associated with decision making and protect their self-esteem (Janis, 1982). The symptoms are of three types. Type I symptoms involve overestimating the group; group members share the illusion that the group is invulnerable and the unquestioned belief that the group's cause is just. Type II symptoms involve closed-mindedness. Group members collectively rationalize away information which is inconsistent with their preferred position and stereotype enemies as weak or stupid. Type III symptoms involve pressures toward uniformity. Members tend to censor their own misgivings about the group's position, contributing to a shared illusion that the group is unanimous in its acceptance of the majority position. The group also puts direct pressure on any member who does express a dissenting view. Finally, members may take on the role of mindguards to protect the group from outside information which could threaten the members' confidence in the correctness of the group's position.

When most, or all, of the symptoms of groupthink are present, the group's decision-making process is likely to be seriously flawed. Janis (1972) listed seven symptoms of the defective decision-making process which groupthink can produce: (1) incomplete survey of alternatives, (2) incomplete survey of objectives, (3) failure to examine risks of the preferred choice, (4) failure to reappraise initially rejected alternatives, (5) poor information search, (6) selective bias in processing available information, and (7) failure to develop contingency plans. The end result of this causal

chain is a greater probability that a poor quality decision will be made.

Several reviews of the groupthink literature (Aldag & Fuller, 1993; Esser, 1998; Hart, 1991; Neck & Moorhead, 1995; Park, 1990) have attempted to assess the validity of groupthink theory. However, at present, the best general conclusion may be that although empirical support for predictions derived from groupthink theory has been mixed, at best, too little empirical research has been reported to allow a complete, point-by-point assessment of the validity of groupthink theory.

PROMOTIONAL LEADERSHIP

Among Janis' antecedents of groupthink perhaps the leader's promotional stance has received the most empirical attention. In the first laboratory test of groupthink, Flowers (1977) trained confederates to lead their groups either by promoting their own preferred solution or by encouraging the members to express all possible viewpoints. As predicted by groupthink, she found that groups whose leaders promoted their personal preferences discussed fewer facts and proposed fewer solutions than groups whose leaders encouraged expression of various viewpoints. However, the Flowers study did not examine the full constellation of dependent measures characterizing the groupthink syndrome (i.e., all eight symptoms of groupthink and all seven symptoms of a defective decision process), nor was the quality of the decision examined.

Two additional laboratory experiments have produced some similar leadership effects in support of groupthink predictions. Leana (1985) trained subjects to lead their groups either by promoting an assigned preference or by encouraging discussion of divergent solutions. As predicted, groups with leaders who promoted their assigned solutions proposed and discussed fewer solutions than groups whose leaders encouraged discussion. Similarly, Fodor and Smith (1982) assigned group leaders on the basis of their need for power. They found that groups whose leaders had high power needs (and who, therefore, were likely to behave in ways which promoted their own points of view) discussed fewer facts, proposed fewer alternatives, and tended to express fewer moral concerns than did groups whose leaders had low power needs. Like the Flowers (1977) study, however, these experiments did not examine most of the measures which identify groupthink.

A final laboratory study (Moorhead & Montanari, 1986) included an attempt to measure the full set of antecedents and consequences of groupthink which Janis (1982) listed. Preestablished teams of business students worked on two decision-making tasks, then completed a questionnaire (Moorhead & Montanari, 1982; Montanari & Moorhead, 1989) designed to measure all antecedents and consequences of groupthink. Factor analyses of the questionnaire reduced the set of measures to three antecedents, four symptoms of groupthink, and two symptoms of a poor decision process. A path analysis revealed that, as predicted by groupthink theory, groups with more promotional leaders were more likely to discourage dissent and adopt an illusion of morality than were groups with less promotional leaders. However, contrary to the groupthink hypothesis, groups with more promotional leaders considered more alternatives than did groups with less promotional leaders.

Unlike most laboratory studies of groupthink, research based on the analysis of historical cases involving important group decisions has typically examined a larger set of variables (i.e., the symptoms of groupthink and the symptoms of a poor decision process). After reviewing this literature, Esser (1998) concluded that there is support for the groupthink hypothesis that promotional leadership is related to the presence of groupthink symptoms, symptoms of poor decision process, and poor decision quality (cf., McCauley, 1989; Neck & Moorhead, 1992; Tetlock, Peterson, McGuire, Chang, & Feld, 1992).

CONFORMITY PREDISPOSITION

The nature of the influence process theorized to produce groupthink has been the subject of debate (McCauley, 1989). Janis (1982), himself, usually seemed to consider groupthink to be the result of a nondeliberate conformity in which group members come to believe that their own misgivings about the group's preferred solution are not correct. This private acceptance of the group's position is consistent with Kelman's (1958) process of internalization. However,

at times, Janis (1982) appeared to include deliberate conformity, based on a fear of recrimination, as at least part of the groupthink influence process. As noted by McCauley (1989), Janis' (1982) inclusion of direct pressure on dissenters as a symptom of groupthink suggests that the groupthink influence process can involve also public compliance (Kelman, 1958) without private acceptance of the group's solution. Thus, McCauley (1989, p. 251) defined groupthink as "premature consensus seeking that may involve internalization, compliance, or both."

It seems reasonable to speculate that certain kinds of individual group members may be more or less susceptible to these influence processes which McCauley (1989) has identified. Indeed, Callaway, Marriott, and Esser (1985) reported results supporting their hypothesis that groups composed of highly dominant members would be able to resist the conformity pressures which characterize groupthink. Conversely, groups composed of individuals who depend upon the approval of others to validate their own actions and, hence, who are predisposed to conform, should be particularly likely to fall victim to groupthink.

One promising way that an individual's conformity predisposition might be measured is to use the Concern for Appropriateness (CFA) scale developed by Lennox and Wolfe (1984). The CFA has been validated in several subsequent studies (Johnson, 1989; Wolfe, Lennox & Cutler, 1986; Wolfe, Welch, Lennox & Cutler, 1985).

HYPOTHESES

The present study was designed to examine the effects of leadership and group composition on a full range of groupthink indicators. The first hypothesis was that groups led by leaders who promoted their own preferred solutions would produce a group process characterized by symptoms of groupthink, symptoms of poor decision making, and a poor quality decision. The second hypothesis was that groups whose members were predisposed to conform would produce a group process characterized by symptoms of groupthink, symptoms of poor decision making, and a poor quality decision.

METHOD

Subjects and Design

The design of the study was a 2 (leadership: promotional or nonpromotional) × 2 (conformity predisposition: high or low). Four hundred and fifty-nine students enrolled in introductory psychology classes were prescreened to determine their conformity predisposition. Students who scored in the top 45 percent on the Concern for Appropriateness scale (CFA; Lennox & Wolfe, 1984) were classified as having a high predisposition to conform and were assigned to groups in the high conformity predisposition conditions. Likewise, students who scored in the bottom 45 percent on the CFA were classified as having a low predisposition to conform and were assigned to groups in the low conformity predisposition conditions. Assignment of subjects to experimental conditions and groups was otherwise random. This procedure produced 16 groups of either four or five members in each of the four cells of the design.

Procedure

To prescreen for conformity predisposition the CFA was administered to students in large groups (*n* = 20–30). The CFA is composed of 20 items, each of which is scored on a 0–5 scale. A higher score was interpreted as indicating a greater predisposition to conform. For the present sample of 459 students the CFA had good internal consistency reliability, alpha = .89. Based on their CFA scores, students were classified as either high (upper 45 percent) or low (lower 45 percent) in conformity predisposition.

Homogeneous groups of high or low conformers were scheduled for each experimental session. Each group was composed of four or five members. Groups were randomly assigned to leadership conditions.

When subjects arrived for their experimental session, they were asked to sign informed consent forms which included the information that their group would be video-recorded. Then the experimenter selected the subject who had arrived first to be the group leader. The group was asked to wait quietly while the experimenter trained the leader. The experimenter then took the leader to a separate room and gave leadership instructions which were adapted from those used by Flowers (1977). *Nonpromotional leaders* were instructed to (1) begin the group decision making with a statement (and later remind the group) that the most important thing was to weigh all viewpoints in order to arrive at the best possible decision; (2) refrain from stating the leader's own preferred solution until all group members had stated their preferred solutions; and (3) encourage discussion of all possible solutions. *Promotional leaders* were instructed to (1) begin the group decision making with a statement (and later remind the group) that the most important thing was for the members to be in total agreement with the group decision; (2) state the leader's preferred solution immediately after the leader's opening statement and before any group members had an opportunity to speak; and (3) discourage discussion of possible alternative solutions.

Next, the leader was returned to the group. The group task was assigned, and a copy of the task materials and a stopwatch were given to the leader. The leader was told to use the stopwatch to keep track of how much time the group took to reach its decision. However, the experimenter kept the official time. After the group completed the decision task, the experimenter collected these materials and distributed two questionnaires to all subjects. Finally, subjects were thanked for their participation, debriefed, and dismissed.

Dependent Variables

The *Black Bear!* task (B. Glaser, 1993) was used to provide two measures of decision quality. The scenario describes a hike in the Smokey Mountains in which the leader is mauled by a black bear. First, the group is to select one best strategy to save the leader's life from a list of five possible strategies. A wilderness-survival expert gave each possible strategy a quality score ranging from zero to 50, with a lower score representing a higher quality decision. Next, a list of 10 backpack items must be rank ordered according to their value for executing this best strategy. The sum of the absolute differences between expert rankings and the group's ranking of backpack items provided a second quality score (a low score represents high decision quality).

Symptoms of groupthink were assessed using a questionnaire called the *Groupthink Index* (R. Glaser, 1993). This questionnaire contains 40 items, five items for each of the eight symptoms of groupthink. Therefore, a total groupthink score and a score for each symptom were obtained. In each case the responses of group members were averaged in order to provide a group score.

Additional measures of the decision process were obtained in two ways. First, the experimenter noted the amount of time the group required to reach its decision. Second, two raters independently viewed the videotapes of the decision-making sessions and counted the number of (1) alternatives discussed, (2) goals discussed, (3) risks discussed, (4) rejected alternatives which were discussed again, (5) contingency plans discussed, (6) different facts discussed, and (7) statements of disagreement.

RESULTS

Leadership Manipulation Check

The leadership manipulation was assessed by having each group member complete a four-item questionnaire about the group leader's behavior. These data were analyzed by first finding the mean for each group for each question. Next, these scores were analyzed using a 2 (leadership: promotional or nonpromotional) × 2 (conformity predisposition: low or high) analysis of variance (ANOVA) for each question.

The first question asked the degree to which the leader suggested his/her own solution to the problem. The ANOVA yielded a significant main effect of leadership, $F(1,60) = 17.77$, $p < .001$, and no other significant effects. As intended, promotional leaders ($M = 3.88$) were seen as suggesting their own solutions to the problem to a greater degree than were nonpromotional leaders ($M = 3.24$).

The remaining three questions asked the degree to which the leader encouraged discussion of every suggested solution, stressed the importance of weighing all viewpoints to reach a good decision, and stressed that the most important thing was for the group to agree on its decision. ANOVAs on these items revealed no significant effects.

Symptoms of Groupthink

The *Groupthink Index* yielded a total score and subscale scores corresponding to each of the eight symptoms of groupthink for each subject. Internal reliabilities for the total scale and for the subscales were estimated by calculating coefficient alphas, using data from the 284 subjects who completed the *Groupthink Index.* Next, means for each decision-making group were obtained. These group means were used in 2 (leadership) × 2 (conformity) ANOVAs performed on the total scale and on the eight subscales.

The internal consistency of the total *Groupthink Index* was acceptable, alpha = .70. The ANOVA revealed a significant main effect of leadership, $F(1,60)$ 4.52, $p < .05$. As hypothesized, groups with promotional leaders ($M = 106.42$) had higher scores on the *Groupthink Index* than did groups with nonpromotional leaders ($M = 102.28$). No other significant effects were found.

The internal consistency reliabilities of the subscales ranged from clearly unacceptable (alphas = .02, .11, and .25 for the belief in the group's morality, rationalization, and pressuring dissenters symptoms, respectively) to marginal (alphas = .32, .36, .40, .45, and .46 for mindguarding, self-censorship, stereotyping, unanimity, and invulnerability respectively). ANOVAs performed on the subscales revealed two significant leadership main effects. As hypothesized, members of groups with promotional leaders reported more self-censorship ($M = 13.27$) than did members of groups with nonpromotional leaders ($M = 12.15$), $F(1,60) = 11.82$, $p < .01$. Also as hypothesized, members of groups with promotional leaders reported more mindguarding ($M = 12.38$) than did members of groups with nonpromotional leaders ($M = 11.62$), $F(1,60) = 4.81$, $p < .05$.

Because the internal consistency reliabilities of the individual groupthink symptom subscales were low, the entire 40-item *Groupthink Index* was subjected to a principal components analysis ($n = 284$). This analysis with a varimax rotation yielded three interpretable factors, which accounted for 28.4 percent of the variance. The first factor accounted for 15.4 percent of the variance and was composed of six items with loadings ranging from .49 to .61. This factor involved an objective attitude, avoiding a closed-minded, self-righteous orientation. The second factor accounted for an additional 7.7 percent of the variance. It was composed of four items with loadings ranging from .49 to .69 and focused on a procedure which encourages intellectual conflict and debate. The third factor accounted for 5.2 percent of the variance and was composed of four items with loadings ranging from .55 to .61. This factor reflected the belief that the majority is correct, and involved pressure on dissenters.

Decision Process

Two raters independently scored videotapes of the group decisions for the number of occurrences of the seven aspects of the group decision process. Interrater reliabilities ranged from .46 for both the number of goals discussed and number of risks discussed to .75 for the number of alternative solutions discussed. (In addition, the raters were in complete agreement that no contingency plans were discussed by any group; because of this lack of variability no reliability coefficient could be computed for this process measure.) Discrepancies between the raters' scores were resolved by averaging them.

ANOVAs on these decision process ratings revealed one significant leadership main effect, $F(1,60)$ = 11,52, $p < .01$. As hypothesized, groups with promotional leaders brought up fewer facts (M = 13.28) than did groups with nonpromotional leaders (M = 18.63).

Time Required to Reach a Decision

The number of minutes required by each group to reach a decision was analyzed by ANOVA. This analysis revealed a main effect of leadership, $F(1,60)$ = 4.04, $p < .05$. As expected, groups with promotional leaders reached a decision more quickly (M = 19.72) than did groups with nonpromotional leaders (M = 22.91).

Decision Quality

The two decision quality scores—the selected strategy for saving the leader's life and the ranking of backpack items—were analyzed by separate ANOVAs. Neither analysis yielded any significant effects.

DISCUSSION

The present study investigated two hypotheses: (1) that groups whose leaders promoted their own preferred solutions would exhibit symptoms of groupthink, symptoms of a poor decision-making process, and poor quality decisions, and (2) that groups whose members were predisposed to conform would exhibit symptoms of groupthink, symptoms of a poor decision-making process, and poor quality decisions. The first hypothesis received partial support, while the second hypothesis received no support.

The present results dovetail with previous laboratory studies of the effects of promotional leadership on groupthink. The authors found that groups with promotional leaders produced more symptoms of groupthink, discussed fewer facts, and reached a decision more quickly than did groups with nonpromotional leadership.

Because it is the first experiment which has examined the effects of promotional leadership on the full range of groupthink indicators, the present study represents an attempt to extend understanding of the leadership-groupthink relationship. However, these results should be interpreted cautiously. Only five analyses of the measures of groupthink consequences (symptoms of groupthink, symptoms of a poor decision-making process, and decision quality) yielded statistically significant effects. Perhaps the authors' manipulation of promotional leadership was not as effective as had been intended. Only one of four manipulation check items indicated that the manipulation was successful.

Another problem in the present study, and in groupthink research, generally, concerns the measurement of groupthink indicators. For example, in the present study the *Groupthink Index* (R. Glaser, 1993) was used to assess the presence of symptoms of groupthink. The estimate of the internal consistency reliability of the overall, 40-item scale was acceptable, but the reliability estimates for the 5-item scales for the individual groupthink symptoms were questionable, at best. A similar concern can be raised regarding the only other groupthink symptom questionnaire which has been reported in the groupthink literature, a 24-item scale developed by Moorhead and Montanari (1982; Montanari & Moorhead, 1989).

The second hypothesis, that groups composed of members who were predisposed to conform would be candidates for groupthink, was based on McCauley's (1989) interpretation of groupthink as sometimes involving compliance—public conformity to the group's preferred position, but without private acceptance. The question remains, however, under what conditions does compliance in groupthink occur? McCauley (1989, p. 258) offered only the "tantalizing hint" that compliance may be most likely when the groupthink antecedent of group homogeneity is absent. The authors believe that, in the present experiment, groups were homogeneous; all participants were students enrolled in introductory psychology classes at a state-supported, regional university. Most grew up and attended high schools within a 60 mile radius of the university campus. Hence, their values and perspectives could be expected to be similar. Thus, they may have been testing for the compliance process in circumstances where it was not to be expected.

In conclusion, the present experiment provides additional support for the groupthink hypothesis regarding the effects of promotional leadership. However, no support was obtained for the hypothesis that groups of people who are predisposed to conform would be more susceptible to groupthink than groups of less conforming people. It is suggested that the further development of better ways to measure groupthink indicators (viz., groupthink symptoms and symptoms of poor decision process) is perhaps the greatest need for future laboratory research on groupthink.

REFERENCES

Aldag, R. J. & Fuller, S. R. (1993). Beyond fiasco: A reappraisal of the groupthink phenomenon and a new model of group decision processes. *Psychological Bulletin, 113,* 533–552.

Callaway, M. R., Marriott, R. G., & Esser, J. K. (1985). Effects of dominance on group decision making: Toward a stress reduction explanation of groupthink. *Journal of Personality and Social Psychology, 49,* 949–952.

Esser, J. K. (1998). Alive and well after 25 years: A review of groupthink research. *Organizational Behavior and Human Decision Processes, 73,* 116–141.

Flowers, M. L. (1977). A laboratory test of some implications of Janis's groupthink hypothesis. *Journal of Personality and Social Psychology, 35,* 888–896.

Fodor, E. M. & Smith, T. (1982). The power motive as an influence on group decision making. *Journal of Personality and Social Psychology, 42,* 178–185.

Glaser, B. (1993). *Black bear!* King of Prussia, PA: Organization Design and Development.

Glaser, R. (1993). *Groupthink index.* King of Prussia, PA: Organization Design and Development.

Hart, P. 't (1991). Irving L. Janis' *Victims of groupthink. Political Psychology, 12,* 247–278.

Janis, I. L. (1972). *Victims of groupthink.* Boston: Houghton-Mifflin.

Janis, I. L. (1982). *Groupthink.* (2nd ed.). Boston: Houghton-Mifflin.

Janis, I. L. & Mann, L. (1977). *Decision making: A psychological analysis of conflict, choice, and commitment.* New York: Free Press.

Johnson, M. A. (1989). Concern for Appropriateness Scale and behavioral conformity. *Journal of Personality Assessment, 53,* 567–574.

Kelman, H. C. (1958). Compliance, identification, and internalization: Three processes of attitude change. *Journal of Conflict Resolution, 2,* 51–60.

Leana, C. R. (1985). A partial test of Janis' groupthink model: Effects of group cohesiveness and leader behavior on defective decision making. *Journal of Management, 11,* 5–17.

Lennox, R. D. & Wolfe, R. N. (1984). Revision of the Self-Monitoring Scale. *Journal of Personality and Social Psychology, 46,* 1349–1364.

McCauley, C. (1989). The nature of social influence in groupthink: Compliance and internalization. *Journal of Personality and Social Psychology, 57,* 250–260.

Montanari, J. R. & Moorhead, G. (1989). Development of the Groupthink Assessment Inventory. *Educational and Psychological Measurement, 49,* 209–219.

Moorhead, G. & Montanari, J. R. (1982). Groupthink: A research methodology. In G. P. White (Ed.), *Proceedings of the 14th Annual Meeting of the American Institute for Decision Sciences* (vol. 1, pp. 380–382).

Moorhead, G. & Montanari, J. R. (1986). An empirical investigation of the groupthink phenomenon. *Human Relations, 39,* 399–410.

Neck, C. P. & Moorhead, G. (1992). Jury deliberations in the trial of U.S. v. John DeLorean: A case analysis of groupthink avoidance and an enhanced framework. *Human Relations,* **48,** 1077–1091.

Neck, C. P. & Moorhead, G. (1995). Groupthink remodeled: The importance of leadership, time pressure, and methodical decision-making procedures. *Human Relations,* **48,** 537–557.

Park, W. (1990). A review of research on groupthink. *Journal of Behavioral Decision Making,* **3,** 229–245.

Tetlock, P. E., Peterson, R. S., McGuire, C., Chang, S. & Feld, P. (1992). Assessing political group dynamics: A test of the groupthink model. *Journal of Personality and Social Psychology,* **63,** 403–425.

Wolfe, R. N., Lennox, R. D. & Cutler, B. L. (1986). Getting along and getting ahead: Empirical support for a theory of protective and acquisitive self-presentation.

Journal of Personality and Social Psychology, **50,** 356–361.

Wolfe, R. N., Welch, L. K.. Lennox, R. D. & Cutler, B. L. (1985). Concern for appropriateness as a moderator variable in the statistical explanation of the self reported use of alcohol and marijuana. *Journal of Personality,* **53,** 1–16.

This article is based on the first author's master's thesis, directed by the second author.

The authors thank Dr. Eileen Russo, Director of Research, Organization Design & Development, Inc. for allowing them to use the *Groupthink Index* and *Black Bear!* materials.

Acknowledgement is due to reviewers including: Michael R. Callaway, Department of Family Medicine, University of Texas Medical Branch, Galveston, TX, USA; and Fred Switzer, III, Department of Psychology, Clemson University, SC, USA.

CRITICAL THINKING QUESTIONS

1. One of the variables investigated in the study was leadership style. To what extent can leadership style be taught? To what extent is leadership style a product of individual personality? Describe the personality characteristics of a leader who would *not* likely try to prevent the development of groupthink. Explain your choices.

2. Consult a social psychology textbook, and read about the different styles of leadership. Which styles might be most prone to the development of groupthink? Design either a laboratory study or a field study to examine how various leadership styles affect the emergence of groupthink.

3. The article concludes by stating that "Further development of better ways to measure groupthink indicators (viz., groupthink symptoms and symptoms of poor decision process) is perhaps the greatest need for future laboratory research on groupthink." Design such a study.

4. Do you think that the homogeneity of the subjects' backgrounds in this experiment had an influence on the outcomes? Discuss how homogeneity, in general, and heterogeneity of backgrounds, in particular, might impact the groupthink process.

Chapter Thirteen

APPLYING
SOCIAL PSYCHOLOGY
Law and Business

Both of the last two chapters in this book of readings have *Applying Social Psychology* in their titles. This heading needs some explaining, however, since it otherwise might create the wrong impression for the reader.

Applying social psychology usually refers to the application of principles and findings generated by research in social psychology to real-world settings. In a sense, this is where social psychology is used to help solve practical problems. But by labeling these chapters *applied*, it might seem to suggest that the preceding 12 chapters were not applied and did not have real-world applications. If you already have read through the preceding chapters, you know that is not the case. Many of the studies in the earlier chapters have direct implications for real-world problems. Although the research may seem abstract and theoretical at times, we need only apply the principles to various social problems to yield applied forms of social psychology.

What distinguishes the research in Chapters 13 and 14 is that it was specifically designed and conducted to address significant real-world issues. Such research has been done in many, many areas. The issues presented here reflect some of the most common areas of concern, but they are by no means the only topics in the domain of applied social psychology.

This chapter addresses the contributions of social psychology to both the forensic (legal) and work arenas. In one form or another, you probably have had some contact with the legal system. Perhaps you (or someone you know) have been arrested and even tried for some offense. Maybe you have been asked to be a juror. More likely, you have watched televised trials or read about real or fictional trials in the media. Does the legal system, as it presently operates, guarantee an objective, unbiased outcome?

Social psychologists working in the forensic field have examined a number of factors that may influence the outcomes in legal settings. Two of the articles in this chapter look at jury trials, which clearly are a major element of the U.S. judicial system. Article 37, "Juries and Justice: Is the System Obsolete?" examines the forces at work in the present legal system that make it difficult to assemble an impartial jury—for instance, extensive pretrial media publicity and the use of courtroom consultants to select specific jurors who will likely favor a certain side. The article tries to make the case that the current system may no longer work.

Article 38, "Beautiful but Dangerous," likewise examines jury trials. However, this article looks at the relationship between the attractiveness of an offender and the nature of the crime and how these two factors may influence the jury's judgment.

You may never have direct contact with the legal system, but it is very likely that a major part of your life will be spent at work. When you apply for a job, what single factor will be most influential in deciding whether you are offered the position? Will it be your GPA? Where you went to school? How well you present yourself during the interview? You only hope that whatever is being evaluated about you has some direct relationship to the job for which you are applying. However, a good deal of evidence suggests that irrelevant characteristics, such as a person's race, may have a subtle yet negative impact on hiring decisions. Article 39, "Aversive Racism and Selection Decisions: 1989 and 1999," examines how this subtle form of racism still exists today and how it may affect hiring decisions.

ARTICLE 37 _____

One cornerstone of the U.S. legal system is the right to a jury trial by one's peers. Perhaps you have already served as a juror. If not, you may very well have that opportunity in the future. As a juror, you are expected to make a conscientious effort to determine a defendant's guilt or innocence based on the weight of the evidence presented in the trial. Your personal biases and beliefs should not come into play. Your decision is supposed to be made objectively.

But is that the way the legal system really works? Is it possible for people to somehow disconnect themselves from their own attitudes and biases and really judge a case objectively? A great deal of social psychological research conducted over the years suggests that achieving this objectivity may be easier said than done. For example, irrelevant factors such as a defendant's physical appearance, gender, and race have been found to impact jurors' decisions.

In the last few years, several new factors have been imposed on the jury trial system that may further limit the objectivity of jurors. First is the amount of media coverage given to trials, especially in high-profile cases. Given the amount of pretrial publicity surrounding many cases, is it possible to find jurors who have not been influenced by what they may have heard or read outside the courtroom? Second, social psychology itself has entered into the jury selection process. Lawyers often employ courtroom consultants to help select jurors who will favor their side, which means that the jurors selected may not be a representative sample of the defendant's peers after all. Barbara Bradley explores these and other issues affecting contemporary jury trials and raises questions as to whether the trial-by-jury system really works anymore.

Juries and Justice
Is the System Obsolete?

■ Barbara Bradley

The murder trial of O. J. Simpson has gripped the country like no other in recent history. Broadcast live over cable's Court TV and recapped nightly on the evening news, it has been more popular than most made-for-TV movies—and the ratings prove it.

But as the trial nears its midpoint, a harsh and nagging question remains: Will the Simpson jury be able to deliver a fair verdict? Or have the months of testimony, the crowds of legal consultants, the confusing technical evidence and the pressure to reach a popular verdict so overwhelmed the jury that delivering justice may just be too much to ask?

"I think there will be skepticism and cynicism about this verdict no matter what happens," says Stephen Adler, a legal editor at the *Wall Street Journal* and author of *The Jury: Trial and Error in the American Courtroom*, one of several new books on the decline of the jury system. "There's a feeling that the system has gotten away from us, that it doesn't belong to the people any more—that lawyers are manipulative, jury consultants manipulate the process and that justice may not be the ultimate result."

The Simpson trial is only the latest in a series of high-profile cases that have contributed to the growing disillusionment. In the widely watched trials of Erik and Lyle Menendez, Lorena Bobbitt and the Los Angeles police officers who beat Rodney King, for example, no one disputed that the defendants actually committed the crimes of which they were accused—yet the juries found none of them guilty.

And the fault for these apparent miscarriages of justice, say many, lies with the jury system itself. "The jury as an institution is an anachronism," says Kate Stith, a criminal-law professor at the Yale Law School and former federal prosecutor in New York. "It's hard to believe that in the 20th century we'd come up with this system."

In fact, the right to a jury of one's peers dates back to 1791, when the Sixth Amendment was ratified. Jurors then were expected to be active participants in a trial, and since they were drawn from the local community, they often knew the defendant, the witnesses and the events surrounding the crime itself. But in the 19th century, jurors began to be seen as "blank slates," and the rules changed.

As modern technology and psychology transform the trial process, jurors today are forced to play by outdated rules. They can't ask questions in court, for example, and often they're barred from taking notes. They aren't allowed to discuss the case as it unfolds. They're selected specifically for their ignorance about the defendant and the crime itself and aren't allowed to gather any information on their own. They are kept from seeing critical evidence. As cases become longer, more complex and involve more technical evidence, jurors are finding they can't keep up. They have remained, in short, abacus users in the age of the computer.

During the last three decades, four seismic events have shaken the jury system to its core: the rise of media interest and courtroom cameras; the advent of racially diverse juries; the use of social psychology in the courtroom; and the increasing complexity of trials. These phenomena have reshaped the trial process, and the system has not made corresponding adjustments to help jurors cope. As a result, the fate of Simpson may have less to do with the evidence than with factors unrelated to his guilt or innocence.

Few, if any, argue that the jury system should be abandoned—and certainly not on the basis of celebrated trials such as Simpson's. Yet, the flaws of that case can be seen in other courtrooms across the country every day. True, few trials take place on prime-time television. But in the age of Court TV, more and more unknowns are candidates for national attention. (Whoever heard of Lorena Bobbitt before her famous slice?) Jury consultants and technical evidence are commonplace. And the race issue, considered to be the wild card in the Simpson trial, permeates trials in almost every part of the country.

Of all the new pressures on the system, the effect of the media is most visible. Shortly after the bodies of Nicole Brown Simpson and Ronald Goldman were found last June 13, the television cameras started filming—and haven't stopped. From the surreal chase of the white Bronco (covered live by helicopter) to the nationally broadcast 911 tape of Nicole Simpson screaming in fear, publicity made it almost impossible to find people who had not formed an opinion of the case. More than 100 candidates were rejected before 12 jurors and 12 alternates were picked.

The publicity of the trial will haunt even those seated, according to Thomas Hafemeister, senior staff attorney and psychoanalyst at the National Center for State Courts in Williamsburg, Va. "Jurors know the community is looking over their shoulders" in any high-publicity case, says Hafemeister, who is conducting a study on juror stress. "They have to face their family and friends, and they have to justify their verdicts."

Moreover, in high-publicity trials, jurors hear both more and less information than the public—which can create outrage with the system when the jury fails to arrive at the same verdict as the public. For example, when William Kennedy Smith was being tried for rape in 1991, the press widely reported Smith's history of aggressive sexual behavior. But the jury heard none of that and acquitted him—leaving many in the public furious.

The King trial demonstrated what can happen when the public has only partial information about a case. Viewers of the famous 81-second videotape had no trouble concluding that the four Los Angeles police officers had used excessive force with King. But many who actually saw the trial said the prosecution did not prove guilt beyond a reasonable doubt—a requirement of law, but not public opinion.

Perhaps more dramatically, says Professor Abraham Goldstein of the Yale Law School, the riots that followed the officers' acquittal raised the stakes for any future jury contemplating a socially unacceptable verdict. And because jurors routinely give interviews to journalists about the deliberations, every juror knows that he or she might become the target of public contempt. "Now jurors know that they will be pursued by the media, that many of their number will talk to the media and be unguarded in their comments," Goldstein tells *Insight*. "This has the potential to destroy the secrecy of the jury room and affect the freedom of the jury to deliberate."

Such concerns were on the mind of Hazel Thornton, a juror in the trial of Erik Menendez—who, with his brother Lyle, shot and killed their parents as they were eating ice cream in front of the television in 1989. During the five-month trial, another high-publicity trial in Los Angeles ended with a jury acquitting Damian Williams of all but one relatively minor charge in the beating of truck driver Reginald Denny during the Los Angeles riots. As in the King trial, the beating of Denny had been videotaped, and the verdict also was met with public dismay. Thornton says all she cared about was reaching the right verdict in the Menendez case—but she felt the pressure nonetheless.

"I wasn't allowed to pay that much attention to the news at that time, but I did know that the verdict was extremely unpopular," Thornton recalls. "What I did hear was the jurors being criticized as idiots, and I was afraid that we would be criticized in the same way when our verdict came out."

Clearly it would be constitutionally risky to muzzle either the news media or the jurors after a verdict is returned, although Goldstein advocates some limits. Still, he and others say, it's time to consider whether a jury operating under a media spotlight is capable of voting according to the facts, without second-guessing the reaction of the public.

Another hot-button issue in both the King and Simpson cases has been race. The very fact that the Simpson jury includes any members of minority groups at all underscores fundamental changes that have rewritten the book on courtroom dynamics. The Supreme Court outlawed discrimination on the basis of race in 1986 and last year extended the protection to gender. Still, race remains a factor: In the Simpson case, the Los Angeles District Attorney's office decided to try Simpson in central Los Angeles rather than the more predominantly white Brentwood area in which the murders took place, to avoid a predominantly white jury. Many court watchers believe that the prosecution is most worried about a hung jury, which they believe would be more likely if African-Americans were a minority in the jury room.

The strategy, of course, is a calculated risk; according to a recent Harris poll, 68 percent of African-Americans believe Simpson is innocent vs. 61 percent of whites who believe him guilty. And after the King beating, some believe that the resentment among many blacks toward the Los Angeles police could tip the scales. In a *Los Angeles Times* poll last fall, 70 percent of African-Americans in that city said they believed police officers commonly lie on the witness stand. That must give the prosecution pause: The star witness in the Simpson case, Mark Fuhrman, is a white detective; the defense is trying to portray him as a racist.

Another factor affecting juries has been the rise of professional trial consultants. About 20 years ago, attorneys began hiring social psychologists and market researchers to help them pick the most sympathetic jurors and tailor their arguments to specific juries. Author Stephen Adler says trial consultants have shaken the credibility of the jury system. "I think that one of the current crises of the jury system is this widening perception that, in fact, we don't have a true cross-section of the community—we have a manipulated, strategically placed jury that may not be there to do justice in the first place."

Jury consultants have been credited with snatching a victory—or a mistrial—from almost certain defeat. For example, in the case of the Menendez brothers, the Los Angeles prosecutors claimed the young men were after an early inheritance. The defense argued they were reacting to years of abuse—not an easy argument to sell, notes Lois Heaney, a trial consultant at the National Jury Project in Minneapolis, which was hired by the Menendez defense team.

"The idea that two young men would kill their parents is, for many, a phenomenon for which there can be no justification," she says. What was needed was a defense similar to battered woman syndrome, in which a wife kills her husband when he is, say, asleep on the couch, because she's afraid of the next beating. "You really need to have people who understand a psychological self-defense, an urgency to act."

To select a jury sympathetic to such a defense, Heaney focused on prospective jurors' attitudes toward psychologists and psychiatrists, who would be the keys to the young men's defense. When the jury for Erik Menendez was seated, it was evenly divided between men and women. Perhaps because women are more often the victims of domestic violence, the six women could accept a self-defense argument and wanted to convict for manslaughter. The six men held out for premeditated murder. "I realized we had a hung jury before we even deliberated," recalls juror Thornton.

Jurors also increasingly face long trials and complex evidence, as is the case with the Simpson trial. Will the jurors be able to remember all the instances in which Judge Lance Ito told them to disregard information, for example, and strike what they heard from their memories? "I say to my students, 'Okay, imagine you have to take a midterm exam,'" explains Valerie Hans, professor of criminal justice and psychology at the University of Delaware and author of *Judging the Jury.* "You have to sit there for several months. You are not allowed to take notes. You cannot ask any questions if you are confused—you have to allow other people to ask questions for you, and of course they may not ask the ones you were concerned about." Her students, she says, look terrified at the idea. "It really brings it home to them how antiquated this system is."

Some attorneys, critics say, use the faults of the system to their advantage by trying to pick the least-capable jurors they can find. "The whole nature of the game right now is to try to strike out people whose views, whose skills you're afraid of," says John Langbein, a legal historian at Yale Law School. "Particularly if you're defense counsel, what you're most concerned about is somebody who's smart enough to see your guy's guilty despite all the tricks you might be employing."

"When you see a lawyer trying to pick a smart jury," famed defense attorney F. Lee Bailey reportedly once said, "you know he's got a strong case. [Defense attorney] Percy Foreman and I once had an argument as to which of us had picked the most stupid jury."

Not surprisingly, the system tends to filter out educated jurors. According to a 1987 study by Joe Cecil at the Federal Judicial Center, the longer and more complex the trial, the less educated the jurors tended to be; while 32 percent of jurors in short cases had college degrees, that figure dropped to 22 percent in long and complex cases. "One thing we didn't do is figure out why the education level decreases," Cecil tells *Insight.* "Is it that attorneys are exercising more peremptories [to get smarter people off the jury]? Or is the judge excusing jurors who weren't able to serve for extended periods?"

Many judges will excuse candidates from a long trial if, for example they cannot take the time off work. What that often leaves, says William Jones, a trial attorney in Phoenix, is a jury pool heavily skewed toward unemployed and less-educated people. And that can have a direct impact on the verdict. Jones recalls one case in which he was defending the city of Phoenix in a personal-injury lawsuit. The issues were complicated, involving road design and questions of liability. The judge told the potential jurors that the trial probably would last eight weeks, and anyone who could not spare that much time could serve on another trial.

When the dust from the stampede settled, Jones was left with "largely unemployed people, people who didn't have any appreciation for what the value of a dollar really is," he says. "It had a horrible effect. There was a very large verdict for the plaintiff—$7 million, and we ultimately settled for $2 million—which didn't surprise me. They didn't understand one issue in the entire case."

Despite the flaws in the jury system, almost no one is suggesting abolishing the Sixth Amendment right to have one's "peers" decide one's fate. The alternative—placing that power solely in the hands of judges—runs counter to the democratic values that define this country.

"One of the most important things about the jury system is it brings credibility to the verdict, if it's working right," Adler concludes. "If you have a jury that's a true cross-section of community, I think the public is much more likely to accept the verdict if it comes from a jury than if it comes from a judge—even if it's unpopular."

The operative phrase, of course, is "if it's working right." With the memory of the Los Angeles riots still fresh and public faith in the system declining, legal experts say there must be some quick and fundamental reforms if justice is to be found in the courthouse and not on the streets.

A growing number of judges and legal scholars are trying to bring the system into the 21st century. Thomas Munsterman, director of the Center for Jury Studies at the National Center for State Courts in Arlington, Va., says that judges are going to profes-

---

DNA: 'Blood Evidence'

Generally, criminal trials are not as intellectually daunting as, say, patent or antitrust civil trials. But one area of criminal law that is perplexing jurors is central to the O. J. Simpson trial—DNA evidence.

"This is a case that really comes down to the blood evidence," says Erwin Chemerinsky, a law professor at the University of Southern California. "If the blood evidence is presented in an understandable, credible way, it could be a conviction. If the blood evidence is undermined by the defense, it could be an acquittal—and then obviously the jury could split all over the place."

Unfortunately, jurors are notoriously bad at understanding blood evidence—in particular the probabilities that there is a match between a blood sample and a defendant. Say that the blood type found on a crime scene is the blood type of 1 percent of the Los Angeles population. The "prosecutor's fallacy" would be that if that blood is the same type as that of the defendant, there's a 99 percent chance it came from that person; therefore, he or she is guilty. The "defense attorney's fallacy" implies innocence: It says that 1 percent of the population—thousands of people—could have committed the crime, so the evidence is worthless. According to DNA expert William Thompson of the University of California at Irvine, both arguments are wrong.

In a study of university students, who might be better-educated than the Simpson jury, Thompson found that the subjects fell into one of the two fallacies—that is, they misinterpreted the evidence 78 percent of the time. "We'd get some hilarious results," Thompson says. "You'd present them with one fallacy, and they'd say, 'Yeah, that sounds right.' And then you'd present them with the other fallacy, and they'd say, 'That sounds right too!'"

Thompson (who also is an adviser to the Simpson defense team) says his study does not indicate that jurors are stupid. Indeed, he found that only the most highly trained professionals, including statisticians and Ph.D. candidates, consistently figured out that both arguments were fallacies. But, he says, the inability of jurors to handle this kind of evidence presents ethical questions for attorneys. "It raises real concerns whether these problems can be dealt with effectively by arguments in front of the jury," he says, "because what it means is that an ethical lawyer who wants to argue for the truth is going to lose in face of these facile fallacies from the opposition. And it looks like the best way to fight one fallacy is with a contrary fallacy."

In the end, it may not matter, says Thomas Munsterman, director of the Center for Jury Studies at the National Center for State Courts. According to exit questionnaires, jurors generally ignore information that is confusing or conflicting. "If there is one expert who says yes and another expert that says no, the jurors basically tune out the experts. They say, if these two learned people, both being recognized by this court as experts, can't agree, what are we to do? Maybe we'll just base it on something else."   —*BB*

sional educators to ask them how people learn. "And they tell you, we permit them feedback, taking notes; every so often we'll stop and review where we've been," he says. "All of the things that we don't do in a jury trial."

According to B. Michael Dann, a superior court judge in Phoenix, several studies have shown that jurors do not understand 50 percent of the judge's instructions at the end of the trial—the equivalent of assembling all the ingredients of a cake but failing to follow the recipe. Dann says that to communicate with jurors, judges and attorneys should adjust their language to a level at which they might speak to sixth-graders because the legal jargon used in the courtroom often leaves jurors befuddled. This creates "frustration and anger" in the jury box, he says, "and it's danger-ous, because an angry, confused jury can distort the outcome, can distort the quality of their decision-making and make the jury more unpredictable than they otherwise are."

So, shortly after donning his robes in 1980, Dann began to experiment. He essentially ran his courtroom like a classroom. He allowed jurors to ask questions and take notes. He asked attorneys to give mini-summations throughout the trial. He also delivered his instructions to the jury at the beginning of the trial, not at the end, as most judges do. Therefore, jurors understood exactly what the prosecutor needed to show to prove manslaughter, for example.

"Most prosecutors don't like jury involvement— even less than defense attorneys," says Michael Kemp, a state prosecutor in Phoenix. "They're afraid the jury will come up with questions they don't want raised" and thus insert an element of doubt. But this situation has worked to his advantage. In a rape case a few years ago, a juror asked a question. "It was something like, 'Was the victim alone with the defendant at the time?'—very down-to-earth stuff, which lawyers al-ways overlook. And we just looked at each other and said, 'Wow, what were we thinking about?'" He won the case in part, he says, because of that question.

Dann's innovations sparked little controversy until last fall, when the Arizona Supreme Court proposed making them standard procedure in courtrooms across the state. The proposal raising the most hackles would allow jurors to discuss the case among them-selves as it goes along. Trial attorney Bill Jones, who supports most of the reforms, says this one will tip the scales toward the prosecution.

Jones says that educational research suggests people remember what they hear repeated most. Since the prosecution presents its case first, he says, jurors would be hearing and discussing the prosecution's evidence for perhaps several weeks before the defense began to tell its side of the story. "And you can instruct them until you're blue in the face not to arrive at any conclusions about what the facts are," Jones says, "but, inevitably, being human beings, they're going to arrive at those conclusions, and it's grossly unfair to the defense."

Despite objections, several states are looking at Arizona's proposals. In addition, New York recently expanded its jury pool to include more people from the welfare and unemployment rolls. California is considering allowing nonunanimous verdicts, as do Louisiana and Oregon. (A hung jury in the Simpson trial likely would give this reform some momentum.)

"I think we're kind of at a historic moment" in the process of jury reform, says Adler. In the last six months alone, he says he has been contacted by "prob-ably 20" state bar associations. "There's just a huge move in that direction."

Most agree that innovation won't come easily in the tradition-bound legal system. But when dealing with the Constitution, it's best to move carefully. "I think any reform has to be tinkering at the edges," says Yale's Stith. "If you tinker at the core, you abolish the jury system altogether."

CRITICAL THINKING QUESTIONS

1. What do you think of the idea expressed in the article that most trials "have a manipu-lated, strategically placed jury that may not be there to do justice in the first place"? What evidence can you find to support or refute this statement?

2. The article was written in 1995, prior to the verdict in the O. J. Simpson criminal trial. Find out what, if anything, has changed in the jury trial system since that time.

3. How can the concepts of social perception (Chapter 2) and social cognition (Chapter 3) be applied to the subjectivity that jurors seem prone to? Is there any way to minimize or eliminate any of these potential sources of bias? Explain.
4. How would you recommend improving the jury trial system? What problems and benefits may result from making such changes? Support your answers.

ARTICLE 38 _____

The previous reading (Article 37) examined some of the biases inherent in jury selection. But what happens after the jury has been formed and the trial has started? What factors may have an impact on determining the defendant's guilt or innocence? Jurors are asked to weigh the evidence presented during the trial. Hopefully, they will not permit irrelevant characteristics of the defendant—such as his or her physical appearance, race, or sex—to affect their judgment. But is it really possible to be totally objective in such situations? Or do irrelevant factors play a role in our beliefs about guilt or innocence?

    The following article by Harold Sigall and Nancy Ostrove is a classic piece of research that investigated the impact of the defendant's physical attractiveness on the severity of sentences given to her. Earlier studies had indicated that physically attractive individuals often have great advantages over less attractive people in a variety of situations. This study not only examined the role of physical attractiveness in a trial-like setting but also how the nature of the crime and attractiveness interact to influence judgments about the defendant. The article also tests two different models that may explain why this particular effect occurs.

Beautiful but Dangerous
Effects of Offender Attractiveness and
Nature of the Crime on Juridic Judgment
■ Harold Sigall and Nancy Ostrove

The physical attractiveness of a criminal defendant (attractive, unattractive, no information) and the nature of the crime (attractiveness-related, attractiveness-unrelated) were varied in a factorial design. After reading one of the case accounts, subjects sentenced the defendant to a term of imprisonment. An interaction was predicted: When the crime was unrelated to attractiveness (burglary), subjects would assign more lenient sentences to the attractive defendant than to the unattractive defendant; when the offense was attractiveness-related (swindle), the attractive defendant would receive harsher treatment. The results confirmed the predictions, thereby supporting a cognitive explanation for the relationship between the physical attractiveness of defendants and the nature of the judgments made against them.

Research investigating the interpersonal consequences of physical attractiveness has demonstrated clearly that good-looking people have tremendous advan-

tages over their unattractive counterparts in many ways. For example, a recent study by Miller (1970) provided evidence for the existence of a physical attractiveness stereotype with a rather favorable content. Dion, Berscheid, and Walster (1972) reported similar findings: Compared to unattractive people, better-looking people were viewed as more likely to possess a variety of socially desirable attributes. In addition, Dion et al.'s subjects predicted rosier futures for the beautiful stimulus persons—attractive people were expected to have happier and more successful lives in store for them. Thus, at least in the eyes of others, good looks imply greater potential.

    Since physical attractiveness hardly seems to provide a basis for an *equitable* distribution of rewards, one might hope that the powerful effects of this variable would occur primarily when it is the only source of information available. Unfair or irrational consequences of differences in beauty observed in some

Reprinted from *Journal of Personality and Social Psychology*, 1975, *31*, 410–414. Copyright © 1975 by the American Psychological Association. Reprinted by permission.

situations would cause less uneasiness if, in other situations given other important data, respondents would tend to discount such "superficial" information. Unfortunately, for the vast majority of us who have not been blessed with a stunning appearance, the evidence does not permit such consolation. Consider, for example, a recent study by Dion (1972) in which adult subjects were presented with accounts of transgressions supposedly committed by children of varying physical attractiveness. When the transgression was severe the act was viewed less negatively when committed by a good-looking child, than when the offender was unattractive. Moreover, when the child was unattractive the offense was more likely to be seen as reflecting some enduring dispositional quality: Subjects believed that unattractive children were more likely to be involved in future transgressions. Dion's findings, which indicate that unattractive individuals are penalized when there is no apparent logical relationship between the transgression and the way they look, underscore the importance of appearance because one could reasonably suppose that information describing a severe transgression would "overwhelm the field," and that the physical attractiveness variable would not have any effect.

Can beautiful people get away with murder? Although Dion (1972) found no differences in the punishment recommended for offenders as a function of attractiveness, Monahan (1941) has suggested that beautiful women are convicted less often of crimes they are accused of, and Efran (1974) has recently demonstrated that subjects are much more generous when assigning punishment to good-looking as opposed to unattractive transgressors.

The previous findings which indicate a tendency toward leniency for an attractive offender can be accounted for in a number of ways. For example, one might explain such results with the help of a reinforcement-affect model of attraction (e.g., Byrne & Clore, 1970). Essentially, the argument here would be that beauty, having positive reinforcement value, would lead to relatively more positive affective responses toward a person who has it. Thus we like an attractive person more, and since other investigators have shown that liking for a defendant increases leniency (e.g., Landy & Aronson, 1969), we would expect good-looking (better liked) defendants to be

punished less than unattractive defendants. Implicit in this reasoning is that the nature of the affective response, which influences whether kind or harsh treatment is recommended, is determined by the stimulus features associated with the target person. Therefore, when other things are equal, benefit accrues to the physically attractive. A more cognitive approach might attempt to explain the relationship between physical appearance and reactions to transgressions by assuming that the subject has a "rational" basis for his responses. It is reasonable to deal harshly with a criminal if we think he is likely to commit further violations, and as Dion's (1972) study suggests, unattractive individuals are viewed as more likely to transgress again. In addition, inasmuch as attractive individuals are viewed as possessing desirable qualities and as having relatively great potential, it makes sense to treat them leniently. Presumably they can be successful in socially acceptable ways, and rehabilitation may result in relatively high payoffs for society.

There is at least one implication that follows from the cognitive orientation which would not flow readily from the reinforcement model. Suppose that situations do exist in which, because of his high attractiveness, a defendant is viewed as more likely to transgress in the future. The cognitive approach suggests that in such instances greater punishment would be assigned to the attractive offender. We might add that in addition to being more dangerous, when the crime is attractiveness related, a beautiful criminal may be viewed as taking advantage of a God-given gift. Such misappropriation of a blessing may incur animosity, which might contribute to severe judgments in attractiveness-related situations.

In the present investigation, the attractiveness of a defendant was varied along with the nature of the crime committed. It was reasoned that most offenses do not encourage the notion that a criminal's attractiveness increases the likelihood of similar transgressions in the future. Since attractive offenders are viewed as less prone to recidivism and as having greater potential worth, it was expected that under such circumstances an attractive defendant would receive less punishment than an unattractive defendant involved in an identical offense. When, however, the crime committed may be viewed as attractiveness-related, as in a confidence game, despite being seen as possessing more potential, the attractive defendant may be regarded as relatively more dangerous, and the effects of beauty could be expected to be cancelled out or reversed. The major hypothesis, then, called for an interaction: An attractive defendant would receive more lenient treatment than an unattractive defendant when the offense was unrelated to attractiveness; when the crime was related to attractiveness, the attractive defendant would receive relatively harsh treatment.

METHOD

Subjects and Overview

Subjects were 60 male and 60 female undergraduates. After being presented with an account of a criminal case, each subject sentenced the defendant to a term of imprisonment. One-third of the subjects were led to believe that the defendant was physically attractive, another third that she was unattractive, and the remainder received no information concerning appearance. Cross-cutting the attractiveness variable, half of the subjects were presented with a written account of an attractiveness-unrelated crime, a burglary, and the rest with an attractiveness-related crime, a swindle. Subjects were randomly assigned to condition, with the restriction that an equal number of males and females appeared in each of the six cells formed by the manipulated variables.

Procedure

Upon arrival, each subject was shown to an individual room and given a booklet which contained the stimulus materials. The top sheet informed subjects that they would read a criminal case account, that they would receive biographical information about the defendant, and that after considering the materials they would be asked to answer some questions.

The case account began on the second page. Clipped to this page was a 5 × 8 inch card which contained routine demographic information and was identical in all conditions.[1] In the attractive conditions, a photograph of a rather attractive woman was affixed to the upper right-hand corner of the card; while in the unattractive conditions, a relatively unat-

tractive photograph was affixed. No photograph was presented in the control conditions.

Subjects then read either the account of a burglary or a swindle. The burglary account described how the defendant, Barbara Helm, had moved into a high-rise building, obtained a pass key under false pretenses, and then illegally entered the apartment of one of her neighbors. After stealing $2,200 in cash and merchandise she left town. She was apprehended when she attempted to sell some of the stolen property and subsequently was charged with breaking and entering and grand larceny. The swindle account described how Barbara Helm had ingratiated herself to a middle-aged bachelor and induced him to invest $2,200 in a nonexistent corporation. She was charged with obtaining money under false pretenses and grand larceny. In both cases, the setting for the offense and the victim were described identically. The information presented left little doubt concerning the defendant's guilt.

The main dependent measure was collected on the last page of the booklet. Subjects were asked to complete the following statement by circling a number between 1 and 15: "I sentence the defendant, Barbara Helm, to ____ years of imprisonment." Subjects were asked to sentence the defendant, rather than to judge guilt versus innocence in order to provide a more sensitive dependent measure.

After sentencing had been completed, the experimenter provided a second form, which asked subjects to recall who the defendant was and to rate the seriousness of the crime. In addition, the defendant was rated on a series of 9-point bipolar adjective scales, including physically unattractive (1) to physically attractive (9), which constituted the check on the attractiveness manipulation. A post-experimental interview followed, during which subjects were debriefed.

RESULTS AND DISCUSSION

The physical attractiveness manipulation was successful: The attractive defendant received a mean rating of 7.53, while the mean for the unattractive defendant was 3.20, $F(1, 108) = 184.29$, $p < .001$. These ratings were not affected by the nature of the crime, nor was there an interaction.

The criminal cases were designed so as to meet two requirements. First, the swindle was assumed to be attractiveness-related, while the burglary was intended to be attractiveness-unrelated. No direct check on this assumption was made. However, indirect evidence is available: Since all subjects filled out the same forms, we obtained physical attractiveness ratings from control condition subjects who were not presented with a photograph. These subjects attributed greater beauty to the defendant in the swindle condition ($X = 6.65$) than in the burglary condition ($X = 5.65$), $F(1, 108) = 4.93$, $p < .05$. This finding offers some support for our contention that the swindle was viewed as attractiveness-related. Second, it was important that the two crimes be viewed as roughly comparable in seriousness. This was necessary to preclude alternative explanations in terms of differential seriousness. Subjects rated the seriousness of the crime on a 9-point scale extending from not at all serious (1) to extremely serious (9). The resulting responses indicated that the second requirement was met: In the swindle condition the mean seriousness rating was 5.02; in the burglary condition it was 5.07 ($F < 1$).

Table 1 presents the mean punishment assigned to the defendant, by condition. Since a preliminary analysis demonstrated there were no differences in responses between males and females, subject sex was ignored as a variable. It can be seen that our hypothesis was supported: When the offense was attractiveness-unrelated (burglary), the unattractive defendant was more severely punished than the attractive defendant; however, when the offense was attractiveness-related (swindle), the attractive defendant was treated more harshly. The overall Attractiveness × Offense interaction was statistically significant, $F(2, 108) = 4.55$, $p < .025$, end this interaction was significant, as well, when the control condition was excluded, $F(1, 108) =$

7.02, $p < .01$. Simple comparisons revealed that the unattractive burglar received significantly more punishment than the attractive burglar, $F(1, 108) = 6.60$, $p < .025$, while the difference in sentences assigned to the attractive and unattractive swindler was not statistically significant, $F(1, 108) = 1.39$. The attractive-swindle condition was compared with the unattractive-swindle and control-swindle conditions also, $F(1, 108) = 2.00$, *ns*. Thus, strictly speaking, we cannot say that for the swindle attractiveness was a great liability; there was a tendency in this direction but the conservative conclusion is that when the crime is attractiveness-related, the advantages otherwise held by good-looking defendants are lost.

Another feature of the data worth considering is that the sentences administered in the control condition are almost identical to those assigned in the unattractive condition. It appears that being unattractive did not produce discriminatory responses, per se. Rather, it seems that appearance had its effect through the attractive conditions: The beautiful burglar got off lightly, while the beautiful swindler paid somewhat, though not significantly, more. It can be recalled that in the unattractive conditions the stimulus person was seen as relatively unattractive and not merely average looking. Therefore, the absence of unattractive-control condition differences does not seem to be the result of a weak manipulation in the unattractive conditions.

Perhaps it is possible to derive a small bit of consolation from this outcome, if we speculate that only the very attractive receive special (favorable or unfavorable) treatment, and that others are treated similarly. That is a less frightening conclusion than one which would indicate that unattractiveness brings about active discrimination.

As indicated earlier, previous findings (Efran, 1974) that attractive offenders are treated leniently can be interpreted in a number of ways. The results of the present experiment support the cognitive explanation we offered. The notion that good-looking people usually tend to be treated generously because they are seen as less dangerous and more virtuous remains tenable. The argument that physical attractiveness is a positive trait and therefore has a unidirectionally favorable effect on judgments of those who have it, would have led to accurate predictions in the burglary

TABLE 1 / Mean Sentence Assigned, in Years (*n* = 20 per cell)

	Defendant Condition		
Offense	Attractive	Unattractive	Control
Swindle	5.45	4.35	4.35
Burglary	2.80	5.20	5.10

conditions. However, this position could not account for the observed interaction. The cognitive view makes precisely that prediction.

Finally, we feel compelled to note that our laboratory situation is quite different from actual courtroom situations. Most important, perhaps, our subjects made decisions which had no consequences for the defendant, and they made those decisions by themselves, rather than arriving at judgments after discussions with others exposed to the same information. Since the courtroom is not an appropriate laboratory, it is unlikely that actual experimental tests in the real situation would ever be conducted. However, simulations constitute legitimate avenues for investigating person perception and interpersonal judgment, and there is no obvious reason to believe that these processes would not have the effects in trial proceedings that they do elsewhere.

Whether a discussion with other jurors would affect judgment is an empirical, and researchable, question. Perhaps if even 1 of 12 jurors notes that some irrelevant factor may be affecting the jury's judgment, the others would see the light. Especially now when the prospect of reducing the size of juries is being entertained, it would be important to find out whether extralegal considerations are more likely to have greater influence as the number of jurors decreases.

REFERENCES

Byrne, D., & Clore, G. L. A reinforcement model of evaluative responses. *Personality: An International Journal,* 1970, *1,* 103–128.

Dion, K. Physical attractiveness and evaluation of children's transgressions. *Journal of Personality and Social Psychology,* 1972, *24,* 207–213.

Dion, K., Berscheid, E., & Walster, E. What is beautiful is good. *Journal of Personality and Social Psychology,* 1972, *24,* 285–290.

Efran, M. G. The effect of physical appearance on the judgment of guilt, interpersonal attraction, and severity of recommended punishment in a simulated jury task. *Journal of Research in Personality,* 1974, *8,* 45–54.

Landy, D., & Aronson, E. The influence of the character of the criminal and victim on the decisions of simulated jurors. *Journal of Experimental Social Psychology,* 1969, *5,* 141–152.

Miller, A. G. Role of physical attractiveness in impression formation. *Psychonomic Science,* 1970, *19,* 241–243.

Monahan, F. *Women in crime.* New York: Washburn, 1941.

ENDNOTE

1. This information as well as copies of the case accounts referred to below, can be obtained from the first author.

This study was supported by a grant from the University of Maryland General Research Board.

CRITICAL THINKING QUESTIONS

1. This article used pictures only of females to show defendants of varying attractiveness. Would the same results be obtained if male defendants were used? In other words, do you think that attractiveness stereotypes operate in the same way for males as for females? Defend your answer.

2. As the authors of the article noted, the methodology of the study differed from real-life jury trials in several ways. For example, subjects made their decisions alone and were presented with a paper description of the person and deed, not a real-life person and crime. Design a study that would investigate the same variables studied in the article in a more natural environment.

3. Would the results of this study be generalizable to situations other than jury trials? Think of a situation in which the attractiveness of a person making a request or performing a certain action may result in his or her being treated differently as a result of his or her attractiveness. Explain your answer.

4. What implications do these findings have for the U.S. legal system? How could the effects of irrelevant factors such as attractiveness somehow be minimized in the real-world

courtroom? For example, would telling the jurors beforehand about the tendency to let attractiveness influence their judgments make any difference? Why or why not?

ADDITIONAL RELATED READINGS

Clark, J. (2000). The social psychology of jury nullification. *Law and Psychology Review, 24,* 39–57.

Perlini, A. H., Marcello, A., Hansen, S. D., and Pudney, W. (2001). The effects of male age and physical appearance on evaluations of attractiveness, social desirability and resourcefulness. *Social Behavior and Personality, 29*(3), 277–287.

ARTICLE 39 _____

Chapter Six, on prejudice and discrimination, contained three articles addressing the historical and contemporary views of racism and other forms of prejudice. In particular, Article 16 focused on ways in which prejudice may be automatically activated in certain situations. Thus, even a self-described liberal, who does not consider himself or herself to be the least bit prejudiced, may unwittingly react to people of a different racial or ethnic group, for example, in ways that would be considered discriminatory.

The term *aversive racism,* which is more fully explained in the following article by John F. Dovidio and Samuel L. Gaertner, has been used to explain the contemporary state of prejudice and discrimination in the United States. According to this perspective, even people who do not overtly express prejudiced attitudes may unconsciously hold negative beliefs and feelings that they will eventually express toward outgroups. These attitudes—the byproducts of normal cognitive information processing—will most likely be expressed indirectly. For example, rather than overtly citing race as the reason for not liking someone, the individual may, instead, unconsciously find some other more socially acceptable reason for disliking the person.

This approach suggests that prejudice and discrimination—at least prejudice and discrimination among whites for people of color—is still part of contemporary U.S. society. The reason this article is included in this chapter, however, is because of the methodology and findings presented. The study has direct applications to issues of subtle racism that still may exist in the hiring process and in the criminal justice system.

Aversive Racism and Selection Decisions: 1989 and 1999

■ John F. Dovidio and Samuel L. Gaertner

Abstract—The present study investigated differences over a 10-year period in whites' self-reported racial prejudice and their bias in selection decisions involving black and white candidates for employment. We examined the hypothesis, derived from the aversive-racism framework, that although overt expressions of prejudice may decline significantly across time, subtle manifestations of bias may persist. Consistent with this hypothesis, self-reported prejudice was lower in 1998–1999 than it was in 1988–1989, and at both time periods, white participants did not discriminate against black relative to white candidates when the candidates' qualifications were clearly strong or weak, but they did discriminate when the appropriate decision was more ambiguous. Theoretical and practical implications are considered.

In part because of changing norms and the Civil Rights Act and other legislative interventions that have made discrimination not simply immoral but also illegal, overt expressions of prejudice have declined significantly over the past 35 years (Schuman, Steeh, Bobo, & Krysan, 1997). Discrimination, however, continues to exist and affect the lives of people of color and women in significant ways (Hacker, 1995). What accounts for this discrepancy? One possibility is that it represents a change in the nature of racial prejudice. Contemporary forms of prejudice may be less conscious and more subtle than the overt, traditional form (Gaertner & Dovidio, 1986; Sears, van Laar, Carillo, & Kosterman, 1997). For these more subtle forms of prejudice, discrimination is expressed

Reprinted from *Psychological Science,* 2000 (July), *11,* 315–319. Copyright © 2000 by the American Psychological Society. Reprinted by permission of Blackwell Publishers.

in indirect and rationalizable ways, but the consequences of these actions (e.g., the restriction of economic opportunity) may be as significant for people of color and as pernicious as the consequences of the traditional, overt form of discrimination (Dovidio & Gaertner, 1998).

In the present research, we examined the issue of changes in expressed prejudice and discrimination from the perspective of one modern form of prejudice, aversive racism. Aversive racism (see Gaertner & Dovidio, 1986) is hypothesized to characterize the racial attitudes of many whites who endorse egalitarian values, who regard themselves as nonprejudiced, but who discriminate in subtle, rationalizable ways. Specifically, the present research explored both the overt expression of racial attitudes and discrimination in simulated employment decisions for two samples across a 10-year period, from 1988–1989 to 1998–1999.

According to the aversive-racism perspective, many people who explicitly support egalitarian principles and believe themselves to be nonprejudiced also unconsciously harbor negative feelings and beliefs about blacks and other historically disadvantaged groups. Aversive racists thus experience ambivalence between their egalitarian beliefs and their negative feelings toward blacks. In contrast to the traditional emphasis on the psychopathological aspects of prejudice, the aversive-racism framework suggests that biases related to normal cognitive, motivational, and sociocultural processes may predispose a person to develop negative racial feelings (see Gaertner & Dovidio, 1986). Nevertheless, egalitarian traditions and norms are potent forces promoting racial equality (e.g., Kluegel & Smith, 1986). As a consequence of these widespread influences promoting both negative feelings and egalitarian beliefs, aversive racism is presumed to characterize the racial attitudes of a substantial portion of well-educated and liberal whites in the United States (Gaertner & Dovidio, 1986).

The aversive-racism framework further suggests that contemporary racial bias is expressed in indirect ways that do not threaten the aversive racist's nonprejudiced self-image. Because aversive racists consciously recognize and endorse egalitarian values, they will not discriminate in situations in which they recognize that discrimination would be obvious to others and themselves—for example, when the appropriate response is clearly dictated. However, because aversive racists do possess negative feelings, often unconsciously, discrimination occurs when bias is not obvious or can be rationalized on the basis of some factor other than race. We have found support for this framework across a range of experimental paradigms (see Dovidio & Gaertner, 1998; Gaertner & Dovidio, 1986).

Because the negative consequences of aversive racism are expressed in ways that are not easily recognizable (by oneself, as well as by others) as racial bias, traditional techniques for eliminating bias by emphasizing the immorality of prejudice and illegality of discrimination are not effective for combating contemporary racism: "Aversive racists recognize prejudice is bad, but they do not recognize that they are prejudiced. . . . Like a virus that has mutated, racism has also evolved into different forms that are more difficult not only to recognize but also to combat" (Dovidio & Gaertner, 1998, p. 25). Thus, direct and overt expressions of prejudice, such as self-reported attitudes, are more amenable to change and pressures of increasingly egalitarian norms (Kluegel & Smith, 1986) than are indirect manifestations of racism because they are more easily recognized as racial biases.

The present research was designed to extend the research on aversive racism by exploring changes, over a 10-year period, in expressed racial attitudes and patterns of discrimination in hiring recommendations for a black or white candidate for a position as a peer counselor. Two measures were taken from two comparable student samples 10 years apart. One measure was self-reported racial prejudice. The other measure involved decisions in a simulated employment context. Participants were asked to use interview excerpts to evaluate candidates for a new program for peer counseling at their university. Three profiles were developed: One reflected clearly strong qualifications (pretested as being accepted 85–90% of the time across two samples), one represented clearly weak qualifications (pretested as being accepted 10–20% of the time), and the third involved marginally acceptable but ambiguous qualifications (pretested as being accepted about 50–65% of the time). Participants evaluated a single candidate who was identifiable as black or white from information in the excerpt.

With respect to expressed racial attitudes, we predicted, on the basis of continued emphasis on egalitarian values in the United States (Schuman et al., 1997), that the general trend toward the expression of less prejudiced attitudes (Dovidio & Gaertner, 1998; Schuman et al., 1997) would be reflected across our two samples. Whereas expressed prejudice was expected to decline, we hypothesized that subtle, covert forms of discrimination would persist. Specifically, we predicted, on the basis of previous work on aversive racism as well as work showing that racial stereotypes are most influential in ambiguous situations (see Fiske, 1998), that discrimination against black applicants would occur when the match between the candidate's qualifications and the position criteria was unclear—in the ambiguous-qualifications condition—but not when candidates were clearly well qualified or unqualified for the position.

METHOD

Participants

Participants were 194 undergraduates at a Northeastern liberal arts college during the 1988–1989 academic year (*n* = 112; 48 white male and 64 white female undergraduates) or the 1998–1999 academic year (*n* = 82; 34 white male and 48 white female undergraduates). Participants were enrolled in the university's introductory psychology class, and admissions data indicated that the student populations were scholastically (e.g., standardized-test scores, high school grades) and demographically (e.g., geographical, sex, and racial distributions, socioeconomic status) comparable across the two time periods. Involvement in the study partially satisfied one option for a course requirement. Self-reported prejudice scores were available for 77% (*n* = 86) of participants in 1988–1989 and 87% (*n* = 71) of participants in 1998–1999.

Procedure

During mass pretesting sessions, participants were administered, along with several other surveys, questionnaires assessing their racial attitudes. For the present study, we examined responses to three racial-attitude items (Weigel & Howes, 1985) that were the same at both testing periods: "Blacks shouldn't push themselves where they are not wanted," "I would probably feel somewhat self-conscious dancing with a black person in a public place," and "I would mind it if a black family with about the same income and education as my own would move next door to my home." Responses were on a scale from 1 *(disagree strongly)* to 5 *(agree strongly)* (Cronbach's alpha = .71 overall).

Later, during an experimental session, participants (from 1 to 8 per session) were informed that they would be asked questions about "the desirability and feasibility of a peer counseling program and the qualities of personnel." They were randomly assigned to one of six conditions in a 3 (qualifications: clearly strong, ambiguous, clearly weak) × 2 (race of candidate) design. Thirty to 34 participants were assigned to each condition. After reading a 120-word description of an ostensibly new program, each participant was asked to evaluate a candidate from a previous round of applicants on the basis of interview excerpts. These excerpts were systematically varied to manipulate the strength of the candidate's qualifications. For the candidate with strong qualifications, leadership experiences included being co-captain of the swim team in high school and being a member of the disciplinary board in college; his self-description was "sensitive, intelligent, and relaxed." In response to the question "If a female student came to you because she was pregnant, what would you do?" this candidate was quoted as saying, "Explain options to her and ask her if she would like the telephone number of the health center." For the candidate with ambiguous qualifications, the candidate's leadership experiences included only being co-captain of the swim team in high school; his self-description was "sensitive, intelligent, and emotional." In response to the question about the female student who might be pregnant, this candidate said, "Ask her if she would like the telephone number of the health center." For the candidate with weak qualifications, the leadership experiences included being co-captain of the chess team in high school; his self-description was "independent, forthright, and intense." This candidate's response to the question about the student's pregnancy was, "Tell her that is too personal and that she must talk with her parents."

The race of the applicant was varied by the list of his activities. Black candidates listed membership in the Black Student Union, whereas white students listed fraternity membership (which was almost exclusively white on campus).

The final versions of the three "interview excerpts" were pretested with 20 undergraduate students from each time period. They were given all three excerpts, in random order and without racially identifying information. Undergraduates at both time periods clearly distinguished among strong, ambiguous, and weak qualifications. The strongly qualified candidate was recommended for the peer counselor program by 85% and 90% of the pretest participants at the two time periods, respectively; the candidate with ambiguous qualifications was recommended by 50% and 65% of these participants; and the candidate with weak qualifications was recommended by 20% and 10% of these students.

In the main study, students evaluated the candidates by rating them on a series of scales. The first item assessed perceptions of whether the candidate was qualified for the position, on a scale from 1 *(not at all)* to 10 *(extremely);* this item served as a check on the manipulation of the interview excerpts. The last two items represented the primary dependent measures. They asked whether participants would recommend the candidate for the position (yes or no) and how strongly they would recommend the candidate (on a scale from 1, *not at all,* to 10, *very strongly*). On the last page of the booklet, participants read, "When reading a resumé or transcript, people often form a visual image of a person. Based on the information provided, what image of the applicant have you formed?" A question about the candidate's race was included among other items about his imagined physical characteristics.

RESULTS

The manipulations of race and qualifications were effective. Participants identified the candidate as being white 100% of the time in the white-candidate condition and as being black 97% of the time in the black-candidate condition. Preliminary analyses of the yes/no recommendations and their strength revealed no systematic effects for the sex of the participant. Conse-

quently, this factor was not included in subsequent analyses. A 3 (qualifications: clearly strong, ambiguous, clearly weak) $\times$ 2 (race of candidate) $\times$ 2 (time: 1988–1989, 1998–1999) analysis of variance demonstrated the expected main effect of manipulated qualifications on perceived qualifications, $F(1, 182) = 62.92$, $p < .001$ ($Ms = 7.21$ vs. 6.38 vs. 3.98; see Table 1). This main effect was uncomplicated by any interactions. Each of the three qualifications conditions differed significantly from the other two according to Scheffé post hoc tests.

The $3 \times 2 \times 2$ analysis of variance performed on the strength of recommendations revealed the anticipated main effect for qualifications, $F(1, 182) = 81.15$, $p < .001$ (see Table 1). Participants recommended candidates in the strong-qualifications condition most highly ($M = 6.85$), candidates in the ambiguous-qualifications condition next most highly ($M = 5.36$), and those in the weak-qualifications condition least highly ($M = 3.15$). Scheffé tests demonstrated that these means differed significantly from each other. There was no main effect for the candidate's race ($F < 1$), but the predicted Qualifications $\times$ Race of Candidate interaction was obtained, $F(2, 182) = 6.08$, $p < .003$. Planned comparisons revealed no significant difference in the strength of recommendations for black and white candidates who had strong qualifications ($Ms = 7.18$ vs. 6.52, $p > .10$) or who had weak qualifications $Ms = 3.50$ vs. 2.81, $p > .10$). However, as predicted, ambiguously qualified black candidates were recommended significantly less strongly than were comparable white candidates ($Ms = 4.82$ vs. 5.91), $t(64) = 2.79$, $p < .001$. In addition, Scheffé tests comparing the strengths of participants' recommendations revealed that when the applicant was white, participants responded to ambiguous qualifications more as if these qualifications were strong (difference between means = 0.61, n.s.; Table 1) than as if they were weak (difference = 3.10, $p < .05$). When the applicant was black, however, participants reacted to ambiguous qualifications more like weak qualifications (difference between means = 1.32, n.s.) than like strong qualifications (difference = 2.36, $p < .05$).

Moreover, the Qualifications $\times$ Race of Candidate interaction was comparable across participants in the 1988–1989 and the 1998–1999 samples: The Qualifications $\times$ Race of Candidate $\times$ Time interaction did

TABLE 1 / Perceived Qualifications and Candidate Recommendations as a Function of the Candidate's Qualifications and Race

Condition	Perceived Qualifications[a]			Strength of Recommendation[a]			Percentage Recommended		
	1988–1989	1998–1999	Both	1988–1989	1998–1999	Both	1988–1989	1998–1999	Both
Clearly strong qualifications									
White candidate	7.32	6.93	7.15	6.74	6.21	6.52	89	79	85
	(1.46)	(2.06)	(1.72)	(1.41)	(2.09)	(1.72)			
Black candidate	7.79	6.60	7.27	7.32	7.00	7.18	95	87	91
	(1.23)	(1.77)	(1.58)	(1.67)	(1.60)	(1.62)			
Ambiguous qualifications									
White candidate	6.45	5.85	6.21	6.05	5.69	5.91	75	77	76
	(1.11)	(1.68)	(1.36)	(1.73)	(1.60)	(1.67)			
Black candidate	6.72	6.33	6.55	5.06	4.53	4.82	50	40	45
	(1.32)	(1.59)	(1.44)	(1.39)	(1.64)	(1.51)			
Clearly weak qualifications									
White candidate	3.90	3.67	3.81	3.05	2.42	2.81	5	8	6
	(2.00)	(2.27)	(2.07)	(1.65)	(1.68)	(1.66)			
Black candidate	4.24	4.08	4.17	3.29	3.77	3.50	12	15	13
	(1.75)	(2.06)	(1.86)	(1.69)	(1.69)	(1.68)			

[a]Table entries are means, with standard deviations in parentheses. Responses were on a scale from 1 (*not at all qualified* or *not at all recommended*) to 10 (*extremely qualified* or *very strongly recommended*).

not approach significance, $F(2, 182) = 0.61$ $p > .54$. The Qualifications × Race of Candidate interaction was marginally significant for participants in 1988–1989, $F(2, 106) = 2.54$, $p < .083$; it was significant for participants in the 1998–1999 sample alone, $F(2, 76) = 3.94$, $p < .024$ (see Table 1).

Log-linear analyses, paralleling those for the strength of recommendations, were conducted on the dichotomous (yes/no) recommendation measure. These analyses yielded the same pattern of results. Overall, candidates in the strong-qualifications condition were recommended most frequently (88%), those in the ambiguous-qualifications condition were recommended next most frequently (61%), and those in the weak-qualifications condition were recommended least frequently (10%), $\chi^2(2, N = 194) = 80.37$, $p < .001$. The Qualifications × Race of Candidate interaction was also obtained, $\chi^2(2, N = 194) = 6.75$, $p < .035$. Black and white candidates were recommended equivalently often in the strong-qualifica-

tions (91% vs. 85%) and weak-qualifications (13% vs. 6%) conditions ($ps > .50$), but blacks were recommended less often than whites in the ambiguous-qualifications condition (45% vs. 76%), $\chi^2(1, N = 66) = 6.35$, $p < .012$. Again, the interaction was not moderated by the time period in which the data were collected; the three-way interaction did not approach significance ($p > .50$). Taken together, the results for the strength of recommendations and the yes/no measure offer support for the hypotheses.

For the participants for whom prejudice scores were available, the 3 (qualifications) × 2 (race of candidate) × 2 (time: 1988–1989, 1998–1999) analysis of variance demonstrated only a main effect for time, $F(1, 145) = 8.31$, $p < .005$. As expected, participants in the 1988–1989 had higher prejudice scores than those in 1998–1999 (*Ms* = 1.84 vs. 1.54). In addition, for both ratings of qualifications and recommendations, 3 × 2 × 2 × 2 (prejudice) analyses of variance, classifying participants in the two samples as high or low in prejudice on the basis of median splits, were performed. There were no significant effects for prejudice qualifying the results reported earlier. However, overall, participants higher in prejudice (as a continuous variable) recommended black candidates less strongly than participants lower in prejudice, $r(79) = -.24$, $p < .05$. The correlation between prejudice and strength of recommendation was nonsignificant for white applicants, $r(74) = .05$, $p > .50$.

DISCUSSION

Overall, the pattern of results supports the hypothesis derived from the aversive-racism framework. As predicted from that framework, and consistent with other theories of modem racism (e.g., McConahay, 1986), and the influence of stereotyping (Fiske, 1998), bias against blacks in simulated hiring decisions was manifested primarily when a candidate's qualifications for the position were ambiguous. When a black candidate's credentials clearly qualified him for the position, or when his credentials clearly were not appropriate, there was no discrimination against him. Moreover, as expected, self-reported expressions of prejudice declined significantly across the 10-year period. Taken together, these contrasting trends for self-reported prejudice and discrimination in simulated employment decisions support our hypothesis that the development of contemporary forms of prejudice, such as aversive racism, may account—at least in part—for the persistence of racial disparities in society despite significant decreases in expressed racial prejudice and stereotypes. However, this finding does not imply that old-fashioned racism is no longer a problem. In fact, the overall negative correlation between expressed prejudice and recommendations for black candidates suggests that traditional racism is a force that still exists and that can operate independently of contemporary forms of racism.

One potential alternative explanation for the results of the employment decision is that the credentials in the clear-qualifications condition were so extreme that ceiling and floor effects suppressed the variance in responses and reduced the likelihood of obtaining differences as a function of the candidate's race. Although plausible, this explanation is not supported empirically. The strength-of-recommendation measure could range from 1 to 10, and the means in the strong-qualifications condition (6.52 for white candidates and 7.18 for black candidates) and the weak-qualifications condition (2.81 for white candidates and 3.50 for black candidates) did not closely approach these scale endpoints. This restricted-range interpretation would also suggest that the within-condition standard deviations would be substantially lower in the clear-qualifications conditions than in the ambiguous-qualifications condition. As illustrated in Table 1, this was not the case. The standard deviations were similar for both white candidates (1.72 and 1.66 vs. 1.67) and black candidates (1.62 and 1.68 vs. 1.51); there was no statistical evidence of heterogeneity of within-group variances. Thus, this extremity explanation cannot readily account for the obtained pattern of results.

In addition, although we had predicted, on the basis of the ambiguity versus clarity of appropriate decisions, that discrimination against blacks would be unlikely to occur when qualifications were either clearly weak or clearly strong, other perspectives could suggest that bias would occur in these conditions. In the weak-qualifications condition, the black candidate's clear lack of credentials could have provided an ostensibly nonracial justification for particularly negative evaluations. Although a floor effect offers one potential explanation for the lack of difference in this condition, as we noted earlier, the within-cell standard deviations do not readily support this interpretation. Another possibility is that because the black candidate did not display obviously negative qualities, but rather insufficiently positive ones, excessive devaluation of this candidate was difficult to rationalize. Contemporary racism is hypothesized to involve sympathy for blacks (Katz, Wackenhut, & Hass, 1986), as well as cautiousness by whites about being too negative in evaluations of blacks (and thus appearing biased); either or both of these factors could have limited the negativity of response to blacks when qualifications were weak and could account for the slightly more positive response to black than to white candidates in this condition (see Table 1). In addition, sympathy and concerns about being too harsh in evaluations are particularly likely to occur when the relevance to the evaluator and the challenge to the status quo are minimal (see Dovidio & Gaertner,

1996; McConahay, 1986). Participants were not led to believe that their responses would directly influence the outcome of the particular candidate's application in the current study. Under conditions of greater relevance to the evaluator, greater bias toward either highly qualified or underqualified blacks may occur as a function of direct or symbolic threats (Dovidio & Gaertner, 1996).

The overall pattern of results obtained in the present study also helps to illuminate some of the processes underlying the effects of aversive racism. In particular, participants' ratings of the candidates' qualifications were not directly influenced by race: Participants rate the objective qualifications of blacks and whites equivalently. The effect of race seemed to occur not in how the qualifications were perceived, but in how they were considered and weighed in the recommendation decisions. We (Gaertner et al., 1997) have proposed, for example, that the effects of aversive racism may be rooted substantially in inter-group biases based on social categorization processes. These biases reflect in-group favoritism as well as out-group derogation. Along these lines, Hewstone (1990) found that people tend to judge a potentially negative behavior as more negative and intentional, and are more likely to attribute the behavior to the person's personality, when the behavior is performed by an out-group member than when it is performed by an in-group member. Thus, when given latitude for interpretation, as in the ambiguous-qualifications condition, whites may give white candidates the "'benefit of the doubt," a benefit that is not extended to out-group members (i.e., to black candidates). As a consequence, as demonstrated in the present study, moderate qualifications are responded to as if they were strong qualifications when the candidate is white, but as if they were weak qualifications when the candidate is black.

The subtle, rationalizable type of bias demonstrated in the present study, which is manifested in terms of in-group favoritism, can pose unique challenges to the legal system. As Krieger (1998) observed, "Title VII is poorly equipped to control prejudice resulting from in-group favoritism" (p. 1325). Identifying the existence and persistence of subtle bias associated with aversive racism can thus help to demonstrate that discrimination is not "a thing of the past" and can encourage renewed efforts to develop techniques to combat contemporary racial bias.

ACKNOWLEDGMENTS

We express our appreciation to Mamie Tobriner and Abby Russin for their assistance in the collection of the data and to Gifford Weary and three anonymous reviewers for their helpful and insightful comments on an earlier version of the manuscript. The research and preparation of this manuscript were supported by National Institute of Mental Health Grant MH48721.

REFERENCES

Dovidio, J.F., & Gaertner, S.L. (1996). Affirmative action, unintentional racial biases, and intergroup relations. *Journal of Social Issues, 52*(4), 51–75.

Dovidio, J.F., & Gaertner, S.L. (1998). On the nature of contemporary prejudice: The causes, consequences, and challenges of aversive racism. In J. Eberhardt & S.T. Fiske (Eds.), *Confronting racism: The problem and the response* (pp. 3–32). Newbury Park, CA: Sage.

Fiske, S. (1998). Stereotyping, prejudice, and discrimination. In D. Gilbert, S. Fiske, & G. Lindzey (Eds.), *The handbook of social psychology* (4th ed., Vol. 2, pp. 357–411). New York: McGraw-Hill.

Gaertner, S.L. & Dovidio, J.F. (1986). The aversive form of racism. In J.F. Dovidio & S.L. Gaertner (Eds.), *Prejudice, discrimination, and racism* (pp. 61–89). Orlando, FL: Academic Press.

Gaertner, S.L., Dovidio, J.F, Banker, B., Rust, M., Nier, J., Mottola, G., & Ward, C. (1997). Does racism necessarily mean anti-blackness? Aversive racism and pro-whiteness. In M. Fine, L. Powell, L. Weis, & M. Wong (Eds.), *Off white* (pp. 167–178). London: Routledge.

Hacker, A. (1995). *Two nations: Black and White, separate, hostile, unequal.* New York: Ballantine Books.

Hewstone, M. (1990). The "ultimate attribution error"? A review of the literature on intergroup attributions. *European Journal of Social Psychology, 20,* 311–335.

Katz, I., Wackenhut, J., & Hass, R.G. (1986). Racial ambivalence, value duality, and behavior. In J.F. Dovidio & S.L. Gaertner (Eds.), *Prejudice, discrimination, and racism* (pp. 35–59). Orlando, FL: Academic Press.

Kluegel, J.R., Smith, E.R. (1986). *Beliefs about inequality: America's views of what is and what ought to be.* New York: Aldine de Gruyter.

Krieger, L.H. (1998). Civil rights perestroika: Intergroup relations after affirmative action. *California Law Review, 86,* 1251–1333.

McConahay, J.B. (1986). Modem racism, ambivalence, and the modem racism scale. In J.F. Dovidio & S.L. Gaertner (Eds.), *Prejudice. discrimination, and racism* (pp. 91–125). Orlando, FL: Academic Press.

Schuman, H., Steeh, C., Bobo, L., & Krysan, M. (1997). *Racial attitudes in America: Trends and interpretations.* Cambridge, MA: Harvard University Press.

Sears, D.O., van Laar, C., Carillo, M., & Kosterman, R. (1997). Is it really racism? The origin of white Americans' opposition to race-targeted policies. *Public Opinion Quarterly, 61,* 16–53.

Weigel, R.H., & Howes, P.W. (1985). Conceptions of racial prejudice: Symbolic racism reconsidered. *Journal of Social Issues, 41*(3), 117–138.

CRITICAL THINKING QUESTIONS

1. The article states, "Aversive racists recognize prejudice is bad, but they do not recognize that they are prejudiced. . . . Like a virus that has mutated, racism has also evolved into different forms that are more difficult not only to recognize but also to combat." Do you agree or disagree with this statement? Why? Conduct an informal survey of minority group members to see if they agree or disagree with the statement and why.

2. Do you think that the aversive racism discussed in the article only applies to whites' reactions to people of color, or does it occur in the reverse situation, as well? How about minorities' perceptions and treatment of each other? Explain your answers, and design a study to test these possibilities.

3. The article concludes by stating that the findings on aversive racism "can encourage renewed efforts to develop techniques to combat contemporary racial bias." What can be done to help eliminate aversive racism in the workplace? In the criminal justice system?

4. The study used simulations of the hiring process, which means the subjects knew that their decisions would have no real consequences. Would the aversive racism effect be stronger or weaker if the consequences were real (i.e., if these were real hiring decisions)? Defend your position. How could this question be addressed? (Be sure to keep in mind the various ethical issues that would be involved in such a study.)

Chapter Fourteen

APPLYING
SOCIAL PSYCHOLOGY
Health and Environment

THE FINAL CHAPTER in this book addresses the contributions of social psychology to both health and environmental issues.

When we think of *health,* often the first thing that comes to mind is the medical, biological component of illness. But what about the behaviors that are linked to illness? Obviously, we can do many things either to increase or decrease the likelihood of illness. Health psychology research examines issues such as personality factors that may be related to health—for instance, the underlying beliefs about health-related issues and how these beliefs can be changed.

Article 40 is a good example of the mounting evidence that psychosocial factors, such as social isolation and anger, are major contributing factors in the occurrence of cardiovascular disease. "Research to the Heart of the Matter" discusses these risk factors along with effective interventions that may help people lead longer and healthier lives.

A second area addressed in this chapter is the environment. The ways in which people are influenced by the environments in which they live, as well as the ways in which people can modify their environments to suit their own desires and needs, is the focus of *environmental psychology.* Once considered an outgrowth of social psychological research, it is now regarded as a discipline in its own right. Article 41, "Territorial Defense and the Good Neighbor," examines the social environment. How people use and define personal space in public settings—and how they protect it from the intrusion of others—is the focus of this classic article.

Finally, "Satisfaction in a Dormitory Building: The Effects of Floor Height on the Perception of Room Size and Crowding," Article 42, looks at how people's satisfaction of living in a given space is mediated by the floor on which it is located. The article highlights the fact that our perceptions of the environment are inherently subjective and that how we perceive two otherwise identical physical spaces may be affected by other factors.

ARTICLE 40 _____

Health psychology is a subdiscipline of social psychology that is concerned with the psychosocial factors affecting prevention, development, and treatment of physical illnesses. Over the years, numerous connections have been made between personality and lifestyle factors and how they may affect health. Perhaps the best-known link is the relationship between stress and health.

But what is *stress?* To a large extent, it is subjective. What is a source of stress for one person may be a neutral or even positive experience for another. Effectively, then, *stress* may be defined as physical, mental, or emotional strain or tension. It has evolved as a shortened version of *distress.*

Many studies have linked the amount of stress people experience with negative health consequences. Sometimes, these negative consequences are the direct result of stress—for instance, developing cardiovascular disease as a result of having elevated blood pressure. In other cases, the health problems may stem from behaviors developed in response to stress, such as smoking out of nervousness and contracting lung cancer. Thus, an important factor in determining the impact of stress on health is one's ability to cope. Someone who has developed effective coping mechanisms in response to stress is less likely to develop stress-related health problems than someone with less effective coping mechanisms.

While the sources and manifestations of stress may be unique to each individual, certain factors seem to predispose most people to health risks. For example, anger and hostility have been linked to cardiovascular disease in numerous studies. Likewise, factors such as social isolation may not only predispose individuals to disease but also impair their recovery from illness. The following article by Rebecca A. Clay examines the mounting evidence that psychosocial factors play a major role in the development of cardiovascular disease. In fact, psychosocial factors are far more malleable than, say, heredity factors, which makes the intervention strategies noted in the article particularly important.

Research to the Heart of the Matter

■ Rebecca A. Clay

The man clutching his heart and falling dead of a heart attack during a fight with his wife has been the stuff of cliché. Now psychologists are producing the science to prove the cliché true—and using that science to design interventions they hope will save lives.

"Although there's still some debate, there is increased recognition among the medical community about the importance of psychosocial factors in cardiovascular disease," says James A. Blumenthal, PhD, a professor of medical psychology at Duke University Medical Center in Durham, N.C. "There are clearly more papers on psychosocial topics being published in the more mainstream medical journals, not just in the psychology journals. We're not just preaching to the converted anymore."

Blumenthal points to the literature review he and colleagues published in the pre-eminent cardiology journal *Circulation* in 1999 (Vol. 99, No. 16). "That the American Heart Association would afford us so much space is a testament to how important they consider psychosocial variables as potentially being," he says.

Today Blumenthal and other psychologists are producing clear evidence that psychosocial factors like hostility, anger, stress, depression and social isolation contribute to cardiovascular disease. They're showing that these factors influence the disease's development both directly and indirectly, through pathophysiological mechanisms and through unhealthy habits such as smoking and bad diets.

And they're beginning to come up with interventions that may help patients live longer, healthier lives.

LINKING PSYCHOSOCIAL FACTORS AND HEART DISEASE

Speculations about the link between psychosocial factors and cardiovascular disease are almost as old as medicine itself. In 1628 William Harvey first described the circulatory, system and noted that emotions affect the heart. In 1897, William Osler—often called the father of internal medicine—described the typical heart disease patient as "a keen and ambitious man, the indicator of whose engine is always at 'full speed ahead.'" In the 1950s, cardiologists Meyer Friedman, MD, and Ray Rosenman, MD, began their work connecting Type-A traits—free-floating hostility, impatience and insecurity—with cardiovascular disease.

Despite this long history, controversy lingers in the medical community. For instance, a study of 630 Army personnel published in the *New England Journal of Medicine* (Vol. 343, No. 18) last year found no link between their levels of anxiety, hostility, depression and stress and their chances of developing clogged arteries.

In recent years, anger in particular has attracted great interest from researchers. In a prospective study published in *Circulation* (Vol. 101, No. 17) last year, for instance, psychologist Janice E. Williams, PhD, explored whether angry dispositions would lead to heart disease among 12,986 white and African-American men and women aged 45 to 64 at baseline. Conducted while Williams was at the University of North Carolina in Chapel Hill, the study used a questionnaire to assess what researchers call "trait" anger—a propensity for frequent, intense, long-lasting rages. Questions included whether study participants considered themselves quick-tempered or whether they felt like hitting someone when they got angry.

During a median follow-up period of about four and a half years, Williams and her colleagues checked to see if participants had had heart attacks or other cardiovascular problems. The results were striking. Among people with normal blood pressure, those with high scores on the anger scale were three times more likely to have suffered heart attacks or sudden cardiac death than were those with low scores. The findings held true even after controlling for risk factors such as smoking, having diabetes or weighing too much.

"This and other studies have shown a positive association between anger and heart attacks or sudden cardiac death," says Williams, who now works in the Cardiovascular Health Branch at the U.S. Centers for Disease Control and Prevention. "The implication is that individuals who find themselves prone to anger might benefit from anger management training."

Other psychologists have also become fixtures in the cardiac field, sharing their expertise in psychosocial factors. One is Karen A. Matthews, PhD, a professor of psychiatry, psychology and epidemiology at the University of Pittsburgh. In a study published in the *Journal of the American Medical Association (JAMA)* last year (Vol. 283, No. 19), she and her colleagues examined the role that hostility—defined as a personality trait marked by cynicism, mistrust, anger and aggression—plays in predisposing young people to cardiovascular disease.

To explore the connection, Matthews and her colleagues assessed the hostility levels of 374 white and African-American men and women aged 18 to 30. A decade later, the researchers used a technique called electron-beam computed tomography to check participants' coronary arteries for calcification—an early sign of the hardening of the arteries known as atherosclerosis.

The researchers discovered that people who scored above the median on the baseline assessment of hostility were twice as likely to have coronary calcification than were those scoring below the median. These results held true even after the researchers controlled for demographic, lifestyle and physiological variables.

"Our study lets us predict really early which individuals are going to be at higher risk down the road," says Matthews. "From a prevention standpoint, that's very helpful. By identifying people early, you can design early interventions to retard further development of coronary artery disease."

Psychologists are also studying the ways psychosocial factors can exacerbate problems in people who already have heart disease. In an article in *JAMA* last year (Vol. 283, No. 14), for instance, psychologist David S. Krantz, PhD, reviewed the evidence he and other researchers have amassed demonstrating that both chronic and acute mental stress can negatively affect patients with coronary artery disease.

Krantz's own work has focused on identifying factors that trigger myocardial ischemia, which occurs when the heart doesn't get the blood supply it needs. In laboratory experiments, for example, he has provoked ischemia via such mental stresses as math exercises and harassment. He has also studied stress's impact on ischemia in everyday life by asking patients to keep detailed diaries of their activities and emotions.

"What surprises me about our findings over the years is that mental stress is about as powerful as strenuous exercise as a trigger for ischemia," says Krantz, professor and chair of the department of medical and clinical psychology at the Uniformed Services University in Bethesda, Md. "This suggests that stress management may be an appropriate addition to rehabilitation programs for patients with coronary disease."

Psychosocial factors also influence patients' recovery from heart attacks and other cardiovascular problems, researchers have found. In a study of 896 heart attack sufferers, for instance, psychologist Nancy Frasure-Smith, PhD, found that patients who were depressed were three times more likely to die in the year following their heart attack than those who were not depressed, regardless of how severe their initial heart disease was. Frasure-Smith, an associate professor of psychiatry at the McGill University School of Medicine and a senior research associate at the Montreal Heart Institute, published her study in *Psychosomatic Medicine* in 1999 (Vol. 61, No. 26).

The study also identified striking gender differences: Women were twice as likely as men to develop depression after a heart attack, with half of women and a quarter of men experiencing at least mild to moderate depression. Yet women's death rates were nonetheless the same as men's.

Social support may influence which depressed patients die, Frasure-Smith found in a study published in *Circulation* (Vol. 101, No. 16) last year. Based on interviews with 887 heart attack patients, the study found that depression's impact on survival was mediated by patient's perceived social support. Depressed patients who felt they didn't get enough support from friends and family members had the highest death rates. In contrast, depressed patients who reported the most support had the same death rates as nondepressed patients.

INTERVENING FOR PATIENTS' HEALTH

Now that researchers have data suggesting causal relationships between psychosocial factors and cardiovascular disease, the next step is to test whether interventions designed to influence those factors can prevent heart disease or improve the prognosis of those who already have it.

Researchers have been working in this area for years and have developed compelling evidence that such interventions cannot only enhance patients' quality of life but also dramatically improve their physical health:

- In the Recurrent Coronary Prevention Project, for example, Friedman and his colleagues randomly assigned 1,013 heart attack patients to receive routine medical care, group counseling about cardiac risk factors or group therapy designed to modify Type-A behavior, plus counseling about risk factors. After four and a half years, patients who received the group therapy intervention had a 44 percent reduction in second heart attacks compared with the other two groups.
- In the Lifestyle Heart Trial, Dean Ornish, MD, and his colleagues assigned 28 patients to a rigorous lifestyle-modification program that included group therapy, meditation and yoga as well as exercise and a lowfat diet. At the one-year follow-up, 82 percent of these patients saw regression in their atherosclerotic lesions compared with only 42 percent of the 20 patients in a control group.

Patients in the experimental group also reported reductions in the frequency, duration and severity of their angina; angina symptoms actually worsened in the control group.

■ In Project New Life, Swedish psychologist Gunilla Burell, PhD, randomly assigned 261 post-bypass patients to receive routine medical care or one year of behaviorally oriented group therapy plus half a dozen "booster" sessions in the project's second and third years. At the follow-up five to six years later, patients in the treatment group were significantly less likely to have undergone further cardiac procedures, spent time in the coronary care unit, had heart attacks or died.

Now a ground-breaking trial called Enhancing Recovery in Coronary Heart Disease is taking this research to a new level. Funded by the National Heart, Lung and Blood Institute, the ongoing eight-center trial will determine whether psychological intervention can reduce heart attack patients' chances of having another heart attack or dying.

Currently in the follow-up stage, the trial randomly assigned about 2,600 heart attack patients to receive treatment as usual or a cognitive-behavioral therapy intervention targeting social isolation and major and minor depression, whether it was related to the illness or other aspects of patients' lives. Patients began with individual therapy, then progressed to group therapy. Results should be available about a year and a half from now.

"This is a landmark study in the field of psychology," says Robert M. Carney, PhD, principal investigator of the St. Louis site and professor of medical psychology and psychiatry at the Washington University School of Medicine. "It's the first opportunity we've had to show that what psychologists do can be potentially very important to the medical outcomes of certain groups of patients. It's very exciting."

Patients aren't the only ones who need interventions, however. Psychologists are also conducting research aimed at physicians and nurses who work with cardiovascular patients. Wayne M. Sotile, PhD, for example, has devoted his career to alerting health-care professionals about the need to pay attention to cardiac patients' psychosocial needs.

With funding from the cardiac device company Medtronic, Sotile and psychologist Samuel F. Sears Jr. recently explored the psychosocial needs of patients with implantable cardioverter defibrillators (ICDs) and also surveyed the family members, doctors and nurses who care for them. Implanted in the chest, the devices provide a lifesaving shock when patients' heart rhythms start going haywire.

The result was a manual called *Brief Psychosocial Interventions for ICD Patients & Their Families,* three audiotapes and patient materials, all designed to help health-care providers meet these patients' psychosocial needs. Since ICD patients will never get better, for example, health-care providers need to replace their usual emphasis on recovery with a new focus on coping skills.

"By choice or by default, physicians, nurses and allied health professionals are the ones who need to take responsibility for systematically and effectively addressing patients' psychosocial needs," says Sotile, director of psychological services for the Wake Forest University Cardiac Rehabilitation Program in Winston–Salem, N.C. "There aren't enough psychologists who are trained in the ins and outs of life with cardiovascular illness. It's a huge area of unmet need."

CRITICAL THINKING QUESTIONS

1. Examine a social psychology textbook to learn more about the psychosocial factors associated with disease. Based on this evidence, what factors may predispose *you* to disease later in life? What interventions can you make now to lower your risk for these factors?

2. Chapter Four of this book dealt with the issues of attitude and attitude change. What role does attitude play in the development of cardiovascular disorders? What techniques of attitude change can be used to help people adapt those behaviors or characteristics that put them at greater risk for disease? Explain your answers.

3. The article notes that social isolation is important both in contributing to cardiovascular disease and in recovering from illness. How can society help decrease the amount of social isolation that some people experience?

4. Numerous books are available dealing with stress management techniques. Review some of them and comment on whether the techniques recommended are effective in reducing cardiovascular risk factors.

ARTICLE 41 _____

Most people are aware that many species of animals claim and mark territory as belonging to them. Another animal, including a human, entering that territory may elicit defensive behaviors on the owner's part.

Humans also tend to claim territory as belonging to them. Some territories, such as our bedrooms, belong exclusively to us. If someone came into your bedroom and rearranged the furniture without your permission, you would most likely be unhappy, to say the least. In contrast with these private territories, we also lay claim, albeit temporarily, to semiprivate spaces. An example of this might be a seat in a classroom. You do not own it, and other people use it when you are not there, yet you most likely sit in the same seat every time you attend a particular class. If, after attending the class for a semester, you arrive one day to find someone else sitting in your seat, you might feel a little annoyed at whomever took your seat. Finally, there also are public spaces, which we use temporarily but over which we lay no claim other than when we actually occupy the space. Seats in a movie theater or in a restaurant are examples of this type of territory.

The following classic article by Robert Sommer and Franklin D. Becker concerns public spaces. When we occupy a public space, it sometimes becomes necessary to leave it for a short time. How can we effectively indicate that the space is already taken? Also, sometimes we want to protect our space from the presence of others. How can we keep people from sitting next to us if we want to be alone? These are but two of the questions addressed in a series of studies presented in the article.

Territorial Defense and the Good Neighbor

■ Robert Sommer and Franklin D. Becker[1]

A series of questionnaire and experimental studies was designed to explore how people mark out and defend space in public areas. The use of space is affected by instructions to defend actively the area or retreat, by room density, and by the location of walls, doors, and other physical barriers. Under light population pressure, most markers are capable of reserving space in a public area, but more personal markers have the greatest effect. As room density increases, the effect of the marker is seen in delaying occupancy of the area and in holding onto a smaller subarea within the larger space. Neighbors play an important part in legitimizing a system of space ownership.

The concept of human territoriality is receiving increased attention. In addition to the popular books by Ardrey (1961, 1966), a number of social scientists have become impressed with the utility of the concept (Altman & Haythorn, 1967; Esser et al., 1965; Hall, 1966; Lipman, 1967; Lyman & Scott, 1967). Hediger (1950) defined a territory as "an area which is first rendered distinctive by its owner in a particular way and, secondly, is defended by the owner." When the term is used by social scientists to refer to human behavior, there is no implication that the underlying mechanisms are identical to those described in animal research. The major components of Hediger's defini-

Reprinted from *Journal of Personality and Social Psychology*, 1969, *11*, 85–92. Copyright © 1969 by the American Psychological Association. Reprinted with permission.

tion are *personalization* and *defense*. Roos (1968) uses the term *range* as the total area an individual traverses, *territory* as the area he defends, *core area* as the area he preponderantly occupies and *home* as the area in which he sleeps. Goffman (1963) makes the further distinction between a territory and a jurisdiction, such as that exercised by a janitor sweeping the floor of an office and keeping other people away. Territories are defended on two grounds, "you keep off" and "this space is mine." Jurisdictions are controlled only on the former ground; no claim of ownership, no matter how transitory, is made.

In a previous study, the reactions to staged spatial invasions were investigated (Felipe & Sommer, 1966). There was no single reaction to a person coming too close; some people averted their heads and placed an elbow between themselves and the intruder, others treated him as a nonperson, while still others left the area when he came too close. The range of defensive gestures, postures, and acts suggested that a systematic study of defensive procedures would contribute materially to our knowledge of human spatial behavior. Following the tradition of ecological research, the studies would be undertaken in naturally occurring environments.

QUESTIONNAIRE STUDIES

During previous observations of library study halls Sommer (1967) was impressed by the heavy concentration of readers at the side-end chairs. Interviewing made it clear that students believed that it was polite to sit at an end chair. Someone who sat, for example, at a center chair of an empty six-chair table (three chairs on each side) was considered to be "hogging the table." There appeared to be two styles by which students gained privacy in the library areas. One method was avoidance, to sit as far away from other people as one could. The other method was offensive ownership of the entire area. To study the two methods of gaining privacy, a brief questionnaire was constructed which presented the student with table diagrams containing 6, 8, and 10 chairs, respectively (Sommer, 1967). Two forms to the questionnaire were distributed randomly within a class of 45 students. Twenty-four students received avoidance instructions: "If you wanted to be as far as possible from

the distraction of other people, where would you sit at the table?" Twenty-one other students in the same class were shown the same diagrams and given the offensive display instructions: "If you wanted to have the table to yourself where would you sit to discourage anyone else from occupying it?" Even though both sets of instructions were aimed at insuring privacy, the two tactics produced a striking difference in seats chosen. Those students who wanted to sit by themselves as far as possible from other people overwhelmingly chose the *end* chairs at the table, while those students who wanted to keep other people away from the table almost unanimously chose the *middle* chair.

When the findings were discussed with architect James Marston Fitch, his first question concerned the location of the door in regards to the table. This seemed a good question, since the preferred location for retreat or active defense should be guided by the path the invaders would take or by the most accessible escape route. The previous diagrams had depicted only a table and chairs, so it seemed necessary to undertake another study in which the entrance to the room was indicated. This conception of the study suggested that additional information could be obtained on the ecology of retreat and active defense by varying the location of walls and aisles and the table size.

Method

The present study involved four diagrams, each one drawn on a separate 8 1/2 × 11-inch sheet.

> *Form G* showed eight rectangular six-chair tables, with a large aisle down the center and two smaller aisles along the walls. (See Figure 1.)
> *Form H* was the same as Form G, only the tables were set against the wall and the center aisle was wider.
> *Form J* was a hybrid of G and H, with the right row of tables against the wall and the left row of tables away from the wall.
> *Form I* contained one row of four-chair tables and one row of eight-chair tables, with aisles in the center and along both walls.

Four different sets of instructions were used with the forms (two defense styles and two densities), but

FIGURE 1 / Arrangement of Tables and Chairs in Form G

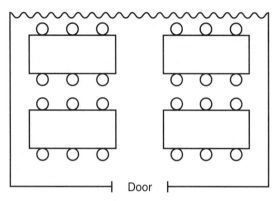

Door

any single subject received only one set. One form asked the subject where he would sit if he wanted to be by himself and away from other people—the retreat instructions. The other form asked where he would sit if he wanted to keep other people away from the table—the active defense instructions. In each case, the prospective room density was also indicated. On half the questionnaires, it was stated that room density was likely to be low throughout the day and very few people would be using the room, while remaining subjects were told that room density was likely to be high and many people would be using the room. All the instructions described the room as a study hall such as that already existing in the campus library, and the respondent was informed that he was the first occupant in the room, so he could take any seat he wanted. Booklets containing some combination of instructional set (Defense Style × Room Density) and two diagrams in random order were passed out randomly among 280 students in introductory psychology classes.

Results

Hypothesis 1 stated that during the retreat condition people gravitate to the end chair closest to the wall. During the active defense condition they make greater use of the center and aisle chairs. Hypothesis 1 was confirmed beyond the .01 level. During the retreat conditions 76% of the subjects occupied a wall chair

compared to 48% during the active defense condition.

Hypothesis 2 stated that with the retreat instructions the subjects face away from the door, while they face towards the door with the active defense instructions. The data disclose a preference in all conditions for a subject to sit with his back to the door—60% of the subjects faced away from the door compared to 40% who faced towards it. However, the results were still in the predicted direction since 44% of the subjects in the active defense condition faced the door compared to 36% in the retreat condition ($p < .05$).

Although the authors had imagined that the use of different-sized tables and the variation in wall placement would influence seating patterns, specific hypotheses had not been formulated. In all conditions there was a marked preference for chairs towards the rear of the room. Overall, 79% selected chairs in the rear half of the room. However, occupancy of the rear was significantly higher with the retreat instructions under high room density than in any of the other conditions ($p < .05$). There was also a highly significant preference for the four-chair tables when they were paired with the eight-chair tables, with 73% selecting a small table compared with 27% selecting a large table. There was a slight trend in the active defense condition to make greater use of the small tables, but this was not statistically significant.

When tables against the wall were paired with tables with aisles on both sides, 62% of the subjects selected a table against the wall compared to 38% who chose a table with aisles on both sides ($p < .001$). As an independent variable, description of the projected room density as high or low made very little difference in where people sat. However, density interacted with the defense instructions on several of the tabulations. With high density *and* retreat instructions, there was significantly greater use of (a) the rear half of the room, (b) a wall compared to an aisle table, and (c) the chair closest to the wall. In essence, the attribution of high room density increased the degree of physical retreat. It had no observable effects on the active defense conditions.

The results make it clear that room dimension and the location of barriers must be considered if we are to understand the ecology of spatial defense. In a library reading room, the best chair for retreat is at the rear, facing away from the door, next to a wall, and at a small table if one is available. Distance from the door protects the person against people simply walking by as well as lazy intruders who are more likely to sit in the first available chair; facing away from the door tends to minimize distraction and also displays an antipathy toward social intercourse; a wall table protects a person's entire left (or right) side; and a small table reduces the number of invaders in close proximity. At this point the authors felt they had derived many useful hypotheses from the questionnaire data which they wanted to extend using an experimental approach under natural conditions. The first experimental studies took place in two soda fountains, and the remainder took place in library areas.

EXPERIMENTAL STUDIES

Most territories are marked and bounded in some clear way. In the animal kingdom, markers may be auditory (bird song), olfactory (glandular secretions by deer), or visual (bear-claw marks on a tree). Since humans rely almost exclusively on visual markers, the authors decided to test the strength of various markers ranging from the physical presence of a person to impersonal artifacts.

Study 1

The first study took place in a popular soda fountain on campus. The soda fountain was located in a converted office building which still contained a number of small rooms. Patrons would obtain their refreshments at a central counter and then repair to one of the smaller rooms to eat and chat informally. Prior to the study, the authors had been struck by the sight of students walking up and down the corridor looking for an empty room. One of the small rooms which contained three square tables, each surrounded by four chairs, was used for the study. A 20-year-old girl who appeared to be studying stationed herself at a table facing the door. On other occasions during the same hours she stationed herself down the hall so she could observe who entered the experimental room. A session took place only when the room was unoccupied at the outset.

If an all-or-none criterion of room occupancy is applied, the experimenter's defense was not very successful. During only 1 of the 10 experimental sessions was she able to keep the entire room to herself. The average length of time before the room was occupied during the experimental sessions was 5.8 minutes compared to 2.6 minutes during the control sessions, but the difference was not statistically reliable. Although the experimenter was unable to keep the room to herself, she was able to protect the table at which she studied. The remaining three seats were occupied only once during the experimental sessions compared to 13 occupancies during the control sessions ($p <$ .01). It seems clear that territorial defense in a public area is not an all-or-none affair. The defender's presence may be seen in a delay in occupancy rather than an absence of invaders and in the avoidance of a subarea within the larger area.

Study 2

The next study took place in a more traditional open-plan soda fountain and, instead of the physical presence of the experimenter, three sorts of objects were used as territorial markers—a sandwich wrapped in cellophane, a sweater draped over a chair, and two paperback books stacked on the table. In each case the experimenter located two adjacent empty tables and arbitrarily placed a marker on one with the other as a control. Seating himself some distance away, he was able to record the duration of time before each table was occupied. The sessions all took place at moderate room density. There were 8 sessions with a sandwich marker, 13 with a sweater, and 20 with the books.

The authors were interested in whether a marker would reserve an entire table as well as the marked chair. The answer for all of the markers was affirmed. The unmarked control tables were occupied significantly sooner than were the marked tables, and the difference was significant for each of the three markers. In fact, in all 41 sessions the control table was occupied sooner or at the same time as the marked table. In only three of the sessions did anyone sit at the marked *chair*. All three were occupied by males, a finding whose significance will be discussed later. It is also interesting to examine the occupancy patterns at the two sorts of tables. The marked tables were eventually occupied by 34 lone individuals and 4 groups of 2 persons, while the unmarked tables were occupied by 18 lone individuals and 20 groups. It can be noted that a group of 2 or 3 could easily be accommodated at a marked table even assuming that the marker represented one person, yet virtually all the groups sat at unmarked tables. It is clear that the markers were able to (a) protect the particular chair almost totally, (b) delay occupancy of the entire table, and (c) divert groups away from the table.

Study 3

A similar study using books and newspapers as markers was undertaken in a dormitory study hall at a time of very light room density. Virtually all the markers proved effective in reserving the marked chair. The only exceptions were two sessions when the school paper which had been used as a marker was treated as litter and pushed aside. After more than 30 individual sessions where virtually all the markers were respected, the authors decided to move the experiments to the main university library where room density was much heavier. It seemed clear that at low densities almost any marker is effective. One qualification is that the object must be perceived as a marker and not as something discarded and unwanted by its former owner. Certain forms of litter such as old newspapers or magazines may, indeed, attract people to a given location.

The locus of study was switched to the periodical room in the university library where room density was high and pressure for seats was great. This room contained rectangular six-chair tables, three chairs to a side. The experimenter arrived at one of the six seats at a designated table at 6:50 P.M., deposited a marker, and then departed to another table at 7:00 P.M. to view any occupancy at the marked position by a student seeking space. During each session, a similarly situated empty chair which was unmarked was used as the control. There were 25 experimental sessions, each lasting 2 hours. The markers included two notebooks and a textbook, four library journals piled in a neat stack, four library journals randomly scattered on the table, a sports jacket draped over the chair, and a sports jacket draped over the chair in addition to the notebooks on the table.

If one compares the average time before occupancy of the marked and the control chairs, it is apparent that all markers were effective. Seventeen of the 25 marked chairs remained vacant the entire 2-hour period, while *all* control chairs were occupied. The average interval before the control chairs were occupied was 20 minutes. Some of the markers were more potent than others. Only one student occupied a chair that was marked either by a sports jacket or a notebook-and-text. Chairs marked by the neatly-piled journals were occupied three of the five sessions, while chairs marked by the randomly placed journals were occupied all five sessions, even though the interval in each case exceeded that of the control chairs. It is clear that the personal markers, such as the sports jacket and notebooks, were able to keep away intruders entirely, while the impersonal library-owned markers (journals) could only delay occupancy of the marked chairs.

An interesting sidelight is that eight of the nine students who sat down despite the markers were males. Since there were more females than males in the control chairs at the same time, the high incidence of males is quite significant. It may be recalled in the previous study that the only three individuals who pushed aside the marker and sat at a marked chair were also males. It is likely that some sort of dominance or risk-taking factor is at work in the decision to disregard a territorial marker. The relationship between personality characteristics and the likelihood of invading someone else's space seems an exciting topic for further investigation.

Another serendipitous finding concerns the role of the neighbor, the person sitting alongside the marked chair, in defending the marked space. In all five trials with the scattered journals, the potential invader questioned the person sitting alongside the marked chair (the neighbor) as to whether the space was vacant. Early in the 2-hour session, the neighbor unknowingly served as the protector of the space. He informed all inquisitive intruders that the space was taken, since he believed the experimenter would return in view of the marker left on the table. As time passed, the neighbor's belief that the experimenter would return to the chair began to wane. At this point he would impart his new conception of the situation to potential invaders, "Yes, somebody was sitting there, but that was over an hour ago. Maybe he's not coming back."

Study 4

Since the role of the neighbor seemed an important aspect of a property-ownership system, the authors decided to investigate it experimentally. The first of such studies involved two experimenters and a person sitting alongside an empty chair. One experimenter seated himself next to a stranger (the neighbor) for 15 minutes and then departed, leaving behind an open book and an open notebook upon the table as territorial markers. After a fixed interval, the second experimenter, in the role of a student looking for a chair, came and inquired about the marked space nonverbally. The nonverbal questioning was a pantomime which included catching the neighbor's eye, pulling out the chair slightly, hesitating, looking at the place markers and at the neighbor, and then back at the markers. The authors had very little experience with such nonverbal cues, but expected that the neighbor's reactions might include verbal defenses ("That seat is taken") and nonverbal defenses (moving the books to reinforce the marker). The independent variable was the length of time between the departure of the first experimenter and the arrival of the second—which was either a 5- or a 20-minute interval. Some sessions had to be terminated when the neighbor departed before the second experimenter arrived on the scene.

Overall the results were discouraging. In only 6 of the 55 trials did the neighbor respond to the nonverbal gestures of the second experimenter in what could be described as a space-defending manner, such as a statement that the seat was taken. Five of the six defensive acts occurred when the experimenter had been away 5 minutes, compared to only one defensive act when he had been away 20 minutes, but considering that there were 55 trials the difference was unimpressive.

Study 5

The authors decided to make another attempt to see if the neighbor could be involved in property defense on a spontaneous basis—that is, if he would defend marked space without being questioned directly. Un-

like in the preceding study, the "owner" attempted to establish a relationship with the neighbor prior to the "owner's" departure. There were two phases of the study; when it seemed that the first approach was not leading anywhere, another approach was used. The markers were a neat stack of three paperback books left on the table in front of a chair. The sessions took place at six-chair tables where there was at least 1 empty seat between the marker and the neighbor. The first experimenter entered the room and found the location meeting the experimental requirements (a person sitting at the end chair of a six-person table with two empty chairs alongside him—O-O-S). The experimenter (a girl) sat down on the same side of the table but one seat away (E-O-S). There were 13 trials in each of the following conditions: (a) The experimenter sat 5 minutes and then departed from the table, leaving her books neatly stacked on the table. During this time she did not interact with her neighbor. (b) Similar to Condition *a,* the experimenter sat for 5 minutes except that during the 5-minute wait, the experimenter asked the neighbor "Excuse me, could you tell me what time it is?" (c) Similar to Condition *a,* the experimenter sat for 5 minutes except that during the 5-minute wait the experimenter engaged the neighbor in conversation four times and, while leaving and placing the stack of three paperback books on the table, declared, "See you later." Fifteen minutes later, the second experimenter (a male) entered the room, walked directly to the marked chair, pushed the books directly ahead of him, and sat down at the table.

The results were again discouraging. In none of the 39 trials involving Conditions *a, b,* and *c* did the neighbor inform the intruder that the seat was taken. The authors therefore decided to strengthen the conditions by having the "owner" return and directly confront the intruder. Seven of such trials were added to Condition *a,* 6 to Condition *b,* and 6 to Condition *c,* making 19 trials in all when the "owner" came back and told the intruder "You are sitting in my chair." Each time she hesitated about 30 seconds to see if the neighbor would intervene, and then she picked up her books and departed. There was no verbal response from the neighbor in any of the 19 sessions. The most that occurred would be a frown or a look of surprise on the part of the neighbor, or some nonverbal communication with someone else at the table. Stated simply, despite a flagrant usurpation of a marked space, all neighbors chose to remain uninvolved. It became clear that if one wanted to study the neighbor's role in such an informal regulatory system one would have to question him directly as to whether the seat was occupied.

Study 6

The next study employed two experimenters, a male and a female, and the same three paperback books as markers. Two different girls were used as experimenters, and the sessions occurred in two different, nearby college libraries. The experimental situation involved six-chair tables where the first experimenter (female) sat down at the same side of a table with a subject, leaving an empty chair between them (E-O-S). The goal of the study was to learn whether a greater amount of interaction between the former occupant and the neighbor would increase the neighbor's likelihood of defending the chair. Unlike in the previous study, the neighbor was questioned directly as to whether the seat was taken. There were three different instructional sets, and these took place according to a prearranged random order. In 14 trials, the first experimenter sat at the chair for 5 minutes without saying anything, deposited the marker (three paperback books), and left. Fourteen other sessions were similar except that at some time during her 5-minute stay, the first experimenter asked the neighbor for the time. Ten other sessions were similar except that the experimenter engaged the neighbor in conversation as to where to get a coke, what was happening on campus, and other minor matters. Fifteen minutes after the first experimenter departed, the second experimenter (a male) entered the room, walked over to the marked chair, and asked the neighbor "Excuse me, is there anyone sitting here ?"

The results differ markedly from those in the previous study. A total of 22 out of the 38 neighbors defended the seat when questioned directly on the matter. The typical defense response was "Yes, there is" or "There is a girl who left those books."[2] However, the amount of contact between the first experimenter and the neighbor made little difference in defensive behavior. When there had been no contact,

or minimal contact, between the first experimenter and neighbor the seat was protected 58% of the time, while the use of several items of conversation between the experimenter and her neighbor raised the percentage of defensive responses only to 66%. The difference between conditions is small and statistically unreliable; what is impressive is the great increase in defensive behavior when the neighbor was questioned directly. Two other parameters of the situation are (a) the time that the first experimenter remained in the seat before depositing her marker, and (b) the length of time that the first experimenter was out of room before the second experimenter approached the marked chair.

Study 7

The final study employed two experimenters, both males, and the same three paperback books. The sessions took place at six-chair tables in the library, where the first experimenter again sat down on the same side of the table with a subject, leaving an empty chair between them (E-O-S). He remained either 5 minutes or 20 minutes, depending upon the experimental condition, and then departed, leaving on the table a neat stack of three paperback books. After a designated interval of either 15 or 60 minutes, the second experimenter entered the room and asked the neighbor whether the (marked) chair was taken. The second experimenter recorded the neighbor's reply verbatim just as soon as he was able to sit down somewhere. Since both experimenters were males, it was decided to use only male neighbors in the experiment.

The independent variables were (a) the length of time the first experimenter had been seated before he left his marker and departed and (b) the length of time the first experimenter was absent before the neighbor was questioned by the second experimenter. Some sessions were unusable since the neighbor departed before the designated time and could not be interviewed. Most of the unusable sessions occurred when the experimenter had been absent for 60 minutes. The sessions took place at times of light-to-moderate room density.

Although the design had not called for comparison of marked and unmarked chairs, it is noteworthy that the markers were effective in keeping people away.

Not one of the 64 marked chairs was ever occupied. Regarding the inclination of the neighbor to defend the marked space when questioned by the second experimenter, a content analysis of the neighbor's responses to the query "Is this seat taken?" into defense and nondefense categories revealed that 44 neighbors defended the marked space by indicating that it was taken, while 20 failed to do so either by pleading ignorance or by stating that the chair was empty. The response to a direct question stands in contrast to the lack of involvement when neighbors were approached nonverbally. The length of time that the first experimenter had originally occupied the chair (his tenure period) had no effect on the willingness of the neighbor to defend the chair. However, the length of time that the previous owner was away—either 15 or 60 minutes—had a significant effect. When the former owner had been absent 15 minutes, 80% of the neighbors defended the space compared to 54% defending it when the former owner had been away a full hour ($p < .05$).

Several aspects of the results require elaboration. It is possible that initial tenure periods of 5 and 20 minutes were not sufficiently different. Yet it seems noteworthy that even with a rather impersonal marker, more than two-thirds of the neighbors defended the marked chair upon direct questioning. Most of those who didn't defend it simply pleaded ignorance ("I don't know if it's taken") rather than indicating that the seat was vacant.

After the experiments had been completed, 15 additional students in the library were interviewed on the question of how personal belongings could reserve space. Each student was asked how he would react if he saw someone intrude into a marked space, particularly if the original owner came back and claimed the space (i.e., the actual experimental situation was described to him). The replies were at variance with what the authors had actually found in such a situation. Most of the respondents maintained that they would indeed protect a marked space, although some of them added qualifications that they would defend the space only if the person were away a short time. Typical responses were: "I would protect the person's books and state (to the intruder) that the place was obviously taken by the presence of the books," and "Yes, I would mention that someone was sitting

there." Although the majority mentioned specifically that they would protect a marked chair, in the actual situation no one had done so unless approached directly. The ethic regarding space ownership in the library exists, but is paid lip service, probably because institutional means of enforcement do not exist.

DISCUSSION

The present article represents a small beginning toward understanding how markers reserve space and receive their legitimacy from people in the area (neighbors) and potential intruders. Psychologists have paid little attention to boundary markers in social interaction, perhaps because such markers were regarded as physical objects relegated to the cultural system (the province of the anthropologist) rather than an interpersonal system which is the true province of the social psychologist. Generally it is the geographers and lawyers who are most concerned with boundaries and markers. Since the present studies took place in public spaces, we are dealing more with norms and customs than with legal statutes. Stated another way, the situations involve an interpersonal system where sanctions are enforced by the individuals immediately present. Goffman (1963) labels the situations the authors used in the experiments *temporary territories*. It is clear that a person placing his coat over the back of a chair desires to reserve the space, and most people in the immediate vicinity will support his claim if questioned (although they will remain uninvolved if they can); such behavior meets Hediger's (1950) definition of territory presented previously as well as the more simple one provided by Noble (1939) that a territory represents "any defended area." The phenomena the present authors have studied do not belong under other available rubrics of spatial behavior, such as home range, biotope, niche, or life space. The major differences between the experimental situations and more enduring territories is that the latter are meshed with a legal-cultural framework and supported in the end by laws, police, and armies. The marked spaces in the present authors' experiments have no legal status and are supported only by the immediate social system. Occasionally it became necessary to articulate the structure of the system by "requiring" neighbors to enter the situation.

People are now spending an increasing portion of their time in public or institutional spaces, including theaters, airport lobbies, buses, schools, and hospitals, where the use of personal belongings to mark out temporary territories is a common phenomenon. The study of territories, temporary as well as enduring ones, deserves study by psychologists. There is some danger that such work will lose much of its force if some semantic clarity is not obtained. While the ethologist's definition of a territory as "any defended area" has considerable heuristic value, there is no need to assume that the mechanisms underlying human and animal behavior are identical. The paucity of data about human territorial behavior makes it most reasonable to assume that the mechanisms are analogous rather than homologous.

In conclusion, the present series of studies suggests that further investigation of spatial markers is feasible and warranted. The physical environment has for too long been considered the background variable in psychological research. The time is past when we can have theories of man that do not take into account his surroundings. Boundary markers not only define what belongs to a person and what belongs to his neighbor, but also who he is and what it means to be a neighbor in a complex society.

REFERENCES

Altman, I., & Haythorn, W. W. The ecology of isolated groups. *Behavioral Science,* 1967, *12,* 169–182.

Ardrey, R. *African genesis.* London: Collins, 1961.

Ardrey, S. *The territorial imperative.* New York: Atheneum, 1966.

Esser, A. H. et al. Territoriality of patients on a research ward. In J. Wortis (Ed.). *Recent advances in biological psychiatry.* Vol. 8. New York Plenum Press, 1965.

Felipe, N., & Sommer. R. Invasions of personal space. *Social Problems,* 1966, *14,* 206–214.

Goffman, E. *Behavior in public places.* New York: Free Press of Glencoe, 1963.

Hall, E. T. *The hidden dimension.* Garden City: Doubleday, 1966.

Hediger, H. *Wild animals in captivity.* London: Butterworths, 1950.

Lipman, A. Old peoples homes: Siting and neighborhood integration. *The Sociological Review,* 1967, *15,* 323–338.

Lyman, S. M., & Scott, M. B. Territoriality: A neglected sociological dimension. *Social Problems,* 1967, *15,* 236–249.

Noble, G. K. The role of dominance in the social life of birds. *Auk,* 1939, 263–273.

Roos, P. D. Jurisdiction: An ecological concept. *Human Relations,* 1968, *21,* 75–84.

Sommer, R. Sociofugal space. *American Journal of Sociology,* 1967, *72,* 654–660.

ENDNOTES

1. The authors are grateful to Harriet Becker, Martha Connell, Ann Gibbs, Lee Mohr, Tighe O'Hanrahan, Pamela Pearce, Ralph Requa, Sally Robison, and Nancy Russo for their assistance.

2. The neighbors' replies to the intruder's question were scored separately by two coders as indicating defense of the space ("Yes, that seat is taken") or nondefense ("No, it isn't taken" or "I don't know"). There was 100% agreement between the two raters in scoring the replies into defense or nondefense categories.

CRITICAL THINKING QUESTIONS

1. The study noted that, in several instances, males were much more likely to ignore territorial markers than were females. Why do you think this was the case? Design a study to determine why males treat territorial markers differently than females do.

2. This article studied various territorial markers in several different settings. What other public spaces might be interesting to study in terms of territorial defense? Besides the markers used in the article, what other ones might be examined?

3. Following the presentation of Study 7, the authors mentioned that they interviewed additional subjects on the question of how personal belongings could reserve space. These subjects' responses differed from what was found in the research. What does this suggest about the relationship between what people do and say? Does it imply that how people respond to a questionnaire also may differ from how they really act? Explain.

ADDITIONAL RELATED READINGS

Rutter, M., Pickles, A., Murray, R., and Eaves, L. (2001). Testing hypotheses on specific environmental causal effects on behavior. *Psychological Bulletin, 127*(3), 291–324.

Stone, N. J. (2001). Designing effective study environments. *Journal of Environmental Psychology, 21*(2), 179–190.

ARTICLE 42 _____

Most social psychological research tends to focus on how people influence and, in turn, are influenced by others. That is to say, the focus is on the *social environment*. Yet every social interaction also takes place in a *physical environment*. The impact of the physical environment on human behavior has become a major research focus of psychologists working in the area of *environmental psychology*.

Over the last few decades, numerous environmental factors have been identified that have direct impact on people's feelings and behaviors. For example, as discussed in Article 33, excessive heat may cause aggression. Likewise, other studies have linked factors such as crowding and loud noise to aggression. To a large extent, however, the impact of these physical factors may be mediated by people's perceptions of the stimuli. That is, one's behavior will be affected only if he or she *perceives* the temperature to be too hot, the room to be too crowded, or the noise to be too loud. What seems crowded to one person, for example, may seem spacious to another.

The fact that our perceptions of the physical environment are, to a large extent, subjective and idiosyncratic may suggest that factors other than the actual physical characteristics of a space may influence our reactions to it. For example, we may perceive two rooms that are identical in size, shape, furnishings, and the like to be very different depending on other factors, such as where they are located. What better place to test this possibility than in an environment known for identically sized and furnished rooms: a college dormitory. The following article by Naz Kaya and Feyzan Erkip examines the impact that floor height may have on people's perception of and satisfaction with living in a dorm room.

Satisfaction in a Dormitory Building
The Effects of Floor Height on the Perception of Room Size and Crowding

■ Naz Kaya and Feyzan Erkip

ABSTRACT: *This article examines the effects of floor height on the perception of room size and crowding as an important aspect of satisfaction with a dormitory building. The analysis was carried out by means of a survey research designed for dormitory residents at Bilkent University, Ankara. Two 5-story dormitory buildings, one housing men and the other women, in which all rooms are of identical size and have equal density, were chosen for the survey. The highest (fifth) and the lowest (ground) floor were included in this research with a sample of an equal number of male and female students for each. As predicted, residents on the highest floor perceive their rooms as larger and feel less crowded than residents of the lowest floor. Overall, when the room is perceived as larger and the feeling of privacy in a room increases, the satisfaction with a dormitory room also increases.*

Satisfaction of users in the built environment is particularly important when the duration of staying is long. Although home is the best example of long-term

Reprinted from N. Kaya and F. Erkip, *Environment and Behavior*, 2001, *33*(1), pp. 35–53, copyright © 2001 by Sage Publications, Inc. Reprinted by permission of Sage Publications, Inc.

environment, public spaces such as dormitories and residences for the elderly are other notable cases in which various aspects of interaction between user and environment can be investigated. Their public nature makes user satisfaction a harder goal to achieve for builders and organizers. Although studies have been conducted in university dormitory buildings as residential settings (Baum, Davis, & Valins, 1979; Mandel, Baron, & Fisher, 1980; Schiffenbauer, 1979; Schiffenbauer, Brown, Perry, Shulack, & Zanzola, 1977; Walden, Nelson, & Smith, 1981), aspects covered need to be extended with further empirical studies. This study measures the effects of a physical characteristic—floor height—on the perception of room size and crowding in a university dormitory. It is assumed that the perception of room size and crowding influence the privacy level and satisfaction of users.

Altman (1975) proposed that crowding occurs when an individual has more social contact than is desired. Westin (1970) defined privacy as the ability to determine the information about oneself that is communicated to others. Westin suggested that there are four basic types of privacy: solitude, intimacy, anonymity, and reserve. Solitude reflects the desire to be alone and free from observation by others, whereas intimacy refers to a need for privacy as a member of a group seeking to form close personal relationships among its members. These two types of privacy are principally considered as they are the most relevant for this study.

Gifford (1987) supports the idea that increasing social density increases the feeling of being crowded in residential settings. Social contact is heightened, the same amount of resources must be distributed to a greater number of people, more physical interference is encountered, and the sense of control is reduced (Jain, 1987). Particularly when social density is undesirable, social outcomes are generally more negative, such as more aggression, less cooperation (Horn, 1990), and more social withdrawal (Sundstrom, 1975).

Social and physical factors affect the spatial perceptions of residents and the feeling of being crowded in dormitory buildings. The social factors include relationships with other residents and with the roommate, the activity taking place, the frequency of encountering strangers, the sharing of bedrooms, and personal characteristics such as sex, family size, and personal background, including the number of people sharing a bedroom at one's home. The physical factors include the room size, characteristics of design such as long or short corridors or suites, intensity of daylight in the room, view from the window, and floor height (Baum et al., 1979).

The effects of social density in a dormitory room were also examined by Walden et al. (1981). When three students had to share a bedroom designed for two, residents felt more crowded. According to Baum and Paulus (1987), students confronted with frequent unwanted interaction with their neighbors experience crowding and avoid contact with unacquainted people even outside of their residential environments.

Second, the physical factors affect the perception of space and crowding. Studies of high-rise dormitories show that when the design involves long corridors as opposed to short corridors or suites, residents experience more crowding and stress (Baum et al., 1979). Long corridors are accompanied by greater competitiveness and social withdrawal and by reduced cooperativeness and lower personal control. In addition, living in a high-rise building may lead to a greater feeling of crowding and other negative attitudes such as less perceived control, safety, privacy, building satisfaction, and lower quality of relationships with other residents (McCarthy & Saegert, 1979).

It is also of interest that perception of crowding varies inversely with the brightness of a room. Mandel et al. (1980) indicates that dormitory rooms receiving more sunlight are perceived as less crowded. They suggest that crowding may be reduced by brightening a room with light colors or graphic designs on walls. Verderber (1986) established that people preferred rooms with windows to rooms lacking a window. In addition, the type of view, whether it is natural or man-made, affects this preference (Butler & Steuerwald, 1991) and personal moods (Stone, 1998). Tennessen and Cimprich (1995) found that university dormitory residents with more natural views from their windows had better performance on attentional measures than those with less natural views.

Among female students in a high-rise dormitory building, rooms on upper floors were perceived as larger than those on the lower floors (Schiffenbauer et al., 1977). Also, perceptions of crowding varied inversely with the brightness of the room. However, an important issue must be pointed out with regard to Schiffenbauer et al.'s (1977) results. That is, only female students participated in their study. Based on empirical research on crowding, it was anticipated that reactions exhibited by males might differ from those shown by females (Kaya, 1997; Rüstemli, 1992; Sears, Peplau, & Freedman, 1988). According to Stokols, Rall, Pinner, and Schopler (1973), males find crowded conditions more emotionally unpleasant than females. Thus, females and males may react to some environmental factors differently.

Moreover, Schiffenbauer (1979) showed that residents of higher floors felt less crowded than residents of lower floors did. This may be because fewer strangers venture to the upper reaches of a building or because views out the windows of higher level dwellings provide more visual expanse or visual escape to the residents than do lower level windows.

This study is designed to investigate the effects of floor height on spatial perceptions of both male and female residents and the feeling of being crowded in a dormitory building. In this research, the dependent variables are perceived room size, the feeling of being crowded, and satisfaction with the room; independent variables are the floor height and the sex of the resident.

HYPOTHESES

To demonstrate the effects of floor height on the spatial perceptions of the residents and the feeling of being crowded in a dormitory room, the following hypotheses are used.

Hypothesis 1: Residents of the highest floor perceive the rooms as larger than residents of the lowest floor.

Hypothesis 2: Perception of room size influences the feeling of crowding and attained privacy.

Hypothesis 3: Residents of the highest floor feel less crowded in their rooms than residents of the lowest floor.

Hypothesis 4: Floor level influences overall satisfaction with the room.

Hypothesis 5: There is a sex difference in the perception of room size and the feeling of being crowded.

METHOD

Setting

The Bilkent University dormitory complex consists of 18 five-story buildings located on a hilltop near the main campus. Eight buildings house two residents in a room, whereas the rest of them either house a single person or are shared by three and four people. In choosing women's and men's dormitory buildings, some criteria were considered. First, only dormitory buildings that have double rooms were included. Therefore, all rooms have equal density. Second, one building houses men and the other women, and all rooms are of identical size. Third, the location of the two buildings with respect to each other is considered. Therefore, we chose women's and men's dormitory buildings that have the same views and visual expanse. Although the rooms are located on the south and north sides of the same dormitory building, their comparative locations are quite alike with similar views and visual expanses from their windows, in both buildings.

According to these criteria, two 5-story dormitory buildings with exactly the same design and configuration were selected. Thus, these two dormitory buildings not only have equal density but also identical room size (3.10 × 2.95 m). Each room consists of a bunk bed, a desk where two people can study, two chairs, and a wardrobe (see Figure 1).

Participants

Of 670 people, the entire population of these two dormitory buildings at Bilkent University, 347 residents are men and 323 are women. Quota sampling was used in this research to obtain an equal number of males and females (Marriott, 1990; Vogt, 1993). To represent the entire population, 80 males and 80 females were sampled. Finally, as the primary concern of this research is to investigate the effects of floor height on the perceptions of room size and crowding,

FIGURE 1 / Floor Plan of the Dormitory Room (Scale: 1/50)

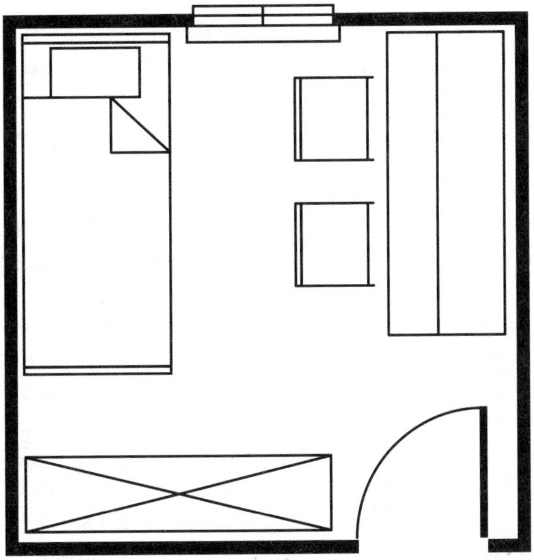

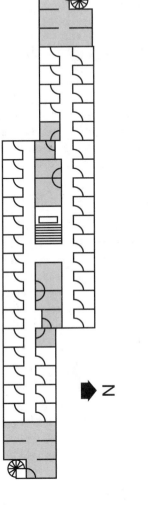

40 residents of the fifth floor and 40 residents of the ground floor were included in each building.

Procedure

On each floor in both dormitory buildings, a total of 38 dormitory rooms are located along two sides of the corridor (see Figure 2). At the time of this survey, some of the rooms were either empty or occupied by only one resident. The residents of those rooms were not included in the survey. Otherwise, the rooms were selected randomly within each floor height. All the participants volunteered with no refusals.

The questionnaire was administered for each room, to be completed individually by each student. It assessed the opinions of residents on the room size, satisfaction with the room, degree of privacy in the room, frequency of encountering strangers on the floor where the resident's room is located, getting along with roommate, frequency of other people (visitors, friends) visiting the room, degree of annoyance with the presence of others visiting the room, and demographic characteristics of the respondents such as years spent in school, duration of staying in a

FIGURE 2 / Floor Plan of the Dormitory Building

Note: Shaded areas indicate semi-public spaces.

dormitory room and with roommate, the number of people sharing a bedroom at home, and family size (see Appendix A for the questionnaire form).

Respondents were also asked their reasons for being satisfied or not with a dormitory room. The residents of the fifth and ground floors were asked to rank their reasons up to four choices. Both positive and negative reasons are grouped into 14 categories involving the physical aspects of the room, degree of privacy, and relations with roommate and visitors. The category named as *other* includes being comfortably hot and uncomfortably cold (see Appendix B and Appendix C for the distribution of positive and negative choices among the ground-floor and fifth-floor residents).

ANALYSIS AND RESULTS

Participants

The sample group consists of 37.5% freshmen, 30% sophomores, 22.5% juniors, and 10% seniors. Responses regarding the duration of staying in a dormitory room and of living with a particular roommate were the same: 41.9% less than 1 year, 37.5% about 1 to 2 years, and 20.6% more than 2 years. At home, 41.9% of the respondents had their own bedroom, 46.2% shared a bedroom with another person, and 11.9% shared a bedroom with more than one person. Half of the respondent group (50.0%) had a family size of 4 people; 13.8%, of 3 people; 22.5%, of 5 people; 9.4%, of 6 people, 3.1%, of 7 people; 0.6%, of 10 people; and 0.6%, of 12 people.

Here it is necessary to mention the assignment procedure to dormitory buildings and to rooms to have a more complete understanding of above-mentioned percentages. Students state their room preferences when they apply to stay in the dormitories. Because there are 18 buildings with different room characteristics, they indicate the room type— single, double, and more crowded rooms are available in different combinations in dormitories with different floor plans—dormitory building, and the friend(s) with whom they would like to share their room. The two dormitories selected for this research have exactly the same floor plan, with double rooms on each floor. Within buildings, regardless of their first choice, students are assigned randomly to available rooms, from the top level to the bottom.

To assure that males and females on different floors in our study were fairly equivalent, a series of chi-square analyses were run. Results showed that neither gender nor floor was related to family size, years of living in the dorm, or number of people sharing the bedroom at home. Family size (grouped as 3, 4, and 5+ people) was tested against sex, $\chi^2(2, N = 160) = 1.735$. Number of years of living in the dorm was tested against the floor, $\chi^2(2, N = 160) = 3.938$, and sex, $\chi^2(2, N = 160) = 4.627$). Number of people sharing the bedroom at home was also tested against floor, $\chi^2(2, N = 160) = 3.107$, and sex, $\chi^2(2, N = 160) = 2.108$. All chi-square tests were insignificant, $p > .05$. Thus, student residents of the first and fifth floors appeared fairly equivalent because of their random assignment from top to bottom floors.

Although the students are given the opportunity to ask for a different room at the end of every academic year, the ratio of such demands is quite low (10%) and two-directional in terms of the desired floor. The main reason to both choose and change a room is the roommate. A slight tendency of moving to lower floors is observed after the first year of residence, the most frequently stated reason being easy access, as the buildings have no elevators. The same reason—easy access—is used to explain the moves toward upper floors, as the stairs cause crowding and noise at the entrance floor. It should also be noted that students can demand to move to other dormitories with single rooms or larger rooms for larger groups, which may be formed within the first years of dormitory residence. Students also leave the dormitories to live in houses. The standard and limited physical qualities of these two buildings serve students with similar backgrounds and expectations.

Chi-Square Tests

Perceived room size was measured as small, medium, and large. Because a categorical scale was used, the chi-square test was applied for data analysis.

For the first hypothesis, the relationship between the perception of room size and residence on the highest and lowest floors was significant, $\chi^2(2, N = 160) = 6.52$, $p = .030$. More residents on the fifth floor perceived their rooms as large (17.5%) than residents on the ground floor (5%). The results indicate that 70% of the fifth-floor residents perceived their room size as small, 12.5% as medium, and 17.5% as large. However, 77.5% of the residents of the ground floor perceived their rooms as small, 17.5% as medium, and 5% as large.

For the second hypothesis, the relationship between the perception of room size and the feeling of privacy was significant, $\chi^2(2, N = 160) = 11.34$, $p = .003$. When the room was perceived as larger, the feeling of privacy also increased, or vice versa. Among residents who perceived their room size as small, 60.2% reported sufficient privacy and 39.8% insufficient privacy. Among residents who perceived their room size as medium, 70.8% reported sufficient privacy and 29.2% insufficient privacy. However, all the residents (100%) who perceived their room size as large reported sufficient privacy in their rooms, a result indicating a strong relationship between perceived room size and privacy level.

For the third hypothesis, the relationship between the feeling of privacy in a room and residence on the highest and lowest floors was significant, $\chi^2(1, N = 160) = 13.52$, $p = .000$. About 80% of the fifth-floor residents said they had sufficient privacy, and 20% did not, whereas 52.5% of the ground-floor residents said they had sufficient privacy and 47.5% did not.

In addition, the relationship between the overall satisfaction with a dormitory room and floor level was significant, $\chi^2(1, N = 160) = 6.41$, $p = 0.010$. Fifth-floor residents (62.5%) were more satisfied with their rooms than ground-floor residents (42.5%). The percentages of unsatisfied residents were 37.5% and 57.5% for the fifth and ground floors, respectively. However, due to the comprehensive character of this hypothesis, we need to develop certain subhypotheses to test the relationships between various factors used in this research, such as satisfaction and the perception of room size, satisfaction and the feeling of privacy, floor level and frequency of encountering strangers, and feeling of privacy and frequency of encountering strangers. The results of these tests are given below.

The relationship between satisfaction with a dormitory room and the perception of room size was also significant, $\chi^2(2, N = 160) = 26.15$, $p = 0.000$. The results indicate that, when the room was perceived as larger, satisfaction also increased, or vice versa. Among residents who were dissatisfied with their rooms, 92.1% perceived the room size as small, 6.6% as medium, and 1.3% as large. For the satisfied residents, the percentages were 57.2%, 22.6%, and 20.2% respectively, indicating a relationship between perceived room size and satisfaction.

The relationship between satisfaction with a dormitory room and the feeling of privacy was also significant, $\chi^2(1, N = 160) = 37.74$, $p = 0.000$. The results indicate that when the feeling of privacy in a room increased, satisfaction also increased. Among residents who were satisfied with their rooms, 88.1% reported sufficient privacy, and only 11.9% reported insufficient privacy. Among residents who were dissatisfied with their rooms, 57.9% had insufficient privacy, and 42.1% had sufficient privacy.

Moreover, the relationship between floor level and the frequency of encountering strangers on the resident's floor was investigated. Encountering strangers is considered as an indication of feeling crowded and losing privacy based on the results of previous research. Results were significant, $\chi^2(2, N = 160) = 42.38$, $p = 0.000$. The results indicate that 46.2% of the fifth-floor residents never encountered strangers, 42.5% sometimes, and only 11.3% frequently. In contrast, only 10% of residents of ground floors never encountered strangers, 35% sometimes, and 55% frequently.

The relationship between the feeling of privacy and the frequency of encountering strangers on the floor was also significant, $\chi^2(2, N = 160) = 33.75$, $p = 0.000$. Residents who frequently encountered strangers claimed that they did not have sufficient privacy in their dormitory rooms. Among residents who said they had insufficient privacy, 63% frequently, 25.9% sometimes, and 11.1% never encountered strangers. However, among residents who said they had sufficient privacy, 17.9% frequently, 45.3% sometimes, and 36.8% never encountered strangers.

Last, for the fifth hypothesis, the perception of room size was significantly related to sex, $\chi^2(2, N = 160) = 7.88$, $p = .010$. About 65% of male residents perceived their room size as small, 17.5% as moderate, and 17.5% as large; whereas 82.5% of female residents perceived their room size as small, 12.5% as moderate, and only 5% as large. Although both male and female residents found their room size small, more females perceived their rooms as small than males. However, the perception of room size could not be statistically tested against sex of the highest and lowest floor residents, due to the limited number of observations in a few room-size categories. Moreover, the relationship between the feeling of privacy and sex was significant, $\chi^2(1, N = 160) = 16.10$, $p = .000$. More males (81.2%) said they had sufficient privacy in their rooms than females (51.2%). About 18.8% of male residents said they had insufficient privacy in their rooms, whereas 48.8% of females reported insufficient privacy. The relationship between floor level and the feeling of privacy in a room was also significant, $\chi^2(3, N = 160) = 30.07$, $p = 0.000$. Female residents of the ground floor (65%) said they had insufficient privacy in their rooms more frequently than male residents (30%) of the same floor. Also, more female residents on the fifth floor (32.5%) said they had insufficient privacy in their rooms, compared to male residents (7.5%) of the same floor.

DISCUSSION

The findings of this research yield strong support for the effects of floor height on the perception of room size and the feeling of crowding. In the current study, even though all the rooms were of the same size and had the same number of individuals living in them (were of equal density), residents of the highest and lowest floors had significantly different ratings of perceived room size and crowding. Residents on the highest floor of the dormitory building perceived their rooms as larger, felt less crowded, and were more satisfied with their rooms than residents of the lowest floor.

These results are interesting for several reasons. First, they provide further empirical support for the effects of floor height on spatial perceptions and crowding in a dormitory building as a residential setting. The significant relationship between floor height and the perception of room size in this research may be because of the windows of higher level dormitory rooms, which provide more visual expanse to residents than lower level dormitory rooms. This study, furthermore, points out the relationship between the perception of room size and the feeling of privacy in a room. When the room size was perceived as larger, the feeling of privacy also increased. Moreover, the relationship between floor height and crowding indicates that density and crowding can be considered conceptually independent concepts. Proshansky, Ittelson, and Rivlin (1970) and Stokols (1972) have established the necessity of viewing density and crowding as different phenomena, which is

supported by this research. The finding that there is a significant difference in crowdedness ratings with no variation in either physical or social density indicates that density is neither a necessary nor a sufficient condition for the perception of crowding to occur. This is clearly evident in the findings on floor height. As mentioned earlier, residents of the highest floor felt less crowded in their rooms than residents of the lowest floor. This may be because fewer strangers venture to the upper reaches of the dormitory building. Also, the findings of this research clearly support that residents of the lowest floor said they more frequently encountered strangers than residents of the highest floor. In addition, the frequency of encountering strangers may affect the feeling of privacy in a room. The findings show that residents who frequently encountered strangers also said they had insufficient privacy and felt more crowded in their dormitory rooms.

The relationship between satisfaction with a dormitory room and the floor height was also found to be statistically significant. Residents of the highest floor were more satisfied with their rooms than residents of the lowest floor. The main reasons for not being satisfied among ground-floor residents were the negative physical aspects of the room, which were perceived as dark, narrow, and noisy, and frequent use of hallways. The noise level on the ground floor was louder than on the fifth floor. This may be as a result of more people using the ground floor. Both residents and visitors who go to the higher floors of the building use the staircase located on the ground floor, as it is the only access (note that these two dormitory buildings, both men's and women's, do not have any elevators). This may cause a problem for residents of the ground floor who want to sleep or study in their rooms. On the other hand, the important reasons for being satisfied with the dormitory room among fifth-floor residents were the positive physical aspects of the room, which were perceived as wide, well-lit, and quiet. The results of this research have also supported that satisfaction with a room is increased when the room is perceived as larger and the feeling of privacy is increased. Thus, residents who perceived their room as large and felt private in their room were more satisfied with their room, or vice versa.

As mentioned before, perception of room size and crowding were influenced by social factors, including relations with other residents and with roommate, and personal characteristics, such as sex, family size, and personal background including the number of people sharing a bedroom at one's home and whether the individual stays alone or shares a bedroom with others. However, these aspects need to be studied further to understand their impact. In this survey, only 5% of the sample group claimed that they could not get along with their roommate, females (3.1%) more than males (1.9%). This may be a result of selecting roommates before applying for a room. It is also interesting that the negative aspects of the dormitory room were mostly associated with physical qualities, whereas relations with roommates were generally positive. The few residents who could not get along with their roommates were not satisfied with their dormitory rooms. In addition, previous research suggests that sharing a residence with more people is correlated with a preference for less privacy (Marshall, 1972). This may be so because the residents who shared a bedroom at home with more than one person were used to living in crowded conditions, so that they might need less privacy than the ones who had a bedroom to themselves at home. Thus, to understand whether residents' personal background influenced their feelings of privacy in a dormitory room, they were asked how many people shared a bedroom at home. However, the chi-square results do not indicate any significant relationship, $\chi^2(2, N = 160) = 2.28, p = 0.318$. Family size (grouped as 3, 4, and 5 or more), however, had a significant relationship with feeling of privacy, $\chi^2(2, N = 160) = 13.78, p = 0.000$, whereas it appeared independent of the perception of room size, $\chi^2(4, N = 160) = 1.71, p = 0.790$. This finding may indicate the effect of long-term crowding on the feeling of privacy, as the expectation of students for privacy differs according to the number of people at home. The number of people sharing a bedroom at home may appear independent because of getting along with the roommate, which also appeared as an important cause of satisfaction in the dormitory room. In addition, the relation between the feeling of privacy and being annoyed with the presence of others, which could partly explain the differences among individuals, is found not to be independent, $\chi^2(1, N = 160) = 11.67, p = 0.001$, as an indication of different effects of familiar and strange people on the perceived privacy level.

It was hypothesized that there would be a sex difference in the perception of room size and the feeling of crowding. Previous research performed in laboratory settings usually finds that males respond to high density more negatively than females; their mood, attitudes toward others, and social behavior are more negative. Females seem to handle the stress of density better than males (Gifford, 1987). However, the results of this study indicate that female residents, both at the highest and lowest floors, felt more crowded than male residents on the same floors do. Also, female residents perceived their rooms as smaller than male residents did, and male residents felt more private in their rooms than female residents did. Thus, the relationship between sex and the feeling of crowding supported the findings of Mandel et al. (1980). Their study provides evidence that women spend more time in their room, and they are more sensitive to the room's physical advantages and disadvantages than men.

There are certain limitations to the present study that should be taken into consideration when interpreting the findings. First, the results of the study are limited by the nature of the sample. The sample group includes only the residents of the two dormitory buildings, one housing men and the other women, at Bilkent University, in Ankara, Turkey. Further research could be carried out in other environments, such as office buildings, hospitals, school buildings, and so forth. Another limitation is that there may be many variations in terms of the personal characteristics of the residents, few of which could be tested in this study. Although this research provided evidence of a positive relationship between floor height and the perception of room size, further research is needed to understand the effects of daylight in a room and the view from the window on the perception of room size. Longitudinal designs with multiple measurements may be needed to provide more comprehensive information on this subject.

APPENDIX A / Questionnaire Form

Sheet #:
Dormitory #:
Floor:
Year:

1. How long have you been staying in your room?
   - ❑ Less than one year
   - ❑ One to two years
   - ❑ More than two years
2. How long have you been staying with your roommate?
   - ❑ Less than one year
   - ❑ One to two years
   - ❑ More than two years
3. How many people did you share your bedroom with at home?
   - ❑ None
   - ❑ One
   - ❑ More than one
4. What is your family size? ____
5. Are you satisfied with your room?
   - ❑ Yes
   - ❑ No
6. Why?
   - ❑ Well-lit
   - ❑ Dark
   - ❑ Large
   - ❑ Small
   - ❑ Noisy
   - ❑ Quiet
   - ❑ Crowded
   - ❑ Privacy: Sufficient
   - ❑ Privacy: Insufficient
   - ❑ Relation with Roommate: Positive
   - ❑ Relation with Roommate: Negative
   - ❑ Relation with Visitors: Positive
   - ❑ Relation with Visitors: Negative
   - ❑ Other _____.

7. How do you find the size of your room?
   - ❑ Small
   - ❑ Medium
   - ❑ Large
8. How do you find the privacy level in your room?
   - ❑ Sufficient
   - ❑ Insufficient
9. How often do you encounter strangers on the floor level where your room is located?
   - ❑ Never
   - ❑ Sometimes
   - ❑ Frequently
10. Do you get along with your roommate?
    - ❑ Yes
    - ❑ No
11. How often do other people (visitors, friends) visit your room?
    - ❑ Never
    - ❑ Sometimes
    - ❑ Frequently
12. Do you get annoyed with the presence of others when they visit your room?
    - ❑ Never
    - ❑ Sometimes
    - ❑ Always
13. Why?
    - ❑ Room size
    - ❑ Noise
    - ❑ Impacts on other activities (studying, sleeping)
    - ❑ Interactions with others

APPENDIX B / Reasons for Being Satisfied or Not with a Dormitory Room and the Priorities for Each Reason among Ground-Floor Residents

	First	Percentage	Second	Percentage	Third	Percentage	Fourth	Percentage	n
Positive responses									
Light	7	8.8	2	2.5					9
Wide	2	2.5	2	2.5					4
Quiet	4	5.0	3	3.8	2	2.5			9
Privacy: Sufficient	11	13.8	5	6.3	3	3.8			19
Relation with roommate, positive	8	10.0	8	10.0	3	3.7	1	1.3	20
Relation with visitors, positive			1	1.3			2	2.5	3

	First	Percentage	Second	Percentage	Third	Percentage	Fourth	Percentage	n
Negative responses									
Dark	5	6.3	6	7.5	4	5.0			15
Narrow	29	36.2	6	7.5	1	1.3			36
Noisy	8	10.0	6	7.5	4	5.0			18
Crowded	5	6.3	9	11.3	4	5.0			18
Privacy: Insufficient	2	2.5	4	5.0	4	5.0			10
Relation with roommate, negative					1	1.3			1
Relation with visitors, negative			1	1.3	1	1.3			2
Other			1	1.3					1

Note: First, second, third, and fourth indicate the respondent's rank for each reason.

APPENDIX C / Reasons for Being Satisfied or Not with a Dormitory Room and the Priorities for Each Reason among Fifth-Floor Residents

	First	Percentage	Second	Percentage	Third	Percentage	Fourth	Percentage	n
Positive responses									
Light	18	22.5	6	7.5	4	5.0			28
Wide	6	7.4	5	6.3	5	6.3	4	5.0	20
Quiet	10	12.5	14	17.5	4	5.0			28
Privacy: Sufficient	6	7.5	7	8.7	3	3.8			16
Relation with roommate, negative	9	11.3	5	6.3	7	8.7	1	1.3	22
Relation with visitors, positive			1	1.3	2	2.5	2	2.5	5
Negative responses									
Dark	1	1.3	1	1.3	4	5.0			6
Narrow	25	31.3	4	5.0	1	1.3			30
Noisy	1	1.3	5	6.3					6
Crowded					1	1.3			1
Privacy: Insufficient	1	1.3	1	1.3					2
Relation with roommate, negative	2	2.5			1	1.3			3
Relation with visitors, negative									
Other	1	1.3	4	5.0					5

REFERENCES

Altman, I. (1975). *The environment and social behavior.* Monterey, CA: Brooks/Cole.

Baum, A., Davis, G. E., & Valins, S. (1979). Generating behavioral data for the design process. In J. R. Aiello & A. Baum (Eds.), *Residential crowding and design* (pp. 175–197). New York: Plenum.

Baum, A., & Paulus, P. B. (1987). Crowding. In I. Altman & D. Stokols (Eds.), *Handbook of environmental psychology* (pp. 533–570). New York: Wiley-Interscience.

Butler, D. L., & Steuerwald, B. L. (1991). Effects of view and rooms size on window size preferences made in models. *Environment & Behavior, 23,* 334–358.

Gifford, R. (1987). *Environmental psychology: Principles and practice.* Boston: Allyn.

Horn, J. L. (1990). Crowding. In R. Corsini (Ed.), *Encyclopedia of psychology* (pp. 365–366). New York: John Wiley.

Jain, U. (1987). Effects of population density and resources on the feeling of crowding and personal space. *Journal of Social Psychology, 127,* 331–338.

Kaya, N. (1997). *The effects of short-term crowding on personal space: A case study on an Automatic Teller Machine.* Unpublished master's thesis, Bilkent University, Ankara, Turkey.

Mandel, D. R., Baron, R. M., & Fisher, J. D. (1980). Room utilization and dimensions of density: Effects of height and view. *Environment & Behavior, 12,* 308–319.

Marriott, F. H. C. (1990). *A dictionary of statistical terms* (5th ed.). New York: John Wiley.

Marshall, N. I. (1972). Privacy and environment. *Human Ecology, 1,* 93–110.

McCarthy, D. P.. & Saegert, S. (1979). Residential density, social overload, and social withdrawal. In J. R. Aiello & A. Baum (Eds.), *Residential crowding and design* (pp. 55–77). New York: Plenum.

Proshansky, H. M., Ittelson, W. H., & Rivlin, L. G. (1970). *An introduction to environmental psychology.* New York: Holt.

Rüstemli, A. (1992). Crowding effects of density on interpersonal distance. *Journal of Social Psychology, 132,* 51–58.

Schiffenbauer, A. I. (1979). Designing for high density living. In J. R. Aiello & A. Baum (Eds.), *Residential crowding and design* (pp. 229–240). New York: Plenum.

Schiffenbauer, A. I., Brown, J. E., Perry, P. L., Shulack, L. K., & Zanzola, A. M. (1977). The relationship between density and crowding: Some architectural modifiers. *Environment & Behavior, 9,* 3–14.

Sears, O. D., Peplau, A., & Freedman, J. (1988). *Social psychology.* Englewood Cliffs, NJ: Prentice Hall.

Stokols, D. (1972). On the distinction between density and crowding: Some implications for further research. *Psychological Review, 79,* 275–277.

Stokols, D., Rall, M., Pinner, B., & Schopler, J. (1973). Physical, social, and personal determinants of the perception of crowding. *Environment & Behavior, 5,* 87–115.

Stone, N. J. (1998). Windows and environmental cues on performance and mood. *Environment & Behavior, 30,* 306–321.

Sundstrom, E. (1975). An experimental study of crowding: Effects of room size. intrusion, self-disclosure, and self-reported stress. *Journal of Personality and Social Psychology, 32,* 645–654.

Tennessen, C. M., & Cimprich, B. (1995). Views to nature: Effects on attention. *Journal of Environmental Psychology, 15,* 77–85.

Verderber, S. (1986). Dimensions of person-window transactions in the hospital environment. *Environment & Behavior, 18,* 450–466.

Vogt, W. P. (1993). *Dictionary of statistics and methodology.* Newbury Park, CA: Sage.

Walden, T. A., Nelson, P. A., & Smith, D. E. (1981). Crowding, privacy, and coping. *Environment & Behavior, 13,* 205–224.

Westin, A. F. (1970). *Privacy and freedom.* New York: Atheneum.

CRITICAL THINKING QUESTIONS

1. This study looked only at residents of the top and bottom floors. Besides the difference in height between the top and the next-to-the-top floors, what other differences might residents of these two floors experience? Test your assumptions by conducting a study using the survey found in Appendix A.

2. The dorms in the study did not have elevators. Would having elevators have made a difference in the results? Why or why not? Design a study to test your hypothesis in a dorm.

3. Do you think any differences would be perceived in crowding and/or satisfaction in a coed dorm as opposed to a single-sex dorm? Why or why not? If possible, conduct a study to test the differences in satisfaction between residents on single-sex versus coed dorm floors.

4. How generalizable are the results of the study to other environments, such as high-rise retirement homes, apartments, and hotel rooms? How about to other populations, such as students in the United States or countries other than Turkey or even older populations? Explain your answers.

5. If applicable, identify other factors of dorm life that may impact the satisfaction of living there. Use your own experiences, if they are relevant. Explain why you think these factors are significant.

Author Index

Subject Index